Webster's

21ST CENTURY™

Dictionary

Walter C. Kidney, Editor
Prepared under the direction
of Laurence Urdang

THOMAS NELSON PUBLISHERS
Nashville

Published in Nashville, Tennessee, by Thomas Nelson, Inc., Publishers and distributed in Canada by Lawson Falle, Ltd., Cambridge, Ontario.

Printed in the United States of America.

Library of Congress Cataloging-in-Publication Data

Webster's 21st century dictionary / Walter C. Kidney, editor ; prepared under the direction of Laurence Urdang.
    p. cm.—(21st century desk reference set)
  ISBN 0-8407-4260-6 (HB—Burgundy)
        0-8407-4229-0 (HB—Navy)
        0-8407-3482-4 (PB)
  1. English language—Dictionaries. I. Kidney, Walter C.
II. Urdang, Laurence. III. Title: Webster's twenty-first century dictionary. IV. Series.
PE1628.W55685 1992b
423—dc20   91–46947
                                            CIP

2 3 4 5 6 7 8 9 10 — 99 98 97 96 95 94 93 92

FOREWORD

Nelson's *Webster's 21st Century™ Dictionary* is the perfect reference companion for everyone whose work may need a quick check for accuracy. Executives, secretaries, proofreaders, students—anyone can have ready answers to common language problems in spelling, hyphenation, and pronunciation.

This compact volume was written specifically to provide the information in an easy-to-use format. Its small size makes it easy to keep within hand's reach on desktop or in drawer. It can be tucked into a briefcase or book bag for work on the go.

This edition has been revised to include new words being introduced into the language, spelling and division guides, brief definitions, and parts of speech are included with each entry. Phonetic spellings have also been added for words which may be difficult to pronounce, such as *negligee,* or where a word may be pronounced in more than one way, such as minute (min′ət) and minute (mī nyoot′). Now you can know quickly whether stationary or stationery is the word you want, whether effect or affect is the right choice. In addition, this practical handbook includes weights and measures equivalents, and U.S. states and their capitals.

A convenient size and accessible format makes Nelson's *Webster's 21st Century™ Dictionary* the primary choice of anyone who wants an accurate working knowledge of the English language.

PRONUNCIATION KEY

Symbol	Key Word	Symbol	Key Word
ă	băt	ŏ	ŏbject
ā	cāpe	ō	ōak
â	târt	ô	ôrb
ȧ	pȧrāde	ȯ	ȯf
a͞u, aͧw	a͞utumn, paͧwn	o͞i	spo͞il
ä	äwful	o͞o	o͞oze
		oͧo	coͧok
		oͧu	oͧur
ĕ	pĕck	oͧw	noͧw
ē	mēal	o͞y	lo͞yal
ê	têrm		
ė	rėply	ŭ	pŭn
e͞w	ne͞ws	ū	trūe
		û	bûrn
ĭ	tĭc		
ī	nīce	ÿ (ē)	merrÿ
î	stîr	y̆ (ĭ)	gly̆cerine
ï	skï	ȳ (ī)	tȳpe
		ẏ (ĭ)	tẏpical

ə (roughly "uh") can symbolize any vowel. Always appears in an unstressed syllable, for instance, *cynicism* (sin′ə siz″əm), *island* (ī′lənd).

A

Ā, a, *n.* **1.** first letter of the English alphabet. **2.** best grade.

ă, *indef. art.* **1.** one. **2.** any single.

ăb′a·cŭs, *n.* calculating device using sliding beads.

a·băft′, *adj., adv. Nautical.* nearer the stern.

a·băn′dŏn, *v.t.* **1.** leave permanently. **2.** give up. —*n.* **3.** freedom from self-restraint. —**a·ban′don·ment,** *n.*

a·băn′doned, *adj.* **1.** left or given up permanently. **2.** without self-restraint; shameless.

a·bāse′, *v.t.,* **abased, abasing.** degrade; humble. —**a·base′ment,** *n.*

a·băsh′, *v.t.* embarrass; shame. —**a·bashed′,** *adj.* —**a·bash′ed·ly,** *adv.*

a·bāte′, *v.t., v.i.,* **abated, abating.** lessen; diminish. —**a′bate·ment,** *n.*

ăb·ăt·tŏir′, *n.* slaughterhouse.

ăb·bé, *n. French.* abbot; priest.

ăb′bĕss, *n.,* nun directing a convent.

ăb′bĕy, *n., pl.* **ab′beys.** monastery or convent.

ăb′bŏt, *n.* monk directing a monastery.

ăb·brē′vi·āte″, *v.t.,* **-ated, -ating.** shorten to essentials. —**ab·bre′vi·a′tion,** *n.*

ăb′dĭ·cāte″, *v.t.,* **-cated, -cating.** give up, as office or power. —**ab″di·ca′tion,** *n.*

ăb′dŏ·mĕn, *n.* **1.** part of the human body between the chest and hips. **2.** part of an animal body in a similar location. —**ab·dom′in·al,** *adj.*

ăb·dŭct′, *v.t.* carry away, esp. by force. —**ab·duc′tion,** *n.* —**ab·duc′tor,** *n.*

a·bēam′, *adv., adj.* across a ship or boat.

a·bĕd′, *adv.* in bed.

ăb″êr·rā′tion, *n.* deviation from what is considered normal.

a·bĕt′, *v.t.,* **abetted, abetting.** aid or encourage. —**a·bet′tor, a·bet′ter,** *n.*

a·bĕy′ànce, *n.* suspension of activity.

ăb·hŏr′, *v.t.,* **abhorred, abhorring.** regard with horror or disgust. —**ab·hor′rence,** *n.* —**ab·hor′rent,** *adj.*

a·bīde′, *v.,* **abode** or **abided, abiding.** *v.i.* **1.** remain. **2.** dwell. —*v.t.* **3.** wait for. **4.** *Informal.* tolerate.

a·bīd′ing, *adj.* enduring; steadfast.

a·bĭl′ĭ·tў, *n., pl.* **-ties. 1.** power. **2.** talent; aptitude.

ăb′jĕct, *adj.* **1.** downcast. **2.** contemptible. —**ab·ject′ly,** *adv.*

ăb·jĕc′tion, *n.* abject state.

ăb·jūre′, *v.t.,* **-jured, -juring.** renounce formally. —**ab″ju·ra′tion,** *n.*

ăb′la·tĭve, *n.* grammatical case of origin, means, location, etc. —**ab′la·tive,** *adj.*

a·blāze′, *adv., adj.* afire.

ā′ble, *adj.,* **abler, ablest. 1.** with the power to do a certain thing. **2.** competent. —**a′bly,** *adv.*

ăb·lū′tion, *n.* washing; cleansing.

ăb′ne·gāte, *v.t.,* **-gated, -gating.** deny or renounce for oneself. —**ab″ne·ga′tion,** *n.*

ăb·nôr′mal, *adj.* not normal. —**ab″nor·mal′i·ty,** *n.*

a·bôard′, *adv.* **1.** onto a ship, train, etc. —*prep.* **2.** on a ship, train, etc.; on board.

a·bōde′, *n.* **1.** home; dwelling. **2.** brief term of residence.

a·bŏl′ĭsh, *v.t.* do away with. —**ab″o·li′tion,** *n.*

ăb″o·lī′tion·ĭst, *n.* person in favor of the abolition of something.

Ā bŏmb, *n.* atomic bomb.

a·bŏm′in·a·ble, *adj.* disgusting; loathsome. —**a·bom′in·a·bly,** *adj.*

a·bŏm′in·āte″, *v.t.,* **-nated, -nating.** hate or loathe. —**a·bom″in·a′tion,** *n.*

ăb″o·rĭg′i·nàl, *adj.* **1.** primitive; original. —*n.* **2.** aborigine.

ă″bo·rĭg′in·ē, *n.* original inhabitant, esp. a savage.

a·bôr′tion, *n.* **1.** termination of pregnancy before full development of a fetus. **2.** wretched piece of work. —**a·bor′tion·ist,** *n.*

a·bôr′tive, *adj.* (of a hope or attempt) frustrated at an early stage.

a·bŏund′, *v.i.* to have or offer something in abundance.

a·bŏut′, *prep.* **1.** concerning; regarding. **2.** around. **3.** near by. **4.** on the point of.

1

—*adv.* **5.** nearly; approximately. **6.** in all directions. **7.** in the opposite direction.

a·bóve', *prep.* **1.** higher than. **2.** greater than. —*adv.*, *adj.* **3.** to or in a higher place. **4.** in a previous part of a text.

a·bóve'bôard'', *adj.*, *adv.* without deception or disguise.

a·bráde', *v.t.*, **-braded, -brading.** scrape or rub. —**a·bra'sion**, *n.* —**a·bra'sive**, *adj.*, *n.*

a·brèast', *adv.*, *adj.* **1.** alongside. **2.** side by side.

a·brídge', *v.t.*, **-bridged, -bridging.** shorten; abbreviate. —**a·bridg'ment**, *n.*

a·bróad', *adv.*, *adj.* **1.** outside one's own country. **2.** outdoors. **3.** over a broad area.

ăb'ró·gāte'', *v.t.*, **-gated, -gating.** end or revoke, as a law. —**ab''ro·ga'tion**, *n.*

ăb·rŭpt', *adj.* **1.** sudden. **2.** steep. —**ab·rupt'ly**, *adv.* —**ab·rupt'ness**, *n.*

ăb'scĕss, *n.* area filled with pus.

ăb·scŏnd', *v.i.* leave secretly and hurriedly.

ăb·sĕnt', *adj.* not present. —*v.t.* remove. —**ab'sence**, *n.* —**ab'sent·ly**, *adv.*

ăb''sĕn·tēe', *n.* absent person. —**ab''sen·tee'ism**, *n.*

ăb·sĕnt-mīnd'ĕd, *adj.* **1.** not paying attention. **2.** forgetful.

ăb'só·lūte, *adj.* **1.** perfect. **2.** pure; unqualified. **3.** unrestricted. —*n.* **4.** that which is perfect, pure, or unmodified. —**ab''so·lute'ly**, *adv.*

ăb·sólve', *v.t.*, **-solved, -solving.** free from blame or guilt. —**ab''so·lu'tion**, *n.*

ăb·sòrb', *v.t.* **1.** take in, as a fluid. **2.** get the attention of; fascinate. —**ab·sorb'ent**, *adj.*, *n.* —**ab·sorp'tive**, *adj.* —**ab·sorp'tion**, *n.*

ăb·stáin', *v.i.* refrain. —**ab·sten'tion**, **ab'sti·nence**, *n.* —**ab'sti·nent**, *adj.*

ăb·stē'mi·óus, *adj.* abstaining from excess.

ăb'străct, *adj.* **1.** reduced to essentials. **2.** non-material; non-specific. —*n.* **3.** summary; abridgment. —*v.t.* (ăb·străct') **4.** remove, esp. in a theft. **5.** summarize; abridge. **6.** cause attention to wander. —**ab·strac'tion**, *n.*

ăb·strūse', *adj.* hard to understand.

ăb·sûrd', *adj.* nonsensical. —**ab·surd'ly**, *adv.* —**ab·surd'i·ty**, **ab·surd'ness**, *n.*

a·bŭn'dánce, *n.* great supply. —**a·bun'dant**, *adj.* —**a·bun'dant·ly**, *adv.*

a·būse', *v.t.*, **-bused, -busing**, *n. v.t.* **1.** use or treat wrongly. —*n.* **2.** wrong use or treatment. **3.** insult. —**a·bus'ive**, *adj.*

a·bŭt', *v.i.*, **-butted, -butting.** meet at an edge or end; border.

a·bŭt'mĕnt, *n.* construction touching or helping to support another construction.

a·bўs'mál, *adj.* measureless in depth; bottomless.

a·bўss', *n.* **1.** great depth; chasm. **2.** hell.

a·cā'cià, *n.* tropical plant with white or yellow flowers.

ăc''à·dĕm'ĭc, *adj.* **1.** pertaining to scholarship. **2.** unconnected with actuality; theoretical.

a·cǎd'e·mў, *n.* **1.** school. **2.** cultural organization. —**a·ca''de·mi'cian**, *n.*

ăc·cēde', *v.i.*, **-ceded, -ceding.** consent.

ăc·cĕl'êr·āte'', *v.* **-ated, -ating.** *v.t.*, *v.i.* increase in speed. —**ac·cel''er·a'tion**, *n.*

ăc·cĕl'êr·ā''tòr, *n.* vehicle speed control.

ăc'cĕnt, *n.* **1.** emphasis. **2.** national or regional manner of pronouncing. —*v.t.* (ăc·cent') **3.** emphasize; stress.

ăc·cĕn'tù·āte'', *v.t.*, **-ated, -ating.** emphasize; stress. —**ac·cen·tu·a'tion**, *n.*

ăc·cĕpt', *v.t.* **1.** receive or take willingly. **2.** agree to. —**ac·cept'a·ble**, *adj.* —**ac·cept'a·bly**, *adv.* —**ac·cept''a·bil'i·ty**, *n.* —**ac·cept'ance**, *n.*

ăc'cĕss, *n.* **1.** means or way of approach. **2.** right of approach. **3.** outburst; attack.

ăc·cĕs'si·blĕ, *adj.* readily approached or reached. —**ac·ces''si·bil'i·ty**, *n.*

ăc·cĕs'sion, *n.* **1.** increase or addition. **2.** assumption of office or position.

ăc·cĕs·sō'rў, *n.*, *pl.* **-ries. 1.** additional working part, decorative object, etc. **2.** companion in a crime.

ăc'ci·dĕnt, *n.* unexpected event, usually undesirable. —**ac''ci·den'tal**, *adj.* —**ac''ci·den'tal·ly**, *adv.*

ăc·clāim', *v.t.* **1.** applaud; cheer. —*n.* **2.** applause. —**ac''cla·ma'tion**, *n.*

ăc'cli·māte'', *v.t.*, **-ated, -ating.** accustom to a new environment. Also, **ac·clim'a·tize''**.

ăc·clĭv'ĭ·tў, *n.*, *pl.* **-ties.** upward slope.

ac·cŏm'mò·dāte'', *v.t.*, **-dated, -dating.**
1. provide with food, lodging, etc. 2. adjust to existing conditions. 3. help with a loan, favor, etc. —**ac·com''mo·da'tion**, *n.* —**ac·com'mo·dat''ing**, *adj.*

ac·cŏm''mò·dā'tions, *n., pl.* lodgings, esp. temporary ones.

ac·cŏm'pà·nì·měnt, *n.* 1. something used with another thing; accessory. 2. music used to supplement that of a singer, soloist, etc.

ac·cŏm'pà·nist, *n.* player of a musical accompaniment.

ac·cŏm'pà·nў, *v.t.*, **-nied, -nying.** 1. travel with. 2. provide a musical accompaniment for.

ac·cŏm'plĭce, *n.* associate, especially in crime.

ac·cŏm'plĭsh, *v.t.* succeed in doing. —**ac·com'plish·ment**, *n.*

ac·cŏm'plĭshed, *adj.* 1. completed. 2. highly skilled.

ac·côrd', *v.t.* 1. grant, as a favor. 2. cause to be in agreement or harmony. —*v.i.* 3. be in agreement or harmony. —*n.* 4. agreement; harmony. 5. consent. —**ac·cord'ance**, *n.* —**ac·cord'ant**, *adj.*

ac·côrd'ing, *adj., adv.* 1. in accordance. 2. **according to, a.** in accordance with. **b.** as stated by.

ac·côrd'ing·lў, *adv.* 1. as is indicated or prescribed. 2. therefore.

ac·côr'dĭ·òn, *n.* reed instrument with keyboard and bellows. —**ac·cor'di·on·ist**, *n.*

ac·cŏst', *v.t.* approach and catch the attention of.

ac·cŏunt', *v.t.* 1. regard as. —*v.i.* 2. **account for, a.** explain or interpret. **b.** justify. **c.** be condemned or punished for. —*n.* 3. story; narrative. 4. explanation. 5. justification. 6. importance. 7. set of business transactions involving one client or customer. 8. business record.

ac·cŏunt'à·ble, *adj.* answerable; responsible.

ac·cŏunt'ĭng, *n.* keeping or interpretation of business accounts. —**ac·count'ant**, *n.* —**ac·count'an·cy**, *n.*

ac·cŏu'têr·měnt, *n.* piece of clothing or equipment carried on the person.

ac·crĕd'ĭt, *v.t.* 1. certify as competent or

valid. 2. attribute. —**ac·cred''it·a'tion**, *n.*

ac·crē'tion, *n.* growth, esp. by accumulation.

ac·crūe', *v.i.* be added, esp. in a regular way. —**ac·cru'al**, *n.*

ac·cū'mū·lāte'', *v.*, **-lated, -lating.** *v.i.* gather; collect. —**ac·cu''mu·la'tion**, *n.* —**ac·cu'mu·la''tive**, *adj.* —**ac·cu'mu·la''tor**, *n.*

ăc'cū·ràte, *adj.* correct; truthful. —**ac'cu·ra·cy, ac'cu·rate·ness**, *n.*

ac·cûrs'ĕd, *adj.* 1. under a curse. 2. damnable.

ac·cū'sà·tĭve, *n.* grammatical case for direct object of verb. —**ac·cu'sa·tive**, *adj.*

ac·cūse', *v.t.*, **-cused, -cusing.** denounce; blame. —**ac·cus'er**, *n.* —**ac''cu·sa'tion**, *n.*

ac·cŭs'tòm, *v.t.* cause to become used to something.

ac·cŭs'tómed, *adj.* usual; customary.

āce, *n.* 1. playing card with one pip. 2. leading expert.

a·cěr'bi·tў, *n.* harshness of temper or speech.

ăc'ē·tāte'', *n.* fiber or fabric derived from cellulose.

a·cět'ў·lēne, *n.* highly inflammable gas.

āche, *v.i.*, **ached, aching**, *v.i.* 1. suffer dull pain. —*n.* 2. dull pain.

a·chiēve', *v.t.*, **-chieved, -chieving.** succeed in reaching, finishing, or fulfilling. —**a·chieve'ment**, *n.*

ăc'ĭd, *n.* 1. chemical compound reacting with base to form salt. 2. sour substance. —*adj.* 4. pertaining to acids. 5. sour. —**a·cid'i·ty**, *n.* —**a·cid'ic**, *adj.*

a·cĭd'ū·loŭs, *adj.* containing or suggesting acid.

ac·knŏwl'ĕdge, *v.t.*, **-edged, -edging.** 1. admit as true or valid. 2. show appreciation or gratitude for. —**ac·knowl'edg·ment**, *n.*

ăc'mē, *n.* summit.

ac'nē, *n.* skin complaint.

ăc'ò·lўte, *n.* priest's assistant; altar boy.

ā'côrn, *n.* nut of an oak tree.

a·coŭs'tĭc, *adj.* pertaining to transmission or reception of sound through air, etc. Also, **a·cous'ti·cal.** —**a·cous'ti·cal·ly**, *adv.*

a·coùs'tics, *n*. **1.** *sing*. science of transmission of sound through air, etc. **2.** *pl*. acoustic properties.

ac·quaint', *v.t.* **1.** make known. **2.** make familiar. —ac·quain'tance, *n*.

ăc''qui·ĕsce', *v.i.*, -esced, -escing. consent or comply. —ac''qui·es'cence, *n*. —ac''qui·es'cent, *adj*.

ac·quire', *v.t.*, -quired, -quiring. obtain; get.

ăc''qui·sĭ'tion, *n*. **1.** act or instance of acquiring. **2.** something acquired.

ăc·quĭs'i·tĭve, *adj*. **1.** pertaining to acquisition. **2.** greedy, grasping.

ac·quĭt', *v.t.*, -quitted, -quitting. **1.** release from blame or detention. **2.** conduct; behave. —ac·quit'tal, *n*.

ā'cre, *n*. land area equal to 43,560 square feet or 4,047 square meters. —a'cre·age, *n*.

ăc'rid, *adj*. harsh and bitter.

ăc'ri·mō''nў, *n*. harshness of manner or expression. —ac''ri·mo'ni·ous, *adj*.

ăc'rō·băt', *n*. gymnastic entertainer, esp. one performing high above the ground. —ac'ro·bat'ic, *adj*.

ăc'rō·nўm, *n*. word formed from the initial letters of a phrase or title, as *NASA*.

a·crŏss', *prep*. **1.** from one side to the other of. **2.** on the other side. —*adv*. **3.** from one side to the other.

ăct, *n*. **1.** something done. **2.** law. **3.** one of the main divisions of a play, etc. —*v.i.* **4.** do something. **5.** conduct oneself. **6.** have an effect on something. **7.** perform in a play or plays.

ăct'ĭng, *n*. **1.** the profession of one who performs in plays. —*adj*. **2.** temporarily performing a specified function.

ăc'tion, *n*. **1.** state of being active. **2.** something done. **3.** *Informal*. interesting activity. **4.** combat. **5.** lawsuit.

ăc'ti·văte'', *v.t.*, -vated, -vating. cause to be active. —ac''ti·va'tion, *n*.

ăc'tĭve, *adj*. **1.** performing actions. **2.** having an effect. **3.** *Grammar*. pertaining to verbs whose subjects act rather than being acted on. —ac'tive·ly, *adv*.

ăc·tĭv'i·tў, *n.*, *pl*. -ties. action, esp. one of a number performed in a sequence.

ăc'tôr, *n*. person, especially a man performing in plays. Also, *fem.*, ac'tress.

ăc'tū·ăl, *adj*. **1.** really existing. **2.** presently existing. —ac''tu·al'i·ty, *n*.

ăc'tū·ăl·lў, *adv*. **1.** really. **2.** presently. **3.** in fact; nevertheless.

ăc''tū·ăr'ў, *n.*, *pl*. -aries. mathematician for an insurance company. —ac''tu·ar'i·al, *adj*.

ăc'tū·āte', *v.t.*, -ated, -ating. cause to act.

a·cū'mĕn, *n*. sharpness of mind.

a·cūte', *adj*. **1.** sharp. **2.** mentally keen. **3.** highly sensitive or perceptive. **4.** severely threatening or distressing. —a·cute'ly, *adv*. —a·cute'ness, *n*.

ăd'age, *n*. old saying.

a·dä'gĭō, *adj. Music*. slow.

ăd'a·mánt, *adj*. unyielding.

a·dăpt', *v.t.* change to suit conditions. —a·dapt'a·ble, *adj*. —a''dap·ta'tion, *n*.

ădd, *v.t.* **1.** join to another or others. **2.** compute as a total. —*v.i.* **3.** constitute an addition. —ad·di'tion, *n*. —ad·di'tion·al, *adj*. —ad·di'tion·al·ly, *adv*.

ăd·dĭct', *v.t.* **1.** make dependent on a drug, etc. —*n*. (a'dikt) **2.** addicted person. —ad·dic'tion, *n*.

ăd'dle, *v.t.*, -dled, -dling. confuse; muddle.

ăd·drĕss', *n*. **1.** speech; oration. **2.** location of a business, residence, etc. **3.** skill. —*v.t.* **4.** speak to formally. **5.** direct as a message. **6.** apply. —ad''dres·see', *n*.

ăd·dūce', *v.t.*, -duced, -ducing. offer as a reason, proof, or example.

ăd'é·noĭd'', *n*. normal growth in the throat behind the nose.

a·dĕpt', *adj*. **1.** skilled. —*n*. **2.** skilled person; expert.

ăd'é·quate, *adj*. suitable or sufficient. —ad'e·quate·ly, *adv*. —ad'e·qua·cy, *n*.

ăd·hēre', *v.i.*, -hered, -hering. **1.** cling. **2.** be loyal or obedient. —ad·her'ent, *adj*. —ad·her'ence, ad·he'sion, *n*. —ad·he'sive, *adj.*, *n*.

ăd''·hŏc'', *adj*. for one special purpose.

a·dieu' (a dyōō'), *interj.*, *n.*, *pl*. -dieux. *French*. good-bye.

ăd'i·pōse'', *adj*. fatty.

ăd·jā'cĕnt, *adj*. near or adjoining.

ăd'jĕc·tĭve, *n*. word qualifying a noun. —ad''jec·tiv'al, *adj*.

ăd·joĭn', *v.t.* be next to.

ad·journ', *v.t.* **1.** suspend operations of (a meeting, court, etc.). —*v.i.* **2.** suspend operations. —**ad·journ'ment**, *n.*

ad·judge', *v.t.*, **-judged, -judging. 1.** decide or declare formally. **2.** award by legal process.

ad·jud'i·cāte'', *v.t.*, **-cated, -cating.** pass judgment regarding. —**ad·jud''i·ca'tion**, *n.*

ad'junct, *n.* something added.

ad·jūre', *v.t.*, **-jured, -juring. 1.** command formally. **2.** request solemnly.

ad·just', *v.t.* **1.** cause to fit or function properly. **2.** settle. —*v.i.* **3.** adapt oneself. —**ad·just'a·ble**, *adj.* —**ad·just'er, ad·just'or**, *n.* —**ad·just'ment**, *n.*

ad'ju·tant, *n.* assistant to military commander.

ad'-lib', *v.*, **-libbed, -libbing.** *Informal.* improvise while talking.

ad·min'is·ter, *v.t.* **1.** direct or manage. **2.** give, esp. according to prescribed rules.

ad·min''is·tra'tion, *n.* **1.** act or process of administering. **2.** term of office. **3.** officials directing or managing. —**ad·min'is·tra''tive**, *adj.* —**ad·min'is·tra''tor**, *n.*

ad'mi·ral, *n.* naval officer of the highest rank.

ad'mi·ral·ty, *n.*, *pl.* **-ies.** naval administrative department.

ad·mīre', *v.t.*, **-mired, -miring.** regard with great respect or pleasure. —**ad'mir·a·ble**, *adj.* —**ad''mi·ra'tion**, *n.* —**ad·mir'er**, *n.*

ad·mis'si·ble, *adj.* **1.** proper for admission. **2.** allowable.

ad·mis'sion, *n.* **1.** act or instance of admitting. **2.** confession. **3.** permission for one to enter a theater, etc.

ad·mit', *v.t.*, **-mitted, -mitting. 1.** allow to enter. **2.** confess or concede. —**ad·mit'tance**, *n.*

ad·mix'ture, *n.* something added to create a mixture.

ad·mon'ish, *v.t.* **1.** urge, esp. as a warning. **2.** reproach. —**ad''mo·ni'tion**, *n.* —**ad·mon'i·to''ry**, *adj.*

a·do', *n.* fussy talk or action.

a·dō'be, *n.* dried, unfired brick.

ad''o·les'cence, *n.* youth between puberty and physical maturity. —**ad''o·les'cent**, *adj.*, *n.*

a·dōpt', *v.t.* take as one's own. —**a·dop'tion**, *n.*

a·dōre', *v.t.*, **-dored, -doring.** worship. —**a''do·ra'tion**, *n.* —**a·dor'a·ble**, *adj.*

a·dôrn', *v.t.* decorate. —**a·dorn'ment**, *n.*

a·drĕn'a·līn, *n.* hormone promoting vigorous bodily action.

a·drīft', *adj.*, *adv.* drifting.

a·droĭt', *adj.* clever. —**a·droit'ly**, *adv.* —**a·droit'ness**, *n.*

ad''u·lā'tion, *n.* excessive praise or respect.

a·dŭlt', *n.* **1.** physically mature person or animal. —*adj.* **2.** physically mature. —**a·dult'hood**, *n.*

a·dŭl'tĕr·āte'', *v.t.*, **-ated, -ating.** add undesirable ingredients to. —**a·dul'ter·a'tion**, *n.*

a·dŭl'tĕr·ĕr, *n.* committer of adultery. Also, *fem.*, **a·dul'ter·ess.**

a·dŭl'tĕr·y̆, *n.*, *pl.* **-ies.** *n.* infidelity of a spouse. —**a·dul'ter·ous**, *adj.*

ad·vănce', *v.*, **-vanced, -vancing**, *n.*, *adj.* *v.t.* **1.** move forward. **2.** suggest for consideration. **3.** pay before earned. —*v.i.* **4.** move forward. —*n.* **5.** motion forward. **6.** act intended to secure favor or friendship. **7.** improvement. **8.** sum to be repaid in money or work. **9.** promotion. —*adj.* **10.** early. —**ad·vance'ment**, *n.*

ad·văn'tage, *n.* **1.** more favorable situation. **2.** benefit. —**ad''van·ta'geous**, *adj.*

ad'vĕnt, **1.** arrival. **2. Advent, a.** coming of Christ. **b.** period before Christmas.

ad''vĕn·tî'tioŭs, *adj.* coming or happening by accident.

ad·vĕn'tūre, *n.*, *v.*, **-tured, -turing.** *n.* **1.** risky undertaking. **2.** thrilling or exciting experience. —*v.t.* undertake with risk. —*v.i.* **4.** seek adventures. —**ad·ven'tur·er**, *n.* —**ad·ven'tur·ous**, *adj.*

ad'vĕrb, *n. Grammar.* word modifying a verb. —**ad·ver'bi·al**, *adj.*

ad'vĕr·sār''y̆, *n.*, *pl.* **-saries.** opponent or enemy.

ad·vĕrse', *adj.* opposing or unfavorable. —**ad·verse'ly**, *adv.*

ad·vĕr'sĭ·ty̆, *n.*, *pl.* **-ties.** difficulty or misfortune.

ad·vĕrt', *v.i.* refer.

ăd'vêr·tīse, v., -tised, -tising. v.t. **1.** call
attention to in order to elicit a public response. —v.i. **2.** request something publicly. —ad'ver·tis''er, n. —ad''ver·
tise'ment, n. —ad'ver·tis''ing, n.

ăd·vīce', n. **1.** opinion urging choice or rejection of a course of action. **2.** piece of
information.

ăd·vīs'a·ble, adj. to be advised; desirable. —ad·vis''a·bil'i·ty, n.

ăd·vīse', v.t., -vised, -vising. **1.** urge to
choose or reject a course of action. **2.**
recommend. **3.** give information. —ad·
vis'er, ad·vis'or, n. —ad·vi'so·ry,
adj.

ăd·vīse'ment, n. thought; consideration.

ăd'vo·cāte, n. **1.** person arguing one side
of a dispute, esp. a lawyer. —v.t. **2.** ăd'
vō·cāte, to argue in favor of. —ad'vo·
ca·cy, n.

ădz, n. long-handled tool for dressing
wood. Also, **adze.**

aē·gĭs, n. sponsorship.

aē·ŏn, n. extremely long time.

āer'āte, v.t., -ated, -ating. expose to air.

āer'ĭ·ăl, adj. **1.** in or of the air. **2.** pertaining to aviation. —n. **3.** antenna for
sending or receiving radio waves.

ā'e·rō''bĭcs, n. exercises to strengthen
circulation and respiration.

āer''ō·dȳ·năm'ĭcs, n. study of the dy-
namics of gases in motion. —aer''o·dy·
nam'ic, adj.

āer''o·nău'tĭcs, n. science of flying.
—aer''o·nau'ti·cal, adj.

āer''ō·sŏl, n. liquid applied by spraying
from a pressurized container.

āer''ō·spāce'', n. all space, including the
earth's atmosphere.

aĕs'thēte'', n. person sensitive to art or
beauty.

aĕs·thĕt'ĭc, adj. **1.** pertaining to beauty.
2. sensitive to art or beauty. —n. **3.** aes·
thet'ics, study of art or beauty.

à·fär', adv. at a great distance.

ăf'fa·ble, adj. cordial; pleasant. —af''
fa·bil'i·ty, n.

ăf·fāir', n. **1.** business matter. **2.** event. **3.**
amorous relationship.

ăf·fĕct', v.t. **1.** have influence on. **2.** move
emotionally. **3.** make an affectation of.

ăf''fĕc·tā'tion, n. pretentious manner-
ism.

ăf·fĕct'ĕd, adj. **1.** characterized by affectation. **2.** moved emotionally.

ăf·fĕct'ĭng, adj. emotionally moving.

ăf·fĕc'tion, adj. **1.** love. **2.** sickness.

ăf·fĕc'tion·āte, adj. loving.

ăf''fĭ·dā'vĭt, n. sworn written statement.

ăf·fĭl'ĭ·āte, v.t., -ated, -ating, n. v.t. **1.**
combine, as independent businesses for
mutual benefit. —n. **2.** ăf·fĭl'ĭ·āte, af-
filiated business, etc. —af·fil'i·a'tion,
n.

ăf·fĭn'ĭ·tȳ, n., pl. -ties. **1.** attraction. **2.**
similarity.

ăf·fĭrm', v.t. **1.** state emphatically. **2.** confirm; ratify. —af''fir·ma'tion, n.
—af·fir'ma·tive, adj.

ăf·fĭx', v.t. attach.

ăf·flĭct', v.t. trouble. —af·flic'tion, n.

ăf'flū·ent, adj. prosperous. —af'flu·
ence, n.

ăf·fôrd', v.t. **1.** have enough money or
other resources. **2.** supply; provide.

ăf·frāy', n. fight.

ăf·frŏnt', v.t. **1.** insult or challenge openly.
—n. **2.** open insult or challenge.

à·fīre', adv., adj. on fire. Also, **a·flame'.**

à·flōat', adv., adj. floating.

à·fŏŏt', adv., adj. **1.** on foot. **2.** in action
or in progress.

à·fôre'said, adj. previously said.

à·frāid', adj. **1.** full of fear. **2.** unable because of fear. **3.** regretful, as because of
inability.

à·frĕsh', adv. from the beginning again.

ăft, adv., adj. Nautical. toward or at the
stern.

ăf'tĕr, prep. **1.** behind. **2.** later than. **3.**
lower in rank or importance. **4.** in
search or pursuit of. **5.** in imitation of.
—adv. **6.** behind. **7.** later.

ăf'tĕr·ĕf·fĕct'', n. later consequence.

ăf'tĕr·māth'', n. consequence, usually
unfavorable.

ăf''tĕr·nŏŏn', n. period after noon and
before evening.

ăf'tĕr·thŏught'', n. belated thought.

ăf'tĕr·wârd, adv. later. Also, **af'ter·
wards.**

à·gain', adv. **1.** once more. **2.** besides.

à·gainst', prep. **1.** toward or into contact
with. **2.** opposed or hostile to.

āge, n., v., aged, aging. n. **1.** remoteness
in time of birth or origin. **2.** distinctive

period of history, geology, etc. **3. of age,** legally mature. —*v.t.* **4.** bring or allow to come to ripeness or maturity. —*v.i.* **5.** become old.

ā'gĕd, *adj.* 1. of a specified age. **2. the aged,** old people.

āge''ĭs·m, *n.* discrimination against the elderly.

āge'lĕss, *adj.* unaffected by time or age.

ā'gĕn·cў, *n., pl.* **-cies. 1.** office handling business for others. **2.** government office. **3.** active force. **4.** means.

a·gĕn'dă, *n., pl.* business matters to be dealt with.

ā'gĕnt, *n.* **1.** person handling business for others. **2.** government official. **3.** active force or substance.

ag·glŏm'ĕr·āte, *v.,* -ated, -ating. *n., adj., v.t., v.i.* **1.** gather into a mass. —*n.* **2. ag·glŏm'ĕr·ăte,** mass of miscellaneous things. —*adj.* **3.** gathered into a mass. —**ag·glom''er·a'tion,** *n.*

ag·grăn'dīze, *v.t.,* -dized, -dizing. increase in power, status, wealth, etc. —**ag·gran'dize·ment,** *n.*

ăg'grā·vāte'', *v.t.,* -vated, -vating. **1.** make worse. **2.** annoy. —**ag''gra·va'tion,** *n.*

ăg'grē·gāte'', *v., -*gated, -gating, *adj., n. v.t., v.i.* **1.** collect or gather. —*adj.* **ăg'grē·gate.** **2.** total; collective. —*n.* **3.** sum; total. —**ag''gre·ga'tion,** *n.*

ag·grĕs'sion, *n.* hostile act or policy. —**ag·gres'sor,** *n.*

ag·grĕs'sĭve, *adj.* **1.** disposed to commit aggressions. **2.** forceful, as in business.

ag·grieve', *v.t.,* -grieved, -grieving. wrong or offend seriously.

a·ghăst', *adj.* horrified.

ă'gĭle, *adj.* nimble; deft. —**a·gil'i·ty,** *n.*

ă'gĭ·tāte'', *v.t.,* -tated, -tating. **1.** shake violently. **2.** disturb emotionally. —**a'' gi·ta'tion,** *n.*

a·glōw', *adj., adv.* glowing.

ăg·nŏs'tĭc, *n.* person regarding the existence of God as unknowable.

a·gō', *adj., adv.* in the past.

a·gŏg', *adj.* eager and excited.

ăg'ō·nīze, *v.t.,* -nized, -nizing. put in agony.

ă'gŏ·nў, *n., pl.* **-ies.** intense suffering.

a·grăr'ĭ·ăn, *adj.* pertaining to farming or the country.

a·grēe', *v.* **agreed, agreeing.** *v.i.* **1.** consent or promise. **2.** be of the same opinion. **3.** be harmonious or in accord. **4.** match exactly. —*v.t.* **5.** concede as true. —**a·gree'ment,** *n.*

a·grēe'a·ble, *adj.* 1 pleasant. **2.** reacting favorably. —**a·gree'a·bly,** *adv.*

ăg'rĭ·cŭl''tūre, *n.* science or occupation of farming. —**ag''ri·cul'tur·al,** *adj.*

a·groŭnd', *adj., adv.* (of a ship) in water too shallow for floating.

a·hĕad', *adv., adj.* **1.** in front. **2.** with an advantage over competitors.

āid, *n., v.* help.

āide-dė-cămp, *n., pl.* **aides-de-camp.** assistant military officer.

ĀIDS, acquired immune deficiency syndrome.

āil, *v.t.* distress or sicken. —**ail'ment,** *n.*

āil'ĕr·ŏn, *n.* the part of an airplane wing that controls rolling.

āim, *v.t.* **1.** point, as for shooting. **2.** intend. —*v.i.* **3.** point a gun, etc. —*n.* **4.** act of pointing a gun, etc. **5.** intention or goal.

āim'lĕss, *adj.* without a goal or purpose.

āin't, *v.i., Dialect.* am, is, or are not.

āir, *n.* **1.** gas compound surrounding the earth. **2.** appearance as derived from action, facial expression, etc. **3.** song or melody. **4. airs,** affectations. —*v.t.* **5.** ventilate.

āir'bôrne'', *adj.* flying.

āir con·dī''tion·ing, treatment of air to control purity, temperature, and humidity. —**air conditioner,** *n.* —**air'con·di'' tion,** *v.t.*

āir'crăft, *n., pl.* **-craft.** flying craft.

āir'field'', *n.* field for taxiing, takeoff, and landing of airplanes.

āir force, flying fighting force.

āir'līne, *n.* company operating regularly scheduled aircraft flights. —**air'lin'' er,** *n.*

āir'plāne, *n.* heavier-than-air flying craft with wings.

āir'pôrt'', *n.* airfield with terminal, storage, and service buildings.

āir'shĭp'', *n.* lighter-than-air flying craft.

āir'tĭght'', *adj.* **1.** preventing passage of air. **2.** unable to be disproven, as an argument.

āir'ў, *adj.,* **airier, airiest. 1.** open to air or

breeze. **2.** loftily situated. **3.** impermanent as air. **4.** flippant; thoughtless. —**air´i·ly,** adv. —**air´i·ness,** n.

aisle, n. **1.** passageway, esp. among seats as in a theater. **2.** a division of a church, esp. between pillars.

a·jâr´, adj., adv. partly open, as a door.

a·kĭm´bō, adj., adv. with hands on hips and elbows out.

a·kĭn´, adj. **1.** of the same family. **2.** of the same sort.

â´´là carte´, with each dish ordered and paid for separately.

a·lăc´ri·tỹ, n. willing readiness.

â´´là mōde´, 1. in fashion. **2.** with ice cream.

a·lârm´, n. **1.** emergency signal. **2.** occasion for fear. **3.** fear —v.t. **4.** startle or frighten.

a·lăs´, interj. exclamation of regret.

ăl·bē´ĭt, conj. even though.

ăl·bĭ´nō, n., pl. **-nos.** person or animal without skin pigmentation.

ăl´bŭm, n. **1.** blank book for mounting photographs, stamps, etc. **2.** blank book for sketching. **3.** booklike container for phonograph records.

ăl·bū´men, n. egg white or similar substance.

ăl´che·mỹ, n. pre-scientific chemistry. —**al´che·mist,** n.

ăl´co·hōl´´, n. colorless liquid used as fuel, intoxicant, etc.

ăl´co·hōl´ĭc, adj. **1.** pertaining to alcohol. —n. **2.** person addicted to alcohol.

ăl´cōve, n. place set back from a larger adjoining space.

ăl´dêr, n. small tree of the birch family.

ăl´dêr·măn, n. city ward representative.

āle, n. strong beerlike drink.

a·lêrt´, adj. **1.** watchful. —v.t., n. **2.** alarm. —**a·lert´ly,** adv. —**a·lert´ness,** n.

ăl´făl´fà, n. fodder plant.

ăl´gaē, n. pl.; sing. **al´ga.** one-celled water plants.

ăl´ge·brà, n. mathematical system based on symbols, not numbers. —**al´´ge·bra´ic,** adj.

ăl´ĭ·às, adv. **1.** otherwise known as. —n. **2.** assumed name.

ăl´ĭ·bī, n., pl. **-bis.** legal plea of absence from the scene of a crime.

ăl´ĭ·èn, adj. **1.** from outside; foreign. —n. **2.** foreigner.

ăl´ĭ·èn·āte´´, v.t., **-ated, -ating. 1.** deprive someone of. **2.** act so as to lose the friendship of. —**al´´i·en·a´tion,** n.

ăl´ĭ·èn·ĭst, n. specialist in mental illness.

a·lĭght´, v.i. **1.** descend, as from a vehicle or animal. —adv., adj. **2.** lighted. **3.** afire.

a·lĭgn, v.t. line up. —**a·lign´ment,** n.

a·līke´, adj. **1.** of the same kind or form. —adv. **2.** in the same way.

ăl´´ĭ·měn·tá·rỹ, adj. pertaining to food or nourishment.

ăl´ĭ·mō´´nỹ, n. allowance paid to one divorced spouse by the other.

a·līve´, adj. **1.** living. **2.** vigorous or lively. **3.** teeming.

ăl´ka·lĭ´´, n., pl. **-lis.** acid-neutralizing chemical. —**al´ka·line´´,** adj.

ăl´ka·lŏĭd´´, n. bitter, alkali-containing chemical.

ăll, adj. **1.** every. **2.** the whole of. —n., pron. **3.** everything or everybody. —adv. **4.** entirely.

Ăl´làh, n. Muslim name for God.

ăl·lāy´, v.t. calm or soothe.

ăl·lēge´, v.t., **-leged, -leging.** assert, esp. without proof. —**al´´le·ga´tion,** n. —**al·leg´ed·ly,** adv.

ăl·lē´gĭance, n. loyalty.

ăl´le·gō´´rỹ, n., pl. **-ies.** story or display using symbols. —**al´´le·gor´i·cal,** adj.

ăl·lêr·gỹ, n., pl. **-gies.** excessive sensitivity to some substance. —**al·ler´gic,** adj.

ăl·lē´vĭ·āte, v.t., **-ated, -ating.** relieve; mitigate. —**al·le´vi·a´´tion,** n.

ăl´lēy, n., pl. **-leys. 1.** narrow service street. **2.** garden walk.

ăl·lī´ánce, n. **1.** combination of independent nations, etc. **2.** treaty for such a combination. **3.** organization or club. **4.** marriage.

ăl·līed´, adj. **1.** joined in an alliance. **2.** closely related.

ăl´´lĭ·gā´tŏr, n. broad-snouted reptile of the southeastern U.S.

ăl·lĭt´´êr·ā´tion, n. use of the same sound to start several succeeding words.

ăl´lō·cāte´´, v.t., **-cated, -cating.** assign or allot. —**al´´lo·ca´tion,** n.

ăl·lŏt´, v.t., **-lotted, -lotting. 1.** distribute

to sharing parties. 2. assign. —**al·lot'ment**, *n*.

all·out', *adj*. without reservation; total.

al·low', *v.t.* 1. permit. 2. give or grant. 3. grant to be true. —**al·low'a·ble**, *adj*. —**al·low'ance**, *n*.

al·loy', *v.t.* 1. mix. 2. weaken; dilute. —*n*. 3. **al'loy**, metal or metals with admixtures.

all'spice'', *n*. spice made from a West Indian berry.

al·lude', *v.i.*, -**luded**, -**luding**. make reference to. —**al·lu'sion**, *n*. —**al·lu'sive**, *adj*.

al·lure', *v.t.*, -**lured**, -**luring**, *n. v.t.* 1. attract temptingly. —*n*. 2. quality of attraction or temptation. —**al·lure'ment**, *n*.

al·lu'vi'um, *n*. soil deposited by moving water. —**al·lu'vi·al**, *adj*.

al·ly', *v.*, -**lied**, -**lying**, *n.*, *pl*. -**lies**. *v.t.*, *v.i.* 1. unite for a common purpose. —*n*. 2. person, country, etc. joined in an alliance.

alma mäter, one's college or secondary school.

al'ma·nac'', *n*. annual publication including a calendar and diverse useful information.

al·might'y, *adj*. 1. totally powerful. —*n*. 2. **the Almighty**, God.

al'mond, *n*. edible nut from a tree.

al'most, *adv*. nearly.

alms, *n.*, *pl*. **alms**. charitable gift or money.

a·loft', *adv.*, *adj*. up high.

a·lone', *adj.*, *adv*. 1. by oneself or itself. 2. only.

a·long', *prep*. 1. in the lengthwise direction of. —*adv*. 2. together with another or others. 3. steadily forward or into the future.

a·long'side'', *prep*. 1. beside. —*adv*. 2. to or at the side.

a·loof'', *adv*. 1. at some distance. —*adj*. 2. showing no interest or concern. —**a·loof'ness**, *n*.

a·loud', *adv*. 1. in the normal volume of voice. 2. loudly.

al'pha·bet'', *n*. all the letters of a language in a customary order. —**al''pha·bet'i·cal**, *adj*. —**al''pha·bet·ize''**, *v.t.*

al·read'y, *adv*. 1. before a stated time. 2. so soon.

al'so, *adv*. additionally.

al'tar, *n*. block or table used for religious ceremonies.

al'ter, *v.t.*, *v.i.* change. —**al''ter·a'tion**, *n*.

al''ter·ca'tion, *n*. quarrel; dispute.

al·ter·nate, *v.*, -**nated**, -**nating**, *adj.*, *n. v.i.* 1. act, appear, etc. in turns. —*v.t.* 2. employ in turns. —*adj*. 3. **al'ter·nate**, acting, appearing, etc. in turns. —*n*. 4. someone or something that acts, appears, etc. in turns. —**al''ter·na'tion**, *n*.

al·ter'na·tive, *n*. 1. other choice. —*adj*. 2. available as another choice.

al·though', *conj*. even though.

al·tim'e·ter, *n*. gauge for measuring altitude.

al'ti·tude'', *n*. height, esp. when considerable.

al'to, *n.*, *pl*. -**tos**. 1. musical range between soprano and tenor. 2. singer, instrument or part with this range.

al''to·geth'er, *adv*. 1. completely. 2. in general.

al'tru·ism'', *n*. concern for others, not oneself. —**al'tru·is'tic**, *adj*. —**al'tru·ist**, *n*.

al'um, *n*. astringent used in medicine.

a·lu'mi·num, *n*. lightweight metal.

a·lum'nus, *n.*, *pl*. -**ni**. school graduate. Also, *fem.*, **a·lum'na**, *pl*. -**nae**.

al'ways, *adv*. 1. all of one's life. 2. forever. 3. continually.

am, *v*. first person present singular indicative of *be*.

a·mal'gam, *n*. a mixture.

a·mal'gam·ate'', *v.*, -**ated**, -**ating**, *v.t.*, *v.i.* form a combination or mixture. —**a·mal''ga·ma'tion**, *n*.

a·mass', *v.t.* gather.

am'a·teur, *n*. 1. non-professional participant. 2. admirer of an art. —*adj*. 3. by or for non-professional participants.

am'a·teur''ish, *adj*. without professional competence.

am'a·to''ry, *adj*. pertaining to love or sex.

a·maze', *v.t.*, -**mazed**, -**mazing**. stun with surprise. —**a·maz'ing**, *adj*. —**a·maze'ment**, *n*.

ăm·băs'sá·dôr, *n.* senior diplomat. —am·bas''sa·do'ri·al, *adj.* —am·bas'sa·dor·ship'', *n.*

ăm'bêr, *n.* **1.** fossil resin. —*adj.* **2.** yellow-brown.

ăm'bêr·grĭs, *n.* whale secretion used for perfume.

ăm''bi·dĕx'trŏus, *adj.* equally able with both hands. —am''bi·dex·ter'i·ty, *n.*

ăm'bĭ·ĕnce, *n.* quality or mood of an environment. Also, am'bi·ance. —am'bi·ent, *adj.*

ăm·bĭg'ŭ·ŏŭs, *adj.* having more than one possible meaning. —am''bi·gu'i·ty, *n.*

ăm·bĭ'tion, *n.* **1.** strong desire for success. **2.** thing whose attainment is strongly desired. —am·bi'tious, *adj.*

ăm'ble, *v.i.,* -bled, -bling, *n. v.i.* **1.** move easily and slowly. —*n.* **2.** easy, slow walk.

ăm·brō'sĭă, *n.* divine food.

ăm'bū·lánce, *n.* vehicle for the sick.

ăm'bū·lá·tō''rŷ, *adj.* able to walk.

ăm'bŭsh, *n.* **1.** concealment for attackers. **2.** attack from a concealed position. —*v.t.* **3.** attack from a concealed position.

á·mēl'iŏ·rāte'', *v.t.,* -rated, -rating. improve. —a·mel''io·ra'tion, *n.*

ă·mĕn', *interj.* so be it.

ă·mĕn'ă·ble, *adj.* agreeable.

á·mĕnd', *v.t.* **1.** alter. **2.** improve. —*n.* **3.** amends, compensation for damage, injury, etc. —a·mend'ment, *n.*

á·mĕn'ĭ·tŷ, *n., pl.* -ties. something agreeable or polite.

Å·mĕr''ĭ·cä''nä, *n. pl.* literature, artifacts, etc. having to do with U.S. history or culture.

Å·mĕr''ĭ·cán·ĭsm, *n.* **1.** partiality to things identified with the U.S. **2.** something characteristic of the U.S.

ăm'é·thŷst, *n.* **1.** violet quartz or corundum. **2.** shade of violet.

ā'mĭ·á·ble, *adj.* creating friendly feelings. —a'mi·a·bly, *adj.* —a''mi·a·bil'i·ty, *n.*

ă'mĭ·cá·ble, *adj.* without hostility or resentment. —a'mi·ca·bly, *adv.*

á·mĭd', *prep.* among. Also, a·midst'.

á·mĭss, *adj.* **1.** not right. —*adv.* **2.** not in the right way.

ăm'ĭ·tŷ, *n.* friendship.

ăm·mō'nĭă, *n.* pungent, water-soluble gas.

ăm''mū·nĭ'tion, *n.* projectiles, together with their charges of gunpowder, etc. fired esp. from guns.

ăm·nē'sĭă, *n.* loss of memory.

ăm'nĕs·tŷ, *n., pl.* -ties. general pardon by a government, esp. for political crimes.

á·mŏk', *adv.* amuck.

á·mòng', *prep.* **1.** surrounded closely by. **2.** in the company or society of. Also, a·mongst'.

á·môr'ăl, *adj.* without a sense of right or wrong.

ăm'ôr·ŏŭs, *adj.* expressing love, esp. sexual love.

á·môr'phoŭs, *adj.* shapeless or formless.

ă'môr·tīze'', *v.t.,* -tized, -tizing. pay off gradually. —am''or·ti·za'tion, *n.*

á·mŏŭnt', *n.* **1.** total. **2.** quantity. —*v.i.* **3.** add up.

á·mour', *n.* love affair.

ăm'pēre, *n.* unit for measuring electric current. —am'per·age, *n.*

ăm·phĭb'ĭ·án, *n.* **1.** animal able to live on land and water. —*adj.* **2.** Also, am·phib'i·ous. able to live on land and water.

ăm'phi·thē''á·têr, *n.* arena or stadium with tiers of seats surrounding the central area. Also, am'phi·the''a·tre.

ăm'ple, *adj.,* ampler, amplest. **1.** copious. **2.** sufficient. —am'ply, *adv.*

ăm'plĭ·fŷ'', *v.t.,* -fied, -fying. **1.** increase in size. **2.** increase in strength, as an electronic signal. —am''pli·fi''er, *n.* —am''pli·fi·ca'tion, *n.*

ăm'plĭ·tŭde'', *n.* **1.** breadth or extent. **2.** abundance.

ăm'pū·tāte', *v.t.,* -tated, -tating. remove, as a limb of a body. —am''pu·ta'tion, *n.* —am''pu·tee', *n.*

á·mŭck', *adv.* in a condition of murderous insanity.

ăm'ū·lĕt, *n.* magical charm worn on the person.

á·mūse', *v.t.,* -mused, -musing. **1.** be funny to. **2.** entertain. —a·muse'ment, *n.*

ăn, *indef. art.* variant of *a,* used when the following word begins with a vowel.

á·năch'rŏn·ĭsm, *n.* something outside its

proper historical period. **—a·nach″**
ron·is′tic, adj.

ăn′á·grăm″, n. word formed from the letters spelling another word.

ā′nàl, adj. pertaining to the anus.

ăn″á·lŏg, n. represented by physical variables.

a·nál′o·gy, n., pl. **-gies.** n. comparison of an unfamiliar thing to a more familiar one. **—a·nal′o·gous,** adj.

a·nál′y·sis, n., pl. **-ses.** 1. separation into component parts. 2. summary of such a separation. 3. psychoanalysis. **—an′a·lyst,** n. **—an″a·lyt′ic, an″a·lyt′ic·al,** adj. **—an′a·lyze′,** v.t.

ăn·âr·chў, n. 1. society without rulers. 2. political or organizational chaos. **—an′ar·chism″,** n. **—an′ar·chist,** n.

a·năth′e·má, n. 1. solemn curse. 2. something hated and despised.

a·năt′o·mў, n. 1. study of the composition of animals and plants. 2. composition of an animal or plant. **—an″a·tom′i·cal,** adj.

ăn″cĕs·tŏr, n. forebear; one from whom a person descends. Also, fem., **an″ces·tress. —an″ces·try,** n.

ăn′chŏr, n. 1. device for mooring a ship or boat. **—v.i.** 2. to secure by anchor.

ăn′chō′vў, n., pl. **-vies.** tiny, salty, herringlike fish.

ān′cient, adj. 1. of the oldest period of human history. 2. very old. **—n.** 3. person, esp. an author or philosopher, of the ancient period. 4. very old person.

ănd, conj. 1. along with. 2. Informal. used instead of the infinitive to.

ănd′ī′·ròn, n. horizontal iron support for firewood, used in pairs.

ăn′ĕc·dōte″, n. true short story.

a·nē′mĭ·á, n. shortage of hemoglobin or red cells in the blood. **—a·ne′mic,** adj.

ăn″es·thē′sïá, n. lack of sensation induced by a gas or drug. **—an″es·thet′ic,** adj., n. **—an·es′the·tize″,** v.t.

a·nēw′, adv. once more.

ān′gĕl, n. messenger or attendant of God. **—an·gel′ic,** adj.

ăn′gêr, n. 1. strong annoyance. **—v.t.** 2. make angry.

ăn·gī′ná pĕc′tó·rĭs, painful heart condition.

ăn′gle, n., v.i., **-gled, gling.** n. 1. divergence of two lines or surfaces that meet. **—v.i.** 2. fish. 3. Informal. use stratagems for personal gain. **—an′gler,** n.

ăn′gle·wŏrm″, n. earthworm.

Ăn′glĭ·căn, n. 1. member of the Church of England or churches in communion with it, e.g. the Episcopal Church. **—adj.** 2. pertaining to the Church of England or churches in communion with it. **—An′gli·can·ism,** n.

Ăn′glō-Săx′ŏn, n. 1. person descended from the Angles and Saxons in England. 2. person of English ancestry. **—adj.** 3. pertaining to or characteristic of the Anglo-Saxons.

ăn′grў, adj. **-grier, -griest.** 1. seriously annoyed. 2. suggesting human anger by action, appearance, etc. **—an′gri·ly,** adv.

ăn′guĭsh, n. intense suffering.

ăn′gū·làr, adj. 1. having angles. 2. conspicuous for angles. **—an″gu·lar′i·ty,** n.

ăn′i·līne, n. benzene derivative used for dyes.

ăn″i·măd·vêrt′, v.i. comment disapprovingly. **—an″i·mad·ver′sion,** n.

ăn′ĭ·mál, n. 1. living thing other than a plant or bacterium. 2. any such thing other than a human being. **—adj.** 3. pertaining to animals.

ăn′i·māte, v.t., **-mated, -mating,** adj. v.t. 1. give life to. 2. make lively. **—adj.** 3. **ăn′i·máte,** having life. **—an″i·ma′tion,** n.

ăn″′ĭ·mŏs′ĭ·tў, n., pl. **-ties.** hostility. Also, **an′i·mus.**

ăn′i·sēed″, n. aromatic seed of the anise plant.

ăn′kle, n. joint between the foot and the leg.

ăn′nàls, n., pl. historical records.

án·nĕx′, v.t. 1. join to a larger existing part. **—n.** 2. **ăn′nĕx,** a part so joined. **—an″nex·a′tion,** n.

án·nī′hĭl·āte″, v.t., **-ated, -ating.** destroy utterly. **—an·ni″hil·a′tion,** n.

ăn″nĭ·vêr′sàr·ў, n., pl. **-ries.** same day of the year as that on which something occurred.

ăn′no·tāte″, v.t., **-tated, -tating.** explain or elaborate with notes. **—an″no·ta′tion,** n.

án·nŏŭnce′, v.t., **-nounced, -nouncing.**

make known, esp. publicly. **—an·noun'·cer,** *n.* **—an·nounce'ment,** *n.*

an·noy', *v.t.* trouble, esp. so as to provoke dislike. **—an·noy'ance,** *n.*

an·nu·al, *adj.* **1.** yearly. **2.** living only one year, as a plant. **—n. 3.** something published once a year. **4.** annual plant. **—an'nu·al·ly,** *adv.*

an·nu'i·ty, *n., pl.* **-ties.** annual income bought from an insurance company.

an·nul', *v.t.,* **-nulled, -nulling.** make legally void. **—an·nul'ment,** *n.*

An·nun''ci·a'tion, *n.* announcement to the Virgin Mary of the impending birth of Christ; celebrated March 25.

an'o·dyne, *n.* pain reliever.

a·noint', *v.t.* put oil, etc. on as part of a ceremony of consecration. **—a·noint'ment,** *n.*

a·nom'a·ly, *n., pl.* **-lies.** something inconsistent or abnormal. **—a·nom'a·lous,** *adj.*

a·non', *adv.* soon.

a·non'y·mous, *adj.* written or spoken by someone whose name is unknown or unpublished. **—an''o·nym'i·ty,** *n.*

an·oth'er, *adj.* **1.** one more. **2.** different. **—n. 3.** one more. **4.** a different one.

an·swer, *n.* **1.** reply to a question. **2.** solution to a problem. **3.** action provoked by something competing. **—v.t. 4.** reply to. **—v.i. 5.** give an answer. **6.** be matching or well-suited. **7.** be accountable or responsible.

an'swer·a·ble, *adj.* **1.** able to be answered. **2.** accountable; responsible.

ant, *n.* small social insect.

an·tag'o·nism, *n.* hostility. **—an·tag'o·nist,** *n.* **—an·tag''o·nis'tic,** *adj.* **—an·tag'o·nize'',** *v.t.*

Ant·arc'tic, *n.* **1.** southernmost zone of the earth. **—adj. 2.** pertaining to this zone.

an''te·cē'dent, *adj.* **1.** coming before. **—n. 2.** something coming before.

an''te·date'', *v.t.,* **-dated, -dating.** precede in time.

an''te·di·lū'vi·an, *adj.* **1.** before the Flood. **2.** from remotest antiquity.

an'te·lope'', *n.* deerlike animal.

an·ten'na, *n., pl.* **—nae** (for 1), **—nas** (for 2). **1.** feeler on the head of an insect.

2. aerial; conductor for sending or receiving radio waves.

an·te'ri·or, *adj.* **1.** previous. **2.** at the front end.

an'te·room'', *n.* room preceding a major room.

an'them, *n.* hymnlike song.

an·thol'o·gy, *n.* book of literary selections.

an'thra·cīte'', *n.* hard coal.

an''thro·poid'', *adj.* **1.** resembling humanity. **—n. 2.** anthropoid animal.

an''thro·pol'o·gy, *n.* study of mankind. **—an''thro·pol'o·gist,** *n.*

an''ti·bi·ot'ic, *n.* substance for destroying or weakening microorganisms.

an''ti·bŏd''y, *n., pl.* **-ies.** blood ingredient that fights foreign substances, e.g. bacteria.

an'tic, *n.* ridiculous or peculiar action.

an·tic'i·pāte'', *v.t.,* **-pated, -pating. 1.** look forward to, esp. with pleasure. **2.** use forethought to deal with. **3.** predict. **—an·tic''i·pa'tion,** *n.*

an''ti·cli'max, *n.* disappointment of increasing expectations. **—an''ti·cli·mac'tic,** *adj.*

an'ti·dōte'', *n.* substance to counteract a poison.

an''ti·his'ta·mine, *n.* substance to counteract allergic reaction.

an·tip'a·thy, *n., pl.* **-thies.** dislike. **—an·tip''a·thet'ic,** *adj.*

an''ti·quar'i·an, *n.* student of antiquities.

an'ti·quar·y, *n., pl.* **-quaries.** *n.* collector or student of antiquities.

an''ti·quat''ed, *adj.* obsolete.

an·tique', *n.* **1.** old manufactured object, esp. a valuable one. **—adj. 2.** ancient.

an·tiq'ui·ty, *n., pl.* **-ties. 1.** ancient times. **2.** something antique.

an''ti·sep'tic, *n.* **1.** substance for destroying harmful bacteria. **—adj. 2.** destroying harmful bacteria.

an''ti·sō'cial, *adj.* **1.** hostile to society. **2.** shunning society.

an·tith'e·sis, *n., pl.* **-ses.** direct opposite. **—an''ti·thet'i·cal,** *adj.*

an''ti·tŏx'in, *n.* substance for counteracting plant, animal, or bacterial toxin.

ant'lêr, *n.* horn of a deer, moose, etc.

ăn′tò·nym″, *n.* word meaning the opposite.

ā′nŭs, *n.* opening at lower end of alimentary canal.

ăn′vĭl, *n.* object on which iron, etc. is rested while being hammered.

ănx·ī·e·tỹ, *n., pl.* **-ies. 1.** fear of possible harm. **2.** eagerness to act. **—anx′ious**, *adj.* **—anx′ious·ly**, *adv.*

an′ỹ, *adj.* **1.** someone, as readily as all others. **2.** every. **—n. 3.** any person or persons.

an′ỹ·bŏd″ỹ, *pron.* some one person, as readily as all others. Also, **an′y·one″**.

an′ỹ·hŏw″, *adv.* **1.** in any way. **2.** whatever the situation is. Also, **an′y·way″**.

an′ỹ·thĭng″, *pron.* **1.** some one thing, as readily as all others. **—n. 2.** something, whatever or how much it may be.

an′ỹ·whĕre″, *adv.* in or into any place. Also, **an′y·place″**.

ā·ôr′ta, *n., pl.* **-as, -ae.** blood vessel from the heart. **—a·or′tic**, *adj.*

a·pärt′, *adv.* **1.** to pieces. **2.** separately.

a·pärt′heid, *n.* racial segregation, esp. in the Union of South Africa.

a·pärt′ment, *n.* series of rooms forming a separate dwelling in a building.

ă′pa·thỹ, *n.* lack of feeling or emotion. **—a″pa·thet′ic**, *adj.* **—a″pa·thet′ic·al·ly**, *adv.*

āpe, *n., v.t.*, **aped, aping.** *n.* **1.** large animal of the monkey family. **—v.t. 2.** imitate.

ăp′ēr·tūre, *n.* opening.

ā′pĕx, *n.* peak.

ăph′o·rĭsm, *n.* brief statement of a truth. **—aph″o·ris′tic**, *adj.*

ăph″rò·dĭs′ĭ·ăc, *n.* drug promoting sexual excitement.

ā′pi·ār″ỹ, *n., pl.* **-ries.** bee farm.

a·piēce′, *adv.* for each.

a·plŏmb′, *n.* self-possession.

Ā·pŏc′a·lỹpse, *n.* revelation to St. John the Apostle. **—a·poc″a·lyp′tic**, *adj.*

Ā·pŏc′rỹ·pha, *n. pl.* biblical books not accepted by Protestants and Jews.

a·pŏc′rỹ·phal, *adj.* highly dubious.

ăp′o·gēe″, *n.* furthest distance of a satellite from its planet.

a·pŏl′″o·gĕt′ĭc, *adj.* confessing oneself to be at fault.

a·pŏl′o·gīze″, *v.i.*, **-gized, -gizing.** confess oneself to be at fault and seek forgiveness.

a·pŏl′o·gỹ, *n., pl.* **-gies. 1.** confession of a fault in search of forgiveness. **2.** statement defending one's actions, etc.

ăp′o·plĕx″ỹ, *n.* bursting of blood vessel with consequent loss of bodily function. **—ap″o·plec′tic**, *adj.*

a·pŏs′tāte″, *n.* renouncer of one's professed faith, etc. **—a·pos′ta·sy**, *n.*

a·pŏs′tle, *n.* **1.** one of the twelve disciples of Christ sent to preach. **2.** preacher of a new faith. **—a″pos·tol′ic**, *adj.*

a·pŏs′trò·phē, *n.* **1.** a sign, ′, used to indicate possessives, omitted letters, plurals involving numerals or initials, etc. **2.** remark made to or as if to some individual in the course of a speech, etc.

a·pŏs′trò·phīze″, *v.t.* **1.** spell with an apostrophe. **2.** address in an apostrophe.

a·pŏth′e·cär″ỹ, *n., pl.* **-ies.** druggist.

ăp·päll′, *v.t.* put in a state of horror or fear. Also, **ap·pal′**. **—ap·pall′ing**, *adj.*

ăp″pa·rā′tŭs, *n.* **1.** instruments, etc. required for an experiment, job, etc. **2.** organizational structure.

ap·păr′ĕl, *n.* **1.** clothes. **—v.t. 2.** clothe.

ap·păr′ĕnt, *adj.* **1.** clear; obvious. **2.** as judged from appearances. **—ap·par′ent·ly**, *adv.*

ăp″pa·rī′tion, *n.* ghost or phantom.

ap·pēal′, *n.* **1.** request for help, mercy, etc. **2.** request for reconsideration. **3.** attractiveness. **—v.t. 4.** request to have reconsidered. **—v.i. 5.** make an appeal. **6.** have appeal.

ap·pēar′, *v.i.* **1.** come into sight. **2.** seem. **—ap·pear′ance**, *n.*

ap·pēase′, *v.t.*, **-peased, -peasing.** satisfy when hostile or demanding. **—ap·pease′ment**, *n.*

ap·pĕl′lànt, *n.* person who appeals, esp. in law.

ap·pĕl′late, *adj.* handling appeals, as a court.

ăp″pĕl·lā′tion, *n.* name given to something or someone.

ap·pĕnd′, *v.t.* add; join. **—ap·pend′age**, *n.*

ăp″pen·dĕc′tò·mỹ, *n., pl.* **-ies.** surgical removal of an appendix.

ap·pĕn″di·cī′tis, *n.* inflammation of the appendix.

ap·pen′dix, *n.*, *pl.* **-dixes, -dices. 1.** supplementary portion at the end of a book, etc. **2.** blind branch of the intestine.

ap·per·tain′, *v.i.* belong.

ap′pe·tite′′, *n.* desire, as for food. **—ap′pe·tiz′′er**, *n.* **—ap′pe·tiz′′ing**, *adj.*

ap·plaud′, *v.t.* show approval of, as by applause.

ap·plause′, *n.* **1.** indications of approval of a dramatic performance, etc. **2.** public recognition and approval.

ap′′ple, *n.* common, crisp fruit, generally red or green.

ap·pli′ance, *n.* machine, etc., esp. for home use.

ap′pli·ca·ble, *adj.* able to be applied.

ap·ply′, *v.*, **-plied, -plying. *v.t.* 1.** place, as on an object or surface. **2.** put to use, as a theory or rule. **3.** devote to a task. **—*v.i.* 4.** make a formal request. **5.** be relevant. **—ap′′pli·ca′tion**, *n.* **—ap′pli·cant**, *n.*

ap·point′ *v.t.* **1.** choose and designate. **2.** provide; furnish. **—ap·poin′tive**, *adj.* **—ap·point′′ee′′**, *n.*

ap·point′ment, *n.* **1.** meeting at a stated time. **2.** selection, as for public office. **3.** provision or furnishing.

ap·por′tion, *v.t.* divide into shares. **—ap·por′tion·ment**, *n.*

ap′po·site, *adj.* appropriate.

ap·praise′, *v.t.*, **-praised, -praising,** estimate the value of. **—ap·prais′er**, *n.* **—ap·prais′al**, *n.*

ap·pre·ci·a·ble, *adj.* **1.** sufficient to be noted. **2.** worthy of note; considerable.

ap·pre′ci·ate′′, *v.*, **-ated, -ating. *v.t.* 1.** be grateful for. **2.** value truly. **—*v.i.* 3.** gain in value. **—ap·pre′′ci·a′tion**, *n.* **—ap·pre′ci·a·tive**, *adj.*

ap′pre·hend′′, *v.t.* **1.** fear. **2.** understand. **3.** capture and arrest. **—ap′′pre·hen′sion**, *n.*

ap′′pre·hen′sive, *adj.* fearful.

ap·pren′tice, *n.*, *v.t.*, **-ticed, -ticing. *n.* 1.** assistant learning a trade. **—*v.t.* 2.** enroll as an apprentice. **—ap·pren′tice·ship′′**, *n.*

ap·prise′, *v.t.*, **-prised, -prising,** inform; notify. Also, **ap·prize′**.

ap·proach′, *v.t.* **1.** come close to. **2.** propose business to. **—*v.i.* 3.** come close. **—*n.* 4.** act or instance of coming close.

5. way of coming close. **6.** manner of taking action.

ap·proach′a·ble, *adj.* willing to be talked with.

ap′′pro·ba′tion, *n.* approval.

ap·pro′pri·ate, *adj.*, *v.t.*, **-ated, -ating. *adj.* 1.** useful or proper. **—*v.t.* 2.** ap·pro′pri′ate′′, reserve for a purpose, as money. **3.** take for oneself. **—ap·pro′′pri·a′tion**, *n.*

ap·prove′, *v.*, **-proved, -proving. *v.t.* 1.** state to be good or suitable. **2.** think favorably of. **—*v.i.* 3.** regard favorably. **—ap·prov′al**, *n.*

ap·prox′i·mate, *adj.*, *v.t.*, **-ated, -ating. *adj.* 1.** reasonably accurate but not precise. **—*v.t.* 2.** amount to as an approximate figure, etc. **—ap·prox′i·mate·ly**, *adv.* **—ap·prox′′i·ma′tion**, *n.*

ap·pur′te·nance, *n.* additional device or feature; accessory.

a′pri·cot′′, *n.* orange-colored peachlike fruit.

A′pril, *n.* fourth month.

a′pron, *n.* covering worn over a dress or trouser front when working.

ap·ro·pos′, *adv.* **1. apropos of,** with regard to. **2.** at the right time. **—*adj.* 3.** to the point; relevant.

apt, *adj.* **1.** displaying a tendency. **2.** likely. **3.** able; intelligent. **—apt′ly**, *adv.* **—apt′ness**, *n.*

ap′ti·tude′′, *n.* talent or ability.

aq′′ua·ma·rine′, *n.* pale bluish-green.

a·quar′i·um, *n.* tank, bowl, etc., usually with glass walls, used for displaying live fish, etc.

a·quat′ic, *adj.* of the water.

aq′ue·duct, *n.* engineering structure for conducting water.

a′que·ous, *adj.* like, of, or created by water.

aq′ui·line′′, *adj.* pertaining to or suggesting eagles.

ar′a·ble, *adj.* good for producing crops.

âr′bit·êr, *n.* judge of controversial matters.

âr′bi·trâr′′y, *adj.* **1.** unreasonable or unjustified. **2.** admitting no discussion or complaint. **3.** chosen at random as a basis for discussion. **—ar′′bi·trar′i·ly**, *adv.*

âr′bi·trāte′′, *v.t.*, **-trated, -trating. 1.**

adjudicate after hearing disputants. **2.** submit for adjudication. —**ar′′bi·tra′tion,** *n.* —**ar′bi·tra′′tor,** *n.*

âr′bor, *n.* shaded walk or garden.

âr·bō′rē·ăl, *adj.* of or inhabiting trees.

âr·bŭ′tŭs, *n.* **1.** shrub with dark green leaves and red berries. **2.** trailing plant with white or pink blossoms.

ârc, *n.* **1.** segment of a circle. **2.** light formed by electricity jumping between electrodes.

âr·cāde′, *n.* **1.** row of arches. **2.** covered walk, esp. one between shops.

ârch, *n.* **1.** curved structure resisting compressive forces. —*v.i.* **2.** bend as an arch does. —*adj.* **3.** chief. **4.** cheerfully mischievous. —**arch′way′′,** *n.*

âr·chā′ĭc, *adj.* **1.** out of date. **2.** ancient.

ârch·ăn·gĕl, *n.* chief angel.

ârch′bĭ′shŏp, *n.* superior bishop.

ârch′dūke′, *n.* Austrian royal prince. Also, *fem.,* **arch′duch′ess.**

âr′′chē·ŏl′ō·gў, *n.* study of ancient cultures through their artifacts. —**ar′′che·ol′o·gist,** *n.* —**ar′′che·o·log′i·cal,** *adj.* Also, **archaeology.**

ârch′êr, *n.* user of a bow and arrow. —**arch′er·y,** *n.*

âr′′chĭ·pĕl′á·gō, *n., pl.* **-gos, -goes. 1.** group of closely spaced islands. **2.** area of water surrounding such a group.

âr′chĭ·tĕct′′, *n.* designer of buildings.

âr′chĭ·tĕc′′tûre, *n.* **1.** art of designing buildings. **2.** a style of building. —**ar′′chi·tec′tur·al,** *adj.*

âr·chĭves, *n. pl.* official records.

Ârc′tĭc, *n.* **1.** northernmost zone of the earth. —*adj.* **2.** pertaining to this zone.

âr′dĕnt, *adj.* eager. —**ar′dent·ly,** *adv.*

âr′dôr, *n.* eagerness; zeal.

âr′dū·oŭs, *adj.* difficult or tedious.

âre, *v.* present indicative plural of *be.*

âr′ē·á, *n.* **1.** surface measure. **2.** region.

ārēá cōde, three-digit code used in telephoning indicating a region.

á·rē′ná, *n.* large space for athletic contests and spectators.

âr′gŏn, *n.* chemical element, an inert gas.

âr′gò·sў, *n., pl.* **-sies.** *Poetic.* large merchant ship or merchant fleet.

âr′gūe, *v.,* **-gued, -guing.** *v.i.* **1.** express a difference or differences of opinion. **2.** offer reasons for or against something.

—*v.t.* **3.** present as true or valid. **4.** express differences of opinion over. —**ar′gu·ment,** *n.* —**ar′′gu·men·ta′tion,** *n.*

âr′′gū·měn′tá·tĭve, *adj.* given to argument or quarreling.

â′rĭ·á, *n.* song, as in an opera.

ā′rĭd, *adj.* dry. —**a·rid′i·ty,** *n.*

á·rīse′, *v.i.,* **arose, arisen, arising. 1.** get up. **2.** happen.

âr′′ĭs·tŏc′rá·cў, *n., pl.* **-cies. 1.** government by a small hereditary or select class. **2.** such a class. —**a·ris′to·crat,** *n.* —**a·ris′′to·crat′ic,** *adj.*

á·rĭth′mě·tĭc, *n.* calculation with numerals. —**ar′′ith·met′i·cal,** *adj.*

ârk, *n.* **1.** vessel of Noah. **2.** wooden chest.

ârm, *n.* **1.** upper human limb. **2.** anything suggesting this by form, position, or function. **3.** weapon. **4. arms,** the military profession. —*v.t.* **5.** equip with weapons.

âr·mâ′dá, *n.* fleet of fighting ships or airplanes.

Âr′′má·gĕd′dòn, *n.* major decisive battle.

ârm′′á·mĕnt, *n.* weapons with which a ship, airplane, etc. is equipped.

ârm′chāir′′, *n.* chair with arm supports.

ârm′fŭl′′, *n., pl.* **-fuls.** amount that can be held in one or both arms.

âr′mi·stice, *n.* suspension of hostilities; truce.

âr′mŏr, *n.* material, usually metal, protecting against weapons and missiles. —**ar′mored,** *adj.*

âr′mŏr·ў, *n., pl.* **-ies. 1.** building for military activities and equipment storage. **2.** place for storing weapons.

ârm′pĭt′′, *n.* area beneath the arm at the shoulder.

âr′mў, *n., pl.* **-mies. 1.** land military force. **2.** large number of persons.

á·rō′má, *n.* scent; odor. —**ar′′o·mat′ic,** *adj.*

á·rŏund′, *prep.* **1.** on all sides of. **2.** in any or all areas of. —*adv.* **3.** on all sides. **4.** in any or all areas. **5.** *Informal.* **a.** nearby. **b.** idly or aimlessly.

á·rŏuse′, *v.t.,* **aroused, arousing. 1.** awaken. **2.** call into activity. —**a·rous′al,** *n.*

âr·rāign′, *v.t.* **1.** bring to court as a defendant. **2.** accuse. —**ar·raign′ment,** *n.*

ar·range', v., **-ranged, -ranging.** v.t. **1.** put in order. —v.t., v.i. **2.** plan; prepare. —**ar·range'ment,** n.

ar'rant, adj. utter; downright.

ar·ray', v.t. **1.** arrange. **2.** dress. —n. **3.** order or arrangement. **4.** clothing.

ar·rears', n. pl. things overdue, esp. payments.

ar·rest', v.t. **1.** seize because of the commission of a crime. **2.** stop. —n. **3.** act or instance of arresting. **4.** state of being arrested.

ar·rive', v.i. **1.** come to a place. **2.** happen. —**ar·riv'al,** n.

ar'ro·gant, adj. proud and insolent. —**ar'ro·gant·ly,** adv. —**ar'ro·gance,** n.

ar'ro·gate'', v.t., **-gated, -gating.** claim or seize unjustly. —**ar''ro·ga'tion,** n.

ar'row, n. missile shot from a bow.

ar·roy'o, n., pl. **-os.** Southwest U.S. gully.

ar'se·nal, n. place for making or storing weapons.

ar'se·nic, n. silvery-white poisonous chemical element.

ar'son, n. crime of burning buildings, etc. —**ar'son·ist,** n.

art, n. **1.** activity of creating things that arouse the emotions through one or more senses. **2.** things so created. **3.** skill or profession. **4.** cunning.

ar'ter·y, n., pl. **-ies. 1.** major blood vessel. **2.** main line of travel or communication. —**ar·te'ri·al,** adj.

ar·te·si·an well, n. well whose opening is lower than the head of water supplying it.

art'ful, adj. cunning.

ar·thri'tis, n. inflammation of a joint of the body. —**ar·thrit'ic,** adj.

ar'ti·choke, n. edible flower head of thistlelike plant.

ar'ti·cle, n. **1.** object for use. **2.** writing on a factual subject. **3.** Grammar. **a, an,** or **the.**

ar·tic'u·late, adj., v., **-lated, -lating.** adj. **1.** readily understood. **2.** able in speech. **3.** jointed. —v.t. (är tĭc'ū läte'') **4.** express clearly. **5.** arrange in a clear and orderly manner. **6.** assemble with joints. —v.i. **7.** speak clearly. —**ar·tic'u·la'tion,** n.

ar'ti·fice, n. **1.** cunning. **2.** cunning action. **3.** insincere behavior.

ar'tif·i·cer, n. craftsman.

ar''ti·fi'cial, adj. **1.** manufactured, esp. in imitation. **2.** contrived or affected. —**ar''ti·fi'cial·ly,** adv. —**ar''ti·fi·ci·al'i·ty,** n.

ar·til'ler·y, n. **1.** guns or other devices for shooting large missiles. **2.** army branch handling such devices.

ar'ti·san, n. craftsman.

art'ist, n. practitioner of an art. —**ar·tist'ic,** adj. —**ar'tist·ry,** n.

art'less, adj. unaffected; natural.

art'y, adj., **-ier, -iest.** feigning artistic sensitivity.

as, adv. **1.** equally. **2.** for example. **3.** if and when. —conj. **4.** equally to. **5.** in the manner that. **6.** while. **7.** because; since. **8.** though. —pron. **9.** that. —prep. **10.** in the guise of.

as·bes'tos, n. fibrous mineral used in fireproofing.

as·cen'dan·cy, n. **1.** domination. **2.** rise to power. Also, **as·cen'den·cy.**

as·cend', v.t., v.i. climb or rise. —**as·cent',** n. —**as·cen'dent,** adj.

As·cen'sion, n. ascent of Christ into heaven, celebrated 40 days after Easter.

as·cer'tain, v.t. find out.

as·cet'ic, adj. **1.** without pleasure or self-indulgence. —n. **2.** one who lives an ascetic life. —**as·cet'i·cism,** n.

as·cribe', v.t., **-scribed, -scribing.** relate to a supposed cause. —**as·crip'tion,** n.

a·sep'sis, n. absence of disease producing germs. —**a·sep'tic,** adj.

ash, n., pl. **ashes. 1.** remainder of something not fully burnt. **2.** tree of the olive family. —**ash'tray'',** n.

a·shamed', adj. feeling shame.

a·shore', adj., adv. on or onto the shore.

a·side', adv. **1.** at or to the side. **2.** apart. **3.** in reserve.

as''i·nine'', adj. silly. —**as''i·nin'ity,** n.

ask, v.t. **1.** seek to know. **2.** seek information of. **3.** seek, as a favor. **4.** invite. —v.i. **5.** seek a favor, information, etc.

a·skance', adv. with suspicion or disapproval.

a·skew', adv., adj. slanted or twisted out of position.

a·sleep', adj., adv. in or into a state of sleep.

as·par'a·gus, n. plant with edible shoots.

ä''spär·tāme, *n.* a synthetic sweetener.

ás'pĕct, *n.* **1.** way of interpreting or understanding something. **2.** appearance or manner. **3.** face or side toward a certain direction.

ás'pĕn, *n.* type of poplar tree.

ás·pêr'ĭ·tў, *n.*, *pl.* -ties. roughness of manner or speech.

ás·pêr'sion, *n.* hostile or accusing remark.

ás'phält, *n.* black tarlike material.

ás·phўx'ĭ·āte'', *v.t.*, -ated, -ating. harm through deprivation of oxygen. —ás·phўx''i·a'tion, *n.*

ás·pīre', *v.i.* -pired, -piring. have ambitious intentions. —as''pi·ra'tion, *n.* —ás·pir'ant, *n.*

ás'pĭ·rĭn, *n.* white crystalline drug used to relieve minor pain and fever.

ăss, *n.* **1.** donkey. **2.** silly person.

ás·sāil', *v.t.* attack. —as·sail'ant, *n.*

ás·săs'sĭn, *n.* murderer, esp. of a statesman. —as·sas'sin·āte'', *v.t.* —as·sas''sin·a'tion, *n.*

ás·säult', *n.*, *v.t.* attack.

ás·sāy', *n.* **1.** chemical evaluation, as of an ore. —*v.t.* **2.** perform an assay upon.

ás·sĕm'ble, *v.t.*, *v.i.*, -bled, -bling. gather. —as·sem'blage, as·sem'bly, *n.*

ás·sĕnt', *v.i.* **1.** agree; consent. —*n.* **2.** agreement; consent.

ás·sêrt', *v.t.* **1.** declare. **2.** claim. **3. assert oneself,** present one's claims, demands, etc. boldly. —as·ser'tion, *n.* —as·ser'tive, *adj.*

ás·sĕss', *v.t.* evaluate. —as·sess'ment, as·ses'sor, *n.*

ás'sĕt, *n.* something contributing to a profit or advantage.

ás·sĭd'ū·oŭs, *adj.* devoted to a task. —ás·sid'u·ous·ly, *adv.* —as''si·du'i·ty, *n.*

ás·sĭgn', *v.t.* **1.** give out as a task or responsibility. **2.** appoint. **3.** transfer possession or enjoyment of. —*n.* **4.** *Law.* person to whom possession or enjoyment of something is transferred. —as·sign'ment, *n.* —as·sign'a·ble, *adj.* —as·sign·ee', *n.*

ás·sĭm'ĭ·lāte'', *v.t.*, -ated, -ating. **1.** absorb. **2.** make like some larger entity. —as·sim''i·la'tion, *n.*

ás·sĭst', *v.t.* help in a task or occupation. —as·sist'ant, *n.* —as·sist'ance, *n.*

ás·sō'cĭ·āte, *v.t.*, -ated, -ating, *adj.*, *n.* *v.t.*, *v.i.* **1.** join in a social or business relationship. —*v.t.* **2.** connect in one's mind. —*adj.* **3.** joined in a social or business relationship. —*n.* **4.** someone or something so joined. —as·so''ci·a'tion, *n.*

ás·sôrt', *v.t.* classify. —as·sort'ment, *n.*

ás·sôrt'ĕd, *adj.* **1.** of various kinds. **2.** classified.

ás·suāge, *v.t.*, -suaged, -suaging. relieve, as suffering.

ás·sūme', *v.t.*, -sumed, -suming. **1.** suppose without knowing. **2.** take upon oneself. **3.** take or receive from another. **4.** begin to cultivate, as a role or affectation. **5.** feign.

ás·sŭmp'tion, *n.* **1.** act or instance of assuming. **2. the Assumption,** ascent of the Virgin Mary to heaven, celebrated August 15.

ás·sūre', *v.t.*, -sured, -suring. **1.** state emphatically. **2.** convince. **3.** make certain or safe. **4.** reassure. —as·sur'ance, *n.* —as·sured', *adj.*

ăs'têr, *n.* daisylike flower.

ăs'têr·ĭsk, *n.* a sign, *, used for footnote references, etc. in print.

á·stêrn', *adv. Nautical.* backwards.

ăs'têr·oīd'', *n.* **1.** small planetlike body. **2.** resembling a star.

ăsth'má, *n.* respiratory disorder. —asth·mat'ic, *adj.*, *n.*

á·stĭg'má·tĭsm, *n.* eye defect which causes imperfect focusing. —a''stig·mat'ic, *adj.*

á·stĭr', *adj.*, *adv.* full of diverse action.

ás·tŏn'ĭsh, *v.t.* surprise greatly. —as·ton'ish·ment, *n.*

ás·toŭnd', *v.t.* surprise very greatly.

á·strāy', *adv.*, *adj.* away from guidance or control.

á·strīde', *prep.*, *adv.*, *adj.* straddling.

á·strĭn''gĕnt, *adj.* **1.** constrictive, styptic. —*n.* **2.** substance which causes contraction of body tissues.

ás·trŏl'ō·gў, *n.* study of stars and planets as influences on events. —as''tro·log'i·cal, *adj.* —as·trol'o·ger, *n.*

ăs'trō·nãūt'', *n.* person exploring or traveling through outer space.

ăs″trȯ·nŏm′ĭ·căl, *adj.* **1.** pertaining to astronomy. **2.** fantastic, as a number of quantity.

ăs·trŏn′ȯ·mў, *n.* study of planets, stars, etc. and space. **—ăs·tron′o·mer**, *n.*

ȧs·tūte′, *adj.* shrewd. **—ȧs·tute′ness**, *n.*

ȧ·sŭn′dēr, *adv., adj.* in parts.

ȧ·sў′lŭm, *n.* home for persons needing protection, e.g., the insane.

ăt, *prep.* in, on, or near (used to specify time, place, or rate).

ā′thē·ĭsm, *n.* belief that no god exists. **—a′the·ist**, *n.* **—a″the·is′tic**, *adj.*

ăth′lēte″, *n.* a person who engages in athletics.

ăth·lĕt′ics, *n. pl.* sports involving vigorous bodily exercise. **—ath·let′ic**, *adj.*

ȧ·thwart′, *adv., prep.* from side to side.

ăt′lăs, *n.* book of maps.

ăt′mȯs·phēre″, *n.* **1.** air closest to the earth. **2.** prevailing mood. **—at″mos·pher′ic**, *adj.*

ăt′ŏll, *n.* ring of coral islands or reefs.

ă′tŏm, *n.* smallest unit constituting a distinct chemical element. **—a·tom′ic**, *adj.*

ȧtŏmĭc bŏmb, bomb acting through atomic energy created by fission. Also, **atom bomb.**

ȧtŏmĭc ĕnêrgў, energy created through fission or fusion of the nuclei of certain atoms.

ăt′ŏm·ĭz″êr, *n.* device creating a fine spray.

ȧ·tōne′, *v.i.* **-atoned, atoning.** make right or show regret for a wrong one has done. **—a·tone′ment**, *n.*

ȧ·tŏp′, *prep., adv.* on top of.

ȧ·trō′cĭoŭs, *adj.* **1.** vicious; outrageous. **2.** wretchedly bad. **—a·troc′i·ty**, *n.*

ă″trŏ·phў, *n.* **1.** a wasting away. **—v.i., v.t.** **2.** to waste away.

ȧt·tăch′, *v.t.* **1.** fasten to something. **2.** bind by ties of affection. **3.** assume legal possession of, as to settle a bad debt. **—at·tach′ment**, *n.*

ăt″ta·ché′, *n.* special member of an embassy staff.

ȧt·tăck′, *v.t.* **1.** act against with physical violence, harsh words, etc. **2.** commence to solve, work out, etc. with vigor. **—n. 3.** act or manner of attacking.

ȧt·tāin′, *n.* arrive at. **—at·tain′a·ble**, *adj.* **—at·tain′ment**, *n.*

ȧt·tär′, *n.* scent extracted from flowers.

ȧt·tĕmpt′, *v.t., n.* try.

ȧt·tĕnd′, *v.t.* **1.** be present at. **2.** accompany. **3.** care for. **—v.i. 4.** be present at a meeting, etc. **5.** give heed. **—at·ten′dance**, *n.*

ȧt·tĕnd′ănt, *n.* **1.** minor assistant. **—adj. 2.** accompanying.

ȧt·tĕn′tion, *n.* **1.** heed. **2.** care, esp. medical care.

ȧt·tĕn′tĭve, *adj.* paying heed or care. **—at·ten′tive·ly**, *adv.*

ȧt·tĕn′ū·āte″, *v.t.,* -**ated, -ating. 1.** thin. **2.** weaken or dilute. **—at·ten″u·a′tion**, *n.*

ȧt·tĕst′, *v.t.* bear witness; certify. **—at″tes·ta′tion**, *n.*

ăt″tĭc, *n.* unfinished floor space beneath the roof of a house.

ȧt·tīre′, *v.t.,* -**tired, -tiring.** *n. v.t.* **1.** dress, esp. showily. **—n. 2.** clothes, esp. showy ones.

ăt′tĭ·tūde″, *n.* **1.** opinion or feeling. **2.** posture.

ăt′tȯr′nĕў, *n., pl.* -eys. lawyer.

ȧt·trăct′, *v.t.* **1.** pull toward oneself. **2.** draw by evoking interest, allure, etc. in. **—at·trac′tive**, *adj.* **—at·trac′tive·ly**, *adv.* **—at·trac′tive·ness**, *n.* **—at·trac′tion**, *n.*

ăt·trĭb′ūte′, *v.t.,* -**uted, -uting.** *n. v.t.* **1.** name something as the cause for. **—n.** (ăt′trib·ūte) **2.** distinguishing quality or feature. **—at″tri·bu′tion**, *n.*

ȧt·trī′tion, *n.* wearing-down.

ȧt·tūne′, *v.t.,* -**tuned, -tuning.** put in harmony.

aŭ′bûrn, *n.* reddish-brown.

aŭc′tion, *n.* **1.** public sale to the highest bidder for each item. **—v.t. 2.** sell at an auction. **—auc″tion·eer′**, *n.*

aŭ·dā′cĭoŭs, *adj.* daring. **—au·da′ci·ty**, *n.*

aŭ′dĭ·ble, *adj.* able to be heard. **—au′di·bly**, *adv.* **—au″di·bil′i·ty**, *n.*

aŭ′dĭ·ĕnce, *n.* **1.** group attending a play, concert, lecture, etc. **2.** persons reached by a book, etc. **3.** formal interview.

aŭ′dĭ·ȯ″ *adj.* pertaining to electronic reproduction of sound.

aŭ′dĭt, *v.t.* **1.** examine financial accounts.

—*n*. **2.** examination of financial accounts. —**au′dit·or,** *n*.

au·di′tion, *n*. **1.** trial of ability for an actor, musician, etc. —*v.t*. **2.** give an audition to. —*v.i*. **3.** perform at an audition.

au′′di·to′ri·um, *n*. room for an audience.

au′di·to′′ry, *adj*. pertaining to hearing.

au′gêr, *n*. drill.

aught, *n*., *Archaic*. **1.** anything. **2.** zero. —*adv*. **3.** in any way.

aug·ment′, *v.t*. add to. —**aug′′men·ta′tion,** *n*.

au′gûr, *v.t*. **1.** predict. —*n*. **2.** prophet. —**au′gu·ry,** *n*.

au·gust′, *adj*. **1.** grand; majestic. —*n*. **2. August,** eighth month.

aunt, *n*. sister of a father or mother, or wife of an uncle.

au′ra, *n*. quality emanating from a particular place or person.

au′ral, *adj*. pertaining to hearing.

au′re·ole′′, *n*. halo.

au re·voir (ō′′rə vwahr′), *French*. until I see you again; good-bye.

au′ri·cle, *n*. **1.** outer ear. **2.** upper chamber of the heart. —**au·ric′u·lar,** *adj*.

au·rif′er·ous, *adj*. gold-bearing.

aus·pice, *n*., *usually pl*. sponsorship.

aus·pi′cious, *adj*. favorable; promising.

aus·tere′, *adj*. **1.** severe in manner. **2.** characterized by abstention. —**aus·ter′i·ty,** *n*.

au·then′tic, *adj*. true or genuine. —**au′′then·ti′ci·ty,** *n*.

au·then′ti·cate′′, *v.t*., **-cated, -ating.** prove the authenticity of. —**au·then′′ti·ca′tion,** *n*.

au′thor, *n*. creator, esp. of a written work. Also, *fem*., **au′thor·ess.** —**au′thor·ship′′,** *n*.

au·thor′′i·tār′i·an, *adj*. characterized by excessive show or use of authority. —**au·thor′′i·tar′i·an·ism,** *n*.

au·thor′i·ta′′tive, *adj*. **1.** confirmed by competent authority. **2.** having authority.

au·thor′i·ty, *n*., *pl*. **-ties. 1.** official power. **2.** person having such power. **3.** proof for a statement. **4.** expert. **5. the authorities,** persons with legal power.

au′thor·ize, *v.t*., **-ized, -izing.** give official consent to. —**au′′thor·i·za′tion,** *n*.

au′tō, *n*. automobile.

au′′to·bi·og′ra·phy, *n*., *pl*. **-ies.** story of one's own life. —**au′′to·bi·o·gra′phi·cal,** *adj*.

au·toc′ra·cy, *n*., *pl*. **-cies.** government by one absolute ruler. —**au′to·crat,** *n*. —**au′′to·crat′ic,** *adj*.

au′to·gräph′′, *n*. one's name in one's handwriting.

au′to·mat′′, *n*. restaurant with coin-operated serving machines.

au′′to·mat′ic, *adj*. controlled by machinery, etc. rather than humans. —**au′′to·mat′ic·al·ly,** *adv*.

au′′to·mā′′tion, *n*. replacement of human beings as controlling elements by automatic devices.

au·tŏm′a·tŏn′′, *n*., *pl*. **-ta.** manlike self-controlled machine; robot.

au′′to·mo·bīle′′, *n*. self-propelled passenger vehicle.

au′′to·mō′tive, *adj*. pertaining to self-propelled road vehicles.

au′′tŏn·ō′mỹ, *n*. self-government. —**au·ton′o·mous,** *adj*.

au′tŏp′′sỹ, *n*., *pl*. **-sies.** examination of a corpse to determine the cause of death.

au′tumn, *n*. season between summer and winter. —**au·tum′nal,** *adj*.

aux·il′ià·rỹ, *adj*., *n*., *pl*. **-ries.** *adj*. **1.** serving to assist. **2.** supplementary. —*n*. **3.** something that assists or supplements. **4.** *Grammar*. verb used in connection with the principal verb of a sentence.

a·vāil′, *v.t*. **1. avail oneself,** take advantage. —*v.i*. **2.** be of help or use. —*n*. **3.** advantage or benefit.

a·vāil′a·ble, *adj*. able to be used or acquired. —**a·vail′′a·bil′i·ty,** *n*.

av′a·lanche′′, *n*. sudden descent down a slope of a mass of snow, rock, etc.

av′a·rīce, *n*. greed. —**av′′a·ri′cious,** *adj*.

a·vâst′, *interj*. *Nautical*. stop.

a·věnge′, *v.t*., **-avenged, avenging.** take revenge for. —**a·veng′er,** *n*.

av′e·nūe′′, *n*. **1.** major street. **2.** approach road.

av′êr·age, *n*., *adj*., *v*., **-aged, -aging,** *n*. **1.** number representing the sum of a group of added figures divided by the number of figures. —*adj*. **2.** typical. **3.**

revealed by an average. —*v.t.* **4.** find the average of. —*v.i.* **5.** form an average.

a·vêrse′, *adj.* opposed; reluctant. —**a·verse·ly**, *adv.*

a·vêr′sion, *n.* strong dislike.

a·vêrt′, *v.t.* **1.** prevent. **2.** turn away, as the eyes.

a′vĭ·âr″ÿ, *n.*, *pl.* **-ies.** place for captive birds.

a″vĭ·ā′tion, *n.* practice of flying aircraft.

a″vĭ·ā″tôr, *n.* person who flies aircraft. Also, *fem.*, **a″vi·a′trix.**

ă·vĭd, *adj.* eager. —**a·vid′i·ty**, *n.*

ă″vō·câ′dō, *n.*, *pl.* **-dos.** pear-shaped tropical fruit.

ăv″ō·cā′tion, *n.* spare-time pursuit; hobby.

a·vōĭd′, *v.t.* keep oneself away or safe from. —**a·void′a·ble**, *adj.* —**a·void′ance**, *n.*

ăv″ōĭr·dù·pōĭs′, *n.* system of weights using a pound of 16 ounces.

a·vōw′, *v.t.* confess. —**a·vow′al**, *n.* —**a·vowed′**, *adj.*

a·wāĭt′, *v.t.* wait for.

a·wāke′, *v.*, **awoke** or **awaked**, **awaking**, *adj. v.t.*, *v.i.* **1.** Also, **a·wak′en**, wake. —*adj.* **2.** not asleep.

a·ward′, *v.t.* **1.** bestow, as a prize, favor, etc. —*n.* **2.** something awarded.

a·wāre′, *adj.* conscious or perceptive. —**a·ware′ness**, *n.*

a·wäsh′, *adj.*, *adv.* just below water level; flooded.

a·wāy′, *adv.* **1.** to or in another place or direction. **2.** from a place. **3.** out of one's possession. **4.** continuously. —*adj.* **5.** absent. **6.** at a specified distance.

äwe, *n.*, *v.t.*, **awed, awing.** *n.* **1.** overwhelming respect, reverence, etc. —*v.t.* **2.** fill with awe. —**awe′some**, *adj.*

äw′fŭl, *adj.* **1.** bad. **2.** awe-inspiring.

äw′fŭl·lÿ, *adv.* **1.** in an awful manner. **2.** *Informal.* very.

a·whīle′, *adv.* for a short time.

äwk′ward, *adj.* **1.** clumsy. **2.** embarrassing. **3.** dangerous or difficult. —**awk′ward·lÿ**, *adv.* —**awk′ward·ness**, *n.*

äwl, *n.* pointed tool.

äwn′ĭng, *n.* device for shading windows, porches, etc. usually made of canvas.

a·wrÿ′, *adv.*, *adj.* **1.** twisted. **2.** not right.

ăx, *n.*, *pl.* **axes.** broad-bladed chopping tool. Also, **axe.**

ăx′ĭ·òm, *n.* statement accepted as a basic truth. —**ax″i·o·mat′ic**, *adj.*

ăx′ĭs, *n.*, *pl.* **axes.** line on which something is centered or rotates. —**ax′i·al**, *adj.*

ăx′le, *n.* shaft on which a wheel turns.

aÿ″à·tōl′läh, *n.* Shi′ite Muslim religious leader.

aÿe, *adv.*, *n.* yes, esp. in voting.

à·zäl′eà, *n.* flowering shrub.

ăz′ūre, *n.* sky blue.

B

B, b, *n.* **1.** second letter of the English alphabet. **2.** second-best grade.

băb′ble, *v.*, **-bled, -bling,** *n. v.t.*, *v.i.* **1.** speak unclearly or meaninglessly. —*n.* **2.** unclear or meaningless spoken words or sounds. —**bab′bler**, *n.*

bābe, *n.* baby.

bă·bōōn′, *n.* large monkey.

bā′bÿ, *n.*, *pl.* **-bies,** *v.t.*, **-bied, -bying.** *n.* **1.** very young child. **2.** infantile person. —*v.t.* **3.** treat with excessive care or indulgence. —**ba′by·ish**, *adj.* —**ba′by·hood**, *n.*

băc′cà·läu′rē·àte, *n.* bachelor's degree.

băch′e·lôr, *n.* **1.** unmarried man. **2.** person holding the lowest academic degree. —**bach′e·lor·hood″**, *n.*

bà·cĭl′lùs, *n.*, *pl.* **bacilli** (bà·cĭl′ī). rod-shaped bacterium.

băck, *n.* **1.** part of a person opposite the face. **2.** uppermost part of an animal. **3.** side of an object opposite that usually faced; rear. **4.** spine. —*adj.* **5.** at the rear. **6.** related to the past. —*adv.* **7.** toward the rear. **8.** into the past. **9.** in return. —*v.t.* **10.** sponsor; support. —*v.t.*, *v.i.* **11.** move backwards. —**back′er**, *n.* —**back′ing**, *n.*

băck′bite″, *v.t.*, *v.i.* slander, esp. someone absent. —**back′bit″er**, *n.*

băck′bōne, *n.* **1.** spine. **2.** strength of character.

băck′fīre, *v.i.* **1.** fire prematurely, as an

engine. **2.** have adverse results, as a plan. —*n.* **3.** premature firing of an engine.

bǎck´grōund, *n.* **1.** area at the rear of a scene. **2.** information generally useful in a given situation. **3.** origin, experience, or environment.

bǎck´lǎsh, *n.* sudden or sharp reaction.

bǎck´lǒg´, *n.* accumulation.

bǎck´slīde´´, *v.i.* -slid, -slidden or -slid, -sliding. forget good resolutions. —**back´slid´´er**, *n.*

bǎck tǎlk, *Informal.* insolent reply.

bǎck´wạrd, *adv.* Also, **back´wards. 1.** toward the rear. **2.** back foremost. **3.** toward the past. —*adj.* **4.** toward the rear or the past. **5.** not sufficiently advanced. —**back´ward·ly**, *adv.* —**back´ward·ness**, *n.*

bǎck´wǒods´, *n. pl.* region of sparsely settled forest. —**back´woods´man**, *n.*

bā´cŏn, *n.* cured meat from the back and sides of a hog.

bǎc·tēr´ĭ·à, *n., pl.* of **bacterium.** microscopic vegetable organism. —**bac·te´ri·al**, *adj.* —**bac·te´ri·al·ly**, *adv.*

bǎc·tē´´rĭ·ŏl´ō·gў, *n.* study of bacteria. —**bac·te´´ri·ol·og´i·cal**, *adj.* —**bac·te´´ri·ol´o·gist**, *n.*

bǎd, *adj.* **worse**, *n., adj.* **1.** unfavorable evil, or unacceptable. —*n.* **2.** condition or realm of that which is bad. —**bad´ly**, *adv.* —**bad´ness**, *n.*

bǎdge, *n.* object worn as a symbol of authority or distinction.

bǎd´gêr, *n.* **1.** burrowing animal. —*v.t.* **2.** torment.

bǎd´´ĭ·nàge´, *n.* teasing conversation or banter.

bǎd´mĭn·tŏn, *n.* game played with rackets and shuttlecocks.

bǎf´fle, *v.t.*, -fled, -fling, *n. v.t.* **1.** confuse. —*n.* **2.** passage made to divert or stop sound, light, etc. —**baf´fling**, *adj.* —**baf´fling·ly**, *adv.*

bǎg, *n., v.*, **bagged, bagging. 1.** flexible container open at one end. **2.** purse. **3.** suitcase. —*v.t.* **4.** put into bags. **5.** kill, esp. in sport. —*v.i.* **6.** bulge.

bǎg´gàge, *n.* containers for things taken on a journey.

bǎg´gў, *adj.* irregularly bulging. —**bag´gi·ness**, *n.*

bǎg´pīpe´´, *n., often pl.* reed musical instrument played with air under pressure in a bag. —**bag´pip´´er**, *n.*

bāil, *n., v. n.* **1.** security for temporary release of a prisoner. **2.** suspension handle. —*v.t.* **3.** have released temporarily by putting up security. **4.** empty of water with a vessel. —*v.i.* **5.** bail out, escape, often by parachute. —**bail´a·ble**, *adj.*

bāil´ĭff, *n.* **1.** deputy sheriff. **2.** officer keeping order in a court.

bāil´ĭ·wĭck, *n.* **1.** area of a bailiff's authority. **2.** any area of authority or competence.

bāit, *n.* **1.** something used as an attraction in trapping or fishing. —*v.t.* **2.** supply with bait. **3.** harass, as with dogs.

bāke, *v.*, -ked, -king. v.t., v.i. cook or harden with dry heat. —**bak´er**, *n.*

bāk´êr·ў, *n., pl.* -eries. **1.** place for baking food made with flour, etc. **2.** place where such food is sold.

bǎl´ance, *n., v.*, -anced, -ancing. *n.* **1.** state of rest due to equal leverage around a point or line. **2.** state of harmony, stability, etc. **3.** weighing device. **4.** remainder from a subtraction. —*v.t.* **5.** put in balance. **6.** compare or contrast. **7.** review, as accounts. —*v.i.* **8.** come into or be in balance.

bǎl´cō·nў, *n., pl.* -ies. **1.** floor area projecting from a building. **2.** interior floor area overlooking a lower floor.

bǎld, *n.* **1.** without hair. **2.** without disguise or mitigation. —**bald´ly**, *adv.* —**bald´ness**, *n.*

bāle, *n., v.t.*, **baled, baling. n. 1.** large compressed or tied bundle. —*v.t.* **2.** make into bales.

bāle´fŭl, *adj.* hostile; evil. —**bale´ful·ly**, *adv.* —**bale´ful·ness**, *n.*

bǎlk, *v.i.* **1.** refuse to act. **2.** be daunted. —*v.t.* **3.** obstruct. —*n.* **4.** obstruction. —**balk´y**, *adj.*

bǎll, *n.* **1.** evenly rounded object; sphere. **2.** game or games played with such an object. **3.** an entertainment of dancing. —*v.t.* **4.** form into spheres.

bǎl´lǎd, *n.* **1.** narrative song or poem. **2.** sentimental song.

bǎl´lǎst, *n.* **1.** weighty material used for stability. —*v.t.* **2.** supply with ballast.

ball bear'ing, machinery bearing rotating on steel balls.

bal''le·rí'na, *n.* leading female ballet dancer.

bal·let', *n.* entertainment by dancers, esp. one acting out a story.

bal·lis'tics, *n.* study of the motion and behavior of projectiles. **—bal·lis'tic,** *adj.*

bal·loon', *n.* **1.** lighter-than-air bag with no engine or steering mechanism. *—v.i.* **2.** travel in balloons. **—bal·loon'ist,** *n.*

bal'lot, *n.* **1.** paper for indicating a vote. **2.** collective vote for a candidate, proposal, etc.

ball'room, *n.* room for social dancing.

bal'ly·hoo'', *n. Informal.* ostentatious publicity.

balm, *n.* **1.** healing or soothing substance. **2.** anything that heals or soothes.

balm'·y, *adj.,* **balmier, balmiest.** soothing or refreshing. **—balm'i·ness,** *n.*

bal'sa, *n.* lightweight wood of a tropical American tree, used for model-making, etc.

bal'sam, *n.* aromatic resin from certain trees. **—bal·sam'ic,** *adj.*

bal'us·ter, *n.* columnlike support for a railing.

bal'us·trade'', *n.* railing supported by balusters.

bam'boo', *n.* tall tropical grass with hollow woodlike stems.

bam·boo'zle, *v.t. Informal.* mystify or cheat.

ban, *v.t.,* **banned, banning,** *n. v.t.* **1.** forbid. *—n.* **2.** act or instance of forbidding.

ba·nal', *adj.* boringly ordinary. **—ba·nal'i·ty,** *n.*

ba·nan'a, *n.* **1.** treelike tropical plant. **2.** fruit from this plant.

band, *n.* **1.** strip of binding material. **2.** stripe. **3.** group of wind and percussion musicians. **4.** informal group, esp. of armed persons. *—v.t.* **5.** mark with bands. *—v.i.* **6.** gather or unite. **—band'mas''ter,** *n.* **—bands'man,** *n.* **—band'stand'',** *n.*

band'age, *n., v.t.,* **-aged, -aging,** *n.* **1.** strip of cloth, etc., for covering a wound. *—v.t.* **2.** tie with a bandage.

ban·dan'na, *n.* printed cloth for the head or neck. Also, **ban·dan'a.**

ban'dit, *n.* armed robber. **—ban'dit·ry,** *n.*

band'wag''on, *n.* **1.** wagon for the musicians in a circus parade. **2.** obviously winning side of a controversy.

ban'dy, *v.t.,* **-died, -dying,** *adj. v.t.* **1.** exchange rapidly, as words. **2.** send back and forth rapidly, as a tennis ball. *—adj.* **3.** bowed, as legs.

bane, *n.* evil or destructive influence.

bang, *n.* **1.** loud noise, as from an explosion or collision. **2.** Often, **bangs,** short hair across the forehead. *—v.i.* **3.** make a loud noise. **4.** strike.

ban'gle, *n.* decorative band for the wrist or ankle.

ban'ish, *v.t.* drive away; exile. **—ban'ish·ment,** *n.*

ban'ister, *n.* stair railing.

ban'jo, *n.* plucked stringed instrument with circular body. **—ban'jo·ist,** *n.*

bank, *n.* **1.** shore of a river or lake. **2.** slope. **3.** long mound. **4.** tilt, as a vehicle or its supporting surface at a turn. **5.** organization for the saving and lending of money. *—v.t.* **6.** heap up. **7.** tilt while turning. **8.** put into a bank. **9.** cover partly, as a fire. *—v.i.* **10.** have a bank account.

bank'er, *n.* proprietor or officer of a bank.

bank'ing, *n.* **1.** operation of a bank or banks. *—adj.* **2.** pertaining to the activities of banks.

bank'rupt'', *adj.* **1.** unable to pay debts. **2.** without resources. *—n.* **3.** bankrupt person. *—v.t.* **4.** make bankrupt. **—bank'rupt·cy,** *n.*

banns, *n. pl.* notice of marriage to be performed. Also, **bans.**

ban'quet, *n., v.i.,* **-queted, -queting.** *n.* **1.** formal dinner or luncheon. *—v.i.* **2.** participate in a banquet. **—ban'quet·er,** *n.*

ban'tam, *n.* **1.** small fowl. *—adj.* **2.** miniature; tiny.

ban'ter, *n.* **1.** teasing. *—v.i.* **2.** exchange teasing remarks. **—ban'ter·er,** *n.*

bap'tism, *n.* rite of initiation, as into a church. **—bap·tis'mal,** *adj.*

bap'tize, *v.t.,* **-ized, -izing.** initiate into a church, esp. by sprinkling with or immersion in water.

bar, *n., v.t.,* **barred, barring,** *prep. n.* **1.**

long round object, used in an enclosure as a lever, etc. 2. stripe. 3. obstruction. 4. drinking place. 5. counter for serving drinks. 6. division of a musical composition. 7. legal profession. —*v.t.* 8. secure with a bar. 9. exclude. 10. obstruct. —*prep.* 11. except for.

bârb, *n.* 1. sharp projection. —*v.t.* 2. furnish with barbs.

bär·bär·i·an, *n.* uncivilized person; savage. —**bar·bar'i·an·ism**, *n.*

bär·bär·ic, *adj.* typical of or suggesting barbarians. —**bar·bar'i·cal·ly**, *adv.*

bär'bär·ism, *n.* barbaric act or state.

bär·bär·ĭ·tỹ, *n., pl.* -ities. 1. cruelty. 2. barbaric state.

bär·bär·oŭs, *adj.* 1. cruel. 2. uncivilized. —**bar'bar·ous·ly**, *adv.* —**bar'bar·ous·ness**, *n.*

bär'be·cūe, *n.* 1. to cook outdoors over an open fire. 2. fireplace or grill used for cooking outdoors. 3. meal cooked over an open fire. 4. meat cooked and basted with sauce.

bärbed, *adj.* 1. having sharp projections. 2. harsh, as a remark; caustic.

bär·bĭ·tū·rāte, *n.* sedative.

bârd, *n.* 1. Celtic poet. 2. any minstrel or poet. —**bard'ic**, *adj.*

bäre, *adj.,* **barer, barest,** *v.t.,* **bared, baring.** *adj.* 1. uncovered or unconcealed. 2. unfurnished. 3. mere. —*v.t.* 4. strip of covering or concealment. —**bare'ness**, *n.*

bäre'bäck'', *adv., adj.* without a saddle.

bäre'fāced'', *adj.* 1. shameless. 2. with an uncovered face.

bäre'lỹ, *adv.* 1. by the smallest possible amount. 2. nakedly.

bär'gāin, *n.* 1. business agreement. 2. advantageous purchase. —*v.i.* 3. reach or attempt to reach a business agreement. —**bar'gain·er**, *n.*

bârge, *n., v.,* **barged, barging.** *n.* 1. slow freight-carrying boat. 2. ceremonial boat carrying royalty, etc. —*v.i.* 3. carry by barge. —*v.i.* 4. barge in, *Informal.* intrude. —**barge'man**, *n.*

bär'ĭ·tōne'', *n.* 1. musical range between tenor and bass. 2. singer, instrument or part with this range.

bârk, *n.* 1. short utterance of a dog. 2. covering of the stem of a tree or shrub. 3.

sailing vessel square-rigged on all but the last of three or more masts. —*v.t.* 4. utter in a barklike tone. 5. utter a bark. 6. strip bark from. 7. skin by accident.

bâr'lěy, *n.* grass with edible grain.

bârn, *n.* building for crop storage, keeping of cows, etc. —**barn'yard''**, *n.*

bär'nå·cle, *n.* shellfish that clings to ship bottoms, whales, etc.

bá·rŏm'ė·tėr, *n.* device for measuring atmospheric pressure and thus foretelling weather changes. —**bar''o·met'ric, bar''o·met'ri·cal**, *adj.*

bär'ŏn, *n.* low-ranking noble. Also, *fem.,* **bar'on·ess**—**bar'on·age**, *n.* —**ba·ro'ni·al**, *adj.*

bär'ŏn·ĕt, *n.* titled British commoner. —**bar'on·et·cy**, *n.*

Bä·rōque', *n.* florid style in architecture, etc. in the 17th century. Also, **ba·roque'**.

bär'råck, *n.* 1. Usually, **barracks**, dormitory for soldiers. —*v.t.* 2. house in barracks.

bär·rá·cu'då, *n., pl.* -da, -das. pikelike tropical fish.

bär'råge, *n.* defensive barrier of artillery fire, captive balloons, etc.

bär'rĕl, *n., v.,* -reled, -reling. *n.* 1. container, usually wood, with circular ends and bulging sides. 2. measure of about 31 gallons. —*v.t.* 3. put into barrels. —*v.i.* 4. *Informal.* move at high speed.

bär'rĕn, *adj.* 1. unable to support plant life. 2. unable to bear children. 3. profitless. —**bar'ren·ness**, *n.*

bär'rĭ·cāde'', *n., v.t.,* -caded, -cading. *n.* 1. obstruction, as to military advance. —*v.t.* 2. defend or shut off with a barricade.

bär'rĭ·êr, *n.* obstruction.

bär'rĭng, *prep.* excepting; aside from.

bär'rŏw, *n.* 1. hand-held frame for carrying loads. 2. wheelbarrow.

bâr'tĕr, *n., v.t., v.i.* trade with goods or services alone.

bá·sält', *n.* dark volcanic rock. —**ba·sal'tic**, *adj.*

bāse, *n., v.t.,* **based, basing,** *adj. n.* 1. part on which a thing rests or stands. 2. basis. 3. principal ingredient. 4. center of military operations. —*v.t.* 5. give a basis or foundation to. —*adj.* 6. contemptible. **7.** inferior, as a metal. —**base′ly,** *adv.* —**base′ness,** *n.*

base′ball′′, *n.* **1.** game played in a diamond-shaped field with a batted ball. **2.** ball used in this game.

base′less, *adj.* unfounded in fact.

base′ment, *n.* **1.** lowermost part of a building. **2.** cellar.

bash, *v.t. Informal.* hit, as with a club.

bash′ful, *adj.* shy. —**bash′ful·ly,** *adv.* —**bash′ful·ness,** *n.*

bas′ic, *adj.* **1.** most important or significant; essential. —*n.* **2. basics,** most important or significant features. —**bas′i·cal·ly,** *adv.*

bas′il, *n.* herb of the mint family.

ba′sin, *n.* **1.** shallow bowl for liquids. **2.** pool. **3.** area drained by a river.

ba′sis, *n., pl.* **-ses. 1.** something on which a thing depends. **2.** main ingredient.

bask, *v.i.* **1.** lie in warmth. **2.** enjoy favor, etc.

bas′ket, *n.* container of woven wood, wire, etc.

bas′ket·ball′′, *n.* **1.** game in which a ball is tossed over a hoop into a suspended net. **2.** ball used in this game.

bass, *n.* **1.** lowermost musical range. **2.** singer, instrument, or part with this range. **3.** *pl.* **basses, bass.** spiny-finned edible fish.

bas′′si·net′, *n.* basketlike bed for a baby.

bas·soon′, *n.* bass woodwind. —**bas′soon′ist,** *n.*

bas′tard, *n.* **1.** person born out of wedlock. **2.** *Informal.* harsh or malicious person. —*adj.* **3.** born out of wedlock. **4.** not authentic. —**bas′tard·y,** *n.*

baste, *v.t.,* **basted, basting. 1.** sew temporarily. **2.** cover with juices, etc. while cooking. —**bast′ing,** *n.*

bat, *n., v.,* **batted, batting.** *n.* **1.** club used for striking a ball, as in baseball or cricket. **2.** nocturnal flying mammal. —*v.t.* **3.** hit with a bat. —*v.i.* **4.** have a turn batting.

batch, *n.* quantity of material prepared or gathered at one time.

bath, *n., pl.* **baths. 1.** complete washing or immersion. **2.** liquid for immersion or washing. —**bath′room′′,** *n.* —**bath′tub′′,** *n.*

bathe, *n.,* bathed, bathing. *v.i.* **1.** take a

bath. **2.** go swimming, esp. in an ocean or lake. —*v.t.* **3.** give a bath to. —**bath′er,** *n.*

ba′thos, *n.* **1.** ridiculous anticlimax. **2.** insincere sentimentality.

bath′robe, *n.* robe used before and after bathing.

ba·ton′, *n.* staff used for directing musicians, as a badge of office, etc.

bat·tāl′ion, *n.* subdivision of a military division.

bat′ten, *n.* **1.** thin strip of wood. —*v.t.* **2.** secure or cover with battens. —*v.i.* **3.** thrive.

bat′ter, *v.t.* **1.** hit or attack repeatedly. —*n.* **2.** person who bats. **3.** cake mixture.

bat′ter·y, *n., pl.* **-ies. 1.** device for storing electricity. **2.** group of cannons used together. **3.** group of any machines, etc. used together. **4.** *Law.* illegal beating.

bat′ting, *n.* fiber packed in sheets.

bat′tle, *n., v.,* **-tled, -tling.** *n.* **1.** major military encounter. **2.** warfare. —*v.t., v.i.* **3.** fight. —**bat′tle·field′′,** *n.*

bat′tle·ment′′, *n.* defensive wall with openings for shooting.

bat′tle·ship′′, *n.* warship with heavy guns and armor.

bau′ble, *n.* trinket.

bawd′y, *adj.,* **-ier, -iest.** obscene. —**bawd′i·ness,** *n.*

bawl, *v.i.* **1.** yell. **2.** weep loudly.

bay, *n.* **1.** distinct area of a wall. **2.** broad inlet, esp. of a sea. **3. at bay, a.** unable to escape. **b.** unable to attack. —*v.i.* **4.** give prolonged howls.

bay′o·net′, *n., v.t.,* **-netted, -netting.** *n.* **1.** sharp thrusting weapon attached to a gun muzzle. —*v.t.* **2.** stab with a bayonet.

bay′ou, *n.* marshy area of a river or lake, esp. in Louisiana.

bay win′dow, *n.* window jutting from a building, esp. a window with its own foundations.

ba·zäar′, *n.* **1.** Near Eastern salesplace. **2.** temporary sale, esp. for charity.

bē, *v.i.,* **was** or **were, been, being. 1.** exist: often refers to an adjective describing the subject. **2.** occur. **3.** continue. **4.** (Used variously as an auxiliary verb).

beach, *n.* **1.** flat shore, esp. a sandy one. —*v.t.* **2.** haul onto a beach.

beach'comb''er, *n.* seaside scavenger.

bea'con, *n.* **1.** signal light. **2.** navigational radio station.

bead, *n.* **1.** small decorative ball. **2.** small drop. **3. draw a bead on**, take aim at.

bead'y̆, *adj.*, **-ier, -iest.** beadlike; small and shiny.

beak, *n.* **1.** pointed mouth, esp. of a bird. **2.** projection suggesting this.

beam, *n.* **1.** horizontal structural member. **2.** shaft of light. **3.** steady radio or radar signal. **4.** width of a ship. —*v.t.* **5.** send as a radio or radar beam. —*v.i.* **6.** shine. **7.** smile kindly.

bean, *n.* any of various edible seeds.

bear, *v.t.* **1.** carry. **2.** endure. **3.** suffer. **4.** give birth to. **5.** produce. —*v.i.* **6.** head or move in a stated direction. **7. bear with**, be patient with. —*n.* **8.** large shaggy mammal. **9.** speculator in the fall of stock prices. —**bear'er**, *n.* —**bear'a·ble**, *adj.*

beard, *n.* **1.** hair on the lower jaw, etc. —*v.t.* **2.** intrude upon and confront. —**beard'ed**, *adj.*

bear'ing, *n.* **1.** posture or attitude. **2.** support for a rotating part. **3. bearings**, orientation.

beast, *n.* **1.** large animal. **2.** cruel or uncouth person.

beast'ly̆, *adj.*, **-lier, -liest.** nasty. —**beast'li·ness**, *n.*

beat, *v.*, **beat, beaten, beating**, *n. v.t.* **1.** hit with force. **2.** win against. **3.** move vigorously back and forth, as arms or wings. —*v.i.* **4.** throb, as the heart. —*n.* **5.** marked rhythm. **6.** unit of such a rhythm. **7.** regular round, as that of a policeman.

be''a·tif'ic, *adj.* **1.** blissful. **2.** imparting blessings.

beat'ing, *n.* **1.** act or instance of hitting, esp. a person or animal. **2.** defeat.

beau, *n.*, *pl.* **beaus, beaux.** suitor.

beau'ti·ful, *adj.* having beauty. Also, **beau'te·ous.** —**beau'ti·ful·ly**, *adv.*

beau'ti·fy, *v.t.*, **-fied, -fying.** make beautiful. —**beau''ti·fi·ca'tion**, *n.*

beau'ty, *n.*, *pl.* **-ties. 1.** quality sensed in that which is in perfect harmony. **2.** beautiful woman.

bea'ver, *n.* broad-tailed, dam-building rodent.

be·calm', *v.t.* halt from a lack of wind in sails.

be·cause', *conj.* **1.** for the reason that. **2. because of**, as a result of.

beck'on, *v.i.* **1.** make a summoning gesture. —*v.t.* **2.** summon with a gesture.

be·come', *v.*, **-came, -come, -coming.** *v.i.* **1.** come to be as specified. —*v.t.* **2.** be suitable to.

be·com'ing, *adj.* **1.** suitable; seemly. **2.** attractively appropriate, as clothing. —**be·com'ing·ly**, *adv.*

bed, *n.*, *v.*, **bedded, bedding.** *n.* **1.** object to lie upon. **2. to bed**, to rest in a lying position. **3. into bed**, beneath the upper bedclothes of a bed. **4.** layer of rock, etc. **5.** layer of surface soil, as for flowers. **6.** foundation for machinery. **7.** bottom of a body of water. —*v.t.* **8.** put into a bed. —*v.i.* **9.** go to or into bed. —**bed'cov''er**, *n.* —**bed'fel''low**, *n.* —**bed'room''**, *n.*; *adj.* —**bed'side''**, *n.*, *adj.* —**bed'spread''**, *n.* —**bed'spring''**, *n.* —**bed'time''**, *n.*

be·daz'zle, *v.t.*, **-zled, -zling.** dazzle; amaze.

bed'clothes'', *n. pl.* sheets, covers, etc. for a bed.

bed'ding, *n.* all movable objects used with a bed.

be·dev'il, *v.t.*, **-iled, -iling.** harass; torment. —**be·dev'il·ment**, *n.*

bed'lam, *n.* chaotic situation.

be''drag'gle, *v.t.*, **-gled, -gling.** soil as by dragging through mud.

bed'rid''den, *adj.* confined to bed by permanent illness or feebleness. Also, **bed'fast''.**

bed'rock'', *n.* uppermost layer of solid rock.

bed'stead'', *n.* framework for bedding.

bee, *n.* **1.** four-winged, pollen-gathering insect. **2.** social meeting for joint work or competition. —**bee'hive''**, *n.* —**bee'keep''er**, *n.* —**bee'keep''ing**, *n.* —**bees'wax''**, *n.*

beech, *n.* hardwood tree.

beef, *n.*, *pl.* **beeves** or **beefs. 1.** meat from cows, steers, etc. **2.** any such animal. —**beef'steak''**, *n.*

beef'y̆, *adj.*, **-ier, -iest.** muscular; brawny.

bee'line'', *n.* straight route.

beer, *n.* **1.** drink of fermented malt, hops, etc. **2.** any of various soft drinks made from plants.

beet, *n.* plant with an edible root.

bee'tle, *n.* **1.** insect with hard wings. **2.** large mallet. —*adj.* **3.** Also, **beet'ling.** overhanging. —**bee'tle-browed''**, *adj.*

be·fall', *v.i.,* **-fell, -fallen.** happen.

be·fit', *v.t.,* **-fitted, -fitting.** be suitable to. —**be·fit'ting**, *adj.* —**be·fit'ting·ly**, *adv.*

be·fore', *prep.* **1.** at an earlier time than. **2.** in front of. **3.** in preference to. —*adv.* **4.** at an earlier time. **5.** in front. —*conj.* **6.** earlier than the time that something happens. **7.** rather than.

be·fore'hand'', *adv.* **1.** in advance. —*adj.* **2.** ahead of time.

be·foul', *v.t.* make foul.

be·friend', *v.t.* act as a friend to.

beg, *v.,* **begged, begging.** *v.t., v.i.* ask as a favor.

beg'gar, *n.* **1.** person who asks strangers for his livelihood. —*v.t.* **2.** impoverish. **3.** render inadequate, esp. any description of a thing. —**beg'gar·y**, *n.*

beg'gar·ly, *adj.* miserably inadequate.

be·gin', *v.,* **began, begun,** *v.t., v.i.* start, commence. —**be·gin'ning**, *n.*

be·gin'ner, *n.* **1.** person who begins. **2.** completely inexperienced person.

be·grudge', *v.t.,* **-grudged, -grudging.** resent another's having or receiving. —**be·grudg'ing·ly**, *adv.*

be·guile', *v.t.,* **-guiled, -guiling.** **1.** charm. **2.** while away pleasantly. —**be·guile'ment**, *n.*

be·half', *n.* **in** or **on behalf of, a.** in the name of **b.** in support of.

be·have', *v.,* **-haved, -having.** *v.i.* **1.** conduct oneself properly —*v.t.* **2.** conduct in a specified way. **3.** conduct properly. —**be·hav'ior**, *n.*

be·hest', *n.* command; urging.

be·hind', *prep.* **1.** at the rear of. **2.** at or to the far side of. **3.** too late or slow for. **4.** in defense or support of. **5.** concealed by. —*adv.* **6.** at the rear. **7.** into a state of lateness or slowness.

be·hold', *v.t.,* **-held, -holding.** see; look at. —**be·hold'er**, *n.*

be·hold'en, *adj.* indebted.

be·hoove', *v.t.,* **-hooved, -hooving.** obligate.

be'ing, *n.* **1.** existence. **2.** essential nature. **3.** something alive.

be·la'bor, *v.t.* attack by or as if by beating.

be·lat'ed, *adj.* later than expected or desirable. —**be·lat'ed·ly**, *adv.*

belch, *v.i.* **1.** emit stomach gas through the mouth. *v.t.* **2.** emit violently, as smoke. —*n.* **3.** act or instance of belching.

be·lea'guer, *v.t.* harass, as by a siege.

bel·fry, *n.,* *pl.* **-fries.** tower or turret for bells.

be·lie', *v.t.,* **-lied, -lying.** **1.** represent deceptively. **2.** prove as false.

be·lieve', *v.t.,* **-lieved, -lieving.** *v.t.* **1.** accept as true or truthful. **2.** guess to be so. —*v.i.* **3.** have faith. **4.** accept the existence of something. —**be·lief'**, *n.* —**be·liev'er**, *n.* —**be·liev'able**, *adj.*

be·lit'tle, *v.t.,* **-tled, -tling.** treat as of minor importance. —**be·lit'tle·ment**, *n.*

bell, *n.* **1.** hollow instrument, usually metal, that sounds when struck. **2.** something having the characteristic flared shape of this. **3.** *Nautical.* half-hour unit of time.

belle, *n.* attractive woman.

belles''let'tres, *n. pl.* literature as an art.

bel·li·cose'', *adj.* warlike. —**bel·li·cos''i·ty**, *n.*

bel·lig'er·ent, *adj.* **1.** eager to fight. **2.** at war. —*n.* **3.** nation, etc. at war. —**bel·lig'er·ence, bel·lig'er·en·cy**, *n.*

bel'low, *v.t., n.* **1.** shout or roar. *n.* **2.** bellows, device for pumping air to a hearth.

bel'ly, *n., pl.* **-lies,** *v.i.,* **-lied, lying.** *n.* **1.** stomach. **2.** human abdomen. **3.** animal's underside. —*v.i.* **4.** swell.

be·long', *v.i.* **1.** be property. **2.** be a member, citizen, etc. of something. **3.** be appropriate.

be·long'ings, *n.,* *pl.* possessions.

be·lov'ed, *adj.* **1.** loved. —*n.* **2.** loved one.

be·low', *prep.* **1.** lower than; under. **2.** inferior in worth or amount to. —*adv.,* *adj.* **3.** to or in some lower place. **4.** later, as in a book. **5.** *Nautical.* on or to a lower deck.

belt, *n.* **1.** strap worn around the waist, over the chest, etc. **2.** long, narrow region, road, etc. **3.** strap for driving machinery. **4.** *Informal.* **a.** hit violently. **b.** sing emphatically.

bē·mōan′, *v.t.* lament.

bē·mūse′, *v.t.*, **-mused, -musing.** put in a thoughtful or bewildered frame of mind. —*v.t.* **5.** put on a bench.

běnch, *n.* **1.** broad seat or stool. **2.** massive worktable. **3.** judge's seat. **4. the bench,** jurisprudence. —*v.t.* **5.** put on a bench.

běnd, *v.*, **bent, bending,** *n. v.t.* **1.** form as a curved or angled shape, esp. by force. **2.** bow or stoop. **3.** submit oneself. —*n.* **4.** bent section. **5.** curve, as in a road or river.

bē·nēath′, *prep.* **1.** under. **2.** unworthy of. —*adj., adv.* **3.** underneath.

běn′e·dic′tion, *n.* blessing.

běn′′e·fǎc′′tion, *n.* act or instance of charity.

běn′′e·fǎc′′tor, *n.* conferrer of benefactions. Also, *fem.,* **ben′e·fac′′tress.**

bē·něf′i·cěnt, *adj.* doing good. —**be·nef′i·cence,** *n.* —**be·nef′i·cent·ly,** *adv.*

běn′′e·fi′cial, *adj.* useful; advantageous. —**be′′ne·fi′cial·ly,** *adv.*

běn′′e·fi′ci·ar·y̆, *n., pl.* **-aries.** enjoyer of a benefit.

běn′e·fit, *n., v.t.,* **-fitted, -fitting.** *n.* **1.** advantage. **2.** entertainment to raise funds for charity, etc. **3.** payment from insurance, etc. —*v.t.* **4.** be of advantage to.

bē·něv′o·lěnt, *adj.* kindly; well-intentioned. —**be·nev′o·lent·ly,** *adv.* —**be·nev′o·lence,** *n.*

bē·night′ed, *adj.* **1.** lacking enlightenment. **2.** hampered or surrounded by darkness.

bē·nīgn′, *adj.* **1.** friendly; well-intentioned. **2.** *Medicine.* not malignant. —**be·nign′ly,** *adv.* —**be·nig′ni·ty,** *n.*

bē·nĭg′nǎnt, *adj.* **1.** benevolent. **2.** beneficial.

bē·quēath′, *v.t.* transfer to heirs. —**be·quest′,** *n.*

bē·rāte′, *v.t.,* **-rated, -rating.** scold.

bē·rēave′, *v.t.,* **-reft, -reaving.** **1.** leave sorrowful, esp. by dying. **2.** deprive; strip. —**be·reave′ment,** *n.*

bē·rĕt′, *n.* soft, flat, visorless cloth cap.

běrm, *n.* earth embankment. Also, **berme.**

běr′ry̆, *n., pl.* **-ies. 1.** juicy cover for a

seed or seeds. **2.** dried seed of a coffee plant, etc.

bēr·sêrk′, *adv., adj.* in violent frenzy.

bêrth, *n.* **1.** shelflike bed. **2.** job. **3.** ship's mooring place.

bēr·yl, *n.* class of hard stone: includes emeralds and aquamarines.

bē·sēech′, *v.t.,* **-sought,** or **-seeched, seeching.** request earnestly. —**be·seech′ing·ly,** *adv.*

bē·sět′, *v.t.,* **-set, -setting.** harass.

bē·sět′tĭng, *adj.* obsessive, as a sin.

bē·sīde′, *prep.* **1.** at the side of. **2.** compared with. **3.** added to. **4.** irrelevant to.

bē·sīdes′, *adv.* **1.** in addition; else. —*prep.* **2.** in addition to; other than.

bē·sīege′, *v.t.,* **-sieged, -sieging.** **1.** lay siege to. **2.** distract repeatedly.

bē·smirch′, *v.t.* mark or soil.

bē·spēak′, *v.t.,* **-spoke, -spoken** or **-spoke, -speaking.** **1.** speak for ahead of time; reserve. **2.** be eloquent of; reveal.

běst, *adj.* **1.** superlative of *good.* **2.** major; greater. —*adv.* **3.** superlative of *well.* **4.** that which is best. **5.** one's utmost.

běs′tĭ·ál, *adj.* savage. —**bes′′ti·al′i·ty,** *n.*

bē·stir′, *v.t.,* **-stirred, -stirring.** rouse to action.

běst mǎn, groom's ring bearer at a wedding.

bē·stōw, *v.t.* give or grant. —**be·stow′al,** *n.*

bět, *n., v.,* **betted, betting.** *n.* **1.** guess on the unpredictable outcome of an event, made to gain money, etc. **2.** money, etc. put up to back one's guess. **3.** possible guess or action regarding an unpredictable matter. —*v.t.* **4.** put up to back one's bet. **5.** guess in betting. —*v.i.* **6.** make a bet.

bē·trāy′, *v.t.* **1.** be treacherous to. **2.** reveal, as a secret. **3.** seduce with a false promise of marriage. **4.** reveal involuntarily. —**be·tray′al,** *n.*

bē·trŏth′al, *n.* engagement to marry.

bē·trŏthed′, *n.* fiancé or fiancée.

bět′têr, *adj.* **1.** comparative of *good.* **2.** major; greater. —*adv.* **3.** comparative of *well.* —*n.* **4.** social superior. **5.** that which is better. **6.** Also, **bet′tor,** person who bets.

bet′ter·ment, *n.* improvement.

be·tween′, *prep.* 1. with two specified persons or things, one on each side. 2. involving or relating two persons or things. 3. as a result of two specified causes. 4. from either one of, in choosing. 5. as a secret shared by two persons.

bev′el, *n.* 1. outer edge formed as a diagonal. —*v.t.* 2. form as such a diagonal.

bev′er·age, *n.* something to drink other than water.

be·ware′, *v.*, *v.i.* 1. be cautious. —*v.t.* 2. be cautious of.

be·wil′der, *v.t.* confuse, esp. with surprise. —**be·wil′der·ment**, *n.*

be·witch′, *v.t.* 1. cast a spell on. 2. charm with delight.

be·yond′, *prep.* 1. on the far side of. 2. too late or advanced for. 3. outside the power or domain of. 4. after; past. —*adv.* 5. further away.

bi·an′nu·al, *adj.* twice a year. —**bi·an′nu·al·ly**, *adv.*

bib, *n.* apronlike cloth to catch dribbles.

bib′′li·og′ra·phy, *n.*, *pl.* **-phies.** list of books, articles, etc. used, recommended, or in existence. —**bib′′li·og′ra·pher**, *n.* —**bib′′li·o·graph′i·cal**, *adj.*

bib′u·lous, *adj.* fond of alcoholic beverages.

bi·cam′er·al, *adj.* composed of two legislative chambers.

bick′er, *v.i.* quarrel about trifles. —**bick′er·er**, *n.*

bi′cy·cle, *n.* two-wheeled vehicle for a balancing rider. —**bi′cy·clist, bi′cy·cler**, *n.*

bid, *n.*, *v.*, **bid** or (for 4 and 6) **bade, bid** or (for 4 and 6) **bidden, bidding.** *n.* 1. offer for an auctioned item. 2. offer to fulfill a contract for a stated sum. 3. attempt to gain victory, favor, notice, etc. —*v.t.* 4. command or ask. 5. offer for an auctioned item. 6. express, esp. a goodbye. —*v.i.* 7. make a bid. —**bid′der**, *n.*

bier, *n.* support for a coffin.

bi·fo′′cals, *n.pl.* spectacles whose lenses have two areas apiece, each with two focuses.

big, *adj.*, **bigger, biggest.** 1. great in size or amount. 2. full-grown. 3. elder. 4. important. —**big′ness**, *n.*

big′a·my̆, *n.* marriage to two spouses in a single period. —**big′a·mous**, *adj.* —**big′a·mist**, *n.*

big′ot, *n.* person with strong, intolerant, unreasoning attitudes. —**big′ot·ry**, *n.* —**big′ot·ed**, *adj.*

bike, *n. Informal.* bicycle.

bi·lat′er·al, *adj.* 1. involving two sides or factions. 2. reciprocal; mutual. —**bi·lat′er·al·ly**, *adv.*

bi·lin′gual, *adj.* 1. familiar with two languages. 2. expressed in two languages.

bil′ious, *adj.* ill-tempered.

bilk, *v.t.* cheat.

bill, *n.* 1. itemized list or statement. 2. written request for payment. 3. printed announcement. 4. piece of paper currency. 5. beak of a bird. —*v.t.* request payment from in writing.

bill′board′′, *n.* large board for advertising posters.

bil′let, *n.* 1. job; position. 2. order to house a soldier. 3. accommodation obtained with such an order. —*v.t.* 4. house with such an order.

bil′′let-doŭx′, *n.*, *pl.* **billets-doux.** love letter.

bill′fold′′, *n.* wallet.

bil′liards, *n.* game using hard balls propelled by a cue.

bil′ling, *n.* public listing of entertainers on a program.

bil′lion, *n.* 1. *U.S.* thousand million. 2. *Great Britain.* million million. —**bil′lionth**, *adj.*

bill of fare, menu.

bil′low, *n.* 1. swelling mass, as of water or smoke. —*v.i.* 2. appear in billows. —**bil′low·y**, *adj.*

bi·month′ly, *adj.* 1. every two months. 2. twice a month.

bin, *n.* large container for loose storage.

bi′′na·ry̆, *adj.* of or pertaining to the mathematical base 2.

bind, *v.*, **bound, binding.** *v.t.* 1. tie or fasten together. 2. obligate. 3. reinforce, as with tape. —*v.i.* 4. stick fast or together. —**bind′er**, *n.* —**bind′ing**, *n.*

bin′na·cle, *n.* housing for a ship's compass.

bin·oc′u·lar, *n.* 1. **binoculars,** twin

telescopelike glasses, one for each eye. —*adj.* **2.** pertaining to both eyes.

bī''ō·chĕm'ĭs·trȳ, *n.* study of life processes as an aspect of chemistry.

bī''ō·dė·grād'ȧble, *adj.* readily decomposed by bacteria.

bī·ŏg'rȧ·phȳ, *n.*, *pl.* **phies.** story of a person's life or career. —**bi''o·graph'i·cal,** *adj.* —**bi·og'ra·pher,** *n.*

bī·ŏl'ȯ·gȳ, *n.* study of animals and plants. —**bi''o·log'i·cal,** *adj.* —**bi·ol'o·gist,** *n.*

bī·ō'nĭcs, *n.* the study of living systems for application to mechanical or electronic systems.

bī''ō·phȳs'ĭcs, *n.* study of biological phenomena as related to physics. —**bi''o·phys'i·cal,** *adj.* —**bi''o·phys'i·cist,** *n.*

bī'pĕd, *n.* two-footed animal.

bîrch, *n.* hardwood tree with smooth bark.

bîrd, *n.* warm-blooded, feathered, flying animal.

bîrd's-eÿe'', *adj.* taken from high above, as a view.

bîrth, *n.* **1.** emergence from a womb, egg, etc. **2.** heredity. **3.** origin or beginning —**birth'mark'',** *n.* —**birth'place'',** *n.* —**birth'rate'',** *n.* —**birth'right'',** *n.*

bîrth'dăy'', *n.* anniversary of one's birth.

bĭs'cuĭt, *n.*, *pl.* **-cuits, -cuit. 1.** small hard-baked cookie or cracker. **2.** breadlike lump eaten esp. with gravy.

bi'sĕct, *v.t.* divide in two parts, esp. equal ones.

bĭsh'ȯp, *n.* **1.** clergyman overseeing a number of local churches or parishes. **2.** chessman moving diagonally an unlimited number of squares. —**bish'op·ric,** *n.*

bi'sŏn, *n.* shaggy, large North American mammal.

bĭt, *n.* **1.** small piece or amount. **2.** boring tool. **3.** metal mouthpiece for controlling a horse. **4.** (computers) one binary digit or piece of data.

bĭtch, *n.* **1.** female dog. **2.** *Informal.* disagreeable woman. —**bitch'y,** *adj.*

bīte, *v.*, **bit, bitten, biting,** *n.* *v.t.* **1.** close one's jaws firmly upon. **2.** cut or eat into. —*v.i.* **3.** make a biting motion. —*n.* **4.** wound from being bitten. **5.** snack. **6.** ability to wound or disturb one's feelings.

bīt'ĭng, *adj.* wounding to the feelings. -**bit'ing·ly,** *adv.*

bĭt'tĕr, *adj.* **1.** harsh-tasting. **2.** causing much suffering. **3.** extremely resentful. —**bit'ter·ly,** *adv.* —**bit'ter·ness,** *n.*

bĭt'tĕr·swēet'', *adj.* **1.** causing both sadness and pleasure. **2.** low-sugar chocolate.

bĭtū̄mĭnoŭs cōal, soft coal, yielding tar when burned.

bī'vălve'', *n.* mollusk with two hinged shells.

bĭv'oŭ·ăc, *n.*, *v.i.*, **-acked, -acking.** *n.* **1.** temporary encampment. —*v.i.* **2.** camp in a bivouac.

bi·wēek'lȳ, *adj.*, *adv.* every two weeks.

bī·zârre', *adj.* odd; grotesque.

blăb, *v.*, **blabbed, blabbing.** *n. v.t.*, *v.i.* **1.** reveal, as a secret. —*v.i.*, *n.* **2.** chatter.

blăck, *n.* **1.** perfectly dark color, opposite to white in shading. **2.** something that is black, e.g. clothes. **3.** person of central African descent; negro. —*adj.* **4.** of the color black. **5.** negro. **6.** dejected or sullen. **7.** evil. —**black'ness,** *n.*

blăck'băll'', *v.t.* exclude or prevent from being a member.

blăck bĕlt, belt denoting highest skill in karate or judo.

blăck'bĕr''rȳ, *n.*, *pl.* **ries.** dark berry of various types of bramble.

blăck'bîrd'', *n.* bird whose male has black plumage.

blăck'bōard'', *n.* board of slate or other material for writing on with chalk.

blăck'ĕn, *v.t.* **1.** make black. **2.** defame. —*v.i.* **3.** become black.

blăck eÿe, 1. discoloration around the eye from a blow. **2.** something causing disrepute.

blăck'jăck'', *n.* **1.** small, flexible club. **2.** card game.

blăck'lĭst, *n.* **1.** list of persons out of favor. —*v.t.* **2.** put on such a list.

blăck'māil'', *n.* **1.** extortion by threats, esp. to reveal harmful information. —*v.t.* **2.** practice blackmail on. —**black'mail''er,** *n.*

blăck mârk, something unfavorable recorded against one.

blăck mârkĕt, unlawful system for selling legally restricted goods. —**black marketeer.**

blăck'ŏut'', *n*. **1.** putting out of lights, as in a play or during an air raid. **2.** sudden loss of consciousness.

blăck shēep, disreputable member, esp. of a family.

blăck'smĭth'', *n*. person who forges iron by hand.

blăd'dĕr, *n*. **1.** sac for collecting and discharging body fluids. **2.** any of various bags for air or liquid.

blāde, *n*. **1.** metal part with a cutting edge or point. **2.** leaf, esp. of grass.

blāme, *v.t.*, **blamed, blaming**, *n*. *v.t.* **1.** accuse for a fault. **2.** put the responsibility for on someone. **3.** fail to sympathize with or understand. —*n*. **4.** responsibility. —**blame'less**, *adj*. —**blame'less·ly**, *adv*. —**blame'less·ness**, *n*. —**blame'wor''thy**, *adj*.

blănch, *v.t.*, *v.i.* **1.** turn pale or white. **2.** scald.

blăn'dĭsh, *v.t.* flatter or coax. —**blan'dish·ment**, *n*.

blănk, *adj*. **1.** free of marks, as paper. **2.** without thought, expression, etc. **3.** unmitigated. —*n*. **4.** blank piece of paper. **5.** blank space. **6.** cartridge without a missile. **7.** lapse of awareness. —**blank'ly**, *adv*. —**blank'ness**, *n*.

blănk'ĕt, *n*. **1.** warm bedcover. **2.** broad or thick cover. —*v.t.* **3.** cover or obscure, as if with a blanket. —*adv*. **4.** covering all or many possibilities.

blāre, *v.*, **blared, blaring**, *n*. *v.i.*, *v.t.* **1.** sound loudly and harshly. —*n*. **2.** loud, harsh sound. **3.** ostentation.

blâr'nĕy, *n*. wheedling, flattering talk.

blă·sé', *adj*. bored from over-familiarity.

blăs·phēme', *v.t.*, **-phemed, -pheming**. speak sacrilegiously of. —**blas·phem'er**, *n*. —**blas'phem·y**, *n*. —**blas'phem·ous**, *adj*.

blăst, *v.t.* **1.** shatter, as with lightning or explosives. **2.** criticize harshly. —*v.i.* **3.** blow violently. —*n*. **4.** explosion or explosive force. **5.** violent rush of air. **6.** loud sound, as on a trumpet.

blăst fûr'năce, furnace for smelting iron, using a blast of air for draft.

blăst'ŏff'', *n*. departure of a rocket.

blā'tănt, *adj*. shamelessly obvious. —**bla'tant·ly**, *adv*. —**bla'tan·cy**, *n*.

blāze, *v.*, **blazed, blazing**, *n*. *v.t.* **1.** indi-cate the route of, esp. by cutting the bark of trees. —*v.i.* **2.** burn brightly. —*n*. **3.** bright fire. **4.** brilliant display. **5.** cut made on tree bark in blazing a trail.

blāz'êr, *n*. jacket in a solid color, often with the badge of a school, etc.

blēach, *v.t.*, *v.i.* **1.** make or become light in color. —*n*. **2.** something used for bleaching.

blēach'êrs, *n. pl.* tiers of benches for spectators.

blēak, *adj*. **1.** barren and gloomy. **2.** unpromising; without hope. —**bleak'ly**, *adv*. —**bleak'ness**, *n*.

blēar'ў, *adj*., **-ier, -iest**. blurred, as the eyes.

blēat, *v.i.* **1.** utter a light cry, as a goat or calf. —*n*. **2.** cry made by such an animal.

blēed, *v.*, **bled, bleeding**, *v.i.* **1.** lose blood. **2.** feel sympathetic grief. —*v.t.* **3.** cause to lose blood. **4.** practice embezzlement or extortion upon.

blĕm'ĭsh, *n*. **1.** skin flaw. **2.** flaw or defacement. —*v.t.* **3.** make or form a blemish upon.

blĕnch, *v.i.* **1.** become pale. **2.** flinch.

blĕnd, *v.*, **blended, blending**, *n*. *v.t.* **1.** mix. **2.** shade into each other. —*v.i.* **3.** mix. **4.** harmonize. —*n*. **5.** mixture. —**blend'er**, *n*.

blĕss, *v.t.*, **blessed, blessing**. **1.** invoke divine favor for. **2.** approve heartily. **3.** confer happiness upon. —**bles'sed**, *adj*. —**bles'sed·ly**, *adv*. —**bles'sed·ness**, *n*.

blĕs'sĭng, *n*. **1.** invocation of divine favor. **2.** approval. **3.** favorable event or circumstance.

blīght, *n*. **1.** plant disease. **2.** deterioration. **3.** source of deterioration. —*v.t.* **4.** put a blight on.

blĭmp, *n*. lighter-than-air vehicle without a rigid frame.

blīnd, *adj*. **1.** without eyesight. **2.** without perception. **3.** closed at the end or rear. **4.** hidden. **5.** beyond human reason or control. —*n*. **6.** device for shutting out light or view. **7.** deceptive ruse. —*v.t.* **8.** make blind. —**blind'ly**, *adv*. —**blind'ness**, *n*.

blīnd'fŏld'', *n*. **1.** device to prevent a person temporarily from seeing. —*v.t.* **2.** put a blindfold on.

blĭnk, *v.i.* **1.** wink repeatedly. **2.** go on and off repeatedly, as a light. —*v.t.* **3.** cause to blink.

blĭss, *n.* intense, tranquil happiness. —**bliss'ful**, *adj.*

blĭs'tẽr, *n.* **1.** raised area of skin enclosing watery matter. **2.** anything similar in form. **3.** form blisters on. —*v.i.* **4.** become blistered.

blīthe, *adj.* cheerful. —**blithe'ly**, *adv.* —**blithe'ness**, *n.*

blĭtz, *n.* sudden, massive attack.

blĭz'zàrd, *n.* heavy storm of snow and wind.

blōat, *v.t.* swell abnormally.

blŏb, *n.* small, round form.

blŏc, *n.* group of organizations or persons united in a common interest.

blŏck, *n.* **1.** thick, short piece of material. **2.** auctioneer's platform. **3.** Also, **blockage**, obstruction. **4.** urban area bounded by streets. —*v.t.* **5.** obstruct.

blŏck·āde', *n., v.t.,* **-aded, -ading.** *n.* **1.** barrier to navigation, created by warships, etc. —*v.t.* **2.** impose such a barrier on.

blŏck'hĕad'', *n.* stupid person.

blŏck'hŏuse'', *n.* fortified retreat.

blŏnd, *adj.* **1.** having light hair and skin. —*n.* **2.** blond person. Also, *fem.,* **blonde.**

blŏod, *n.* **1.** fluid in the arteries of animals. **2.** lineage. **3.** temperament. **4.** kinship. **5.** bloodshed. —**blood'less**, *adj.*

blŏod'cûrd''lĭng, *adj.* horrifying.

blŏod'hŏund'', *n.* large hound tracking by scent.

blŏod'shĕd'', *n.* killing.

blŏod'shŏt'', *adj.* reddened from broken veins, as the eyes.

blŏod'thĭrst''ȳ, *adj.* eager to kill. —**blood'thirst''i·ness**, *n.*

blŏod'ȳ, *adj.* **-ier, -iest. 1.** covered with blood. **2.** involving much bloodshed.

blŏom, *v.i.* **1.** put forth flowers. **2.** be full of health or youth. —*n.* **3.** flower. **4.** period or state of flowering.

blŏs'sòm, *n.* **1.** flower, esp. of a fruit. —*v.i.* **2.** put forth blossoms.

blŏt, *n., v.,* **blotted, blotting.** *n.* **1.** stain, as from ink. **2.** something that mars or discredits. —*v.t.* **3.** stain. **4.** efface **5.**

dry, as writing in ink. —*v.i.* **6.** make blots.

blŏtch, *n.* **1.** skin discoloration. —*v.t.* **2.** mark with blotches. —**blotch'y**, *adj.*

blŏt'tẽr, *n.* **1.** sheet for blotting up excess ink. **2.** log of events, esp. in a police station.

blŏuse, *n.* loose shirt.

blōw, *v.,* **blew, blown, blowing,** *n. v.i.* **1.** move, as wind. **2.** exhale with force. **3.** **blow over, a.** pass by, as a storm. **b.** cease to be troublesome, as a scandal. —*v.t.* **4.** drive with wind or breath. **5.** cause to sound with the breath, as a horn. **6. blow up, a.** inflate. **b.** explode. **c.** enlarge. —*n.* **7.** stroke, as with a fist or club. **8.** saddening shock. —**blow'er**, *n.*

blōw'ŏut'', *n.* rupture of an automobile tire.

blōw'tôrch'', *n.* lamp for burning or melting.

blŭb'bẽr, *n.* **1.** whale fat. —*v.i.* **2.** weep noisily. —**blub'ber·y**, *adj.* —**blub'ber·er**, *n.*

blŭd'geon, *n.* **1.** short club. —*v.t.* **2.** beat with a bludgeon. **3.** coerce.

blūe, *n.* **1.** primary color, that of a clear sky. **2. blues, a.** jazz tune with a slow tempo, and words, and a certain harmonic pattern. **b.** mental depression. —*adj.* **3.** of the color blue. **4.** sad.

blūe'bẽr''rȳ, *n., pl.* **-ries.** shrub with blue-black berries.

blūe'blŏod'', *n.* person of distinguished ancestry. —**blue'blood''ed**, *adj.*

blūe'-cŏl'làr, *adj.* pertaining to manual workers.

blūe'jāy'', *n.* blue North American bird.

blūe lāw, law restricting commerce or recreation on a quasi-religious basis.

blūe'prĭnt'', *n.* **1.** photographic reproduction of a measured drawing, appearing as white on blue. **2.** any plan or project. —*v.t.* **3.** reproduce or present as a blueprint.

blūe'stŏck''ĭng, *n.* female pedant.

blŭff, *v.t.* **1.** deceive with an air of frankness or assurance. —**blue 2.** frank or abrupt in manner. **3.** rising steeply. —*n.* **4.** steep cliff or ridge. **5.** act or instance of bluffing.

blŭn'dẽr, *n.* **1.** avoidable error. —*v.i.* **2.**

make such an error. **3.** move unthinkingly or awkwardly. **—blun'der·er,** *n.*

blŭnt, *adj.* **1.** with a dull edge. **2.** plainspoken. **—v.t. 3.** dull the edge of. **—blunt'ly,** *adv.* **—blunt'ness,** *n.*

blûr, *v.,* **blurred, blurring,** *n. v.t.* **1.** cause to lose sharpness or clarity. **—v.i. 2.** become indistinct. **—n. 3.** something that blurs; smear. **4.** indistinct image or impression. **—blur'ry,** *adj.* **—blur'ri·ness,** *n.*

blûrt, *v.t.* say impulsively.

blŭsh, *v.i.* **1.** become red in the face with embarrassment or anger. **2.** be ashamed. **—n. 3.** redness in the face. **4.** pink tone.

blŭs'têr, *v.i.* **1.** roar, as the wind. **2.** pretend rage, bravery, etc. **—n. 3.** pretense of rage, bravery, etc. **—blus'ter·er,** *n.*

bōar, *n.* **1.** ungelded male pig. **2.** wild hog.

bōard, *n.* **1.** long, flat piece of wood. **2.** sheet of fibrous material. **3.** meals as part of one's accommodations. **4.** administrative group. **5. on board,** on or onto a ship, airplane, train, etc. **—v.t. 6.** go on or onto, as a ship. **7.** pay for the accommodations, with meals, of. **—v.i. 8.** live as a boarder. **—board'er,** *n.*

bōard'ing hōuse, house offering lodgings with board.

bōast, *v.i.* **1.** talk to excess about one's merits or accomplishments. **—n. 2.** boasting remark. **3.** something boasted about. **—boast'er,** *n.* **—boast'ful,** *adj.* **—boast'ful·ly,** *adv.* **—boast'ful·ness,** *n.*

bōat, *n.* **1.** small vessel or craft. **2.** loosely, any ship. **3.** container with curved sides converging at the ends. **—v.i. 4.** travel in a boat, esp. for recreation. **—boat'man,** *n.*

bōat·swain, (bō'sun), *n.* petty officer in charge of a deck crew.

bŏb, *v.,* **bobbed, bobbing,** *n. v.t.* **1.** cut in a short hairdo. **—v.i. 2.** sink, then rise again quickly. **—n. 3.** short hairdo. **4.** quick sinking and rising movement. **5.** weight hung from a line or pendulum.

bŏb'slĕd'', *n., v.i.,* **sledded, sledding.** *n.* **1.** long high-speed sled. **—v.i. 2.** ride in such a sled.

bŏck, *n.* dark beer.

bōde, *v.t.,* **boded, boding. bode ill** or **well;** foretell bad or good events.

bŏd'ĭ·lÿ, *adj.* **1.** pertaining to the body. **—adv. 2.** physically.

bŏd'ÿ, *n., pl.* **-ies.** *n.* **1.** physical part of a man or animal. **2.** corpse. **3.** part of a vehicle that encloses passengers or freight. **4.** distinct area of water or land. **5.** object in outer space. **6.** group or organization. **7.** richness or favor.

bŏd'ÿ·guârd', *n.* person or group protecting against attack.

bŏg, *n., v.* **bogged, bogging.** *n.* **1.** marshy or spongy area. **—v.t., v.i. 2.** sink into a bog. **3.** slow or halt, as in accomplishing something. **—bog'gy,** *adj.*

bŏg'gle, *v.i.,* **-gled, -gling. 1.** overwhelmed. **2.** hesitate.

bō'gŭs, *adj.* false.

bō'gÿ·măn', *n., pl.* **-men.** imaginary demon. Also, **bo'gey·man''.**

bŏil, *v.t.* **1.** heat in water that bubbles from being heated. **2.** heat to bubbling. **—v.i. 3.** be heated in either of these ways. **4.** seethe, as with rage. **—n. 5.** enough heat for boiling. **6.** inflamed, pus-filled swelling.

bŏil'êr, *n.* **1.** container for boiling things. **2.** container for making steam or heating water.

bŏis'têr·oŭs, *adj.* **1.** rowdy. **2.** stormy. **—bois'ter·ous·ly,** *adv.*

bōld, *adj.* **1.** daring. **2.** presumptuous. **3.** conspicuous. **—bold'ly,** *adv.* **—bold' ness,** *n.*

bō·lō'gná, *n.* smoked sausage.

bōl'stêr, *n.* **1.** long pillow. **—v.t. 2.** prop up.

bōlt, *n.* **1.** fastener with a thread; screw. **2.** sliding device for securing a door, etc. **3.** arrow for a crossbow. **4.** stroke of lightning. **5.** sudden dash. **6.** roll, as of cloth. **—v.t. 7.** fasten or secure with a bolt. **8.** swallow hastily. **—v.i. 9.** flee or start suddenly.

bŏmb, *n.* **1.** explosive or incendiary device. **—v.t. 2.** destroy or attack with bombs.

bŏm·bârd', *v.t.* **1.** attack with bombs or shells. **2.** direct atomic particles against the nuclei of. **—bom·bard'ment,** *n.*

bŏm''bâr·dïer', *n.* person who bombs from an airplane.

bŏm′bāst, *n.* grandiose, empty language. —**bom·bas′tic,** *adj.*

bŏmb′ĕr, *n.* **1.** military plane for dropping bombs. **2.** person who plants bombs.

bŏmb′shĕll′′, *n.* **1.** bomb. **2.** someone or something sensational.

bōnä fīde, in good faith.

bō·năn′zä, *n.* source of prosperity.

bŏn′bŏn′′, *n.* piece of candy.

bŏnd, *n.* **1.** something that binds. **2.** business obligation. **3.** certificate of money lent at interest to an organization. **4.** monetary guarantee from a bailed prisoner, employee, etc.

bŏnd′age, *n.* servitude.

bōne, *n., v.t.,* **boned, boning,** *n.* **1.** part of a skeleton. —*v.t.* **2.** remove the bones from.

bŏn′fīre′′, *n.* large outdoor fire.

bon mot (bäw′ mō′), *pl.* **bons mots.** witty or pithy remark.

bŏn′nĕt, *n.* woman's cloth hat with a chin strap.

bō′nŭs, *n., pl.* **-nuses.** payment in addition to that customary.

bon voyage (bäw vwah yahj′) good journey; said to someone departing.

bōn′ÿ, *adj.,* **-ier, -iest.** with bones much in evidence. —**bon′i·ness,** *n.*

bōo, *inter., n., pl.* **boos,** *v.t.,* **booed, booing.** *interj., n.* **1.** sound made to startle or show disapproval. —*v.t.* **2.** disapprove of with boos.

bōo′bÿ, *n., pl.* **-bies.** fool. Also, **boob.**

bŏŏk, *n.* **1.** long piece of writing, etc., published or kept as a distinct entity. **2.** major subdivision of such a piece. **3.** libretto. **4. books,** business accounts. **5.** something suggesting a bound book in form. —*v.t.* **6.** record. **7.** make a reservation for. —**book′bind′′er,** *n.* — **book′bind′′ing,** *n.* —**book′case′′,** *n.* —**book′keep′′er,** *n.* —**book′keep′′ ing,** *n.* —**book′let,** *n.* —**book′shelf′′,** *n.* —**book′shop′′, book′store′′,** *n.*

bŏŏk′ĕnd′′, *n.* device for holding books upright on a shelf.

bŏŏk′māk′′ĕr, *n.* person who takes bets. Also, *Informal,* **book′ie.**

bŏŏk′worm′′, *n.* person fond of reading.

bŏŏm, *n.* **1.** loud, deep, hollow sound. **2.** spar hinged at one end. **3.** flurry of business or industrial activity. —*v.i.* **4.** make a booming noise. **5.** enjoy a boom, as a town or industry.

bōo′mêr·ăng′′, *n.* **1.** Australian throwing stick that returns to the thrower. —*v.i.* **2.** be harmful to the originator, as a plot.

bōon, *n.* favor or blessing.

bōon′dŏg′′gle, *n.* piece of meaningless, contrived work.

bôor, *n.* uncouth person. —**boor′ish,** *adj.*

bōost, *v.t.* **1.** lift from below. **2.** add to the power of. **3.** speak in praise of. —*n.* **4.** act or instance of boosting.

bōot, *n.* **1.** shoe with tall sides. —*n., v.t.* **2.** kick. —*v.t.* **3.** (computers) to load operating system software.

bōoth, *n.* small shelter or enclosure.

bōot′lĕg′′, *v.,* **-legged, -legging,** *adj. v.t.* **1.** make or sell unlawfully, esp. liquor. —*v.i.* **2.** act as a bootlegger. —*adj.* **3.** made or sold by bootleggers. —**boot′ leg′′ger,** *n.*

bōo′tÿ, *n., pl.* **-ties.** plunder; spoils.

bōoze, *n., v.i.,* **boozed, boozing.** *Informal.* *n.* **1.** liquor. —*v.i.* **2.** drink liquor heavily.

bô′răx, *n.* **1.** crystalline salt. **2.** *Informal.* cheap, showy furniture.

bôr′dĕr, *n.* **1.** edge. **2.** special area along an edge. **3.** political boundary. —*v.t.* **4.** give a border to. **5.** adjoin the edge of. —*v.i.* **6.** border on, **a.** adjoin. **b.** nearly belong to. —**bor′der·land′′,** *n.* —**bor′ der·line′′,** *n.*

bôre, *v.,* **bored, boring,** *n. v.t., v.i.* **1.** penetrate with a rotating movement. —*v.t.* **2.** dig by boring. **3.** weary by being uninteresting. **4.** cylindrical hollow, e.g. in the barrel of a cannon. **5.** uninteresting person or thing. **6.** petty annoyance. —**bore′dom,** *n.*

bôr′ough, *n.* incorporated town.

bŏr′rōw, *v.t.* **1.** take and later return. **2.** take for use in one's own creative work. —**bor′row·er,** *n.*

bŏs′ŏm, *n.* **1.** human breast, esp. as the seat of emotion. **2.** midst.

bŏss, *n.* **1.** employer or manager. **2.** rounded projection. —*v.t.* **3.** *Informal.* order or control firmly.

bŏs′sÿ, *adj., Informal.* domineering.

bō′sŭn, *n.* boatswain.

bŏt'á·nȳ, *n.* study of plants. —**bo·tan'i·cal, bo·tan'ic,** *adj.* —**bot'a·nist,** *n.*

bŏtch, *v.t.* **1.** ruin, as work. —*n.* **2.** clumsy or ineffectual work.

bŏth, *adj., pron.* **1.** one and the other. —*conj., adv.* **2.** equally.

bŏth'ĕr, *v.t.* **1.** annoy or worry. —*v.i.* **2.** take the trouble to do something. —*n.* **3.** source of annoyance or worry. —**both'er·some,** *adj.*

bŏt'tle, *n., v.t.,* **-tled, -tling.** *n.* **1.** container, usually glass and with a stoppable narrow outlet, for liquids and gases. **2.** capacity of such a container, used as a measure. —*v.t.* **3.** put into a bottle. —**bot'tler,** *n.*

bŏt'tle·nĕck'', *n.* obstruction to a flow of work, traffic, water, etc.

bŏt'tŏm, *n.* **1.** lowermost part. **2.** ground under a body of water. **3.** cause or meaning. —**bot'tom·less,** *adj.*

boû·doir', *n.* woman's private sitting room or bedroom.

bŏugh, *n.* limb of a tree.

bouïl·lŏn, *n.* clear broth.

bŏul·dĕr, *n.* large, rounded stone.

bŏul'e·vârd'', *n.* major city street, often tree-lined.

bŏunce, *v.,* **bounced, bouncing,** *n. v.i.* **1.** jump in a new direction after striking a hard surface. —*v.t.* **2.** cause to jump in this way. —*n.* **3.** act or instance of bouncing. **4.** ability to bounce.

bŏund, *v.i.* **1.** jump. **2.** run with jumping steps. **3.** bounce. —*v.t.* **4.** adjoin or determine the boundaries of. —*n.* **5.** act or instance of jumping or bouncing. **6. bounds,** limits. —*adj.* **7.** tied or joined. **8.** obligated. **9.** certain. **10.** headed for a specified goal. —**bound'less,** *adj.*

bŏund'a·rȳ, *n., pl.* **-ries.** border of an area of land.

bŏu·quet', *n.* **1.** bunch or arrangement of flowers. **2.** aroma of wine.

boûr·bŏn, *n.* American whiskey made from corn mash.

bour·geois (boŏr'ʒhwä), *n., pl.* **-geois,** *adj.* *n.* **1.** member of the bourgeoisie. —*adj.* **2.** concerned with money, possessions, social conventions, etc. **3.** pertaining to the bourgeoisie.

bour·geoi·sie (boŏr'ʒhwä zē), *n., sing.* or *pl.* social class of merchants, busi-

nessmen, professionals, clerks, etc.; middle class.

bŏut, *n.* **1.** fight or contest. **2.** period or spell.

boû·tïque, *n.* small shop for fashionable goods.

bow (bō for 1–3, 6; boū for 4, 5, 7–9). *n.* **1.** springy length of wood for shooting arrows. **2.** length of wood for playing various stringed instruments. **3.** Also, **bow knot,** knot with two loops. **4.** front part of a ship, etc. **5.** forward bend of the upper body as a mark of respect or acceptance. —*v.t.* **6.** play with a bow. **7.** cause to stoop, as beneath a burden. —*v.i.* **8.** bend the upper body forward. **9.** agree or submit.

bŏw'ĕl, *n.* **1.** intestine. **2. bowels,** inner depths.

bŏwl, *n.* **1.** deep, wide-topped container. —*v.t.* **2.** roll with an underhanded motion. **bowl'er,** *n.*

bŏw'lĕg''gĕd, *adj.* with legs curved outward at the knees.

bŏx, *n.* **1.** container, usually rectangular and with a lid. **2.** compartment suggesting this in form. **3.** blow of the hand. —*v.t.* **4.** put into a box. **5.** have a fistfight with. —**box'er,** *n.*

bŏȳ, *n.* young male. —**boy'hood''**, *n.* —**boy'ish,** *adj.*

bŏȳ'cŏtt, *n.* **1.** refusal to deal or associate with a person or persons in order to coerce them. —*v.t.* **2.** practice a boycott on.

brāce, *v.t.,* **braced, bracing,** *n. v.t.* **1.** stiffen. **2.** prepare for an emotional shock. **3.** stimulate. —*n.* **4.** stiffening device. **5.** pair. **6.** hand tool for drilling with a bit.

brāce'lĕt, *n.* decorative armband.

brăck'ĕt, *n.* **1.** brace for a corner. **2.** horizontally projecting support. **3.** classification —*v.t.* **4.** support with brackets.

brăd, *n.* thin, small-headed nail.

brăg, *v.i.,* **bragged, bragging,** *n. v.i.* **1.** boast. —*n.* **2.** boasting talk. —**brag'ger, brag'gart,** *n.*

brāid, *n.* **1.** interweaving of three strands of fiber. —*v.t.* **2.** make into a braid.

brāin, *n.* **1.** organ of thought, control of actions, etc. **2. brains, a.** intelligence. **b.** cleverness. —**brain'y,** *adj.*

brāin'stôrm, *n. Informal.* sudden idea or impulse.

brāin'wăsh'', *v.t.* change the attitudes or beliefs of through psychological conditioning.

brāise, *v.t.,* **braised, braising.** brown. then simmer, esp. meat.

brāke, *n., v.,* **braked, braking.** *n.* **1.** device for slowing or stopping machinery. —*v.t., v.i.* **2.** slow down or stop with a brake.

brāke'măn, *n.* assistant to a railroad conductor.

brăm'ble, *n.* prickly shrub.

brăn, *n.* grain husks separated from flour in milling.

brănch, *n.* **1.** woodlike extension from the body of a tree, etc. **2.** anything derived or extending from a main body, system, etc. —*v.i.* **3.** put forth branches. **4.** extend as a branch.

brănd, *n.* **1.** identifying mark or symbol of a company's merchandise. **2.** merchandise so identified. **3.** identifying mark burned into hide or skin. **4.** piece of burning wood. —*v.t.* **5.** put a brand on.

brăn'dĭsh, *v.t.* wave, as a sword or club.

brănd-nēw, *adj.* wholly new.

brăn'dy, *n., pl.* **-dies,** *v.t.,* **-died, -dying.** *n.* **1.** distilled grape or other wine. —*v.t.* **2.** preserve in brandy.

brăsh, *adj.* **1.** hot-headed. **2.** noisy and uncouth. —**brash'ness,** *n.*

brăss, *n.* **1.** alloy of copper and zinc. **2.** **brasses,** wind instruments of brass. **3.** *Informal.* high military officers.

brás·siēre', *n.* supporter for women's breasts.

brăt, *n.* ill-behaved child.

brȧ·vȧ'dō, *n.* false courage or confidence.

brāve, *adj., n., v.t.,* **braved, braving.** *adj.* **1.** courageous. **2.** fine-looking. —*n.* **3.** American Indian warrior. —*v.t.* **4.** encounter defiantly. —**brave'ly,** *adv.* —**brav'er·y, brave'ness,** *n.*

brȧ'vō, *interj.* well done!

brȧ·vū'rȧ, *n.* brilliance or daring.

brăwl, *v.i.* **1.** fight noisily. —*n.* **2.** noisy fight. —**brawl'er,** *n.*

brăwn, *n.* muscular strength. —**brawn'y,** *adj.*

brāy, *n.* **1.** cry of a donkey. —*v.i.* **2.** make this or a similar sound.

brā'zĕn, *adj.* **1.** made of brass. **2.** shameless. **3.** strident. —**bra'zen·ly,** *adv.* —**bra'zen·ness,** *n.*

brēach, *n.* **1.** opening broken through. **2.** violation. **3.** rift, as in a friendship. —*v.t.* **4.** make a breach in or through.

brĕad, *n.* **1.** food of baked flour, water, etc. **2.** livelihood. —*v.t.* **3.** coat before cooking with bread crumbs.

brĕadth, *n.* **1.** width. **2.** range, as of knowledge.

brĕad'wĭn''nĕr, *n.* sole support of a family.

brēak, *v.,* **broke, broken, breaking,** *n.* *.v.t.* **1.** force to divide into pieces. **2.** put out of repair. **3.** terminate. **4.** violate. **5.** end of the effectiveness of. **6.** reduce in health, wealth, rank, etc. —*v.i.* **7.** force one's way. **8.** end a relationship. **9.** appear or begin suddenly. **10.** change in activity. **11.** be broken. **12.** **break down,** **a.** fail in health or operation. **b.** abandon self-restraint. —*n.* **13.** act or instance of breaking. **14.** stroke of luck or mercy. **15.** pause in activity. **16.** change. —**break'age,** *n.* —**break'a·ble,** *adj.*

break dănc·ing, *n.* style of dancing characterized by acrobatic spins and robotic movement.

break'dŏwn'', *n.* **1.** failure of health or operation. **2.** detailed analysis.

break'ĕr, *n.* **1.** wave that breaks on the shore. **2.** device or person that breaks.

break'fȧst, *n.* morning meal.

break'nĕck'', *adj.* reckless, as speed.

break'through'', *n.* **1.** act or instance of forcing a way against opposition. **2.** major accomplishment or discovery.

break'wȧ''tĕr, *n.* wall for breaking the force of waves.

brĕast, *n.* **1.** upper forward part of the body. **2.** this part regarded as the seat of emotions. **3.** female milk-secreting gland. —*v.t.* **4.** oppose or head into forcefully. —**breast'bone'',** *n.* —**breast'-feed'',** *v.t.*

brĕath, *n.* **1.** air going into and out of the lungs. **2.** manner of breathing. **3.** ability to breathe readily. —**breath'less,** *adj.* —**breath'less·ly,** *adv.* —**breath'y,** *adj.*

brēathe, *v.,* **breathed, breathing.** *v.i.* **1.** move air into and out of the lungs. —*v.t.* **2.** speak or sing, esp. quietly.

breath´tāk´´ĭng, *adj.* astonishing or exciting.

breech, *n.* **1.** buttocks. **2.** loaded end of a gun. **3. breeches,** trousers.

breed, *v.,* **bred, breeding,** *n. v.t.* **1.** give birth to. **2.** raise, as animals. **3.** be a source of. —*v.i.* **4.** give birth to offspring. **5.** emerge or proliferate. —*n.* **6.** strain, as of animals. **7.** type, esp. of person. —**breed´er,** *n.*

breed´ing, *n.* **1.** act of one who breeds. **2.** manners or character.

breeze, *n., v.i.,* **breezed, breezing.** *n.* **1.** light wind. —*v.i.* **2.** become a breeze. **3.** move briskly or jauntily. —**breez´y,** *adj.*

brĕth´rĕn, *n. Archaic.* **1.** brothers. **2.** monks.

brĕv´ĭ·tў, *n.* briefness.

brew, *v.t.* **1.** make by fermenting malt and hops, as beer. **2.** make by any of various means, as beverages or other liquids. **3.** plot. —*v.i.* **4.** begin to appear or take shape. —*n.* **5.** something brewed. —**brew´er,** *n.*

brew´ĕr·ў, *n., pl.* **-ies.** place for brewing malt beverages.

brīăr, *n.* brier.

brïbe, *v.t.,* **bribed, bribing,** *n. v.t.* **1.** pay to abuse a position of trust. —*n.* **2.** payment offered for this. —**brib´er·y,** *n.*

brĭc´·ȧ-brăc´´, *n.* miscellaneous decorative objects.

brick, *n.* **1.** oblong object of baked or unbaked clay, etc., used in construction. **2.** oblong object of any material. —*v.t.* **3.** enclose or cover with brickwork. —**brick´lay´´er,** *n.* —**brick´-work´´,** *n.*

brīde, *n.* woman at the time of her wedding. —**brid´al,** *adj.* —**brides´maid´´,** *n.*

brīde´grōōm´´, *n.* man at the time of his wedding.

bridge, *n., v.t.,* **bridged, bridging.** *n.* **1.** structure for crossing a stream, valley, etc. **2.** any of various connecting structures, etc. **3.** control post of a ship. **4.** card game for four players. —*v.t.* **5.** cross with or as with a bridge.

bridge´hĕad´´, *n.* fortified position of invaders.

brī´dle, *n., v.t.,* **-dled, -dling.** *n.* **1.** harness for a horse's head. **2.** means of restraint. —*v.t.* **3.** put a bridle on. **4.** restrain.

brief, *adj.* **1.** short or concise. —*n.* **2.** legal summary —*v.t.* **3.** supply with useful information. —**brief´ly,** *adv.* —**brief´-ness,** *n.* —**brief´ing,** *n.*

brief´cāse, *n.* handle-held case for business papers.

brī´êr, *n.* thorny bush.

brig, *n.* **1.** two-masted square-rigged ship. **2.** navy or marine position.

bri·gāde´, *n.* **1.** military unit formed of battalions. **2.** pseudo-military organization.

brĭg´ȧ·dĭer gĕnĕrȧl, military officer between a colonel and a major general. Also, **brig´´a·dier´.**

brĭght, *adj.* **1.** shedding or reflecting much light. **2.** intelligent or mentally active. **3.** cheerful. **4.** promising. —**bright´ly,** *adv.* —**bright´ness,** *n.* —**bright´en,** *v.t., v.i.*

brĭl´lĭant, *adj.* very bright. —**bril´liant-ly,** *adv.* —**bril´liance, bril´lian·cy,** *n.*

brĭm, *n., v.i.,* **brimmed, brimming.** *n.* **1.** rim. —*v.i.* **2.** run or run over with liquid.

brĭn´dled, *adj.* gray or tawny with darker spots. Also, **brin´dle.**

brīne, *n.* salty water.

brĭng, *v.t.,* **brought, bringing. 1.** carry or escort to a place. **2.** cause as a consequence. **3. bring about,** cause. **4. bring out,** make apparent. **5. bring up,** raise, as children.

brĭnk, *n.* edge or verge.

brĭsk, *adj.* **1.** lively or abrupt. **2.** forceful, as the wind. —**brisk´ly,** *adv.* —**brisk´-ness,** *n.*

brĭs´kĕt, *n.* breast meat.

brĭs´tle, *n., v.i.,* **-tled, -tling.** *n.* **1.** stiff hair, as on a pig. **2.** fiber on the head of a brush. —*v.i.* **3.** stand up stiffly. **4.** be tense with annoyance, etc.

brĭt´tle, *adj.* easily shattered. —**brit´tle-ness,** *n.*

brōach, *v.t.* bring forth as a subject of discussion.

brōad, *adj.* **1.** wide. **2.** diverse. **3.** not strict. **4.** not detailed. —**broad´ly,** *adv.* —**broad´ness,** *n.* —**broad´en,** *v.t., v.i.*

brōad´cȧst´´, *v.t.,* **-cast,** or (for 1) **-casted, -casting,** *n. v.t.* **1.** send by radio or television. **2.** scatter widely.

—*n.* **3.** radio or television program. —**broad'cast''er**, *n.*

brôad'-mind''ed, *adj.* not strict or opinionated. —**broad'-mind'ed·ly**, *adv.* —**broad'-mind'ed·ness**, *n.*

brō·chûre'', *n.* pamphlet.

brōgue, *n.* Irish accent, esp. in speaking English.

brōil, *v.t.* cook with direct heat from a fire, etc. —**broil'er**, *n.*

brōke, *adj. Informal.* without money; bankrupt.

brōk'ĕn, *adj.* **1.** past participle of *break,* used adjectivally. **2.** deprived of spirit, health, etc. **3.** badly pronounced, as by a foreigner. **4.** discontinuous. —**brok'en·ly**, *adv.*

brōk'ĕr, *n.* agent for buying and selling. —**brok'er·age**, *n.*

brŏn'cō, *n., pl.* **-cos**, wild or half-wild horse of the West. Also, **bron'cho.**

brŏn'tó·saŭr''ŭs, *n.* large herbivorous dinosaur.

brŏnze, *n., v.t.* **bronzed, bronzing.** *n.* **1.** alloy of copper and tin. **2.** reddish-brown. —*v.t.* **3.** color like or coat with bronze.

brōoch, *n.* large ornamental pin.

brōod, *n.* **1.** group of children or baby chickens. —*v.i.* **2.** worry or sulk at length.

brōok, *n.* **1.** small stream. —*v.t.* **2.** endure.

brōom, *n.* bundle of straws, etc. attached to a stick and used for sweeping. —**broom'stick''**, *n.*

brŏth, *n.* soup from boiled meat.

brŏth'ĕl, *n.* house of prostitution.

brŏth'ĕr, *n.* **1.** son of one's father. **2.** fellow-human as an object of love, etc. **3.** fellow-member of a religious order, lodge, etc. —**broth'er·hood**, *n.* —**broth'er·ly**, *adj.*

brŏth'ĕr-ĭn-lâw'', *n., pl.* **broth'ers-in-law''.** **1.** brother of a spouse. **2.** husband of a sister or sister-in-law.

brŏw, *n.* **1.** eyebrow. **2.** forehead. **3.** edge of a cliff.

brōw'bēat'', *v.t.* **-beat, -beaten, -beating.** bully.

brōwn, *n.* **1.** color combining red, yellow, and black. —*v.t., v.i.* **2.** make or become brown.

brōwse, *v.i.,* **browsed, browsing.** look idly through things for sale. —**brows'er**, *n.*

brŭise, *v.,* **bruised, bruising.** *n. v.t.* **1.** injure the skin or surface of with a blow or pressure. **2.** hurt, as the feelings. —*v.i.* **3.** become bruised. —*n.* **4.** mark made by bruising.

brŭnch, *n. Informal.* meal part-breakfast, part-lunch.

brŭ·nĕt', *n.* person with dark hair, esp. when with dark eyes. Also, *fem.,* **brunette'.**

brŭnt, *n.* shock or stress, as of an attack.

brŭsh, *n.* **1.** device for cleaning, painting, etc. consisting of bristles on a handle. **2.** act or instance of brushing. **3.** something suggesting a brush in form. **4.** Also, **brush'wood''**, underbrush. —*v.t.* **5.** remove or apply with a brush. **6.** apply a brush to. **7.** graze lightly in passing.

brŭsh'ŏff'', *n. Informal.* tactless act of dismissing or ignoring someone.

brŭsque, *adj.* abrupt in manner. —**brusque'ly**, *adv.* —**brusque'ness**, *n.*

brŭ'tál, *adj.* extremely cruel or harsh. —**bru'tal'i·ty**, *n.*

brŭ'tál·īze, *v.t.,* **-ized, -izing.** **1.** make brutal. **2.** treat brutally. —**bru''tal·i·za'tion**, *n.*

brŭte, *adj.* **1.** beastlike, esp. in force or lack of intelligence. —*n.* **2.** beast. **3.** brutal person. —**brut'ish**, *adj.*

bŭb'ble, *n., v.i.,* **-bled, -bling.** *n.* **1.** void or body of gas surrounded by a liquid. **2.** something bubblelike in roundness and thinness. **3.** something insubstantial. —*v.i.* **4.** give off bubbles. —**bub'bly**, *adj.*

bŭc''cà·nēer', *n.* pirate, esp. in the Caribbean Sea.

bŭck, *n.* **1.** grown male deer, goat, etc. **2.** act or instance of bucking. **3.** *Informal.* dollar. —*v.t.* **4.** oppose with force. —*v.i.* **5.** rear upward, as a horse.

bŭck'ĕt, *n.* open watertight container.

bŭck'le, *n., v.,* **-led, -ling.** *n.* **1.** fastener for two ends of a belt, etc. —*v.t.* **2.** fasten with a buckle. **3.** cause to bulge or bend, as sheet metal. —*v.i.* **4.** bulge or bend.

bŭck'tōoth'', *n.* projecting front tooth. —**buck'toothed'**, *adj.*

bŭck'whēat'', *n.* wheat with triangular seeds.

bū·cŏl'ĭc, *adj.* pastoral; serene and countrylike.

bŭd, *n.*, *v.i.*, **budded, budding**, *n.* **1.** swelling from which a flower, leaf, etc. grows. —*v.i.* **2.** put forth such swellings.

bŭdge, *v.*, **budged, budging**. *v.t.*, *v.i.* move by or because of force.

bŭdg'ĕt, *n.* **1.** allotment of money, time, etc. for various purposes. —*v.t.* **2.** submit to a budget. —**budg'et·ar''y**, *adj.*

bŭff, *n.* **1.** dull tan color. —*v.t.* **2.** polish with a soft surface.

bŭf'fà·lō'', *n.*, *pl.* -**loes. 1.** any of various wild oxen. **2.** American bison.

bŭf'fêr, *n.* something that prevents or lessens the shocks of collision.

bŭf·fĕt', *n.* **1.** sideboard. **2.** meal for eaters helping themselves.

bŭf·fōōn', *n.* clownish person. —**buf·foon'er·y**, *n.*

bŭg, *n.*, *v.t.*, **bugged, bug·ging**, *n.* **1.** insect. **2.** (computers) an error in programming. *v.t.* **3.** *Informal.* **a.** plant listening devices in. **b.** pester.

bŭg'gy, *n.*, *pl.* -**gies. 1.** light one-horse carriage. **2.** baby carriage.

bū'gle, *n.* trumpetlike brass instrument. —**bu'gler**, *n.*

bŭild, *v.*, **built, building**, *n. v.t.* **1.** assemble, as a structure. **2.** found or base. **3.** bring into being or develop. **4.** establish or base something. **5.** accumulate. —*n.* **6.** frame of the body. —**build'er**, *n.*

build'ing, *n.* habitable construction.

bŭilt'-īn', *adj.* integral or inherent.

bŭilt'-ŭp', *adj.* made from a number of parts.

bŭlb, *n.* **1.** any of various underground plant stems, roots, or buds. **2.** something swelling toward the end. —**bulb'ous**, *adj.*

bŭlge, *n.*, *v.i.*, **bulged, bulging**. *n.* **1.** swelling. —*v.i.* **2.** swell.

bŭlk, *n.* **1.** size or weight. **2.** greater or principal part. —*v.i.* **3.** be massive or important. —*adj.* **4.** shipped without containers. —**bulk'y**, *adj.*

bŭll, *n.* **1.** male ox, elephant, etc. **2.** speculator in the rise of stock prices. **3.** papal decree. —**bul'lish**, *adj.*

bŭll'dŏg'', *n.* small, heavy-built fighting dog.

bŭll'dōze'', *v.t.*, -**dozed, -dozing. 1.** push or level earth. **2.** *Informal.* force with aggressiveness. —**bull'doz·er**, *n.*

bŭl'lĕt, *n.* pointed projectile from a firearm. —**bul'let-proof''**, *adj.*

bŭl'lė·tĭn, *n.* **1.** announcement, esp. of news. **2.** official publication.

bŭl'liŏn, *n.* ingots of precious metal.

bŭlls'eÿe'', *n.* **1.** center of a target. **2.** direct hit.

bŭl'lÿ, *n.*, *pl.* -**lies**, *v.t.*, -**lied, -lying**, *n.* **1.** person who injures or threatens weaker persons. —*v.t.* **2.** act as a bully toward.

bŭl'wârk, *n.* defensive wall or barrier.

bŭm, *n.*, *v.*, **bummed, bumming**. *n.* **1.** poor person who refuses to work. —*v.i.* **2.** live as a bum. —*v.t.* **3.** obtain by begging.

bŭm'ble·bēe'', *n.* yellow-and-black bee.

bŭmp, *v.t.* **1.** collide with, esp. not violently. —*v.i.* **2.** move over a bumpy surface. **3.** bump into, **a.** collide with. **b.** *Informal.* meet by chance. —*n.* **4.** act or instance of bumping or of being bumped. **5.** surface unevenness or swelling. —**bump'y**, *adj.*

bŭmp'êr, *n.* **1.** device to receive the shock of collisions. —*adj.* **2.** especially abundant, as a crop.

bŭmp'tioŭs, *adj.* annoyingly self-assertive. —**bump'tious·ly**, *adv.*

bŭn, *n.* small baked roll.

bŭnch, *n.* **1.** small cluster. **2.** *Informal.* group of persons. —*v.t.*, *v.i.* **3.** gather into a bunch.

bŭn'dle, *n.*, *v.t.*, -**dled, -dling**. *n.* **1.** group of things bound or wrapped together. —*v.t.* **2.** make into a bundle.

bŭn'gà·lōw'', *n.* one-storied cottage.

bŭn'gle, *v.*, -**gled, -gling**, *n. v.t.*, *v.i.* **1.** do or act stupidly. —*n.* **2.** act or instance of bungling. —**bun'gler**, *n.*

bŭn'iŏn, *n.* inflamed swelling at the joint of the big toe.

bŭnk, *n.* **1.** flat frame serving as a bed, esp. in barracks, camps, or ships. **2.** *Informal.* false statements. —*v.i.* **3.** sleep in a bunk. —**bunk'house''**, *n.*

bŭnk'êr, *n.* **1.** storage space for coal, etc. **2.** underground shelter against bombs or shells.

bŭn′nў, *n.*, *pl.* **-nies.** *Informal.* rabbit.

bŭn′tĭng, *n.* cloth for making flags or flaglike decorations.

bŭoŷ, *n.* **1.** floating signal or marker. **2.** life preserver. —*v.t.* **3.** lift up, as the spirits. **4.** keep afloat.

bŭoŷ′ănt, *adj.* **1.** a tendency to float. **2.** cheerful or optimistic. —**buoy′an·cy**, *n.*

bŭr, *n.* **1.** seed capsule with sharp, clinging extensions. **2.** burr.

bŭr′dĕn, *n.* **1.** heavy load. **2.** theme. **3.** chorus or refrain. —*v.t.* **4.** put a load upon. —**bur′den·some**, *adj.*

bū′reau, *n.*, *pl.* **-reaus**, **-reaux.** **1.** official agency or department. **2.** chest of drawers.

bū·reâu·crã′cў, *n.*, *pl.* **-cies.** **1.** government by officials. **2.** government departments as a source of political power, obstruction to progress, etc. —**bu′reau·crat″**, *n.* —**bu″reau·crat′ic**, *adj.*

bŭr′glăr, *n.* person who breaks into buildings, esp. to steal. —**bur′gla·ry**, *n.* —**bur′glar·ize″**, *v.t.*

bŭr′ĭ·ăl, *n.* burying of the dead.

bŭr′lăp, *n.* coarse jute or hemp cloth.

bŭr·lĕsque′, *n.*, *v.t.*, **-lesqued**, **-lesquing.** *n.* **1.** sexually allusive vaudeville. **2.** satirical parody. —*v.t.* **3.** make the subject of a burlesque.

bŭr′lў, *adj.*, **-lier**, **-liest.** big and strong. —**bur′li·ness**, *n.*

bŭrn, *v.*, **burned** or **burnt**, **burning.** *v.t.* **1.** use as fuel. **2.** damage with heat. **3.** create or finish with fire or intense heat. **4.** damage with acids, etc. —*v.i.* **5.** be on fire. **6.** give out light or heat. **7.** be damaged by heat. **8.** be full of eagerness or passion. —*n.* **9.** burned place. —**burn′a·ble**, *adj.*

bŭr′nêr, *n.* device for applying intense heat.

bŭr′nĭsh, *v.t.* rub to a polish.

bŭrn′′ôut, *n.* lethargy resulting from excess stress.

bŭrp, *n.*, *v.i. Informal.* **1.** belch. —*v.t.* **2.** cause to burp.

bŭrr, *n.* **1.** rough edge on cut metal. **2.** rough trilling of the sound *r*, as by a Scot.

bŭr′rŏw, *n.* **1.** hole of a digging animal. —*v.i.* **2.** dig deep holes. **3.** hide in or as if in a burrow.

bŭrst, *v.*, **burst**, **bursting**, *n.* *v.i.* **1.** be torn apart, as from pressure. **2.** make a sudden and vehement beginning into song, tears, etc. —*v.t.* **3.** cause to be torn apart. —*n.* **4.** act or instance of bursting. **5.** sudden show of energy. **6.** volley of shots.

bŭrў, *v.t.*, **-ied**, **-ying.** **1.** put under earth or other material. **2.** entomb. **3.** put out of sight or notice. **4.** immerse, as in work.

bŭs, *n.*, *pl.* **-es**, **-ses**, *v.t.*, **-ed** or **-sed**, **-ing** or **-sing.** *n.* **1.** vehicle for many passengers. **2.** (computers) a circuit for connecting two components. —*v.t.* **3.** transport by bus.

bŭsh, *n.* **1.** low, spreading woody plant. **2.** land overgrown with bushes. —**bush′y**, *adj.*

bŭsh′ĕl, *n.* dry measure of 4 pecks or 32 quarts.

bus′i·ly (bĭz′ĭ·lў), *adv.* in a busy manner.

busi′ness (bĭz′nĕs), *n.* **1.** type of work or commerce. **2.** duty or task. **3.** rightful concern. **4.** commerce. **5.** event or affair. **6. mean business**, have earnest intentions. —**busi′ness·man**, *n.* —**busi′ness·wom″an**, *n.*

busi′ness·like″ (bĭz′nes·līk″), *adj.* efficient.

bŭst, *n.* **1.** head, neck, and upper part of the chest. **2.** sculpture of these parts. **3.** *Informal.* **a.** failure. **b.** bankruptcy. —*v.t.*, *v.i.* **4.** *Informal.* break or burst.

bŭs′tle, *n.*, *v.i.*, **-tled**, **-tling.** *n.* **1.** activity, as of a crowd. —*v.i.* **2.** move hurriedly.

bus′y (bĭz′ў), *adj.*, **-ier**, **-iest**, *v.t.*, **-ied**, **-ying.** *adj.* **1.** with much to do. **2.** in action or use. **3.** full of distracting elements, as a decoration. —*v.t.* **4.** cause to be busy. —**bus′y·ness**, *n.*

bus′y·bod′′y (bĭz′ў·bŏd′′ў), *n.*, *pl.* **-ies.** gossipy or meddlesome person.

bŭt, *prep.* **1.** except for. —*conj.* **2.** and yet. **3.** on the other hand. —*adv.* **4.** only; merely. **5.** just; only.

bŭtch′êr, *n.* **1.** slaughterer or seller of meat. —*v.t.* **2.** slaughter. —**butch′er·y**, *n.*

bŭt′lêr, *n.* head male house servant.

bûtt, *n.* **1.** thick end. **2.** remnant of a smoked cigarette or cigar. **3.** target. **4.** act or instance of butting. —*v.t.* **5.** ram with the head. **6.** join without overlapping.

bütte, *n.* steep hill isolated in flat land.

bŭt′têr, *n.* **1.** solid product made from churned cream. —*v.t.* **2.** spread with butter. **3. butter up,** *Informal.* ingratiate oneself with. —**but′ter·fat″,** *n.*

bŭt′têr·flÿ″, *n., pl.* **-flies.** slender-bodied four-winged insect.

bŭt′têr·milk″, *n.* liquid remaining after butter is made of cream.

bŭt′têr·scŏtch″, *n.* candy of brown sugar, butter, etc.

bŭt′tŏcks, *n., pl.* part on which one sits.

bŭt′tŏn, *n.* **1.** broad object passed through holes or loops in cloth as a fastener. **2.** object pushed to operate a control mechanism. **3.** large badge with a slogan, etc. —*v.t., v.i.* **4.** fasten with buttons. —**but′ton·hole″,** *n.*

bŭt′trĕss, *n.* **1.** heavy mass resisting a thrust, as that of an arch. —*v.t.* **2.** give stability or support to.

bŭx′ŏm, *adj.* attractively plump.

buÿ, *v.t.,* **bought, buying,** *n. v.t.* **1.** get in return for money. **2.** *Informal.* accept as true or wise. —*n.* **3.** *Informal.* something cheap at the price. —**buy′er,** *n.*

bŭzz, *v.i.* **1.** make a deep, rough hum. —*n.* **2.** hum of this sort. —**buzz′er,** *n.*

bŭz′zârd, *n.* **1.** type of slow hawk. **2.** type of vulture.

bÿ, *prep.* **1.** close to. **2.** past. **3.** a multiplier or other dimension being. **4.** in measures or units of. **5.** after. **6.** during the time of day or night. **7.** not later than. **8.** through the agency of. **9.** according to. **10. by way of, a.** past or through. **b.** as a means or form of. **11.** in readiness. **12.** aside. **13.** past. —**by′stand″er,** *n.*

bÿ′gŏne″, *adj.* in the past.

bÿ′läw″, *n.* rule for an organization's internal affairs.

bÿ′līne, *n.* printed line identifying author of news story, article, etc.

bÿ′păss″, *n.* route, etc. serving as an alternate way between two points.

bÿ′-prŏd′ŭct, *n.* product incidental to a main one. Also, **by′prod″uct.**

bÿte, *n.* (computers) a group of eight bits of data.

C

C, c, *n.* **1.** third letter of the English alphabet. **2.** third best grade or rating. **3.** centigrade.

căb, *n.* **1.** chauffeured vehicle for hire. **2.** shelter for the operator of a locomotive, etc.

ca·băl′, *n.* **1.** group of intriguers. **2.** intrigue of such a group.

căb′a·ret (kab″a·rā′), *n.* restaurant with musical entertainment.

căb′bage, *n.* vegetable with a head of thick leaves.

căb′ĭn, *n.* **1.** primitive house. **2.** passenger room on a ship. **3.** passenger space in an airplane.

căb′ĭ·nĕt, *n.* **1.** boxlike piece of furniture. **2.** body of officials reporting to a head of state. —**cab′i·net·mak″er,** *n.* —**cab′i·net·work″,** *n.*

cā′ble, *n., v.t.,* **-bled, -bling.** *n.* **1.** heavy rope. **2.** heavy electric wire. **3.** cablegram. —*v.t.* **4.** send a cablegram to.

cā′ble·grăm″, *n.* transoceanic telegraph message.

ca·bōōse′, *n.* car for the conductor and brakemen of a freight train.

căche, *n., v.t.,* **cached, caching.** *n.* **1.** hiding place, esp. for food and supplies. **2.** goods hidden in such a place. —*v.t.* **3.** put in a cache.

căck′le, *v.i.,* **-led, -ling,** *n. v.i.* **1.** make henlike noises. —*n.* **2.** henlike noise. **3.** *Informal.* busy, meaningless talk.

ca·cŏph′o·nÿ, *n., pl.* **-nies.** harsh, disagreeable sound. —**ca·coph′o·nous,** *adj.*

căc′tŭs, *n., pl.* **-tuses, -ti.** prickly desert plant.

căd, *n.* violator of a gentlemanly code. —**cad′dish,** *adj.*

ca·dăv′êr, *n.* corpse. —**ca·dav′er·ous,** *adj.*

căd′diē, *n.* person who carries a golfer's clubs. Also, **cad′dy.**

ca'dence, n. **1.** rise and fall of a speaking voice. **2.** marching rhythm. **3.** end of a musical phrase.

ca·dĕt', n. **1.** military student. **2.** trainee.

cădge, v., **cadged, cadging**. v.t., v.i. **1.** beg. —v.t. **2.** get by begging. —**cadg'er**, n.

cǎ'drĕ, n. organizational nucleus, esp. of military officers.

ca·fe (ka fā'), n. small restaurant. Also, **ca·fé'**.

cǎf''ė·tė'rǐ·à, n. self-service restaurant.

cǎf·fēine', n. stimulant in coffee or tea. Also, **caf·fein'**.

cāge, n., v.t., **caged, caging**. n. **1.** openwork structure for confinement. **2.** openwork structure of any kind. —v.t. **3.** confine in a cage.

ca·hoots', *Informal*. **in cahoots with**, in a conspiracy with.

cais'son, n. **1.** watertight chamber for work under water. **2.** ammunition wagon.

cā·jōle', v.t., **-joled, -joling**. coax or wheedle. —**ca·jol'er·y**, n.

cāke, n., v., **caked, caking**. n. **1.** sweetened piece of baked dough. **2.** flat piece of food, fried, or baked. **3.** piece of soap. —v.t., v.i. **4.** cover with or form a solid crust.

cà·lăm'ĭ·tў, n., pl. **-ties**. disaster. —**ca·lam'i·tous**, adj.

cǎl'cū·lāte'', v., **-lated, -lation**. v.t. **1.** ascertain through rational means. **2.** plan methodically. —v.i. **3.** reckon. **4.** rely. —cal'cu·la''tor, n. —cal''cu·la'tion, n. —cal'cu·la·ble, adj.

cǎl'cū·lāt''ĕd, adj. intended to produce the actual result.

cǎl'cū·lāt''ĭng, adj. scheming.

cǎl'cū·lŭs, n. method used in higher mathematics.

cǎl'drŏn, n. large kettle.

cǎl'en·dàr, n. **1.** printed object or device for determining the day of the month, etc. **2.** system for reckoning the years. **3.** schedule of agenda.

cǎl'en·dêr, n. **1.** machine for giving a smooth finish. —v.t. **2.** smooth in a calender.

cǎlf, n., pl. **calves**. n. **1.** young cow or bull. **2.** fleshy part of the lower leg. —**calf'skin''**, n.

cǎl'ĭ·bêr, n. **1.** diameter of a bullet, gun bore, etc. **2.** quality of character. Also, **cal'i·bre**.

cǎl'ĭ·brāte'', v.t., **-brated, -brating**. **1.** establish the scale of measurements of. **2.** determine the caliber of. —**cal''i·bra'tion**, n.

cǎl'ĭ·cō'', n., pl. **-coes, -cos**. printed cotton.

cǎl'ĭ·pêr, n. device for measuring outside or inside diameters. Also, **cal'i·pers**.

cǎl''ĭs·thĕn'ĭcs, n. pl. athletic exercises.

cǎlk, v.t. caulk.

cǎll, v.t. **1.** utter loudly. **2.** summon. **3.** name or describe. **4.** telephone. **5.** awaken. —v.i. **6.** make an order or request. **7.** impose a demand. **8.** make a visit. **9.** cry, as an animal. **10.** shout. —n. **11.** act or instance of calling. **12.** urge or appeal. —**call'er**, n.

cǎl·lǐg''rà·phў'', n. handwriting, penmanship, often ornamental.

cǎll'ĭng, n. vocation.

cǎl·lǐ'ó·pē'', n. organ of steam whistles.

cǎl'loŭs, adj. insensitive to the sufferings of others. —**cal'lous·ly**, adv. —**cal'lous·ness, cal·los'i·ty**, n.

cǎl'lŏw, adj. immature or inexperienced. —**cal'low·ness**, n.

cǎl'lŭs, n., pl. **-luses**. hard thickening on the skin.

cǎlm, adj. **1.** without strong emotion. **2.** undisturbed. —n. **3.** state of quiet. —v.t. **4.** make quiet or tranquil. —**calm'ly**, adv. —**calm'ness**, n.

cǎl'ó·rĭē, n. unit of heat measurement.

cǎl'ŭm·nў, n., pl. **-nies**. slander.

cǎm, n. rotating machine part producing reciprocating motion.

câ''mà·râ·dė·rĭē, n. cheerful companionship.

cǎm'bêr, n. shallow upward curve.

cǎm'brĭc, n. fine linen or cotton.

cǎm'côr·dêr, n. combined portable video camera and recorder.

cǎm'ĕl, n. desert animal storing water in one or two humps.

cǎm'ē·ō, n., pl. **-os**. gem of contrasting layers of stone.

cǎm'ĕr·à, n. **1.** boxlike device for taking photographs, shooting movie film, etc. **2.** optical device for copying a view. —**cam'er·a·man**, n.

căm·ou·fläge, *n.*, *v.t.* **-flaged, -flaging.** *n.* **1.** paintwork, etc. making something hard to see or interpret. —*v.t.* **2.** apply camouflage to.

cămp, *n.* **1.** temporary residence in the open. **2.** recreation area in the country. —*v.i.* **3.** establish or live in a camp. —**camp'fire''**, *n.* —**camp'site''**, *n.* —**camp'er**, *n.*

căm·päign', *n.* **1.** series of operations to attain a planned goal. —*v.i.* **2.** act in a campaign. —**cam·paign'er**, *n.*

căm'phŏr, *n.* aromatic crystalline substance.

căm'pŭs, *n.*, *pl.* **-puses. 1.** open area of lawn and trees, esp. the grounds of a school. **2.** academic community.

căn, *v.i.*, past tense **could** for 1 and 2, **canned, canning** for 3, *v.i.* **1.** be able or know how to. **2.** have the right to. **3.** preserve in sealed cans or jars. —*n.* **4.** metal container sealed to preserve food, etc. **5.** cylindrical container, esp. of sheet metal. —**can'ner**, *n.*

cá·năl', *n.* artificial waterway.

cá·nârd', *n.* rumor, esp. a malicious one.

cá·när'ÿ, *n.*, *pl.* **-ies.** yellow songbird.

căn'cĕl, *v.t.*, **-celed, -celing. 1.** cover with marks, esp. in order to invalidate. **2.** invalidate or terminate. **3.** *Math.* remove from both sides of an equation. —**can'' cel·la'tion**, *n.*

căn'cĕr, *n.* spreading malignant tumor. —**can'cer·ous**, *adj.*

căn''dè·lá'brŭm, *n.*, *pl.* **-bra.** branched candlestick.

căn'dĭd, *adj.* **1.** frank. **2.** unposed, as a snapshot. —**can'did·ly**, *adv.* —**can' dor, can'did·ness**, *n.*

căn'dĭ·däte'', *n.* competitor for public office, an honor, etc. —**can'di·da·cy**, *n.*

căn'dle, *n.*, *v.t.*, **-dled, -dling.** *n.* **1.** cylinder of wax, etc. with a central wick for burning. —*v.t.* **2.** inspect against a light, as eggs.

căn'dle·stĭck'', *n.* holder for candles.

căn'dÿ, *n.*, *pl.* **-dies**, *v.t.*, **-died, -dying.** *n.* **1.** flavored sweet. —*v.t.* **2.** cook in sugar. **3.** form into sugar crystals.

căne, *n.*, *v.t.*, **caned, caning.** *n.* **1.** hollow, jointed plant stalk. **2.** stick held while walking. —*v.t.* **3.** stretch with split rattan, as a chair seat. **4.** beat with a cane.

cā'nīne, *adj.* **1.** pertaining to dogs. **2.** pertaining to wolves or foxes. —*n.* **3.** dog, wolf, or fox. **4.** sharp human tooth.

căn'ĭs·têr, *n.* small storage can used in a kitchen.

căn'kêr, *n.* ulcerous sore.

căn'nêr·ÿ, *n.*, *pl.* **-ries.** plant for canning food.

căn'nĭ·bàl, *n.* person or animal that eats its own kind. —**can'ni·bal·ism**, *n.*

căn'nĭ·bàl·īze'', *v.t.*, **-ized, -izing.** strip in order to reuse parts.

căn'nŏn, *n.*, *pl.* **-nons, -non.** heavy gun.

căn''nŏn·āde', *n.* continuous firing of cannon.

căn·nŏt', *v.i.* can not.

căn'nÿ, *adj.*, **-nier, -niest.** shrewd. —**can'ni·ly**, *adv.* —**can'ni·ness**, *n.*

ca·noe (kà nōō'), *n.*, *v.i.*, **-noed, -noing.** *n.* **1.** narrow paddled boat. —*v.i.* **2.** travel by canoe.

căn'ŏn, *n.* **1.** basic principle or law. **2.** church official. **3.** official list of writings. —**ca·non'i·cal**, *adj.*

căn''ŏn·īze'', *v.t.*, **-ized, -izing.** declare to be a saint. —**can''on·i·za'tion**, *n.*

căn'ŏ·pÿ, *n.*, *pl.* **-pies. 1.** light, rooflike covering supported by poles. **2.** rooflike projection, as over a window.

cănt, *n.* **1.** hypocritical jargon. **2.** slang or jargon of a group. —*v.t.*, *v.i.* **3.** slant.

càn·tâ'tá, *n.* setting of a narrative for chorus.

căn·tēen', *n.* **1.** portable container for water. **2.** recreation center, as for soldiers.

căn'têr, *n.* easy gallop.

căn'tĭ·lē''vêr, *n.* **1.** projecting structural member secured at one end. —*v.t.* **2.** support with or treat as a cantilever.

căn'tō, *n.*, *pl.* **-tos.** division of a long poem.

căn'tŏr, *n.* singer at a Jewish service.

căn'vàs, *n.* **1.** tightly woven heavy cloth of hemp, cotton, etc. **2.** painting on canvas.

căn'vàss, *v.t.*, *v.i.* solicit for votes, opinions, sales orders, etc.

căp, *n.*, *v.t.*, **capped, capping.** *n.* **1.** soft, close-fitting hat. **2.** anything for capping. —*v.t.* **3.** cover the upper end of.

cā'pá·ble, *adj.* **1.** competent. **2.** **capable of,** with the ability, personality, etc. for.

—ca''pa·bil'i·ty, *n.* —ca'pa·bly, *adv.*

cá·pā'cioŭs, *adj.* spacious.

cá·păc'ĭ·tў, *n.*, *pl.* -ties. 1. ability to contain a quantity of material, number of persons, etc. 2. amount that can be produced. 3. role or function. 4. capability.

cāpe, *n.* 1. cloak. 2. projection of land seaward.

cā'pêr, *v.i.* 1. leap about playfully. —*n.* 2. playful leap.

căp'ĭl·lār''ў, *adj.* pertaining to the attraction of liquids in narrow tubes to above normal levels.

căp'ĭ·tál, *n.* 1. location of a national or state government. 2. money for investing or lending. 3. upper feature of a column or pier. 4. letter of the form used to begin a sentence or proper name. —*adj.* 5. excellent. 6. large, as letters. 7. pertaining to the death penalty.

căp'ĭ·tál·ĭsm, *n.* economic system based on investment or lending at interest of privately owned money. —cap'i·tal·ist, *n.* —cap''i·tal·is'tic, *adj.*

căp'ĭ·tál·īze'', *v.*, -ized, -izing. *v.t.* 1. spell with an initial capital. 2. use as or change into capital (2). 3. furnish with capital (2). —*v.i.* 4. **capitalize on**, exploit. —cap''i·tal·i·za'tion, *n.*

căp'ĭ·tŏl, *n.* legislative building.

cá·pĭt'ŭ·lāte, *v.i.*, -lated, -lating. cease to fight or resist. —ca·pit''u·la'tion, *n.*

cá·prīce', *n.* whim or whimsy. —ca·pri'cious, *adj.*

căp'sīze, *v.*, -sized, -sizing. *v.t.*, *v.i.* overturn, as a boat.

căp'stán, *n.* upright drum for winding cables.

căp'sŭle, *n.* sealed container.

căp'taïn, *n.* 1. military or naval officer. 2. master of a ship. 3. leader. —cap'tain·cy, *n.*

căp'tiŏn, *n.* title, explanation, etc. for a printed picture.

căp'tioŭs, *adj.* argumentative or faultfinding. —cap'tious·ly, *adv.* —cap'tious·ness, *n.*

căp'ti·vāte'', *v.t.*, -vated, -vating. fascinate, as with charm. —cap''ti·va'tion, *n.*

căp'tĭve, *n.* captured person or animal. —cap·tiv'i·ty, *n.*

căp'tŏr, *n.* person who takes a captive.

căp'tūre, *v.t.*, -tured, -turing. *n.* *v.t.* 1. prevent from fleeing, fighting, etc. by force. 2. express through art or speech. —*n.* 3. act or instance of capturing.

câr, *n.* 1. automobile. 2. wheeled vehicle of any kind. 3. elevator compartment.

cá·rāfe', *n.* bottle for serving beverages, usually water or wine.

căr'á·mèl, *n.* 1. burnt sugar, used as a flavor or color. 2. type of candy.

căr'ăt, *n.* 1. unit of 200 milligrams for weighing gems. 2. karat.

căr'á·văn'', *n.* group of travelers, beasts of burden, etc. in a desert.

câr'bīne, *n.* 1. short-barreled rifle. 2. light automatic military rifle.

câr''bŏ·hў'drāte, *n.* starch or sugar.

câr'bŏn, *n.* nonmetallic element found in organic compounds.

câr'bŭn·cle, *n.* 1. subcutaneous inflammation. 2. type of gem.

câr'bŭ·ret''ôr, *n.* device for making explosive mixtures of air and gasoline.

câr'căss, *n.* 1. dead animal body. 2. rough frame or shell, as of a building.

cârd, *n.* 1. stiff paper bearing writing, etc. 2. one of such papers used in games. 3. postcard. 4. **cards**, game played with cards.

cârd'bôard'', *n.* thick, papery sheeting.

câr'dĭ·ăc'', *adj.* pertaining to the heart.

câr'dĭ·gán, *n.* sweater buttoning in front.

câr'dĭ·nál, *n.* 1. Roman Catholic ecclesiastic second to the pope. 2. red American songbird. 3. cardinal number. —*adv.* 4. primary.

cârdĭnál nŭmbêr, basic number, as 1, 2, 3, etc.

câr'dĭ·ŏ·grăm'', *n.* electrocardiogram. —car'di·o·graph'', *n.*

câr''dĭ·ŏl'ŏ·gў, *n.* branch of medicine concerned with the heart.

cāre, *n.*, *v.*, **cared, caring.** *n.* 1. responsibility. 2. charge or protection 3. caution or heed. 4. worry. —*v.i.* 5. have responsibility. 6. feel liking or desire. 7. feel affection. 8. feel concern. —*v.t.* 9. have as a subject of concern.

cāre'fŭl, *adj.* 1. cautious. 2. with attention to accuracy.

cāre'lĕss, *adj.* not properly careful.

cá·rĕss', *v.t.* 1. touch lightly and affectionately. —*n.* **2.** gesture or touch indicating affection.

cär′gö, *n., pl.* **-goes, -gos.** freight.

cär′i·ca·tûre″, *n., v.t.,* **-tured, -turing.** *n.* **1.** exaggerated rendering of a person's peculiarities. —*v.t.* **2.** render in caricature. —**car′i·ca·tur″ist,** *n.*

cär′ies, *n.* decay of teeth or bones.

cär′il·lŏn, *n.* set of bells tuned to a scale. —**car″il·lon·neur′,** *n.*

cär′mïne, *n.* purplish red or crimson.

cär′nàge, *n.* slaughter.

cär′nàl, *n.* pertaining to the body or its appetites.

cär′nï·val, *n.* **1.** time of merrymaking before Lent. **2.** fair with entertainments.

cär′nï·vŏre″, *n.* flesh-eating animal or plant. —**car·niv′o·rous,** *adj.*

cär′ŏl, *n., v.,* **-oled, -oling.** *n.* **1.** song of praise, esp. at Christmas. —*v.i., v.t.* **2.** sing exuberantly. —**car′ol·er, car′ol·ler,** *n.*

cà·rŏuse′, *v.i.,* **-roused, -rousing,** *n. v.i.* **1.** drink together boisterously. —*n.* **2.** Also, **ca·rous′al,** period of carousing.

cä″roü·sël′, *n.* merry-go-round.

cärp, *v.i., n., pl.* **carp** or **carps.** *v.i.* **1.** find fault unjustly. —*n.* **2.** edible freshwater fish. —**carp′er,** *n.*

cär′pén·tēr, *n.* builder in wood. —**car′pen·try,** *n.*

cär′pét, *n.* **1.** cloth floor covering. —*v.t.* **2.** cover with or as if with a carpet. —**car′pet·ing,** *n.*

cär′pôrt″, *n.* open-ended shelter for an automobile.

cär′rïage, *n.* **1.** large animal-drawn passenger vehicle. **2.** any of various moving and carrying devices. **3.** posture.

cär′rï·êr, *n.* **1.** thing or person that carries. **2.** aircraft carrier.

cär′rï·òn, *n.* dead, decaying flesh.

cär′rŏt, *n.* vegetable with an edible orange root.

cär′rÿ, *v.,* **-ried, -rying.** *v.t.* **1.** support or suspend. **2.** take the weight of and move. **3.** transmit. **4.** win or attain. **5.** prosecute or develop. —*v.i.* **6.** be transmitted.

cärt, *n.* **1.** small wagon. —*v.t.* **2.** transport in a small wagon.

cär·tël′, *n.* monopolistic association of businesses.

cär′tï·làge, *n.* tough, elastic skeletal tissue.

cär′tòn, *n.* cardboard or plastic box.

cär·töön′, *n.* **1.** amusing or satirical drawing. **2.** motion picture of such drawings. **3.** artist's design for a fresco, tapestry, etc. —**car·toon′ist,** *n.*

cär′trïdge, *n.* **1.** unit of ammunition for a handgun, rifle, etc. **2.** any unit loaded or fitted into a machine.

cärt′wheel″, *n.* sidewise handspring.

cärve, *v.t.,* **carved, carving. 1.** form by cutting parts from. **2.** cut into parts, as meat. —**carv′er,** *n.* —**carv′ing,** *n.*

căs·cäde′, *n., v.i.,* **-caded, -cading.** *n.* **1.** chain of shallow waterfalls. —*v.i.* **2.** falling or as if in a cascade.

cäse, *n., v.t.,* **cased, casing.** *n.* **1.** box. **2.** instance. **3.** predicament. **4.** rational argument. **5.** form of a noun, etc. that shows its role in a sentence. —*v.t.* **6.** put in a case.

cäse′mént, *n.* window hinged on one side.

cäsh, *n.* **1.** money as opposed to checks, etc. **2.** money or check given in payment. —*v.t.* **3.** exchange for money, as a check or coupon.

cäsh·iër′, *n.* **1.** person in charge of cash in a bank, etc. —*v.t.* **2.** dismiss, as from the military.

cäs′ïng, *n.* outer cover.

cà·sï′nō, *n., pl.* **-nos. 1.** place for dances, entertainments, etc. **2.** place for gambling.

cäsk, *n.* barrel for liquids.

cäs′két, *n.* **1.** box for jewels, etc. **2.** ornate coffin.

căs′se·rŏle″, *n.* **1.** dish for baking. **2.** food baked in such a dish.

căs·sëtte′, *n.* a compact, ready-to-use case containing audio or video tape.

căs′sŏck, *n.* clergyman's long, loose garment.

cäst, *v.t.,* **cast, casting,** *n., v.t.* **1.** throw. **2.** directs or projects. **3.** form in a mold. —*n.* **4.** act or instance of casting. **5.** something formed in a mold. **6.** casing of a broken limb. **7.** group performing a play, etc. **8.** air or appearance.

cäst′à·wäy″, *n.* shipwrecked person.

cäste, *n.* rigid social division, esp. in India.

cäst′êr, *n.* **1.** small wheel supporting a furniture leg, etc. **2.** table pitcher for vinegar, etc. Also, **cast′or.**

căs′tĭ·gāte″, *v.t.,* **-gated, -gating.** rebuke severely. **—cas″ti·ga′tion,** *n.* **—cas′ti·ga″tor,** *n.*

căst′ĭng, *n.* something cast in a mold.

căs′tle, *n.* **1.** heavily fortified residence. **2.** chess rook.

căst′-ŏff″, *adj.* discarded.

căs′trāte, *v.t.,* **-trated, -trating.** remove the testicles of. **—cas·tra′tion,** *n.*

căs′ū·al, *adj.* **1.** occurring by chance. **2.** not regular. **3.** informal. **4.** relaxed. **—cas′u·al·ly,** *adv.* **—cas′u·al·ness,** *n.*

căs′ū·al·tў, *n., pl.* **-ties. 1.** victim of an accident or military action. **2.** serious accident.

căs′ū·ĭst·rў, *n., pl.* **-tries.** sophistry. **—cas′u·ist,** *n.*

căt, *n.* **1.** small, furry, four-footed animal. **2.** any feline.

căt′a·clўsm, *n.* sudden, drastic change. **—cat″a·clys′mic,** *adj.*

căt′a·cŏmb″, *n.* underground passage with burial places.

căt′a·lŏg″, *n., v.t.,* **-loged, -loging.** *n.* **1.** list of things acquired, to be sold, etc. **—v.t. 2.** list in a catalog. Also, **cat′a·logue″.**

căt′a·lўst, *n.* something that affects the speed of a chemical reaction without being altered in the process. **—cat″a·lyt′ic,** *adj.*

căt″a·ma·răn′, *n.* boat with two parallel hulls.

căt′a·pŭlt″, *n.* **1.** machine for hurling missiles, launching airplanes, etc. **—v.t. 2.** hurl or launch from or as if from a catapult.

căt′a·răct″, *n.* **1.** large waterfall. **2.** opacity in the eye causing blindness.

că·târrh′, *n.* inflammation of mucous membranes in the nose or throat.

că·tăs′trŏ·phē, *n.* major disaster. **—cat″a·stroph′ic,** *adj.*

căt′căll″, *n.* shrill noise expressing contempt.

cătch, *v.,* **caught, catching,** *n. v.t.* **1.** capture or seize. **2.** discover or surprise. **3.** become infected with. **—v.i. 4.** become caught or entangled. **5.** take or retain hold. **—n. 6.** act or instance of catching. **7.** number of things caught, esp. fish. **8.**

something for catching hold. **9.** desirable spouse or acquaintance. **10.** *Informal.* drawback. **catch′er,** *n.*

cătch′ăll″, *n.* place, category, etc. for miscellaneous things.

cătch′ĭng, *adj.* **1.** contagious. **2.** attractive.

cătch′ŭp, *n.* ketchup.

cătch′ў, *adj.* **-ier, -iest.** memorable, as a tune.

căt′ė·chĭsm (kat′ə kism), *n.* set of questions and answers, esp. on religious doctrine.

căt′ė·chīze″, *v.t.,* **-chized, -chizing.** question in detail. Also, **cat′e·chise″.**

căt″ė·gôr′ĭ·căl, *adj.* **1.** pertaining to categories. **2.** specific, as a statement. **—cat″e·gor′i·cal·ly,** *adv.*

căt′ė·ĝo·rīze″, *v.t.,* **-rized, -rizing.** put into categories.

căt′ė·ĝô″rў, *n., pl.* **-ries.** classification.

cā′tĕr, *v.t.* **1.** supply food, drink, tableware, etc. to parties for a fee. **2.** be overly accommodating. **—ca′ter·er,** *n.*

căt′ĕr·côr″nėred, *adj., adv.* on diagonally opposite corners. Also, **cat′er·cor″ner** or **cat′ty·cor″ner.**

căt′ĕr·pĭl″lår, *n.* crawling larva of a butterfly, moth, etc.

căt′gŭt″, *n.* tough string made from dried intestines of sheep, etc.

că·thär′sĭs, *n.* purging, esp. of morbid emotions.

că·thär′tĭc, *n.* **1.** medicine for clearing the bowels. **—adj. 2.** pertaining to cathartics. **3.** pertaining to a catharsis.

că·thē′drál, *n.* church in which a bishop normally officiates.

căth′ô·lĭc, *adj.* **1.** universal. **2. Catholic,** pertaining to the Roman Catholic Church. **—n. 3. Catholic,** member of the Roman Catholic Church. **—cath″o·lic′i·ty,** *n.* **—Ca·thol′i·cism,** *n.*

căt′năp″, *n., v.i.,* **-napped, -napping.** *n.* **1.** brief nap. **—v.i. 2.** take such a nap.

căt′s′-păw″, *n.* person used by another as a tool.

căt′sŭp, *n.* ketchup.

căt′tle, *n. pl.* cows, bulls, etc. **—cat′tle·man,** *n.*

căt′wălk″, *n.* narrow elevated walk, esp. for industrial workers.

cau′cŭs, *n., v.i.,* **-cused** or **-cussed,**

-cusing or **-cussing** *n*. **1.** business meeting of political leaders. —*v.i.* **2.** meet in a caucus.

caul·dron, *n*. caldron.

cau·li·flow´´êr, *n*. edible white head of a vegetable of the cabbage family.

caulk, *v.t.* make watertight, esp. a seam.

cau·sal, *adj*. pertaining to or involving the relation of cause and effect. —**cau·sal´i·ty**, *n*.

cause, *n., v.t.*, **caused, causing.** *n*. **1.** something to which a later event or condition is attributed. **2.** reason or motivation. **3.** goal or purpose, esp. political or religious. **4.** case for advocacy. —*v.t.* **5.** be the cause of. —**caus´er**, *n*. —**caus´a·tive**, *adj*.

cause´way´´, *n*. raised roadway.

caus´tic, *adj*. **1.** burning. **2.** bitterly sarcastic.

cau´têr·īze´´, *v.t.*, **-ized, -izing.** *Medicine*. burn or sear, as the flesh of a wound, to seal it. —**cau´´ter·i·za´tion**, *n*.

cau´tion, *n*. **1.** care, as to avoid danger. **2.** warning. —*v.t.* **3.** warn. —**cau´tion·ar´´y**, *adj*.

cau´tious, *adj*. careful to avoid danger.

căv´al·cāde´´, *n*. procession, esp. on horseback.

căv´´a·liêr´´, *n*. **1.** horseman, esp. a knight. **2.** gallant. —*adj*. **3.** casual. **4.** arrogant.

căv´al·ry, *n., pl.* **-ries.** *n*. **1.** fighting force on horseback. **2.** fighting force in motor vehicles. —**căv´al·ry·man**, *n*.

căve, *n., v.*, **caved, caving.** *n*. **1.** covered opening in the earth. —*v.i., v.t.*, **2. cave in**, collapse. —**cave´-in´´**, *n*.

căv´êrn, *n*. spacious cave. —**cav´ern·ous**, *adj*.

căv´i·âr´´, *n*. roe, esp. that of sturgeon. Also, **cav´i·are´**.

căv´il, *n., v.i.*, **-iled, -iling.** quibble. -**cav´il·er, cav´il·ler**, *n*.

căv´i·ty, *n., pl.* **-ities.** hollow place.

ca·vôrt´, *v.i.* frolic.

cay´·ênne´, *n*. extremely hot red pepper.

cay´·ūse´, *n*. small cowboy horse.

cēase, *v.*, **ceased, ceasing.** *v.i., v.t.*, *n*. stop. —**cease´less**, *adj*.

cē´dâr, *n*. type of fragrant pine.

cēde, *v.t.*, **ceded, ceding.** yield possession of.

cēil´ing, *n*. **1.** structure or surface forming the upper part of a room, etc. **2.** upper limit.

cěl´e·brāte´´, *v.*, **-brated, -brating.** *v.t.* **1.** perform ritually. **2.** mark or commemorate with festivity. **3.** do honor to. —*v.i.* **4.** have festivities. —**cel´´e·bra´tion**, *n*. —**cel´e·brant**, *n*. —**cel´e·brat´´ed**, *adj*.

ce·lěb´ri·ty, *n., pl.* **-ties.** **1.** fame. **2.** currently famous person.

ce·lěr´i·ty, *n*. swiftness.

cěl´êr·ÿ, *n*. plant with edible leaf stalks.

ce·lěs´tial, *adj*. pertaining to heaven or outer space.

cěl´i·bàte´´, *n*. **1.** unmarried person. **2.** sexually abstinent person. —*adj*. **3.** pertaining to celibates or celibacy. —**cel´i·ba·cy**, *n*.

cěll, *n*. **1.** unit of protoplasm. **2.** unit of space. **3.** habitable space in a prison, monastery, etc. **4.** electric battery. **5.** local unit of an organization. —**celled**, *adj*. —**cel´lu·lar**, *adj*.

cěl´lâr, *n*. **1.** basement. **2.** storage space totally or partly underneath a building. **3.** collection of wine.

cěl´lo·phāne´´, *n*. transparent wrapping material.

cěl·lō (chellō), *n., pl.* **-los.** large stringed instrument. —**cel´list**, *n*.

Cěl´lu·loīd´´, *n*. *Trademark*. plastic made from nitrocellulose and camphor.

Cěl´sĭus, *adj*. centigrade.

ce·měnt´, *n*. **1.** mixture of burned lime and clay, used for building. **2.** adhesive substance. —*v.t.* **3.** join with cement. **4.** cover with cement.

cěm´e·těr´´ÿ, *n., pl.* **-ies.** area of land for burying the dead.

cěn´sör, *n*. **1.** person who eliminates unauthorized material from writings, etc. **2.** official who criticizes the state of government, society, etc. —**cen´sor·ship´´**, *n*.

cěn·sô´ri·oŭs, *adj*. given to harsh criticism.

cěn´sûre, *n., v.t.*, **-sured, -suring.** *n*. rebuke or condemnation. *v.t.* **2.** rebuke or condemn.

cĕn′sŭs, *n.* counting and analysis of population, etc.

cĕnt, *n.* hundredth part of a dollar.

cĕn′täur′′, *n. Greek Mythology.* creature with the body of a horse and the head and trunk of a man.

cĕn′′tė·năr′ĭ·ȧn, *n.* person 100 years old.

cĕn′tė·nӑr′′ÿ, *adj., n., pl.* -ies. centennial.

cĕn·tĕn′nĭ·ȧl, *adj.* 1. pertaining to or marking a period of 100 years. —*n.* 2. hundredth anniversary. 3. celebration of such an anniversary.

cĕn′têr, *n.* 1. point or area equidistant from all outer points. 2. place of concentration. 3. area of political moderation. —*v.t.* 4. put or concentrate at a center.

cĕn′tĭ·grăde′′, *adj.* pertaining to a system of temperature measurement in which the range between the freezing and boiling points of water is 100 degrees; Celsius.

cĕn′tĭ·grăm′′, *n.* hundredth part of a gram. Also, **cĕn′tĭ·gramme′′.**

cĕn′tĭ·mē′′têr, *n.* hundredth part of a meter. Also, **cĕn′tĭ·me′′tre.**

cĕn′tĭ·pēde′′, *n.* many-legged crawling insect.

cĕn′trȧl, *adj.* 1. located at the center. 2. accessible from all points. 3. fundamental; basic. —**cĕn′trȧl·ly,** *adv.*

cĕn′trȧl·īze′′, *v.t.,* -ized, -izing. 1. unite under or control from a single authority. 2. place at a center. —**cen′′tral·i·za′tion,** *n.*

cĕn·trĭf′ŭ·gȧl fôrce, force tending to pull a mass away from a point around which it moves.

cĕn·trĭp′e·tȧl fôrce, force tending to pull a mass toward a point around which it moves.

cĕn·tû′rÿ, *n., pl.* -ries. 1. period of 100 years. 2. such a period as a unit, reckoned from A.D. 1.

cė·răm′ĭc, *n.* 1. ceramics, making of objects from baked clay or similar materials. 2. object so made. —*adj.* 3. pertaining to ceramics. 4. made as a ceramic.

cē′rē′′ȧl, *n.* 1. grain used as food. 2. food manufactured from such grain. —*adj.* 3. pertaining to grain.

cĕr·ē′brȧl, *adj.* reasoned rather than felt.

cĕr′′ė·mō′nĭ·ȧl, *adj.* 1. formal. —*n.* 2. ceremony.

cĕr′ė·mō′′nÿ, *n., pl.* -nies. 1. ordered set of actions for a formal occasion. 2. formality. —**cer′′e·mo′ni·ous,** *adj.*

cĕr′tȧin, *adj.* 1. without doubt. 2. without error. 3. inevitable. 4. unspecified. —**cer′tain·ly,** *adv.* —**cer′tain·ty,** *n.*

cĕr·tĭf′ĭ·cȧte, *n.* document that certifies.

cĕr′tĭ·fÿ′′, *v.t.,* -fied, -fying. 1. declare formally to be competent, valid, true, etc. 2. issue a certificate to. —**cer′′ti·fi·ca′tion,** *n.*

cĕr′tĭ·tūde′′, *n.* inevitability.

cĕs·sä′tion, *n.* stop.

cĕs′sion, *n.* act or instance of ceding.

cĕss′pōōl, *n.* receptacle for plumbing wastes.

chäfe, *v.,* **chafed, chafing.** *v.t.* 1. wear by rubbing. 2. warm by rubbing, as the skin. —*v.i.* 3. become restless and annoyed.

chăff, *n.* 1. waste from threshed grain. 2. worthless stuff. —*n. v.i.* 3. banter.

chäfĭng dĭsh, metal dish with a heating lamp underneath.

chȧ·grĭn′, *n., v.t.,* -grined, -grining. *n.* 1. embarrassment at failure or disappointment. —*v.t.* 2. cause chagrin in.

chäin, *n.* 1. flexible length formed of connected pieces. 2. related series of events, arguments, etc. 3. **chains,** bondage. —*v.t.* 4. fasten with a chain.

chäin rėäction, series of reactions each caused by one immediately previous.

chäir, *n.* 1. seat with a back. 2. official post or position, esp. a chairmanship or professorship. 3. chairman. —*v.t.* 4. preside over as chairman.

chäir′mӑn, *n.* person who presides over a meeting. —**chäir′man·ship′′,** *n.* Also, **chair′per′′son.**

chäise longue, *pl.* **chaise longues.** daybed with a chairlike back at one end. Also, **chaise lounge.**

cha·let (sha lā′), *n.* Swiss farmhouse with a low, jutting roof.

chăl′ĭce, *n.* wine goblet used in religious communions.

chälk, *n.* 1. soft white limestone. 2. white or dyed stonelike material for writing or drawing. —*v.t.* **3.** write or mark with chalk. —**chalk′y,** *adj.*

chǎl′lěnge, *v.t.,* -**lenged,** -**lenging,** *n. v.t.* **1.** call upon to fight, compete, or act bravely. **2.** demand identification of. **3.** demand proof from or for. **4.** reject as a juror. —*n.* **5.** act or instance of challenging. **6.** demand for one's best effort. —**chal′leng·er,** *n.*

chǎm′běr, *n.* **1.** room, esp. a bedroom. **2.** enclosed space, as in a machine, gun, or part of the body. **3.** legislative or official body. **4. chambers,** judge's office. —**cham′bered,** *adj.* —**cham′ber·maid′′,** *n.*

chǎmbêr mǔsǐc, music written for small groups and intended for small gatherings.

chá·mē·lē·ôn (kȧ mē′lē ŏn), *n.* lizard able to change the color of its skin.

cham·ois (shǎm′ē), *n.* **1.** small European mountain antelope. **2.** Also, **cham′my,** soft leather of a chamois or other animal, used for polishing.

chǎmp, *v.t., v.i.* bite or chew noisily.

chǎm·págne, *n.* sparkling white wine, originally from northern France.

chǎm′pǐ·ŏn, *n.* **1.** person who fights in another's behalf. **2.** athlete winning or getting first place in a series of competitions. **3.** advocate of a cause. —*v.t.* **4.** defend or advocate. —**cham′pi·on·ship′′,** *n.*

chánce, *n., adj., v.,* **chanced, chancing.** *n.* **1.** possibility of becoming, doing, or getting something desired. **2.** the unpredictable. **3.** unpredictable event. **4.** risk. **5.** lottery ticket. —*adj.* **6.** accidental. —*v.t.* **7.** risk. —*v.i.* **8.** transpire or come by accident.

chǎn′cěl, *n.* area of a church around the altar.

chǎn′cel·lòr, *n.* high government or academic official. —**chan′cel·lor·ship′′,** *n.*

chǎnc′ỹ, *adj.,* -**ier,** -**iest.** risky or uncertain.

chǎn′′dè·lïér′, *n.* lighting fixture suspended from a ceiling.

chǎnd′lêr, *n.* supplier, esp. to ships. —**chand′ler·ry,** *n.*

chǎnge, *v.,* **changed, changing,** *n. v.t.* **1.** make into a different form. **2.** give up

one for the other, as articles of clothing, vehicles, etc. **3.** give lower denominations of money in exchange for. —*v.i.* **4.** become different. **5.** leave one vehicle for another. —*n.* **6.** act or instance of changing. **7.** variety. **8.** money returned from that offered in payment. **9.** money in small denominations, esp. coins. —**change′less,** *adj.* —**change′a·ble,** *adj.*

chǎn′něl, *n., v.t.,* -**neled,** -**neling.** *n.* **1.** deeper part of a watercourse. **2.** body of water linking two larger ones. **3.** groove. **4.** *Television and radio.* frequency band. **5. channels,** offices in an official sequence for a given purpose. —*v.t.* **6.** send through or as through a channel. **7.** make grooves in.

chǎnt, *n.* **1.** sung liturgical music. **2.** heavily rhythmical song or speech. —*v.t.* **3.** sing or utter in a chant.

chǎn′tēy, *n., pl.* -**teys.** rhythmical work song of a sailor. Also, **chan′ty.**

chá·ŏs (kā′os), *n.* utter disorder. —**chaot′ic,** *adj.*

chǎp, *v.,* **chapped, chapping.** *v.t., v.i.* roughen or crack, as the skin or lips.

chǎp′ěl, *n.* **1.** small church. **2.** private church, as in a school or house.

chǎp′êr·ŏn (shǎp′ēr ŏn), *n., v.t.,* -**oned,** -**oning.** *n.* **1.** person who accompanies young unmarried persons to ensure propriety. —*v.t.* **2.** accompany as a chaperon. Also, **chap′er·one′′.**

chǎp′lǎin, *n.* **1.** clergyman employed by an institution, military force, etc. **2.** clergyman attached to a chapel.

chǎps, *n., pl.* leather leggings worn by cowboys.

chǎp′těr, *n.* **1.** division of a book. **2.** local branch of an association. **3.** council of a religious community.

chár, *v.,* **charred, charring.** *v.t., v.i.* **1.** burn on the surface. **2.** burn to charcoal.

chǎr′ác·těr, *n.* **1.** personality. **2.** moral strength. **3.** person as judged by his actions. **4.** eccentric or conspicuous person. **5.** reputation. **6.** person in a work of fiction. **7.** any symbol used in forming writing.

chǎr′′ác·těr·ǐs′tǐc, *adj.* **1.** typical. —*n.* **2.** typical or distinguishing quality. —**char′′ac·ter·is′tic·al·ly,** *adv.*

chăr′ăc·tēr·īze″, *v.t.*, **-ized**, **-izing**. **1.** attribute or give characteristics to. **2.** be characteristic of. —**char″ac·ter·i·za′ tion**, *n.*

chá·rāde′, *n.* pantomime offering clues to guessing a secret word.

chár′cŏal″, *n.* wood partially burned in the absence of air.

chârge, *v.*, **charged**, **charging**, *n. v.t.* **1.** supply or load. **2.** electrify. **3.** accuse. **4.** make responsible. **5.** ask as a price or fee. **6.** enter as a debt. **7.** attack with swift movement. **8.** require payment. **9.** move swiftly in an attack. —*n.* **10.** act or instance of charging. **11.** that with which something is charged. **12.** care or responsibility. **13.** object of one's care or responsibility. —**charge′a·ble**, *adj.*

chăr′ĭ·ŏt, *n.* two-wheeled horse-drawn vehicle. —**char″i·o·teer′**, *n.*

chá·rĭs′má (ká riz′má), *n.* quality of leadership derived from the personality. —**char″is·mat′ic**, *adj.*

chăr′ĭ·tá·ble, *adj.* **1.** kindly. **2.** generous. **3.** pertaining to charities.

chăr′ĭ·tў, *n.*, *pl.* **-ties**. **1.** love for mankind. **2.** generosity to the needy. **3.** organization for helping the needy. **4.** kindness in judging others.

châr·là·tán (shahr′lä tán), *n.* perpetrator of frauds. —**char′la·tan·ism, char′la·tan·ry**, *n.*

chârm, *n.* **1.** attractive or delightful quality. **2.** trinket. **3.** magic spell. —*v.t.* **4.** exercise charm or a charm upon. —**charm′er**, *n.* —**charm′ing**, *adj.*

chârt, *n.* **1.** map, esp. for navigation. **2.** graph or table. —*v.t.* **3.** make a chart of. **4.** map or plan.

châr′tēr, *n.* **1.** license or franchise. **2.** statement of fundamental organizational principles. **3.** hire of a vehicle. —*v.t.* **4.** grant a charter to. **5.** hire, as for a trip.

chár′ў, *adj.* **-ier**, **-iest**. **1.** cautious. **2.** sparing.

chāse, *v.*, **chased**, **chasing**. *n. v.t.* **1.** go after to overtake or capture. **2.** drive away. **3.** hunt. **4.** engrave, as metal. —*v.i.* **5.** *Informal.* rush. —*n.* **6.** pursuit. **7.** hunting of game.

chăsm (kas′m), *n.* abyss.

chăs′sĭs (chas′ē), *n.*, *pl.* **-sis.** frame and running gear of an automobile, not including the engine.

chāste, *adj.* **1.** pure, esp. of sexual desire or activity. **2.** tastefully restrained. —**chas′ti·ty**, *n.*

chās′tĕn, *v.t.* correct or subdue, esp. by punishment or scolding.

chăs·tīse′, *v.t.*, **-tised**, **-tising**. punish or scold.

chăt, *n.*, *v.i.*, **chatted**, **chatting**. *n.* **1.** light, informal conversation. —*v.i.* **2.** have such a conversation.

chă·teau′, *n.*, *pl.* **-teaux**, **-teaus.** castle or country house in France. Also, **châ·teau′**.

chăt′tĕl, *n.* piece of movable personal property.

chăt′tĕr, *v.i.* **1.** make rapid sounds with the voice. **2.** talk foolishly. **3.** make rapid clashing sounds, as the teeth of a chilled person. —*n.* **4.** chattering noise. **5.** foolish talk.

chauf·feŭr′, *n.* person hired to drive an automobile.

chau·vĭn·ĭsm, *n.* fanatical devotion to one's country, etc. —**chau′vin·ist**, *n.* —**chau″vin·is′tic**, *adj.*

chēap, *adj.* **1.** low in price. **2.** low in worth. **3.** despicable. **4.** *Informal.* stingy. —*adv.* **5.** at low cost. —**cheap′ly**, *adv.* —**cheap′ness**, *n.* —**cheap′en**, *v.t.*, *v.i.*

chēat, *v.t.* **1.** deceive, esp. for money. **2.** evade. —*v.i.* **3.** be deceptive. —*n.* **4.** deception. **5.** deceiver.

chĕck, *n.* **1.** precaution. **2.** inspection. **3.** halt or frustration. **4.** identification slip. **5.** document transferring money. **6.** bill, as in a restaurant. **7.** square in a checkered pattern. **8.** *Chess.* danger to a king. —*v.t.* **9.** halt or restrain. **10.** verify or investigate. **11.** place with another for shipment or storage. —**check′book″**, *n.* —**check′room″**, *n.*

chĕck′ēr, *n.* **1.** person or thing that checks. **2. checkers, a.** pattern of squares in alternating colors. **b.** game played on a board with this pattern. **3.** disk used in playing checkers. —**check′er·board″**, *n.*

chĕck′māte″, *n.*, **-mated**, **-mating**. *n.* **1.** *Chess.* inevitable capture of a king. **2.**

total defeat or ruin. —*v.t.* **3.** impose a checkmate on.

chĕck′ŭp″, *n.* medical examination.

chĕd′dår, *n.* hard cheese, often sharp.

chēek, *n.* **1.** side of the face below the eye. **2.** impudence.

chēer, *n.* **1.** happiness. **2.** shout of delight, encouragement, etc. **3.** food and entertainment. —*v.i.* **4.** shout cheers. **5.** become less unhappy. —*v.t.* **6.** encourage, etc. with cheers. **7.** make less unhappy. —**cheer′ful,** *adj.* —**cheer′less,** *adj.*

chēese, *n.* food made from milk curds.

chēese′bürg″ēr, *n.* hamburger cooked with cheese.

chēese′cāke″, *n.* cake made with cheese.

chēese′clŏth″, *n.* loosely woven cotton.

chĕf, *n.* cook, esp. a supervising cook.

chĕm′ĭ·cál, *adj.* **1.** pertaining to, or produced or operated by, chemistry. —*n.* **2.** substance produced by or used in chemistry. —**chem′ĭ·cál·ly,** *adv.*

chē·mīse′, *n.* loose-fitting woman's dress or slip.

chĕm′ĭs·trў, *n.* study of substances and their production or conversion. —**chem′ist,** *n.*

chē·nĭlle′, *n.* fabric woven from a soft, tufted yarn.

chĕr′ĭsh, *v.t.* regard as dear or precious.

chĕr′rў, *n.,* *pl.* **-ries.** tree bearing a small, red fruit.

chĕr′ŭb, *n.,* *pl.* **-ubs, -ubim.** angel often shown as a chubby, winged child. —**che·ru′bic,** *adj.*

chĕss, *n.* game played on a checkerboard with 16 pieces on each of two sides. —**chess′board″,** *n.* —**chess′man,** *n.*

chĕst, *n.* **1.** any of various boxlike containers for storage. **2.** part of the body within the ribs.

chĕst′nŭt, *n.* tree of the beech family with an edible nut.

chĕv′rŏn, *n.* sign like a V or inverted V, used for military insignia, heraldry, etc.

chēw, *v.t.* reduce with the teeth, as for swallowing. —**chew′y,** *adj.*

Chi·an·ti (kē ähn′tē), *n.* dry red table wine.

chĭc, *n.* elegance; smartness.

chī·cān′ĕr·ў, *n.,* *pl.* **-ries.** trickery.

chĭ·cä″nō, *n.,* *fem.* a person of Mexican descent.

chĭck, *n.* young bird, esp. a chicken.

chĭck′ĕn, *n.* hen or rooster.

chĭck′ĕn-heârt″ĕd, *adj.* cowardly.

chĭckĕn pŏx, contagious virus disease of children.

chĭck′pēa″, *n.* edible seed of a bushy plant.

chĭc′o·rў, *n.* plant with leaves used in salad and roots used as a coffee substitute.

chīde, *v.,* **chided** or **chid** or **chidden,** **chiding.** *v.t., v.i.* scold; rebuke.

chief, *n.* **1.** principal person —*adj.* **2.** main. —**chief′ly,** *adv.*

chief′táin, *n.* leader of a tribe or clan.

chif·fo·nier (shif′ō nēr′), *n.* chest of drawers. Also, **chif″fon·nier′.**

Chi·hua·hua (tshǐ wä′wä), *n.* small dog.

child, *n.,* *pl.* **children. 1.** human before puberty. **2.** offspring. —**child′birth″,** *n.* —**child′hood″,** *n.* —**child′less,** *adj.* —**child′like″,** *adj.*

chīld′ĭsh, *adj.* characteristic of children, esp. as regards behavior or judgment.

chĭl′ĭ, *n.* dish of beef, red pepper, etc. Also, **chili con car′ne.**

chĭll, *n.* **1.** perceptible cold. **2.** shiver from cold. —*adj.* **3.** chilly. —*v.t.* **4.** cause to be cold. —*v.i.* **5.** become cold.

chĭll′ў, *adj.,* **-ier, -iest.** cold.

chīme, *n.,* *v.,* **chimed, chiming.** *n.* **1.** bell, esp. in a clock. **2. chimes,** tuned bells. —*v.t., v.i.* **3.** sound with chimes.

chī·mē′rå (kǐ mē′rå), *n.* fantastic, imaginary thing. —**chi·mer′i·cal,** *adj.*

chĭm′nĕy, *n.,* *pl.* **-nies.** passage for smoke or heat.

chĭm″păn·zēe′, *n.* medium-sized ape.

chĭn, *n.* part of the face at the lower jaw.

chī′nå, *n.* **1.** porcelain. **2.** vitrified earthenware. **3.** dishes, etc. Also, **chi′na·ware.**

chĭnk, *n.* **1.** narrow crack. **2.** clinking sound.

chĭntz, *n.* printed cotton, usually glazed.

chĭp, *n.,* *v.,* **-ped, -ping.** *n.* **1.** small cut or broken piece. **2.** token used in gambling, etc. **3.** (computers) the basic component of miniaturized electronic circuitry. —*v.t.* **4.** knock chips from. —*v.i.* **5.** break into chips.

chĭp′mŭnk″, *n.* small North American squirrel.

chĭp′pêr, *adj.* lively in spirit.

chi·rŏp′o·dy̆, *n.* podiatry. **—chi·rop′o·dist,** *n.*

chi′′ro·prăc′tic, *n.* treatment of illness through manipulation of the joints. **—chi′ro·prac′′tor,** *n.*

chĭrp, *v.i.* make short, shrill, birdlike noises.

chĭs′el, *n., v.t.,* **-eled** or **-eling.** *n.* **1.** cutting tool narrow at one end. **—***v.t.* **2.** cut with a chisel. **—***v.i.* **3.** *Informal.* cheat, esp. on small matters. **—chĭs′el·er,** *n.*

chĭt′chăt′′, *n.* light conversation or gossip.

chĭt′tẽr·lĭngs, *n. pl.* small intestines of pigs as a food. Also, **chit′lins, chit′lings.**

chĭv′ăl·ry̆, *n.* **1.** medieval institution of knighthood. **2.** courage, gallantry, etc. **—chiv·al′ric,** *adj.* **—chiv′al·rous,** *adj.*

chlō′rĭne (klō′rēn), *n.* greenish chemical used for disinfection. **—chlo′ri·nate′′,** *v.t.*

chlō′ro·fŏrm′′, *n.* **1.** volatile liquid anaesthetic. **—***v.t.* **2.** kill or anaesthetize with chloroform.

chlō′ro·phy̆ll, *n.* green substance in plants. Also, **chlo′ro·phyl.**

chŏck, *n.* **1.** wedge stopping wheels from rolling. **—***v.t.* **2.** stop with chocks.

chŏck′-fŭll′, *adj.* absolutely full.

chŏc′o·làte, *n.* **1.** dark-brown substance made from or flavored with cacao seeds. **2.** reddish brown.

chōĭce, *n., adj.,* **choicer, choicest.** *n.* **1.** fact or instance of choosing. **2.** thing chosen. **—***adj.* **3.** superior in quality.

choir (kwīr), *n.* **1.** chorus, esp. one singing religious music. **2.** part of a church for such a chorus.

chōke, *v.,* **choked, choking,** *n. v.t.* **1.** cut off the breath of. **2.** clog. **—***v.i.* **3.** suffer from the cutting-off of breath. **—***n.* **4.** act, instance, or sound of choking.

cho·lĕs·tẽr·ŏl, *n.* solid found in bile, etc.

chōōse, *v.,* **chose, chosen, choosing.** *v.t.* **1.** decide upon as best to take, do, etc. **—***v.i.* **2.** make a choice.

chōōs′y̆, *adj.,* **-ier, -iest.** *Informal.* taking great care or trouble over purchases, etc. Also, **choos′ey.**

chŏp, *v.,* **chopped, chopping,** *n. v.t., v.i.* **1.** cut with small blows. **—***n.* **2.** small cutting blow. **3.** meat cut from the rib, shoulder, or loin. **4.** small, distinct waves of water. **5. chops,** mouth and lower cheeks. **—chop′per,** *n.* **—chop′py,** *adj.*

chŏp′stĭcks′′, *n. pl.* twin sticks used in eating, esp. in the Far East.

chŏp sū′ey, meat, bean sprouts, bamboo shoots, etc.

chó·răle′, *n.* **1.** hymn tune. **2.** choral composition. **3.** chorus or choir.

chor·al (kōr′əl), *adj.* pertaining to or for a chorus.

chord (kōrd), *n.* **1.** combination of musical tones. **2.** straight line intercepting an arc at two points.

chôre, *n.,* routine or hard task.

chor·e·og·ra·phy (kōr′′ē ahg′ra fē), *n.* art of planning or executing ballets or dances. **—chor′′e·o·graph′ic,** *adj.* **—chor′e·o·graph′′,** *v.t.* **—chor′′e·og′ra·pher,** *n.*

chôr′tle, *v.,* **-tled, -tling.** *v.i., v.t.* speak with chuckles.

cho·rus (kō′rus), *n.* **1.** singing group. **2.** composition for such a group. **3.** repeated part of a song composed in stanzas. **4.** unison. **—***v.t.* **5.** utter in chorus.

chŏw, *n.* **1.** medium-sized dog. **2.** *Informal.* food.

chŏw′dẽr, *n.* soup of milk, clams, fish, etc.

chow mein (chŏw mān), fried noodles, meat, bean sprouts, etc.

chrĭs′tĕn, *v.t.* **1.** baptize. **2.** name formally. **—chris′ten·ing,** *n.*

Chrĭs′tĕn·dŏm, *n.* Christian part of the world or of humanity.

Chrĭs′tiàn, *n.* **1.** believer in Christ. **—***adj.* **2.** pertaining to believers in Christ or to their churches. **3.** consistent with the teachings of Christ, esp. regarding charity or salvation. **—Chris′ti·an′i·ty,** *n.*

Chrĭstiàn nàme, *n.* name given to a person, as at baptism.

Chrĭst′màs, *n.* celebration of the birth of Christ, usually December 25.

chrō·măt′ic, *adj.* **1.** pertaining to color. **2.** *Music.* composed of semitones, as a scale.

chrōme, *n., adj., v.t.,* **chromed, chroming.** *n.* **1.** chromium or a chromium al-

loy. —*adj.* **2.** made with chromium. —*n.*
3. plate with chrome.

chro′mi·ŭm, *n.* corrosion-resistant metallic element.

chro′mŏ·sōme″, *n.* gene-bearing body.

chron′ĭc, *adj.* **1.** long-lasting or recurrent. **2.** suffering from a chronic ailment. —**chron′i·cal·ly,** *adv.*

chron′i·cle, *n., v.t.,* **-cled, -cling.** *n.* **1.** chronological record. —*v.t.* **2.** put into such a record. —**chron′i·cler,** *n.*

chrŏ·nŏl′ŏ·gў, *n., pl.* **-gies. 1.** measurement of time. **2.** recording of events in order of occurrence. **3.** dating of event. —**chron′′o·log′i·cal,** *adj.*

chrŏ·nŏm′ĕ·têr, *n.* highly accurate timepiece.

chrўs′ȧ·lĭs, *n.* pupa or cocoon of a butterfly.

chrўs·ăn′thė·mŭm, *n.* showy late-blooming flower.

chŭb′bў, *adj.* **-bier, -biest.** plump.

chŭck, *v.t.* **1.** toss. **2.** tap, esp. under the chin. —*n.* **3.** neck and shoulder cut of beef. **4.** act or instance of chucking.

chŭck′le, *v.i.,* **-led, -ling,** *n.* *v.i.* **1.** laugh softly. —*n.* soft laugh.

chŭg, *n., v.i.,* **chugged, chugging.** *n.* **1.** sound of an engine exhaust. —*v.i.* **2.** move with chugs.

chŭm, *n. Informal.* friend. **chum′my,** *adj.*

chŭmp, *n. Informal.* person with bad judgment.

chŭnk, *n.* thick fragment.

chŭnk′ў, *adj.* **-ier, -iest.** short and thick.

chûrch, *n.* **1.** religious organization. **2.** religious building. **3.** whole community of Christians. —**church′go′′er,** *n.* —**church′ly,** *adj.* —**church′man,** *n.*

chûrch′yârd″, *n.* grounds of a church, esp. when used as a cemetery.

chûrl, *n.* surly, ill-mannered person. —**churl′ish,** *adj.*

chûrn, *n.* **1.** device for shaking cream to form butter. —*v.t., v.i.* **2.** stir or shake.

chŭte (shōōt), *n.* slide for transferring materials, etc.

chŭt′nёў, *n.* Indian relish.

chutz′pah (hŏŏtz′päh), *n. Yiddish.* impudence; audacity. Also, **chutz′pa.**

ci·că·dȧ (si kä′dȧ), *n.* large insect making

a shrill rasping sound; often called a locust.

ci′dêr, *n.* apple juice, usually fermented.

ci·gâr′, *n.* rolled tobacco for smoking.

cĭg′′ȧ·rĕtte′, *n.* tobacco rolled in paper for smoking.

cĭnch, *n.* **1.** *Informal.* something easy. **2.** strap for securing a saddle.

cĭn′dêr, *n.* ash.

cĭn′ė·mȧ, *n.* motion picture or pictures. —**cin′′e·mat′ic,** *adj.*

cĭn′nȧ·mŏn, *n.* East Indian spice.

ci′phêr, *n.* **1.** code. **2.** zero.

cîr′cȧ, *prep.* around; used with dates.

cîr′cle, *n., v.t.,* **-cled, -cling.** *n.* **1.** closed two-dimensional curve with one center. **2.** something formed like such a curve. **3.** group of friends, persons with common interests, etc. —*v.t.* **4.** go around in a circle.

cîr′cuĭt, *n.* **1.** continuous path of movement. **2.** regular round of professional visits. **3.** path of an electric current.

cîr·cū′i·toŭs, *adj.* roundabout.

cîr′cuĭt·rў, *n.* components of an electrical circuit.

cîr′cū·lȧr, *adj.* **1.** shaped like a circle. —*n.* **2.** pamphlet, etc. for general distribution.

cîr′cū·lȧr·ize″, *v.t.,* **-ized, -izing. 1.** solicit from or notify by means of circulars. **2.** make circular.

cîr′cū·lāte″, *v.,* **-ated, -ating.** *v.i.* **1.** move in a closed, continuous path. **2.** move from person to person or place to place. —*v.t.* **3.** cause to move in either of these ways. —**cir′cu·la·to′′ry,** *adj.*

cîr′′cū·lā′tion, *n.* **1.** act or instance of circulating. **2.** normal movement of blood. **3.** readership of a periodical.

cîr′cŭm·cīse″, *v.t.,* **-cised, -cising.** cut away the foreskin of. —**cir′′cum·ci′sion,** *n.*

cîr′cŭm·fêr′ence, *n.* dimension along the line of a circle. —**cir·cum′fer·en′′tial,** *adj.*

cîr′′cŭm·lō·cū′tion, *n.* wordy, evasive speech.

cîr′′cŭm·năv′ĭ·gāte, *v.t.,* **-gated, gating.** sail or fly entirely around.

cîr′cŭm·scrībe″, *v.t.,* **-scribed, -scribing. 1.** draw a circle around. **2.** confine.

cîr′cŭm·spĕct″, *adj.* cautious. —**cir″ cum·spec′tion,** *n.*

cîr·cŭm·stănce″, *n.* **1.** accompanying condition. **2.** chance. **3.** **circumstances,** state of material welfare.

cîr″cŭm·stăn′tial, *adj.* **1.** pertaining to circumstances or circumstance. **2.** pertaining to legal evidence implying but not proving something. **3.** detailed.

cîr′cŭm·vĕnt″, *v.t.* prevent or overcome with cunning. —**cir″cum·ven′tion,** *n.*

cîr′cŭs, *n.* **1.** traveling show of animals, acrobats, etc. **2.** ancient show of human and animal combats, etc.

cîr′rŭs, *n.* feathery cloud formation.

cîs′têrn, *n.* tank for water storage.

cĭt′a·dĕl, *n.* fortress, esp. in a city.

cīte, *v.t.,* **cited, citing. 1.** mention as a scholarly authority. **2.** mention as an example. **3.** mention officially as meritorious. **4.** summon before a court. —**ci·ta′tion,** *n.*

cĭt′ĭ·zĕn, *n.* member of a state or other political entity. —**cit′i·zen·ry,** *n.* —**cit′i·zen·ship″,** *n.*

cĭt′rŏn, *n.* lemonlike fruit whose rind is candied.

cĭt″rŏn·ĕl′là, *n.* oil used to repel mosquitoes, etc.

cĭt′rŭs, *adj.* of or pertaining to lemons, oranges, limes, etc. —**cit′ric,** *adj.*

cĭt′ÿ, *n., pl.* **-ies. 1.** large community. **2.** government of such a community. **3.** civilized part of the world.

cĭv′ĭc, *adj.* pertaining to cities or their citizens.

cĭv′ĭcs, *n., pl.* study of the relation of citizens to political entities.

cĭv′ĭl, *adj.* **1.** not military or religious. **2.** polite. —**ci·vil′i·ty,** *n.*

cĭvĭl ĕngĭnēerĭng, engineering of public works or the like. —**civil engineer.**

cĭ·vĭl′ián, *n.* person outside any military or police organization.

cĭv″ĭ·lĭ·zā′tion, *n.* **1.** lawful, orderly state of society. **2.** society characterized by order. **3.** civilized part of the world.

cĭv′ĭ·līze″, *v.t.,* **-ized, -izing.** cause to adopt civilization.

cĭvĭl sêrvĭce, non-military, non-police government service. —**civil servant.**

cĭvĭl war, war between factions of the same nation.

clăd, *adj.* dressed.

clāim, *v.t.* **1.** designate for oneself. **2.** assert as true. **3.** require. —*n.* **4.** act or instance of claiming. **5.** something claimed. —**claim′ant, claim′er,** *n.*

clāir·vŏy′ànce, *n.* sensitivity to things not usually seen, esp. the supernatural. —**clair·voy′ant,** *adj., n.*

clăm, *n.* bivalve mollusk.

clăm′bêr, *v.i.* climb laboriously.

clăm′mÿ, *adj.,* **-mier, -miest.** cold and moist.

clăm′ôr, *n.* **1.** loud outcry. —*v.i.* **2.** make such an outcry, as in demanding or complaining. —**clam′or·ous,** *adj.*

clămp, *n.* **1.** mechanical device for holding things together. —*v.t.* **2.** fasten with a clamp.

clăn, *n.* group of families with a common ancestor. —**clans′man,** *n.*

clăn·dĕs′tĭne, *adj.* secret; stealthy.

clăng, *n.* loud ringing noise.

clăng′ŏr, *n.* clanging, as of bells.

clănk, *n.* dull metallic sound.

clăn′nĭsh, *adj.* sociable together but excluding others.

clăp, *v.t.,* **1.** strike together, as the palms of the hands. —*v.i.* **2.** clap the palms together. —*n.* **3.** sound of clapping. **4.** act or instance of clapping.

clăp·bôard (klə′bərd), *n.* board used as a siding for buildings.

clăp′pêr, *n.* object for striking a bell.

clăque, *n.* group for the purpose of applauding a performer, esp. for pay.

clăr′ĕt, *n.* dry red table wine.

clăr′ĭ·fÿ″, *v.t.,* **-fied, -fying.** make clear. —**clar″i·fi·ca′tion,** *n.*

clăr″ĭ·nĕt, *n.* reed woodwind instrument. —**clar″i·net′ist,** *n.*

clăr′ĭ·tÿ, *n.* clearness, esp. to the understanding.

clăsh, *v.i.* **1.** strike together violently. **2.** be in violent disagreement. —*n.* **3.** act or instance of clashing.

clăsp, *n.* **1.** folding fastener. **2.** embrace. **3.** grasp, as of the hand. —*v.t.* **4.** hold with or in a clasp.

clăss, *n.* **1.** category or grade. **2.** social or economic level. **3.** *Informal.* stylishness. **4.** group of students taught or graduating together. —*v.t.* **5.** classify. —**class′less,** *adj.* —**class′mate″,** *n.* —**class′room″,** *n.*

clăs´sĭc, *adj.* **1.** excellent of its kind. **2.** completely typical. **3.** harmonious. **4.** pertaining to Greco-Roman antiquity or art. —*n.* **5.** something excellent of its kind. **6.** Greek or Roman author.

clăs´sĭ·cal, *adj.* **1.** pertaining to Greco-Roman antiquity or art. **2.** *Music.* serious and of permanent value. **3.** traditional.

clăs´sĭ·cĭsm, *n.* adherence to forms or principles deemed classic. **clas´si·cist,** *n.*

clăs´sĭ·fȳ˝, *v.t.,* **-fied, -fying. 1.** put into meaningful categories. **2.** designate officially as secret. **clas˝si·fi·ca´tion,** *n.*

clăt´tẽr, *n.* **1.** loud rattling noise. —*v.i.* **2.** make a clatter. —*v.t.* **3.** cause to clatter.

claūse, *n.* **1.** unit of a sentence. **2.** unit of a document.

claus˝trŏ·phō´bĭ·à, *n.* morbid fear of enclosure. —**claus˝tro·pho´bic,** *adj.*

clăv´ĭ·chôrd˝, *n.* pianolike keyboard instrument.

clăv´ĭ·cle, *n.* collarbone.

clăw, *n.* **1.** hooked paw or foot. —*v.t., v.i.* **2.** scratch or grasp with or as with a claw.

clāy, *n.* earth in a readily molded state.

clēan, *adj.* **1.** free of dirt, germs, impurities, etc. **2.** keeping things clean. **3.** irreproachable. **4.** thorough. —*v.t.* **5.** make clean. —**clean´er,** *n.* —**clean´up˝,** *n.*

clēan´lȳ, *adj.,* **-lier, -liest.** free of or avoiding dirt, etc. —**clean´li·ness,** *n.*

clĕanse, *v.t.,* **cleansed, cleansing.** make clean.

clēar, *adj.* **1.** perfectly transparent. **2.** lucid. **3.** unambiguous. **4.** obvious. **5.** unobstructed. **6.** free of blame, danger, debt, etc. —*adv.* **7.** clearly. —*v.t.* **8.** make clear. **9.** pass without colliding with. **10.** net a profit of. —**clear´ly,** *adv.* —**clear´ness,** *n.*

clēar´ánce, *n.* **1.** space between two obstructions. **2.** official approval to proceed.

clēar´ĭng, *n.* forest area free of trees.

clēat, *n.* object attached to a surface to improve traction, give reinforcement, etc.

clēave, *v.,* **cleaved** or (for 1) **cleft** or **clove, cleaved** or (for 1) **cleft** or **cloven, cleaving.** *v.t., v.i.* **1.** split. —*v.i.* **2.** adhere or be faithful. —**cleav´er,** *n.* —**cleav´age,** *n.*

clĕf, *n.* *Music.* symbol establishing pitch.

clĕft, *n.* narrow opening; crack.

clĕm´ént, *n.* **1.** merciful. **2.** mild, as the weather. —**clem´en·cy,** *n.*

clĕnch, *v.t.* press or bind firmly together.

clẽr´gẙ, *n., pl.* **-gies.** priests, ministers, and other religious leaders. —**cler´gy·man,** *n.*

clĕr´ĭ·cal, *adj.* **1.** pertaining to clerks. **2.** pertaining to clergy.

clẽrk, *n.* **1.** record keeper. **2.** retail employee.

clĕv´ẽr, *adj.* able in understanding, contriving, etc. —**clev´er·ly,** *adv.* —**clev´er·ness,** *n.*

clĭ·ché, *n.* trite metaphor or phrase.

clĭck, *n.* **1.** sharp noise from striking, buckling, etc. —*v.t., vi.* **2.** move with a click.

clĭ´ént, *n.* person who buys professional services.

clī˝´ĕn·tēle´, *n.* clients of a professional merchant, etc.

clĭff, *n.* abrupt rise of land.

clĭ·măc´tẽr·ĭc, *n.* critical period of life, esp. in middle age.

clĭ·māte, *n.* characteristic weather. **cli·mat´ic,** *adj.*

clĭ´măx, *n.* point of greatest interest, emotion, tension, etc. —**cli·mac´tic,** *adj.*

clĭmb, *v.t.* **1.** move upward upon or within. —*v.i.* **2.** climb something. **3.** grow or become higher. —*n.* **4.** act or instance of climbing. **5.** something climbed. —**climb´er,** *n.*

clĭnch, *v.t.* **1.** establish firmly. **2.** bend to secure firmly, as a driven nail. —*n.* **3.** act or instance of clinching.

clĭng, *v.i.,* **clung, clinging. 1.** hold firmly. **2.** stay close.

clĭn´ĭc, *n.* **1.** session of medical treatment as a form of instruction. **2.** association of medical specialists. **3.** place for treating outpatients.

clĭn´ĭ·cál, *adj.* **1.** pertaining to clinics. **2.** pertaining to medical education and treatment involving actual cases. **3.** impersonally analytical.

clĭnk, *n.* **1.** high, muted ringing. —*v.i.* **2.** make such a sound. —*v.t.* **3.** strike so as to make such a sound.

clĭnk′êr, *n.* lump of coal ash, etc.

clĭp, *v.*, **clipped**, **clipping**. *v.t.* **1.** cut, as with scissors. **2.** fasten. **3.** *Informal.* hit sharply. —*v.i.* **4.** move swiftly. —*n.* **5.** fastener. **6.** *Informal.* sharp blow.

clĭp′pêr, *n.* **1.** fast sailing vessel. **2.** **clippers**, device for cutting hair.

clĭp′pĭng, *n.* article cut from a periodical.

clĭque, *n.* exclusive social group. —**cliqu′ish**, *adj.*

cloak, *n.* **1.** long, loose garment worn over the shoulders. —*v.t.* **2.** cover with a cloak. **3.** obscure.

clŏb′bêr, *v.t. Informal.* beat.

clŏck, *n.* **1.** machine for measuring time. **2.** narrow sock ornament. —*v.t.* **3.** time. —**clock′work′′**, *n.*, *adj.*

clŏck′wīse′′, *adv.*, *adj.* as the hands of a clock move, i.e. from left to right through 12 o'clock.

clŏd, *n.* **1.** lump of earth. **2.** *Informal.* stupid person.

clŏg, *v.*, **clogged**, **clogging**, *n. vt.* **1.** stop flow through; choke. —*v.i.* **2.** become stopped up. —*n.* **3.** act or instance of clogging. **4.** thick-soled shoe.

clŏis′têr, *n.* **1.** covered walk in a monastery, etc. **2.** monastic institution.

clōne, *n.*, *v. Biology.* a genetic duplicate of an organism.

clōse, *v.*, **closed**, **closing**, *adj.*, **closer**, **closest**, *n. v.t.* (klōz) **1.** block or fill, as with a door. **2.** move so as to block or fill. **3.** deny public access to. **4.** conclude. —*v.i.* **5.** become closed. —*n.* **6.** conclusion. —*adj.* (klōs) **7.** near; not far. **8.** confined. **9.** intimate. **10.** stuffy. **11.** careful. **12.** secretive. —**close′ly**, *adv.* —**close′ness**, *n.* —**clo′sure**, *n.*

clŏs′ĕt, *n.* **1.** small storage room. —*v.t.* **2.** put in a small room for privacy.

clōse′-ŭp′′, *n.* photograph at close range.

clŏt, *n.*, *v.i.*, **clotted**, **clotting**. *n.* **1.** lump, esp. of coagulated blood. —*v.i.* **2.** form a clot.

clŏth, *n.*, *pl.* **cloths**. **1.** material of interwoven fibers. **2.** piece of such material. **3. the cloth**, the clergy.

clōthe, *v.t.*, **clothed**, **clothing**. **1.** put clothes on. **2.** give clothes to.

clōthes, *n.*, *pl.* things to cover the human body. Also, **cloth′ing**.

clŏud, *n.* **1.** mass of vapor in the sky. **2.** mass of airborne material. **3.** something marring happiness, reputation, etc. —*v.t.* **4.** make indistinct, as from vapor. **5.** mar. —*v.i.* **6.** become cloudy. —**cloud′less**, *adj.* —**cloud′y**, *adj.*

clŏud′bûrst′′, *n.* sudden, violent rainstorm.

clŏut, *n.* **1.** blow. —*v.t.* **2.** hit.

clōve, *n.* **1.** tropical spice. **2.** section of a head of garlic, etc.

clō′vĕn, *adj.* divided or split.

clō′vêr, *n.* three-leafed herb.

clō′vêr-lēaf′′, *n.* system of curved ramps between roads crossing at different grades.

clŏwn, *n.* **1.** entertainer with funny antics. —*v.i.* **2.** act like a clown.

clŏy′ĭng, *adj.* repulsively sweet, sentimental, etc.

clŭb, *n.*, *v.* **clubbed**, **clubbing**. *n.* **1.** stick, etc. for striking blows. **2.** similar object used in exercises or sports. **3.** social group. **4.** suit of playing cards. —*v.t.* **5.** strike with a club. —*v.i.* **6.** unite for a purpose. —**club′foot′′**, *n.* —**club′house′′**, *n.*

clŭck, *n.* **1.** henlike sound. —*v.i.* **2.** make such a sound.

clūe, *n.* **1.** indication of the solution to a puzzle.

clŭmp, *n.* cluster, as of trees.

clŭm′sy̆, *adj.*, **-sier**, **-siest**. without skill or care. —**clum′si·ly**, *adv.* —**clum′si·ness**, *n.*

clŭs′têr, *n.* **1.** loose group. —*v.t.*, *v.i.* **2.** gather in a group.

clŭtch, *v.t.*, *v.i.* **1.** grasp violently. —*n.* **2.** grasp. **3.** **clutches**, unrightful possession or power. **4.** device for engaging a machine with its mover.

clŭt′têr, *v.t.* **1.** fill with unwanted things. —*n.* **2.** disorderly accumulation.

cōach, *n.* **1.** enclosed horse-drawn carriage. **2.** bus. **3.** railroad passenger car. **4.** trainer, as in sports or performing arts. —*v.t.* **5.** train, rehearse, or prompt. —**coach′man**, *n.*

cō·ăg′ū·lāte′′, *v.*, **-ated**, **-ating**. *v.i.*, *v.t.* turn from a liquid to a semi-solid. —**co·ag′′u·la′tion**, *n.* —**co·ag′u·lant**, *n.*

cōal, *n.* **1.** combustible mineral. **2.** ember. —*v.t.* **3.** supply with coal.

cō''a·lĕsce', *v.i.*, -**lesced, lescing.** unite. —**co''a·les'cence,** *n.*

cō''a·li'tion, *n.* act of uniting for a specific purpose.

cōal ŏil, kerosene.

cōarse, *adj.* **1.** composed of large grains, fibers, etc. **2.** roughly made. **3.** unrefined, as manners or language. —**coarse'ly**, *adv.* —**coarse'ness**, *n.* —**coars'en**, *v.t., v.i.*

cōast, *n.* **1.** land by a sea, etc. —*v.i.* **2.** move by gravity or momentum. **3.** sail along a coast. —**coast'al**, *adj.* —**coast'line''**, *n.*

cōast'ĕr, *n.* **1.** person or thing that coasts. **2.** mat or stand for wet glasses. **3.** ship on a coastal run.

cōat, *n.* **1.** cold-weather garment. **2.** jacket. **3.** Also, **coat'ing**, layer of material. —*v.t.* **4.** cover with a coat.

cōat ŏf ärms, *Heraldry.* arms of a person, state, etc.

cōax, *v.t.*, persuade with flattery or wheedling.

cō·ăx'ĭ·ål, *adj.* having a common axis.

cŏb, *n.* corncob.

cŏb'ble, *v.t.*, -**bled, -bling**, *n.* **1.** repair, as shoes. **2.** assemble clumsily. —*n.* **3.** Also, **cob'ble·stone''**, large pebble used for paving.

cŏb'blĕr, *n.* **1.** person who cobbles. **2.** fruit-filled pastry.

cō'brá, *n.* poisonous Asian and African snake.

cŏb'wĕb'', *n.* web of a spider.

cō·cāine,', *n.* narcotic from the coca plant.

cŏck, *n.* **1.** rooster. **2.** faucet. —*v.t.* **3.** tilt. **4.** make ready for firing, as a gun.

cŏck·āde', *n.* hat badge or ribbon.

cŏck'á·tōō'', *n.* crested East Indian parrot.

cŏckĕr spănĭel, small, droopy-eared spaniel.

cŏck'eÿed'', *adj. Informal.* awry; wrong.

cŏck'le, *n.* edible shellfish.

cŏck'nĕy, *n., pl.* -**nies. 1.** native of London's East End. **2.** dialect of such a native.

cŏck'pĭt'', *n.* **1.** place for a cockfight. **2.** space for an airplane crew.

cŏck'rŏach'', *n.* crawling insect found in buildings.

cŏck'sūre'', *adj.* foolishly self-assured.

cŏck'tāil'', *n.* **1.** mixed alcoholic drink. **2.** mixed appetizer.

cŏck'ÿ, *adj.*, -**ier, -iest.** *Informal.* showily self-assured.

cō'cōa, *n.* drink made from roasted cacao powder.

cō'cō·nŭt, *n.* fruit of a palm tree, whose flesh and juice are consumed. Also, **co'coa·nut.**

cŏ·cōōn', *n.* case of certain insect pupas, made of a thread.

cŏd, *n., pl.* **cod, cods.** edible northern saltwater fish. Also, **cod'fish''.**

cŏd'dle, *v.t.*, -**dled, -dling. 1.** cook in water just below boiling. **2.** take excessive care of; pamper.

cōde, *n., v.t.*, **coded, coding.** *n.* **1.** set of laws or principles. **2.** formula for secret messages. **3.** formula for transcription by telegraph, wigwag, etc. —*v.t.* put into code.

cō'dēine, *n.* pain reliever derived from opium. Also, **co'dein.**

cŏd'ĭ·cĭl, *n.* appendix to a will.

cŏd'ĭ·fÿ'', *v.t.*, -**fied, -fying.** put into systematic form, esp. in writing. —**cod''i·fi·ca'tion**, *n.*

cō'-ēd'', *n. Informal.* woman in a coeducational school. Also, **co'ed''.**

cō·ĕd''ū·cā'tion, *n.* enrollment of men and women in the same school. —**co·ed''u·ca'tion·al**, *adj.*

cō''ĕf'fĭ'cĭĕnt, *n.* multiplier.

cō·ērce', *v.t.*, -**erced, -ercing.** compel by force or threats. —**co·er'cion**, *n.*

cō·ē'vál, *adj.* at or of the same age.

cō''ĕx·ĭst', *v.i.* **1.** exist together. **2.** live together without dispute. —**co''ex·ist'ence**, *n.*

cŏf'fēe, *n.* drink made from the roasted seed of a tropical shrub.

cŏf'fĕr, *n.* chest for valuables.

cŏf'fĭn, *n.* burial chest.

cŏg, *n.* gear tooth.

cō·gĕnt, *adj.* forcefully convincing, as an argument. —**co'gen·cy**, *n.*

cŏg'ĭ·tāte'', *v.*, -**tated, -tating.** *v.t., v.i.* ponder. —**cog''i·ta'tion**, *n.* —**cog'i·ta''tor**, *n.*

co·gnac (kōn'yăk), *n.* a French brandy.

cŏg'nāte'', *adj.* **1** related. —*n.* **2.** someone or something related.

cŏg·nĭ′tion, *n.* knowledge or perception. —cog′ni·tive, *adj.*

cŏg′nĭ·zănce, *n.* official notice. —cog′ni·zant, *adj.*

cŏg·nō′měn, *n.* nickname.

cŏg′whēel′′, *n.* gear wheel, esp. in a clock, toy, etc.

cō·hăb′ĭt, *v.i.* live together, esp. out of wedlock. —co·hab′′i·ta′tion, *n.*

cō·hēre′, *v.i.*, -hered, -hering. 1. stick together. 2. be rationally connected. —co·her′ent, *adj.* —co·her′ence, *n.*

cō·hē′sion, *n.* tendency of particles, etc. to hold together. —co·he′sive, *adj.*

cŏif·fūre′, *n.* hair style.

cŏĭl, *n.* 1. spiral or helix. —*v.t.*, *v.i.* 2. wind into a coil.

cŏin, *n.* 1. piece of metal used as money. 2. metal money. —*v.t.* 3. stamp as money. 4. invent as a new expression. —coin′age, *n.*

cō′′ĭn·cīde′, *v.i.*, -cided, -ciding. 1. happen at the same time. 2. be in the same space. 3. be in agreement. —co·in′ci·dence, *n.* —co·in′′ci·den′tal, co·in′ci·dent, *adj.*

cō·ĭ′tŭs, *n.* sexual intercourse. Also, co·i′tion, *n.*

cŏke, *n.* 1. fuel derived from coal. 2. slang for cocaine.

cŏl′ăn·dẽr, *n.* large strainer.

cōld, *adj.* 1. having a temperature lower than normal or working temperature. 2. having a relatively low temperature. 3. feeling a lack of warmth. 4. unemotional. 5. hostilely unexpressive. 6. *Informal.* a. unprepared. b. unconscious. c. fully memorized. —*n.* 7. cold conditions, weather, etc. 8. illness associated with cold weather. —cold′ly, *adv.* —cold′ness, *n.*

cōld′blŏŏd′′ĕd, *adj.* 1. having a temperature of the environment. 2. without emotion, conscience, etc.

cōld wãr, prolonged hostile situation without fighting.

cōle′slăw′′, *n.* salad of shredded raw cabbage.

cŏl′ĭc, *n.* abdominal cramp.

cŏl′lăb′o·rāte′′, *v.i.*, -rated, -rating. 1. work together, as on a project. 2. assist the invaders of one's country. —col-

lab′′o·ra′tion, *n.* —col·lab′o·ra′′tor, *n.* —col·lab′′o·ra′tion·ist, *n.*

cŏl·lăpse′, *v.*, -lapsed, -lapsing, *n. v.i.* 1. fall because of weakness. 2. fold when not in use. 3. fail suddenly in bodily or mental health. —*v.t.* 4. cause to collapse. —*n.* 5. act or instance of collapsing. —col·laps′i·ble, *adj.*

cŏl′lãr, *n.* 1. band worn around the neck. 2. band of material applied to a shaft, etc. —*v.t.* 3. seize by the neck. 4. put a collar on.

cŏl′lãr·bōne′′, *n.* bone between the breastbone and shoulder blade; clavicle.

cŏl·lăt′ẽr·ăl, *n.* 1. security for a loan. —*adj.* 2. accompanying. 3. related through a remote ancestor.

cŏl′lēague, *n.* professional associate.

cŏl·lĕct′, *v.t.*, *v.i.* 1. gather together. —*v.t.* 2. acquire to enjoy permanently. 3. enforce payment of. —*adv.*, *adj.* 4. with the receiver paying the charges. —col·lect′a·ble, col·lect′i·ble, *adj.*, *n.* —col·lect′or, *n.* —col·lec′tion, *n.*

cŏl·lĕct′ĕd, *adj.* with one's emotions under control.

cŏl·lĕc′tĭve, *adj.* 1. involving cooperation. —*n.* 2. collective enterprise or workplace. —col·lec′tive·ly, *adv.*

cŏl·lĕc′tĭv·ĭsm, *n.* adoption of collective working methods. —col·lec′tiv·ist, *n.*, *adj.* —col·lec′tiv·ize′′, *v.t.*

cŏl′lēge, *n.* 1. generalized institution of higher learning. 2. specialized school. 3. official organization. —col·le′giate, *adj.*

cŏl·līde′, *v.i.*, -lided, -liding. strike together with direct impact. —col·li′sion, *n.*

cŏl′lĭe, *n.* large, long-haired dog.

cŏl·lō′quĭ·ăl, *adj.* pertaining to or used in informal conversation only. —col·lo′qui·al·ism, *n.*

cŏl·lō′quý, *n.*, *pl.* -quies. discussion.

cŏl·lū′sion, *n.* unlawful conspiracy. —col·lu′sive, *adj.*

cŏ·lŏgne′, *n.* perfumed toilet water.

cō′lŏn, *n.*1. part of the large intestine. 2. punctuation mark written thus : .

colo′nel (kẽr′něl), *n.* military officer between a lieutenant colonel and a brigadier general. —colo′nel·cy, *n.*

cŏl′ō·nīze, *v.*, -nized, -nizing. *v.t.* 1. establish colonies in. —*v.i.* **2.** settle in or as a colony.

cŏl″ŏn·nāde′, *n.* row of columns, esp. before a porch.

cŏl′o·nў, *n., pl.* **-nies. 1.** region in the possession of a foreign nation. **2.** community of settlers. **3.** group of social insects, etc. —**co·lon′i·al**, *adj., n.* —**col′on·ist**, *n.*

cŏl′ŏr, *n.* **1.** property deriving from specific wavelengths of light. **2.** pigment. **3.** vividness. **4.** colors, **a.** national flag. **b.** uniform, badge, etc. distinctively colored. —*v.t.* **5.** give color to. —*v.i.* **6.** blush. —**col″or·a′tion**, *n.* —**col′or·ful**, *adj.* —**col′or·ing**, *n.*

cŏl′′ŏr·à·tū′rà, *n.* soprano capable of brilliant effects.

cŏl′ŏr·lĕss, *adj.* not vivid.

co·lŏs′sàl, *adj.* gigantic; enormous.

co·lŏs′sŭs, *n., pl.* **-si, -suses.** something gigantic.

cŏlt, *n.* young male horse.

cŏl′ŭmn, *n.* **1.** narrow, upright structural support. **2.** stack of printed or written lines read together. **3.** regular series of articles by a journalist. **4.** file of troops. —**col′um·nist**, *n.*

co′mà, *n.* pathological unconsciousness. —**co′ma·tose′′**, *adj.*

cŏmb, *n.* **1.** pronged device for arranging the hair or other fibers. **2.** crest of a rooster, etc. **3.** honeycomb. —*v.t.* **4.** use a comb on. **5.** search exhaustively.

cŏm′băt, *n., v.t.,* **-bated, -bating.** *n.* **1.** battle. —*v.t.* (kăm băt′) **2.** fight or oppose. —**com′bat′ant**, *n., adj.* —**com′bat′ive**, *adj.*

cŏm′′bī·nā′tion, *n.* **1.** act or instance of combining. **2.** group of successive settings of a lock dial that open the lock.

cŏm·bīne, *v.t., v.i.* **1.** join together. —*n.* (cŏm′bīne) **2.** machine that harvests and threshes grain. **3.** syndicate.

cŏm′bō, *n., pl.* **-bos.** *Jazz.* small instrumental group.

cŏm·bŭs′tion, *n.* act of burning. —**com·bus′ti·ble**, *adj.*

cŏme, *v.i.,* **came, come, coming,** *interj.* *v.i.* **1.** move to this place. **2.** attend; be present. **3.** occur; happen. —*interj.* **4.** be truthful, reasonable, etc.

co·mē′dĭ·àn, *n.* humorous performer. Also, *fem.,* **co·me′′di·enne′**.

cŏm′e·dў, *n., pl.* **-dies. 1.** drama with a happy ending. **2.** amusing situation.

cóme′lў, *adj.,* **-lier, -liest.** physically attractive.

co·mĕs′tĭ·ble, *n., adj.* edible.

cŏm′ĕt, *n.* cloud of fine dust in orbit around the sun.

cóm′fŏrt, *n.* **1.** feeling of physical wellbeing. **2.** consolation. —*v.t.* **3.** console or reassure.

cóm′fŏrt·à·ble, *adj.* **1.** enjoying comfort. **2.** promoting comfort. —**com′fort·a·bly**, *adv.*

cóm′fŏrt·êr, *n.* **1.** source of comfort. **2.** quilt.

cŏm′ĭc, *adj.* **1.** Also, **com′i·cal**, amusing. **2.** pertaining to comedy. **3. comics,** comic strip. —*n.* **4.** comedian. —**com′i·cal·ly**, *adv.*

cŏm′ĭng, *adj.* **1.** on the way. **2.** destined for preeminence. —*n.* **3.** approach or arrival.

cŏm′mà, *n.* a mark, used especially to separate phrases or clauses in a sentence.

cóm·mănd′, *v.t.* **1.** order or direct. **2.** have authority over. **3.** have the use or enjoyment of. **4.** overlook. —*n.* **5.** order. **6.** authority or control.

cŏm′măn·dănt′′, *n.* commanding officer.

cŏm′′măn·dēer′, *v.t.* take control of by authority or force.

cóm·măn′dêr, *n.* naval officer between a lieutenant commander and a captain in rank.

cómmănder ĭn chiêf, *n., pl.* **commanders in chief.** supreme military commander.

cóm·mănd′mĕnt, *n.* order, esp. a standing one from a deity.

cŏm·măn′dō, *n., pl.* **-dos, -does.** member of a raiding force.

cóm·mĕm′ô·rāte′′, *v.t.,* **-rated, -rating.** honor or preserve the memory of. —**com·mem′′o·ra′tion**, *n.* —**com·mem′o·ra·tive**, *adj.*

cóm·mĕnce′, *v.,* **menced, -mencing.** *v.t., v.i.* begin.

cóm·mĕnce′mĕnt, *n.* **1.** beginning. **2.** high-school graduation ceremony.

cóm·mĕnd′, *v.t.* **1.** praise. **2.** recommend.

3. entrust. —**com′mend′a·ble,** *adj.*
—**com′′men·da′tion,** *n.* —**com′mend′a·to′′ry,** *adj.*

com·měn′sûr·a·ble, *adj.* able to be measured or evaluated in the same way.

com·měn′sû·rate, *adj.* equal or in proportion.

com′měnt, *n.* **1.** remark or remarks on something observed. **2.** opinion or explanation regarding something. —*v.i.* **3.** make a comment.

com′měn·tār′′y, *n., pl.* **-ries.** set of explanatory notes.

com′měn·tā′′tor, *n.* person who comments on current events.

com′mêrce, *n.* purchasing and sale of merchandise.

com·měr′ciàl, *adj.* **1.** pertaining to commerce. —*n.* **2.** television or radio advertisement.

com·měr′ciàl·ĭsm, *n.* emphasis on ready mass saleability rather than on quality, taste, etc.

com·měr′ciàl·īze′′, *v.t.* **-ized, izing.** make, sell, etc. for maximum profit.

com·mĭn′gle, *v.,* **-gled, -gling.** *v.t., v.i.* blend.

com·mĭs′êr·āte′′, *v.t.* **-ated, -ating.** feel sympathetic sorrow. —**com·mĭs′′er·a′tion,** *n.*

com′′mĭs·sär′ĭ·ăt, *n.* military department in charge of food.

com′mĭs·sär′′y, *n., pl.* **-ries.** *n.* **1.** military food shop. **2.** factory canteen.

com·mĭs′sion, *n.* **1.** entrusted task. **2.** formal authorization. **3.** military officership. **4.** committee. **5.** salesman's percentage of the amount of a sale. —*v.t.* **6.** entrust or authorize. **7.** put in service, as a ship.

com·mĭs′sion·êr, *n.* head of a municipal department or commission.

com·mĭt′, *v.t.* **-mitted, -mitting. 1.** obligate. **2.** state the position of in a controversy. **3.** do, esp. a crime. **4.** send for confinement. —**com·mĭt′ment,** *n.* —**com·mĭt′al,** *n.*

com·mĭt′tēe, *n.* chosen group of persons with specified responsibilities. —**com·mĭt′tee·man,** *n.* —**com·mĭt′tee·wom′′an,** *n.*

com·mōde′, *n.* **1.** chest of drawers. **2.** water closet.

com·mō′dĭ·oǔs, *adj.* roomy.

com·mŏd′ĭ·tў, *n., pl.* **-ties.** *Commerce.* material or article, as opposed to a service.

com′mó·dôre′′, *n.* **1.** naval officer ranking between a captain and a rear admiral. **2.** head of a yacht squadron.

com′mŏn, *adj.* **1.** pertaining to many or to all. **2.** not unusual. **3.** low in rank or status. **4.** vulgar. —*n.* **5.** area of public land in a village. —**com′mon·ly,** *adv.*

com′mŏn·êr, *n.* citizen not of the nobility.

cŏmmŏn lăw, law based on custom and court decision.

com′mŏn·plăce′′, *adj.* **1.** completely or tritely familiar. —*n.* **2.** something commonplace.

cŏmmŏn sĕnse, ordinary good judgment. —**com′′mon-sense′′, com′′mon·sen′′si·cal,** *adj.*

com′mŏn·wēal′′, *n.* general good.

com′mŏn·wēalth′′, *n.* **1.** federation of states. **2.** state.

com·mō′tion, *n.* uproar.

com·mū′nàl, *adj.* pertaining to or shared by a community or group.

com·mūne′, *v.i.,* **-muned, -muning.** *n. v.i.* **1.** be in intimate communication or sympathy. —*n.* (kom′yōōn) **2.** community sharing goods, responsibilities, etc.

com·mūn′ĭ·cà·ble, *adj.* **1.** able to be communicated. **2.** able to be transferred, as an illness.

com·mūn′ĭ·cànt, *n.* partaker of the Eucharist.

com·mūn′ĭ·căte, *v.,* **-cated, -cating.** *v.t.* **1.** make understood to others. —*v.i.* **2.** exchange messages. **3.** be in communion. **4.** be connected, as rooms. —**com·mun′′i·ca′tion,** *n.*

com·mūn′ĭ·cà·tĭve, *adj.* talkative or confiding.

com·mūn′ion, *n.* **1.** state of intimacy. **2.** *Christianity.* sharing of bread and wine in remembrance of Christ. **3.** religious denomination.

com·mūn′′ĭ·qué, *n.* official message or news release.

com′mū′nĭsm, *n.* **1.** political theory demanding public ownership of economic resources. **2. Communism.** socialism derived from the theories of Karl Marx.

—com′′mu·nis′tic, *adj.* —com′mu·nist, *n., adj.*

com·mūn′i·tÿ, *n., pl.* **-ties. 1.** town, etc. **2.** group with common interests, etc. **3.** sharing in common.

com·mūte′, *v.,* **-muted, -muting.** *v.t.* **1.** alter, as a prison sentence. —*v.i.* **2.** travel regularly, as between home and work. —com′mut′er, *n.* —com′′mu·ta′tion, *n.*

com·păct′, *adj.* **1.** occupying a minimal space. **2.** succinct. —*n.* (kom′pakt) **3.** small cosmetic case. **4.** small-bodied car. **5.** mutual agreement. —com·pact′ly, *adv.* —com·pact′ness, *n.*

com·păn′ion, *n.* **1.** person who keeps one company. **2.** one of a pair or set. —com·pan′ion·ship′′, *n.*

com·păn′ion·a·ble, *adj.* willing to keep one company.

com·păn′ion·wāy′′, *n.* stair in a ship.

com′pa·nÿ, *n., pl.* **-nies. 1.** fellowship; companionship. **2.** group of persons. **3.** group of persons assembled for social purposes. **4.** guests. **5.** business organization or association. **6.** military unit.

com′pa·ra·ble, *adj.* allowing comparison.

com·păr′a·tĭve, *adj.* **1.** involving comparison. **2.** in comparison to other cases. —com·par′a·tive·ly, *adv.*

com·pāre′, *v.,* **-pared, -paring.** *n. v.t.* **1.** examine for similarities and differences. **2.** regard or describe as similar. —*v.i.* **3.** be similar to, esp. in worth. —*n.* **4. beyond compare,** without equal.

com·păr′ĭ·sŏn, *n.* **1.** act or instance of comparing. **2.** similarity.

com·părt′ment, *n.* division of a larger space.

com′păss, *n.* **1.** instrument for establishing or indicating direction. **2.** scope. **3.** **compasses,** instrument for drawing circles.

com·păs′sion, *n.* sympathy, esp. with suffering or weakness. —com·pas′sion·ate, *adj.*

com·păt′ĭ·blĕ, *adj.* **1.** content together. **2.** logically consistent. —com·pat′′i·bil′i·ty, *n.*

com·pā′trĭ·ŏt, *n.* fellow national.

com·pĕl′, *v.t.,* **-pelled, -pelling.** force.

com·pĕn′dĭ·ŭm, *n., pl.* **-ums, -a.** detailed summary. —com·pen′di·ous, *adj.*

com′pĕn·sāte′′, *v.,* **-sated, -sating.** *v.t.* **1.** pay, as for work or damage. —*v.i.* **2.** serve to offset or make up for something else. —com′′pen·sa′tion, *n.* —com·pen′sa·to′′ry, *adj.*

com·pēte′, *v.i.,* **-peted, -peting.** act in rivalry. com′′pe·ti′tion, *n.* —com·pet′i·tive, *adj.* —com·pet′i·tor, *n.*

cŏm′pé·tĕnt, *adj.* **1.** normal in mental ability. **2.** able to work, etc. adequately. **3.** adequately done. **4.** legally authorized. —com′pe·tent·ly, *adv.* —com′pe·tence, com′pe·ten·cy, *n.*

com·pīle′, *v.t.,* **-piled, -piling.** gather or publish together, as documents. —com·pil′er, *n.* —com′′pi·la′tion, *n.*

com·plā′cĕn·cÿ, *n.* satisfaction, esp. with oneself. —com·pla′cent, *adj.*

com·plāin′, *v.i.* **1.** discuss one's grievance with others. —*v.t.* **2.** state as a grievance. —com·plain′er, *n.*

com·plāint′, *n.* **1.** act or instance of complaining. **2.** wording in which one complains. **3.** distressing illness.

com·plāi′sănt, *adj.* willing or eager to please. —com·plai′sance, *n.*

cŏm′plĕ·mĕnt, *n.* **1.** something that completes. **2.** wholeness. —*v.t.* **3.** complete. —com′′ple·men′ta·ry, *adj.*

com·plēte′, *adj., v.t.,* **-pleted, -pleting.** *adj.* **1.** entire; with nothing missing. **2.** accomplished. **3.** utter. —*v.t.* **4.** perfect. **5.** finish. —com·plete′ly, *adv.* —com·plete′ness, *n.* —com·ple′tion, *n.*

com·plĕx′, *adj.* **1.** not readily analyzed or understood. —*n.* (kom′pleks) **2.** something complex. **3.** *Psychology.* **a.** group of impulses controlling behavior. **b.** obsessive attitude. —com·plex′i·ty, *n.*

com·plĕx′ion, *n.* color and texture of the skin.

com·plī·cāte′′, *v.t.,* **-cated, -cating. 1.** make difficult to do or understand. **2.** make unnecessarily complex. —com′′pli·ca′tion, *n.*

com·plĭc′i·tÿ, *n., pl.* **-ties.** association, esp. in crime.

cŏm′plĭ·mĕnt, *n.* **1.** expression of praise. —*v.t.* **2.** pay a compliment to.

cŏm″plĭ·mĕn′tàr·y̆, *adj.* **1.** serving as a compliment. **2.** granted free of charge.

cŏm·plȳ′, *v.i.*, **-plied, -plying.** act as ordered or urged. **—com·pli′ance**, *n.* **—com·pli′ant**, *adj.*

cŏm·pō′nĕnt, *n.* **1.** part of a whole. **—adj.** **2.** serving as a component.

cŏm·pôrt′, *v.t.* conduct or behave. **—com·port′ment**, *n.*

cŏm·pōse′, *v.t.*, **-posed, -posing. 1.** create or organize artistically. **2.** constitute. **3.** put in order. **4.** make calm.

cŏm·pōsed′, *adj.* apparently calm.

cŏm·pŏs′ĭte, *adj.* made of many constituents.

cŏm″pò·sĭ′tion, *n.* **1.** something composed. **2.** method of composing. **3.** nature, as of constituents or traits.

cŏm·pŏst, *n.* decayed matter for use as fertilizer.

cŏm·pō′sûre, *n.* apparent calm.

cŏm′pōte″, *n.* dish of stewed fruits.

cŏm·pŏŭnd, *adj.* **1.** not simple; complex. **—n. 2.** substance of mixed elements. **3.** building enclosure. **—v.t.** (cŏm′pound′) **4.** mix or make by mixing. **5.** permit unlawfully.

cŏm″prĕ·hĕnd′, *v.t.* **1.** have a conception or understanding of **2.** include. **—com″pre·hen′sion**, *n.* **—com″pre·hen′si·ble**, *adj.*

cŏm″prĕ·hĕn′sĭve, *adj.* including all or most elements. **—com″pre·hen′sive·ly**, *adv.* **—com″pre·hen′sive·ness**, *n.*

cŏm·prĕss′, *v.t.* **1.** press to lessen volume. **2.** put under pressure. **—n.** (kahm′pres) **3.** pad of cloth applied as an aid to medicine. **—com·pres′sion**, *n.* **—com·pres′sor**, *n.*

cŏm·prīse′, *v.t.*, **-prised, -prising. 1.** include. **2.** consist of.

cŏm″prò·mīse″, *n.*, *v.*, **-mised, -mising.** *n.* **1.** expedient but not fully satisfactory agreement. **2.** something with disparate elements. **—v.i. 3.** make a compromise. **—v.t. 4.** endanger in reputation, etc.

cŏmp·trŏl′lĕr, *n.* financial manager.

cŏm·pŭl′sĭon, *n.* act or instance of compelling. **—com·pul′sive**, *adj.* **—com·pul′so·ry**, *adj.*

cŏm·pŭnc′tion, *n.* uneasy, guilty feeling.

cŏm·pūte′, *v.t.*, **-puted, -puting.** determine by calculation. **—com″pu·ta′tion**, *n.*

cŏm·pūt′êr, *n.* electronic device for rapid calculation or data comparison. **—com·put′er·ize**, *v.t.* **—com·put″er·i·za′tion**, *n.*

cŏm′rāde″, *n.* **1.** close friend. **2.** associate. **—com′rade·ship″**, *n.*

cŏmsăt, *n.* communications satellite.

cŏn, *v.t.*, **conned, conning**, *adj.*, *n.* *v.t.* **1.** survey carefully. **—n. 2.** person or argument opposed. **—v.t. 3.** swindle. **—n. 4.** convict.

cŏn·cāve′, *adj.* curving inward. **—con·cav′i·ty**, *n.*

cŏn·cēal′, *v.t.* hide or keep secret. **—con·ceal′ment**, *n.*

cŏn·cēde′, *v.t.*, **-ceded, -ceding. 1.** admit as true. **2.** acknowledge defeat in. **3.** grant.

cŏn·cēit′, *n.* **1.** excessive pride. **2.** fanciful idea or expression.

cŏn·cēit′ĕd, *adj.* full of conceit.

cŏn·cēive′, *v.*, **-ceived, -ceiving.** *v.i.* **1.** form an idea. **2.** become pregnant. **—v.t. 3.** imagine as possible or true. **4.** become pregnant with. **—con·ceiv′a·ble**, *adj.* **—con·ceiv′a·bly**, *adv.*

cŏn′cĕn·trāte″, *v.*, **-trated, -trating.** *n.* *v.t.* **1.** focus. **2.** increase in strength. **—v.i. 3.** focus attention or effort. **—n. 4.** something concentrated. **—con″cen·tra′tion**, *n.*

cŏn·cĕn′trĭc, *adj.* having a common or identical center.

cŏn′cĕpt, *n.* idea of something possible. **—con·cep′tu·al**, *adj.*

cŏn·cĕp′tion, *n.* act or instance of conceiving.

cŏn·cêrn′, *v.t.* **1.** be the business of. **2.** cause care or anxiety in. **3.** have as a subject. **—n. 4.** business or affair. **5.** care or anxiety. **6.** business organization. **7.** importance.

cŏn·cêrned′, *adj.* **1.** anxious. **2.** interested. **3.** engaged in political or social problems.

cŏn·cêrn′ing, *prep.* on the subject of.

cŏn′cêrt, *n.* **1.** series of musical compositions performed at one time. **2.** harmony.

cŏn·cêrt′ĕd, *adj.* performed in an agreed manner.

cŏn''cêr·tï'ná, *n.* small accordion.

con·cer'to (kŏn chêr'tō), *n., pl.* **-tos, -ti.** orchestral composition, usually with soloists.

con·cĕs'sion, *n.* **1.** act or instance of conceding. **2.** something conceded. **3.** trade conducted on another person's property.

con·cĕs'sion·âire'', *n.* person allowed to engage in trade on another's property.

con·cil'ĭ·āte'', *v.t.,* **-ated, -ating.** pacify or appease. —**con·cil'i·a''tor**, *n.* —**con·cil'i·a·to''ry**, *adj.* —**con·cil'i·a'tion**, *n.*

con·cise', *adj.* confined to essentials, as a piece of writing. —**con·cise'ly**, *adv.* —**con·cise'ness**, *n.*

con·clāve, *n.* private meeting.

con·clūde', *v.,* **-cluded, cluding.** *v.t.* **1.** end. **2.** reach an opinion or decision. —*v.i.* **3.** bring a meeting, etc. to an end. —**con·clu'sion**, *n.*

con·clū'sive, *adj.* compelling a certain opinion or decision.

con·cŏct', *v.t.* **1.** make of varied ingredients. **2.** devise. —**con·coc'tion**, *n.*

con·cŏm'ĭ·tant, *adj.* **1.** accompanying. —*n.* **2.** something that accompanies. —**con·com'i·tant·ly**, *adv.*

con'cŏrd, *n.* harmonious agreement.

con·cŏrd'ánce, *n.* list of occurrences in a book of certain words, etc.

con'côurse, *n.* **1.** crowd. **2.** space or hall for accommodating crowds.

con·crēte', *adj.* (kon krēt') **1.** real; material. **2.** specific. —*n.* (kon'krēt) **3.** material of cement and stone, etc. —*v.t., v.i.* **4.** solidify. —**con·cre'tion**, *n.*

con'cū·bīne'', *n.* mistress.

con''cū·pis'cence, *n.* lust. —**con''cu·pis'cent**, *adj.*

con·cūr', *v.i.,* **-curred, -curring. 1.** agree. **2.** cooperate. **3.** coincide. —**con·cur'rent**, *adj.* —**con·cur'rence**, *n.*

con·cŭs'sion, *n.* **1.** shock, as from a blow. **2.** malfunctioning of the mind or body from a blow.

con·dĕmn', *v.t.* **1.** disapprove of strongly. **2.** reject as unfit. **3.** acquire by legal authority. **4.** sentence, as to prison. —**con''dem·na'tion**, *n.*

con·dĕnse', *v.,* **-densed, -densing.** *v.t., v.i.* **1.** turn from a gas to a liquid. —*v.t.*

2. put in succinct form. —**con''den·sa'tion**, *n.* —**con·dens'er**, *n.*

con''dè·scĕnd', *v.i.* **1.** show patronizing affability to an inferior. —*v.t.* **2.** do with a good grace despite superior status. —**con''de·scen'sion**, *n.*

con'dĭ·mĕnt, *n.* flavor or seasoning.

con·dĭ'tion, *n.* **1.** state of health, repair, etc. **2.** good state of health, etc. **3.** something necessary or required. —*v.t.* **4.** put in condition. **5.** accustom.

con·dĭ'tion·ál, *adj.* subject to certain conditions.

con·dōle', *v.i.,* **-doled, -doling.** express sorrowful sympathy. —**con·dol'ence**, *n.*

con''dō·mĭn'ĭ·ŭm, *n.* **1.** multi-unit group of privately owned dwellings. **2.** territory under a joint rule.

con·dōne', *v.t.,* **-doned, -doning.** to voluntarily fail to forbid or disapprove.

con·dūce', *v.i.,* **-duced, -ducing.** tend or lead. —**con·duc'ive**, *adj.*

con·dŭct', *v.t.* **1.** lead or direct. **2.** transmit. **3.** behave. —*n.* (kahn'duct) **4.** behavior.

con·dŭc'tör, *n.* **1.** leader of a band or orchestra. **2.** person in charge of a train, etc. **3.** thing that transmits electricity, heat, etc.

con'duĭt, *n.* channel for wiring or fluids.

cōne', *n.* **1.** solid generated by rotating an isosceles triangle around its centerline. **2.** fruit of an evergreen.

con·fĕc'tion, *n.* food made with sugar. —**con·fec'tion·er**, *n.* —**con·fec'tion·er·y**, *n.*

con·fĕd'êr·a·cў, *n., pl.* **-cies.** alliance.

con·fĕd'êr·āte, *n., adj., v.,* **-ated, -ating.** *n.* **1.** ally or accomplice. —*adj.* **2.** allied. —*v.t., v.t.* (con·fĕd'êr·āte'') **3.** ally. —**con·fed''er·a'tion**, *n.*

con·fêr', *v.,* **-ferred, -ferring.** *v.t.* **1.** bestow. —*v.i.* **2.** consult or discuss. —**con·fer'ment**, *n.* —**con'fer·ence**, *n.*

con·fĕss', *v.t.* **1.** admit as true. **2.** profess belief in. **3.** hear the confession of.

con·fĕs'sion, *n.* **1.** act or instance of confessing. **2.** admission of sins by a penitent. **3.** creed or sect.

con·fĕs'sion·ál, *n.* place where a priest hears confessions.

còn·fĕs'sör, *n.* priest who hears confessions.

còn·fĕt'tĭ, *n.* finely chopped colored paper thrown about in celebration.

cŏn'fĭ·dănt'', *n.* person in whom one confides. Also, *fem.*, **con'fi·dante''**.

còn·fīde', *v.*, **-fided, -fiding.** *v.i.* 1. place trust, esp. by relating secrets. —*v.t.* 2. entrust to someone's care or hearing.

cŏn'fĭ·dĕnce, *n.* 1. trust. 2. self-assurance. —**con'fi·dent**, *adj.* —**con'fi·dent·ly**, *adv.*

cŏn''fĭ·dĕn'tĭal, *adj.* 1. to be kept a secret. 2. entrusted with secrets. —**con''fi·den'tial·ly**, *adv.*

còn·fĭg''ŭ·rā'tion, *n.* outline or contour.

còn·fīne', *v.t.*, **-fined, -fining**, *n. v.t.* 1. keep within limits or boundaries. 2. keep as if a prisoner. —*n.* 3. confines (khan'fīnz), boundaries. —**con·fine'ment**, *n.*

còn·fĭrm', *v.t.* 1. certify as true. 2. approve formally. 3. admit fully to a church. —**con''fir·ma'tion**, *n.*

còn'fĭs·cāte, *v.t.*, **-cated, -cating**. seize by authority. —**con''fis·ca'tion**, *n.*

còn·flā·grā'tion, *n.* fire causing major damage.

cŏn'flĭct, *n.* (kahn'flikt) 1. fight. 2. disagreement. 3. emotional malaise or quandary. —*v.i.* (kən flikt') 4. be hostile or in disagreement.

cŏn·flū'ence, *n.* place where two rivers, etc. meet.

còn·fōrm', *v.i.* 1. form one's appearance, manners, etc. according to prevailing standards. 2. act or be in accordance with a law, rule, etc. 3. be similar. —*v.t.* 4. cause to conform. —**con·form'i·ty**, *n.*

còn·fōrm'ĭst, *n.* person who conforms unquestioningly.

còn·foŭnd', *v.t.* confuse.

còn·frŏnt', *v.t.* 1. approach or face hostilely. 2. to force to meet. —**con''fron·ta'tion**, *n.*

còn·fūse', *v.t.*, **-fused, -fusing**. 1. hamper in the powers of perception, analysis, decision, etc. 2. embarrass. 3. mistake for another. —**con·fu'sion**, *n.*

cŏn·fūte', *v.t.*, **-futed, -futing**. show as wrong. —**con''fu·ta'tion**, *n.*

còn·gēal', *v.t.*, *v.i.* thicken or freeze. —**con·geal'ment**, *n.*

còn·gĕn'ĭ·ăl, *adj.* agreeable. —**con·gen''i·al'i·ty**, *n.*

còn·gĕn'ĭ·tăl, *adj.* from the time of birth. —**con·gen'i·tal·ly**, *adv.*

còn·gĕst', *v.t.* fill to excess. —**con·ges'tion**, *n.*

còn·glŏm'·ẽr·āte'', *v.*, **-ated, -ating**, *adj.*, *n. v.t.*, *v.i.* 1. form into a mass. —*adj.* (còn glŏm'ẽr āte) 2. formed as a mass. —*n.* 3. mass of small elements. 4. corporation composed of diverse subsidiaries. —**con·glom''er·a'tion**, *n.*

còn·grăt'ŭ·lāte'', *v.t.*, **-lated, -lating**. show sympathetic pleasure, as for success or good luck. —**con·grat''u·la'tion**, *n.* —**con·grat'u·la·to''ry**, *adj.*

cŏn'grĕ·gāte'', *v.*, **-gated, -gating**. *v.t.*, *v.i.* gather into a group or assembly. —**con''gre·ga'tion**, *n.* —**con''gre·ga'tion·al**, *adj.*

cŏn'grĕss, *n.* 1. legislative body. 2. formal gathering. —**con·gres'sion·al**, *adj.*

Cŏn'grĕss·măn, *n.* member of the U.S. Congress, esp. the House of Representatives.

cŏn'grŭ·ent, *adj.* in correspondence or harmony. —**con'gru·ence**, *n.*

cŏn'grŭ·oŭs, *adj.* 1. congruent. 2. appropriate. —**con·gru'i·ty**, *n.*

cŏn'ĭc, *adj.* 1. Also, **con'i·cal**, coneshaped. 2. derived from a cone.

cŏn'ĭ·fẽr, *n.* tree or shrub bearing cones. —**co·nif'er·ous**, *adj.*

còn·jĕc'tūre, *n.*, *v.* **-tured, -turing**. *n.*, *v.t.*, *v.i.*, guess. —**con·jec'tur·al**, *adj.*

còn·jŏĭn', *v.t.*, *v.i.* join together.

cŏn'jŭ·gal, *adj.* marital.

cŏn'jŭ·gāte'', *v.t.*, **-gated, -gating**. give the inflections of a verb. —**con''ju·ga'tion**, *n.*

còn·jŭnc'tion, *n.* 1. union or combination. 2. coincidence. 3. word linking others in a sentence. —**con·junc'tive**, *adj.*

cŏn·jŭnc'tūre, *n.* combination of events.

cŏn'jūre, *v.t.*, **-jured, -juring**. cause to appear as by magic. —**con'jur·er, con'jur·or**, *n.*

còn·nĕct', *v.t.* 1. join. —*v.i.* 2. adjoin. —**con·nec'tor, con·nec'ter**, *n.* —**con·nec'tive**, *adj.* —**con·nec'tion**, *n.*

còn·nïve', *v.i.*, **-nived, -niving. 1.** conspire. **2.** permit crime, etc. to occur by ignoring it. **—con·niv'er**, *n.* **—con·niv'ance**, *n.*

còn''nóis·sëur', *n.* person with refined knowledge.

còn·nöte', *v.t.*, **-noted, -noting.** imply through wording, etc. **—con''no·ta'tion**, *n.*

còn·nü'bï·àl, *adj.* marital.

còn'quêr, *v.t.* overcome, as in war. **—con'quer·or**, *n.*

còn'quëst, *n.* **1.** act or instance of conquering. **2.** something conquered.

còn''sän·guïn'ï·tÿ, *adj.* blood relationship.

còn'scïënce, *n.* inner prompting to do good or repent evil. **—con''sci·en'tious**, *adj.*

còn'scioùs, *adj.* **1.** aware of the surrounding world. **2.** aware of some specific thing. **3.** deliberate. **—con'scious·ness**, *n.*

còn·scrïpt', *v.t.* **1.** enroll forcibly in an army, labor force, etc. **—n. 2.** conscripted person. **—con·scrip'tion**, *n.*

còn'se·crâte'', *v.t.*, **-crated, -crating.** dedicate, as to deity. **—con''se·cra'tion**, *n.*

còn·sêc'ü'tïve, *adj.* one after the other. **—con·sec'u·tive'ly**, *adv.*

còn·sën'süs, *n.* general agreement on a question.

còn·sënt', *n.* **1.** permission. **2.** agreement. **—v.i. 3.** give permission.

còn'se·quënce'', *n.* **1.** result. **2.** importance.

còn'se·quënt, *adj.* resulting.

còn''se·quën'tial, *adj.* **1.** important. **2.** consequent.

còn·sêrv'a·tïve, *n.* **1.** person skeptical of change. **2.** pertaining to conservatives. **3.** avoiding excesses. **—con·serv'a·tive·ly**, *adv.* **—con·serv'a·tism**, *n.*

còn·sêr'vä·tô''rÿ, *n.*, *pl.* **-ries. 1.** greenhouse. **2.** art or music school.

còn·sêrve', *v.t.*, **-served, -serving.** keep from decaying, being squandered, etc. **—con''ser·va'tion**, *n.* **—con''ser·va'tion·ist**, *n.*

còn·sïd'êr, *v.t.* **1.** think of the importance, implications, etc. of. **2.** regard; believe. **3.** be considerate of.

còn·sïd'êr·à·ble, *adj.* extensive or significant.

còn·sïd'êr·äte, *adj.* respectful of the feelings of others.

còn·sïd''êr·à'tion, *n.* **1.** state of being considerate. **2.** act of considering. **3.** something to be considered. **4.** fee.

còn·sïgn', *n.* **1.** deliver. **2.** entrust. **—con·sign'ment**, *n.*

còn·sïst', *v.i.* **1.** be composed. **2.** have essential nature.

còn·sïs'tèn·cÿ, *n.* **1.** agreement with something already done, stated, or implied. **2.** ability to hold together, as of a liquid. **—con·sis'tent**, *adj.* **—con·sis'tent·ly**, *adv.*

còn·söle', *v.t.*, **-soled, -soling.** *n. v.t.* **1.** soothe or cheer in grief or annoyance. **—n.** (kahn'söl) **2.** television set, etc. standing on the floor. **3.** instrument panel. **—con''so·la'tion**, *n.*

còn·söl'ï·däte'', *v.*, **-dated, -dating.** *v.t., v.i.* unite into a solid; whole. **—con·sol''i·da'tion**, *n.*

còn'sòm·mé'', *n.* soup based on a clear meat broth.

còn'só·nànt, *adj.* **1.** in harmony. **—n. 2.** speech sound other than a vowel. **—con'so·nance**, *n.*

còn·sôrt', *v.i.* **1.** be in company or association. **—n.** (kahn'sort) **2.** spouse of a sovereign.

còn·sôr'tï·ùm, *n.*, *pl.* **-tia.** international business alliance.

còn·spïc'ü·oùs, *adj.* **1.** readily observed. **2.** compelling observation. **—con·spic'u·ous·ly**, *adv.* **—con·spic'u·ous·ness**, *n.*

còn·spïre', *v.t.*, **-spired, -spiring.** plan secretly as a group. **—con·spir'a·cy**, *n.* **—con·spir'a·tor**, *n.*

còn·stä'ble, *n.* policeman. **—con·stab'u·lar''y**, *n.*

còn·stànt, *adj.* **1.** continual. **2.** faithful. **—n. 3.** unvarying element. **—con'stant·ly**, *adv.* **—con'stan·cy**, *n.*

còn''stël·lä'tion, *n.* pattern of stars.

còn''stêr·nä'tion, *n.* horrified shock.

còn''stï·päte'', *v.t.*, **-pated, -pating.** impair the movement of the bowels. **—con''sti·pa'tion**, *n.*

còn·stït'ü·ènt, *adj.* **1.** forming an essential part. **2.** electing. **—n. 3.** voter. **4.**

constituent thing. —con·stit'u·en·cy, *n.*

cŏn·sti·tūte'', *v.t.*, -tuted, -tuting. 1. combine to form. 2. be tantamount to.

cŏn''sti·tū'tion, *n.* 1. act or instance of constituting. 2. fundamental law. 3. body, esp. as regards health.

cŏn''sti·tū'tion·ăl, *adj.* 1. pertaining to a constitution. 2. permitted by a constitution. 3. pertaining to health. —*n.* 4. health-promoting walk.

cŏn·strāin', *v.t.* 1. compel. 2. restrain. —con·straint', *n.*

cŏn·strĭct', *v.t.* force to be narrow. —con·stric'tion, *n.*

cŏn·strŭct', *v.t.* build. —con·struc'tor, *n.* —con·struc'tion, *n.*

cŏn·strŭc'tĭve, *adj.* useful or helpful.

cŏn·strūe', *v.t.*, -strued, -struing. interpret.

cŏn'sŭl, *n.* government agent in a foreign city who assists his nationals there. —con'sul·ar, *adj.* —con'sul·ate, *n.*

cŏn·sŭlt', *v.t.* 1. seek advice or information from. —*v.i.* 2. discuss business matters. —con''sul·ta'tion, *n.*

cŏn·sŭl'tănt, *n.* 1. person who is consulted. 2. person who seeks advice.

cŏn·sūme', *v.t.*, -sumed, -suming. 1. use up in the process of living, etc. 2. destroy, as by fire.

cŏn·sūm'ẽr, *n.* person who uses goods or services for himself rather than in business.

cŏn·sŭm'măte, *adj.*, *v.t.* -mated, -mating. *adj.* 1. perfect. —*v.t.* (kahn səm āt') 2. complete, esp. the state of marriage by sexual intercourse. —con''sum·ma'tion, *n.*

cŏn·sŭmp'tion, *n.* 1. act or instance of consuming. 2. tuberculosis of the lungs. —con·sump'tive, *adj.*

cŏn'tăct, *n.* 1. touch. 2. communication. 3. connection.

cŏn·tā'gious, *adj.* distributed by personal contact, as disease. —con·ta'gion, *n.*

cŏn·tāin', *v.t.* 1. enclose; include. 2. restrain. —con·tain'er, *n.*

cŏn·tăm'ĭn·āte'', *v.t.*, -ated, -ating. spoil the purity of. —con·tam''in·a'tion, *n.* —con·tam'in·ant, *n.*

cŏn·tĕm·plāte'', *v.t.*, -plated, -plating. 1. regard or think of intently. 2. anticipate. —con''tem·pla'tion, *n.* —con'tem·pla·tive, *adj.*

cŏn·tĕm'pô·rär''ÿ, *adj.*, *n.*, *pl.* -ries, *adj.* 1. Also, con·tem''po·ra'ne·ous, of the same time. 2. modern. —*n.* 3. person or thing of the same age.

cŏn·tĕmpt', *n.* 1. disapproval involving a feeling of one's own superiority. 2. defiance, as of a court order. —con·tempt'i·ble, *adj.*

cŏn·tĕnd', *v.t.* 1. assert forcibly. —*v.i.* 2. fight or be in opposition. —con·tend'er, *n.*

cŏn·tĕnt, *n.* 1. something contained. 2. meaning or message. (cŏn·tĕnt') 3. contentment. —*adj.* 4. satisfied. 5. willing. —*v.t.* 6. satisfy. —con·tent'ed, *adj.* —con·tent'ed·ly, *adv.* —con·tent'ed·ness, *n.*

cŏn·tĕn'tious, *adj.* quarrelsome.

cŏn·tĕnt'mĕnt, *n.* contented state.

cŏn'tĕst, *n.* 1. competition or fight. —*v.i.* (cŏn·tĕst') 2. dispute. 3. fight to gain or hold. —con·test'ant, *n.*

cŏn'tĕxt, *n.* circumstances giving exact meaning. —con·tex'tu·al, *adj.*

cŏn·tĭg'ū·oŭs, *adj.* 1. in touch. 2. adjacent. —con''ti·gu'i·ty, *n.*

cŏn'tĭ·nĕnt, *n.* 1. major land mass. 2. the Continent, European mainland. —*adj.* 3. exercising restraint. —con''ti·nen'tal, *adj.* —con'ti·nence, *n.*

cŏn·tĭn'gĕn·cÿ, *n.*, *pl.* -cies. chance occurrence.

cŏn·tĭn'gĕnt, *adj.* 1. depending on chance. —*n.* 2. chance occurrence. 3. group of recruits.

cŏn·tĭn'ū·ăl, *adj.* 1. repeated without pause. 2. continuous. —con·tin'u·al·ly, *adv.*

cŏn·tĭn'ūe, *v.*, -ued, -uing. *v.t.*, *v.i.* 1. not stop. 2. recommence. 3. extend. —*v.i.* 4. remain. —con·tin'u·a'tion, con·tin'u·ance, *n.*

cŏn·tĭn'ū·oŭs, *adj.* uninterrupted. —con·tin'u·ous·ly, *adv.* —con''tin·u'i·ty, *n.*

cŏn·tôrt', *v.t.* twist out of shape. —con'tor'tion, *n.*

cŏn·toûr, *n.* outline of a form.

cŏn'tră·bănd'', *n.* 1. goods unlawful to import or export. —*adj.* 2. constituting such goods.

cŏn′′trȧ·cĕp′tion, *n.* prevention of pregnancy. —**con′′tra·cep′tive**, *adj., n.*

cŏn′trăct, *n.* **1.** formal business agreement. —*v.t.* (con tract′) **2.** undertake or establish by contract. **3.** be afflicted with. **4.** make smaller. —*v.i.* **5.** make a contract. **6.** become smaller. —**con·trac′tion**, *n.*

cŏn′trăc·tŏr, *n.* **1.** person who undertakes work by contract. **2.** builder.

cŏn′′trȧ·dĭct′, *v.t.* **1.** declare to be falsely stated. **2.** declare to have not spoken the truth. **3.** be inconsistent with. —**con′′tra·dic′tion**, *n.* —**con′′tra·dic′to·ry**, *adj.*

cȯn·trăl′tō, *n., pl.* **-tos.** lowest female singing voice.

cŏn·trăp′tion, *n. Informal.* gadget.

cȯn·trȧ·ry, *n., pl.* **ries**, *adj. n.* **1.** (con′trȧ ry) something opposite. —*adj.* **2.** opposite. **3.** (con trȧ′ry) stubborn; perverse. —**con·trar′i·ly**, *adv.*

cȯn·trăst′, *v.t.* **1.** show the differences of from another or others. —*v.i.* **2.** reveal differences from another or others. —*n.* (con′trast) **3.** act or instance of contrasting. **4.** something notably different.

cŏn′trȧ·vēne′, *v.t., v.* -vened, -vening. act in violation of. —**con′′tra·ven′tion**, *n.*

cȯn·trĭb′ūte, *v.* -uted, -uting. *v.t., v.i.* give toward a desired total. —**con·trib′u·tor**, *n.* —**con′′tri·bu′tion**, *n.* —**con·trib′u·to′ry**, *adj.*

cȯn·trīte′, *adj.* repentant. —**con·trite′ness**, **con·tri′tion**, *n.*

cȯn·trīve′, *v.t., v.* -trived, -triving. **1.** devise or invent. **2.** bring about. —**con·triv′ance**, *n.*

cȯn·trōl′, *v.t., v.* -trolled, -trolling. *n. v.t.* **1.** govern or direct. **2.** restrain. —*n.* **3.** ability to control. **4.** Often, **controls**, means of controlling. —**con·trol′la·ble**, *adj.*

cȯn·trōl′lĕr, *n.* financial manager.

cŏn′trȯ·vĕr′′sў, *n., pl.* **-sies.** earnest debate. —**con′′tro·ver′sial**, *adj.*

cŏn′trȯ·vĕrt′′, *v.t.* **1.** dispute. **2.** debate.

cŏn·tū′mé·lў, *n., pl.* **-lies.** scornful abuse.

cȯn·tū′sion, *n.* bruise.

cȯ·nŭn′drŭm, *n.* riddle answered with a pun.

cŏn′′ûr·bā′tion, *n.* area of urban density resulting from unchecked growth.

cŏn′′vȧ·lĕsce′′, *v.i.* **-lesced, -lescing.** become better after illness. —**con′′va·les′cent**, *n., adj.* —**con′′va·les′cence**, *n.*

cȯn·vĕc′tion, *n.* movement of heated or cooled gases or liquids.

cȯn·vēne′, *v.,* -vened, -vening. *v.i., v.t.* assemble in a meeting.

cȯn·vēn′ience, *n.* **1.** ease or handiness. **2.** something promoting this. —**con·ven′ient**, *adj.*

cŏn′vĕnt, *n.* community of nuns.

cȯn·vĕn′tion, *n.* **1.** assembly of a political party, professional association, etc. **2.** something customary.

cȯn·vĕn′tion·ăl, *adj.* **1.** ordinary. **2.** customary.

cȯn·vērge′, *v.,* -verged, -verging. *v.t., v.i.* to come together. —**con·ver′gence**, *n.* —**con·ver′gent**, *adj.*

cȯn·vēr′sȧnt, *adj.* familiar; skilled.

cŏn′′vêr·sā′tion, *n.* **1.** informal talk. **2.** ability to carry on such talk. —**con′′ver·sa′tion·al**, *adj.* —**con′′ver·sa′tion·al·ist**, *n.*

cȯn·vērse′, *v.i.,* -versed, -versing. *adj., n. v.i.* **1.** carry on a conversation. —*adj.* (con′verse) **2.** in reverse order or position. —*n.* **3.** something converse. —**con·verse′ly**, *adv.*

cȯn·vērt′, *v.t.* **1.** change from one thing or state to another. **2.** acquire a new religion. —*v.i.* **3.** be converted. —*n.* (con′vert) **4.** person with a new religion. —**con·vert′er**, **con·vert′or**, *n.* —**con·vert′i·ble**, *adj.*

cŏn·vĕx′, *adj.* curving outward. —**con·vex′i·ty**, *n.*

cȯn·vey′, *v.t.* **1.** transport. **2.** transmit. **3.** succeed in expressing. —**con·vey′er**, **con·vey′or**, *n.* —**con·vey′ance**, *n.*

cȯn·vict′, *v.t.* **1.** find guilty. —*n.* (con′vict) **2.** person found guilty.

cȯn·vic′tion, *n.* **1.** act or instance of convicting or being convicted. **2.** strongly held belief.

cȯn·vince′, *v.t.,* -vinced, -vincing. cause to believe.

cȯn·vĭv′i·ăl, *adj.* **1.** fond of company. **2.** festive.

cȯn·vōke′, *v.t.,* -voked, -voking. call to an assembly. —**con′′vo·ca′′tion**, *n.*

cŏn''vo·lū'tion, *n.* **1.** twist, fold, etc. **2.** formation of these.

cŏn'voy, *n.* **1.** ships, etc. with a protective escort. **2.** protective escort. **3.** several military, etc. vehicles traveling together. —*v.t.* (con voy') **4.** escort protectively.

cŏn·vŭlse', *v.t.*, -vulsed, -vulsing. **1.** agitate. **2.** rack with laughter or anger. —con·vul'sion, *n.* —con·vul'sive, *adj.*

cōo, *v.i.*, cooed, cooing. **1.** make a dove-like sound. —*n.* **2.** dovelike sound.

cŏok, *v.t.* **1.** prepare (food) by heating. —*v.i.* **2.** act as a cook. **3.** become cooked or heated. —*n.* **4.** person who cooks. —cook'er·y, *n.* —cook'book'', *n.*

cŏok'ie, *n.* small baked sweet biscuit.

cōol, *adj.* **1.** slightly cold; not warm. **2.** not adding to body heat. **3.** showing no emotion. **4.** unenthusiastic. —*n.* **5.** cool condition. —*v.t.* **6.** make cool. —*v.i.* **7.** become cool. —cool'er, *n.* —cool'ly, *adv.* —cool'ness, *n.*

cōon, *n.* racoon. —coon'skin'', *n.*

cŏop, *n.* **1.** shelter for chickens, etc. —*v.t.* **2.** confine.

cōop'ĕr, *n.* barrel maker.

cō''ŏp'ĕr·āte'', *v.i.*, -ated, -ating. act in harmony or together with others. Also, co''·op''er·ate''. —co''op''er·a'tion, *n.*

cō''ŏp'ĕr·a·tĭve, *adj.* **1.** willing to cooperate. **2.** jointly owned by the users. —*n.* **3.** cooperative store, apartment house, etc. Also, co''-op''er·a·tive.

cō·ôr'di·nāte, *adj.*, *n.*, *v.t.*, -nated, -nating. *adj.* **1.** equal in importance. **2.** pertaining to coordination. —*n.* **3.** something coordinate. *v.t.* (ko''or'də nāt'') **4.** put in proper interaction. **5.** make coordinate.

cō''ôr'di·nā''tion, *n.* **1.** act or instance of coordinating. **2.** proper interaction, esp. of the limbs or muscles.

cŏp, *n.*, *v.t.*, copped, copping. *Informal.* *n.* **1.** policeman. **2.** arrest. —*v.t.* **3.** seize. **4.** inform.

cōpe, *v.i.*, coped, coping. attack and overcome a problem or emergency.

cŏp'ĭng, *n.* uppermost course of an unroofed masonry wall.

cō'pi·oŭs, *adj.* abundant.

cŏp'pĕr, *n.* reddish metallic element.

cŏp'pêr·hĕad'', *n.* poisonous North American snake.

cŏpse, *n.* thicket. Also, cop'pice.

cŏp'ū·lāte'', *v.i.*, -lated, -lating. have sexual intercourse. —cop''u·la'tion, *n.*

cŏp'ỹ, *n.*, *pl.* -ies, *v.t.*, -ied, -ying. *n.* **1.** imitation of an original. **2.** individual published book. **3.** words to be printed. —*v.t.* **4.** make or be a copy of. —cop'y·ist, *n.*

cŏp'ỹ·rīght'', *n.* **1.** exclusive right to publish a book, etc. or license its publication. —*v.t.* **2.** obtain a copyright for.

cō·quĕtte', *n.* flirtatious woman.

côr'ăl, *n.* **1.** hardened skeletons of a marine animal. **2.** yellowish red.

côrd, *n.* **1.** strong string. **2.** electric wire. **3.** 128 cubic feet of chopped wood.

côr'diăl, *adj.* **1.** warmly friendly. —*n.* **2.** liqueur. —cor'dial·ly, *adv.* —cor''di·al'i·ty, *n.*

côr'dŏn, *n.* **1.** circle of guards. —*v.t.* **2.** put a cordon around.

côr'dò·vàn, *n.* soft, dark leather.

côr'du·rŏy'', *n.* **1.** ribbed cotton. **2.** felled tree trunks used as a paving.

côre, *n.*, *v.t.*, cored, coring. *n.* **1.** central part or element. —*v.t.* **2.** remove the core from.

côrk, *n.* **1.** bark of an oak tree. **2.** stopper made of this bark. —*v.t.* **3.** stop with a cork.

côrk'scrĕw'', *n.* augerlike device for pulling corks.

côrn, *n.* **1.** American plant with kernels on a cob. **2.** small hard seed of a cereal plant. **3.** *Informal.* trite or sentimental art. **4.** painful growth on the foot. —*v.t.* **5.** pickle in brine. —corn'starch'', *n.*

côr'nē·à, *n.* outer coating of the eyeball.

côr'nêr, *n.* **1.** angular junction. **2.** intersection of two streets. **3.** monopoly of a commodity or stock. —*v.t.* **4.** trap in a corner. **5.** get a monopoly on.

côr'nêr·stōne'', *n.* stone at the corner of a building with its date, etc.

côr·nĕt', *n.* trumpetlike musical instrument.

côr'nĭce, *n.* major horizontal molding on or at the top of a wall.

côr''nŭ·cō'pi·à, *n.* hornlike container

with fruits, flowers, etc. spilling from it.

côr'ŏl·lǎr'' y̆, n., pl. -ies. statement deduced from one already proven.

côr'ŏ·nǎr'' y̆, adj., n., pl. -ies. adj. 1. pertaining to the arteries supplying the heart. —n. 2. coronary thrombosis.

côr''ŏ·nā'tion, n. installation of a monarch.

côr'ŏ·nêr, n. official who investigates suspicious deaths.

côr''ŏ·nĕt, n. crown of a noble.

côr'pŏ·ral, adj. 1. bodily. —n. 2. lowest noncommissioned military officer.

côr'pŏ·rāte, adj. pertaining to organizations.

côr'pŏ·ra''tion, n. 1. business organization existing as an entity apart from its members. 2. municipal government.

côr·pō'rē·ǎl, adj. physical.

côrps (kor), n., pl. corps (korz). military branch.

côrpse, n. dead body.

côr'pŭ·lĕnce, n. fatness. —cor'pu·lent, adj.

côr·pŭs·cle, n. blood or lymph cell.

côr·rǎl', n., v.t., -ralled, -ralling. n. 1. enclosure for cattle, horses, etc. —v.t. 2. enclose in a corral.

côr·rĕct'', adj. 1. accurate. 2. according to rules. —v.t. 3. make correct. 4. punish. —cor·rect'ly, adv. —cor·rect'ness, n. —cor·rec'tion, n. —cor·rec'tive, adj.

côr'rĕ·lāte'', v., -lated, -lating. v.t. 1. put into a mutual relationship. —v.i. 2. have a mutual relationship. —cor''re·la'tion, n. —cor'rel·a'tive, adj.

côr''rĕ·spŏnd'', v.i. 1. write or exchange letters, news, etc. 2. match. —cor''re·spond'ence, n. —cor''re·spond'ent, n.

côr'rĭ·dôr, n. narrow passageway.

côr·rŏb'ŏ·rāte'', v.t., -rated, -rating. support or confirm with evidence, etc. —cor·rob''o·ra'tion, n. —cor·rob'o·ra'tive, adj.

côr·rōde', v., -roded, -roding. v.t., v.i. decay, esp. by chemical action. —cor·ro'sion, n. —cor·ro'sive, adj., n.

côr'rŭ·gāte'', v.t., -gated, -gating. v.t., v.i. bend into parallel ridges and furrows. —cor''ru·ga'tion, n.

côr·rŭpt', adj. 1. impure. 2. depraved.

—v.t. 3. make corrupt. —v.i. 4. become corrupt. —cor·rupt'ly, adv. —cor·rupt'i·ble, adj. —cor·rup'tion, n.

côr·sāge', n. small bouquet for a party dress.

côr'sĕt, n. garment for shaping the torso.

côr'tēge', n. ceremonial procession. Also, cor·tège'.

côr'ŭs·cāte'', v.i., -cated, -cating. glitter. —cor''us·ca'tion, n.

cŏs·mĕt'ĭc, n. 1. preparation applied to the body to improve its appearance. —adj. 2. improving outer appearance.

cŏs'mĭc, adj. pertaining to the cosmos.

cŏs'mŏ·nāut'', n. astronaut.

cŏs''mŏ·pŏl'ĭ·tán, n. 1. Also, cos·mop'o·lite'', person regarding the entire world as his home. —adj. 2. characteristic of such persons.

cŏs'mŏs, n. the entire universe.

cŏst, v.t., cost, costing. n. v.t. 1. require or exact as specified. —n. 2. something given up in exchange. 3. loss; grief.

cŏst'ly̆, adj., -lier, -liest. costing much.

cŏs'tūme, n., v.t., -tumed, -tuming. n. 1. dress, esp. of a special or unusual kind. —v.t. 2. supply with such dress.

cŏt, n. narrow folding bed.

cō'tē·rĭē, n. small, exclusive group of friends.

cŏt'tāge, n. small house. —cot'tag·er, n.

cŏt'tĕr pĭn'', split fastener passed through the things to be attached, then bent open.

cŏt'tŏn, n. fiber from a plant of the mallow family. —cot'ton·y, adj. —cot'ton·seed, n.

cŏt'tŏn·mŏuth'', water moccasin.

cŏt'tŏn·tāil'', n. white-tailed American rabbit.

cŏt'tŏn·wŏod'', n. poplar with hairy seeds.

cŏuch, n. 1. bedlike article of furniture. —v.t. 2. put into words.

cŏu'gár, n. tawny American wildcat.

cŏugh, n. 1. loud expulsion of breath from the lungs, as to clear the throat. —v.i. 2. emit a cough. —v.t. 3. expel with a cough.

cŏun'cĭl, n. body of legislators, advisors, etc. —coun'cil·man, coun'cil·or, coun'cil·lor, n.

cŏun'sel, v.t., -seled, -seling. n. v.t. 1. advise. —*n*. 2. legal representative. 3. advice. —**coun′se·lor, coun′sel·lor,** *n*.

count, *v.t.* 1. note one by one to get a total. 2. include in a total or group. 3. consider as being. —*v.i.* 4. count numbers or items. 5. be important. 6. depend. —*n*. 7. act or instance of counting. 8. total. 9. legal accusation. 10. continental European nobleman equal to an earl.

count′down′, *n*. count of seconds in reverse order before an action.

coun′te·nance, *n*., *v.t.*, **-nanced, -nancing.** *n*. 1. face, esp. with regard to expression. 2. approval. —*v.t.* 3. approve.

count′er, *n*. 1. person or thing that counts. 2. tablelike surface for serving, displaying goods, etc. 3. token used in games.

coun′ter, *v.i.* 1. act in retaliation. —*v.t.* 2. oppose. —*adj*. 3. opposed. —*adv*. 4. in opposition. —**coun′′ter·act′,** *v.t.* —**coun′′ter·at·tack′′,** *v.t.*, *v.i.*, *n*. —**coun′ter·bal′′ance,** *v.t.*, *n*. —**coun′′ter·clock′wise,** *adj., adv.* —**coun′′ter·rev′′o·lu′tion,** *n*. —**coun′′ter·rev′′o·lu′tion·ar′′y,** *adj., n.* —**coun′′ter·weight′′,** *n., v.t.*

coun′ter·feit′′, *v.t.* 1. imitate closely, esp. money. 2. pretend. —*adj*. 3. having been counterfeited. —*n*. 4. something counterfeit. —**coun′ter·feit′′er,** *n*.

coun′ter·mand′′, *v.t.* cancel with a contrary order.

coun′ter·part′′, *n*. 1. similar person or thing. 2. duplicate.

coun′ter·point′′, *n*. *Music.* interaction of melodies.

coun′ter·sign′′, *n*. 1. reply to a password establishing identity. 2. secret sign. 3. confirming signature. —*v.t.* 4. sign as a confirmation.

coun′ter·sink′′, *v.t.*, **-sunk, -sinking.** 1. drive or set flush with or below a surface. 2. cut to receive the head of a countersunk part.

count′ess, *n*. wife of a count or earl.

count′less, *adj*. innumerable.

coun′try, *n.*, *pl.* **-tries.** 1. rural area. 2. land of which one is a citizen. 3. region. —**coun′try·man,** *n*.

coun′try·side′′, *n*. rural terrain.

coun′ty, *n*. 1. political division of a U.S.

state. 2. political division of a European country.

coup (kōō), *n.*, *pl.* **coups** (kōōz). bold, adroit, successful act.

coup de grace (kōō′′de grahs′), something putting an end to a miserable existence.

coupé (kōō pā′), *n*. two-door hard-top car.

cou′ple, *n.*, *v.*, **-pled, -pling.** *n*. pair. —*v.t.*, *v.i.* 2. join one to another. —**coup′ling,** *n*.

coup′let, *n*. pair of verses that rhyme.

cou′pon, *n*. valuable certificate to be cut or detached from a bond, advertisement, etc.

cour′age, *n*. bravery or fortitude. —**cou·ra′geous,** *adj*.

cou′ri·er, *n*. messenger.

course, *n.*, *v.i.*, **coursed, coursing.** *n*. 1. path or direction of a moving thing. 2. natural progress or outcome. 3. way of acting. 4. phase of a meal. 5. program of instruction in one subject. 6. layer of stones, shingles, etc. in a building. —*v.i.* 7. run or race.

court, *n*. 1. Also, **court′yard,** area surrounded by buildings. 2. agency for trying civil or criminal cases. 3. group immediately attached to a sovereign. 4. act of wooing. 5. place to play ball games. —*v.t.* 6. woo. 7. ingratiate oneself with. 8. seek to obtain. —*v.i.* 9. engage in courtship. —**court′house′′,** *n*. —**court′room′′,** *n*.

cour′te·ous, *adj*. polite.

cour′te·san, *n*. prostitute.

cour′te·sy, *n.*, *pl.* **-sies.** politeness.

cour′ti·er, *n*. member of a royal court.

court′ly, *adj.*, **-lier, -liest.** worthy of a royal court, esp. in manner.

court′-mar′′tial, *n.*, *pl.* **courts-martial,** *v.t.*, **-tialed, -tialing.** *n*. 1. military court or trial. —*v.t.* 2. try before such a court.

court′ship′′, *n*. wooing.

cous′in, *n*. offspring of an uncle or aunt.

cove, *n*. small inlet or bay; small valley.

cov′e·nant, *n*. agreement.

cov′er, *v.t.* 1. put a lid, shelter, etc. over. 2. conceal. 3. protect or shield. 4. clothe. 5. hold at bay with a gun, etc. 6. investigate or watch. —*n*. 7. something that covers. 8. means of concealing actions, identity, etc. —**cov′er·age**, *n*. —**cov′er·ing**, *n*.

cóv′êr·lèt, *n*. bedspread.

cóv′êrt, *adj*. concealed. —**cov′ert·ly**, *adv*.

cóv′êr-ŭp′′, *n*. plot to conceal guilt or guilty actions.

cóv′ét, *v.t.* desire enviously. —**cov′et·ous**, *adj*.

cóv′ēy, *n., pl.* **-ies.** flock of quail or partridge.

cŏw, *n*. **1.** four-footed milk-giving bovine animal. **2.** female elephant, whale, etc. —*v.t.* **3.** intimidate. —**cow′hide′′**, *n*.

cŏw′ard, *n*. person without courage. —**cow′ard·ly**, *adj., adv.* —**cow′ard·ice**, *n*.

cŏw′bŏy′′, *n*. ranch worker. Also, **cow′hand′′**.

cŏw′êr, *v.i.* cringe.

cŏwl, *n*. hood or hooded cloak.

cō′wôrk′′êr, *n*. fellow worker.

cox·swain (kok′sán), *n*. steerer of a boat.

cŏy, *adj*. affectedly shy.

coy·ō′tē, *n*. small North American wolf.

cō′zy, *adj*., **-zier, -ziest.** snug and comfortable. —**coz′i·ly**, *adv*. —**coz′i·ness**, *n*.

crăb, *n*. four-legged crustacean.

crăb ăp′ple, *n*. small, sour apple.

crăbbed, *n*. **1.** Also, **crab′by**, ill-tempered. **2.** hard to read.

crăb′′grăss′′, *n*. grass regarded as a weed.

crăck, *v.i., v.t.* **1.** break across abruptly. —*n*. **2.** act or instance of cracking. **3.** narrow break or opening.

crăck′êr, *n*. **1.** crisp wafer. **2.** firecracker.

crăck′le, *v.i., v.t.,* **-led, -ling.** *n*. **1.** make rapid snapping sounds in bending. —*n*. **2.** irregular cracked pattern.

crăck′pŏt′′, *n*. *Informal.* person with delusions.

crā′dle, *n., v.t.,* **-dled, -dling.** *n*. **1.** rocking, high-sided bed for a baby. **2.** concave support, as for a boat. —*v.t.* **3.** place or rock in a cradle. **4.** support in or as in a cradle.

crăft, *n., pl.* **crafts** (for 1 and 2), **craft** (for 3). **1.** cunning. **2.** skilled trade. **3.** vehicle for movement through water or air.

crăfts′män, *n*. **1.** skilled handworker. **2.** skilled, conscientious worker of any kind. —**crafts′man·ship′′**, *n*.

crăft′ȳ, *adj.,* **-ier, -iest.** cunning. —**craft′i·ly**, *adv*.

crăg, *n*. abruptly rising rock formation. —**crag′gy**, *adj*.

crăm, *v.,* **crammed, cramming.** *v.t.* **1.** pack tightly or excessively. —*v.i.* **2.** *Informal.* study in a hasty, superficial way.

crămp, *n*. **1.** painful muscular contraction. **2.** Often, **cramps**, abdominal spasm. —*v.t.* **3.** afflict with cramp. **4.** hamper or confine.

crăn′bĕr′′rȳ, *n., pl.* **-ries.** sour red berry from an evergreen.

crāne, *n., v.t.,* **craned, craning.** *n*. **1.** long-legged, long-billed water bird. **2.** hoisting machine. —*v.t.* **3.** stretch and bend, as the neck.

crā′nì·ŭm, *n., pl.* **-niums, -nia. 1.** bone covering the brain. **2.** skull. —**cra′ni·al**, *adj*.

crănk, *n*. **1.** rotating device incorporating a lever. **2.** *Informal.* person with an ill temper or delusion. —*v.t.* **3.** move with a crank. —**crank′case′′**, *n*. —**crank′shaft′′**, *n*.

crănk′ȳ, *adj.,* **-ier, -iest.** ill-tempered. —**crank′i·ly**, *adv*.

crăn′nȳ, *n., pl.* **-nies.** crevice.

crăps, *n*. dice game. —**crap′shoot′′er**, *n*.

crăsh, *n*. **1.** destructive collision, fall, etc. **2.** noise of this. **3.** business failure. **4.** coarse linen. —*v.i.* **5.** suffer a crash. —*v.t.* **6.** cause to have or produce a crash. **7.** batter one's way through.

crăss, *adj*. stupid and coarse.

crāte, *n., v.t.,* **crated, crating.** *n*. **1.** wooden shipping case. —*v.t.* **2.** pack in a crate.

crā′têr, *n*. pit in the ground made by volcanic eruption, meteors, bombs, etc.

crá·văt′, *n*. necktie.

crāve, *v.t.,* **craved, craving.** desire or request eagerly. —**crav′ing**, *n*.

crā′vèn, *n*. **1.** coward. —*adj*. **2.** cowardly.

crăw, *n*. **1.** sac in a bird's gullet. **2.** stomach.

crăwl, *v.i.* **1.** move slowly with the body horizontal. **2.** move slowly. **3.** feel as if crawled on. —*n*. **4.** crawling movement. **5.** swimming stroke.

crăy′fish′′, *n*. small lobsterlike crustacean. Also, **craw′fish′′**.

crāy′ŏn, *n*. stick of pigmented material for making lines or tones.

crāze, *v*., **crazed, crazing**, *n., v.t.* **1.** make insane. **2.** cause to crack in random patterns. —*v.i.* **3.** become crazed. —*n.* **4.** fad.

crā′zȳ, *adj.*, **-zier, -ziest. 1.** insane. **2.** rickety. —**cra′zi·ly**, *adv.*

crēak, *v.t.* **1.** make a squeak or groan from bending or rubbing. —*n.* **2.** sound from such a cause. —**creak′y**, *adj.*

crēam, *n*. **1.** richer part of milk. **2.** substance with a creamlike or salvelike consistency. **3.** yellowish white. **4.** finest part or element. —*v.t.* **5.** make with cream. **6.** beat to a creamlike consistency. —**cream′y**, *adj.*

crēam′ẽr, *n*. cream pitcher.

crēam′ẽr·ȳ, *n., pl.* **-ies.** place for processing or selling dairy products.

crēase, *n., v.t.*, **creased, creasing.** *n.* **1.** ridge made by pressing. **2.** furrow. —*v.t.* **3.** make a crease or creases in.

crē·āte′, *v.t.* **-ated, -ating. 1.** bring into existence. **2.** bring about. —**cre·a′tion**, *n.*

crē·ā′tĭve, *adj.* **1.** pertaining to creation. **2.** of an original mind; inventive. —**cre′′a·tiv′i·ty**, *n.*

crē·ā′tŏr, *n*. **1.** person who creates. **2. the Creator,** God.

crē′dênce, *n*. belief, as in the truth of a statement.

crè·dēn′tiăls, *n.* documentation proving authority, identity, etc.

crĕd′ĭ·ble, *adj.* able to be believed. —**cred′′i·bil′i·ty**, *n.*

crĕd′ĭt, *n.* **1.** deference of payment. **2.** money paid or owed to one. **3.** praise or good reputation. **4.** source of this. **5.** acknowledgment for participation. **6.** unit of academic accomplishment. —*v.t.* **7.** believe. **8.** give a credit or credits to.

crĕd′ĭt·a·ble, *adj.* deserving of credit.

crĕd′ĭ·tŏr, *n.* person to whom a debt is owed.

crē′dō, *n., pl.* **-dos.** creed.

crĕd′ū·loŭs, *adj.* too ready to believe things. —**cre·du′li·ty**, *n.*

crēed, *n*. formally stated belief.

crēek, *n*. small stream.

crēep, *v.i.*, **crept, creeping. 1.** crawl. **2.** move stealthily. **3.** grow along the ground.

crē′māte′′, *v.t.*, **-mated, -mating.** burn a body, etc. to ashes. —**cre·ma′tion**, *n.* —**cre′ma·to′′ry, cre′′ma·to′ri·um**, *n.*

Crē′ōle, *n*. descendant of the original settlers of Louisiana.

crē′ò·sōte′′, *n*. wood preservative distilled from coal or coal tar.

crēpe, *n*. **1.** thin, crinkled cloth. **2.** rolled, filled pancake. Also, **crêpe.**

crē·scĕn′dō, *adj., n., pl.* **-dos.** *adj., adv.* **1.** increasing in loudness. —*n.* **2.** increase in loudness.

crĕs′cent, *n*. shape like that of a new moon.

crĕst, *n*. **1.** uppermost edge or feature. **2.** feature surmounting a heraldic escutcheon.

crĕst′fäl′′lèn, *adj.* abashed.

crē′tĭn, *n*. mentally deficient person resulting from a thyroid condition.

crē′tŏnne, *n*. heavy, printed upholstery or curtain material.

crē·vässe′, *n*. crevice, esp. in a glacier.

crĕv′ĭce, *n*. deep, narrow gap.

crēw, *n*. labor force, esp. on a ship. —**crew′man**, *n.*

crĭb, *n., v.t.*, **cribbed, cribbing.** *n.* **1.** small child's bed with high slatted sides. **2.** receptacle for corn, animal fodder, etc. **3.** stall for cattle. **4.** *Informal.* aid to cheating in school. —*v.t.* **5.** confine as in a crib. **6.** *Informal.* copy dishonestly.

crĭb′bāge, *n*. card game.

crĭck, *n*. cramp in the neck or back.

crĭck′ĕt, *n*. **1.** grasshopperlike insect. **2.** game played with wide bats, esp. in England.

crī′êr, *n*. maker of vocal announcements.

crīme, *n*. violation of the law.

crĭm′ĭn·ăl, *adj.* **1.** pertaining to or guilty of crime. —*n.* **2.** committer of crimes.

crĭm′′ĭn·ŏl′ó·gȳ, *n*. study of crime. —**crim′′in·ol·o′gist**, *n.*

crĭmp, *n., v.t.* pleat.

crĭm′sòn, *n*. deep red.

crĭnge, *v.i.*, **cringed, cringing. 1.** crouch or draw back out of fear. **2.** behave servilely.

crĭn′kle, *v.* **-kled, -kling,** *v.t., v.i.* **1.** wrinkle. 2. rustle, as crisp paper. —**crin′kly,** *adj.*

crip′ple, *v.t.,* **-pled, -pling,** *n., v.t.* 1. deprive of the use of arms or legs. 2. render ineffective. —*n.* 3. crippled person.

cri′sis, *n., pl.* **-ses.** point that determines a good or bad outcome.

crisp, *n.* 1. brittle. 2. clear; fresh. 3. briskly abrupt in manner.

criss′cross′′, *n.* 1. pattern of crossed lines. —*adj., adv.* 2. in this pattern. —*v.t.* 3. mark with this pattern. —*v.i.* 4. move in or bear this pattern.

cri·tēr′i·on, *n., pl.* **-ions, ia.** basis for judgment.

crit′ic, *n.* person who evaluates good and bad qualities.

crit′i·cal, *adj.* 1. pertaining to critics. 2. pertaining to crises. 3. fault-finding. —**crit′i·cal·ly,** *adv.*

crit′i·cīze′, *v.t.,* **-cized, -cizing.** 1. evaluate. 2. find fault with. —**crit′i·cism,** *n.*

cri·tique′, *n.* evaluation by a critic.

croak, *v.i.* 1. make a deep froglike noise. —*n.* 2. croaking sound.

cro·chet (krō shā′), *v.t.,* **-cheted, -cheting.** make with a hooked needle and thread.

crōck, *n.* earthenware vessel. —**crock′er·y,** *n. Informal.* nonsense.

croc′o·dīle′′, *n.* large tropical river reptile.

crō′cŭs, *n., pl.* **-cuses.** early-blooming flower of the iris family.

crōne, *n.* shriveled old woman.

crō′nў, *n., pl.* **-nies.** close friend.

crook, *n., v.,* **crooked, crooking.** *n.* 1. hooked staff. 2. curve. 3. *Informal.* thief. —*v.i., v.t.,* 4. bend.

crook′ed, *adj.* 1. full of bends. 2. dishonest.

croon, *v.i., v.t.* sing or hum in low, sweet sounds. —**croon′er,** *n.*

crŏp, *n., v.t.,* **cropped, cropping.** *n.* 1. yield at a harvest. 2. whip. 3. craw of a bird. —*v.t.* 4. cut short.

cro·quet (krō kā′), *n.* lawn game with balls driven by mallets.

crō·quĕtte′, *n.* deep-fried piece of ground meat, etc.

crŏss, *n.* 1. upright with a side-to-side beam used in Roman crucifixions. 2. this form as a symbol of Christianity. 3.

modification of this symbolizing Christian saints, sects, etc. 4. source of trouble or unhappiness. 5. mixture of breeds. —*v.t.* 6. go across. 7. thwart. 8. mix with another breed. —*adj.* 9. illtempered. —**cross′road′′,** *n.* —**cross′roads′′,** *n. sing.* —**cross′wise′′, cross′ways′′,** *adv.* —**cross′ly,** *adv.*

crŏss′bow′′, *n.* weapon with a short bow mounted on a guide for a type of arrow.

cross′′-ĕx·ăm′ine, *v.t. Law.* examine after examination by an opposing attorney. Also, **cross′′-quĕs′tion.** —**cross′′-ex·am′i·na′′tion.** *n.*

cross′-eyēd′′, *adj.* with eyes not properly aligned.

cross-rĕf′ĕr·ence, *n.* reference to another part of a book. **cross′-re·fer′,** *v.i., v.t.*

crŏtch, *n.* 1. place where a tree limb branches from a larger one. 2. place where the legs meet.

crŏtch′et, *n.* eccentric whim or attitude. —**crotch′et·y,** *adj.*

crŏuch, *v.i., n.* stoop or squat.

croup, *n.* inflammation of respiratory passages.

crow, *v.i.,* **crowed,** or (for 1) **crew, crowed, crowing,** *n. v.i.* 1. cry like a rooster. 2. boast or exult. —*n.* 3. crowing sound. 4. shiny dark bird.

crow′băr′′, *n.* heavy metal lever.

crŏwd, *n.* 1. large, random group. —*v.t.* 2. fill with a crowd. 3. force into a restricted space. —*v.i.* 4. push one's way. 5. gather in a crowd.

crŏwn, *n.* 1. symbol of sovereignty. 2. royalty as the head of state. 3. upper part. —*v.t.* 4. give a crown to. 5. reward or fulfill.

cru′ciăl, *adj.* 1. decisive. 2. trying. —**cru′cial·ly,** *adv.*

cru′cĭ·ble, *n.* melting pot.

cru′cĭ·fĭx′′, *n.* image of the Christian cross.

cru′cĭ·fў′′, *v.t.,* **-fied, fying.** 1. nail to a cross as punishment. 2. ruin the reputation, happiness, etc. of. —**cru′′cĭ·fix′ion,** *n.*

crūde, *adj.* 1. unrefined or unfinished. 2. boorish. —**crude′ly,** *adv.* —**crud′i·ty, crude′ness,** *n.*

cru′ĕl, *adj.* 1. causing suffering. 2. desiring to cause suffering. —**cru·el'ly,** *adv.* —**cru·el'ty,** *n.*

cru·et, *n.* small bottle for oil, vinegar, etc.

cruise, *v.,* **cruised, cruising.** *n. v.i.* **1.** travel slowly, as for recreation or inspection. **2.** move at normal speed, as a ship. —*v.t.* **3.** cruise in or over. —*n.* **4.** act or instance of cruising.

cruis·er, *n.* large, lightly armored warship.

crul·ler, *n.* piece of twisted deep-fried dough.

crumb, *n.* small fragment, esp. from dough.

crum'ble, *v.,* **-bled, -bling.** *v.t., v.i.* break or drop in pieces.

crum'ple, *v.,* **-pled, -pling,** *v.i., v.t.* collapse into wrinkles.

crunch, *v.t.* **1.** crush, chew, grind, etc. with a brittle sound. —*v.i.* **2.** emit such a sound.

cru·sade', *n., v.i.,* **-saded, -sading.** *n.* **1.** Christian campaign to recover the tomb of Christ from the Muslims. **2.** idealistic campaign. —*v.i.* **3.** engage in a crusade. —**cru·sad'er,** *n.*

crush, *v.t.* **1.** break or squeeze with pressure. **2.** reduce to helplessness or despair through an attack. —*v.i.* **3.** become crushed. —*n.* **4.** crowd. **5.** *Informal.* infatuation. —**crush'er,** *n.*

crust, *n.* **1.** hardened outer surface. —*v.t.* **2.** cover with a crust. —**crust'y,** *adj.*

crus·ta'cean, *n.* sea animal with jointed feet and a hard outer shell.

crutch, *n.* prop for a lame person.

crux, *n., pl.* **cruxes, cruces.** decisive feature or aspect.

cry, *v.,* **cried, crying,** *n., pl.* **cries.** *v.i.* **1.** weep loudly. **2.** utter a call. **3.** ask for something loudly. —*v.t.* **4.** announce in a shout. —*n.* **5.** act or instance of crying.

crypt, *n.* underground church vault, esp. for burial.

cryp'tic, *adj.* defying interpretation.

cryp'to·gram'', *n.* code message.

cryp·tog'ra·phy, *n.* encoding and decoding of messages, etc. —**cryp·tog'ra·pher,** *n.*

crys'tal, *n.* **1.** clear quartz. **2.** geometrically formed fused mineral, sugar, etc. **3.** brilliant glass or glassware. **4.** window of a watch dial. —**crys'tal·line,** *adj.* —**crys'ta·lize'',** *v.t., v.i.*

cub, *n.* young animal.

cub'by·hole'', *n.* small enclosure.

cube, *n., v.t.,* **cubed, cubing.** *n.* **1.** solid with six square sides. **2.** *Math.* third power of a number. —*v.t.* **3.** divide into cubes. **4.** *Math.* multiply to the third power. —**cu'bic,** *adj.* —**cu'bic·al,** *adj.*

cu'bi·cle, *n.* small alcove.

cu'bit, *n.* measure of about 18 inches.

cuck'old, *n.* **1.** husband of an unfaithful wife. —*v.t.* **2.** make a cuckold of. —**cuck'old·ry,** *n.*

cuck'oo'', *n.* **1.** bird with a two-note call. —*adj.* **2.** *Informal.* crazy.

cu'cum''ber, *n.* long, green fruit used in salads or as pickles.

cud, *n.* food chewed by cows, etc. after regurgitation.

cud'dle, *v.,* **-dled, -dling.** *v.t.* **1.** hold and caress. —*v.i.* **2.** lie or curl up snugly.

cudg'el, *n., v.t.,* **-eled, -eling.** *n.* **1.** short club. —*v.t.* **2.** beat with a cudgel.

cue, *n., v.t.,* **cued, cuing** or **cueing.** *n.* **1.** signal for speech or action. **2.** stick used in billiards or pool. —*v.t.* **3.** give a cue to.

cuff, *n.* **1.** feature terminating a sleeve or trouser leg. **2.** slap. —*v.t.* **3.** slap.

cui·sine', *n.* manner of cooking.

cul'·de·sac'', *n.* blind street with a turning circle at the end.

cu·li·nar''y, *adj.* pertaining to cooking.

cull, *v.t.* select.

cul'mi·nate'', *v.i.,* **-nated, -nating.** reach a final development. —**cul''mi·na'tion,** *n.*

cul'pa·ble, *adj.* at fault. —**cul''pa·bil'i·ty,** *n.*

cul'prit, *n.* **1.** accused person. **2.** guilty person.

cult, *n.* **1.** religious sect. **2.** religious practice or devotion. —**cult'ist,** *n.*

cul'ti·vate, *v.t.,* **-vated, -vating.** **1.** work on to grow crops. **2.** develop, as personal qualities. **3.** seek to make a friend or associate. —**cul'ti·va''tor,** *n.*

cul''ti·va'tion, *n.* **1.** development of culture, manners, etc. **2.** act or instance of cultivating.

cul'ture, *n.* **1.** familiarity with the arts, etc. **2.** society, esp. with regard to its art or technology. **3.** development through special care. **—cul′tur·al,** *adj.*

cŭl′vĕrt, *n.* drain under an embankment.

cŭm′bĕr·sŏme, *adj.* heavy; burdensome.

cū′mū·lā′′tĭve, *adj.* increasing from additions.

cū′mū·lŭs, *n., pl.* **-li.** dense cloud with domelike upper parts.

cŭn′nĭng, *adj.* **1.** crafty; sly. **2.** clever; skillful. **—n. 3.** craftiness; slyness. **4.** skill.

cŭp, *n., v.t.,* **cupped, cupping,** *n.* **1.** small bowl-like drinking utensil. **2.** contents of a cup. **—v.t. 3.** form into a cuplike shape.

cŭp′bôard, *n.* storage cabinet, esp. for dishes or food.

cŭp′căke′′, *n.* small cup-shaped cake.

Cū′pĭd, *n.* mythological god of love, represented as a naked boy with a bow and arrow.

cū·pĭd′ĭ·tў, *n.* greed; avarice.

cū′pŏ·là, *n.* windowed structure on top of a roof.

cŭr, *n.* mongrel dog.

cū′rāte, *n.* clergyman with a parish. **—cu′ra·cy,** *n.*

cū·rā′tŏr, *n.* custodian or director of a museum department.

cŭrb, *n.* **1.** Also, **curb′ing,** edge of a sidewalk. **2.** wall at the top of a well. **3.** border or framework. **4.** something that restrains. **—v.t. 5.** check or restrain.

cŭrd, *n.* coagulated milk substance, used esp. to make cheese.

cûr′dle, *v.,* **-dled, dling.** *v.t., v.i.* form into curds.

cūre, *n.* **1.** method of remedial treatment, esp. for disease. **2.** recovery from disease. **—v.t. 3.** restore to health; heal. **4.** preserve, as food.

cûr′fĕw, *n.* ban on being out late.

cū′rĭ·ō, *n.* small beautiful or rare object.

cū′rĭ·oŭs, *adj.* **1.** inquisitive. **2.** odd. **—cu′ri·ous·ly,** *adv.* **—cu′′ri·os′i·ty,** *n.*

cûrl, *v.t., v.i.* **1.** form into spiral shapes; coil. **—v.i. 2.** become curved, spiraled or undulated. **3.** move in a curving direction. **—n. 4.** something with a curved or twisted form. **—curl′y,** *adj.*

cûr′lĕw, *n., pl.* **-lews** or **-lew.** shore bird with a downcurved beak.

cûrl′ĭ·cūe′′, *n.* fancifully curved ornamental figure.

cûr′rănt, *n.* **1.** small seedless raisin. **2.** acid edible berry of a wild shrub.

cûr′rĕn·cў, *n.* **1.** money. **2.** general acceptance or use.

cûr′rĕnt, *adj.* **1.** happening in the present. **2.** practiced or accepted. **—n. 3.** continuous movement of a fluid. **4.** flow of electricity. **—cur′rent·ly,** *adv.*

cŭr·rĭc′ū·lŭm, *n., pl.* **-lums, -la.** program of studies. **—cur·ric′u·lar,** *adj.*

cûr′rў, *n., pl.* **-ries,** *v.t.,* **-ried, -rying.** *n.* **1.** spicy condiment. **2.** food made with this. **—v.t. 3.** brush, as a horse. **4.** make with curry.

cûrse, *n., v.t.,* **cursed** or **curst, cursing.** *n.* **1.** prayer, etc. invoking harm to another. **2.** blasphemy, etc. **3.** source of constant trouble. **—v.t. 4.** make the object of a curse. **—curs′ed,** *adj.*

cûr′sŏr, *n.* indicator on a computer monitor showing where the next input will appear.

cûr′sŏ·rў, *adj.* hasty or superficial.

cûrt, *adj.* rude; abrupt. **—curt′ly,** *adv.*

cûr·tāil′, *v.t.* cut short. **—cur·tail′ment,** *n.*

cûr′tăin, *n.* cloth hanging before a window, theater stage, etc.

cûrt′sў, *n., pl.* **-sies,** *v.i.,* **-sied, sying.** *n.* **1.** woman's bow in which the knees are bent. **—v.i. 2.** make such a bow. Also, **curt′sey.**

cûr′và·tûre, *n.* **1.** curve. **2.** degree of curving. **3.** abnormal curve, as of the spine.

cûrve, *n., v.,* **curved, curving.** *n.* **1.** continuous line continually changing direction. **2.** anything formed along such a line. **—v.t., v.i. 3.** bend along a curve.

cŭsh′ĭŏn, *n.* **1.** soft pad for support. **—v.t. 2.** preserve from a shock, as from impact.

cŭsp, *n.* pointed projection.

cŭs′pĭd, *n.* single pointed tooth; canine tooth.

cŭs′pĭ·dôr′′, *n.* spittoon.

cŭs′tàrd, *n.* sweet milk and egg mixture that sets after cooking.

cŭs′tŏ·dў, *n., pl.* **-dies. 1.** guardianship; care. **2.** legal restraint; imprisonment. **—cus·to′di·an,** *n.* **—cus·to′di·al,** *adj.*

cŭs'tóm, *n.* **1.** habitual practice or manner of thinking. **2. customs,** revenue on foreign goods. —*adj.* **3.** made to personal order. —**cus'tom·ar''y,** *adj.* —**cus'' tom·ar'i·ly,** *adv.*

cŭs'tò·mêr, *n.* buyer; purchaser.

cŭt, *v.,* **cut, cutting,** *n.* *v.t.* **1.** divide or penetrate with something sharp. **2.** form with sharp tools. **3.** terminate abruptly. **4.** *Informal.* **a.** shun ostentatiously. **b.** be absent from. —*v.i.* **5.** become cut. **6.** swerve. —*n.* **7.** wound from cutting. **8.** act or instance of cutting. **9.** wounding or snubbing remark. **10.** illustration for printing.

cū·tā''nē·oŭs, *adj.* pertaining to the skin.

cūte, *adj.,* **-ter, -test, 1.** attractive; pretty. **2.** clever; shrewd.

cū'ti·cle, *n.* outer layer of skin.

cŭt'lăss, *n.* short, heavy-edged sword.

cŭt'lêr·ў, *n.* cutting tools, esp. for food.

cŭt'lĕt, *n.* slice or patty food for frying or broiling.

cût'têr, *n.* **1.** person or implement for cutting. **2.** ship's boat with oars. **3.** Coast Guard ship.

cy'á·nīde'', *n.* potassium- or sodium-based poisonous substance.

cy''bêr·nĕt'ĭcs, *n.* study of human control systems and functions and of mechanical systems that can be used to replace them. —**cy''ber·net'ic,** *adj.*

cy'clá·māte'', *n.* artificial sweetening agent.

cy'cle, *n., v.i.,* **-cled, -cling.** *n.* **1.** repeated series. **2.** repeated period of time. **3.** two-wheeled vehicle. —*v.i.* **4.** ride a cycle. —**cy'clic, cy'cli·cal,** *adj.* —**cy'clist,** *n.*

cy'clōne, *n.* storm with rotating winds.

cy'clò·pē'dĭá, *n.* encyclopedia. Also, **cy''clo·pae'di·a.**

cy'clò·tròn'', *n.* machine for giving acceleration to charged particles by electric and magnetic forces.

cyl'ĭn·dêr, *n.* **1.** solid generated by a rectangle turned on its centerline. **2.** expansion chamber in an engine. —**cy·lin' dri·cal,** *adj.*

cym'bál, *n.* one of a pair of concave brass or bronze plates struck together to produce a sound.

cyn'ĭc, *n.* person who sees all actions as selfishly motivated. —**cyn'i·cal,** *adj.* —**cyn·i·cism** (sin'ə siz''əm), *n.*

cy'nò·sûre'', *n.* center of attraction.

cy'prĕss, *n.* scaly-leaved evergreen tree.

cyst, *n.* abnormal sac or growth, usually filled with fluid.

czâr (zar), *n.* Slavic emperor. Also, *fem.,* **cza·ri'na.**

D

D, d, *n.* **1.** fourth letter of the English alphabet. **2.** fourth-best grade.

dăb, *v.,* **dabbed, dabbing,** *n.* *v.t.* **1.** touch or apply lightly. —*n.* **2.** small moist lump.

dăb'ble, *v.i.,* **-bled, -bling. 1.** play in water. **2.** be superficially active. —**dab' bler,** *n.*

dăft, *adj.* **1.** insane. **2.** silly.

dăg'gêr, *n.* short-pointed weapon.

dăhl'iá, *n.* showy perennial-flowering plant.

dāi'lў, *adj., n., pl.* **-lies.** *adj.* **1.** happening each day. —*n.* **2.** daily periodical.

dāin'tў, *adj.,* **-tier, -tiest,** *n., pl.* **-ties.** *adj.* **1.** delicate; fine. —*n.* **2.** delicacy. —**dain'ti·ly,** *adv.* —**dain'ti·ness,** *n.*

dāir'ў, *n., pl.* **-ies.** place where milk and milk products are processed. —**dair'y· man,** *n.*

dā'ĭs, *n., pl.* **-ises.** raised platform.

dāi'sў, *n., pl.* **-sies.** flower with a yellow diskshaped center and white petals.

dāle, *n.* valley.

dăl'lў, *v.i.,* **-lied, -lying. 1.** play in a loving way. **2.** delay; waste time. —**dal'li· ance,** *n.*

dăm, *n., v.t.,* **dammed, damming.** *n.* **1.** barrier to hold back water. **2.** female parent, esp. of quadrupeds. —*v.t.* **3.** obstruct, as with a dam.

dăm'áge, *n., v.t.,* **-aged, -aging.** *n.* **1.** injury. **2. damages,** compensation for injury. —*v.t.* **3.** injure; harm. —**dam'age· a·ble,** *adj.*

dăm'ăsk, *n.* **1.** fabric woven in patterns. —*adj.* **2.** pink.

dămn, *v.t.* condemn. **—dam′na·ble,** *adj.* **—dam·na′tion,** *n.*

dămp, *adj.* **1.** moist. *—n.* **2.** moisture. *—v.t.* **3.** make moist. **4.** deaden, as a shock. **—damp′ness,** *n.*

dămp′ĕn, *v.t.* **1.** make damp. **2.** deaden or depress, as the spirits. *—v.i.* **3.** become damp.

dămp′ĕr, *n.* **1.** something that deadens or depresses. **2.** valve in a flue to regulate draft.

dăm′sĕl, *n. Archaic.* girl.

dănce, *v.,* **danced, dancing,** *n. v.i.* **1.** move one's body and feet in rhythm, esp. to music. *—v.t.* **2.** execute as a dance. **3.** cause to dance. *—n.* **4.** social gathering for dancing. **—danc′er,** *n.*

dăn′dē·lī′′ŏn, *n.* weedy plant with yellow flowers.

dăn′drŭff, *n.* scales that form on the scalp and fall off.

dăn′dў, *n. pl.,* **-dies,** *adj.,* **-dier, -diest.** *n.* **1.** man overly particular about his appearance. *—adj.* **2.** *Informal.* very good.

dăn′gĕr, *n.* exposure to harm; risk. **—dan′ger·ous,** *adj.*

dăn′gle, -gled, -gling. *v.i., v.t.* hang loosely.

dănk, *adj.* unpleasantly moist.

dăp′pĕr, *adj.* **1.** neat. **2.** small and active.

dăp′ple, *adj., n., v.,* **-pled, -pling.** *adj.* Also, **dap′pled,** spotted. *—n.* **2.** spot or marking. *—v.t.* **3.** mark with spots.

dāre, *v.,* **dared, daring.** *n. v.i.* **1.** have the necessary courage or audacity. *—v.t.,* **2.** challenge. **—dar′ing,** *adj., n.*

dârk, *adj.* **1.** having little or no light. **2.** tending in color toward black. **3.** gloomy. **4.** ignorant. *—n.* **5.** absence of light. **—dark′en,** *v.t., v.i.* **—dark′ness,** *n.*

dâr′lĭng, *n.* **1.** person dear to another. *—adj.* **2.** very dear; cherished.

dârn, *v.t.* mend by weaving rows of stitches.

dârt, *n.* **1.** small pointed missile usually thrown by hand. **2.** sudden motion. *—v.t., v.i.* **3.** move suddenly and swiftly.

dăsh, *v.t.* **1.** hurl violently. **2.** smash. **3.** frustrate. *—v.i.* **4.** rush; sprint. *—n.* **5.** small amount shaken from a bottle, etc.

6. short race. **7.** punctuation mark (—) indicating a break.

dăsh′bôard′′, *n.* instrument panel.

dăsh′ĭng, *adj.* **1.** lively. **2.** showy; stylish. **—dash′ing·ly,** *adv.*

dăs′tărd, *n.* coward; sneak. **—das′tard·ly,** *adj.*

dā′′tă, *n. pl.* **1.** facts; figures. **2.** (computers) information stored in a memory.

dā′′tă·băse, *n.* (computers) a structured file facilitating data access and manipulation.

dāte, *n., v.,* **dated, dating.** *n.* **1.** particular time. **2.** day of the month. **3.** appointment. **4.** sweet, fleshy fruit of a palm tree. *—v.t.* **5.** give a date to. *—v.i.* **6.** belong to a specific time.

dāt′ĕd, *adj.* **1.** antiquated. **2.** showing a date.

daŭb, *v.t.* **1.** cover or smear with a soft, muddy substance. *—v.t., v.i.* **2.** paint clumsily. *—n.* **3.** something daubed. **—daub′er,** *n.*

daŭgh′tĕr, *n.* female child. **—daugh′ter·ly,** *adj.*

daŭgh′tĕr-ĭn-lăw′′, *n. pl.,* **daughters-in-law.** son's wife.

daŭnt, *v.t.* frighten; dishearten. **—daunt′less,** *adj.*

dăv′ĕn·pôrt′′, *n.* large couch.

dăw′dle, *v.i.,* **-dled, -dling.** waste time. **—daw′dler,** *n.*

dăwn, *v.i.* **1.** begin to grow light in the morning. *—n.* **2.** break of day.

dāy, *n.* **1.** period between sunrise and sunset. **2.** period of earth's rotation on its axis. **3.** era; period of time.

dāy′drēam′′, *n.* **1.** period of pleasant, dreamy thought. *—v.t.* **2.** have daydreams.

dāy′lĭght′′, *n.* **1.** light of day. **2.** openness.

dāy′tīme′′, *n.* period between sunrise and sunset.

dāze, *v.t.,* **dazed, dazing,** *n., v.t.* **1.** stun; bewilder. *—n.* **2.** stunned condition.

dăz′zle, *v.t.,* **-zled, -zling. 1.** overwhelm with intense light. **2.** impress with brilliance.

dēa′cŏn, *n.* **1.** cleric just below a priest in rank. **2.** lay church officer. **—dea′con·ry,** *n.*

dĕad, *adj.* **1.** no longer alive. **2.** without life. **3.** obsolete. **4.** accurate; unerring.

—*adj.*, *adv.* 5. straight. —*n.* 6. **the dead**, persons no longer living. **dead'en**, *v.t.*

dead'line'', *n.* latest time by which something must be completed.

dead'lock'', *n.* 1. frustrated standstill. —*v.t.*, *v.i.* 2. bring or come to a deadlock.

dead'ly, *adj.* -**lier**, -**liest**. 1. likely to cause death. 2. typical of death. —**dead'li·ness**, *n.*

deaf, *adj.* incapable of hearing. —**deaf'ness**, *n.* —**deaf'en**, *v.t.*

deal, *v.*, **dealt, dealing**, *n.* *v.t.* 1. portion out. 2. administer, as a blow. —*v.i.* 3. do or have business. 4. portion out cards, etc. —*n.* 5. business transaction or agreement. —**deal'er**, *n.*

dean, *n.* 1. college official who supervises students or faculty. 2. presiding cleric in a cathedral.

dear, *adj.* 1. beloved. 2. expensive. —*n.* 3. beloved person. —**dear'ly**, *adv.*

dearth, *n.* scarcity; lack.

death, *n.* 1. act of dying. 2. state of being dead. —**death'less**, *adj.* —**death'like''**, *adj.* —**death'ly**, *adj.*, *adv.*

de·bâ'cle, *n.* ruinous collapse.

de·bar', *v.t.*, -**barred**, -**barring**. exclude; prohibit.

de·base', *v.t.*, -**based**, -**basing**. lower in value. —**de·base'ment**, *n.*

de·bate', *v.* -**bated**, -**bating**. *n.* *v.t.* 1. discuss; argue. 2. consider. —*v.i.* 3. take part in discussion. —*n.* 4. discussion of opposing views. —**de·bat'a·ble**, *adj.* —**de·bat'er**, *n.*

de·bauch'', *v.t.* 1. corrupt; seduce. —*n.* 2. seduction. —**de·bauch'er·y**, *n.*

de·bil'i·tâte, *v.t.*, -**tated**, -**tating**. weaken. —**de·bil''i·ta'tion**, *n.*

de·bil'i·ty, *n.*, *pl.* -**ties**. weakness.

deb'it, *n.* 1. recorded debt. —*v.t.* 2. charge with a debt.

deb''o·nair', *adj.* 1. courteous; pleasantly mannered. 2. carefree.

de·bris' (dé brē), *n.* rubbish; remains.

debt, *n.* 1. something owed. 2. condition of owing. —**debt'or**, *n.*

de·but' (dā byōō'), *n.* 1. first public appearance. 2. formal introduction into society.

déb'ü·tânte'', *n.* girl making a society debut.

dec'āde, *n.* ten-year period.

dec'a·dence, *n.* decay; deterioration. —**dec'a·dent**, *adj.*, *n.*

dec''a·hē'dron, *n.*, *pl.* -**drons**, -**dra**. ten-sided solid.

de·cal', *n.* transfer of a picture or design from paper to glass, wood, etc. Also, **de·cal''co·ma'ni·a**.

Dec'a·lôgue'', *n.* Ten Commandments. Also, **Dec'a·log''**.

de·camp', *v.i.* 1. break camp. 2. depart suddenly.

de·cant', *v.t.* pour gently so as not to disturb sediment.

de·cant'êr, *n.* ornamental bottle, esp. for wine.

de·cap'i·tâte'', *v.t.*, -**tated**, -**tating**. behead. —**de·cap''i·ta'tion**, *n.*

de·câth'lôn, *n.* contest consisting of ten track and field events.

de·cay', *v.i.*, *v.t.* 1. deteriorate; rot. —*n.* 2. deterioration.

de·cease', *n.*, *v.i.* -**ceased**, -**ceasing**. *n.* 1. death. —*v.i.* 2. die. —**de·ceased'**, *adj.*, *n.*

de·ceit', *n.* lying; fraud. —**de·ceit'ful**, *adj.*

de·ceive', *v.t.* -**ceived**, -**ceiving**. mislead.

De·cem'bêr, *n.* twelfth and final month.

de'cent, *adj.* 1. appropriate. 2. not offensive to modesty. 3. respectable. 4. adequate. —**de'cent·ly**, *adv.* —**de'cen·cy**, *n.*

de·cen'tral·ize'', *v.t.*, -**ized**, -**ising**. free from dependency on a central authority, source, etc. —**de·cen''tral·i·za'tion**, *n.*

de·cep'tion, *n.* 1. act or instance of deceiving. 2. fraud. —**de·cep'tive**, *adj.*

de·cide', *v.*, -**cided**, -**ciding**. *v.t.* 1. reach a decision regarding. —*v.i.* 2. make a judgment or choice.

de·cid'ed, *adj.* 1. clear-cut. 2. determined. —**de·cid'ed·ly**, *adv.*

de·cid'u·ous, *adj.* shedding leaves at a particular season, as a tree or shrub.

dec'i·mal, *adj.* 1. based on the number ten. 2. pertaining to fractions whose denominators are ten or some power of ten. —*n.* 3. decimal fraction.

děc'ǐ·māte'', *v.t.*, **-mated, -mating.** destroy a sizable number of.

dè·cì'phêr, *v.t.* determine the meaning of.

dè·cì'sion, *n.* **1.** choice or judgment. **2.** emphasis; firmness.

dè·cì'sǐve, *adj.* **1.** determining an outcome or conclusion. **2.** emphatic; firm. —de·ci'sive·ly, *adv.* —de·ci'sive·ness, *n.*

děck, *n.* **1.** floor of a ship, bridge, etc. **2.** pack of playing cards. —*v.t.* **3.** adorn.

dè·clàim', *v.i., v.t.,* speak or utter rhetorically. —de''clam·a'tion, *n.* —de·clam'a·to''ry, *adj.*

dè·clâre', *v.t.* **-clared, -claring. 1.** make known. **2.** say emphatically. —de·clar'a·tive, de·clar'a·to''ry, *adj.* —dec''la·ra'sion, *n.*

dè·clēn'sion, *n.* **1.** grammatical inflection of nouns, pronouns, or adjectives. **2.** decline.

dè·clīne', *v.,* **-clined, -clining,** *n. v.t., v.i.* **1.** bend or slope downward. **2.** deteriorate. **3.** refuse. —*v.i.* **4.** give grammatical inflections. —*n.* **5.** deterioration. **6.** downward slope.

dè·clǐv'ǐ·tȳ, *n., pl.* **-ties.** downward slope.

dè·cōde', *v.t.* **-coded, -coding.** decipher from code.

dē''còm·pōse', *v.,* **-posed, -posing.** *v.t., v.i.* **1.** break up into parts. **2.** decay. —de''com·po·si'tion, *n.*

dè·côr', *n.* style of decoration.

děc'ò·rāte'', *v.t.,* **-rated, -rating. 1.** adorn. **2.** give a medal to. —dec'o·ra·tive, *adj.* —dec'o·ra''tor, *n.* —dec''o·ra'tion, *n.*

děc'ò·roǔs, *adj.* proper.

dè·cō'rǔm, *n.* propriety.

dè·coỹ', *n.* **1.** artificial bird used as a lure in hunting. **2.** lure. —*v.t.* **3.** lure into a trap.

dè·crēase', *v.,* **-creased, -creasing,** *n. v.t., v.i.* **1.** gradually lessen. —*n.* **2.** lessening.

dè·crēe', *n., v.,* **-creed, -creeing.** *n.* **1.** edict. —*v.t.* **2.** ordain by decree.

dè·crěp'ǐt, *adj.* worn by old age or long use. —de·crep'i·tude'', *n.*

dè·crȳ', *v.t.,* **-cried, -crying.** denounce. —de·cri'al, *n.*

děd'ǐ·cāte'', *v.t.,* **-cated, -cating. 1.** set apart; devote. **2.** inscribe. —ded''i·ca'tion, *n.*

dè·dūce', *v.t.,* **-duced, -ducing.** infer; derive. —de·duc'i·ble, *adj.*

dè·dǔct', *v.t.* subtract; take away. —de·duct'i·ble, *adj.*

dè·dǔc'tion, *n.* **1.** act or result of reasoning from the general to the specific. **2.** amount deducted. —de·duc'tive, *adj.*

dēed, *n.* **1.** something that is done; an act. **2.** legal conveyance esp. of land. —*v.t.* **3.** transfer by deed.

dēem, *v.t., v.i.* believe; adjudge.

dēep, *adj.* **1.** extending far downward or inward. **2.** difficult to understand. **3.** profound; serious. **4.** dark and rich, esp. a color. **5.** low in pitch. —*n.* **6.** deep place. —*adv.* **7.** far down. —deep'en, *v.t., v.i.* —deep'ly, *adv.*

dēer, *n., pl.* **deer, deers.** ruminant animal, the male of which have antlers or horns.

dè·fáce', *v.t.,* **-faced, -facing.** mar; disfigure. —de·face'ment, *n.*

dè·fǎc'tō, actually existing but not lawfully authorized.

dè·fāme', *v.t.* **-famed, -faming.** attack the reputation of; slander. —def''am·a'tion, *n.* —de·fam'a·to''ry, *adj.*

dè·fâult', *n.* **1.** failure, esp. to pay a debt. —*v.t., v.i.* **2.** fail, esp. to pay, when required.

dè·fēat', *v.t.* **1.** overthrow; conquer. —*n.* **2.** act or instance of defeating.

dè·fēat'ǐst, *n.* person who accepts defeat. -de·feat'ism, *n.*

dě''fè·cāte'', *v.i.,* **-cated, -cating.** *v.i.* excrete waste from the bowels. —def''e·ca'tion, *n.*

dě''fěct', *n.* **1.** imperfection; fault. —*v.i.* (dē fekt') **2.** desert a cause, esp. to join another. —de·fec'tive, *adj.* —de·fec'tion, *n.* —de·fec'tor, *n.*

dè·fěnd', *v.t.* **1.** protect; guard against attack. **2.** support with one's words. —de·fend'er, *n.*

dè·fěnd'ànt, *n. Law.* accused person.

dè·fěnse', *n.* **1.** protection against attack. **2.** justification. **3.** *Law.* reply to a charge. —de·fense'less, *adj.* —de·fen'si·ble, *adj.*

dè·fěn'sǐve, *adj.* **1.** pertaining to defense.

2. anxious to justify oneself. —*n.* 3. situation of a defender.

de·fer', *v.*, **-ferred**, **-ferring**. *v.t.*, *v.i.* 1. postpone. —*v.i.* 2. yield politely. —**de·fer'ment**, *n.* —**def'er·ence**, *n.* —**def''er·en'tial**, *adj.*

de·fi'ance, *n.* open disregard of or bold resistance to authority. —**de·fi'ant**, *adj.*

de·fi'cien·cy, *n.*, *pl.* **-cies.** lack; inadequate amount. —**de·fi'cient**, *adj.*

def'i·cit, *n.* deficiency, esp. of assets.

de·file', *v.*, **-filed**, **-filing**. *v.t.* 1. desecrate. 2. make filthy. —*v.i.* 3. march in file. —*n.* 4. narrow passage. —**de·file'ment**, *n.*

de·fine', *v.t.*, **-fined**, **-fining**. 1. state the meaning of. 2. determine. —**def''i·ni'tion**, *n.* —**de·fin'a·ble**, *adj.*

def'i·nite, *adj.* 1. exact. 2. within precise limits. —**def'i·nite·ly**, *adv.*

de·fin'i·tive, *adj.* 1. conclusive. 2. defining.

de·flate', *v.*, **-flated**, **-flating**. *v.t.*, *v.i.* 1. collapse by releasing air. 2. increase in purchasing power. —**de·fla'tion**, *n.* —**de·fla'tion·ar''y**, *adj.*

de·flect', *v.t.*, *v.i.* turn from a course; swerve. —**de·flec'tion**, *n.*

de·form', *v.t.* 1. mar the form of. 2. make ugly. —**de''for·ma'tion**, *n.* —**de·form'i·ty**, *n.*

de·fraud', *v.t.* cheat; take rights or property of by fraud.

de·fray', *v.t.* pay, as expenses.

de·frost', *v.t.*, *v.i.* free or be freed of ice.

deft, *adj.* skillful. —**deft'ly**, *adv.* —**deft'ness**, *n.*

de·funct', *adj.* no longer alive or in existence.

de·fy', *v.t.*, **-fied**, **-fying**. 1. openly resist. 2. challenge.

de·gen'er·ate, *adj.*, *n.*, *v.*, **-ated**, **-ating**. *adj.* 1. deteriorated. 2. depraved. *n.* 3. depraved person. —*v.i.* (de gen''er ate') 4. deteriorate. —**de·gen''er·a'tion**, *n.* —**de·gen'er·a·cy**, *n.* —**de·gen'er·a·tive**, *adj.*

de·grade', *v.t.*, **-graded**, **-grading**. reduce in quality or rank. —**deg''ra·da'tion**, *n.*

de·gree', *n.* 1. stage or point, as in a process. 2. extent or intensity. 3. title

conferred by a college. 4. unit of temperature. 5. 360th of a circle.

de·hu'man·ize'', *v.t.*, **-ized**, **-izing**. deny human qualities to.

de·hy'drate, *v.*, **-drated**, **-drating**. *v.t.* *v.i.* remove or lose water. —**de''hy·dra'tion**, *n.*

de'i·fy'', *v.t.*, **-fied**, **-fying**. make a god of. —**de''i·fi·ca'tion**, *n.*

deign, *v.t.*, *v.i.* condescend.

de'ism, *n.* belief that a god created the world but has had no control over it. —**de'ist**, *n.*

de'i·ty, *n.*, *pl.* **-ties.** god or goddess

de·ject', *v.t.* dishearten. —**de·jec'tion**, *n.*

de·lay', *v.t.* 1. postpone. 2. hinder; make late. —*v.i.* 3. linger; procrastinate. —*n.* 4. act or instance of delaying.

de·lec'ta·ble, *adj.* delightful; delicious. —**de''lec·ta'tion**, *n.*

del'e·gate, *n.*, *v.t.*, **-gated**, **-gating**. *n.* 1. representative. —*v.t.* (del' ə gāt) 2. send as a representative. 3. entrust to another, as authority. —**del''e·ga'tion**, *n.*

de·lete', *v.t.*, **-leted**, **-leting**. remove from a text. —**de·le'tion**, *n.*

del''e·te'ri·ous, *adj.* injurious to health;

de·lib'er·ate, *v.*, **-ated**, **-ating**, *adj.* *v.t.*, *v.i.* 1. ponder. —*adj.* 2. intentional. 3. unhurried. —**de·lib'er·ate·ly**, *adv.* —**de·lib''er·a'tion**, *n.* —**de·lib'er·a·tive**, *adj.* —**de·lib'er·a''tor**, *n.*

del'i·ca·cy, *n.*, *pl.* **-cies.** 1. fineness of quality. 2. choice food.

del'i·cate, *adj.* 1. fine in quality or texture. 2. easily damaged. 3. considerate; tactful. 4. functioning precisely. —**del'i·cate·ly**, *adv.*

del''i·ca·tes'sen, *n.* store selling food specialties.

de·li'cious, *adj.* 1. pleasing to taste. 2. delectable. —**de·li'cious·ly**, *adv.*

de·light', *v.t.*, *v.i.* 1. give great pleasure. —*n.* 2. joy or great pleasure. —**de·light'ed**, *adj.* —**de·light'ful**, *adj.*

de·lin'e·ate'', *v.t.*, **-ated**, **-ating**. trace the outline of. —**de·lin''e·a'tion**, *n.*

de·lin'quent, *adj.* 1. neglectful of duty or law. 2. late, as a debt. —*n.* 3. delinquent person. —**de·lin'quen·cy**, *n.*

de·lir'i·um, *n.* temporary excited mental disorder. —**de·lir'i·ous**, *adj.*

de·liv′er, *v.t.* **1.** set free or save. **2.** hand over. **3.** assist at the birth of. **4.** present to an audience. **5.** distribute. —**de·liv′er·ance**, *n.* —**de·liv′er·y**, *n.*

del·phin′i·um, *n.* tall blue garden flower.

del′ta, *n.* deposit of soil formed at a divided river mouth.

de·lude′, *v.t.*, -**luded**, -**luding**. mislead.

del·uge′, *n.*, *v.t.*, -**uged**, -**uging**. *n.* **1.** flood. **2.** heavy rainfall. —*v.t.* **3.** flood. **4.** overwhelm.

de·lu′sion, *n.* false conception, esp. one persistent and opposed to reason. —**de·lu′sive**, *adj.*

de·luxe′, *adj.* of specially fine quality.

delve, *v.i.*, **delved**, **delving**. dig.

dem′a·gogue′′, *n.* unscrupulous player on popular emotion. Also, **dem′a·gog′′**. —**dem′a·gog′′y**, **dem′a·gogu′′er·y**, *n.*

de·mand′, *v.t.* **1.** ask for boldly; claim as a right. **2.** require. —*v.i.* **3.** make a demand. —*n.* **4.** act or instance of demanding. **5.** thing demanded. —**de·mand′ing**, *adj.*

de·mean′, *v.t.* **1.** debase; humble. **2.** behave; conduct.

de·mean′or, *n.* behavior or conduct.

de·ment′ed, *adj.* mentally deranged.

de·mer′it, *n.* **1.** fault. **2.** mark against a person for a fault.

dem′i·god′, *n.* **1.** mythological being who is divine and human. **2.** godlike human.

de·mil′i·tar·ize′′, *v.t.*, -**ized**, -**izing**. free from military control. **de·mil′′i·tar·i·za′tion**, *n.*

de·mise′, *n.*, *v.t.*, -**mised**, -**mising**. *n.* **1.** death. —*v.t.* **2.** transfer by lease.

de·mo′bi·lize′′, *v.t.*, -**lized**, -**lizing**. free from military service; disband. —**de·mo′′bi·li·za′tion**, *n.*

de·moc′ra·cy̆, *n.* **1.** government by the people. **2.** country with such government. **3.** social equality. —**dem′o·crat′′**, *n.* —**dem′′o·crat′ic**, *adj.* —**de·moc′ra·tize′′**, *v.t.*

De′′mo·crat′, *n.* member of the Democratic party.

de·mol′ish, *v.t.* destroy. —**dem′′o·li′tion**, *n.*

de′mon, *n.* **1.** evil spirit; devil. **2.** person regarded as evil. —**de·mon′ic**, **de·mo′ni·ac′′**, **de′′mo·ni′a·cal**, *adj.*

dem′on·strate′′, *v.* -**strated**, -**strating**. *v.t.* **1.** prove in detail. **2.** explain by example. **3.** reveal. —*v.i.* **4.** call public attention to one's attitude. —**dem′′on·stra′tion**, *n.* —**dem′on·stra′′tor**, *n.* —**de·mon′stra·ble**, *adj.*

de·mon′stra·tive, *adj.* **1.** self-expressive. **2.** illustrative or explanatory. **3.** conclusive.

de·mor′al·ize′′, *v.t.*, -**ized**, -**izing**. lower the morale of. —**de·mor′′al·i·za′tion**, *n.*

de·mote′, *v.t.*, -**moted**, -**moting**. lower in rank. —**de·mo′tion**, *n.*

de·mur′, *v.i.*, -**murred**, -**murring**, *n.* *v.i.* **1.** object. —*n.* **2.** objection.

de·mure′, *adj.* modest; coy. —**de·mure′ly**, *adv.*

den, *n.* **1.** cave of a wild animal. **2.** vile place. **3.** small, private room for a man.

de·ni′al, *n.* **1.** refusal of consent. **2.** contradiction. **3.** refusal to believe.

den′i·grate′′, *v.t.*, -**grated**, -**grating**. blacken or malign the character of. —**den′′i·gra′tion**, *n.*

den′im, *n.* heavy twill cotton cloth.

den′i·zen, *n.* inhabitant.

de′nom′i·nate′′, *v.t.*, -**nated**, -**nating**. name.

de·nom′′i·na′tion, *n.* **1.** name. **2.** act of naming. **3.** religious sect. —**de·nom′′i·na′tion·al**, *adj.*

de·nom′i·na′′tor, *n.* *Math.* term below the line in a fraction; divisor.

de·note′, *v.t.*, -**noted**, -**noting**. indicate; mean. —**de′′no·ta′tion**, *n.*

de-noue·ment (dā nōō mäh′), *n.* *Literature.* resolution of a conflict.

de·nounce′, *v.t.*, -**nounced**, -**nouncing**. **1.** accuse openly. **2.** inform against. —**de·nounce′ment**, *n.*

dense, *adj.* **1.** thick. **2.** stupid. —**dense′ly**, *adv.* —**dense′ness**, *n.* —**den′si·ty**, *n.*

dent, *n.* **1.** hollow area made by a blow. —*v.t.*, *v.i.* **2.** make or receive a dent.

den′tal, *adj.* pertaining to teeth or dentistry.

den′ti·frice, *n.* preparation used in brushing the teeth.

den′tist, *n.* doctor specializing in teeth and gums. —**den′tist·ry**, *n.*

den′ture, *n.* set of false teeth.

dė·nūde′, *v.t.*, **-nuded, -nuding.** strip. —den′′u·da′tion, *n.*

dė·nŭn′′ci·ā′tion, *n.* **1.** condemnation. **2.** accusation.

dė·nȳ′, *v.t.*, **-nied, -nying. 1.** reject as untrue. **2.** refuse to give or allow. **3.** refuse something to.

dē·ō′dŏr·ănt, *n.* **1.** preparation for destroying odors. —*adj.* **2.** destroying odors.

dė·pärt′, *v.i.* **1.** leave; go away. **2.** die. —de·par′ture, *n.*

dė·pärt′mĕnt, *n.* **1.** part or section. **2.** field of activity. —de·part′′men′tal, *adj.*

dė·pĕnd′, *v.i.* **1.** look outside oneself for support, help, etc. **2.** be according to conditions. —de·pend′a·ble, *adj.* —de·pend′a·bly, *adv.* —de·pend′a·bil′i·ty, *n.* —de·pend′ent, *adj.*, *n.* —de·pend′ence, de·pend′en·cy, *n.*

dė·pict′, *v.t.* **1.** portray; delineate. **2.** describe. —de·pic′tion, *n.*

dė·plēte′, *v.t.*, **-pleted, -pleting.** exhaust or reduce in amount. —de·ple′tion, *n.*

dė·plōre′, *v.t.*, **-plored, -ploring.** regret strongly. —de·plor′a·ble, *adj.*

dē·pŏp′ū·lāte′′, *v.t.*, **-lated, -lating.** remove the population of. —de·pop′′u·la′tion, *n.*

dė·pȯrt′, *v.t.* expel from a country. —de′′por·ta′tion, *n.*

dė·pȯrt′mĕnt, *n.* conduct or behavior.

dė·pōse′, *v.t.*, **-posed, -posing. 1.** remove from office or power. **2.** testify. —dep′′o·si′tion, *n.*

dė·pŏs′ĭt, *v.t.* **1.** put in a bank, etc. **2.** give in partial payment. **3.** drop or cause to settle. —*n.* **4.** something deposited. —de·pos′i·tor, *n.*

dē′·pōt, *n.* **1.** bus or railroad station. **2.** storage place for military supplies.

dė·prāve′, *v.t.* **-praved, -praving.** corrupt. —de·prav′i·ty, *n.*

dėp′′rė·cāte′′, *v.t.*, **-cated, -cating. 1.** express disapproval of. **2.** belittle. —dep′′re·ca′tion, *n.* —dep′re·ca·to′′ry, *adj.*

dė·prē′ci·āte′′, *v.*, **-ated, -ating.** *v.t.*, *v.i.* **1.** lessen in value or seeming importance. —*v.t.* **2.** belittle. —de·pre′′ci·a′tion, *n.*

dĕp′′rė·dā′tion, *n.* robbery.

dė·prĕss′, *v.t.* **1.** deject; sadden. **2.** push down. **3.** weaken. —de·pressed′, *adj.* —de·press′ant, *n.*

dė·prĕs′sion, *n.* **1.** act of depressing or being depressed. **2.** depressed state. **3.** period when business and employment decline. —de·pres′sive, *adj.*

dė·prīve′, *v.t.*, **-prived, -priving.** withhold from. —de·pri·va′tion, *n.*

dĕpth, *n.* **1.** distance downward or inward. **2.** quality of being deep. **3.** intensity or profundity. **4.** profundity. **5. depths,** deepest part.

dĕp′′u·tā′tion, *n.* delegation.

dĕp′ū·tȳ, *n.*, *pl.* **-ties.** person appointed to act as a substitute for another.

dė·rāil′, *v.t.*, *v.i.* run off the rails. —de·rail′ment, *n.*

dė·rānge′, *v.t.*, **-ranged, -ranging. 1.** disturb the arrangement of. **2.** make insane. —de·range′ment, *n.*

dĕr′bȳ, *n.* stiff hat with a round crown.

dĕr′é·lĭct′, *adj.* **1.** abandoned by its owner. **2.** negligent. —*n.* **3.** something abandoned, esp. a ship. **4.** destitute person.

dĕr′′é·lĭc′tion, *n.* **1.** negligence of a duty. **2.** forsakenness.

dė·rīde′, *v.t.*, **-rided, -riding.** mock. —de·ri′sion, *n.* —de·ri′sive, *adj.*

dė·rīve′, *v.* **-rived, -riving.** *v.t.* **1.** obtain from a source. **2.** trace to or from a source. **3.** deduce; infer. —*v.i.* **4.** originate or be derived. —der′′i·va′tion, *n.* —de·riv′a·tive, *adj.*, *n.*

dĕr′ȯ·gāte′′, *v.*, **-gated, -gating.** *v.t.*, *v.i.*, detract. —der′′o·ga′tion, *n.* —de·rog′a·to′′ry, *adj.*

dĕr′rĭck, *n.* **1.** crane for lifting and moving heavy objects. **2.** tall framework over an oil well.

dĕs′cănt, *n.* **1.** melody. —*v.i.* (des cant′) **2.** sing. **3.** discourse.

dė·scĕnd′, *v.t.* **1.** move down, along or through. —*v.i.* **2.** move downward. **3.** slope downward. **4.** make a sudden attack, etc. **5.** be derived from specified ancestors. —des·cent′, *n.* —de·scen′dant, *n.*

dė·scrībe′, *v.t.*, **-scribed, -scribing. 1.** give a conception or account of. **2.** trace by movement. —de·scrib′a·ble, *adj.* —de·scrip′tion, *n.* —de·scrip′tive, *adj.*

dė·scrȳ′, v.t., -scried, -scrying. perceive.

dĕs′ė·crāte′′, v.t., -crated, -crating. profane. —**des′′e·cra′tion**, n.

dė·sĕg′′rė·gāte′′, v., -gated, -gating. v.t., v.i. eliminate racial segregation in. —**de·seg′′re·ga′tion**, n.

dė·sĕrt′, v.t. **1.** abandon. **2.** abscond from permanently, as duty. —n. **3.** Often, **deserts**, something deserved. **4.** (des′ ert) wasteland, esp. a sandy one. —adj. **5.** desolate; barren. —**de·sert′er**, n. —**de·ser′tion**, n.

dė·sĕrve′, v., -served, -serving. v.t. **1.** have as a rightful outcome or reward. —v.i. **2.** be worthy. —**de·serv′ing**, adj., n.

dĕs′ic·cāte′′, v., -cated, -cating. v.t., v.i. dry completely. —**des′′ic·ca′tion**, n.

dė·sīgn′, v.t. **1.** plan the form and making of. **2.** contrive. **3.** intend. —n. **4.** plan or pattern. **5.** designing of artistic objects. **6.** scheme or intention.

dĕs′ig·nāte′′, v.t., -nated, -nating. **1.** specify; indicate. **2.** name. **3.** appoint. —**des′′ig′na′tion**, n.

dė·sīgn′ẽr, n. **1.** one who designs. —adj. **2.** of or pertaining to clothing, etc. styled by a designer, as *designer jeans*.

dė·sīgn′ing, adj. scheming.

dė·sīre′, v. -sired, -siring, n. v.t. **1.** long for. **2.** request. —v.i. **3.** have a desire. —n. **4.** craving. **5.** request. **6.** lust. **7.** thing desired. —**de·sir′a·ble**, adj. —**de·sir′a·bly**, adv. —**de·sir′′a·bil′i·ty**, n. —**de·sir′ous**, adj.

dė·sīst′, v.i. stop; cease.

dĕsk, n. table with drawers used for writing.

dĕs′ȯ·lȧte, adj., v. -lated, -lating. adj. **1.** barren. **2.** lonely. **3.** uninhabited. —v.t. (des′o late′′) **4.** make barren. —**des′′o·la′tion**, n.

dė·spāir′, v.i. **1.** lose hope. —n. **2.** hopelessness.

dĕs′′pẽr·â′dō, n., pl. -does, -dos. reckless criminal.

dĕs′pẽr·ȧte, adj. **1.** reckless due to despair. **2.** having an urgent need. **3.** very serious. **4.** extreme or drastic. —**des′′per·a′tion**, n.

dĕs′pĭ·ca·ble, adj. contemptible. —**des′pi·ca·bly**, adv.

dė·spīse′, v.t., -spised, -spising. scorn; loathe.

dė·spīte′, prep. in spite of.

dė·spŏil′, v.t. rob; pillage.

dė·spŏnd′, v.i. lose hope or courage. —**despond′en·cy, de·spond′ence**, n. —**de·spond′ent**, adj.

dĕs′pŏt, n. tyrant or absolute ruler. —**des·pot′ic**, adj. —**des′pot·ism**, n.

dės·sĕrt′, n. sweet course ending a meal.

dĕs′′tĭ·nā′tion, n. place to be reached.

dĕs′tīne, v.t., -tined, -tining. **1.** intend. **2.** predetermine.

dĕs′tĭn·ȳ, n., pl. -nies. **1.** predetermined course of events. **2.** rate.

dĕs′tĭ·tūte′′, adj. **1.** deprived. **2.** without means of existence. —**des′′ti·tu′tion**, n.

dė·strŏy′, n. **1.** damage so as to eliminate. **2.** kill.

dė·strŏy′ẽr, n. **1.** light, fast warship. **2.** person or thing that destroys.

dė·strŭc′tion, n. **1.** act or instance of destroying. **2.** agency by which one is destroyed. —**de·struct′i·ble**, adj. —**de·struc′tive**, adj.

dĕs′ŭl·tô′′rȳ, adj. **1.** random. **2.** disconnected. —**des′′ul·to′ri·ly**, adv.

dė·tăch′, v.t. separate; disconnect. —**de·tach′a·ble**, adj.

dė·tăched′, adj. **1.** separate; not connected. **2.** disinterested.

dė·tăch′ment, n. **1.** state of being detached. **2.** military unit on a special mission.

dė·tāil′, n. **1.** subordinate part or feature. **2.** soldiers for a specific duty. —v.t. **3.** make, plan, or relate the details of. **4.** assign to a duty.

dė·tāin′, v.t. **1.** keep from going on; delay. **2.** keep in custody. —**de·ten′tion**, n.

dė·tĕct′, v.t. discover. —**de·tec′tion**, n. —**de·tec′tor**, n. —**de·tect′a·ble, de·tect′i·ble**, adj.

dė·tĕc′tĭve, n. investigator seeking private or hidden information.

de·tente (dā tahnt′), n. lessening of tension, esp. internationally.

dė·tẽr′, v.t., -terred, -terring. discourage or prevent. —**de·ter′ment**, n. —**de·ter′rent**, n.

dė·tẽr′gĕnt, adj. **1.** cleansing. —n. **2.** preparation used for cleaning.

de·te'ri·o·rate'', v., -rated, -rating. v.t., v.i. worsen. —de·te''ri·o·ra'tion, n.

de·ter''mi·na'tion, n. 1. act or instance of determining. 2. firmness of resolve. 3. firm intention.

de·ter'mine, v., -mined, -mining. v.t. 1. settle. 2. ascertain. 3. direct; impel. 4. set limits to. —v.i. 5. decide. —de·ter'mi·na·ble, adj. —de·ter'mi·nate, adj.

de·ter'mined, adj. showing determination.

de·test', v.t. hate. —de·test'a·ble, adj. —de·test'a·bly, adv. —de''tes·ta'tion, n.

de·throne', v.t., -throned, -throning. remove from sovereign power.

det'o·nate'', v., -nated, -nating. v.t., v.i. explode. —det''o·na'tion, n. —det''o·na'tor, n.

de·tour', n. 1. roundabout course. —v.t., vi. 2. go or route on a detour.

de·tract', v.t. 1. take away. —v.i. 2. take a desirable quality. —de·trac'tion, n.

det'ri·ment, n. 1. injury or loss. 2. something that causes injury or loss. —det''ri·men'tal, adj.

de·val'u·ate'', v.t., -ated, -ating. lessen in value. Also, de·val'ue. —de·val''u·a'tion, n.

dev'as·tate'', v.t., -tated, -tating. destroy everywhere. —dev''as·ta'tion, n.

de·vel'op, v.t. 1. bring to maturity or completeness. 2. elaborate. 3. fall ill with. 4. Photography. bring out the picture on. —v.i. 5. be developed. —de·vel'op·ment, n. —de·vel''op'men'tal, adj.

de''vi·ate'', v.i., -ated, -ating. adj., n. v.i. 1. turn aside; digress. —adj. (de'vi ate) 2. deviant. —n. 3. deviant person. 4. sexual pervert. —de''vi·a'tion, n.

de·vice', n. 1. tool, etc. 2. plan. 3. symbol or representation.

dev'il, n., v.t., -iled or -illed, -iling or -illing. n. 1. fiend of hell. 2. the Devil, Satan. 3. malicious or formidable person. —v.t. 4. torment. —dev'il·ish, adj. —dev'il·try, dev'il·try, n.

de'vi·ous, adj. 1. indirect; circuitous. 2. shifty; not straightforward. —de'vi·ous·ly, adv.

de·vise', v.t., -vised, -vising. n. v.t. 1. contrive. 2. bequeath. —n. 3. bequest. —de·vis'er, n.

de·void', adj. empty of something specified.

de·volve', v., -volved, -volving. v.i., v.t. pass to another, as a duty.

de·vote', v.t., -voted, -voting. dedicate. —de·vot'ed, adj.

dev''vo·tee', n. admirer or enthusiast.

de·vo'tion, n. 1. dedication. 2. devout act, esp. a prayer. —de·vo'tion·al, adj.

de·vour', v.t. 1. eat hungrily. 2. consume or take in greedily.

de·vout', adj. pious; very religious.

dew, n. moisture condensed at ground level. —dew'drop'', n. —dew'y, adj.

dex'ter·ous, adj. skillful; cunning. Also, dex'trous. —dex·ter'i·ty, n.

dex'trose, n. type of sugar found in plants and animals.

di''a·be'tes, n. disease characterized by the body's inability to use sugar properly. —di''a·be'tic, adj., n.

di''a·bol'ic, adj. devilish. Also, di''a·bol'i·cal.

di''a·dem'', n. crown.

di''ag·nose'', v.t., -nosed, -nosing. 1. make a diagnosis of. 2. establish by diagnosis.

di''ag·no'sis, n., pl. -ses. determination of the nature of an illness or situation. —di''ag·nos'tic, adj.

di·ag'o·nal, adj. 1. connecting two nonadjacent angles. 2. oblique. —n. 3. something that is diagonal.

di'a·gram'', n., v.t., -gramed, -graming. n. 1. chart or plan that explains something simply. —v.t. 2. make a diagram of. —di''a·gram·mat'ic, adj.

di'al, n., v.t., -aled or -aling. n. 1. disk or strip with a calibrated edge, as on a clock or gauge. 2. disk turned to get radio frequencies, make telephone calls, etc. —v.t. 3. obtain or reach by turning a dial.

di'a·lect'', n. variety of a language peculiar to a region or class. —di''a·lec'tal, adj.

di'a·logue'', n. conversation between two or more people. Also, di'a·log''.

di·am'e·ter, n. 1. straight line passing through the center of a circle. 2. length of such a line. —di''a·met'ri·cal, adj.

dī′a·mònd, *n.* **1.** hard, transparent crystallization of carbon. **2.** parallelogram. **3. diamonds,** suit of playing cards. **4.** baseball field.

dia′pêr, *n.* **1.** piece of absorbent material that forms a baby's undercloth. —*v.t.* **2.** put a diaper on.

dī·a·phrägm (dī′ə fram″), *n.* **1.** muscular wall, esp. between the chest and abdomen. **2.** vibrating disk in a microphone etc. **3.** contraceptive device for women.

dī″ár·rhē′á, *n.* intestinal disorder characterized by too frequent and too loose bowel movements.

dī′á·rÿ, *n.* daily record of experiences. —**dī′a·rist,** *n.*

dī·ăs′to·lē, *n.* normal rhythmic expansion of the heart. —**dī″a·stol′ic,** *adj.*

dī′á·trībe′, *n.* bitter denunciation.

dīce, *n. pl., sing.* **die,** *v.,* **diced, dicing.** *n.* **1.** small cubes commonly marked on each side with one to six spots, used in games. —*v.i.* **2.** play with dice. —*v.t.* **3.** cut into small cubes.

dī′chŏt′o·mÿ, *n.* division into two parts.

dĭck′êr, *v.i.* bargain.

dĭc′tāte′, *v.,* **-tated, -tating.** *v.t., v.i.* **1.** speak for preservation in writing. **2.** impose on others, as terms. —**dic·ta′tion,** *n.*

dĭc′tā·tör, *n.* de facto absolute ruler. —**dic′ta·tor·ship″,** *n.* —**dic″ta·to′ri·al,** *adj.*

dĭc′tion, *n.* **1.** choice of words. **2.** enunciation.

dĭc′tion·ār″ÿ, *n., pl.* **-ies.** book explaining the meanings, etc. of alphabetically listed words.

dĭc′tŭm, *n.* authoritative statement; pronouncement.

dĭ·dăc′tĭc, *adj.* intended for instruction. —**dĭ·dac′ti·cism,** *n.*

dīe, *v.i.,* **died, dying,** *n.* *v.i.* **1.** cease to live. **2.** lose vigor or strength. —*n.* **3.** shaping device.

dī·êr′é·sis, *n., pl.* **-ses.** mark placed over a vowel to show that it is pronounced separately.

diē′sèl, *n.* internal-combustion engine in which fuel is ignited by air compression. Also, **diesel engine.**

dī′ét, *n.* **1.** food normally eaten. **2.** selection of food for purposes of health. **3.** legislature. —*v.i.* **4.** be on a diet. —**dī′e·tar″y,** *adj.* —**dī″e·ti′tian, di″e·ti′cian,** *n.* —**dī″e·tet′ic,** *adj.*

dĭf′fêr, *v.i.* **1.** be different. **2.** disagree.

dĭf′fêr·ence, *n.* **1.** unlikeness. **2.** disagreement. **3.** amount after subtraction. —**dif′fer·ent,** *adj.* —**dif′fer·ent·ly,** *adv.*

dĭf″fêr·ĕn′tiăl, *adj.* **1.** pertaining to difference. —*n.* **2.** difference. **3.** Also, **differential gear,** gear turning axles at individual speeds.

dĭf″fêr·ĕn′ti·āte′, *v.,* **-ated, -ating.** *v.t.* **1.** make unlike. **2.** distinguish between or from another. —*v.i.* **3.** make a distinction.

dĭf′fĭ·cŭlt, *adj.* **1.** hard to do or understand. **2.** hard to deal with or satisfy. —**dif′fi·cul″ty,** *n.*

dĭf′fĭ·dėnt, *adj.* shy; self-conscious. —**dif′fi·dence,** *n.*

dĭf·frăc′tion, *n.* breaking of light, sound, etc. into separate components.

dif·fuse, *v.* **-fused, -fusing,** *adj. v.t., v.i.* (dif fyōoz′) **1.** disseminate; spread. —*adj.* (dif fyōos′) **2.** not concentrated. **3.** wordy. —**dif·fu′sion,** *n.*

dĭg, *v.,* **dug, digging,** *n. v.t.* **1.** cut into or turn over. **2.** form by digging. **3.** discover or remove by or as if by digging. —*v.i.* **4.** break up earth, etc. by digging. —*n.* **5.** act or instance of digging. **6.** taunting remark.

dĭ·gĕst′, *v.t.* **1.** transform food in the body so it is absorbable. **2.** absorb mentally. —*n.* (di′gest). **3.** abridged and systematic collection of information; summary. —**di·gest′i·ble,** *adj.* —**di·ges′tion,** *n.* —**di·ges′tive,** *adj.*

dĭg′ĭt, *n.* **1.** finger or toe. **2.** any Arabic figure: 0 to 9. —**dig′it·al,** *adj.*

dĭg′ĭ·tăl, *adj.* represented by numerals.

dĭg″ĭ·tăl′ĭs, *n.* dried leaves of a plant, used as a heart stimulant.

dĭg′nĭ·fīed″, *adj.* showing dignity; stately.

dĭg′nĭ·fÿ″, *v.t.,* **-fied, -fying.** honor; give dignity to.

dĭg′nĭ·tăr″ÿ, *n., pl.* **-ies.** eminent person, esp. because of rank.

dĭ·grĕss′, *v.i.* wander away from the main

subject or purpose. —di·gres′sion, n. —di·gres′sive, adj.

dike, n. dam made to prevent flooding.

di·lap′i·dat′ed, adj. ruined; broken down. —di·lap′i·da′tion, n.

di·late′, v., -lated, -lating. v.t., v.i. 1. widen; expand. 2. speak at length. —di·la′tion, dil′′a·ta′tion, n.

dil′a·to′′ry̆, adj. delaying.

di·lĕm′ma, n. predicament requiring a puzzling choice between two alternatives.

dil′′et·tănte′, n., pl. -tantes, -tanti. amateur, superficial artist, thinker, etc.

dil′i·gént, adj. hard-working. —dil′i·gence, n.

dill, n. plant with aromatic leaves and seeds used for flavoring.

di·lūte′, v.t., -luted, -luting. water down; thin out. —di·lu′tion, n.

dĭm, adj., dimmer, dimmest, v., dimmed, dimming. adj. 1. not bright; indistinct. 2. not clearly seeing or understanding. —v.t., v.i. 3. make or grow dim. —dim′ly, adv.

dime, n. ten-cent coin.

di·měn′sion, n. 1. length, breadth, or height. 2. coordinate used in locating something in space and/or time. —di·men′sion·al, adj.

di·min′ish, v.t., v.i. lessen in size or importance. —dim′′i·nu′tion, n.

di·min′ù·tĭve, adj. 1. very small. —n. 2. suffix or variant modifying a word to indicate smallness.

dim′i·ty̆, n. thin woven cloth.

dĭm′ple, n., v., -pled, -pling. n. 1. small, natural hollow, esp. on the cheek or chin. —v.t., v.i. 2. form dimples.

dĭn, n., v.t., dinned, dinning. n. 1. confused or continuous noise. —v.t. 2. repeat insistently.

dine, v., dined, dining. v.i. 1. eat dinner. —v.t. 2. provide dinner for.

di′ner, n. 1. person eating. 2. railroad dining car. 3. restaurant resembling such a car.

dĭn·ghy̆, n. small boat belonging to a larger boat.

dĭn·gy̆, adj., -gier, -giest. dark; grimy. —din′gi·ness, n.

dĭn′ner, n. main meal of the day.

di′no·sâur′′, n. large reptile of prehistoric times.

dĭnt, n. 1. exertion. 2. dent.

di′o·cése, n. district under a bishop. —di·oc′e·san, adj., n.

dĭp, v., dipped, dipping, n. v.t. 1. lower briefly and raise. 2. remove with a scoop. —v.i. 3. be dipped. 4. plunge abruptly. —n. 5. short swim or bath. 6. abrupt plunge or slope.

diph·thong (dif′thong, dip′thong), n. sound containing two vowels.

di·plō′ma, n. certificate conferring a degree.

di·plō′măt′, n. 1. official representing a state. 2. person of tact. —di·plo′ma·cy, n. —dip′′lo·mat′ic, adj.

dĭp′pêr, n. 1. ladle. 2. **Dipper,** either of two constellations in the shape of a dipper.

dĭp′′sò·mā′nĭ·à, n. irresistible craving for alcohol. —dĭp′′so·ma′ni·ac′′, n.

dire, adj., direr, direst. 1. Also, dire′ful, dreadful. 2. urgent.

di·rĕct′, adj. 1. straight. 2. straightforward. 3. unbroken; continuous. 4. faithful to an original. —v.t. 5. guide. 6. supervise or command. 7. address. —di·rect′ly, adv. —di·rect′ness, n. —di·rec′tor, n.

di·rĕc′tion, n. 1. line toward a place, point of the compass, etc. 2. instruction. 3. act, instance, or responsibility of directing. —di·rec′tion·al, adj.

di·rĕc′tĭve, n. general order.

di·rĕc′tò·ry̆, n., pl. -ries. book with names, addresses, etc.

dîrge, n. funeral song.

dĭr′i·gĭ·ble, n. maneuverable airship.

dîrk, n. dagger.

dîrt, n. 1. any unclean substance; filth. 2. soil.

dîrt′y̆, adj., -ier, -iest, v., -ied, -ying. adj. 1. not clean; soiled. 2. indecent. —v.t., v.i. 3. make or become dirty. —dirt′i·ness, n. —dirt′i·ly, adv.

dĭs·ā′ble, v.t., -bled, -bling. make incapable or unfit. —dis′′a·bil′i·ty, n.

dĭs′′à·būse′, v.t., -bused, -busing. rid of false ideas; set right.

dĭs′′ăd·van·tàge, n. 1. unfavorable circumstance. 2. injury or detriment.

—**dis''ad·van'taged,** *adj.* —**dis·ad''van·ta'geous,** *adj.*

dis''af·fěct', *v.t.* make unfriendly; antagonize. —**dis''af·fec'tion,** *n.*

dis''a·gree', *v.i.* **-greed, -greeing. 1.** fail to agree. **2.** quarrel. —**dis''a·gree'ment,** *n.*

dis''a·gree'a·ble, *adj.* not agreeable; unpleasant. —**dis''a·gree'a·bly,** *adv.*

dis''ap·pear', *v.i.* **1.** vanish. **2.** cease to exist. —**dis''ap·pear'ance,** *n.*

dis''ap·point', *v.t.* thwart the expectations or hopes of. —**dis''ap·point'ment,** *n.*

dis''ap·prove', *v.,* **-proved, -proving.** *v.t., v.i.* not to approve. —**dis''ap·prov'al,** *n.*

dis·arm', *v.t.* **1.** take away or deprive of weapons. **2.** make friendly. —*v.i.* **3.** reduce armed forces. —**dis·ar'ma·ment,** *n.*

dis''ar·range', *v.t.,* **-ranged, -ranging.** put in disorder. —**dis''ar·range'ment,** *n.*

dis''ar·ray', *v.t.* **1.** throw into disorder. —*n.* **2.** disorder; confusion.

dis·ăs'têr, *n.* cause of much damage. —**dis·as'trous,** *adj.*

dis''a·vow', *v.t.* disclaim knowledge of or responsibility for. —**dis''a·vow'al,** *n.*

dis·bănd', *v.t., v.i.* break up, as an organization. —**dis·band'ment,** *n.*

dis·bâr', *v.t.,* **-barred, -bar·ring.** expel from the legal profession. —**dis·bar'ment,** *n.*

dis·bē''lieve', *v.,* **-lieved, -lieving.** *v.t., v.i.* refuse to believe. —**dis''be·lief',** *n.*

dis·bûrse', *v.t.,* **-bursed, -bursing. 1.** pay out. **2.** scatter. —**dis·burse'ment,** *n.*

disc, *n.* disk.

dis·cârd', *v.t.* **1.** throw away. —*n.* (dis'card) **2.** state of being thrown away. **3.** something thrown away.

dis·cêrn', *v.t.* perceive; recognize; distinguish. —**dis·cern'i·ble,** *adj.* —**dis·cern'ment,** *n.* —**dis·cern'ing,** *adj.*

dis·chârge', *v.,* **-charged, -charging,** *v.t.* **1.** emit. **2.** shoot or fire. **3.** unload. **4.** perform. **5.** release or dismiss from service. —*v.i.* **6.** release a load, etc. —*n.* (dis'charge) **7.** act, instance, or means of discharging. **8.** something discharged.

dis·cī'ple, *n.* follower of a teacher or teaching.

dis·ci·pline, *n., v.,* **-plined, -plining.** *n.* **1.** training that develops self-control. **2.** punishment. **3.** set or system of rules and regulations. **4.** branch of learning. —*v.t.* **5.** train. **6.** punish. —**dis·ci·pli·na''ry,** *adj.* —**dis·ci·pli·nar''i·an,** *n.*

dis·clăim', *v.t.* disown.

dis·clăim'êr, *n.* disavowal or renunciation.

dis·clōse', *v.t.,* **-closed, -closing.** reveal or uncover. —**dis·clo'sure,** *n.*

dis·cō, *n.* **1.** discotheque; a club featuring dancing to rock music. **2.** a style of dance music with a pronounced beat.

dis·col'ôr, *v.t., v.i.* fade or stain. —**dis·col''or·a'tion,** *n.*

dis·com'fĭt, *v.t.* frustrate the plans of; disconcert. —**dis·com'fi·ture,** *n.*

dis·com'fôrt, *n.* lack of comfort.

dis''con·cêrt', *v.t.* upset; disarrange; perturb.

dis''con·nĕct', *v.t.* finish the connection of; separate. —**dis''con·nec'tion,** *n.*

dis''con·sò·late, *adj.* unhappy; dejected.

dis''con·tĕnt', *adj.* **1.** Also, **dis''con·tent'ed,** dissatisfied with something; not content. —*n.* **2.** dissatisfaction; lack of content.

dis''con·tĭn'ūe, *v.,* **-ued, -uing.** *v.t., v.i.* stop. —**dis''con·tin'u·ance, dis''con·tin''u·a'tion,** *n.*

dis'côrd, *n.* **1.** lack of harmony. **2.** disagreement. —**dis·cord'ance,** *n.* —**dis·cord'ant,** *adj.*

dis·cò·thèque, *n.* place where people dance to recorded music.

dis·cŏunt, *n.* **1.** reduction in price. —*v.t.* **2.** deduct from a bill. **3.** advance with deduction or interest. **4.** sell at less than the regular price. **5.** disregard. —**dis·count·a·ble,** *adj.*

dis·coûr'age, *v.t.,* **-aged, -aging.** hamper or stop with predictions of failure, disapproval, etc. —**dis·cour'age·ment,** *n.*

dis·coûrse', *n., v.i.,* **-coursed, -coursing.** *n.* **1.** conversation. **2.** essay or lecture. —*v.i.* **3.** converse.

dis·coûr'te·sў, *n., pl.* **-sies.** lack of courtesy; rudeness. —**dis·cour'te·ous,** *adj.*

dis·cŏv'êr, *v.t.* perceive for the first time.

—dĭs·cŏv'er·er, *n.* —dĭs·cŏv'er·y, *n.*
—dĭs·cŏv'er·a·ble, *adj.*

dĭs·crĕd'ĭt, *v.t.* 1. cast doubt on. 2. injure the reputation of. —*n.* 3. state of being discredited.

dĭs·crēet', *adj.* prudent. —dis·creet'ly, *adv.*

dĭs·crĕp'an·cў, *n.* inconsistency.

dĭs·crēte', *adj.* separate; distinct.

dĭs·crē'tion, *n.* 1. prudence. 2. freedom of choice in actions. —dis·cre'tion·ary'', *adj.*

dĭs·crĭm'ĭ·nāte'', *v.i.,* -nated, -nating, *adj. v.i.* 1. make careful distinctions. 2. show unjust favor or disfavor. —*adj.* (dis crim'i nate) 3. making careful distinctions. —dis·crim''i·na'tion, *n.* —dis·crim'i·nat''ing, *adj.* —dis·crim'i·na·to''ry, *adj.*

dĭs·cûr'sĭve, *adj.* rambling; wandering from topic to topic.

dĭs·cŭss', *v.t.* talk or write about. —dis·cus'sion, *n.*

dĭs·dāin', *v.t.* 1. scorn; despise. —*n.* 2. scorn. —dis'dain'ful, *adj.*

dĭs·ēase', *n., v.t.,* -eased, -easing. *n.* 1. ailment; sickness. —*v.t.* 2. affect with sickness.

dĭs''em·bärk', *v.i.* leave a ship or aircraft. —dis''em·bar·ka'tion, dis''em·bark'ment, *n.*

dĭs''em·bŏd'ў, *v.t.,* -ied, -ying. free from the body. —dis''em·bŏd'i·ment, *n.*

dĭs''en·chänt', *v.t.* destroy the enthusiasm of. —dis''en·chant'ment, *n.*

dĭs''en·gāge', *v.,* -gaged, -gaging. *v.t., v.i.* disconnect. —dis''en·gage'ment, *n.*

dĭs·fā'vŏr, *n.* 1. disapproval. —*v.t.* 2. treat with disfavor.

dĭs·fĭg'ûre, *v.t.,* -ured, -uring. mar. —dis·fig'ure·ment, *n.*

dĭs·frăn'chīse, *v.t.,* -chised, -chising. deprive of a right or privilege, esp. voting. Also, dis''en·fran'chise.

dĭs·gôrge', *v.,* -gorged, -gorging. *v.t., v.i.* pour out.

dĭs·grāce', *n., v.t.,* -graced, -gracing. *n.* 1. state or cause of shame. —*v.t.* 2. bring shame upon. —dis·grace'ful, *adj.*

dĭs·grŭn'tle, *v.t.,* -tled, -tling. make discontent or sulky.

dĭs·guīse', *v.t.,* -guised, -guising. *n. v.t.*

1. render temporarily unrecognizable. 2. misrepresent. —*n.* 3. something that disguises. —dis·guise'ment, *n.*

dĭs·gŭst', *v.t.* 1. offend the good taste or senses of. —*n.* 2. sickening dislike.

dĭsh, *n.* 1. shallow container for food. 2. food that is served.

dĭs·heärt'ĕn, *v.t.* discourage.

dĭ·shĕv'ĕl, *v.t.,* -eled, -eling. cause disarray in.

dĭs·hŏn'ĕst, *adj.* not honest. —dis·hon'est·ly, *adv.* —dis·hon'es·ty, *n.*

dĭs·hŏn'ŏr, *n.* 1. lack of respect; disgrace. —*v.t.* 2. disgrace. —dis·hon'or·a·ble, *adj.*

dĭs''ĭl·lū'sion, *v.t.* free from illusion. —dis''il·lu'sion·ment, *n.*

dĭs''ĭn·clīne', *v.t.,* -clined, -clining. make unwilling or averse. —dis·in''cli·na'tion, *n.*

dĭs''ĭn·fĕct', *v.t.* rid of infection. —dis''in·fect'ant, *n., adj.*

dĭs''ĭn·hĕr'ĭt, *v.t.* deprive of inheritance.

dĭs·ĭn'tè·grāte'', *v.,* -grated, -grating. *v.t., v.i.* separate. —*v.t., v.i.* separate into elements. —dis·in''te·gra'tion, *n.*

dĭs·ĭn'têr·ĕst, *n.* indifference.

dĭs·ĭn'têr·ĕst·ĕd, *n.* 1. impartial. 2. indifferent.

dĭs·jŏīnt'ĕd, *adj.* 1. separated at the joints. 2. incoherent.

dĭsk, *n.* 1. thin, flat, round object. 2. phonograph record.

dĭsk·ĕtte', *n.* (computers) a 5¼-inch magnetic disk or a 3½-inch disk used for data storage.

dĭs·līke', *v.t.,* -liked, -liking, *n. v.t.* 1. regard with aversion or distaste. —*n.* 2. aversion; distaste.

dĭs'lŏ·cāte'', *v.t.,* -cated, -cating. put out of the proper or customary place. —dis''lo·ca'tion, *n.*

dĭs·lŏdge', *v.t.,* —lodged, -lodging. force from a place. —dis·lodg'ment, *n.*

dĭs·lŏy'al, *adj.* not loyal; unfaithful. —dis·loy'al·ty, *n.*

dĭs'mȧl, *adj.* 1. gloomy; dreary. 2. causing dreariness or misery.

dĭs·măn'tle, *v.t.,* -tled, -tling. 1. deprive or strip of equipment. 2. take apart.

dĭs·māy', *v.t.* 1. dishearten. —*n.* 2. disheartenment.

dis·mem′bêr, *v.t.* deprive of limbs. —**dis·mem′ber·ment**, *n.*

dis·miss′, *v.t.* **1.** direct or allow to leave. **2.** discharge from employment. **3.** put out of consideration. —**dis·mis′sal**, *n.*

dis·mount′, *v.i.* **1.** alight from a horse, bicycle, etc. —*v.t.* **2.** take from a mounting. **3.** dismantle.

dis″o·bē′di·ent, *adj.* not obedient. —**dis″o·be′di·ence**, *n.* —**dis″o·bey′**, *v.t.*

dis·ôr′dêr, *n.* **1.** confusion. **2.** ailment. **3.** riot. —*v.t.* **4.** create disorder in. —**dis·or′der·ly**, *adj.*

dis·ôr′gan·ize″, *v.t.*, **-ized, -izing.** throw into confusion. —**dis·or″gan·i·za′tion**, *n.*

dis·own′, *v.t.* repudiate.

dis·pâr′age, *v.t.*, **-aged, -aging.** belittle. —**dis·par′age·ment**, *n.*

dis′pa·râte, *adj.* distinct in kind. —**dis·par′i·ty**, *n.*

dis·pãs′sion·âte, *adj.* impartial. —**dis·pas′sion·ate·ly**, *adv.*

dis·pâtch′, *v.t.* **1.** send off. **2.** kill. **3.** transact quickly. —*n.* **4.** sending-off. **5.** killing. **6.** promptness. **7.** message. —**dis·patch′er**, *n.*

dis·pĕl′, *v.t.*, **-pelled, -pelling.** scatter; drive off.

dis·pĕn′sa·rȳ, *n.*, *pl.* **-ries.** place where medical aid is given.

dis″pĕn·sā′tion, *n.* **1.** act or instance of dispensing. **2.** something dispensed. **3.** release from obligation. **4.** divine ordering of events.

dis·pĕnse′, *v.*, **-pensed, -pensing.** *v.t.* **1.** distribute. **2.** prepare and give out as medicine. —*v.i.* **3.** **dispense with, a.** forgo **b.** get rid of. —**dis·pen′sa·ble**, *adj.*

dis·pêrse′, *v.*, **-persed, -persing.** *v.t.*, *v.i.* scatter. —**dis·per′sal, dis·per′sion**, *n.*

dis·plãce′, *v.t.*, **-placed, -placing. 1.** put out of place. **2.** take the place of. —**dis·place′ment**, *n.*

dis′plãy, *v.t.*, *n.* exhibit.

dis·plēase′, *v.t.*, **-pleased, -pleasing.** offend. —**dis·pleas′ure**, *n.*

dis·pōse′, *v.*, **-posed, -posing.** *v.t.* **1.** arrange. **2.** incline or make willing. —*v.i.* **3.** rid oneself. —**dis·pos′a·ble**, *adj.* —**dis·pos′al**, *n.*

dis″pō·sǐ′tion, *n.* **1.** temperament. **2.** tendency. **3.** arrangement. **4.** settlement. **5.** disposal.

dis″pòs·sěss′, *v.t.* deprive of possession. —**dis″pos·ses′sion**, *n.*

dis″prō·pôr′tion, *n.* lack of proportion. —**dis″pro·por′tion·ate**, *adj.*

dis·prōve′, *v.t.*, **-proved, -proving.** prove false. —**dis·proof′**, *n.*

dis·pūte′, *v.*, **-puted, -puting.** *n. v.i.*, *v.t.* **1.** argue. —*v.t.* **2.** express doubt regarding. **3.** oppose or fight. —*n.* **4.** act or instance of disputing. **5.** state of being disputed. —**dis·pu′tant**, *n.*, *adj.* —**dis·put′a·ble**, *adj.* —**dis″pu·ta′tion**, *n.* —**dis″pu·ta′tious**, *adj.*

dis·quäl′i·fȳ″, *v.t.*, **-fied, -fying.** make or declare unqualified. —**dis·qual″i·fi·ca′tion**, *n.*

dis·quī′et, *v.t.* **1.** disturb; make uneasy. —*n.* **2.** Also, **dis·qui′e·tude**, restlessness.

dis″quǐ·sǐ′tion, *n.* formal discourse.

dis″rē·gârd′, *v.t.* **1.** ignore. **2.** treat with little or no respect. —*n.* **3.** neglect. **4.** lack of respect.

dis″rē·pâir′, *n.* impaired condition.

dis″rē·pūte′, *n.* bad reputation. —**dis·rep′u·ta·ble**, *adj.*

dis″rē·spĕct′, *n.* lack of respect. —**dis″re·spect′ful**, *adj.*

dis·rōbe′, *v.*, **-robed, -robing.** *v.t.*, *v.i.* undress.

dis·rŭpt′, *v.t.*, *v.i.* **1.** break up. **2.** disturb. —**dis·rup′tion**, *n.* —**dis·rup′tive**, *adj.*

dis·sǎt′is·fȳ″, *v.t.*, **-fied, -fying.** fail to satisfy; displease. —**dis·sat″is·fac′tion**, *n.*

dis·sēct′, *v.t.* **1.** cut apart. **2.** examine closely. —**dis·sec′tion**, *n.*

dis·sĕm′ble, *v.*, **-bled, -bling.** *v.t.*, *v.i.* disguise. —**dis·sem′blance**, *n.* —**dis·sem′bler**, *n.*

dis·sĕm′i·nâte″, *v.t.*, **-nated, -nating.** distribute widely. —**dis·sem″i·na′tion**, *n.*

dis·sĕn′sion, *n.* disagreement or quarreling.

dis·sĕnt′, *v.i.* **1.** disagree. —*n.* **2.** disagreement. —**dis·sent′er**, *n.*

dis″sêr·tā′tion, *n.* formal essay; thesis.

dis·sǐm′i·lár, *adj.* not similar. —**dis·sim″i·lar′i·ty**, *n.*

dis·sĭm′ŭ·lāte″, *v.*, **-lated, -lating.** *v.t.*, *v.i.* dissemble. **—dis·sim″u·la′tion,** *n.*

dĭs′sĭ·pāte″, *v.*, **-pated, -pating.** *v.t.* **1.** scatter. **2.** squander. **—v.i. 3.** live in extravagance or vice. **—dis″si·pa′tion,** *n.*

dĭs′sĭ·pāt″ĕd, *adj.* living in extravagance or vice.

dĭs·sō′cĭ·āte″, *v.t.*, **-ated, -ating.** break the connection between.

dĭs′sŏ·lūte″, *adj.* dissipated. **—dis′so·lute″ly,** *adv.* **—dis″so·lu′tion,** *n.*

dĭs·sŏlve′, *v.*, **-solved, -solving.** *v.t.*, *v.i.* **1.** melt; combine with a liquid. **2.** terminate. **3.** destroy. **—dis″so·lu′tion,** *n.*

dĭs′sŏ·nánce, *n.* musical discord. **—dis′so·nant,** *adj.*

dĭs·suāde′, *v.t.*, **-suaded, -suading.** deter by persuasion. **—dis·sua′sion,** *n.*

dĭs′tánce, *n.* **1.** interval of space or time. **2.** remoteness. **3.** reserve; aloofness. **—dis′tant,** *adj.*

dĭs·tāste′, *n.* dislike. **—dis·taste′ful,** *adj.*

dĭs·tĕm′pĕr, *n.* infectious disease of dogs.

dĭs·tĕnd′, *v.t.*, *v.i.* expand. **—dis·ten′tion,** *n.*

dĭs·tĭll′, *v.t.* **1.** make or purify by evaporation and condensation. **—v.t. 2.** become distilled. **—dis·till′er,** *n.* **—dis·till′er·y,** *n.* **—dis″til·la′tion,** *n.*

dĭs·tĭnct′, *adj.* **1.** individual. **2.** clearly noticeable or understandable. **—dis·tinct′ly,** *adv.*

dĭs·tĭnc′tion, *n.* **1.** act or instance of distinguishing. **2.** difference. **3.** eminence. **4.** something that gives or betokens eminence.

dĭs·tĭnc′tĭve, *adj.* characteristic.

dĭs·tĭn′guĭsh, *v.t.* **1.** characterize as individual. **2.** perceive. **3.** make eminent or excellent. **—dis·tin′guish·a·ble,** *adj.* **—dis·tin′guished,** *adj.*

dĭs·tôrt′, *v.t.* **1.** alter from a normal shape. **2.** corrupt the true meaning of. **—dis·tor′tion,** *n.*

dĭs·trăct′, *v.t.* **1.** prevent from concentrating. **2.** bewilder. **—dis·trac′tion,** *n.*

dĭs·trăct′ĕd, *adj.* frantic. Also, **dis·traught′.**

dĭs·trĕss′, *n.* **1.** pain or need. **2.** source of this. **3.** danger. **—v.t. 4.** cause distress in.

dĭs·trĭb′ute, *v.t.*, **-uted, -uting. 1.** give out in portions. **2.** disperse. **—dis″tri·bu′tion,** *n.* **—dis·trib′u·tor,** *n.*

dĭs′trĭct, *n.* distinct geographical area.

dĭs·trŭst′, *n.* **1.** lack of trust. **—v.t. 2.** place no trust in. **—dis·trust′ful,** *adj.*

dĭs·tûrb′, *v.t.* **1.** end the quiet state of. **2.** upset or trouble. **3.** interrupt. **—dis·turb′ance,** *n.*

dĭs·ūse′, *n.* absence of use.

dĭtch, *n.* channel dug in the ground.

dĭt′tō, *n.*, *pl.* **-tos. 1.** the same as before. **2.** Also, **ditto mark,** a mark, ″, used to indicate that the word or line above is repeated.

dĭt′tÿ, *n.*, *pl.* **-ties.** simple tune.

dĭ·ûr′nál, *adj.* **1.** daily. **2.** pertaining to the day.

dĭ·văn′, *n.* long, low couch.

dīve, *v.i.,* **dived** or **dove, dived, diving,** *n.* *v.i.* **1.** fall intentionally. **2.** descend below the water. **3.** lose altitude quickly. **—n. 4.** act, instance, or form of diving. **—div′er,** *n.*

dĭ·vêrge′, *v.i.*, **-verged, -verging. 1.** part in two or more directions. **2.** become of unlike opinion, etc. **—di·ver′gent,** *adj.* **—di·ver′gence,** *n.*

dī′vêrs, *adj.* *Archaic.* various.

dĭ·vêrse′, *adj.* **1.** different. **2.** various. **—di·verse′ly,** *adv.* **—di·vers′i·ty,** *n.*

dĭ·vêr′sĭ·fÿ″, *v.t.*, **-fied, -fying.** vary. **—di·ver″si·fi·ca′tion,** *n.*

dĭ·vêrt′, *v.t.* **1.** turn aside from a path or course. **2.** entertain; amuse. **—di·ver′sion,** *n.*

dĭ·vĕst′, *v.t.* **1.** deprive or strip. **2.** rid.

dĭ·vīde′, *v.*, **-vided, -viding.** *v.t.* **1.** separate into parts or classes. **2.** prevent from uniting. **—v.i. 3.** separate. **—n. 4.** line separating two drainage areas. **—di·vid′er,** *n.*

dĭv′ĭ·dĕnd″, *n.* **1.** number to be divided. **2.** sum allotted to a stockholder.

dĭ·vīne′, *adj.*, *v.t.*, **-vined, -vining.** *adj.* **1.** godly or godlike. **2.** religious. **—v.t. 3.** prophesy. **4.** perceive intuitively. **—div″i·na′tion,** *n.*

dĭ·vĭn′ĭ·tÿ, *n.*, *pl.* **-ties. 1.** deity. **2.** theology.

di·vis′i·ble, *adj.* able to be divided, esp. evenly.

di·vi′sion, *n.* **1.** act or instance of dividing. **2.** element or component. **3.** *Math.* process of determining the ratio of one number to another. **4.** military unit.

di·vi′sive, *adj.* causing disunity.

di·vi′sor, *n. Math.* number used to divide another.

di·vorce′, *n., v.t.,* **-vorced, -vorcing.** *n.* **1.** legal dissolution of a marriage. **2.** conceptual separation. —*v.t.* **3.** separate oneself from by a divorce. **4.** separate by a divorce. **5.** separate conceptually. —**di·vorce′ment,** *n.*

di·vor′cee′, *n.* divorced woman.

di·vulge′, *v.t.,* **-vulged, -vulging.** reveal. —**di·vulg′ence,** *n.*

Dix′ie, *n.* southern part of the U.S.

diz′zy, *adj.,* **-zier, -ziest. 1.** unsteady. **2.** causing unsteadiness, as a height.

do, *v.,* **did, done, doing.** *v.t.* **1.** be at work upon or occupied with. **2.** complete. **3.** cause. —*v.i.* **4.** act. **5.** succeed in or accomplish something. **6.** suffice. **7.** happen.

doc′ile, *adj.* readily disciplined. —**do·cil′i·ty,** *n.*

dock, *n.* **1.** place for ships between voyages. **2.** pier or wharf. **3.** fleshy part of an animal's tail. —*v.t.* **4.** put into a dock. **5.** deduct from the wages of. —*v.i.* **6.** enter a dock.

dock′et, *n.* **1.** list of agenda, esp. of a court. —*v.t.* **2.** put on a docket.

doc′tor, *n.* **1.** person who practices medicine, etc. **2.** person with a high academic degree. —*v.t.* **3.** *Informal.* heal or fix. —**doc′tor·al,** *adj.* —**doc·tor·ate,** *n.*

doc′′tri·naire′, *adj.* rigidly adhering to or following doctrine.

doc′trine, *n.* body of teaching, esp, in religion or politics. —**doc′trin·al,** *adj.*

doc′u·ment, *n.* **1.** writing, etc. used as a proof. —*v.t.* **2.** prove or support with documents. —**doc′′u·men·ta′tion,** *n.*

doc′′u·men′ta·ry, *adj., n., pl.* **-ries.** *adj.* **1.** pertaining to documents. **2.** serving as a record of events. —*n.* **3.** film, etc. serving as a record of events.

dodge, *v.,* **dodged, dodging.** *n. v.t.* **1.** avoid by moving quickly. **2.** evade by a

trick. —*v.i.* **3.** dodge something. —*n.* **4.** act or instance of dodging. **5.** trick.

doe, *n.* female of certain animals, as deer or rabbits.

doff, *v.t. Archaic.* remove, as a hat.

dog, *n., v.t.,* **dogged, dogging.** *n.* **1.** four-legged domestic animal. —*v.t.* **2.** track; follow.

dog·ged, *adj.* stubborn in difficulty.

dog′ger·el, *n.* simple verse.

dog′ma, *n.* doctrine, esp. in religion, regarded as unquestionable.

dog·mat′ic, *adj.* **1.** pertaining to or published as dogma. **2.** offering personal opinions as dogma. —**dog′ma·tism,** *n.*

dog′wood′′, *n.* tree with white or pink blossoms.

doi′ly, *n., pl.* **-lies.** small mat, often of lace.

dol′drums, *n. pl.* **1.** equatorial region with little wind. **2.** period of depression or inactivity.

dole, *n., v.t.,* **doled, doling.** *n.* **1.** money, food, etc. given to the unemployed. —*v.t.* **2.** portion out sparingly.

dole′ful, *adj.* sad.

doll, *n.* toy shaped like a baby or other human being.

dol′lar, *n.* currency unit of the U.S., Canada, etc.

do′lor·ous, *adj.* sorrowful or painful.

dol′phin, *n.* aquatic mammal.

dolt, *n.* oaf. —**dolt′ish,** *adj.*

do·main′, *n.* **1.** territory of a ruler. **2.** area of influence or power.

dome, *n.* structure like an upcurved segment of a sphere.

do·mes′tic, *adj.* **1.** pertaining to the home. **2.** belonging to or originating in one's own country. **3.** tamed. —**do′′mes·ti′ci·ty,** *n.*

do·mes′ti·cate′′, *v.t.,* **-cated, -cating.** adapt to domestic conditions. —**do·mes′′ti·ca′tion,** *n.*

dom′i·cile′′, *n., v.t.,* **-ciled, -ciling.** *n.* **1.** residence. —*v.t.* **2.** house.

dom′i·nant, *adj.* prevailing. —**dom′i·nance,** *n.*

dom′i·nate′′, *v.t.,* **-nated, -nating. 1.** master. **2.** be most conspicuous in. —**dom′′i·na′tion,** *n.*

dom′′i·neer′, *v.t., v.i.* tyrannize.

do·min′ion, *n.* **1.** sovereign power. **2.** territory reigned over or ruled by a sovereign.

dŏm'ĭ·nō, *n., pl.* **-noes. 1.** small plaque marked with spots. **2. dominoes,** a game played with these plaques. **3.** mask.

dŏn, *n., v.t.,* **donned, donning.** *n.* **1.** title of respect for a Spanish gentleman. —*v.t.* **2.** *Archaic.* put on, as clothes.

dō'nāte, *v.,* **-nated, -nating.** *v.t., v.i.* give, esp. in charity or friendship. —**do·na'tion,** *n.* —**do'nor,** *n.*

dŏn'kēy, *n., pl.* **-keys.** domesticated ass.

doŏ'dle, *v.i.,* **-dled, -dling,** *n. v.i.* **1.** scribble or draw absentmindedly. —*n.* **2.** product of doodling.

dōōm, *n.* **1.** death or annihilation. **2.** fate. —*v.t.* **3.** predestine or sentence to death, damnation, etc.

dŏor, *n.* **1.** movable partition for barring access. **2.** Also, **door'way'',** entrance. **3. out of doors,** outdoors.

dōpe, *n., v.t.,* **doped, doping.** *n.* **1.** *Informal.* **a.** habit-forming drug. **b.** fool. **c.** information. **2.** thick liquid used for industrial purposes. —*v.t.* **3.** *Informal.* drug.

dôr'mănt, *adj.* **1.** asleep or at rest. **2.** not active. —**dor'man·cy,** *n.*

dôr'mĕr, *n.* window structure in a roof.

dôr'mĭ·tô''rȳ, *n., pl.* **-ries.** place for residents of an institution to sleep.

dō'rȳ, *n., pl.* **-ries.** flat-bottomed rowboat used for fishing, etc.

dōse, *n., v.t.,* **dosed, dosing.** *n.* **1.** amount of medicine taken at one time. —*v.t.* **2.** give medicine to. —**dos'age,** *n.*

dos·si·er (dos'sē ā'), *n.* file of documents on one subject.

dŏt, *n., v.t.,* **dotted, dotting.** *n.* **1.** tiny round mark. —*v.t.* **2.** mark or make with dots.

dōte, *v.i.,* **doted, doting. 1.** show excessive fondness. **2.** be senile. —**dot'ing,** *adj.* —**dot'age,** *n.*

doŭ'ble, *adj., adv., n., v.,* **-bled, -bling.** *adj.* **1.** twice as much. **2.** intended for two. **3.** having two aspects. —*adv.* **4.** twice. —*n.* **5.** duplicate. —*v.t.* **6.** fold over. **7.** make twice as much or as many of. —*v.i.* **8.** fold in two. **9.** reverse one's direction. —**doub'ly,** *adv.*

doŭ''ble-crŏss', *v.t. Informal.* cheat or betray.

doŭbt, *v.t.* **1.** be unsure or skeptical of. —*n.* **2.** uncertainty or distrust. **3.** something unsettled or uncertain. —**doubt'ful,** *adj.* —**doubt'less,** *adv.*

dōugh, *n.* pastry mixture of flour and water for baking. —**dough'y,** *adj.*

dōugh'nŭt'', *n.* deep-fried ring-shaped cake.

dŏur, *adj.* gloomily severe.

dōuse, *v.t.,* **doused, dousing.** plunge into or drench with liquid.

dŏve, *n.* cooing pigeonlike bird.

dŏve'tāil'', *n.* **1.** interlocking carpentry joint. —*v.t.* **2.** join with dovetails.

dŏw'a·gĕr, *n.* widow endowed with a title or property.

dŏw'dȳ, *adj.,* **-dier, -diest.** plainly or untidily dressed, made up, etc.

dŏw'el, *n., v.t.,* **-eled, -eling.** *n.* **1.** round length of wood, used as a fastening between two joined pieces. —*v.t.* **2.** fasten with dowels.

dŏwn, *adv., adj.* **1.** to or at a lower place. **2.** to or in a lower condition, amount, etc. **3.** in writing. **4.** in advance. **5.** out of operation. —*adv.* **6.** to a later period. **7.** dejected. **8.** completed. —*prep.* **9.** descending along, through, etc. **10.** soft feathers or hair. —*v.t.* **11.** put down. —**down'stairs',** *adv., adj., n.* —**down'ward, down'wards,** *adv.* —**down'y,** *adj.*

dŏwn'fäll'', *n.* **1.** fall, as of snow. **2.** fall, as from power or eminence.

dŏwn'grāde'', *v.t.,* **-graded, -grading,** *adv., adj., n. v.t.* **1.** demote. —*adv., adj.* **2.** downward. —*n.* **3.** downward slope.

dŏwn''heärt'ĕd, *adj.* discouraged. —**down'heart'ed·ly,** *adv.*

dŏwn'hĭll'', *adv., adj.* downward.

dŏwn'pôur'', *n.* heavy rainstorm.

dŏwn'rĭght'', *adj.* **1.** utter. —*adv.* **2.** utterly.

dŏwn'stāirs'', *adv.* to or at a lower level.

dŏwn''-tò-êarth', *adj.* realistic.

dŏwn'tŏwn', *adv., adj.* toward or in the business district of a town.

dŏwn'trŏd''dèn, *adj.* oppressed.

dŏw'rȳ, *n., pl.* **-ries.** property bestowed on a bride by her family.

dŏx·ŏl'o·gȳ, *n., pl.* **-gies.** hymn of praise.

dōze, *v.i.,* **dozed, dozing,** *n. v.i.* **1.** sleep lightly. —*n.* **2.** light sleep.

dŏz'ĕn, *n., pl.* **-ens** or (after a number) **-en.** group of twelve. —**doz'enth,** *adj.*

drăb, *n., adj.,* **drabber, drabbest.** *n.* **1.** yellow-brown. —*adj.* **2.** dreary. —**drab'ly,** *adv.* —**drab'ness,** *n.*

drăft, *n.* **1.** act or amount of drawing. **2.** swallowing or inhalation. **3.** current of air. **4.** tentative version of writing. **5.** order to pay. **6.** selection for conscription. —*v.t.* **7.** make a draft of. **8.** conscript. —**draft'ee,** *n.* —**draft'y,** *adj.*

drăfts'măn, *n.* person who makes working drawings or sketches.

drăg, *v.,* **dragged, dragging.** *v.t.* **1.** pull with effort. **2.** search with a dragnet. —*v.t.* **3.** move slowly or with effort. —*n.* **4.** act or instance of dragging. **5.** *Informal.* something or someone dreary or obstructive.

drăg'nĕt'', *n.* **1.** net for fishing up submerged objects. **2.** methodical police search.

drăg'ŏn, *n.* mythical large reptile.

drăg'ŏn·flȳ'', *n.* large, stiff-winged insect.

drāin, *n.* **1.** channel for carrying away liquids. **2.** steady depletion. —*v.t.* **3.** remove through a channel. **4.** deplete steadily. —*v.i.* **5.** be drained. —**drain'age,** *n.*

drăm, *n.* **1.** eighth part of an apothecary's ounce or fluid ounce. **2.** small drink.

drä'mà, *n.* **1.** play. **2.** theater as an art. **3.** sensational event. **4.** emotionalism. —**dram'a·tist,** *n.* —**dram'a·tize'',** *v.t.* —**dra·mat'ic,** *adj.*

drāpe, *n., v.,* **draped, draping.** *n.* **1.** cloth hanging or curtain. —*v.t., v.i.* **2.** hang loosely or in folds. —**drap'er·y,** *n.*

drăs'tĭc, *adj.* severe or extreme.

drăught, *n., v.t., adj.* draft.

drăw, *v.,* **drew, drawn, drawing.** *n. v.t.* **1.** pull, attract, or take in. **2.** elicit or provoke. **3.** receive. **4.** sketch with a pencil, pen, etc. **5.** *Nautical.* need a depth of. —*v.i.* **6.** exert a pulling force. **7.** move. **8.** pass smoke, etc. readily. **9.** make demands. **10.** lessen in size. —*n.* **11.** act or instance of drawing. **12.** even final score. —**draw'ing,** *n.*

drăw'băck'', *n.* lessening of advantage.

drăw'brĭdge'', *n.* bridge that can be lifted or pulled.

drăw'·er, *n.* **1.** person or thing that draws. (drôr) **2.** sliding compartment in a piece of furniture. **3. drawers.** underpants.

drăwl, *n.* **1.** slow speech. —*v.t., v.i.* **2.** speak in a drawl.

drăwn, *adj.* haggard.

drāy, *n.* heavy freight wagon.

drĕad, *n.* **1.** fearful anticipation. **2.** awe. —*adj.* **3.** awesome. —*v.t.* **4.** anticipate fearfully.

drĕad'fŭl, *adj.* **1.** very bad. **2.** inspiring dread.

drēam, *n., v.,* **dreamed** or **dreamt, dreaming.** *n.* **1.** succession of images appearing in sleep or reverie. **2.** vision of something possible or desirable. —*v.t.* **3.** imagine in a dream. —*v.i.* **4.** have a dream. **dream'er,** *n.* —**dream'less,** *adj.* **dream'like'',** *adj.* —**dream'y,** *adj.*

drēar'ȳ, *adj.,* **-ier, -iest.** causing sadness or boredom.

drĕdge, *v.,* **dredged, dredging.** *n. v.t.* **1.** dig, esp. under water. **2.** coat with flour. —*n.* **3.** digging device.

drĕgs, *n., pl.* sediment, as of wine.

drĕnch, *v.t.* soak with falling liquid.

drĕss, *v.t.* **1.** put clothing on. **2.** prepare or finish. —*v.i.* **3.** put on clothing. **4.** wear formal clothing. —*n.* **5.** clothing. **6.** skirt. —**dress'mak''er,** *n.*

drĕs'sĕr, *n.* **1.** person who dresses. **2.** chest of drawers with a mirror.

drĕs'sing, *n.* **1.** material applied to wounds, bruises, etc. **2.** sauce for salad. **3.** stuffing for fowl.

drĭb'ble, *v.,* **-bled, -bling,** *n. v.t.* **1.** let drip untidily. —*n.* **2.** act or instance of dribbling.

drī'ĕr, *n.* thing or substance for drying.

drĭft, *v.i.* **1.** be carried by a current. **2.** move or live aimlessly or passively. —*n.* **3.** drifting motion. **4.** force or gist, as of an argument. **5.** pile of wind-driven snow.

drĭft'wŏŏd'', *n.* wood weathered and driven ashore by the sea.

drĭll, *n.* **1.** boring tool. **2.** system of exercises. **3.** seed-planting machine. **4.** coarse fabric. —*v.t.* **5.** bore with a drill. **6.** train or exercise with a drill.

drī'lў, *adv.* in a dry manner.

drĭnk, *n., v.,* **drank, drunk, drinking.** *n.*
1. liquid for swallowing. **2.** alcoholic
liquor. —*v.t.* **3.** swallow as a drink.
—*v.i.* **4.** swallow liquid. **5.** take alcoholic liquor. —**drĭnk'er,** *n.*

drĭp, *v.,* **dripped, dripping,** *n. v.i.* **1.** fall
in drops. —*v.t.* **2.** let liquid fall in drops.
3. let fall in drops. —*n.* **4.** act, instance,
or sound of dripping.

drĭve, *v.,* **drove, driven, driving,** *n. v.t.* **1.**
force along. **2.** compel. **3.** control, as a
vehicle. **4.** transport in a road vehicle.
—*v.i.* **5.** operate a road vehicle. **6.** advance forcefully. —*n.* **7.** forceful campaign. **8.** energy. **9.** motivation. **10.**
pleasure trip in an automobile. **11.** road
for pleasure driving. —**drĭv'er,** *n.*
—**drive'way,** *n.* —**drive'-in'',** *adj., n.*

drĭv'ĕl, *n., v.i.,* **-eled, -eling.** *n.* **1.** stupid,
nonsensical utterance. —*v.i.* **2.** write or
talk drivel.

drĭz'zle, *n., v.,* **-zled, -zling.** *n.* **1.** fine
rain. —*v.i., v.t.* **2.** rain in fine drops.

drŏll, *adj.* **1.** oddly amusing. —*n.* **2.** oddly
amusing person. —**drŏl'lў,** *adv.*
—**drŏll'ness, drol'ler·y,** *n.*

drŏm'ė·dār''ў, *n., pl.* **-ies.** single-
humped camel.

drōne, *n., v.i.,* **droned, droning.** *n.* **1.**
low hum. **2.** nonworking male bee. **3.**
idler. —*v.i.* **4.** emit a drone.

drōōl, *v.i.* **1.** drip saliva. —*n.* **2.** saliva that
drips.

drōōp, *v.i.* **1.** hang loosely. **2.** lose energy
or hope. —*n.* **3.** act or instance of drooping. —**droop'y,** *adj.*

drŏp, *v.t.,* **dropped, dropping,** *n. v.t.* **1.**
allow to fall. **2.** abandon. **3.** put down.
—*v.i.* **4.** fall. —*n.* **5.** globule of liquid
that falls or is about to fall. **6.** descent.
7. small drink. —**drop'per,** *n.*

drŏp'sў, *n.* edema.

drŏss, *n.* **1.** waste on top of molten metal.
2. waste matter.

drŏught, *n.* long dry spell. Also, **drouth.**

drōve, *n.* group of driven cattle. —**drov'
er,** *n.*

drŏwn, *v.t., v.i.* **1.** suffocate in water.
—*v.i.* **2.** flood.

drŏwse, *v.i.,* **drowsed, drowsing,** *n. v.i.*
1. be close to sleep. —*n.* **2.** sleepy state.
—**drows'y,** *adj.*

drŭb, *v.t.,* **drubbed, drubbing.** beat.
—**drub'bing,** *n.*

drŭdge, *v.i.,* **drudged, drudging,** *n. v.i.*
1. do dull, hard work. —*n.* **2.** a person
who drudges. —**drudg'er·y,** *n.*

drŭg, *n., v.t.,* **drugged, drugging.** *n.* **1.**
medicinal substance. **2.** narcotic, hallu-
cinogen, etc. —*v.t.* **3.** stupefy with a
drug. —**drug'gist,** *n.* —**drug'store'',**
n.

drŭm, *n., v.,* **drummed, drumming.** *n.*
1. percussion musical instrument. **2.**
eardrum. **3.** cylindrical object. —*v.i.* **4.**
beat rhythmically. —*v.t.* **5.** play on a
drum. —**drum'mer,** *n.* —**drum'
stick'',** *n.*

drŭnk, *adj.* **1.** overcome by alcohol. —*n.*
2. *Informal.* **a.** drunken person. **b.** alcoholic.

drŭnk'ärd, *n.* alcoholic.

drŭnk'ĕn, *adj.* drunk.

drў, *adj.,* **drier, driest,** *v.,* **dried, drying.**
adj. **1.** free of moisture. **2.** thirsty. **3.** not
sweet. **4.** not emotional or expressive.
—*v.t.* **5.** free of moisture. —*v.i.* **6.** become dry. —**dry'lў,** *adv.* —**dry'ness,** *n.*

drў'-clēan'', *v.t.* clean with chemicals
rather than water. —**dry cleaner,** *n.*

drў gōōds, cloth or things made of cloth.

dū'ăl, *adj.* **1.** pertaining to two. **2.** two-
fold. —**du·al'i·tў,** *n.*

dŭb, *v.t.,* **dubbed, dubbing.** **1.** make a
knight of. **2.** give a name to.

dū'bĭ·oŭs, *adj.* doubtful.

dū'căl, *adj.* pertaining to dukes.

dŭch'ĕss, *n.* woman equal in rank to a
duke.

dŭch'ў, *n., pl.* **-ies.** area ruled by a duke or
duchess.

dŭck, *n.* **1.** flat-billed waterfowl. **2.** can-
vaslike cloth. —*v.i.* **3.** stoop or crouch to
avoid a blow. —*v.t., v.i.* **4.** plunge into
water briefly. —**duck'ling,** *n.*

dŭct, *n.* passage for fluids. —**duct'less,**
adj.

dŭc'tĭle, *adj.* able to be stretched. —**duc·
til'i·tў,** *n.*

dūde, *n. Informal.* **1.** fancy dresser. **2.**
man from the city.

dūe, *adj.* **1.** owed. **2.** proper. **3.** adequate.
4. expected to arrive. —*adv.* **5.** directly.
—*n.* **6.** something due.

dū'ĕl, *n., v.,* **-eled, -eling.** *n.* **1** formal

mortal combat between two persons.
—*v.t.*, *v.i.* **2.** fight in a duel. —**du·el·ist**,
duel´er.

dū·ĕt´, *n.* **1.** musical composition for two.
2. pair of musicians.

dūke, *n.* nobleman next in rank to a prince.
—**duke´dom**, *n.*

dŭll, *adj.* **1.** not vivid. **2.** not interesting. **3.**
not intelligent. **4.** not sharp. —*v.t.*, *v.i.*
5. make or become dull. —**dul´ly**, *adv.*
—**dull´ness**, **dul´ness**, *n.*

dū´lỹ, *adv.* in a due manner.

dŭmb, *adj.* **1.** unable to speak or make
sound. **2.** silent. **3.** *Informal.* stupid.

dŭmb´bĕll´, *n.* weight for exercising the
arms.

dŭmb´fŏund´, *v.t.* render speechless with
astonishment. Also, **dum´found´**.

dŭmb´´wāit´ẽr, *n.* **1.** hoist for food. **2.**
small serving table.

dŭm´mỹ, *n.*, *pl.* **-ies**, *adj.* **1.** lifesized object in human form. **2.** imitation or
mockup. —*adj.* **3.** serving as an imitation.

dŭmp, *v.t.* **1.** throw down or away and
abandon. **2.** unload in a heap. —*n.* **3.**
place for refuse. **4.** military storage
place.

dŭmp´lĭng, *n.* rounded piece of baked
dough, sometimes with a fruit filling.

dŭmp´stẽr, *n.* a large, metal bin for holding garbage until pick-up.

dŭmp´ỹ, *adj.*, **-ier**, **-iest**. squat.

dŭn, *n.*, *v.t.*, **dunned**, **dunning**. *n.* **1.** dull
gray-brown. —*v.t.* **2.** attempt to recover
a debt from.

dŭnce, *n.* poor learner.

dūne, *n.* mound of wind-driven sand.

dŭng, *n.* manure. —**dung´heap´´**, **dung´
hill**, *n.*

dŭn´´gà·rēes´, *n.*, *pl.* blue cotton work
pants or overalls.

dŭn´geŏn, *n.* dark prison, as in a castle.

dŭnk, *v.t.* dip into a drink.

dū´ō, *n.*, *pl.* **-os**. duet.

dūpe, *v.t.*, **duped**, **duping**, *n.* *v.t.* **1.**
cheat. —*n.* **2.** person who is cheated.
—**dup´er**, *n.*

dū´plĕx, *adj.* **1.** double. —*n.* **2.** two-
floored apartment. **3.** two-family
house.

dū·plĭ·cāte´´, *v.t.*, **-cated**, **-cating**, *adj.*,
n. *v.t.* **1.** imitate exactly. —*n.* (dū´plĭ-

cate) **2.** exact imitation. —*adj.* **3.** serving as a duplicate. —**du´´pli·ca´tion**, *n.*
—**du´´pli·ca´´tor**, *n.*

dū·plĭc´ĭ·tỹ, *n.*, *pl.* **-ties**. deceit.

dū´rà·ble, *adj.* long-lasting; sturdy. —**du´
ra·bly**, *adv.* —**dura·bil´i·ty**, *n.*

dū·rā´tion, *n.* period of existence.

dū·rĕss´, *n.* coercion.

dūr´ĭng, *prep.* in or throughout the period
of.

dŭsk, *n.* **1.** darker part of twilight. **2.**
gloom. —**dusk´y**, *adj.*

dŭst, *n.* **1.** powder, esp. of earth. **2.** disin-
tegrated human remains. —*v.t.* **3.** re-
move dust from. **4.** put powder on. —*v.i.*
5. remove dust from furniture, etc.
—**dust´y**, *adj.*

dū´tē·oŭs, *adj.* dutiful.

dū´tĭ·à·ble, *adj.* subject to customs duty.

dū´tĭ·fŭl, *adj.* faithful to duty. —**du´ti-
ful·ly**, *adv.*

dū´tỹ, *n.*, *pl.* **-ties**. **1.** moral requirement.
2. requirement by authority. **3.** action,
conduct, etc. required by morality or
authority. **4.** tax on an import.

dwärf, *n.*, *pl.* **dwarfs**, **dwarves**. *v.t.* **1.** abnormally small living thing. —*v.t.* **2.**
make abnormally small. **3.** make seem
small.

dwĕll, *v.i.*, **dwelled** or **dwelt**, **dwelling**. **1.**
have one's habitation. **2.** linger, as in
speech or thought. —**dwel´ler**, *n.*
—**dwel´ling**, *n.*

dwĭn´dle, *v.i.*, **-dled**, **-dling**. diminish.

dỹe, *n.*, *v.t.*, **dyed**, **dying**. *n.* **1.** stain for
cloth, etc. —*v.t.* **2.** stain with dye. —**dy´
er**, *n.* —**dye´stuff**, *n.*

dỹ·năm´ĭc, *adj.* **1.** pertaining to motion.
2. vigorous, as a person. —**dy·nam´i·
cal·ly**, *adv.* —**dy´na·mism**, *n.*

dỹ´nà·mō´´, *n.*, *pl.* **-mos**. electrical generator.

dỹ´nàs·tỹ, *n.*, *pl.* **-ties**. succession of rulers in one family. —**dy·nas´tic**, *adj.*

dỹs´´en·tĕr´´ỹ, *n.* intestinal inflammation.

dỹs·pĕp´sĭ·à, *n.* indigestion. —**dys·pep´
tic**, *adj.*, *n.*

E

E, e, *n.* **1.** fifth letter of the English alphabet. **2.** fifth-best grade.

each, *adj.* **1.** every one individually. —*adv.* **2.** apiece.

ea′gĕr, *adj.* full of desire. —**ea′ger·ly,** *adv.* —**ea′ger·ness,** *n.*

ea′gle, *n.* large bird of prey.

ĕar, *n.* **1.** part of the body for hearing. **2.** grain-bearing part of a plant. —**ear′drum″,** *n.* —**ear′muffs″,** *n., pl.*

ĕarl, *n.* British nobleman equal to a count. —**earl′dom,** *n.*

ĕar′lў, *adj., adv.,* **-lier, -liest. 1.** before the expected time. **2.** in good time. **3.** toward the beginning.

ĕar′mârk″, *v.t.* note for the future.

ĕarn, *v.t.* work or deserve to acquire. —**earn′ings,** *n., pl.*

ĕar′nest, *adj.* **1.** sincere; serious. —*n.* **2.** pledge. —**ear′nest·ly,** *adv.*

ĕar′ring″, *n.* ornament hung from an ear lobe.

ĕar′shŏt″, *n.* hearing distance.

ĕarth, *n.* **1.** this planet. **2.** ground level. **3.** regions below ground level. **4.** soil. —**earth′en,** *adj.* —**earth′en·ware″,** *n.* —**earth′ly,** *adj.* —**earth′quake″,** *n.*

ĕarth′lў, *adj.* pertaining to this world.

ĕarth′wŏrm″, *n.* worm living in soil.

ĕarth′ў, *adj.,* **-ier, -iest.** matter-of-fact.

ĕase, *n., v.t.,* **eased, easing. 1.** freedom from toil, pain, etc. —*v.t.* **2.** make easy.

ĕa′sĕl, *n.* stand for a painting, etc.

ĕast, *n.* **1.** direction to the right of north. **2.** eastern area. —*adj., adv.* **3.** toward, in, or from the east. —**east′er·ly,** *adj.* —**east′ern,** *adj.* —**east′ern·er,** *n.* —**east′ward,** *adv., adj.* —**east′wards,** *adv.*

Ĕast′êr, *n.* celebration of the resurrection of Christ.

ĕas′ў, *adj.,* **-ier, -iest. 1.** not difficult. **2.** free of pain, etc. —**eas′i·ly,** *adv.* —**eas′i·ness,** *n.*

ĕat, *v.t.,* **ate, eaten, eating. 1.** consume as food. **2.** dissolve, erode, etc.

ĕaves, *n., pl.* projecting edge of a roof.

ĕaves′drŏp″, *v.i.,* **-dropped, -dropping.** overhear conversation, esp. intentionally.

ĕbb, *n.* **1.** going out of a tide. **2.** decline or lessening. —*v.i.* **3.** go out, as the tide. **4.** decline or lessen.

eb′o·nў, *n.* **1.** hard, dark wood. **2.** very deep brown or black.

e·bŭl′liĕnt, *adj.* **1.** exuberant. **2.** bubbling. —**e·bul′lience,** *n.*

ec·cĕn′tric, *adj.* **1.** peculiar in manner. **2.** off center. —*n.* **3.** eccentric person. **4.** eccentric machine part. —**ec″cen′tric′i·ty,** *n.*

ec·cle″si·ăs′tĭc, *adj.* **1.** Also, **ec·cle″si·as′ti·cal.** pertaining to churches. —*n.* **2.** clergyman.

ech·e·lon (ĕsh′è lŏn″), *n.* **1.** formation of troops, etc., each line being to the right or left of that preceding it. **2.** level of responsibility.

ĕch′ō, *n., pl.* **-oes,** *v.t.,* **-oed, -oing.** *n.* **1.** reflected sound. —*v.t.* **2.** reflect as an echo.

e·clàir′, *n.* custard-filled pastry.

e·clĕc′tic, *adj.* using those thought best, regardless of source.

e·clipse′, *n., v.t.,* **-clipsed, -clipsing.** *n.* **1.** obscuring of the sun or moon. —*v.t.* **2.** obscure.

e·clĭp′tĭc, *n.* apparent annual path of the sun.

ē·cŏl′o·gў, *n., pl.* **-gies. 1.** study of the relation of living things to their environment. **2.** system permitting living things to exist. —**e′co·log′i·cal,** *adj.* —**e·col′o·gist,** *n.*

ē″cò·nŏm′i·căl, *adj.* thrifty.

ē″cò·nŏm′ics, *n.* **1.** *sing.* study of wealth. **2.** *pl.* resources and demands on wealth. —**e″co·nom′ic,** *adj.* —**e·con′o·mist,** *n.*

e·cŏn′o·mў, *n., pl.* **-mies. 1.** thrift. **2.** system of producing and dividing wealth. —**e·con′o·mize″,** *v.i.*

ĕc′stá·sў, *n., pl.* **-sies.** state of overwhelming emotion. —**ec·stat′ic,** *adj., n.*

ĕc″ū·mĕn′i·căl, *adj.* **1.** universal. **2.** promoting universal accord, esp. in religion.

ĕc′zĕ·má, *n.* scaly skin disease.

ĕd′dў, *n., pl.* **-dies, -died, -dying.** *n.* **1.** turbulence of water or wind. —*v.i.* **2.** move in a circular current.

ĕdge, *n., v.,* **edged, edging.** *n.* **1.** outer

limit. **2.** sharp intersection. —*v.t.* **3.** border. —*v.i.* **4.** side. —**edge′wise″, edge′ways″,** *adv.* —**edg′ing,** *n.*

ĕd′ĭ·ble, *adj.* suitable for eating. —**ed′′i·bil′i·ty,** *n.*

ē′dĭct, *n.* decree.

ĕd′ĭ·fĭce, *n.* building.

ĕd′ĭ·fȳ″, *v.t.,* **-fied, -fying.** educate or improve the mind of. —**ed′′i·fi′ca′tion,** *n.*

ĕd′′ĭt, *v.t.* prepare for publication or presentation. —**ed′′i·tor,** *n.* —**ed′′i·tor′ial,** *n., adj.*

é·dī′tion, *n.* printing of a book.

ĕd′′ĭ·tôr′ĭ·al, *n.* **1.** periodical′s commentary on public issues. —*adj.* **2.** pertaining to editing.

ĕd′ŭ·cāte, *v.t.,* **-cated, -cating.** develop the mind, knowledge or skill of. —**ed′′u·ca′tion,** *n.* —**ed′′u·ca′tion·al,** *adj.* —**ed′u·ca′′tor,** *n.*

ēel, *n.* long, snakelike fish.

ēe′rĭĕ, *adj.,* **-rier, -riest.** weird; uncanny.

éf·fāce′, *v.t.,* **-faced, -facing.** eliminate all trace of. —**ef·face′ment,** *n.*

éf·fĕct′, *n.* **1.** result. **2.** influence. **3.** effects, personal property. —*v.t.* **4.** cause. —**ef·fec′tive,** *adj.* —**ef·fec′tu·al,** *adj.*

éf·fĕm′ĭ·nāte, *adj.* having feminine qualities. —**ef·fem′i·na·cy,** *n.*

ĕf′′fĕr·vĕsce′, *v.i.,* **-vesced, -vescing.** bubble. —**ef′′fer·ves′cent,** *adj.* —**ef′′fer·ves′cence,** *n.*

éf·fēte′, *adj.* decadent.

ĕf′′fĭ·cā′cĭoŭs, *adj.* producing the desired result. —**ef·fi′ca·cy,** *n.*

éf·fĭ′cĭĕnt, *adj.* efficacious without waste. —**ef·fi′cient·ly,** *adv.* —**ef·fi′cien·cy,** *n.*

ĕf′′fĭ·gȳ, *n., pl.* **-gies.** copy or image, esp. in three dimensions.

ĕf′fôrt, *n.* **1.** expenditure of strength, thought, etc. **2.** attempt.

ĕf·frŏnt′ĕr·ȳ, *n., pl.* **-ies.** impudence.

ĕf·fū′sion, *n.* outpouring of enthusiasm. —**ef·fu′sive,** *adj.*

ē·gäl′ĭ·tār′′ĭ·ăn, *adj.* believing that all people should be equal.

ĕgg′hĕad′′, *n. Informal.* intellectual.

ĕgg′plänt′′, *n.* purple-skinned vegetable.

ē′gō, *n.* self. —**e′′go·cen′tric,** *adj., n.*

ē′gō·ĭsm, *n.* selfishness. —**e′go·ist,** *n.* —**e′′go·is′tic, e′′go·is′ti·cal,** *adj.*

ē′gō·tĭsm, *n.* self-conceit; vanity. —**e′go·tist′′,** *n.* —**e′′go·tis′tic, e′′go·tis′ti·cal,** *adj.*

é·grē′gĭoŭs, *adj.* conspicuous in a bad way.

eight (āt), *n.* seven plus one. —**eighth,** *adj.*

eight·ēen′, *n.* seventeen plus one.

eight′ȳ, *n.* eight times ten. —**eight′i·eth,** *adj.*

ei·ther (ēthèr, ī′thèr), *adj.* **1.** one or the other but not both. **2.** each. —*pron.* **3.** one or the other. *conj.* **4.** (used to emphasize choice). —*adj.* **5.** as well.

é·jĕct′, *v.t.* hurl or force out. —**e·jec′tion,** *n.*

ēke, *v.t.,* **eked, eking. eke out,** gain with difficulty.

ē·lăb′ō·rate, *adj., v.t.,* **-rated, -rating.** *adj.* **1.** having many parts or aspects. —*v.t.* (ē lab′ō rāte′) **2.** plan in detail. —**e·lab′′o·ra′tion,** *n.*

é·lăpse′, *v.i.,* **-lapsed, -lapsing.** pass, as time.

é·lăs′tĭc, *adj.* able to recover from stretching or bending. —*n.* elastic material or object. —**e·las′′tic′i·ty,** *n.*

é·lāte′, *v.t.,* **-lated, -lating.** raise in spirits. —**e·la′tion,** *n.*

ĕl′bōw, *n.* joint halfway up the arm. —*v.t., v.i.* push with the elbows.

ĕl′dẽr, *adj.* **1.** senior. —*n.* **2.** senior. **3.** shrub with red or purple berries. —**eld′est,** *adj.* —**eld′er·ly,** *adj.*

é·lĕct′, *v.t.* **1.** choose, esp. by a vote. —*adj.* **2.** chosen. **3.** elected to but not yet in public office. —**e·lec′tion,** *n.* —**e·lec′tor,** *n.* —**e·lec′tor·al,** *adj.* —**e·lec′tor·ate,** *n.* —**e·lec′tive,** *adj.*

é·lĕc′′trĭc′ĭ·tȳ, *n.* **1.** property of motion in certain particles composing matter. **2.** current created by such motion. —**e·lec′tric, e·lec′tri·cal,** *adj.* —**e·lec′tri·fy′′,** *v.t.*

é·lĕc′′trō·cūte′′, *v.t.,* **-cuted, -cuting.** injure or kill with electricity. —**e·lec′′tro·cu′tion,** *n.*

é·lĕc′trōde, *n.* object conducting electricity into or out of a battery, etc.

é·lĕc′trŏl′y·sĭs, *n.* decomposition of a material by the passage of electricity. —**e·lec′′tro·lyt′ic,** *adj.*

é·lĕc′′trō·măg′nĕt, *n.* magnet operating

through an electric current. —e·lec'' tro·mag·net'ic, *adj.*

é·lĕc'trŏn, *n.* negatively charged particle of an atom.

é·lĕc''trŏn'ĭcs, *n., sing.* study of the action of electrons and its application to technology. —e·lec''tron'ic, *adj.*

ĕl'é·gănt, *adj.* tasteful and dignified. —el'e·gance, *n.*

ĕl'é·gў, *n., pl.* -gies. poem of lament, esp. for the dead. —el''e·gi'ac, el''e·gi'a·cal, *adj.*

ĕl'é·mĕnt, *n.* 1. major or basic component. 2. natural environment. 3. elements, natural forces, esp. of weather. —el''e·men'tal, *adj.*

ĕl''é·mĕn'tá·rў, *n.* fundamental; rudimentary.

ĕl'é·phănt, *n.* large four-legged animal with a long prehensile nose.

ĕl·é·vāte', *v.t.,* -vated, -vating. 1. raise to a greater height. 2. raise in rank, spirits, etc.

ĕl''é·vā'tion, *n.* 1. height. 2. drawing of one side of a building, etc., in its true dimensions.

ĕl'é·vā''tŏr, *n.* 1. cabinet or platform for raising or lowering persons or goods. 2. storage place for grain.

é·lĕv'ĕn, *n.* ten plus one.

ĕlf, *n., pl.* elves. small fairy. —elf'in, elf'ish, *adj.*

é·lĭc'ĭt, *v.t.* draw forth, as a reaction or comment.

ĕl'ĭ·gĭ·ble, *adj.* suitable for choice. —el''i·gi·bil'i·ty, *n.*

é·lĭm'ĭ·nāte', *v.t.,* -nated, -nating. get rid of. —e·lim''i·na'tion, *n.*

é·līte, *n.* choice element. —e·lit'ism, *n.*

é·lĭx'îr, *n.* medicine in a solution of alcohol.

ĕlk, *n., pl.* elks, elk. large mooselike deer.

ĕl·lĭpse', *n.* oval symmetrical about two axes. —el·lip'ti·cal, *adj.*

ĕlm, *n.* tall deciduous tree.

ĕl''ŏ·cū'tion, *n.* public speaking.

é·lŏn'gāte'', *v.t., v.i.,* -gated, -gating. lengthen. —e''lon·ga'tion, *n.*

é·lōpe', *v.i.,* -loped, -loping. flee, esp. in order to marry. —e·lope'ment, *n.*

ĕ'lŏ·quĕnt, *adj.* convincing in speech. —e'lo·quence, *n.*

ĕlse, *adj.* 1. other. 2. more. —*adv.* 3. otherwise.

ĕlse'whêre'', *adv.* somewhere else.

é·lū'cĭ·dāte'', *v.t.,* -dated, -dating. clarify; explain. —e·lu''ci·da'tion, *n.*

é·lūde', *v.t.,* -luded, -luding. escape or evade. —e·lu'sive, *adv.*

é·mā'cĭ·āte'', *v.t.,* -ated, -ating. make abnormally thin. —e·ma''ci·a'tion, *n.*

ĕm'á·nāte'', *v.i.,* -nated, -nating. come forth; issue. —em''a·na'tion, *n.*

é·măn'cĭ·pāte'', *v.t.,* -pated, -pating. free, as from bondage. —e·man''ci·pa'tion, *n.* —e·man'ci·pa''tor, *n.*

é·măs'cū·lāte'', *v.t.,* -lated, -lating. castrate.

ĕm·bălm', *v.t.* preserve against decay after death.

ĕm·bănk', *v.t.* support, strengthen, etc., with piled earth, etc. —em·bank'ment, *n.*

ĕm·bâr'gō, *n., pl.* -goes, *n.* ban on shipping or commerce.

ĕm·bârk', *v.i.* 1. set forth, esp. on a ship. —*v.t., v.i.* 2. board, esp. a ship. —em''bar·ka'tion, *n.*

ĕm·băr'răss, *v.t.* 1. make ashamed or self-conscious. 2. put at a loss for money. —em·bar'rass·ment, *n.*

ĕm'băs·sў, *n., pl.* -sies. permanent mission to a foreign government.

ĕm·bĕd', *v.t.,* -bedded, -bedding. sink and fix firmly.

ĕm·bĕl'lĭsh, *v.t.* decorate. —em·bel'lish·ment, *n.*

ĕm'bêr, *n.* red-hot piece of fuel.

ĕm·bĕz'zle, *v.t.,* -zled, -zling. steal from an employer, client, etc. —em·bez'zler, *n.* —em·bez'zle·ment, *n.*

ĕm·bĭt'têr, *v.t.* make bitter.

ĕm'blĕm, *n.* symbolic design. —em''blem·at'ic, *adj.*

ĕm·bŏd'ў, *v.t.,* -died, -dying. 1. realize in bodily form. 2. incorporate. —em·bod'i·ment, *n.*

ĕm·bŏss', *v.t.* mark with raised designs or lettering.

ĕm'brāce', *v.,* -braced, -bracing. *n. v.t.* 1. put the arms around. 2. accept readily. —*v.i.* 3. embrace each other. —*n.* 4. act or instance of embracing.

ĕm·brōī'dêr, *v.t.* decorate with applied colored yarns. —em·broi'der·y, *n.*

ĕm'brÿ·ō'', *n., pl.* -oes. animal or plant in the first stage of development. —em'' bry·on'ic, *adj.*

e·mĕnd', *v.t.* correct; edit. —e''men·da' tion, *n.*

ĕm'ẽr·ald, *n.* vivid green gem.

e·mẽrge', *v.i.,* -merged, -merging. appear into notice. —e·mer'gence, *n.*

e·mẽr'gĕn·cÿ, *n., pl.* -cies. mishap demanding prompt action.

e·mĕt'ĭc, *adj.* 1. causing vomiting. —n. 2. emetic substance.

ĕm'ĭ·grāte'', *v.i.,* -grated, -grating. leave one's country to settle elsewhere. —em''i·gra'tion, *n.* —em''i·grant, *n., adj.*

ĕm'ĭ·nĕnt, *adj.* high in standing or rank. —em'i·nence, *n.* —em'i·nent·ly, *adv.*

ĕm'ĭs·sãr''ÿ, *n., pl.* -ies. person sent on a mission.

e·mĭt', *v.t.,* -mitted, -mitting. send out or forth; discharge. —e·mis'sion, *n.*

e·mō'tion, *n.* 1. natural feelings and reactions. 2. specific feeling or reaction. —e·mo'tion·al, *adj.*

ĕm'pẽr·ör, *n.* ruler of an empire.

ĕm'pha·sĭs, *n., pl.* -ses. force or stress. —em·phat'ic, *adj.* —em'pha·size'', *v.t.*

ĕm'pīre, *n.* number of countries or regions under one monarch.

ĕm·pĭr'ĭ·cál, *adj.* derived from experience.

ĕm·plŏy', *v.t.* 1. hire or use. —n. 2. hire. —em·ploy'er, *n.* —em·ploy'ee, *n.* —em·ploy'ment, *n.*

ĕm·pô'rĭ·ŭm, *n., pl.* -ums, -a. store with varied merchandise.

ĕm·pŏw'ẽr, *v.t.* give official power to.

em'press, *n.* woman married to or with the rank of an emperor.

ĕmp'tÿ, *adj.,* -tier, -tiest, *v.,* -tied, -tying. *adj.* 1. lacking contents. —v.t. 2. make empty. —v.i. 3. become empty. —emp'ti·ness, *n.*

ĕm'ū·lāte'', *v.t.,* -lated, -lating. imitate, esp. in excellence. —em''u·la'tion, *n.* —em'u·lous, *adj.*

e·mŭl'sion, *n.* mixture of two liquids made possible by addition of a third. —e·mul'si·fy'', *v.t., v.i.*

ĕn·ā'ble, *v.t.,* -bled, -bling. make able.

en·ăct', *v.t.* 1. make into law. 2. represent in a play. —en·act'ment, *n.*

en·ăm'el, *n., v.t.,* -eled or -elled, -eling or -elling. *n.* 1. glassy, fused coating. 2. hard, glossy paint. 3. exterior material of teeth. —v.t. 4. cover with enamel.

en·ăm'öred, *adj.* full of love.

en·cămp', *v.i., v.t.* camp. —en·camp' ment, *n.*

en·câse', *v.t.,* -cased, -casing. enclose.

en·chănt', *v.t.* 1. charm. 2. put a magic spell on. —en·chant'ment, *n.*

en·cĭr'cle, *v.t.,* -cled, -cling. surround.

en·clôse', *v.t.,* -closed, -closing. 1. surround. 2. put into a container, envelope, etc. —en·clo'sure, *n.*

en·cŏm'păss, *v.t.* 1. surround. 2. include.

en·core (ahn'kör), *interj.* 1. again: request to a musician. —n. 2. repetition of a musical performance.

en·coŭn'tẽr, *v.t.* 1. happen to meet. 2. meet in combat. —n. 3. act or instance of encountering.

en·coŭr'âge, *v.t.,* -aged, -aging. give courage or resolution to. —en·cour' age·ment, *n.*

en·crōach', *v.i.* trespass. —en·croach' ment, *n.*

en·cŭm'bẽr, *v.t.* burden or hinder. —en· cum'brance, *n.*

en·cÿ''clō·pē'dĭ·à, *n.* reference work dealing at length with all areas of knowledge. Also, en·cy''clo·pae'di·a. —en· cy''clo·pe'dic, *adj.*

ĕnd, *n.* 1. far or final part. 2. result. 3. purpose. —v.t. 4. put an end to. —v.i. 5. come to an end. —end'less, *adj.*

en·dăn'gẽr, *v.t.* put in danger.

en·dēar', *v.t.* make dear. —en·dear'ing, *adj.* —en·dear'ment, *n.*

en·dĕav'ör, *v.t., n.* attempt.

ĕnd'ĭng, *n.* conclusion.

ĕnd'mōst'', *adj.* farthest.

en·dôrse', *v.t.,* -dorsed, -dorsing. 1. write on the back of, esp. a signature. 2. approve. —en·dors'er, *n.* —en·dorse' ment, *n.*

en·dŏw', *v.t.* 1. provide with personal resources or qualities. 2. give money for. —en·dow'ment, *n.*

en·dūre', *v.,* -dured, -during. *v.t.* 1. tolerate. 2. suffer. —v.i. 3. survive. —en· dur'able, *adj.* —en·dur'ance, *n.*

ĕn′e·mў, *n., pl.* **-mies. 1.** person who wishes one harm. **2.** hostile nation or military force.

ĕn′ẽr·gў, *n., pl.* **-gies. 1.** force able to produce motion, heat, light, etc. **2.** vigor. —**en′′er·get′ic,** *adj.*

ĕn′ẽr·vāte′′, *v.t.,* **-vated, -vating.** deprive of vitality. —**en′′er·va′tion,** *n.*

ĕn·fēe′ble, *v.t.,* **-bled, -bling.** make feeble.

ĕn·fōld′, *v.t.* wrap.

ĕn·fôrce′, *v.t.,* **-forced, -forcing.** administer forcefully, as a law. —**en·force′ment,** *n.*

ĕn·gāge′, *v.t.,* **-gaged, -gaging. 1.** commit. **2.** commit to marriage. **3.** hire. **4.** hold or connect with. **5.** meet and fight. —**en·gage′ment,** *n.*

ĕn·gāg′ing, *adj.* charming. —**en·gag′ing·ly,** *adv.*

ĕn·gĕn′dẽr, *v.t.* bring into being.

ĕn′gĭne, *n.* **1.** machine producing mechanical force, esp. by means of heat energy. **2.** locomotive.

ĕn′′gĭ·nēer′, *n.* **1.** person who designs systems or structures applying static or dynamic forces or various sources of energy. **2.** skilled operator of machines, etc. —**en′′gi·neer′ing,** *n.*

ĕn·grāve′, *v.t.,* **-graved, -graving.** form designs or letters with shallow cuts on wood, steel, etc. —**en·grav′er,** *n.* —**en·grav′ing,** *n.*

ĕn·grŏss′, *v.t.* capture the attention of.

ĕn·gŭlf′, *v.t.* swallow up; submerge.

ĕn·hănce′, *v.t.,* **-hanced, -hancing.** increase or improve.

e′·nĭg′mà, *n., pl.* **-mas.** puzzle. —**e′′nig·mat′ic,** *adj.*

ĕn·jŏin′, *v.t.* forbid.

ĕn·jŏy′, *v.t.* **1.** get pleasure from. **2.** have the benefit of. —**en·joy′a·ble,** *adj.* —**en·joy′ment,** *n.*

ĕn·lārge′, *v.,* **-larged, -larging.** *v.t.* **1.** make larger. —*v.i.* **2.** become larger. —**en·large′ment,** *n.*

ĕn·līght′ĕn, *v.t.* free of ignorance or wrong attitudes. —**en·light′en·ment,** *n.*

ĕn·lĭst′, *v.t., v.i.* enroll. —**en·list′ment,** *n.*

ĕn·lĭv′ĕn, *v.t.* make lively.

ĕn′mĭ·tў, *n., pl.* **-ties.** hostility.

ĕn·nui′ (ahn wē′), *n.* boredom.

e·nôr′mĭ·tў, *n., pl.* **-ties. 1.** wickedness. **2.** outrage.

e·nôr′mŏŭs, *adj.* beyond normal size or extent. —**e·nor′mous·ly,** *adv.*

e·noŭgh′, *n., adj., adv. n.* **1.** as much as is wanted; sufficiency. —*adj.* **2.** adequate; sufficient. —*adv.* **3.** sufficiently.

ĕn·quīre′, *v.t., v.i.,* **-quired, -quiring.** inquire. —**en·quir′y,** *n.*

ĕn·rāge′, *v.t.,* **-raged, -raging.** put in a rage.

ĕn·rĭch′, *v.t.* make rich or richer. —**en·rich′ment,** *n.*

ĕn·rōll′, *v.t.* name on a list or record. —**en·roll′ment,** *n.*

ĕn roŭte, on the way.

ĕn·scŏnce′, *v.t.* put in a snug or secure place.

ĕn·sĕm′ble (ŏn sŏm′bŭl), *n.* related group.

ĕn·shrīne′, *v.t.,* **-shrined, -shrining.** put in or as if in a shrine.

ĕn′sĭgn, *n.* **1.** flag, as on a ship. **2.** lowest commissioned naval officer.

ĕn·slāve′, *v.t.,* **-slaved, -slaving.** make a slave of. —**en·slave′ment,** *n.*

ĕn·sūe′, *v.i.,* **-sued, -suing.** follow, esp. as a consequence.

ĕn·sūre′, *v.t.,* **-sured, -suring.** make sure.

ĕn·tāil′, *v.t.* necessitate.

ĕn·tăn′gle, *v.t.,* **-gled, -gling.** trap or impede. —**en·tan′gle·ment,** *n.*

ĕn′tẽr, *v.t.* **1.** go into. **2.** have enrolled in or admitted to something. **3.** list or record.

ĕn′tẽr·prīse′′, *n.* **1.** project with some risk. **2.** willingness to undertake such projects. —**en′ter·pris′′ing,** *adj.*

ĕn′′tẽr·tāin′, *v.t.* **1.** have as a guest. **2.** amuse. **3.** consider. —**en′′ter·tain′er,** *n.* —**en′′ter·tain′ment,** *n.*

ĕn·thū′sĭ·ăsm, *n.* intense approval, or favor. —**en·thu′si·ast,** *n.* —**en·thu′′si·as′tic,** *adj.*

ĕn·tīce′, *v.t.,* **-ticed, -ticing.** tempt, esp. deceitfully. —**en·tice′ment,** *n.*

ĕn·tīre′, *adj.* complete. —**en·tire′ly,** *adv.* —**en·tire′ty,** *n.*

ĕn·tī′tle, *v.t.,* **-tled, -tling.** give a right or claim.

ĕn′tĭ·tў, *n., pl.* **-ties.** one that exists.

ĕn''tŏ·mŏl'ŏ·gў, *n.* study of insects. —en''to·mol'o·gist, *n.*

en·tou·rage (ahn''tŏŏ rahzh'), *n.* followers of an important person.

ĕn'trāils, *n. pl.* internal organs, esp. viscera.

ĕn'trănce, *n., v.t.,* -tranced, -trancing. *n.* 1. way of entering. 2. right to enter. 3. act of entering. —*v.t.* (en trans'). 4. fill with wonder.

ĕn·trăp', *v.t.* catch, as if in a trap. —en·trap'ment, *n.*

ĕn·trēat', *v.t., v.i.* ask earnestly. en·treat'y, *n.*

en·tree (ahn trā'), *n.* main dinner course.

ĕn·trĕnch', *v.t.* secure the position of.

en''trĕ·pre·neûr', *n.* undertaker of business ventures.

ĕn·trŭst', *v.t.* 1. give to someone in trust. 2. trust with something.

ĕn'trў, *n., pl.* -tries. 1. entrance. 2. something noted. 3. competitor.

e·nū'mêr·āte'', *v.t.,* -ated, -ating. 1. cite one by one. 2. count. —e·nu''mer·a'tion, *n.*

é·nŭn'cĭ·āte'', *v.,* -ated, -ating. *v.t., v.i.* speak distinctly. —e·nun''ci·a'tion, *n.*

ĕn·vĕl'ŏp, *v.i.* wrap up.

ĕn'vĕ·lōpe'', *n.* 1. paper cover for letters, papers, etc. 2. outer covering.

ĕn·vĭ'rŏn·mĕnt, *n.* 1. surroundings. 2. conditions. —en·vi''ron''men'tal, *adj.*

ĕn·vĭ'rŏns, *n., pl.* surrounding area.

ĕn·vĭs'ăge, *v.t.,* -aged, -aging. visualize; contemplate

ĕn·vĭ'sĭŏn, *v.t.* contemplate as likely.

en·vŏў, *n.* diplomatic representative.

ĕn'vў, *n., v.t.,* -vied, -vying. *n.* 1. resentment over another's good luck. —*v.t.* 2. feel envy toward. —en'vi·a·ble, *adj.* —en'vi·ous, *adj.*

ē'ŏn, *n.* very long period.

é·phĕm'êr·ăl, *n.* short-lived.

ĕp·ĭc, *adj.* 1. heroic. —*n.* 2. long poem about heroism.

ĕp'ĭ·cūre'', *n.* person with refined tastes, esp. for food and drink. —ep''i·cu·re'an, *adj., n.*

ĕp''ĭ·dĕm'ĭc, *adj.* 1. spreading through a community. —*n.* 2. epidemic disease.

ĕp''ĭ·dêr'mĭs, *n.* outer layer of skin. —ep''i·der'mal, ep''i·der'mic, *adj.*

ĕp'ĭ·grăm'', *n.* short witty observation. —ep''i·gram·mat'ic, *adj.*

ĕp'ĭ·lĕp''sў, *n.* nervous disease with convulsions and unconsciousness. —ep''i·lep'tic, *adj., n.*

ĕp'ĭ·lŏgue'', *n.* final statement of a play, etc.

É·pĭph'á·nў, *n.* revelation of Jesus as the Christ, celebrated January 6.

é·pĭs'cŏ·pál, *adj.* pertaining to or governed by a bishop.

ĕp'ĭ·sōde'', *n.* occurrence. —ep''i·sod'ic, *adj.*

é·pĭs'tle, *n.* letter; written message.

ĕp'ĭ·tăph'', *n.* inscription on a tomb.

ĕp'ĭ·thĕt'', *n.* characterizing name.

é·pĭt'ŏ·mē'', *n., pl.* -mes. 1. summary. 2. ideal example. —e·pit'o·mize'', *v.t.*

ĕp'ŏch, *n.* distinct historical or geological period. —ep'och·al, *adj.*

ēq'uá·ble, *adj.* emotionally steady.

ē'quál, *adj., n., v.t.,* -qualed, -qualing. *adj.* 1. of the same amount, rank, etc. 2. competent; adequate. —*n.* 3. equal person or thing. —*v.t.* 4. be equal to. —e'qual'i·ty, *n.* —e'qual·ize'', *v.t.*

ĕ''quá·nĭm'ĭ·tў, *n.* calm.

ē·quāte', *v.t.,* -quated, -quating. regard as equal. —e·qua'tion, *n.*

é·quá'tŏr, *n.* imaginary line bisecting the earth. —e''qua·to'ri·al, *adj.*

ē''quĭ·dĭs'tánt, *adj.* equally far.

ē''quĭ·lăt'êr·ál, *adj.* with equal sides.

ē''quĭ·lĭb'rĭ·ŭm, *n.* balance.

ē'quĭ·nŏx'', *n.* time of equal day and night periods, marking the beginning of spring or autumn. —e''qui·noc'ti·al, *adj.*

é·quĭp', *v.t.,* -quipped, -quipping. furnish with what is necessary. —e·quip'ment, *n.*

ĕ''quĭ·tá·ble, *adj.* just; fair. —e'qui·ta·bly, *adv.*

ĕ'quĭ·tў, *n.* 1. fairness. 2. value of something in excess of money owed for it.

é·quĭv'á·lĕnt, *adj., n.* equal. —e·quiv'a·lence, *n.*

é·quĭv'ŏ·cál, *adj.* of doubtful meaning or nature.

é·quĭv'ŏ·cāte, *v.i.,* -cated, -cating. speak equivocally. —e·quiv''o·ca'tion, *n.*

ĕr'á, *n.* distinctive historical period.

e·răd′i·cāte″, *v.t.*, -cated, -cating. eliminate by destroying. —e·rad″i·ca′tion, *n.*

e·rāse′, *v.t.*, -rased, -rasing. obliterate. —e·ras′er, *n.* —e·ra′sure, *n.*

e·rĕct′, *adj.* **1.** upright. —*v.t.* **2.** build. —e·rec′tion, *n.*

er′mīne, *n.* weasel with white winter fur.

e·rōde′, *v.*, -roded, -roding. *v.t., v.i.* wash away or out. —e·ro′sion, *n.*

e·rŏt′ic, *adj.* pertaining to or arousing sexual desire. —e·rot″i·cism, *n.*

êrr, *v.i.* be in error.

er′rănd, *n.* journey for some purpose.

êr′rănt, *adj.* wandering.

êr·răt′ic, *adj.* unreliable.

êr·răt′ŭm, *n., pl.* -a. printing or writing error.

er·rō′ne·oŭs, *adj.* in error.

êr′rŏr, *n.* mistaken belief or action.

êrst′whīle″, *adj.* former.

êr′ū·dīte″, *adj.* informed; scholarly. —er″u·di′tion, *n.*

e·rŭpt′, *v.i.* break forth. —e·rup′tion, *n.*

ĕs′ca·lāte″, *v.i.*, -lated, -lating. **1.** rise on an escalator. **2.** increase rapidly, as in intensity.

ĕs′ca·lā″tor, *n.* endless moving stair.

ĕs′ca·pāde″, *n.* reckless adventure.

es·cāpe′, *v.*, -caped, -caping. *v.i.* **1.** flee. —*v.t.* **2.** evade the notice of. —*n.* **3.** act or instance of escaping.

es·cāp′ism, *n.* tendency to attempt to escape reality. —es·cap′ist, *n., adj.*

ĕs·chĕw′, *v.t.* shun; do without.

es·côrt′, *v.t.* **1.** take charge of and accompany. —*n.* **2.** person or thing that escorts.

ĕs′crōw, *n. Law.* state of property that is temporarily held in trust for another.

ĕs·cŭtch′eŏn, *n.* symbolic shield holding a coat of arms.

ĕs″ō·tĕr′ic, *adj.* reserved for an understanding few.

ĕs·pē′ciàl, *adj.* special. —es·pe′cial·ly, *adv.*

ĕs′pī·o·nāge″, *n.* practice of spying.

es·pōuse′, *v.t.*, -poused, -pousing. **1.** marry. **2.** devote oneself to. —es·pous′al, *n.*

es·prit de corps (es prē′de kor′), morale of an organization.

es·pȳ, *v.t.*, -pied, -pying. discern.

ĕs′sāy, *n.* **1.** writing on some theme. —*v.t.* (es sāy′) **2.** attempt. —es′say·ist, *n.*

ĕs′sĕnce, *n.* **1.** basic nature. **2.** concentrated substance.

ĕs·sĕn′tial, *adj.* **1.** indispensable. —*n.* **2.** something indispensable. —es·sen′tial·ly, *adv.*

ĕs·tăb′lĭsh, *v.t.* **1.** bring into being. **2.** prove. —es·tab′lish·ment, *n.*

és·tāte′, *n.* **1.** personal property. **2.** grounds belonging to a house.

ĕs·tēem′, *n.* **1.** evaluation. —*v.t.* **2.** deem. —es′tim·a·ble, *adj.*

ĕs′thēte″, *n.* aesthete.

ĕs·thĕt′ics, *n.* aesthetics.

ĕs′ti·māte, *n., v.t.*, -mated, -mating. *n.* **1.** rough calculation or appraisal. —*v.t.* (es′ti māte″) **2.** make an estimate of. —esti·ma′tion, *n.*

és·trānge′, *v.t.*, -tranged, -tranging. lose the affection of.

ĕs′tū·ārў, *n., pl.* -ies. tidal river mouth.

ĕt cētêrä, and other persons or things. Abbreviated etc.

ĕtch, *v.t.* make or mark by the corrosion of acid. —etch′ing, *n.*

e·têr′nàl, *adj.* lasting or valid forever. —e·ter′nal·ly, *adv.* —e·ter′ni·ty, *n.*

ē′thêr, *n.* **1.** upper part of the atmosphere. **2.** volatile, flammable anesthetic or solvent.

e·thē′rē·àl, *adj.* **1.** delicate. **2.** unearthly.

ĕth′ics, *n.* **1.** study of right and wrong in actions. **2.** *pl.* **a.** Also, eth′ic, personal standards of right and wrong action. **b.** standards of conduct adopted by professionals. —eth′i·cal, *adj.*

ĕth′nic, *adj.* **1.** pertaining to distinct nations or tribes. —*n.* **2.** member of a minority national group. —eth·nic′i·ty, *n.*

ĕt′i·quĕtte, *n.* code of acceptable conduct.

ē″tў·mŏl′o·gў, *n.* study of word origins.

Eū′cha·rĭst, *n.* **1.** Holy Communion. **2.** bread and wine used at Holy Communion. —Eu·cha·ris′tic, *adj.*

Eū·clĭd′ē·àn, *adj.* pertaining to traditional geometry. Also, Eu·clid′i·an.

eū·gĕn′ics, *n.* attempt to improve humanity by controlled mating. —eu·gen′ic, *adj.*

eū′lo·gў. *n., pl.* -gies. praise in speech or writing. —eu″lo·gize′, *v.t.*

eū′nŭch, *n.* castrated man.

eū′phē·mĭsm, *n.* expression substituted for a less agreeable one. —euphe·mis′tic, *adj.*

eū·phō′nĭ·oŭs, *adj.* pleasant-sounding. —eu′pho·ny, *n.*

eū·phō′rĭ·a, *n.* sensation of well-being. —eu·phor′ic, *adj.*

eū·rē′ka, *interj.* I have found it!

eū′′thā·nā′sĭ·a, *n.* killing to prevent or end suffering.

e·văc′ū·āte′′, *v.t.*, -ated, -ating. 1. empty. 2. send to a place of security. —e·vac′′u·a′tion, *n.* —e·vac′′u·ee′, *n.*

e·vāde′, *v.t.*, -vaded, -vading. avoid or escape from. —e·va′sion, *n.* —e·va′sive, *adj.*

e·văl′ū·āte′′, *v.t.*, -ated, -ating. estimate the worth of. —e·val′′u·a′tion, *n.*

ē′′văn·gĕl′ĭ·cal, *adj.* 1. pertaining to the New Testament. 2. emphasizing salvation through Jesus.

ē·văn′gĕl·ĭst, *n.* 1. author of a Gospel. 2. itinerant preacher. —e·van′gel·ism, *n.*

e·văp′ó·rāte′′, *v.t.*, *v.i.*, -rated, -rating. turn into vapor. —e·vap′′o·ra′tion, *n.*

ēve, *n.* time just before.

ē′vĕn, *adj.* 1. level or smooth. 2. unvarying. 3. equal. 4. divisible by two. 5. with nothing owed. —*adv.* 6. although improbable. 7. yet; still. —*v.t.* 8. make even. —e′ven·ness, *n.*

ēve′nĭng, *n.* time between afternoon and night.

e·vĕnt′, *n.* something that happens. —e·vent′ful, *adj.*

e·vĕn′tū·al, *adj.* at some future time. —e·ven′tu·al·ly, *adv.*

e·vĕn′′tū·ăl′ĭ·tў, *n.*, *pl.* -ties. possible occurrence.

ĕv′êr, *adv.* at any time.

ĕv′êr·grēen′′, *adj.* 1. with green leaves all the year round. —*n.* 2. evergreen tree or plant.

ĕv′′êr·lăst′ĭng, *adj.* eternal or lifelong.

ĕv′êr·ў, *adj.* 1. each individual. 2. any possible. —ev′er·y·one′′, *pron.* —ev′er·y·thing′′, *n.*

ĕv′êr·ў·bŏd′′ў, *n.* every person.

ĕv′êr·ў·whêre′, *adv.* at or to every place.

e·vĭct′, *v.t.* drive out, as from rented lodgings. —e·vic′tion, *n.*

ĕv′ĭ·dénce, *n.*, *v.t.*, -denced, -dencing. *n.* 1. matter supporting an argument. —*v.t.* 2. make evident.

ĕv′ĭ·dént, *adj.* obvious. —ev′i·dent·ly, *adv.*

ē′vĭl, *adj.* 1. wrong or wicked. 2. injurious. —e′vĭl·ly, *adv.*

e·vĭnce′, *v.t.*, -vinced, -vincing. make obvious.

e·vōke′, *v.t.*, -voked, -voking. call forth. —e·voc′a·tive, *adj.* —ev′′o·ca′tion, *n.*

e·vŏlve′, *v.*, -volved, -volving. *v.t.*, *v.i.* develop gradually. —ev′′o·lu′tion, *n.*

ex·ăc′êr·băte, *v.t.*, -bated, -bating. aggravate.

ex·ăct′, *adj.* 1. accurate. 2. precise. —*v.t.* 3. extort or demand. —ex·act′ly, *n.* —ex·act′ing, *adj.* —ex·ac′tion, *n.*

ex·ăg′gêr·āte′′, *v.t.*, -ated, -ating. overstate the importance of. —ex·ag′′ger·a′tion, *n.*

ex·ält′, *v.t.* 1. raise in status. 2. praise. —ex′′al·ta′tion, *n.*

ex·ăm′ĭne, *v.t.*, -ined, -ining. 1. inspect. 2. test for knowledge. —ex·am′′i·na′tion, *n.* —ex·am′in·er, *n.*

ex·ăm′ple, *n.* 1. sample. 2. illustrative instance.

ex·ăs′pêr·āte′′, *v.t.*, -ated, -ating. anger or annoy seriously. —ex·as′′per·a′tion, *n.*

ĕx′ca·vāte′′, *v.t.*, -vated, -vating. dig, as in or from earth. —ex′′ca·va′tion, *n.*

ex·cēed′, *v.t.* 1. be in excess of. 2. surpass.

ex·cēed′ing·lў, *adv.* extremely.

ex·cĕl′, *v.*, -celled, -celling. *v.t.*, *v.i.* surpass.

ĕx′cĕl·lént, *adj.* among the finest of its kind. —ex′cel·lent·ly, *adv.* —ex·cel′lence, *n.*

ex·cĕpt′, *prep.* 1. Also, ex·cept′ing, aside from. —*v.t.* 2. exclude or disregard. —ex·cep′tion, *n.*

ex·cĕp′tion·a·ble, *adj.* objectionable.

ex·cĕp′tion·ăl, *adj.* highly unusual. —ex·cep′tion·al·ly, *adv.*

ĕx′cêrpt, *n.* quotation, esp. printed.

ex·cĕss′, *n.* 1. lack of self-restraint or moderation. 2. surplus. —*adj.* 3. surplus. —ex·ces′sive, *adj.*

ex·chānge′, *v.t.*, -changed, -changing, *n.*

v.t. **1.** give in return for something else. —*n.* **2.** act or instance of exchanging.

ex·cīse′, *n.*, *v.t.*, **-cised, -cising.** *n.* **1.** tax on merchandise. —*v.t.* **2.** cut out. —**ex·ci′sion,** *n.*

ex·cīte′, *v.t.*, **-cited, -citing. 1.** stimulate. **2.** rouse emotionally. —**ex·cit′a·ble,** *adj.* —**ex·cite′ment,** *n.* —**ex·cit′ed·ly,** *adv.* —**ex·cit′ing,** *adj.*

ex·clāim′, *v.i.*, *v.t.* shout or speak loudly and emotionally. —**ex′′cla·ma′tion,** *n.*

ex·clūde′, *v.t.*, **-cluded, -cluding.** leave or keep out. —**ex·clu′sion,** *n.* —**ex·clu′sive,** *adj.*

ex·cō′′ri·āte′′, *v.t.*, **-ated, -ating.** denounce bitterly. —**ex·co′′ri·a′tion,** *n.*

ex′cré·mént, *n.* excreted matter.

ex·crēs′cénce, *n.* abnormal outgrowth.

ex·crēte′, *v.t.*, **-creted, -creting.** eliminate as waste from the body. —**ex·cre′tion,** *n.* —**ex′cre·to′′ry,** *adj.*

ex·crū′ci·ăt′′ĭng, *adj.* racking.

ex′′cŭl·pāte′′, *v.t.*, **-pated, -pating.** prove guiltless. —**ex′′cul·pa′tion,** *n.*

ex·cûr′siŏn, *n.* short pleasure journey. —**ex·cur′sion·ist,** *n.*

ex·cūse′, *v.t.*, **cused, -cusing,** *n.* *v.t.* **1.** remove or mitigate the blame of or for. **2.** forgive. **3.** permit to leave. —*n.* **4.** something that excuses. —**ex·cus′a·ble,** *adj.* —**ex·cus′a·bly,** *adv.*

ĕx′′e·crāte′′, *v.t.*, **-crated, -crating. 1.** denounce. **2.** detest. —**ex′e·cra·ble,** *adj.*

ĕx′′e·cūte′′, *v.t.*, **-cuted, -cuting. 1.** perform. **2.** kill after condemnation. —**ex′′e·cu′tion,** *n.* —**ex′′e·cu′tion·er,** *n.*

ex·ĕc′ū·tĭve, *adj.* **1.** concerned with administration of laws, policies, etc. —*n.* **2.** person in an executive capacity.

ex·ĕc′ū·tŏr, *n.* person who administers a will. Also, *fem.,* **ex·ec′u·trix.**

ex·ĕm′plâ·rў, *adj.* serving as a good example.

ex·ĕm′plĭ·fў′′, *v.t.*, **-fied, -fying.** be an example of. —**ex·em′′pli·fi·ca′tion,** *n.*

ex·ĕmpt′, *v.t.*, *adj.* free from an obligation. —**ex·emp′tion,** *n.*

ĕx′′ër·cīse′′, *n.*, *v.*, **-cised, -cising.** *n.* **1.** activity developing skill, knowledge, strength, etc. **2.** performance. **3.** **exercises,** ceremony. —*v.t.* **4.** cause to do exercises. **5.** put into effect.

ex· êrt′, *v.t.* put into action. —**ex·er′tion,** *n.*

ex·hāle′, *v.*, **-haled, -haling.** *v.t.*, *v.i.* breathe out. —**ex′′ha·la′tion,** *n.*

ex·haŭst′, *v.t.* **1.** empty; deplete. **2.** tire thoroughly. —*n.* **3.** waste gas, etc. from machinery. —**ex·haus′tion,** *n.*

ex·haŭs′tĭve, *adj.* omitting nothing.

ex·hĭb′ĭt, *v.t.*, *n.* display. —**ex′′hi·bi′tion,** *n.* —**ex·hib′i·tor,** *n.*

ĕx′′hĭ·bĭ′tion·ĭsm, *n.* ostentation; self-display. —**ex′′hi·bi′tion·ist,** *n.*

ex·hĭl′′á·rāte′′, *v.t.*, **-rated, -rating. 1.** fill with delight. **2.** stimulate. —**ex·hil′′a·ra′tion,** *n.*

ex·hôrt′, *v.t.* urge strongly. —**ex′′hor·ta′tion,** *n.*

ex·hūme′, *v.t.*, **-humed, -huming.** dig up after burial. —**ex′′hu·ma′tion,** *n.*

ĕx′ĭ·gén·cў, *n.*, *pl.* **-cies.** urgency. —**ex′i·gent,** *adj.*

ĕx′īle, *v.t.*, **-iled, -iling.** *n.* *v.t.* **1.** banish from a country. —*n.* **2.** state of banishment. **3.** exiled person.

ex·ĭst′, *v.i.* **1.** have being. **2.** be alive. —**ex·ist′ence,** *n.* —**ex·ist′ent,** *adj.*

ĕx′ĭt, *n.* **1.** departure. **2.** means of departure.

ĕx ŏf·fĭ′ci·o, by virtue of his or her office.

ex·ŏn′ẽr·āte′′, *v.t.*, **-ated, -ating.** declare guiltless. —**ex·on′′er·a′tion,** *n.*

ex·ôr′bĭ·tánt, *adj.* beyond reason or moderation. —**ex·or′bi·tance,** *n.*

ĕx′′ŏr·cīze′′, *v.t.*, **-cized, -cizing.** expel with incantations. —**ex′or·cism,** *n.*

ĕx·ŏt′ĭc, *adj.* markedly foreign.

ex·pănd′, *v.t.*, *v.i.* widen. —**ex·pan′sion,** *n.* —**ex·pan′sive,** *adj.*

ex·pănse′, *n.* broad, unbroken area.

ĕx·pā′tĭ·āte′′, *v.i.*, **ated, -ating.** talk or write at length.

ex·pā′trĭ·āte, *n.* person living outside his country.

ex·pĕct′, *v.t.* **1.** regard as going to happen. **2.** regard as obligatory. —**ex′′pec·ta′tion, ex·pect′an·cy,** *n.* —**ex·pec′tant,** *adj.*

ex·pĕc′tŏ·rāte′′, *v.t.*, *v.i.* **-rated, -rating.** spit.

ex·pē′dĭ·ént, *adj.* **1.** useful on a given occasion. **2.** determined by self-interest alone. —*n.* **3.** something expedient. —**ex·pe′di·en·cy,** *n.*

ex'pe·dīte'', *v.t.*, **-dited, -diting. 1.** make faster or easier. **2.** do quickly.

ex''pe·dī'tion, *n.* journey for exploration or invasion. —**ex''pe·di'tion·ar''y**, *adj.*

ex''pe·dī'tious, *adj.* prompt.

ex·pĕl', *v.t.*, **-pelled, -pelling. 1.** oust. **2.** emit.

ex·pĕnd', *v.t.* **1.** spend. **2.** use up. —**ex·pend'i·ture**, *n.*

ex·pĕnd'a·ble, *adj.* able or intended to be sacrificed, as in war.

ex·pĕnse', *n.* **1.** act or instance of spending. **2.** cost.

ex·pĕn'sīve, *adj.* high in price.

ex·pĕr'ī·ence, *n.*, *v.t.*, **-enced, -encing.** *n.* **1.** something lived through. **2.** knowledge from life, work, etc. —*v.t.* **3.** have experience of.

ex·pĕr'ī·mĕnt, *n.* **1.** test establishing facts. —*v.i.* **2.** engage in experiments. —**ex·per''i·men·ta'tion**, *n.* —**ex·per''i·men'tal**, *adj.*

ex'pĕrt, *n.* **1.** person with specialized knowledge or skill. —*adj.* **2.** pertaining to such persons. —**ex'pert·ly**, *adv.* —**ex''per·tise', ex'pert·ness**, *n.*

ex'pī·āte'', *v.t.*, **-ated, -ating.** atone for. —**ex''pi·a'tion**, *n.* —**ex'pi·a·to''ry**, *adj.*

ex·pīre', *v.i.*, **-pired, -piring. 1.** die. **2.** cease to be in effect. **3.** breathe out. —**ex''pi·ra'tion**, *n.*

ex·plāin', *v.t.* **1.** make understandable or meaningful. **2.** account for. —**ex''pla·na'tion**, *n.* —**ex·plan'a·to''ry**, *adj.*

ex'plē·tīve, *n.* exclamation.

ex·plī'ca·ble, *adj.* able to be explained.

ex·plĭc'ĭt, *adj.* **1.** clear. **2.** outspoken.

ex·plōde', *v.*, **-ploded, -ploding.** *v.t.*, *v.i.* burst from internal pressure. —**ex·plo'sive**, *adj.*, *n.* —**ex·plo'sion**, *n.*

ex'plŏĭt, *n.* **1.** daring deed. —*v.t.* (ex ploit') **2.** take advantage of. —**ex''ploi·ta'tion**, *n.* —**ex·ploit'a·tive**, *adj.*

ex·plōre', *v.*, **-plored, -ploring.** *v.t.*, *v.i.* investigate thoroughly. —**ex·plor'er**, *n.* —**ex''plo·ra'tion**, *n.* —**ex·plor'a·to''ry**, *adj.*

ex·pō'nent, *n.* **1.** expounder of a principle. **2.** *Math.* number indicating how many times a quantity is to be multiplied by itself.

ex·pôrt', *v.t.* **1.** ship out of the country. —*n.* (eks'pōrt) **2.** something exported.

ex·pōse', *v.t.*, **-posed, -posing. 1.** reveal. **2.** make vulnerable. —**ex·pos'ure**, *n.*

ex''po·sī'tion, *n.* **1.** event presenting manufactures, processes, etc. to the public. **2.** explanation.

ex pōst făc'tō, retroactive; retroactively.

ex·pŏs'tū·lāte'', *v.i.*, **-lated, -lating.** argue in objection. —**ex·pos''tu·la'tion**, *n.*

ex·pōund', *v.t.* state or explain.

ex·prĕss', *v.t.* **1.** communicate adequately. **2.** squeeze. —*adj.* **3.** precise; definite. —*n.* **4.** vehicle on a fast, direct schedule. **5.** agency for sending things. —**ex·press'ive**, *adj.*

ex·prĕs'sion, *n.* **1.** means of expressing. **2.** facial attitude. **3.** revelation of feeling.

ex·prō'prī·āte'', *v.t.*, **-ated, -ating.** seize for public use.

ex·pŭl'sion, *n.* act or instance of being expelled.

ex·pŭnge', *v.t.*, **-punged, -punging.** erase.

ex'pŭr·gāte'', *v.t.*, **-gated, -gating.** censor.

ex'quī·sīte, *adj.* of extreme refinement.

ex·tant', *adj.* alive; present.

ex·tĕm''po·rā'ne·ous, *adj.* without prior preparation.

ex·tĕnd', *v.t.* **1.** stretch or expand. **2.** offer. —*v.i.* **3.** be extended. —**ex·ten'sion**, *n.*

ex·tĕn'sīve, *adj.* large in extent or scope.

ex·tĕnt', *n.* amount or degree of extending.

ex·tĕn'ū·āte'', *v.t.*, **-ated, -ating.** prompt leniency for.

ex·tē'rī·ôr, *adj.* **1.** outer or outward. —*n.* **2.** outside.

ex·tĕr'mĭ·nāte'', *v.t.*, **-nated, -nating.** destroy wholly. —**ex·ter''mi·na'tion**, *n.* —**ex·ter'mi·na''tor**, *n.*

ex·tĕr'nàl, *adj.* exterior; outward.

ex·tĭnct', *adj.* no longer in existence.

ex·tĭnc'tion, *n.* dying-out or destruction.

ex·tĭn'guĭsh, *v.t.* put out of existence, as a flame.

ex·tĭr'pāte'', *v.t.*, **-pated, -pating.** uproot; exterminate.

ex·tōl', *v.t.*, **-tolled, -tolling.** praise highly.

ex·tôrt', *v.t.* obtain by threats or force.

—**ex·tor′tion,** *n.* —**ex·tor′tion·ist,** *n.*
—**ex·tor′tion·ate,** *adj.*

ĕx′trà, *adj.* additional.

ĕx·trăct′, *v.t.* **1.** draw out. —*n.* (ek′strakt)
2. something extracted. —**ex·trac′tion,**
n.

ĕx′trà·dīte′, *v.t.,* **-dited, -diting.** surrender for prosecution to a foreign country.
—**ex′tra·di′′tion,** *n.*

ĕx·trä′nē·oŭs, *adj.* **1.** from outside. **2.** irrelevant.

ĕx·traôr′di·när′′ÿ, *adj.* **1.** remarkable.
2. out of the ordinary.

ex·trăv′a·gànt, *adj.* beyond economy,
reason, etc. —**ex·trav′a·gance,** *n.*

ex·trēme′, *adj.* **1.** farthest. **2.** ultimate. **3.**
immoderate. —*n.* **4.** farthest point, position, etc. —**ex·treme′ly,** *adv.*

ex·trĕm′i·tÿ, *n., pl.* **-ties.** *n.* **1.** something
extreme. **2.** end. **3.** extremities, hands
and feet.

ĕx′tri·cāte′, *v.t.,* **-cated, -cating.** free.

ĕx′trō·vêrt′′, *n.* person oriented toward
the outside world. —**ex′′tro·ver′sion,**
n.

ex·ū′bêr·ànt, *adj.* full of health and spirits. —**ex·u′ber·ance,** *n.*

ex·ūde′, *v.,* **-uded, -uding.** *v.t., v.i.* **1.**
pass through the pores. **2.** seem to radiate. —**ex·u·da′tion,** *n.*

ex·ŭlt′, *v.i.* rejoice. —**ex′′ul·ta′tion,** *n.*

eÿe, *n.* **1.** organ of sight. **2.** eyelike opening. **3.** visual sensitivity. —**eye′brow′′,**
n. —**eye′ball′′,** *n.* —**eye′lid′′,** *n.* —**eye′**
sight′′, *n.*

eÿe′lăsh′′, *n.* row of stiff hairs over the
eye.

eÿe′sôre′′, *n.* unpleasant sight.

F

F, f., *n.* **1.** sixth letter of the English alphabet. **2.** failing grade.

fā′ble, *n.* **1.** moralizing story. **2.** legend.

făb′rĭc, *n.* cloth.

făb′rĭ·cāte, *v.t.,* **-cated, -cating. 1.** assemble. **2.** invent for deception. —**fab′′**
ri·ca′tion, *n.*

făb′ū·loŭs, *adj.* wonderful.

fà·cäde (fa sahd′), *n.* **1.** decorative building front. **2.** false appearance. Also, **fa·**
çade′.

fāce, *n., v.,* **faced, facing.** *n.* **1.** front of
the human head. **2.** main surface. **3.**
outer appearance. —*v.t.* **4.** confront.
—*v.i.* **5.** look or be turned toward. —**fa′**
cial, *adj.*

făc′ĕt, *n.* **1.** plane surface of a gem, etc. **2.**
aspect.

fà·cē′tioŭs, *adj.* joking; impish; frivolous.

făc′ile, *adj.* revealing no effort.

fà·cĭl′i·tāte′′, *v.t.,* **-tated, -tating.** make
easy.

fà·cĭl′i·tÿ, *n., pl.* **-ties. 1.** ease. **2.** skill. **3.**
facilities, equipment, staff, etc.

făc·sĭm′i·lė, *n.* copy; reproduction.

făct, *n.* objective truth. —**fac′tu·al,** *adj.*

făc′tion, *n.* group promoting its own interests. —**fac′tion·al,** *adj.*

făc′tör, *n.* **1.** influential thing. **2.** quantity
multiplied by another.

făc′tö·rÿ, *n., pl.* **-ries.** place of manufacture.

făc·tō′tŭm, *n.* person who does odd jobs.

făc′ŭl·tÿ, *n., pl.* **-ties. 1.** aptitude or ability. **2.** teaching staff.

făd, *n.* brief fashion or whim.

fāde, *v.,* **faded, fading.** *v.i.* **1.** lose color or
freshness. **2.** disappear slowly.

făg, *v.t.,* **fagged, fagging.** tire.

Fähr′en·heit′′, *adj.* pertaining to a temperature scale with the freezing point of
water at 32 degrees and the boiling point
at 212 degrees.

fāil, *v.t.* **1.** attempt without success. **2.** not
to do. **3.** disappoint. —*v.i.* **4.** have no
success. **5.** die away. —**fail′ing,** *n.*
—**fail′ure,** *n.*

fāint, *adj.* **1.** weak. —*n.* **2.** temporary loss
of consciousness. —*v.i.* **3.** go into a
faint. —**faint′ly,** *adv.* —**faint′ness,** *n.*

fäir, *adj.* **1.** honest; just. **2.** beautiful or
handsome. **3.** light. **4.** mediocre. **5.**
sunny. **6.** gathering for sales or display.
—**fair′ly** *adv.*

fäir′ÿ, *n., pl.* **-ies.** creature with magic
powers.

faith, *n.* **1.** belief; confidence. **2.** loyalty.
3. religion. —**faith′ful,** *adj.* —**faith′**
less, *adj.*

fāke, *adj., n., v.t.,* **faked, faking.** *adj.* **1.**

false. —*n.* **2.** something false. —*v.t.* **3.** give a false appearance of. —**fak'er,** *n.*

fal'con, *n.* small hawk.

fall, *v.i.,* **fell, fallen, falling,** *n. v.i.* **1.** descend without support. —*n.* **2.** act or instance of falling. **3.** autumn.

fal'la·cy, *n., pl.* **-cies.** instance of false reasoning. —**fal·la'cious,** *adj.*

fal'li·ble, *adj.* capable of mistakes. —**fal''li·bil'i·ty,** *n.*

fal'low, *adj.* unplanted.

false, *adj.,* **falser, falsest. 1.** not true. **2.** untruthful or unfaithful. —**false'ly,** *adv.* —**false'hood'',** *n.* —**fal'si·fy'',** *v.t.* —**fal'si·ty,** *n.*

fal·set'tō, *n., pl.* **-tos.** artificially high voice.

fal'ter, *v.i.* act, speak, etc. hesitantly or unsteadily.

fame, *n.* widespread reputation. —**fa'mous, famed,** *adj.*

fa·mil'iar, *adj.* **1.** well known. **2.** well acquainted. —**fa·mil'iar·ly,** *adv.* —**fa·mil''i·ar'i·ty,** *n.* —**fa·mil'iar·ize'',** *v.t.*

fam'i·lỹ, *n., pl.* **-lies. 1.** group of relatives. **2.** group of related things. —**fa·mil'ial,** *adj.*

fam'ine, *n.* severe food shortage.

fam'ish, *v.t.* starve.

fan, *n., v.t.,* **fanned, fanning.** *n.* **1.** device for moving air. **2.** *Informal.* devotee. —*v.t.* **3.** cool or move with a fan.

fa·nat'ic, *n.* irrational enthusiast or hater. —**fa·nat'i·cal,** *adj.* —**fa·nat'i·cism,** *n.*

fan'ci·êr, *n.* breeder of animals or plants.

fan'cỹ, *adj.,* **-cier, -ciest,** *n., v.t.,* **-cied, -cying.** *adj.* **1.** elaborate. —*n.* **2.** imagination. **3.** liking. —*v.t.* **4.** take a liking to. —**fan'ci·ful,** *adj.* —**fan'ci·ly,** *adv.*

fan'fare', *n.* **1.** introductory call of trumpets, etc. **2.** publicity.

fang, *n.* long, pointed tooth.

fan·tās'tic, *adj.* odd and extravagant.

fan'ta·sỹ, *n., pl.* **-sies. 1.** imagination. **2.** something imagined.

far, *adj., adv.,* **farther, farthest.** at or to a great distance.

farce, *n.* ridiculous comedy. —**far'ci·cal,** *adj.*

fare, *n., v.i.,* **fared, faring.** *n.* **1.** money paid to travel. **2.** food. —*v.i.* **3.** prosper or succeed.

fare·wĕll', *interj., n., adj.* good-bye.

far'-fĕtched', *adj.* implausible.

farm, *n.* **1.** place for raising plants or animals. —*v.t.* **2.** cultivate. —**farm'er,** *n.* —**farm'hand'',** *n.* —**farm'house'',** *n.* —**farm'yard'',** *n.*

far'-ŏff', *adj.* remote.

far'-rēach'ing, *adj.* with extensive effects.

far'sīght''ĕd, *adj.* **1.** provident. **2.** seeing distant objects better than close ones.

fas'ci·nāte', *v.t.,* **-nated, -nating.** hold the entire attention of. —**fas''ci·na'tion,** *n.*

Făs'cism, *n.* authoritarian, militaristic system of government. —**Fas'cist,** *n., adj.* —**Fas·cis'tic,** *adj.*

fash'ion, *n.* **1.** manner of acting. **2.** prevailing style. —*v.t.* **2.** make. —**fash'ion·a·ble,** *adj.*

fast, *adj.* **1.** speedy. **2.** firm; fixed. —*adv.* **3.** firmly. —*v.i.* **4.** abstain from food or drink. *n.* **5.** act or instance of fasting.

fast'en, *v.t.* attach; make secure. —**fas'ten·er,** *n.* —**fast'en·ing,** *n.*

fas·tĭd'i·oŭs, *adj.* not readily pleased. —**fas·tid'i·ous·ly,** *adv.*

fat, *adj.,* **fatter, fattest,** *n. adj.* **1.** having much fat. —*n.* **2.** greasy material. —**fat'ness,** *n.* —**fat'ty,** *adj.*

fā'tàl, *adj.* causing death or destruction. —**fa'tal·ly,** *adv.*

fā'tàl·ism, *n.* **1.** belief in fate. **2.** resignation. —**fa'tal·ist,** *n.* —**fa''tal·is'tic,** *adj.* —**fa''tal·is'ti·cal·ly,** *adv.*

fa·tăl'i·tỹ, *n., pl.* **-ties. 1.** deadliness. **2.** death by accident.

fāte, *n.* **1.** power determining events. **2.** death.

fā'thêr, *n.* **1.** male parent. **2.** founder or originator. **3.** Christian priest. —**fa'ther·hood'',** *n.* —**fa'ther·ly,** *adj.*

fā'thêr-ĭn-lăw'', *n., pl.* **fathers-in-law.** father of a spouse.

făth'ŏm, *n.* *Nautical.* unit of 6 linear feet. —*v.t.* **2.** probe to understand.

fa·tigue', *n., v.t.,* **-tigued, -tiguing.** *n.* **1.** weariness. **2.** **fatigues,** military work clothes. —*v.t.* **3.** tire thoroughly.

făt'ten, *v.t.* **1.** make fat. —*v.i.* **2.** become fat.

făt′tў, *adj.* containing fat.

făt′ū·oŭs, *adj.* foolishly self-satisfied. **—fa·tu′i·ty,** *n.*

faū′cet, *n.* valve for running water; tap.

fault, *n.* defect. **—fault′y,** *adj.*

faū′na, *n. pl.* animals.

faux pas (fō′pah′), *n., pl.* **faux pas.** social mistake.

fā′vŏr, *n.* **1.** act of kindness. **2.** approval. **—***v.t.* **3.** do a favor for. **4.** treat as a favorite. **5.** advocate or support. **—fa′vor·a·ble,** *adj.* **—fa′vor·ite,** *adj., n.*

fā′vŏr·ĭt·ĭsm, *n.* preferential treatment for favorites.

fawn, *v.i.* **1.** show servility. **—***n.* **2.** young deer.

fāze, *v.t.,* **fazed, fazing.** daunt.

fear, *n.* **1.** desire to escape danger. **2.** awe. **—***v.t.* **3.** have fear of. **4.** believe with regret. **—fear′ful,** *adj.* **—fear′less,** *adj.*

fea′sĭ·ble, *adj.* able to be done; practical. **—fea″si·bil′i·ty,** *n.*

feast, *n.* **1.** religious festival. **2.** lavish meal. **—***v.i.* **3.** have a feast.

feat, *n.* act of skill or daring.

feath′er, *n.* part of a bird's covering. **—feath′er·y,** *adj.*

fea′tūre, *n., v.t.,* **-tured, turing.** *n.* **1.** distinct aspect. **2. features,** face. **—***v.t.* **4.** present as a feature.

Feb′rū·ăr″y, *n.* second month.

fē′cēs, *n., pl.* solid excrement. **—fe′cal,** *adj.*

fĕck′lĕss, *adj.* **1.** ineffectual. **2.** irresponsible.

fē′cŭnd, *adj.* fertile. **—fe·cun′di·ty,** *n.*

fĕd′ĕr·al, *adj.* **1.** composed of federated states. **2.** pertaining to a federation.

fĕd″ĕr·ā′tion, *n.* union of states or organizations under a central government or authority.

fēe, *n.* charge for services.

fēe′ble, *adj.,* **-bler, -blest.** without energy or force. **—fee′bly,** *adv.* **—fee′bleness,** *n.*

fēed, *v.,* **fed, feeding,** *n., v.t.,* **1.** nourish with food. **—***v.i.* **2.** eat. **—***n.* **3.** animal food.

fēed′băck″, *n.* **1.** noise caused by a microphone picking up its own amplified signal. **2.** reactions to an idea or course of action.

fēel, *v.,* **felt, feeling.** *n. v.t.* **1.** sense by touch. **2.** be aware of. **3.** believe. **—***v.i.* **4.** be sensed as specified. **—***n.* **5.** feeling; sensation. **—feel′ing,** *n.*

feign (fān), *v.t.* pretend.

feint (fānt), *n.* **1.** false attack made as a diversion. **—***v.i.* **2.** make a feint.

fē·lĭc′ĭ·tāte″, *v.t.,* **-tated, -tating.** congratulate. **—fe·lic″i·ta′tion,** *n.*

fē·lĭc′ĭ·toŭs, *adj.* appropriate. **—fe·lic′i·tous·ly,** *adv.*

fē·lĭc′ĭ·tў, *n., pl.* **-ties.** happiness.

fē′line, *adj.* pertaining to the cat family.

fĕll, *v.t.* cause to fall.

fĕl′lŏw, *n.* **1.** man. **2.** companion. **—fel′low·ship″,** *n.*

fĕl′ŏn, *n.* committer of a major crime. **—fel′on·y,** *n.* **—fe·lo′ni·ous,** *adj.*

fĕlt, *n.* fabric of compacted wool, etc.

fē′māle, *adj.* **1.** pertaining to the sex bearing offspring. **—***n.* **2.** someone or something female.

fĕm′ĭ·nine, *adj.* characteristic of girls and women. **—fem″i·nin′i·ty,** *n.*

fĕnce, *n., v.,* **fenced, fencing.** *n.* **1.** light barrier. **—***v.i.* **2.** fight with thrusting swords.

fĕnd, *v.t.* drive or ward.

fĕnd′ĕr, *n.* cover for a wheel on a vehicle.

fĕr·mĕnt′, *v.t.* **1.** break down, as through bacterial action. **—***v.i.* **2.** be broken down, as an organic substance. **—***n.* (fer′ment) **3.** anticipatory excitement. **—fer″men·ta′tion,** *n.*

fêrn, *n.* fronded plant reproduced by spores.

fē·rō′cioŭs, *adj.* savage. **—fe·ro′cious·ly,** *adv.* **—fe·roc′i·ty,** *n.*

fĕr′rĕt, *n.* **1.** weasellike animal. **—***v.i.* **2.** hunt; search.

fĕr′roŭs, *adj.* pertaining to iron. Also, **fer′ric.**

fĕr′rў, *n., pl.* **-ries,** *v.t.,* **-ried, -rying.** *n.* **1.** Also, **fer′ry·boat″,** boat on a shuttle service. **2.** service running such a boat. **—***v.t.* **3.** transport by or as by a ferry.

fĕr′tile, *adj.* yielding offspring, crops, etc. **—fer·til′i·ty,** *n.* **—fer′til·ize″,** *v.t.*

fĕr′vĕnt, *adj.* passionate. Also, **fer′vid. —fer′vent·ly,** *adv.* **—fer′ven·cy, fer′vor,** *n.*

fĕs′tĭ·văl, *n.* occasion of celebration or merrymaking. **—fes′tive,** *adj.* **—fes·tiv′i·ty,** *n.*

fĕs·tōōn′, *n*. **1**. decorative hanging suspended between two supports. —*v.t*. **2**. drape.

fĕtch, *v.t*. **1**. get. **2**. summon.

fete (fāt), *n., v.t*., **feted, feting**. *n*. **1**. festive entertainment. —*v.t*. **2**. honor with a fete. Also, **fête**.

fĕt′id, *adj*. evil-smelling.

fĕt′ĭsh, *n*. subject of obsessive concern.

fĕt′tēr, *n., v.t*. shackle or chain.

fĕt′tle, *n*. **in fine fettle**, in excellent state.

fē′tŭs, *n., pl*. **-tuses**, unborn young in its later state. —**fe′tal**, *adj*.

feud, *n*. murderous rivalry between families.

feu′dal·ĭsm, *n*. system of serfs and overlords. —**feu′dal**, *adj*.

fē′vēr, *n*. excess of body temperature. —**fe′ver·ish**, *adj*.

fē′vēr blĭs′tēr, *n*. a cold sore.

fĕw, *adj., pron., n*. some but not many.

fi·an·cé (fē″ahn sā′), *n*. man engaged to be married. Also, *fem.*, **fi″an·cée′**.

fī·ăs′cō, *n., pl*. **-coes, -cos**. ridiculous failure.

fī′ăt, *n*. decree.

fī′bēr, *n*. long thin piece of material. Also, **fi′bre**.

fĭck′le, *adj*. capricious and untrustworthy.

fĭc′tion, *n*. **1**. not factually true. **2**. novels, etc. —**fĭc′tion·al**, *adj*.

fĭc·tĭ′tĭoŭs, *adj*. not factually true.

fĭd′dle, *n., v.i*., **-dled, -dling**. *n*. **1**. violin. —*v.i*. **2**. play a fiddle. **3**. fumble. —**fĭd′dler**, *n*.

fi·dĕl′ĭ·tў, *n*. faithfulness.

fĭd′gĕt, *v.i*. move or fumble nervously. —*n*. **2**. nervous state. —**fĭd′get·y**, *adj*.

fi·dü′cĭ·ār″ў, *adj., n., pl*. **-ies**. *adj*. **1**. pertaining to a trust. —*n*. **2**. trustee.

field, *n*. **1**. area of open land. **2**. area of work or knowledge.

fiend, *n*. **1**. evil spirit. **2**. vicious person. —**fiend′ish**, *adj*.

fierce, *adj*., **fiercer, fiercest**. **1**. savage. **2**. violent. —**fierce′ly**, *adv*.

fiēr′ў, *adj*., **-ier, -iest**. **1**. covered or filled with fire. **2**. passionate.

fi·ĕs′tà, *n*. festival in a Spanish-speaking region.

fife, *n*. small flute.

fif·tēen′, *n*. ten plus five. —**fif′teenth′**, *adj*.

fĭfth, *adj*. **1**. following the fourth. —*n*. **2**. fifth thing, person, or part.

fĭf′tў, *n., adj*. five times ten. —**fĭf′ti·eth**, *adj*.

fĭg, *n*. small sweet tree fruit.

fĭght, *n., v*., **fought, fighting**. *n*. **1**. dispute or competition with violence. **2**. angry argument. —*v.t*. **3**. make a fight against. —*v.i*. **4**. engage in a fight.

fĭg′mĕnt, *n*. something merely imaginary.

fĭg′ū·rà·tĭve, *adj*. using or forming a figure of speech.

fĭg′ūre, *n., v.t*., **-ured, -uring**. *n*. **1**. shape. **2**. numeral. **3**. sum. —*v.t., v.i*. **4**. calculate.

fĭgūre of spēech, word or idiom not to be taken literally or in the usual way.

fĭl′à·mĕnt, *n*. narrow thread or wire.

fĭl′bērt, *n*. hazelnut.

fĭlch, *v.t*. steal.

file, *n., v.t*., **-filed, -filing**. *n*. **1**. group of documents. **2**. tool for rubbing. **3**. front-to-rear row. —*v.t*. **4**. preserve in a file. **5**. rub with a file.

fĭl′ĭ·ăl, *adj*. pertaining to or appropriate in a son or daughter.

fĭl′ĭ·bŭs″tēr, *n*. meaningless speech hindering legislation.

fĭl′ĭ·grēe″, *n*. lace-like gold or silver wirework.

fĭll, *v.t*. **1**. cause to be completely occupied. **2**. satisfy the requirements of. —*v.i*. **3**. become full. —*n*. **4**. enough to fill.

fĭl·let (fil ā′), *n*. boneless lean cut of meat or fish.

fĭl′lip, *n*. stimulus.

fĭlm, *n*. **1**. thin coating. **2**. strip or sheet for registering photographic images. —*v.t*. **3**. make a motion picture or photograph of.

fĭl′tēr, *n*. **1**. something screening out unwanted things. —*v.i*. **2**. pass through a filter. —*v.t*. **3**. exclude with a filter.

fĭlth, *n*. foul matter. —**filth′y**, *adj*.

fĭn, *n*. bladelike extension.

fī′nàl, *adj*. at the end. —**fi′nal·ly**, *adv*. —**fi·nal′i·ty**, *n*.

fī·nā′lē, *n*. concluding feature.

fī′nàl·ĭst, *n*. competitor in a final contest.

fi·nance (fĭ năns′, fī′năns), *n., v.t*.,

-nanced, -nancing. *n.* **1.** management of money. **2. finances,** resources of money. —*v.t.* **3.** lend or obtain money for. —**fi·nan'cial,** *adj.* —**fi''nan·cier',** *n.*

find, *v.t.,* **found, finding,** *n. v.t.* **1.** come upon by chance. **2.** succeed in a search for. —*n.* **3.** valuable discovery. —**find'er,** *n.* —**find'ing,** *n.*

fine, *adj.,* **finer, finest,** *n., v.t.,* **fined, fining.** *adj.* **1.** in tiny pieces. **2.** excellent. —*n.* **3.** money penalty. —*v.t.* **4.** impose a fine on. —**fine'ly,** *adv.* —**fine'ness,** *n.*

fin'er·y, *n.* fine costume.

fi·nesse', *n.* skill, esp. in human relations.

fine'-tune', *v.* to make minor adjustments.

fin'ger, *n.* extension of the hand.

fin'ick·y, *adj.* too particular or demanding. Also, **fin'i·cal, fin'ick·ing.**

fi'nis, *n., pl.* **-nises.** end; finish.

fin'ish, *v.t.* **1.** bring to an end. **2.** give a desired surface to. —*v.i.* **3.** end an activity.

fi'nite, *adj.* not endless.

fir, *n.* cone-bearing evergreen tree.

fire, *n., v.* **fired, firing.** *n.* **1.** burning. **2.** deep feeling. **3.** discharge of guns. —*v.t.* **4.** set fire to. **5.** discharge, as of a gun. —**fire'proof'',** *adj.*

fire'arm', *n.* weapon operated by explosives.

fire'crack''er, *n.* a firework.

fire'man, *n.* **1.** person who extinguishes fires. **2.** person who tends fires.

fire'trap'', *n.* building dangerous in fires.

fire'works'', *n., pl.* explosive and burning devices used in celebrations.

firm, *adj.* **1.** unyielding. **2.** steady. —*n.* **3.** business organization. —**firm'ly,** *adv.* **firm'ness,** *n.*

fir'ma·ment, *n.* heavens.

first, *adj., adv.* **1.** at the very front or beginning. **2.** before all others. —*n.* **3.** first person or thing.

first'-hand', *adj., adv.* without intermediaries.

fis'cal, *adj.* pertaining to income and expense; financial.

fish, *n., pl.* **fish,** *v.i. n.* **1.** cold-blooded water animal, breathing with gills.

—*v.i.* **2.** attempt to catch fish. —**fish'er·man,** *n.*

fis'sion, *n.* splitting; cleaving. —**fis'sion·a·ble,** *adj.*

fis'sûre, *n.* crack.

fist, *n.* ball of the hand and fingers for striking.

fit, *v.,* **fitted, fitting,** *adj.,* **fitter, fittest,** *n. v.i.* **1.** be suitable, esp. in size. —*v.t.* **2.** be suitable for. **3.** cause to be suitable. —*adj.* **4.** suitable. **5.** healthy. —*n.* **6.** manner of fitting. **7.** bodily seizure.

fit'ful, *adj.* intermittent; spasmodic. —**fit'ful·ly,** *adv.* —**fit'ful·ness,** *n.*

fit'ting, *adj.* suitable.

five, *adj., n.* four plus one.

fix, *v.t.,* **fixed, fixing. 1.** repair or adjust. **2.** prepare. **3.** establish firmly. —**fix'i·ty,** *n.*

fix·a'tion, *n.* psychological obsession.

fix'tûre, *n.* attached piece of equipment.

fizz, *v.i.,* **fizzed, fizzing,** *n. v.i.* **1.** emit a buzzing bubbling sound. —*n.* **2.** such a sound.

fiz'zle, *v.i.,* **-zled, -zling,** *n. v.i.* **1.** fail. —*n.* **2.** failure.

flab'by, *adj.,* **-bier, -biest.** fat, soft, and weak.

flac'cid, *adj.* flabby.

flag, *n., v.* **flagged, flagging.** *n.* **1.** emblem-bearing cloth. **2.** Also, **flag'stone'',** flat paving stone. —*v.t.* **3.** signal with a flag.

fla'grant, *adj.* outrageously evident. —**fla'grant·ly,** *adv.* —**fla'gran·cy,** *n.*

flail, *n.* **1.** hand-held threshing device. —*v.t.* **2.** beat or move in a flaillike manner.

flair, *n.* shrewd perceptiveness or talent.

flake, *n., v.* **flaked, flaking.** *n.* **1.** thin piece. —*v.i.* **2.** fall off in flakes.

flam·boy'ant, *adj.* brashly ostentatious. —**flam·boy'ance,** *n.*

flame, *n., v.* **flamed, flaming.** *n.* burning gas. —*v.i.* **2.** be burned with flames.

fla·min'go, *n., pl.* **-gos.** pink tropical wading bird.

flam'ma·ble, *adj.* burnable.

flange, *n.* perpendicular edge.

flank, *n.* **1.** side. —*v.t.* **2.** be beside. **3.** attack or get around the flank of.

flan'nel, *n.* loosely woven wool or cotton.

flap, *n., v.,* **-flapped, flapping.** *n.* **1.**

hinged panel. **2.** sound of flapping. —*v.i.*, *v.i.* **3.** move to and fro.

flāre, *v.i.*, **flared, flaring**, *n. v.i.* **1.** blaze. **2.** curve outward. —*n.* **3.** torchlike signal.

flăsh, *n.* **1.** momentary bright light. **2.** moment. —*v.i.* **3.** emit a flash. —*v.t.* **4.** cause to flash.

flăsh′lĭght′′, *n.* hand-held battery-operated light.

flăsh′ỹ, *adj.*, **-ier, -iest.** showy. —**flash′i·ness,** *n.*

flăsk, *n.* bottle, often flat.

flăt, *adj.*, **flatter, flattest,** *n. adj.* **1.** without rises or hollows. **2.** absolute. **3.** featureless. **4.** *Music.* slightly low in pitch. —*n.* **5.** apartment. **6.** something flat. —**flat′ly,** *adv.* —**flat′ten,** *v.t.*, *v.i.*

flăt′tẽr, *v.t.* compliment, as in order to wheedle. —**flat′ter·y,** *n.*

flăunt, *v.t.* display proudly.

flā′vŏr, *n.* **1.** taste. **2.** Also, **fla′vor·ing,** something giving a certain taste. —*v.t.* **3.** add a flavor to.

flăw, *n.* shortcoming; fault. —**flaw′less,** *adj.*

flăx, *n.* threadlike plant fiber for linen.

flēa, *n.* bloodsucking, wingless jumping insect.

flĕck, *n.* spot or flake.

flĕdg′lĭng, *n.* beginner at a profession, etc.

flēe, *v.*, **fled, fleeing.** *v.t.*, *v.i.* escape; run.

flēece, *n.* **1.** covering of a sheep, etc. —*v.t.* **2.** cheat. —**fleec′y,** *adj.*

flēet, *n.* **1.** ships under one command. —*adj.* **2.** swift.

flēet′ĭng, *adj.* passing quickly.

flĕsh, *n.* **1.** muscle tissue. **2.** soft part of a plant. **3.** animal meat. —**flesh′y,** *adj.*

flĕx, *v.t.*, *v.i.* bend. —**flex′i·ble,** *adj.*

flĕx′tīme, flex′i·time, *n.* system in which work hours are flexible.

flĭck, *n.* **1.** quick, light motion. —*v.t.* **2.** throw, etc. with such a motion.

flĭck′ẽr, *v.i.* have a wavering light or appearance.

flī′ẽr, *n.* **1.** aviator. **2.** advertising paper.

flĭght, *n.* **1.** act or instance of flying or fleeing. **2.** stair between floors.

flĭght′ỹ, *adj.*, **-ier, -iest.** overly emotional or whimsical. —**flight′i·ness,** *n.*

flĭm′sỹ, *adj.*, **-ier, -iest.** readily torn or broken. —**flim′si·ly,** *adv.*

flĭnch, *v.i.* hold back or retreat, as from a blow.

flĭng, *v.t.*, **flung, flinging,** *n. v.t.* **1.** hurl. —*n.* **2.** act or instance of flinging. **3.** brief indulgence.

flĭnt, *n.* spark-producing gray siliceous rock. —**flint′y,** *adj.*

flĭp, *v.t.*, **flipped, flipping,** *n. v.t.* **1.** toss jerkily. —*n.* **2.** act or instance of flipping.

flĭp′pănt, *adj.* cheerfully disrespectful. —**flip′pan·cy,** *n.*

flĭp′pẽr, *n.* flat limb for paddling.

flĭrt, *v.i.* **1.** make mild erotic advances. **2.** consider something unseriously. —**flir·ta′tion,** *n.* —**flir·ta′tious,** *adj.*

flĭt, *v.i.*, **flitted, flitting.** move quickly and lightly.

flōat, *v.i.* **1.** be carried on water, etc. —*n.* **2.** something that floats.

flŏck, *n.* **1.** group of sheep, etc. —*v.i.* **2.** join in a flock.

flŏg, *v.t.*, **flogged, flogging.** whip.

flŏod, *n.* **1.** overflow, as of a river. —*v.t.*, *v.i.* **2.** fill to excess.

flŏod′lĭght′′, *n.* lamp casting a directed light.

flōor, *n.* **1.** supporting interior surface. **2.** bottom surface. **3.** right to speak. —*v.t.* **4.** supply with a floor. —**floor′ing,** *n.*

flōor ĕx′ẽr·cīse′, *n.* tumbling maneuvers performed on a mat in a competitive gymnastics event.

flŏp, *v.*, **flopped, flopping,** *n. v.t.*, *v.i.* **1.** overturn heavily. —*v.i.* **2.** move clumsily. **3.** *Informal.* fail. —*n.* **4.** act or instance of flopping.

flō′rá, *n. pl.* plants.

flō′rál, *adj.* pertaining to flowers.

flŏr′ĭd, *adj.* **1.** ruddy. **2.** gaudy.

flō′rĭst, *n.* flower merchant.

flŏss, *n.* soft down or twisted thread. —**flos′sy,** *adj.*

flō·tĭl′là, *n.* small fleet.

flŏunce, *v.i.*, **flounced, flouncing,** *n. v.i.* **1.** move quickly and jerkily. —*n.* **2.** act or instance of flouncing.

flŏun′dẽr, *n.* **1.** edible flat fish. —*v.i.* **2.** struggle.

flŏur, *n.* powdered grain, etc.

flŏur′ĭsh, *v.i.* **1.** thrive. —*v.t.* **2.** wave.

flōw, *v.i.* **1.** move steadily, as a liquid. —*n.* **2.** act or instance of flowing.

flōw′ẽr, *n.* **1.** petaled seed-producing part of a plant; blossom. —*v.i.* **2.** produce blossoms. —**flow′er·y**, *adj.*

flū, *n.* influenza.

flŭc′tū·āte″, *v.i.*, **-ated**, **-ating.** change rate or quantity irregularly. —**fluc″tu·a′tion**, *n.*

flūe, *n.* passage for smoke, etc.

flū′ent, *adj.* speaking or writing readily. —**flu′en·cy**, *n.*

flŭff, *n.* soft fibrous material. —**fluf′fy**, *adj.*

flū′ĭd, *adj.* **1.** flowing. —*n.* **2.** liquid or gas.

flūke, *n.* **1.** barb. **2.** stroke of luck.

flūme, *n.* chute carrying water.

flŭnk, *v.t.*, *v.i. Informal.* fail at school.

flŭr′rÿ, *n.*, *pl.* **-ries.** brief spells of activity, weather, etc.

flŭsh, *v.t.* **1.** wash out. **2.** frighten from cover. —*v.i.* **3.** be flushed. **4.** blush. —*n.* **5.** act or instance of flushing. —*adj.* **6.** even. **7.** wealthy.

flŭs′tẽr, *v.t.* confuse.

flūte, *n.* **1.** high-pitched wind instrument. **2.** Also **flut′ing**, longitudinal concavity. —**flut′ist**, *n.*

flŭt′tẽr, *v.t.*, *v.i.* **1.** oscillate rapidly. —*n.* **2.** excited state. —**flut′ter·y**, *adj.*

flŭx, *n.* **1.** fluid state. **2.** substance aiding metal fusion.

flÿ, *v.*, **flew, flown, flying**, *n.*, *pl.* **flies.** *v.i.* **1.** move in the air. **2.** go quickly. —*v.t.* **3.** cause to move in the air. **4.** flee from. —*n.* **5.** two-winged insect.

flÿ′ing côlõrs, great success.

flÿ′whēel″, *n.* heavy wheel regulating a machine by inertia.

fōam, *n.* **1.** fine bubbles. —*v.i.* **2.** emit or break into foam. —**foam′y**, *adj.*

fō′cŭs, *n.*, *pl.* **-cuses, -ci**, *v.*, **-cused, -cusing.** *n.* **1.** point of concentration. **2.** state of sharpness or clarity. —*v.t.* **3.** bring into focus.

fŏd′dẽr, *n.* food for horses, cows, etc.

fōe, *n.* enemy.

fœ′tŭs, *n.* fetus.

fŏg, *n.*, *v.*, **fogged, fogging**. *n.* **1.** water vapor obscuring vision. —*v.t.*, *v.i.* **2.** obscure with fog. —**fog′gy**, *adj.*

fō′gÿ, *n.*, *pl.* **-gies.** reactionary. Also, **fo′gey.**

foī′ble, *n.* weakness.

foīl, —*v.i.* **1.** frustrate. —*n.* **2.** thin metal sheeting. **3.** pointed sword. **4.** contrasting feature.

foīst, *v.t.* get accepted by trickery.

fōld, *v.t.*, *v.i.* **1.** double over. **2.** wrap. —*n.* **3.** folded place.

fōld′ẽr, *n.* **1.** bent sheet for holding papers. **2.** folded, unbound pamphlet.

fōl′ĭ·âge, *n.* leaves.

fōlk, *n.* **1.** folks, **a.** people. **b.** relatives. —*adj.* **2.** pertaining to ethnic groups. —**folk′lore″**, *n.*

fōlk′sÿ, *adj.*, **-sier, -siest.** *Informal.* characteristic of ordinary people.

fŏl′lōw, *v.t.* **1.** go after or along. **2.** happen after. **3.** conform to. **4.** learn from or understand. —*v.i.* **5.** go or happen after. **6.** be logically deductible.

fŏl′lōw·ẽr, *n.* disciple or adherent.

fŏl′lōw·ĭng, *adj.* **1.** happening afterwards. —*prep.* **2.** after. —*n.* **3.** group of followers.

fŏl′lÿ, *n.*, *pl.* **-lies.** mad or foolish thing or disposition.

fō·mĕnt′, *v.t.* incite, as trouble.

fŏnd, *adj.* full of affection. —**fond′ly**, *adv.* —**fond′ness**, *n.*

fŏn′dle, *v.t.*, **-dled, -dling.** handle fondly.

fŏnt, *n.* baptismal basin.

fōod, *n.* material that nourishes. —**food′stuff″**, *n.*

fōol, *n.* **1.** person of bad judgment. —*v.t.* **2.** deceive. —*v.i.* **3.** act like a fool. —**fool′ish**, *adj.*

fōol′hârd″ÿ, *adj.*, **-dier, -diest.** unwisely audacious.

fōol′prŏŏf″, *adj.* proof against failure.

fōot, *n.* **1.** extremity of a leg. **2.** lower-most feature; bottom; pedestal. **3.** unit of 12 inches. —**foot′hold″**, *n.* —**foot′step″**, *n.*

fōot′bäll″, *n.* **1.** game with a kicked ball. **2.** ball used.

fōot′ĭng, *n.* **1.** support for a foot. **2.** basis.

fōot′prĭnt″, *n.* **1.** mark left by a foot. **2.** area required for an office machine.

fŏp, *n.* foolish or vain person. —**fop′pish**, *adj.*

fôr, *prep.* **1.** in favor of. **2.** in place of. **3.** in order to reach, etc. **4.** to be used, etc. by.

5. during. **6.** obtaining in exchange. **7.** considering the nature of. —*conj.* **8.** because.

for´age, *v.i.*, **-aged, -aging**, search, as for food.

for´ay, *n.* plundering expedition.

for·bear´, *v.*, **-bore, -borne, -bearing.** *v.t.* **1.** refrain. —*v.i.* **2.** control oneself. —**for·bear´ance,** *n.*

for·bid´, *v.t.*, **-bade** or **-bad, -bidden, -bidding. 1.** give an order against. **2.** prevent.

for·bid´ding, *adj.* formidable or unapproachable.

force, *n.*, *v.t.*, **forced, forcing.** *n.* **1.** agency influencing events. **2.** power. **3.** compulsion. **4.** organization or group. —*v.t.* **5.** compel. —**force´ful,** *adj.* —**for´ci·ble,** *adj.*

ford, *n.* **1.** wadeable part of a stream. —*v.t.* **2.** wade across.

fore, *adj., adv.* **1.** forward. —*n.* **2.** front.

fore´arm´, *n.* **1.** arm between the elbow and wrist. —*v.t.* (fore arm´) **2.** arm in advance.

fore´bear´´, *n.* ancestor.

fore´bod´´ing, *n.* premonition.

fore·cast´, *v.t.*, **-cast** or **-casted, -casting,** *n.* *v.t.* **1.** predict. —*n.* **2.** prediction.

fore·cas·tle (fōk´səl), *n.* upper forward part of a ship.

fore·close´, *v.t.*, **-closed, -closing.** deprive a mortgagor of the right of redeeming. —**fore·clos´ure,** *n.*

fore´fa´´ther, *n.* ancestor.

fore´fin´´ger, *n.* finger nearest the thumb.

fore´front´´, *n.* extreme forward position.

fore·gath´er, *v.i.* come together.

fore´go´´ing, *adj.* preceding.

fore·gone´, *adj.* **1.** determined in advance. **2.** previous.

fore´ground´´, *n.* area nearest the viewer.

fore´head, *n.* front of the head between the eyebrows and hair.

for´eign, *adj.* **1.** belonging to an area outside the country. **2.** not belonging where found. —**for´eign·er,** *n.*

fore´man, *n.* supervising worker.

fore´most´´, *adj., adv.* first.

fore´noon´´, *n.* morning after sunrise.

fo·ren´sic, *adj.* pertaining to legal proceedings or public debate.

fore´´or·dain´, *v.t.*, predestine. —**fore·or´´di·na´tion,** *n.*

fore´´run´´ner, *n.* predecessor.

fore·see´, *v.t.*, **-saw, -seen, -seeing.** anticipate. —**fore·see´a·ble,** *adj.* —**fore´sight´´,** *n.*

fore·shad´ow, *v.t.* hint at in advance.

for´est, *n.* area of trees. —**for´´es·ta´tion,** *n.* —**for´est·ry,** *n.*

fore·stall´, *v.t.* prevent by early action.

fore·tell´, *v.t.*, **-told, -telling.** predict.

fore´thought´´, *n.* planning, etc. in advance.

for·ev´er, *adj.* **1.** eternally. **2.** ceaselessly.

fore·warn´, *v.t.* warn beforehand.

fore´word´´, *n.* book introduction.

for´feit, *v.t.* **1.** have taken away because of a misdeed, etc. —*n.* **2.** something forfeited. —*adj.* **3.** forfeited. —**for´fei·ture,** *n.*

forge, *n., v.*, **forged, forging.** *n.* **1.** place for hammering hot metal. —*v.t.* **2.** shape or assemble by hammering. **3.** counterfeit. —*v.i.* **4.** move against obstacles. —**forg´er,** *n.* —**forg´er·y,** *n.*

for·get´, *v.t.*, **-got, -gotten, -getting. 1.** lose the memory of. **2.** ignore. —**for·get´ful,** *adj.*

for·give´, *v.t.*, **-gave, -given, -giving.** regard without ill will despite an offense. —**for·giv´a·ble,** *adj.* —**for·giv´ing·ly,** *adv.*

for·go´, *v.t.*, **-went, -gone, -going.** do without.

fork, *n.* **1.** pronged lifting instrument. **2.** division into two branches from one. —*v.i.* **3.** divide into two branches.

for·lorn´, *adj.* forsaken. —**for·lorn´ly,** *adv.*

form, *n.* **1.** outline or contour. **2.** basic organizing principle. **3.** information blank. —*v.t.* **4.** give form to. **5.** develop. —**for·ma´tion,** *n.* —**form´a·tive,** *adj.*

for´mal, *adj.* **1.** emphasizing rules or customs. **2.** explicit. **3.** correct in manner. —**for´mal·ly,** *adv.* —**for·mal´i·ty,** *n.*

for´mat, *n.* basic design or plan.

for´mer, *adj.* **1.** past. **2.** being the first of two mentioned. —**for´mer·ly,** *adv.*

for´mi·da·ble, *adj.* **1.** awe-inspiring. **2.** difficult.

for´mu·la, *n., pl.* **-las, lae. 1.** rule to be followed. **2.** words to be uttered. **3.** ingredients to be used. —**for·mu·late**'', *v.t.*

for·ni·cāte'', *v.i.*, -**cated**, -**cating**. have illicit sexual intercourse. —**for**''**ni·ca**''**tion**, *n.* —**for**''**ni·ca**''**tor**, *n.*

for·sāke', *v.t.*, -**sook**, -**saken**, -**saking**. 1. desert. 2. give up.

fort, *n.* 1. strongly fortified place. 2. army post.

for·te (fôr'tā), *adj., adv. Music.* loud; loudly.

forte, *n.* special ability.

forth, *adv.* 1. forward. 2. outward.

forth·cóm''**ĭng**, *adj.* soon to appear.

forth·rĭght'', *adj.* frank.

forth''**wĭth**', *adj.* without delay.

for·tĭ·fy'', *v.t.*, -**fied**, -**fying**. 1. make resistant to attack. 2. strengthen. —**for**''**ti·fi·ca**''**tion**, *n.*

for·tĭs''**sĭ·mō**'', *adj., adv. Music.* with extreme loudness.

for·tĭ·tūde'', *n.* persistent courage.

fort'**nĭght**'', *n.* two-week period. —**fort**'**night**''**ly**, *adj., adv.*

for·tréss, *n.* large fort.

for·tū·ĭ·toŭs, *adj.* happening by chance.

for·tū·nāte, *adj.* lucky. —**for**'**tu·nate·ly**, *adv.*

for·tūne, *n.* 1. luck. 2. riches.

for·tў, *adj., n.* four times ten. —**for**'**ti·eth**, *adj.*

fō'**rŭm**, *n.* place for or occasion of public discussion.

for'**wárd**, *adv.* 1. Also, **for**'**wards**, to the front. —*adj.* 2. at the front. 3. presumptuous.

fŏs'**sĭl**, *n.* hardened or petrified plant or animal. —**fos**'**sil·ize**'', *v.t.*

fŏs'**tẽr**, *v.t.* 1. raise, as young. 2. promote. —*adj.* 3. in a family relationship of adoption rather than blood.

foul, *adj.* 1. dirty. 2. disgusting. 3. unethical. —*v.t.* 4. make foul. 5. obstruct or tangle. —*n.* 6. illicit act. —**foul**'**ly**, *adv.* —**foul**'**ness**, *n.*

fŏund, *v.t.* establish.

fŏund'**ẽr**, *v.i.* 1. sink. 2. break down. —*n.* 3. person who founds.

fŏund'**lĭng**, *n.* child abandoned by unknown parents.

fŏun'**drў**, *n., pl.* -**dries**. place for casting metal.

fŏun'**taĭn**, *n.* source of flowing water.

fôur, *adj., n.* three plus one. —**fourth**, *adj., n.*

fôur·tēen', *adj., n.* ten plus four.

fŏwl, *n., pl.* **fowl**. 1. any bird. 2. domestic bird eaten as food.

fŏx, *n.* 1. small canine predatory animal. —*v.t.* 2. cheat; trick.

fŏx'**ў**, *adj.* cunning.

fŏy'**ẽr**, *n.* lobby, esp. of a theater.

frā'**cás**, *n.* brawl.

frăc'**tion**, *n.* portion. —**frac**'**tion·al**, *adj.*

frăc'**tioŭs**, *adj.* rebellious.

frăc'**tûre**, *n., v.t., v.i.*, -**tured**, -**turing**. break.

frăg'**ĭle**, *adj.* readily broken. —**fra·gil**'**i·ty**, *n.*

frăg'**mént**, *n.* 1. broken or torn-away piece. —*v.t., v.i.* 2. break into pieces. —**frag**'**men·tar**'**y**, *adj.*

frā'**gránt**, *adj.* sweet-smelling. —**fra**'**grance**, *n.*

frāil, *adj.* 1. fragile. 2. weak, physically or morally. —**frail**'**ty**, *n.*

frāme, *n., v.t.*, **framed**, **framing**. *n.* 1. open structure. 2. border. —*v.t.* 3. make a frame for. 4. put into words or concepts. —**frame**'**work**'', *n.*

frănc, *n.* currency unit in French-speaking countries.

frăn'**chīse**, *n.* 1. right to vote. 2. right to do business.

frănk, *adj.* 1. not deceitful or evasive. —*n.* 2. right to mail without postage. —**frank**'**ly**, *adv.* —**frank**'**ness**, *n.*

frănk'**fûrt·ẽr**, *n.* wiener.

frăn'**tĭc**, *adj.* wild with emotion. —**fran**'**ti·cal·ly**, *adv.*

frá·tẽr'**nàl**, *adj.* brotherly.

frá·tẽr'**nĭ·tў**, *n., pl.* -**ties**. male social organization.

frăt'**ẽr·nīze**'', *v.i.*, -**ized**, -**izing**. be in friendly association.

frăud, *n.* 1. deceit for gain. 2. impostor. —**fraud**'**u·lent**, *adj.* —**fraud**'**u·lent·ly**, *adv.* —**fraud**'**u·lence**, *n.*

frăught, *adj.* filled, as with some quality.

frāy, *v.t., v.i.* 1. wear thin. —*n.* 2. fight.

frăz'**zle**, *v.t., v.i.*, -**zled**, -**zling**. *n. Informal.* fatigue.

frēak, *n.* oddity, esp. of nature.

frĕck'**le**, *n.* brownish skin spot.

frēe, *adj.*, **freer**, **freest**, *adv., v.t.*, **freed**, **freeing**. *adj.* 1. not bound or controlled.

2. without charge. 3. without obstructions. —*adv.* 4. without charge. —*v.t.* 5. make free. —**free′ly**, *adv.* —**free′dom**, *n.*

free′hănd′′, *adj., adv.* without rulers, compasses, etc.

free′lănce′′, *n., v.i.*, **-lanced**. *n.* 1. person paid by the assignment. —*v.i.* 2. work as a freelancer.

free′thĭnk′′ĕr, *n.* person without standard religious beliefs.

freeze, *n., froze, frozen, freezing, n. v.t., v.i.* 1. harden from cold. —*v.i.* 2. suspend all visible motion. —*n.* 3. suspension of change.

freight (frāt), *n.* 1. merchandise, etc. in transit. —*v.t.* 2. load with freight.

freight′ĕr, *n.* freight ship.

Frĕnch hôrn, coiled wind instrument with a flaring bell.

frĕ·nĕt′ĭc, *adj.* frantic.

frĕn′zў, *n., pl.* **-zies.** wild excitement. —**fren′zied**, *adj.*

frē′quĕn·cў, *n., pl.* **-cies.** number of occurrences in a given period.

frĕ′quĕnt, *adj.* 1. occurring often. —*v.t.* 2. be often present at. —**fre′quent·ly**, *adv.*

frĕsh, *adj.* 1. in good, new condition. 2. rested and energetic. 3. inexperienced. —**fresh′ly**, *adv.* —**fresh′ness**, *n.* —**fresh′en**, *v.t., v.i.*

frĕsh′ĕt, *n.* flooded stream.

frĕsh′măn, *n.* person in his first year, esp. in school or Congress.

frĕt, *v.*, **fretted, fretting,** *n. v.i.* 1. be anxious. —*v.t.* 2. fray or gnaw. —*n.* 3. state of anxiety. 4. repeated geometrical design. —**fret′ful**, *adj.* —**fret′work′′**, *adj.*

Freud′ĭ·ăn, *adj.* 1. pertaining to the theories of Sigmund Freud. —*n.* 2. follower of Freud.

frī′a·ble, *adj.* readily crumbled.

frī′ăr, *n.* monk.

frĭc′ăs·sēe′′, *n., v.t.*, **-seed, -seeing.** *n.* 1. cut and stewed meat. —*v.t.* 2. make a fricassee of.

frĭc′tion, *n.* 1. rubbing. 2. resistance to sliding. 3. conflict; antagonism. —**fric′tion·al**, *adj.*

Frī′dăy, *n.* sixth day.

friĕnd, *n.* 1. person who likes or is helpful to one. 2. supporter or sympathizer.

—**friend′less**, *adj.* —**friend′ly**, *adj.* —**friend′ship**, *n.*

frieze, *n.* horizontal decorative band.

frĭg′ăte, *n.* 1. sailing warship with one gun deck. 2. medium-sized modern warship.

frĭght, *n.* sudden fear. —**fright′en**, *v.t.* —**fright′ful**, *adj.*

frĭg′ĭd, *adj.* 1. cold. 2. sexually unresponsive. —**fri·gid′i·ty**, *n.*

frĭll, *n.* 1. minor ornament. 2. something unnecessary. —**fril′ly**, *adj.*

frĭnge, *n., v.t.*, **fringed, fringing.** *n.* 1. border. 2. edging or parallel loose strands. —*v.t.* 3. supply or constitute a fringe for.

frĭsk, *v.i.* 1. gambol; frolic. —**frisk′y**, *adj.*

frĭt′tĕr, *v.t.* 1. waste gradually. —*n.* 2. fried cake.

frĭv′o·loŭs, *adj.* without proper seriousness. —**friv′o·lous·ly**, *adv.* —**fri·vol′i·ty**, *n.*

frō, *adv.* **to and fro,** away and back again.

frŏck, *n.* robe; dress.

frŏg, *n.* leaping amphibian.

frŏ′lĭc, *v.i.*, **-icked, -icking,** *n. v.i.* 1. romp. 2. make merry. —*n.* 3. occasion of frolicking. —**frol′ick·er**, *n.* —**frol′ic·some**, *adj.*

frŏm, *prep.* 1. beginning or originating at. 2. with no opportunity or use of. 3. as unlike. 4. because of.

frŏnd, *n.* branchlike leaf.

frŏnt, *n.* 1. foremost part or surface. 2. vertical side. 3. pretense; mask. 4. forward battle area. —*v.i.* 5. face. —**front′age**, *n.* —**front′al**, *adj.*

frŏn·tier′, *n.* outer limit. —**fron′′tiers′man**, *n.*

frŏn′tĭs·pĭece′′, *n.* illustration beginning a book.

frŏst, *n.* 1. frozen vapor. 2. freezing temperature. —*v.t.* 3. cover with frost. 4. cover with frosting. —**frost′y**, *adj.*

frŏst′bīte′′, *n.* injury to the body from freezing.

frŏst′ĭng, *n.* sweetened coating for a cake; icing.

frŏth, *n., v.i.* foam. —**froth′y**, *adj.*

frō′ward, *adj.* willful.

frŏwn, *n.* 1. expression of displeasure.

—*v.i.* **2.** assume such an expression. **3.** look with disapproval.

fru·gal′, *adj.* **1.** thrifty. **2.** meager. —**fru′gal·ly**, *adv.* —**fru·gal′i·ty**, *n.*

fruit, *n.* **1.** juicy, seedbearing growth. **2.** reward of endeavor. —**fruit′ful**, *adj.* —**fru·i′tion**, *n.* —**fruit′less**, *adj.*

frump, *n.* dowdy woman. —**frump′ish**, **frump′y**, *adj.*

frus′trate′, *v.t.*, **-trated, -trating.** prevent from succeeding. —**frus·tra′tion**, *n.*

frus′tum, *n.* lower part of a severed cone.

fry, *v.t.* cook in grease, over direct heat. —**fry′er**, *n.*

fuch·sia (fyōō′shə), *n.* shrub with pink-to-purple flowers.

fud′dle, *v.t.*, **-dled, -dling.** stupefy, as with liquor.

fudge, *n.* **1.** soft candy made of butter, milk, sugar and flavoring. —*v.i.* **2.** cheat.

fu′el, *n.*, *v.*, **-eled** or **-elled, -eling** or **-elling.** *n.* **1.** substance for burning. —*v.t.* **2.** supply with fuel. —*v.i.* **3.** take on fuel.

fu′gi·tive, *n.* **1.** person who flees. —*adj.* **2.** fleeing. **3.** transitory.

ful′crum, *n.* support for a lever.

ful′′fill′, *v.t.*, **-filled, -filling. 1.** satisfy. **2.** accomplish. —**ful·fill′ment, ful·fil′ment**, *n.*

full, *adj.* **1.** completely occupied. **2.** complete. **3.** broad or ample. —*adv.* **4.** completely. **5.** directly. —**ful′ly**, *adv.* —**full′ness, ful′ness**, *n.*

full′-scale′, *adj.* unreduced.

ful′some, *adj.* annoyingly excessive.

fum′ble, *v.*, **-bled, -bling**, *n.* *v.i.* **1.** grope. —*v.t.* **2.** handle clumsily. —*n.* **3.** act or instance of fumbling.

fume, *n.*, *v.*, **fumed, fuming.** *n.* **1.** odor, smoke, etc. —*v.t.* **2.** treat with fumes. —*v.i.* **3.** show petulance. **4.** give off fumes.

fum′i·gate′, *v.t.*, **-gated, -gating.** expose to fumes, as to kill vermin. —**fum′′i·ga′tion**, *n.*

fun, *n.* **1.** enjoyment. **2.** source of enjoyment.

func′tion, *n.* **1.** purpose. **2.** ceremony. —*v.i.* **3.** operate; work. —**func′tion·al**, *adj.*

func′tion·ar′′y, *n.*, *pl.* **-ries.** official.

fund, *n.* **1.** money for a purpose. **2.** **funds,** ready money. —*v.t.* **3.** supply money.

fun′′da·men′tal, *adj.* **1.** basic; essential. —*n.* **2.** something fundamental. —**fun′′da·men′tal·ly**, *adv.*

fun′′da·men′tal·ism, *n.* literal belief in a sacred text. Also, **Fun′′da·men′tal·ism.** —**fun′′da·men′tal·ist**, *n.*, *adj.*

fu′ner·al, *n.* ceremony of farewell to the dead.

fu·ne′re·al, *adj.* mournful; solemn.

fun′gus, *n.*, *pl.* **-gi** or **-guses.** spore-reproduced plant without chlorophyll. —**fun′gous**, *adj.*

fun′nel, *n.* **1.** tapered channel used to help pouring. **2.** smokestack.

fun′ny, *adj.*, **-nier, -niest. 1.** comical. **2.** peculiar.

fur, *n.* thick animal hair with its hide. —**fur′ry**, *adj.*

fu′ri·ous, *adj.* **1.** wildly angry. **2.** wild. —**fu′ri·ous·ly**, *adv.*

furl, *v.t.* bundle up.

fur′long, *n.* eighth of a mile.

fur′lough, *n.* **1.** military leave of absence. —*v.t.* **2.** grant a furlough to.

fur′nace, *n.* heating chamber.

fur′nish, *v.t.* **1.** supply. **2.** put furniture in.

fur′nish·ings, *n. pl.* **1.** furniture and decorative objects. **2.** minor clothing, etc.

fur′ni·ture, *n.* tables, chairs, etc.

fu′ror, *n.* frenzied excitement.

fur′ri·er, *n.* dealer in furs.

fur′row, *n.* **1.** groove or wrinkle. —*v.t.* **2.** make furrows in.

fur′ther, *adv.* **1.** to a greater distance or extent. **2.** in addition. —*adj.* **3.** additional. **4.** farther. —*v.t.* **5.** promote. —**fur′ther·ance**, *n.*

fur′ther·more′′, *adv.* in addition.

fur′thest, *adj.* **1.** most distant. —*adv.* **2.** to the greatest distance or extent.

fur′tive, *adj.* sneaking. —**fur′tive·ly**, *adv.*

fu′ry, *n.*, *pl.* **-ries. 1.** extreme rage. **2.** violence.

fuse, *n.*, *v.t.*, **fused, fusing.** *n.* **1.** Also, **fuze,** detonating device. **2.** device of fusible metal for preventing electrical overloads. —*v.t.*, *v.i.* **3.** melt. —**fu′si·ble**, *adj.* —**fu′sion**, *n.*

fu·sil·lade′′, *n.* discharge of massed guns.

fŭss, *n*. **1**. unreasonable show of concern. —*v.i.* **2**. make a fuss. —**fus'sy**, *adj.*

fu'tĭle, *adj.* vain; useless. —**fu·til'i·ty**, *n*.

fu'tûre, *n*. **1**. time to come. **2**. what will happen. **3**. promise of success.

fŭzz, *n*. fine hair or fibers. —**fuz'zy**, *adj.*

G

G, g, *n*. seventh letter of the English alphabet.

găb, *v.i.*, **gabbed, gabbing**, *n*. chatter.

găb'ble, *v.*, **-bled, -bling**, *v.i.*, *v.t.*, *n*. babble.

gā'ble, *n*. wall area perpendicular to a roof ridge.

gădg'ĕt, *n*. mechanical contrivance. —**gadg'et·ry**, *n*.

găff, *n*. **1**. spar for the head of a fore-and-aft sail. **2**. hook for landing fish.

găffe, *n*. social blunder.

găg, *n*., *v.*, **gagged, gagging**. *n*. **1**. device to prevent speech by stopping the mouth. **2**. joke. —*v.t.* **3**. silence with a gag. —*v.i.* **4**. retch.

gai'e·tў, *n*., *pl*. **-ties**. **1**. quality of being gay. **2**. merrymaking.

gai'lў, *adv.* in a gay manner.

gāin, *v.t.* **1**. acquire. **2**. reach. —*v.i.* **3**. profit. —*n*. **4**. profit. —**gain'ful**, *adj.*

gāin''sāy', *v.t.*, **-said, -saying**. **1**. deny. **2**. contract.

gāit, *n*. manner of walking or running.

gā'là, *adj.* **1**. festive. —*n*. **2**. celebration.

gā'lăx·ў, *n.*, *pl*. **-ies**. vast cluster of stars. —**ga·lac'tic**, *adj.*

gāle, *n*. high wind.

găll, *n*. **1**. liquid secreted by the liver. **2**. *Informal*. impudence.

găl'lănt, *adj.* **1**. brave; high-spirited. **2**. polite to women. —**gal'lant·ry**, *n*.

găl'lêr·ў, *n.*, *pl*. **-ies**. **1**. covered passage. **2**. uppermost theater balcony. **3**. place for the display of art.

găl'lēy, *n.*, *pl*. **-leys**. **1**. rowed ship. **2**. ship's kitchen.

găl'lŏn, *n*. liquid measure of 4 quarts or 128 fluid ounces.

găl'lŏp, *n*. **1**. fastest gait of a horse. —*v.i.* **2**. move at a gallop.

găl'lŏws, *n.*, *pl*. **-lowses, -lows**. frame for hanging condemned persons.

găll'stōne', *n*. stony mass in the gall bladder.

ga·lôre', *adv.* in abundance.

ga·lŏsh', *n*. rubber or rubberized boot.

găl·văn'ĭc, *adj.* pertaining to electric currents, esp. from batteries.

găl'và·nīze'', *v.t.*, **-nized, -nizing**. **1**. apply electricity to. **2**. plate with zinc. **3**. stimulate.

găm'bĭt, *n*. opening in chess involving a sacrifice.

găm'ble, *v.*, **-bled, -bling**, *n*. *v.i.* **1**. stake money on the outcome of a game, race, etc. —*v.t.* **2**. stake by gambling. —*n*. **3**. risky undertaking. —**gam'bler**, *n*.

găm'bŏl, *v.i.*, **-boled** or **-bolled, -boling** or **-bolling**, *n*. romp.

gāme, *n.*, *adj.*, **gamed, gaming**. *n*. **1**. contest decided by skill or chance. **2**. hunted animals or birds. —*adj.* **3**. *Informal*. willing to meet a challenge.

gāme'cŏck'', *n*. rooster used in cockfights.

găm'ŭt, *n*. **1**. musical scale. **2**. complete range.

găn'dêr, *n*. male goose.

găng, *n*. group of workers, criminals, etc. acting or associating together.

găn'glĭng, *adj.* awkwardly tall. Also, **gan'gly**.

găn'glĭ·ŏn, *n.*, *pl*. **-a, -ons**. mass of nerve cells.

găn'grēne, *n*. decay of body tissue deprived of blood. —**gan'gre·nous**, *adj.*

găng'stêr, *n*. member of a criminal gang.

găng'wăy'', *n*. **1**. entrance to a ship. —*interj*. **2**. clear the way!

găp, *n*. opening; hiatus.

gāpe, *v.i.*, **gaped, gaping**. **1**. open the mouth wide. **2**. stare with stupefied astonishment. **3**. open wide.

ga·râge', *n*. place for keeping automobiles.

gârb, *n*. clothing.

gâr'bàge, *n*. food refuse, etc.

gâr'ble, *v.t.*, **-bled, -bling**. confuse.

gâr'dĕn, *n*. **1**. area for growing plants. —*v.i.* **2**. work in a garden. —**gar'den·er**, *n*.

gâr·dē'nĭ·à, *n.* white fragrant flower.

gär·găn'tū·àn, *adj.* gigantic.

gâr'gle, *v.i.* -gled, -gling. rinse the throat with liquid and air bubbles.

gâr'goÿle, *n.* grotesque, carved waterspout.

gâr'ĭsh, *adj.* vulgarly showy.

gâr'lànd, *n.* wreath.

gâr'lĭc, *n.* strong-flavored material from a plant bulb.

gâr'mènt, *n.* article of clothing.

gâr'nèt, *n.* deep-red gemstone.

gâr'nĭsh, *v.t.* 1. decorate. —*n.* 2. decoration.

gâr''nĭsh·ēe', *v.t.,* -eed, -eeing. *Law.* attach (money or property) to settle a bad debt.

gâr'rèt, *n.* attic.

gär'rĭ·sòn, *n.* 1. resident body of troops. —*v.t.* 2. station as a defensive force.

gàr·rŏte', *n., v.t.,* -roted, -roting. *n.* 1. device for strangling. —*v.t.* 2. kill with a garrote.

gâr'rŭ·loŭs, *adj.* talkative. —**gar·ru'li·ty,** *n.*

gâr'tẽr, *n.* band for holding up a stocking.

găs, *n., v.t.,* gassed, gassing. *n.* 1. expansive fluid. 2. *Informal.* gasoline. —*v.t.* 3. injure or kill with a gas. —**gas'e·ous,** *adj.* —**gas'sy,** *adj.*

găsh, *n.* 1. long, deep cut. —*v.t.* 2. make a gash in.

găs'kèt, *n.* seal against leakage.

găs'ò·hŏl, *n.* a mixture of gasoline and alcohol.

găs'ò·līne'', *n.* engine fuel derived from petroleum.

găsp, *v.i.* 1. sudden, short breath. —*n.* 2. act or instance of gasping.

găs'trĭc, *adj.* pertaining to the stomach.

găs·trŏn'ò·mÿ, *n.* cooking as an art. —**gas''tro·nom'ic, gas''tro·nom'i·cal,** *adj.*

gāte, *n.* 1. open-air door. 2. Also **gate' way'',** structure holding such a door.

găth'ẽr, *v.t.* 1. bring together. 2. infer. —*v.i.* 3. come together. 4. increase. —**gath'er·ing,** *n.*

gauche (gōsh), *adj.* socially awkward.

gaŭd'ÿ, *adj.,* -ier, -iest. bright and showy. —**gaud'i·ly,** *adv.*

gâuge, *n., v.t.,* gauged, gauging. *n.* 1. measuring instrument. 2. standard mea-

sure. —*v.t.* 3. measure. 4. estimate the amount of. Also, **gage.**

gäunt, *adj.* lean; bony.

gäunt'lèt, *n.* 1. glove with a flaring cuff. 2. hazardous passage.

gäuze, *n.* loosely woven cloth. —**gauz'y,** *adj.*

gäv'èl, *n.* hammerlike noisemaker.

gâwk, *v.i.* stare stupidly.

gâwk'ÿ, *adj.,* -ier, -iest. ungainly.

gäy, *adj.* 1. cheerful. —*n., adj.* 2. homosexual. —**gay''e·ty, gai''e·ty,** *n.* —**gay''ly,** *adv.*

gāze, *v.i.,* gazed, gazing. look steadily.

gà·zètte', *n.* published official record.

găz''èt·tēer', *n.* geographical reference work.

gēar, *n.* 1. Also, **gear'wheel'',** toothed machine wheel. 2. mechanical assembly. 3. equipment. —*v.t.* 4. furnish with gears or a gear.

gee (jē), *interj.* exclamation of surprise.

gĕl'à·tĭn, *n.* jellylike substance from bones or various vegetable substance. Also, **gel'a·tine.** —**ge·lat'i·nous,** *adj.*

gĕld, *v.t.,* gelded, gelding. castrate.

gĕl'ĭd, *adj.* icy.

gĕm, *n.* jewel. Also, **gem'stone''.**

gĕn'dẽr, *n.* classification into masculine, feminine, and neuter.

gēne, *n.* entity by which hereditary characteristics are transmitted.

ge''nē·äl'ò·gÿ, *n., pl.* -gies. study of ancestry. —**ge''ne·a·log'i·cal,** *adj.* —**ge''ne·al'o·gist,** *n.*

gĕn'ẽr·àl, *adj.* 1. pertaining to a whole group. 2. unspecific. 3. common. —*n.* 4. military officer ranking above a colonel. —**gen'er·al·ly,** *adv.*

gĕn''ẽr·ăl'ĭ·tÿ, *n., pl.* -ties. statement supposed to be generally true.

gĕn'ẽr·ȧl·īze'', *v.i.,* -ized, -izing. infer or speak in generalities —**gen''er·al·i·za'tion,** *n.*

gĕn'ẽr·āte'', *v.t.,* -ated, -ating. bring into being. —**gen'er·a·tive,** *adj.*

gĕn''ẽr·ā'tion, *n.* 1. group of persons of about the same age. 2. period of about 30 years. 3. production, esp. of electricity.

gĕn'ẽr·ā''tŏr, *n.* machine for producing electricity.

gé·nêr'ĭc, *adj.* pertaining to a group. —ge·ner'i·cal·ly, *adv.*

gĕn'ẽr·oŭs, *adj.* 1. giving freely. 2. ample. —gen'er·ous·ly, *adv.* —gen''er·os'i·ty, *n.*

gė·nĕt'ĭcs, *n.* study of heredity. —ge·net'i·cal·ly, *adv.* —ge·net'ic, *adj.* —ge·net'i·cist, *n.*

gė'nĭ·ȧl, *adj.* warmly outgoing. —ge''ni·al'i·ty, *n.*

gĕn'ĭ·tȧls, *n., pl.* sexual organs. Also, gen''i·ta'li·a. —gen'i·tal, *adj.*

gēn·iŭs, *n.* 1. presiding spirit. 2. great mental power. 3. person with such powers.

gĕn'ȯ·cīde'', *n.* willful killing of a whole race or nation.

gĕn·tēel', *adj.* overrefined. —gen·til'i·ty, *n.*

gĕn'tīle, *n.* 1. non-Jew. —*adj.* 2. non-Jewish.

gĕn'tle, *adj.* mild in manner or effect. —gen'tly, *adv.*

gĕn'tle·mȧn, *n.* 1. Also, *fem.,* gen'tle·wom''an, man of the upper class. 2. well-mannered man.

gĕn'trȳ, *n.* persons of the upper class.

gĕn'ū·flĕct'', *v.i.* bend the knee in homage. —gen''u·flec'tion, *n.*

gĕn'ū·ine, *adj.* 1. true; real. 2. sincere. —gen'u·ine·ly, *adv.* —gen'u·ine·ness, *n.*

gē'nŭs, *n., pl.* genera, genuses. 1. type. 2. *Biology.* distinctive group of plant or animal species.

gė·ŏg'rȧ·phȳ, *n., pl.* -phies. 1. study of the earth or its features. 2. terrain. —ge''o·graph'i·cal, ge''o·graph'ic, *adj.* —ge·og'ra·pher, *n.*

gė·ŏl'ȯ·gȳ, *n.* study of the earth's crust. —ge''o·log'ic, ge''o·log'i·cal, *adj.*

gė·ŏm'e·trȳ, *n., pl.* -tries. study of points, lines, planes, and solids. —ge''o·met'ric, ge''o·met'ri·cal, *adj.*

gē''ō·phŷs'ĭcs, *n.* study of the effects of climate, etc. on the earth.

gĕr''ĭ·ăt'rĭcs, *n.* branch of medicine dealing with old age. —ger''i·at'ric, *adj.*

gêrm, *n.* 1. disease-causing organism. 2. origin.

gêr·māne', *adj.* relevant.

gêr'mĭ·cīde'', *n.* destroyer of germs. —ger''mi·ci'dal, *adj.*

gêr'mĭ·nāte'', *v.,* -nated, -nating. *v.i., v.t.* sprout. —ger''mi·na'tion, *n.*

gĕr'rȳ·măn''dêr, *v.t.* manipulate election districts so as to favor one side.

gĕs'tāte, *v.t.,* -tated, -tating. bear in the uterus. —ges·ta'tion, *n.*

gĕs·tĭc'ū·lāte'', *v.i.,* -lated, -lating. make gestures. —ges·tic·u·la'tion, *n.*

gĕs'tūre, *v.i.,* -tured, -turing, *n. v.i.* 1. move the hands, arms, etc. as a signal. —*n.* 2. act or instance of gesturing. 3. act intended to impress others.

gĕt, *v.,* got, gotten, getting. *v.t.* 1. take or receive. 2. cause to be or do. —*v.i.* 3. become. 4. go or arrive.

geȳ'sêr, *n.* natural eruption of water or steam.

ghăst'lȳ, *adj.,* -lier, -liest. 1. horrible. 2. ghostlike. —ghast'li·ness, *n.*

ghêr'kĭn, *n.* small pickle.

ghĕt'tō, *n., pl.* -tos, -toes. neighborhood populated by particular minority ethnic group.

ghŏst, *n.* spirit from the dead. —ghost'ly, *adj.*

ghoŭl, *n.* 1. robber of the dead. 2. person morbidly fascinated by disasters. —ghoul'ish, *adj.*

GI, *n., pl.* GI's, GIs, *adj. n.* enlisted man. —*adj.* 2. government issue.

gī'ȧnt, *n.* 1. greatly oversized creature or thing. —*adj.* 2. gigantic. Also, *fem.,* gi'ant·ess.

gĭb'bêr, *v.i.* make incoherent utterances. —gib'ber·ish, *n.*

gībe, *v.i.,* gibed, gibing, *n.* jeer.

gĭb'lĕt, *n.* internal organ of fowl.

gĭd'dȳ, *adj.,* -dier, -diest. 1. dizzy. 2. frivolous.

gĭft, *n.* 1. something given. 2. natural ability.

gĭft'ĕd, *adj.* intelligent or talented.

gī·găn'tĭc, *adj.* huge.

gĭg'gle, *v.i.,* -gled, -gling, *n. v.i.* 1. laugh in a quick, high-pitched way. —*n.* 2. act or instance of giggling.

gĭld, *v.t.,* gilded or gilt, gilding. cover with gold leaf. —gilt, *adj.*

gĭll, *n.* 1. (jil) quarter of a pint; 4 fluid ounces. 2. (gill) breathing apparatus of a fish, etc.

gĭm′lĕt, *n.* small boring tool.

gĭm′mick, *n. Informal.* gadget.

gĭn, *n., v.t.*, **ginned, ginning**. *n.* 1. distilled grain liquor. 2. cotton seed remover. —*v.t.* 3. process with a cotton gin.

gĭn′gêr, *n.* tropical spice. —**gin′ger·y**, *adj.*

gĭn′gêr·lў, *adj.* 1. cautious. —*adv.* 2. cautiously.

gĭng′hăm, *n.* checked or striped cotton.

gĭ·răffe′, *n.* long-necked, long-legged African animal.

gîrd, *v.t.*, **girded** or **girt, girding**. surround, as with a belt.

gîrd′êr, *n.* major structural beam.

gîr′dle, *n., v.t.*, **-dled, -dling**. *n.* 1. woman's undergarment. 2. belt. —*v.t.* 3. encircle.

gîrl, *n.* young female. —**girl′hood**″, *n.* —**girl′ish**, *adj.*

gîrth, *n.* circumference.

gĭst, *n.* basic meaning or content.

gĭve, *v.*, **gave, given, giving**, *n. v.t.* 1. transfer. 2. make a present of. 3. supply or afford. 4. concede. —*v.i.* 5. yield, as to force. —*n.* 6. compressibility. —**giv′er**, *n.*

gĭv′ĕn, *adj.* 1. specified. 2. granted. 3. habituated.

glā′cĭal, *adj.* icy.

glā′cĭer, *n.* broad, moving mass of ice.

glăd, *adj.*, **gladder, gladdest**. 1. happy. 2. quite willing. —**glad′ly**, *adv.* —**glad′ness**, *n.* —**glad′den**, *v.t., v.i.*

glāde, *n.* open space in a forest.

glăd′ĭ·ā′tŏr, *n.* swordsman in ancient Roman contests.

glăd″ĭ·ō′lŭs, *n., pl.* **-luses, -li**. flower with spikes of funnel-shaped blossoms. Also, **glad″i·o′la**.

glăm′ŏr, *n.* mysterious charm. Also, **glam′our**. —**glam′or·ous**, *adj.* —**glam′or·ize**, *v.t.*

glănce, *v.t.*, **glanced, glancing**, *n. v.i.* 1. look briefly. 2. ricochet. —*n.* 3. act or instance of glancing.

glănd, *n.* bodily organ that extracts and processes elements in the blood. —**glan′du·lar**, *adj.*

glāre, *n., v.i.*, **glared, glaring**. *n.* 1. dazzling brightness. 2. furious look. —*v.i.* 3. cast a glare.

glâr′ĭng, *adj.* 1. dazzlingly bright. 2. ostentatious; loud. 3. flagrant.

glăss, *n.* 1. substance of fused silicates. 2. object of this substance. 3. object with a lens or lenses. 4. **glasses**, lenses in a frame, used to aid vision. —**glass′ful**, *n.* —**glas′sy**, *adj.*

glāze, *v.t.*, **glazed, glazing**, *n. v.t.* 1. fill with glass, as a window. 2. put a glassy coating on. —*v.i.* 3. become glassy. —*n.* 4. glassy coating.

glā′zĭer, *n.* person who glazes windows.

glēam, *n.* 1. beam of light. —*v.i.* 2. emit a gleam.

glēan, *adj.* gather.

glēe, *n.* joy. —**glee′ful**, *adj.*

glĕn, *n.* isolated, small valley.

glĭb, *adj.*, **glibber, glibbest**. unconvincingly ready with explanations. —**glib′ly**, *adv.* —**glib′ness**, *n.*

glīde, *v.*, **glided, gliding**, *n. v.i., v.t.* slider. —*n.* 2. act or instance of gliding.

glīd′êr, *n.* unpowered aircraft.

glĭm′mêr, *n., v.i.* gleam.

glĭmpse, *v.t.*, **-glimpsed, glimpsing**, *n. v.t.* 1. see briefly or in part. —*n.* 2. act or instance of glimpsing.

glĭnt, *v.i., n.* gleam or glitter.

glĭs′tĕn, *v.i.* reflect with a dull shine.

glĭtch, *n.* (computers) a problem or error in a program.

glĭt′têr, *v.i.* 1. shine or reflect brightly. —*n.* 2. act or instance of glittering.

glōam′ĭng, *n.* evening twilight.

glōat, *v.i.* experience proud or malicious pleasure.

glōbe, *n.* 1. the earth. 2. model of the earth. 3. spherical object. —**glob′al**, *adj.*

glŏb′ūle, *n.* tiny ball or drop. —**glob′u·lar**, *adj.*

glōōm, *n.* 1. darkness. 2. sadness or dreariness. —**gloom′y**, *adj.*

glō′rĭ·fў″, *v.t.*, **-fied, -fying**. 1. give glory to. 2. exaggerate the importance or worth of. —**glo″ri·fi·ca′tion**, *n.*

glō′rў, *n., pl.* **-ries**, *v.i.*, **-ried, -rying**. *n.* 1. high honor. 2. splendor or splendid feature. —*v.i.* 3. take pride. —**glo′ri·ous**, *adj.*

glŏss, *n.* 1. sheen. 2. explanation. —**glos′sy**, *adj.*

glŏs'sà·rў, *n., pl.* **-ries.** list of terms with definitions.

glŏve *n.* garment for the hand.

glŏw, *v.i.* **1.** give off soft light or color. —*n.* **2.** act or instance of glowing.

glŏw'êr, *v.i.* stare threateningly.

glŭ'cōse, *n.* sugar in fruit and honey.

glŭe, *n., v.t.*, **glued, gluing.** *n.* **1.** adhesive substance. —*v.t.* **2.** fasten with glue.

glŭm, *adj.*, **glummer, glummest.** gloomy; moody. —**glum'ly**, *adv.*

glŭt, *v.*, **glutted, glutting**, *n., v.i.* **1.** eat to excess. —*v.t.* **2.** satiate. **3.** oversupply. —*n.* **4.** act or instance of glutting.

glŭ'tĭ·noŭs, *adj.* sticky.

glŭt'tón, *n.* person who overeats. —**glut'ton·ous**, *adj.* —**glut'ton·y**, *n.*

glў'cêr·ĭn, *n.* liquid derived from fats and oils. Also, **gly'cer·ine.**

gnârled, *adj.* twisted or knotted, like a tree trunk.

gnăsh, *v.t.* grind together, as the teeth, with anger or frustration.

gnăt, *n.* small, stinging insect.

gnăw, *v.t., v.i.* bite away gradually.

gnōme, *n.* dwarf who guards treasure. —**gnom'ish**, *adj.*

gō, *v.i.*, **went, going**, *n., pl.* **goes.** *v.i.* **1.** leave. **2.** operate. **3.** belong. **4.** become.

gōad, *n., v.t.* prod.

gōal, *n.* **1.** object to be reached or attained. **2.** *Sports.* area to be defended.

gōat, *n.* horned, cud-chewing mammal.

gōat·ēe', *n.* small, pointed beard.

gŏb'ble, *v.*, **-bled, -bling**, *n. v.t.* **1.** eat greedily. —*v.i.* **2.** make turkeylike sounds. —*n.* **3.** sound of a turkey.

gŏb'ble·dў·gōok', *n. Informal.* jargon.

gō'-bè·twēen'', *n.* arranger of bargains between others.

gŏb'lĕt, *n.* stemmed, deep-bowled drinking vessel.

gŏb'lĭn, *n.* evil supernatural being.

gŏd, *n.* **1.** one of the supreme beings. **2.** **God**, the Supreme Being. Also, *fem.*, **god'dess.** —**god'hood''**, *n.* —**god'less**, *adj.*

gŏd'chĭld'', *n.* child sponsored in religion by a godparent.

gŏd'hĕad'', *n.* **1.** godhood. **2.** **the Godhead**, God.

gŏd'lў, *adj.*, **-lier, -liest.** devout. —**god'li·ness**, *n.*

gŏd'păr''ènt, *n.* sponsor of a godchild. Also, *masc.*, **god'fa''ther**, *fem.*, **god'mother.**

gŏd'sĕnd'', *n.* piece of good luck.

gŏg'gle, *v.i.*, **-gled, -gling** *n. v.i.* **1.** stare with eyes bulging. —*n.* **2.** **goggles**, protective glasses.

gō'ĭng, *adj.* **1.** current. **2.** operative. —*n.* **3.** departure. **4.** conditions.

goī'têr, *n.* enlargement of the thyroid gland. Also, **goi'tre.**

gōld, *n.* soft, yellow, precious metallic element. —**gold'en**, *adj.*

gōld'èn·rŏd'', *n.* plant with tiny yellow flowers.

gōldèn rūle, do unto others as you would have others do unto you.

gōld'fĭsh'', *n.* small yellow-orange fish.

gŏlf, *n.* outdoor game played with balls knocked from ground level with clubs. —**golf'er**, *n.*

gō'nǎd, *n.* animal reproductive organ.

gŏn'dō·là, *n.* **1.** one-oared Venetian boat. **2.** low-sided railroad freight car. **3.** airship cabin. —**gon''do·lier'**, *n.*

gŏng, *n.* thin brass disk beaten to produce sound.

gŏn''ôr·rhē'à, *n.* a venereal disease.

gŏŏd, *adj.*, **better, best**, *n. adj.* **1.** right; proper. **2.** kind. **3.** beneficial. —*n.* **5.** good purpose or result. **6. goods**, valuable objects or material.

gŏŏd''-bye', *interj.* **1.** (departing salutation). —*n.* **2.** saying of good-bye. Also, **good'-by'.**

Gŏŏd Frĭdǎy, Friday before Easter.

gŏŏd'lў, *adj.*, **-lier, -liest. 1.** considerable in amount. **2.** good. **3.** good-looking.

gŏŏf, *Informal. n.* **1.** blunderer. **2.** blunder. —**goof'y**, *adj.*

gōose, *n., pl.* **geese.** web-footed ducklike bird.

gō'phêr, *n.* **1.** burrowing rodent. **2.** prairie squirrel.

gōre, *n., v.t.*, **gored, goring.** *n.* **1.** blood. **2.** triangular segment. —*v.t.* **3.** pierce, as with a horn. —**gor'y**, *adj.*

gŏrge, *n., v.*, **gorged, gorging.** *n.* **1.** narrow canyon. **2.** gullet. —*v.t.* **3.** glut. —*v.i.* **4.** eat greedily.

gŏr'geoŭs, *adj.* dazzlingly attractive.

gȯ·rĭl'là, *n.* powerful manlike African ape.

Gŏs′pĕl, *n.* **1.** teachings of Jesus and the Apostles.

gŏs′să·mĕr, *adj.* **1.** light and frail. —*n.* **2.** cobweb.

gŏs′sĭp, *n.* **1.** rumors and conjectures about others. **2.** person who originates or spreads these. —*v.i.* **3.** engage in gossip. —**gos′sip·y**, *adj.*

gŏuge, *n.*, *v.t.*, **gouged, gouging.** *n.* **1.** chisel for cutting grooves. —*v.t.* **2.** cut out with a scooping motion.

goŭ′lăsh, *n.* stew seasoned with paprika.

gôurd, *n.* decorative fruit of the squash or melon family.

goŭr′mănd, *n.* heavy eater and drinker.

gour′met (gŏōr mā′), *n.* connoisseur of food and drink.

gŏut, *n.* illness causing pain in the joints. —**gout′y**, *adj.*

gŏv′ĕrn, *v.t.* **1.** have authority over. **2.** guide. **3.** determine.

gŏv′ĕrn·mĕnt, *n.* **1.** system for running a country. **2.** group in political control. —**gov″ern·men′tal**, *adj.*

gŏv′ĕr·nŏr, *n.* **1.** supreme local official. **2.** device for controlling machinery speed. —**gov′er·nor·ship**, *n.*

gŏwn, *n.* long outer garment.

grăb, *v.t.*, *v.i.*, **grabbed, grabbing**, *n.* snatch.

grāce, *n.*, *v.t.*, **graced, gracing.** *n.* **1.** beauty of form, movement or manner. **2.** kindness or favor. **3.** prayer before a meal. —*v.t.* **4.** add grace to, as by being present. —**grace′ful**, *adj.* —**grace′less**, *adj.*

grā′cioŭs, *adj.* **1.** charming in manner. **2.** kind. **3.** discriminatingly luxurious.

grăck′le, *n.* crowlike blackbird.

grā·dā′tion, *n.* succession of increasing or decreasing amounts, etc.

grāde, *n.*, *v.t.*, **graded, grading.** n. **1.** step in a progressive series. **2.** Also, **gra′di·ent**, slope. —*v.t.* **3.** assign a grade to. **4.** give a level to, as a road.

grăd′u·ăl, *adj.* in small amounts. —**grad′u·al·ly**, *adv.*

grăd′u·āte″, *v.*, **-ated, -ating**, *n.*, *adj.* *v.t.* **1.** leave after satisfying academic requirements. **2.** certify as having satisfied requirements. **3.** divide into grades. —*n.* (grad′yŏŏ et) **4.** person

who has graduated. —*adj.* **5.** postbaccalaureate. —**grad″u·a′tion**, *n.*

grăf·fi·tō, *n.*, *pl.* **-ti.** writing or drawing by a passer-by.

grăft, *n.* **1.** transplant of organic material. **2.** dishonest use of public funds. —*v.t.* **3.** transplant. **4.** obtain by graft.

grāin, *n.* **1.** hard seed, as of wheat. **2.** hard particle. **3.** pattern of fiber, as in wood.

grăm, *n.* metric unit of weight, about ¹⁄₂₈ of an ounce. Also, **gramme.**

grăm′măr, *n.* forms and arrangement of words. —**gram·mat′i·cal**, *adj.*

grăn′á·rÿ, *n.*, *pl.* **-ries.** place for storing grain.

grănd, *adj.* **1.** impressive. **2.** illustrious. —**grand′ly**, *adv.* —**gran′deur**, *n.*

grănd′chĭld″, *n.* child of a son or daughter. Also, *masc.*, **grand′son″**, *fem.*, **grand′daugh″ter.**

grăn·dĭl′ó·quĕnt, *adj.* pretentious in speech. —**gran·dil′o·quence**, *n.*

grăn′dī·ōse″, *adj.* **1.** full of grandeur. **2.** pompous.

grănd′păr″ĕnt, *n.* parent of a parent. Also, *masc.*, **grand′fa″ther**, *fem.*, **grand′moth″er.**

grănd′stănd″, *n.* stand for spectators at sporting events.

grăn′īte, *n.* grainy igneous rock.

grănt, *v.t.* **1.** give. **2.** admit. —*n.* **3.** something granted.

grăn′ū·lāte″, *v.t.*, **-lated, -lating.** form as or in granules.

grăn′ūle, *n.* small particle. —**gran′u·lar**, *adj.*

grāpe, *n.* small juicy fruit.

grāpe′frŭit″, *n.* large, sharp-tasting citrus fruit.

grăph, *n.* two-dimensional visual representation of interrelated data.

grăph′ĭc, *adj.* **1.** pertaining to two-dimensional visual art. **2.** vividly realistic.

grăph′īte, *n.* soft carbon used as a writing material or lubricant.

grăp′ple, *v.*, **-pled, -pling.** *v.i.* **1.** wrestle; struggle. —*v.t.* **2.** grasp and hold.

grăsp, *v.t.* **1.** take hold of with the hand; clutch. **2.** comprehend. —*v.i.* **3.** make clutching motions. —*n.* **4.** act or instance of grasping. **5.** ability to grasp.

grăsp′ĭng, *adj.* avaricious.

grâss, *n*. 1. narrow-leafed green plant with seedlike fruit. **—gras'sy**, *adj*.

grâss'hŏp''pêr, *n*. jumping, plant-eating insect.

grâte, *v*., **grated, grating**, *n*. *v.t*. 1. scrape into particles. 2. grind. **—***v.i*. 3. grind or rasp. 4. be irritating. **—***n*. 5. Also, **grat' ing**, framework of metal, etc. bars. **—grat'er**, *n*.

grāte'fŭl, *adj*. 1. appreciative of favors. 2. welcome.

grăt'ĭ·fy'', *adj*. **-fied, -fying**. be pleasing to. **—grat''i·fi·ca'tion**, *n*.

grā'tĭs, *adj*. free of charge.

grăt'ĭ·tūde'', *n*. appreciation for favors.

grá·tū'ĭ·toŭs, *adj*. 1. gratis. 2. uncalled-for.

grá·tū'ĭ·tỹ, *n*., *pl*. **-ties**. gift, esp. a tip.

grāve, *adj*. 1. solemn. 2. important; serious. **—***n*. 2. place of burial.

grăv'ĕl, *n*. mixture of stone fragments. **—grav'el·ly**, *adj*.

grăv'ĭ·tāte'', *v.i*., **-tated, -tating**. 1. move by gravity. 2. move or tend naturally. **—grav''i·ta'tion**, *n*. **—grav''i·ta'tion·al**, *adj*.

grăv'ĭ·tỹ, *n*. 1. seriousness. 2. pull toward the center of the earth.

grā'vỹ, *n*., *pl*. **-ies**. meat juice, or a sauce from this.

grāy, *adj*. 1. mixed black and white. 2. dreary.

grāy măttêr, 1. brain tissue. 2. *Informal*. intelligence.

grāze, *v*., **grazed, grazing**. *v.t*. *v.i*. 1. scrape in passing. **—***v.i*. 2. feed on grasses.

grēase, *n*., *v.t*., **greased, greasing**. *n*. (grēs). 1. thick, fatty or oily substance. **—***v.t*. (grēz) 2. coat or lubricate with grease. **—greas'y**, *adj*.

grēat, *adj*. 1. large. 2. eminent. **—great' ly**, *adv*.

grēed, *n*. excessive passion for money, food, etc. **—greed'y**, *adj*.

grēen, *n*. 1. color of leaves and plants. 2. **greens**, leafy vegetables. **—***adj*. 3. of the color green. 4. unripened or unprocessed.

grēen'êr·ỹ, *n*. plant life.

grēen'hoŭse'', *n*. glazed building for growing plants.

grēet, *v.t*. 1. acknowledge meeting. 2. re-

ceive in a specified way. **—greet'ing**, *n*.

grē·gär'ĭ·oŭs, *adj*. associating with others of one's kind.

grē·nāde'', *n*. small hand bomb.

grĕn'á·dĭne'', *n*. pomegranate syrup.

grey, *adj*. gray.

grey'hoŭnd'', *n*. fast, slender hound.

grĭd, *n*. system of crisscrossed elements.

grĭd'dle, *n*. pan for cooking pancakes, etc.

grĭd'ĭrŏn'', *n*. 1. broiling frame. 2. football field.

grĭd'lŏck, *n*. severe, urban traffic jam.

grĭef, *n*. 1. great unhappiness. 2. ruin; failure.

grĭev'ánce, *n*. 1. cause for complaint. 2. complaint.

grĭeve, *v*., **grieved, grieving** *v.i*. 1. suffer grief. **—***v.t*. 2. cause grief to.

grĭev'oŭs, *adj*. 1. seriously injurious. 2. being in grief.

grĭll, *n*. 1. gridiron. 2. broiled dish. **—***v.t*. 3. broil. 4. *Informal*. question severely.

grĭlle, *n*. open screen; grating. **—grille'work''**, *n*.

grĭm, *adj*., **grimmer, grimmest**. 1. harsh. 2. menacing. **—grim'ly**, *adv*.

grĭ'măce, *n*., *v.i*., **-maced, -macing**. *n*. 1. smirk, esp. of displeasure. **—***v.i*. 2. give such a smirk.

grĭme, *n*. clinging dirt. **—grim'y** *adj*.

grĭn, *n*. *v.i*., **grinned, grinning**. *n*. 1. broad, toothy smile. **—***v.i*. 2. give such a smile.

grĭnd, *v.t*., **ground, grinding**. 1. wear down with pressure or friction. 2. turn the crank of. **—grind'er**, *n*.

grĭp, *v.t*., **gripped, gripping**, *n*. *v.t*. 1. grasp firmly. **—***n*. 2. firm grasp. 3. handle. 4. small piece of luggage.

grĭpe, *v*., **griped, griping**, *n*. *v.t*. 1. produce pain in the bowels. **—***v.i*. 2. *Informal*. complain. **—***n*. 3. pain in the bowels. 4. *Informal*. complaint.

grĭs'lỹ, *adj*., **-lier, -liest**. horrible.

grĭst, *n*. grain for grinding. **—grist'mill''**, *n*.

grĭs'tle, *n*. cartilage. **—gris'tly**, *adv*.

grĭt, *n*., *v.t*., **gritted, gritting**. *n*. 1. rough, hard particles. 2. fortitude. **—***v.t*. 3. grind together, as the teeth. **—grit'ty**, *adj*.

grĭts, *n*. *pl*. coarsely ground grain.

grĭz'zlĕd, *adj*. with gray hair.

grĭz'zlў, *adj*. **-zlier, -zliest**, *n. adj*. **1**. grayish. —*n*. **2**. Also, **grizzly bear**, large, ferocious American bear.

grōan, *n*. **1**. deep utterance, as of pain. —*v.i*. **2**. give such an utterance.

grō'cêr, *n*. food merchant. —**gro'cer·y**, *n*.

grŏg'gў, *adj*. **-gier, -giest**. befuddled.

grōĭn, *n*. junction of the abdomen and thighs.

grŏm'mĕt, *n*. eyelet.

grōōm, *n*. **1**. man at his wedding. **2**. tender of horses. —*v.t*. **3**. comb, etc. to make tidy.

grōōve, *n., v.t.,* **grooved, grooving**. *n*. **1**. long, shallow depression. —*v.t*. **2**. make a groove in.

grōpe, *v.i.,* **groped, groping**. feel for something blindly.

grŏss, *adj*. **1**. coarse. **2**. flagrant. **3**. before deductions. —*n*. **4**. *pl*. **gross**, quantity of 144.

grō·tĕsque', *adj*. fantastically distorted.

grŏt'tō, *n., pl*. **-tos, -toes**. cave.

grōŭch, *v.i*. **1**. sulk. —*n*. **2**. sulky mood. **3**. person who sulks. —**grouch'y**, *adj*.

grōŭnd, *n*. **1**. solid surface of the earth. **2**. earth. **3**. **grounds**, **a**. basis. **b**. land of an estate or institution. **c**. dregs of coffee, etc. —*v.t*. **4**. instruct in rudiments.

grōŭnd'hŏg'', *n*. woodchuck.

grōŭnd'lĕss, *adj*. without reason.

grōŭnd'wŏrk'', *n*. basic or preparatory work.

grōŭp, *n*. **1**. number of persons or things considered together. *v.t., v.i*. **2**. form into a group or groups.

grōŭse, *n., pl*. **grouse**, *v.i.,* **groused, grousing**. *n*. **1**. plump game bird. —*v.i*. **2**. complain.

grōve, *n*. cluster of trees.

grŏv'ĕl, *v.i.,* **-eled, -eling**. **1**. crouch low or crawl. **2**. behave servilely.

grōw, *v.,* **grew, grown, growing**. *v.i*. **1**. become. **2**. develop. —*v.t*. **3**. cause to live, as plants. —**grow''er**, *n*. —**growth**, *n*.

grōwl, *n*. **1**. low, rumbling vocal noise. —*v.i*. **2**. make such a noise.

grōwn'-ŭp', *adj., n*. adult.

grŭb, *v.,* **grubbed, grubbing**, *n. v.i., v.t*.

1. dig. —*n*. **2**. beetle larva. **3**. drudge. **4**. *Informal*. food.

grŭb'bў, *adj*. **-bier, -biest**. nastily dirty.

grŭdge, *n., v.t.,* **grudged, grudging**. *n*. **1**. long-held resentment. —*v.t*. **2**. begrudge. —**grudg'ing·ly**, *adv*.

grŭ'el·ing, *adj*. exhausting; very tiring.

grŭe'sŏme, *adj*. horrifying or loathsome.

grŭff, *adj*. curt.

grŭm'ble, *v.i*. **-bled, -bling**. complain in a suppressed manner.

grŭm'pў, *adj*. **-pier, -piest**. surly.

grŭnt, *n*. **1**. throaty sound caused by exertion, etc. —*v.i*. **2**. utter such a sound.

guăr''ăn·tēe', *n., v.t.,* **-teed, -teeing**. *n*. **1**. firm assurance. **2**. promise to make good if necessary. —*v.t*. **3**. assure with a guarantee. Also, **guar'an·ty**. —**guar'an·tor''**.

guârd, *v.t., v.i*. **1**. watch, esp. in order to protect or confine. —*n*. **2**. person or group that guards. **3**. protection. **4**. protective device.

guârd'ĕd, *adj*. cautious.

guârd'ĭ·ăn, *n*. **1**. person who guards. **2**. person responsible for a minor or incompetent. —**guard'ian·ship''**, *n*.

gū''bêr·nȧ·tô'rĭ·ăl, *adj*. pertaining to governors.

guêr·rĭl'lȧ, *n*. irregular soldier using surprise tactics.

guĕss, *v.t*. **1**. form an opinion about without knowing. —*n*. **2**. act or instance of guessing. —**guess'work''**, *n*.

guĕst, *n*. **1**. enjoyer of hospitality. **2**. customer of a hotel, etc.

gŭf·făw', *n*. **1**. raucous laugh. —*v.i*. **2**. emit such a laugh.

guīde, *v.t.,* **guided, guiding**, *n. v.t*. **1**. tell how to proceed. —*n*. **2**. person or thing that guides. —**guid'ance**, *n*.

guīle, *n*. unscrupulous cunning.

guĭlt, *n*. **1**. responsibility for a wrong action. **2**. shame. —**guilt'y**, *adj*.

guĭn'ĕa pĭg, **1**. small, fat rodent. **2**. subject of an experiment.

guīse, *n*. semblance; false face.

guĭ·târ', *n*. six-stringed plucked instrument. —**gui·tar'ist**, *n*.

gŭlch, *n*. deep narrow ravine.

gŭlf, *n*. **1**. ocean area partly surrounded by land. **2**. wide deep void.

gŭll, *n*. light-colored soaring water bird.

gŭl′lĕt, *n.* throat.

gŭl′li·ble, *adj.* credulous. **—gul″li·bil′i·ty,** *n.*

gŭl′lў, *n., pl.* **-lies.** narrow ravine.

gŭlp, *v.t., v.i.* **1.** swallow hastily. **—n. 2.** act or instance of gulping.

gŭm, *n., v.t.,* **gummed, gumming.** *n.* **1.** sticky, semisolid substance. **2.** area of flesh surrounding teeth. *—v.t.* **3.** stick with gum.

gŭmp′tion, *n.* **1.** enterprise. **2.** common sense.

gŭn, *n., v.,* **gunned, gunning.** *n.* **1.** weapon shooting a missile by means of an explosive charge. *—v.t., v.i.* **2.** hunt with a gun. **—gun′ner·y,** *n.*

gŭnk, *n. Informal.* viscous substance.

gŭn′nў, *n.* coarse cloth of jute or hemp.

gŭn′pŏw″dĕr, *n.* explosive used in guns.

gun·wale (gun′l), *n.* upper edge of a ship's side.

gûr′gle, *v.i.,* **-gled, -gling,** *n. v.i.* **1.** emit a bubbling sound in flowing. *—n.* **2.** such a sound.

gū′rū, *n.* Hindu spiritual teacher.

gŭsh, *v.i.* **1.** flow out abundantly. **2.** express oneself effusively. *—n.* **3.** act or instance of gushing. **—gush′y,** *adj.*

gŭs′sĕt, *n.* triangular reinforcement.

gŭst, *n.* **1.** strong puff of air. **2.** sudden outburst. **—gust′y,** *adj.*

gŭs′tà·tô″rў, *adj.* pertaining to the sense of taste.

gŭs′tō, *n.* great enjoyment or vigor.

gŭt, *n., v.t.,* **gutted, gutting.** *n.* **1.** intestine. **2.** guts, *Informal.* courage. *—v.t.* **3.** destroy the inside of.

gŭt′tĕr, *n.* **1.** channel for rain water. **2.** realm of sordidness. *—v.t.* **3.** splutter before being extinguished, as a candle.

gŭt′tŭr·ȧl, *adj.* pertaining to or produced in the throat.

guў, *n.* **1.** *Informal.* male person. **2.** Also, **guy′wire″,** steadying wire.

gŭz′zle, *v.i., v.t.,* **-zled, -zling.** drink greedily.

gỹm′nā′sǐ·ŭm, *n., pl.* **-ums, -a.** place for physical exercise. Also, *Informal.* **gym.**

gỹm′nǎs′tǐcs, *n. pl.* physical exercises. **—gym′nast**, *n.* **—gym·nas′tic,** *adj.*

gỹ″′nĕ·cŏl′ȯ·gỹ, *n.* branch of medicine concerned with women's diseases. **—gy″ne·col′o·gist,** *n.*

gўp, *n., v.t.,* **gypped, gypping.** *Informal.* swindle.

gўp′sŭm, *n.* sulfate of calcium, used to make plaster of Paris.

gȳ·rāte′, *v.i.,* **-rated, -rating.** whirl. **—gy·ra′tion** *n.*

gȳ′rȯ·scōpe″, *n.* object maintaining its position by the inertia of a rapidly turned wheel. **—gy″ro·scop′ic,** *adj.*

H

H, h, *n.* eighth letter of the English alphabet.

hăb′ĭt, *n.* **1.** custom, esp. one hard to depart from. **2.** distinctive costume. **—ha·bit′u·ȧl,** *adj.* **—ha·bit′u·ate″,** *v.t.*

hăb′ĭt·à·ble, *adj.* able to be lived in.

hăb″ĭ·tät″, *n.* usual area of habitation.

hăb″ĭ·tā′tion, *n.* home.

hăck, *v.i., v.t.* **1.** chop roughly. *—v.i.* **2.** cough hoarsely. *—n.* **3.** artistic drudge.

hăck′ĕr, *n.* a computer enthusiast.

hăck′sǎw″, *n.* frame-mounted metal-cutting saw.

hăd′dock, *n., pl.* **-dock, -docks.** Atlantic codlike fish.

Hā′dēs, *n.* hell. Also, **ha′dēs.**

hăft, *n.* knife or ax handle.

hăg, *n.* ugly old woman.

hăg′gȧrd, *adj.* weary-looking.

hăg′gle, *v.i.,* **-gled, -gling.** dispute over a price.

hāil, *v.t.* **1.** greet loudly. **2.** shout to. **3.** welcome as desirable. **4.** shower heavily. *—n.* **5.** frozen rain in small balls. **—hail′stone″,** *n.*

hāir, *n.* **1.** slender growth from the skin. **2.** these growths collectively. **—hair′y,** *adj.* **—hair′i·ness,** *n.*

hāir′rāis″ĭng, *adj.* terrifying.

hāir′splĭt″tĭng, *n.* making of trivial distinctions.

hăl′cỹ″ŏn, *adj.* idyllic.

hāle, *adj., v.t.,* **haled, haling.** *adj.* **1.** full of health and vigor. *—v.t.* **2.** summon forcibly.

hȧlf, *n., pl.* **halves,** *adj., adv. n.* **1.** one of two equal divisions. —*adj.* **2.** being a half. —*adv.* **3.** as far as a half.

hälf'-brēed'', *n.* child of parents from different races.

hälf-heärt'ed, *adj.* without enthusiasm or determination. —**half'-heart'ed·ly**, *adv.*

hälf'wāy', *adj.*, *adv.* **1.** at or to a midpoint. **2.** to a partial extent.

hälf'wĭt'', *n.* person of subnormal intelligence. —**half'wit'ted**, *adj.*

häl'ĭ·bŭt, *n.*, *pl.* **-but, -buts.** northern saltwater flatfish.

häl''ĭ-tō'sĭs, *n.* bad breath.

häll, *n.* **1.** large room, as for meetings. Also, **hall'way''**, corridor or vestibule.

häl''lĕ·lū'jäh, *interj.* praise the Lord! Also, **hal''le·lu'iah.**

häl'lōw, *v.t.* sanctify.

Häl''lōw·ēen', *n.* eve of All Saints' Day, celebrated October 31. Also, **Hal''low·e'en'.**

häl·lū''cĭ·nā'tion, *n.* deluded perceptions of a nonexistent sight, sound, etc. —**hal·lu'ci·nate''**, *v.i.* —**hal·lu'ci·na·to''ry**, *adj.*

hā'lō, *n.*, *pl.* **-los, -loes.** ring of light, as around the portrayed head of a holy person.

hält, *v.t.*, *v.i.*, *n.* stop.

häl'têr, *n.* line for securing an animal.

hälve, *v.t.*, **halved, halving. 1.** divide into halves. **2.** reduce by half.

häm, *n.* upper part of a hog's hind leg.

häm'bûr''gêr, *n.* sandwich of ground beef in a bun. Also, **ham'burg.**

häm'lĕt, *n.* small village.

häm'mêr, *n.* **1.** device for beating or driving with blows. —*v.t.*, *v.i.* **2.** strike with repeated blows.

häm'mŏck, *n.* flexible bed suspended at the ends.

häm'pêr, *v.t.*, **1.** encumber. —*n.* **2.** covered basket.

händ, *n.* **1.** extremity of the arm. **2.** active part. **3.** hired worker. **4.** handwriting. **5.** side or direction. —*v.t.* **6.** give with the hand. —**hand'ful**, *n.*

händ'bäll'', *n.* game with a thrown rubber ball.

händ'bŏŏk'', *n.* manual.

händ'cläsp'', *n.* handshake.

händ'gŭn'', *n.* pistol.

händ'ĭ·căp, *n.*, *v.t.*, **-capped, -capping.** *n.* **1.** hindrance. —*v.t.* **2.** hinder. **3.** disability.

händ'ĭ·wörk'', *n.* **1.** work done by hand. **2.** work done personally.

händ'kêr·chĭef'', *n.* small wiping cloth.

hän'dle, *n.*, *v.t.*, **-dled, -dling.** *n.* **1.** something to be grasped. —*v.t.* **2.** grasp, as in order to wield. **3.** manage or dominate. **4.** sell.

händ'ōut'', *n.* **1.** charitable gift. **2.** news release.

händ'-pĭck', *v.t.* **1.** pick by hand. **2.** choose carefully and individually.

händ'shāke'', *n.* friendly gripping and shaking of another's hand.

händ'sŏme'', *adj.* **1.** good-looking. **2.** generous.

händs'-ōn', *adj.* practical; making actual use of, as *hands-on training.*

händ'wrīt''ĭng, *n.* freehand writing. —**hand'writ''ten**, *adj.*

händ'ӯ, *adj.*, **-ier, -iest.** convenient. —**hand'i·ly**, *adv.* —**hand'i·ness**, *n.*

händ'ӯ·măn, *n.* man who does odd jobs.

häng, *v.*, **hung** or (for 2) **hanged, hanging**, *n. v.t.* **1.** hold up from above. **2.** kill by suspending from a rope around the neck. —*v.i.* **3.** be hung or hanged. —**hang'man**, *n.*

häng'är, *n.* aircraft shelter.

häng'dŏg'', *adj.* abject.

hän'kêr, *v.i.* yearn.

Hä'nŭ·kä'', *n. Judaism.* festival of the rededication of the Temple at Jerusalem. Also, **Ha'nuk·kah''.**

häp''häz'ärd, *adj.* **1.** random. —*adv.* **2.** by chance.

häp'lĕss, *adj.* unlucky.

häp'pĕn, *v.i.* come about by chance. —**hap'pen·ing**, *n.*

häp'pӯ, *adj.*, **-pier, -piest. 1.** feeling pleased. **2.** fortunate. —**hap'pi·ly**, *adv.* —**hap'pi·ness**, *n.*

hä·răngue', *n.*, *v.t.*, **-rangued, -ranguing.** *n.* **1.** long vehement speech. —*v.t.* **2.** deliver a harangue to.

hä·răss', *v.t.* trouble persistently. —**ha·rass'ment**, *n.*

här'bĭn·gêr, *n.* forerunner.

här'bôr, *n.* **1.** sheltered place for shipping. —*v.t.* **2.** shelter.

hârd, *adj.* **1.** unyielding. **2.** difficult.

—*adv.* 3. energetically. —**hard'en,** *v.t.,*
v.i.

hârd'-heârt'éd, *adj.* callous.

hârd'lў, *adv.* barely; scarcely.

hârd'ship, *n.* something hard to endure.

hârd'wāre, *n.* 1. tools, fasteners, etc. 2.
(computers) equipment, as microchips,
disk drives, printers, etc.

hâr'dў, *adj.* -**dier,** -**diest.** *n.* 1. of much
endurance. 2. vigorous. —**har'di·ly,**
adv.

hāre, *n.* rabbitlike mammal.

hā'rém, *n.* 1. women's quarters of a
Muslim house. 2. its inhabitants.

hârk, *v.i.* listen.

hârk'én, *v.i.* hearken.

hâr'lót, *n.* prostitute.

hârm, *n.* 1. injury. —*v.t.* 2. injure.
—**harm'ful,** *adj.* —**harm'ful·ly,** *adv.*
—**harm'less,** *adj.* —**harm'less·ly,** *adv.*

hâr·mŏn'ĭ·cà, *n.* mouth organ.

hâr'mŏ·nў, *n.* 1. pleasant combination. 2.
agreement; accord. —**har·mo'ni·ous,**
adj. —**har'mo·nize'',** *v.t., v.i.*

hâr'nĕss, *n.* 1. straps, etc. on an animal
that pulls or carries. —*v.t.* 2. put a harness on. 3. control the energy of.

hârp, *n.* 1. large plucked stringed instrument. —*v.i.* 2. speak tediously. —**harp'**
ist, *n.*

hâr·pōŏn, *n.* 1. spear for whales, etc.
—*v.t.* 2. spear with a harpoon.

hâr'rŏw, *n.* 1. device for breaking and lev-
eling plowed ground. —*v.t.* 2. work on
with a harrow. 3. cause anxiety to.

hâr'rў, *v.t.,* -**ried,** -**rying.** harass.

hârsh, *adj.* 1. unpleasantly rough. 2. severe. —**harsh'ly,** *adv.* —**harsh'ness,**
n.

hâr'vĕst, *n.* 1. occasion of gathering
crops. 2. crop gathered. —*v.t.* 3. gather
as a harvest. —**har'vest·er,** *n.*

hăsh, *v.t.* 1. chop finely for cooking. —*n.*
2. chopped mixture of meat and vegetables.

hăsp, *n.* bolted fastening fitted over a
shackle.

hăs'sle, *n., v.i.,* -**sled,** -**sling.** *Informal.*
squabble.

hăs'sŏck, *n.* cushionlike seat.

hāste, *n.* speed, esp. when excessive.
—**hast'y,** *adj.* —**hast'i·ly,** *adv.*

hās'tén, *v.t., v.i.* hurry.

hăt, *n.* head garment, esp. a formal one.

hătch, *v.t.* 1. bring forth from eggs. —*v.i.*
2. open to release young. —*n.* 3. Also,
hatch'way'', opening serving as a door
or window.

hătch'ét, *n.* short-handled chopping tool.

hāte, *v.t.,* **hated, hating.** *n. v.t.* 1. dislike
violently. *n.* 2. Also, **hat'red,** feeling of
hating.

hāte'fŭl, *adj.* to be hated.

hăugh'tў, *adj.* -**tier,** -**tiest.** arrogant.
—**haugh'ti·ness,** *n.* —**haugh'ti·ly,**
adv.

hāŭl, *v.t., v.i.* 1. pull. —*n.* 2. act or instance of hauling.

hăunch, *n.* area from upper thigh to but-
tock.

hăunt, *v.t.* 1. be often present at. —*n.* 2.
favorite place or resort.

hăve, *v.t.,* **had, having.** 1. own or possess.
2. acquire. 3. experience or engage in.
4. cause. 5. be obliged.

hā'vén, *n.* place of shelter.

hăv'ŏc, *n.* vast destruction.

hăwk, *n.* 1. bird of prey. —*v.t.* 2. peddle.

hăw'sér, *n.* mooring or towing rope.

hāy, *n.* grass, etc. dried as fodder.

hāy fēvér, allergy to pollen.

hāy'wīre'', *adv. Informal.* awry.

hăz'árd, *n., v.t.* risk. —**haz'ard·ous,**
adj.

hāze, *n., v.t.,* **hazed, hazing.** *n.* 1. light
mist or vapor. —*v.t.* 2. harass or humiliate, as in an initiation. —**haz'y,** *adj.*
—**haz'i·ly,** *adv.*

hāz'él, *n.* tree of the birch family. —**haz'**
el·nut'', *n.*

hē, *pron., pl.* **they,** *n., pl.* **they.** *pron.* 1.
the male person or animal mentioned.
—*n.* 2. often used when gender is not
known.

hĕad, *n.* 1. part of the body for thinking,
eating, seeing, etc. 2. director. 3. uppermost or working feature. —*adj.* 4. at or
against the head. —*v.t.* 5. direct. —*v.i.*
6. direct oneself. —**head'ache'',** *n.*

hĕad'ĭng, *n.* title or subtitle.

hĕad'līne'', *n.* title of a newspaper article.

hĕad'lŏng'', *adv., adj.* 1. with the head
first. 2. at reckless speed.

hĕad'-ŏn', *adj., adv.* with the front end or
ends foremost.

hĕad′quâr′′tẽrs, *n. pl.* main center of command.

hĕad′strŏng′′, *adj.* willful and impulsive.

hĕad′wāy′′, *n.* forward motion.

hĕad′ÿ, *adj.,* **-ier, -iest.** intoxicating.

hēal, *v.t.* **1.** return to health. **2.** make whole again.

hĕalth, *n.* **1.** well-being. **2.** condition of the body or mind. —**health′ful**, *adj.* —**health′y**, *adj.*

hēap, *n.* **1.** loose pile. —*v.t.* **2.** pile up.

hẽar, *v.,* **heard, hearing.** *v.t.* **1.** perceive through the ears. **2.** understand from others. **3.** listen to. —**hear′ing**, *n.*

hẽark′ĕn, *v.i.* listen carefully.

hẽar′sāy′′, *n.* rumor.

hẽarse′, *n.* funeral car.

hẽart, *n.* **1.** organ that pumps blood. **2.** compassion or sensitivity. **3.** courage. **4.** enthusiasm. **5.** center. **6.** essence. —**heart′less**, *adj.*

hẽart′brēak′′, *n.* great sorrow. —**heart′bro′′ken**, *adj.*

hẽart′ĕn, *v.t.* encourage.

hẽart′fĕlt′′, *adj.* deeply sincere.

hẽarth, *n.* floor of a fireplace, furnace.

hẽart′ÿ, *adj.,* **-ier, -iest.** enthusiastic. —**heart′i·ly**, *adv.* —**heart′i·ness**, *n.*

hēat, *n.* **1.** warmth. **2.** strong feeling. —*v.t.,* *v.i.* **3.** warm. —**heat′er**, *n.*

hēa′thĕn, *n., pl.* **-thens, -then**, *adj. n.* **1.** person not Christian, Jewish, or Muslim. —*adj.* **2.** pertaining to such persons.

hēave, *v.,* **heaved** or **hove, heaving**, *n. v.t.* **1.** lift, or lift and throw, with effort. —*v.i.* **2.** rise and fall in rhythm. —*n.* **3.** act or instance of heaving.

hĕav′ĕn, *n.* **1.** heavens; sky. **2. Heaven**, dwelling of God, the angels, and the blessed. —**heav′en·ly**, *adj.*

hĕav′ÿ, *adj.,* **-ier, -iest. 1.** with much weight. **2.** with much difficulty. —**heav′i·ly**, *adv.*

hĕav′ÿ-hănd′ĕd, *adj.* **1.** clumsy. **2.** tyrannical.

hĕck′le, *v.t.,* **-led, -ling.** harass verbally.

hĕc′tăre, *n.* area of 10,000 square meters.

hĕc′tic, *adj.* **1.** feverish. **2.** hasty and confused.

hĕdge, *n., v.,* **hedged, hedging.** *n.* **1.** barrier of close-growing shrubs. —*v.t.* **2.**

partition off with a hedge. —*v.i.* **3.** refuse to commit oneself.

hĕdge′hŏg′′, *n.* American porcupine.

hē′dŏn·ism, *n.* doctrine that pleasure is the highest good. —**he′don·ist**, *n.* —**he′′do·nis′tic**, *adj.*

hēed, *v.t.* **1.** pay attention to. —*n.* **2.** attention. —**heed′ful**, *adj.* —**heed′less**, *adj.*

hēel, *n.* **1.** rear of the foot. **2.** something similar in form or location. —*v.i., v.t.* **3.** lean; list. **4.** a contemptible person.

hĕft, *v.t.* pick up in order to weigh.

hĕft′ÿ, *adj.,* **-ier, -iest. 1.** heavy. **2.** large.

hēif′ẽr, *n.* young cow.

hēight, *n.* **1.** dimension from bottom to top. **2.** raised area. **3.** highest point.

hēight′ĕn, *v.t.* **1.** make higher. —*v.i.* **2.** increase.

hēi′noŭs, *adj.* outrageously wicked.

hēir, *n.* person who inherits. Also, *fem.,* **heir′ess.**

hēir′lōom′′, *n.* family possession.

hĕl′i·cŏp′′tẽr, *n.* aircraft flying by means of a propellerlike rotor.

hē′li·ŭm, *n.* light gaseous chemical element.

hē′lix, *n., pl.* **-lixes, -lices.** rising curve. —**hel′i·cal**, *adj.*

hĕll, *n.* Also **Hell**, place of confinement for those not redeemed. —**hel′lish**, *adj.*

hĕl·lō′, *interj.* exclamation of greeting.

hĕlm, *n.* means of steering a ship. —**helms′man**, *n.*

hĕl′mĕt, *n.* protective head covering.

hĕlp, *v.t.* **1.** assist. **2.** rescue. **3.** prevent or mitigate. —*v.i.* **4.** be useful. —*n.* **5.** assistance. **6.** rescue. —**help′ful**, *adj.*

hĕlp′ing, *n.* portion of food.

hĕlp′lĕss, *adj.* unable to act. —**help′less·ly**, *adv.* —**help′less·ness**, *n.*

hĕlp′māte′′, *n.* helpful companion. Also, **help′meet′′.**

hĕm, *n., v.t.,* **hemmed, hemming.** *n.* **1.** edge formed on a cloth. —*v.t.* **2.** make a hem on.

hĕm′i·sphēre′′, *n.* **1.** half a sphere. **2.** half of the earth. —**hem′′i·spher′i·cal**, *adj.*

hĕm′lŏck′′, *n.* **1.** pinelike evergreen. **2.** poisonous plant related to parsley.

hĕm′ŏr·rhăge, *n.* massive loss of blood.

hĕmp, *n.* Asiatic plant used for rope and hashish.

hĕn, *n.* female bird, esp. a chicken.

hĕnce, *adv.* 1. away. 2. from this time. 3. therefore.

hĕnce'fôrth'', *adv.* from now on.

hĕnch'măn, *n.* assistant villain.

hêr, *pron.* 1. objective of *she*. —*adj.* 2. pertaining to a female previously mentioned.

hĕr'ăld, *n.* 1. officer who announces. 2. signifier of what is to come. —*v.t.* 3. signify in advance.

hĕr'ăld·rў, *n.* study of coats of arms, etc. —**he·ral'dic**, *adj.*

hĕrb (êrb), *n.* annual, biennial, or perennial seed plant used in cookery or medicine. —**her·ba'cious**, *adj.* —**herb'age**, *n.* —**herb'al**, *adj.*

hĕr''cū·lē'ăn, *adj.* with immense effort.

hĕrd, *n.* 1. group of cows, sheep, etc. 2. person who tends such a group. —*v.i.*, *v.t.* 3. gather or move as a herd.

hêre, *adv.* 1. in or to this place. 2. now.

hêre·ăf'têr, *adv.* 1. after this. —*n.* 2. next world.

hêre'bў, *adv.* by this means.

he·rĕd'ĭ·tār''ў, *adj.* so by inheritance or heredity.

hêre·ĭn', *adv.* in this.

hêre·ŏf', *adv.* of or concerning this.

hĕr'e·sў, *n.*, *pl.* **-sies.** contradiction of a dogma. —**her'e·tic**, *n.* —**he·ret'i·cal**, *adj.*

hêre'to·fôre'', *adv.* until now.

hêre·wĭth', *adv.* 1. with this. 2. by this means.

hĕr'ĭt·age, *n.* traditions, etc. from predecessors.

hĕr·mĕt'ĭc, *adj.* airtight. Also, **her·met'i·cal.** —**her·met'i·cal·ly**, *adv.*

hĕr'mĭt, *n.* person willingly living alone. —**her'mit·age**, *n.*

hĕr'nĭ·à, *n.* abdominal rupture.

hē'rō, *n.*, *pl.* **-roes.** 1. person of courage and accomplishment. 2. protagonist. Also, *fem.*, **he'ro·ine.** —**he·ro'ic**, *adj.* —**he'ro·ism**, *n.*

hē'rō·ĭn, *n.* morphine-based narcotic.

hĕr'ŏn, *n.* wading bird.

hĕr'pēs, *n.* a viral infection causing sores.

hĕr'rĭng, *n.* North Atlantic fish.

hêrs, *pron.* something belonging or pertaining to *her*.

hêr·sĕlf', *pron.* 1. intensive and reflexive of *she*. 2. her true self.

hêrtz, *n.* *Physics.* one cycle per second.

hĕs'ĭ·tāte'', *v.i.*, **-tated, -tating.** 1. be unresolved. 2. pause briefly. 3. be reluctant. —**hes''i·ta'tion**, *n.* —**hes'i·tant**, *adj.*

hĕt'êr·ö·dŏx'', *adj.* unorthodox. —**het'er·o·dox''y**, *n.*

hĕt''êr·ö·gē'nē·oŭs, *adj.* 1. dissimilar. 2. of dissimilar components. —**het''er·o·ge·ne'i·ty**, *n.*

hĕt''êr·ö·sĕx'ū·ăl, *adj.* 1. attracted solely to the opposite sex. —*n.* 2. heterosexual person. —**het''er·o·sex''u·al'i·ty**, *n.*

hĕw, *v.t.*, **hewed, hewed** or **hewn, hewing.** chop.

hĕx, *v.t.* 1. put an evil spell on. —*n.* 2. evil spell.

hĕx'à·gŏn'', *n.* six-sided plane figure. —**hex·ag'o·nal**, *adj.*

hī·ā'tŭs, *n.*, *pl.* **-tuses, -tus.** interruption.

hī'bêr·nāte'', *v.i.*, **-nated, -nating.** be dormant through winter. —**hi''ber·na'tion**, *n.*

hĭc'cŭp, *n.*, *v.i.*, **-cuped, -cuping.** *n.* 1. sharp sound due to involuntary contraction of the diaphragm. —*v.i.* 2. emit such a sound. Also, **hic'cough.**

hĭck'ö·rў, *n.*, *pl.* **-ries.** tree of the walnut family.

hīde, *v.*, **hid, hidden, hiding,** *n.* *v.t.* 1. keep from being seen. —*v.i.* 2. conceal oneself. —*n.* 3. animal skin.

hĭd'ē·oŭs, *adj.* horribly ugly.

hī'êr·ār''chў, *n.*, *pl.* **-ies.** organization of higher officials.

hī''êr·ö·glўph'ĭc, *n.* picture representing a word or sound.

hīgh, *adj.* 1. being or reaching far up. 2. of a specified height. 3. superior. 4. notably large in amount. —*adv.* 5. in or to a high place or situation. —**high'ly**, *adv.*

hīgh'-flōwn'', *adj.* pretentious, as speech.

hīgh'-hănd'ĕd, *adj.* overbearing. —**high'-hand'ed·ly**, *adv.* —**high'-hand'ed·ness**, *n.*

hīgh'lănd, *n.* hilly or mountainous region.

hīgh'līght'', *n.* 1. brilliant reflection. 2. salient fact. —*v.t.* 3. emphasize.

high'ness, *n.* **1.** height. **2. Highness,** title of respect for royalty.

high'rise', *n.* multistoried building. Also, **high'rise''.**

high'-strung', *adj.* nervous.

high'way'', *n.* major road.

hi'jack'', *v.t. Informal.* take in transit by robbery. **—hi'jack''er,** *n.*

hike, *v.i.,* **hiked, hiking,** *n. v.i.* **1.** go for a long walk. **—n.** **2.** long walk.

hi·lār'i·ous, *adj.* **1.** merry. **2.** very funny. **—hi·lar'i·ty,** *n.*

hill, *n.* distinctive area of rising ground. **—hill'y,** *adj.*

hil'lock, *n.* small hill.

hilt, *n.* handle of a sword, etc.

him, *pron.* objective of *he.*

him·sĕlf', *pron.* **1.** intensive or reflexive of *him.* **2.** his true self.

hind, *adj.,* **hinder, hindmost** or **hinder-most.** *adj.* behind.

hin'dêr, *v.t.* **1.** stop or slow down. **—adj.** **2.** rear. **—hin'drance,** *n.*

hind'sight'', *n.* belated perception.

hinge, *n., v.i.,* **hinged, hinging.** *n.* **1.** support allowing the supported part to turn. **—v.i.** **2.** depend.

hint, *n.* **1.** something that allows an inference to be made. **—v.t.** **2.** imply. **—v.i.** **3.** make a hint.

hip, *n.* area around the upper leg joints.

hip''piē, *n., pl.* **-pies.** *Informal.* person alienated from conventional society.

hip''pó·pŏt'á·mŭs, *n., pl.* **-muses, -mi.** large river-loving African mammal.

hire, *v.t.,* **hired, hiring,** *n. v.t.* **1.** employ or use for wages or a fee. **—n.** **2.** amount paid in hiring.

hire'ling, *n.* unscrupulous mercenary.

hîr'sūte, *adj.* hairy.

his, *pron.* **1.** something belonging or pertaining to him. **—adj.** **2.** pertaining to him.

hiss, *n.* **1.** prolonged s-like sound. **—v.i.** **2.** emit a hiss. **—v.t.** **3.** hiss at to show disapproval.

his'tó·rў, *n., pl.* **-ries. 1.** study of the past. **2.** account of the past. **3.** known or recorded past. **4.** determining forces as inferred from past events. **—his·to'ri·an,** *n.* **—his·tor'ic, his·tor'i·cal,** *adj.*

hit, *v.,* **hit, hitting,** *n. v.t.* **1.** come against or send something against with force.

—v.i. **2.** come by chance. **3.** strike a blow. **—n.** **4.** accurate discharge of a missile. **5.** successful song, etc.

hitch, *v.t.* **1.** tie or harness. **—n.** **2.** simple knot. **3.** obstacle or drawback.

hitch'hike'', *v.i.* **-hiked, -hiking.** solicit a free automobile ride.

hith'êr, *adv.* **1.** to this place. **—adj.** **2.** nearer.

hith'êr·to'', *adv.* until now.

hive, *n.* **1.** beehive. **2. hives,** itchy skin condition.

hôard, *n.* **1.** precious hidden accumulation. **—v.t.** **2.** accumulate and secrete.

hôarse, *adj.* emitting or having a harsh, grating sound.

hôar'ў, *adj.* **-ier, -iest. 1.** gray-haired from age. **2.** very old.

hôax, *n.* **1.** fraud. **—v.t.** **2.** perpetrate a hoax on.

hŏb'ble, *v.,* **-bled, -bling.** *v.i.* **1.** limp. **—v.t.** **2.** hamper.

hŏb'bў, *n., pl.* **-bies.** spare-time activity. **—hob'by·ist,** *n.*

hŏb'nŏb'', *v.i.,* **-nobbed, -nobbing.** be on social terms.

ho'bō, *n., pl.* **-bos, -boes. 1.** migrant worker. **2.** transient.

hŏck'ey, *n.* game played on ice with long, clublike sticks and a puck.

ho'cŭs-po'cŭs, *n.* **1.** meaningless jargon. **2.** trickery.

hŏd, *n.* **1.** trough for bricks or mortar. **2.** coal scuttle.

hŏdge'pŏdge'', *n.* random mixture.

hŏe, *n., v.t.,* **hoed, hoeing.** *n.* **1.** long-handled tool for loosening earth. **—v.t.** **2.** dig with a hoe.

hŏg, *n.* **1.** pig raised for meat. **2.** *Informal.* greedy person.

hŏgs'hĕad'', *n.* **1.** large cask. **2.** measure of 63 liquid gallons.

hŏī'pŏl·lŏī', the common people.

hŏīst, *v.t.* **1.** lift, as by a crane. **—n.** **2.** hoisting device.

hōld, *v.,* **held, holding,** *n. v.t.* **1.** have in the hand. **2.** keep from moving or changing. **3.** embrace. **4.** contain. **5.** possess. **6.** carry on. **7.** consider. **—v.i.** **8.** remain firm or fixed. **—n.** **9.** act or instance of holding. **10.** means of holding. **11.** cargo space. **—hold'er,** *n.* **—hold'ing,** *n.*

hōle, *n.* opening, esp. a deep one.

hŏl'ĭ·dāy'', n. 1. day specially celebrated. 2. day of no work.

hŏl'ĭ·nĕss, n. 1. quality of being holy. 2. **Holiness**, title of respect for a pope.

hŏl'lŏw, adj. 1. empty inside. 2. worthless; vain. 3. booming. —v.t. 4. make hollow.

hŏl'lў, n., pl. -ies. evergreen shrub with red berries.

hŏl'lў·hŏck'', n. tall plant with showy flowers.

hŏ'lō·caŭst'', n. widely destructive fire.

hŏl'stēr, n. pistol holder.

hō'lў, adj., -lier, -liest. 1. dedicated to religion. 2. spiritually pure.

Hōlў Commūnion, n. Christian ritual of bread and wine.

Hōlў Spĭrĭt, n. spirit of God. Also, **Holy Ghost**.

hŏm'āge, n. reverent respect.

hōme, n. 1. place of residence. 2. one's own place. —adv. 3. to one's home. 4. into the proper place. —**home'land**'', n. —**home'ward**, adv.

hōme'lў, adj., -lier, -liest. 1. commonplace. 2. not handsome or beautiful.

hōme'sĭck'', adj. sad at being away from home.

hōme'wŏrk', n. schoolwork done at home.

hōme'ў, adj., -ier, -iest. cozy.

hŏm'ĭ·cīde'', n. killing of one person by another. —**hom''i·cid'al**, adj.

hŏm'ĭ·lў, n., pl. -lies. sermon or moral lecture.

hō''mō·gē'nē·oŭs, adj. of uniform composition or content. —**ho·mo''ge·ne'i·ty**, n.

hō·mŏg'é·nīze'', v.t., -nized, -nizing. make homogeneous.

hŏm'ō·nўm, n. word like another in pronunciation but not in other ways.

Hō'mō sä'pĭ·ĕns'', man.

hō''mō·sĕx''ū·ăl, adj. 1. sexually attracted to one's own sex. —n. 2. homosexual person. —**ho''mo·sex''u·al'i·ty**, n.

hōne, v.t., **honed, hone**. bring to a fine, sharp edge.

hŏn'ĕst, adj. 1. without desire to steal, lie, etc. 2. genuine. 3. frank. —**hon'est·ly**, adv. —**hon'es·ty**, n.

hŏn'ĕy, n., pl. -neys. syrup made by bees from flowers.

hŏn'ĕy·cŏmb'', n., 1. structure with hexagonal cells made by bees to store honey. 2. openwork geometrical pattern.

hŏn'ĕy·dĕw'' melon, n. sweet, green melon.

hŏn'ĕy·mōōn'', n. vacation of newlyweds. —**hon'ey·moon''er**, n.

hŏn'ĕy·sŭck''le, n. climbing plant with small, sweet blossoms.

hŏn'ōr, n. 1. high respect. 2. good reputation. 3. integrity. 4. chastity. 5. conferred distinction. —v.t. 6. hold in honor. 7. confer distinction or praise on. 8. accept as valid. —**hon'or·a·ble**, adj. —**hon'or·ar''y**, adj.

hŏn''ör·ĭf'ĭc, adj. conferring honor.

hōōd, n. 1. cloth covering for the head and nape. 2. engine cover of an automobile, etc.

hōōd'lŭm, n. violent criminal.

hōōd'wĭnk'', v.t. cheat.

hōōf, n., pl. **hoofs, hooves**. hard foot covering of a horse, etc.

hōōk, n. 1. curved object for hanging or attaching things. —v.t. 2. attach with a hook. —v.i. 3. curve as a hook does.

hōōp, n. circular band.

hōōt, n. 1. loud, shrill sound. —v.i. 2. utter a hoot. —v.t. 3. show scorn for by hooting.

hŏp, v.i., **hopped, hopping**, n. vi. 1. jump on one foot or with both feet together. —n. 2. act or instance of hopping.

hōpe, n., v., **hoped, hoping**. n. 1. belief that something good may happen. 2. source or cause of such a belief. —v.t., v.i. 3. entertain hopes. —**hope'ful**, adj., n. —**hope'less**, adj.

hŏp'pêr, n. funnel-like chute.

hôrde, n., v.i., **horded, hording**, n. 1. swarm; multitude. —v.i. 2. gather in a horde.

hō·rī'zŏn, n. apparent edge of a scene.

hŏ''rī·zŏn'tăl, adj. running across, like a featureless horizon. —**ho''ri·zon'tal·ly**, adv.

hŏr'mōne'', n. substance influencing one part of the body but made in another. —**hor·mo'nal**, adj.

hôrn, n. 1. hard, pointed protuberance from an animal head. 2. substance of this. 3. pointed projection. 4. wind instrument. —**horn'y**, adj.

hôr′nĕt, *n.* yellow and black wasp.

hôr′ó·scōpe″, *n.* chart of zodiacal signs.

hôr·rĕn′dŏus, *adj.* horrible.

hôr′rĭ·ble, *adj.* 1. causing horror. 2. *Informal.* very bad. —**hôr′ri·bly**, *adv.*

hôr′rĭd, *adj.* 1. causing horror. 2. very unpleasant.

hôr′rĭ·cŭl″, *v.t.*, -fied, -fying. fill with horror.

hôr′rör, *n.* strong fear and disgust.

hors de com·bat (ôr′dĕ kŏm bä′), out of action.

hors d'oeuvre (ôr dêrv′), *n.*, *pl.* hors d'oeuvres, appetizer.

hôrse, *n.* 1. four-footed grass eating animal. 2. supporting frame. —**horse′back″**, *adv.*, *n.* —**horse′man**, **horse′wom″an**, *n.*

hôrse chĕstnŭt, large-leaved flowering tree.

hôrse′lăugh″, *n.* loud, open laugh.

hôrse′plăy″, *n.* rough play.

hôrse′pŏw″êr, *n.* unit of power equalling 33,000 foot-pounds/minute or 746 watts.

hôrse′răd″ĭsh, *n.* plant with a pungent root used as a relish.

hôrse′shoe″, *n.* iron reinforcement for a hoof in the form of an open loop.

hôr′tĭ·cŭl″tūre, *n.* gardening. —**hor″ti·cul′tur·al**, *adj.* —**hor″ti·cul′tur·ist**, *n.*

hō·săn′nà, *interj.* exclamation of praise to God.

hōse, *n.*, *pl.* (for 1) hoses, (for 2) hose. 1. flexible tube for water, etc. 2. long stocking.

hō′sier·ȳ, *n.* stockings.

hŏs′pĭce, *n.* facility for terminally ill persons.

hŏs′pĭ·tà·ble, *adj.* readily offering hospitality.

hŏs′pĭ·tàl, *n.* place for healing. —**hos′pi·tal·ize″**, *v.t.*

hŏs″pĭ·tăl′ĭ·tȳ, *n.* generosity and friendship toward visitors.

hŏst, *n.* 1. Also, *fem.*, **hos′tess**, person who entertains guests. 2. organism supporting parasites. 3. multitude. 4. wafer eaten in Holy Communion.

hŏs′tàge, *n.* prisoner kept to enforce demands.

hŏs′tĕl, *n.* institution providing lodgings.

hŏs′tīle, *adj.* in a state of enmity. —**hos·til′i·ty**, *n.*

hŏt, *adj.*, hotter, hottest. 1. very warm. 2. very spicy. 3. intense, as in emotion. —**hot′ly**, *adv.*

hŏt′bĕd″, *n.* 1. miniature greenhouse. 2. prolific source.

hŏt′-blŏod″ĕd, *adj.* impetuous.

hō·tĕl′, *n.* place renting rooms and often serving food.

hŏt′-hĕad″ĕd, *adj.* quick-tempered. —**hot′head″**, *n.*

hŏt rŏd, standard automobile with a supercharged engine. —**hot rod′der**.

hŏund, *n.* 1. hunting dog. —*v.t.* 2. persecute.

hŏur, *n.* twenty-fourth of a day. —**hour′ly**, *adv.*, *adj.*

house, *n.*, *pl.* houses, *v.t.*, housed, housing. *n.* (hŏws). 1. building to live in. 2. family. 3. business firm. 4. legislative body. —*v.t.* (hŏwz) 5. provide lodgings or shelter for.

hŏuse′flȳ″, *n.* ordinary fly.

hŏuse′hŏld″, *n.* inhabitants of a house.

hŏuse′hŏld″êr, *n.* 1. head of a household. 2. owner of a house.

hŏuse′kēep″êr, *n.* person responsible for keeping a house in order.

hŏuse′wife″, *n.* wife who runs a home.

hŏus·ing, *n.* 1. complex of dwellings. 2. provision of dwellings.

hŏv′êr, *v.i.* 1. remain poised in the air. 2. linger near by. 3. waver.

hŏw, *adv.* 1. in what way. 2. in what state. 3. for what reason. 4. to what extent.

hŏw·ĕv′êr, *adv.* 1. regardless of how. —*conj.* 2. nevertheless.

hŏw′ĭtz·êr, *n.* short-barreled, high-trajectory cannon.

hŏwl, *v.i.* 1. raise a loud, animal-like cry. 2. laugh uproariously. 3. complain bitterly. —*n.* 4. act or instance of howling.

hŭb, *n.* center of a wheel.

hŭb′bŭb, *n.* confusion; disorder.

hŭck′le·bĕr″rȳ, *n.*, *pl.* -ries. dark blue shrub berry.

hŭck′stêr, *n.* peddler.

hŭd′dle, *n.*, *v.*, -dled, -dling. *n.* 1. close, irregular group. —*v.t.*, *v.i.* 2. gather in a huddle.

hūe, *n.* 1. color. 2. tint.

huff, n. mood of silent resentment. —**huf′fy**, adj.

hug, v., **hugged**, **hugging**, n. v.t., v.i. 1. embrace. —v.t. 2. keep close to. —n. 3. embrace.

huge, adj. very large. —**huge′ness**, n. —**huge′ly**, adv.

hulk, n. hull of a ship deprived of masts, etc.

hulk′ing, adj. large and bulky.

hull, n. 1. shell of a seed, etc. 2. body of a ship. —v.t. 3. remove the hulls from.

hul′la·ba·loo″, n. clamor.

hum, v., **hummed**, **humming**, n. v.i. 1. make an inarticulate sound between closed lips. —v.t. 2. render by humming. —n. 3. low, continuous murmur.

hu′man, adj. 1. being a man, woman, or child. 2. characteristic of man. —**hu′man·ly**, adv. —**hu′man·kind″**, n.

hu·mane′, adj. 1. merciful. 2. civilizing.

hu′man·ism, n. intellectual movement centered around man. —**hu′man·ist**, n. —**hu″man·is′tic**, adj.

hu·man″i·tār′i·an, n. 1. philanthropist. —adj. 2. philanthropic. —**hu·man″i·tar′i·an·ism**, n.

hu·man′i·tÿ, n. 1. human beings collectively. 2. quality of being humane.

hum′ble, adj., **-bler**, **-blest**, v.t., **-bled**, **-bling**. adj. 1. unpretentious, unconceited. 2. low in rank. —v.t. 3. make humble. —**hum′bly**, adv.

hum′drum″, adj. drearily ordinary.

hu′mid, adj. moist. —**hu·mid′i·fy″**, v.t. —**hu·mid′i·ty**, n.

hu·mil′i·āte″, v.t., **-ated**, **-ating**. cause to feel shame. —**hu·mil″i·a′tion**, n.

hu·mil′i·tÿ, n. humble quality.

hum′ming·bĭrd, n. tiny bird with fast-moving wings.

hū′mŏr, n. 1. mood. 2. comical quality. 3. bodily fluid. —**hu′mor·ist**, n. —**hu′mor·ous**, adj.

hump, n. high lump on a back of a camel.

hū′mŭs, n. soil with decayed leaf matter, etc.

hŭnch, n. 1. Informal. intuitive feeling. 2. hump.

hunch′băck″, n. person with a hump on the back. Also, **hump′back″**.

hŭn′drĕd, adj., n. ten times ten. —**hun′dredth**, adj.

hŭn′drĕd·weight″, n. U.S. 100 pounds.

hŭn′gêr, n. 1. desire to eat. 2. deprivation of food. 3. strong desire. —v.i. 4. be hungry. —**hun′gry**, adj. —**hun′gri·ly**, adv.

hŭnk, n. Informal. large piece.

hŭnt, v.t. 1. pursue to kill or harass. —v.i. 2. hunt game. 3. search. —n. 4. act or instance of hunting. —**hunt′er**, **hunts′man**, fem. **hunt′ress**, n.

hûr′dle, n., v.t., **-dled**, **-dling**. n. 1. barrier to be leapt. —v.t. 2. leap over.

hûrl, n. throw with force.

hûr′lÿ-bûr′lÿ, n., pl. **-lies**. turmoil.

hûr·räh″, interj. n. shout of approval. Also **hur·ray′**.

hûr′rī·cāne″, n. tropical cyclone.

hûr′rÿ, v., **-ried**, **-rying**, v.i. 1. move or act quickly. —v.t. 2. cause to hurry. —n. 3. reason for hurrying. 4. eagerness to hurry. —**hur′ried·ly**, adv.

hûrt, v., **hurt**, **hurting**, v.t. 1. damage; injure. 2. feeling of pain. —v.i. 3. cause pain. 4. do harm. —n. 5. damage; injury. —**hurt′ful**, adj.

hûr′tle, v.i., **-tled**, **-tling**. move at high speed.

hŭs′bănd, n. 1. woman's spouse. —v.t. 2. manage economically.

hŭs′bănd·rÿ, n. 1. farming. 2. management.

hŭsh, n., v.t. silence.

hŭsk, n. 1. outer covering. —v.t. 2. remove the husk from.

hŭs′kÿ, adj. 1. hoarse. 2. robust.

hŭs′tle, v., **-tled**, **-tling**, n. v.t. 1. jostle. 2. force roughly. —v.i. 3. move or act energetically. —n. 4. act or instance of hustling. 5. Informal. enterprise.

hŭt, n. small, crude dwelling.

hŭtch, n. 1. cupboard. 2. coop for rabbits, etc.

hÿ′a·cĭnth″, n. bell-shaped flower of the lily family.

hÿ′brĭd, n. 1. offspring or product of mixed species or varieties. —**hy′brid·ize″**, v.t.

hÿ·drăn′gē·à, n. shrub with clusters of white, blue, or pink flowers.

hÿ′drănt, n. valved pipe from a water main.

hÿ·drău′lĭc, adj. 1. operated by liquid pressure. —n. 2. **hydraulics**, study of the mechanical properties of liquids. —hy′·drau′li·cal·ly, adv.

hȳ″·dró·cãr′bon, n. compound of hydrogen and carbon.

hȳ″·drō·ė·lĕc′trĭc, adj. pertaining to electricity produced by water power.

hȳ′dró·gén, n. flammable gaseous element.

hȳ″·dró·phō′bĭ·a, n. rabies.

hȳ′dró·plāne″, n. 1. seaplane. 2. motorboat with hydrofoils or a planing hull.

hȳ″dró·pŏn′ĭcs, n. growing of plants in liquids.

hȳ·ē′nà, n. wolflike African or Asian animal.

hȳ′giène, n. 1. system of health preservation. 2. cleanliness. —hy″·gi·en′ic, adj. —hy″·gi·en′i·cal·ly, adv.

hȳmn, n. poem or song of praise, as to God. —hymn′book″, hym′nal, n.

hȳpe, n. exaggerated publicity.

hȳ·pêr′bó·lē″, n. exaggeration for the rhetorical effect. —hy″per·bol′ic, adj.

hȳ″·pêr·crĭt′ĭ·cál, adj. over-critical.

hȳ″·pêr·sĕn′sĭ·tĭve, adj. too sensitive.

hȳ″·pêr·tĕn′sion, n. excessive blood pressure.

hȳ′phĕn, n. dash, -, used to join words or syllables. —hy′phen·ate″, v.t. —hy″phen·a′tion, n.

hȳp·nō′sĭs, n., pl. -ses. sleeplike, obedient condition induced by suggestion from another. —hyp·not′ic, adj. —hyp′no·tism, n. —hyp′no·tist, n. —hyp′no·tize″, v.t.

hȳ″pó·chŏn′drĭ·à, n. fear of imaginary illness. —hy″po·chon′dri·ac″, n., adj.

hy·pŏc′rĭ·sỹ, n., pl. -sies. false pretension to virtue, affection, etc. —hy′po·crite, n. —hy″po·crit′i·cal, adj.

hȳ″pó·dĕr′mĭc, adj. 1. under the skin. —n. 2. hypodermic injection or injecting device. —hy″po·der′mi·cal·ly, adv.

hȳ·pŏt′ė·nūse″, n. side of a right triangle opposite the right angle.

hȳ·pŏth′ė·sĭs, n., pl. -ses. unproved theory. —hy″po·thet′i·cal, adj.

hỹs·tē′rĭ·à, n. 1. pathologically excitable condition. 2. Also, hys·ter′ics, outbreak of uncontrolled emotion. —hyster′i·cal, adj.

I

I, i, n. 1. ninth letter of the English alphabet. —pron. 2. I (first person singular as a subject).

ĭbĭd., in the same place: used in scholarly notes.

ïce, n., v., iced, icing. n. 1. water frozen solid. 2. frozen dessert. —v.t. 3. put ice over or around. 4. put icing over. —v.i. 5. freeze or form ice. —ice′box″, n. —ice′skate″, n. —ic′y, adj.

ïce′bêrg″, n. floating fragment from a polar icecap.

ïce′cap″, n. polar mass of ice.

ĭch″·thȳ·ŏl′ó·gȳ, n. study of fish. —ich″thy·ol′o·gist, n.

ï′cĭ·cle, n. conical hanging mass of frozen water.

ïc′ing, n. sweet cover for a cake.

ï′cŏn, n. religious image, esp. in an Eastern Orthodox church.

ï′cŏn·ó·clãst″, n. destroyer of long-held values. —i·con″o·clas′tic, adj.

ï·dē′à, n. image in the mind; conception.

ï·dē′àl, adj. 1. perfect. 2. imaginary. —n. 3. something perfect. —i·de′al·ly, adv. —i·de′al·ize″, v.t.

ï·dē′àl·ĭsm, n. conformity to or belief in ideals. —i·de′al·ist, n. —i″′de·al·is′tic, adj.

ï·dĕn′tĭ·cál, adj. exactly alike or the same. —i·den′ti·cal·ly, adv.

ï·dĕn′tĭ·fỹ″, v.t., -fied, -fying. 1. establish the identity of. 2. associate with another person or thing. —i·den″ti·fi·ca′tion, n.

i·dĕn′tĭ·tỹ, n., pl. -ties. 1. state of being identical. 2. individuality.

ï″·dē·ŏl′ó·gỹ, n., pl. -gies. political or social doctrine. —i″de·o·log′i·cal, adj.

ĭd′ĭ·ŏm, n. 1. dialect. 2. combination of words with a nonliteral meaning. —id″i·o·mat′ic, adj.

ĭd″·ĭ·ó·sỹn′crà·sỹ, n., pl. -sies. personal trait.

ĭd'ĭ·ŏt, *n.* feeble-minded person. —id''i·ot'ic, *adj.* —id'i·o·cy, *n.*

ī'dle, *adj.*, idler, idlest, *v.i.*, idled, idling. *adj.* 1. not at work or in use. 2. lazy. 3. frivolous. —*v.i.* 4. be idle. —id'ly, *adv.* —id'ler, *n.*

ī'dŏl, *n.* 1. statue of a god. 2. idealized person. —i'dol·ize'', *v.t.*

ĭ·dŏl'ā·trў, *n.*, *pl.* -tries. worship of idols. —i·dol'a·ter, *n.* —i·dol'a·trous, *adj.*

ī'dўll, *n.* 1. poem of pastoral life. 2. beautiful episode. Also, i'dyl. —i·dyl'ic, *adj.*

ī.ē., that is.

ĭf, *conj.* 1. on condition that. 2. supposing that. 3. whether.

ĭg'lŏō, *n.*, *pl.* -loos. domed Eskimo snow house.

ĭg'nē· oŭs, *adj.* resulting from intense heat.

ĭg·nīte', *v.*, -nited, -niting. *v.t.*, 1. set on or catch fire. —*v.i.* 2. catch fire. —ig·ni'tion, *n.*

ĭg·nō'ble, *adj.* base; mean.

ĭg'nŏ·mĭn''ў, *n.* shame. —ig''no·min'i·ous, *adj.*

ĭg''nŏ·rā'mŭs, *n.*, *pl.* -muses. ignorant person.

ĭg'nŏ·rănt, *adj.* 1. uneducated. 2. unaware. —ig'no·rance, *n.* —ig'no·rant·ly, *adv.*

ĭg·nōre', *v.t.*, -nored, -noring. take no heed of.

ĭll, *adj.*, worse, (for 1) worst, *adv.*, worse, worst, *n.* *adj.* 1. bad. 2. sick. —*adv.* 3. badly. 4. scarcely. —*n.* 5. harm.

ĭll'ad·vīsed', *adj.* showing bad judgment.

ĭl·lē'găl, *adj.* unlawful. —il·le'gal·ly, *adv.* —il''le·gal'i·ty, *n.*

ĭl·lĕg'ĭ·ble, *adj.* unable to be read. —il·leg''i·bil'i·ty, *n.*

ĭl''lė·gĭt'ĭ·māte, *adj.* 1. not legitimate. 2. born out of wedlock. —il''le·git'i·ma·cy, *n.*

ĭl·lĭc'ĭt, *adj.* not allowed. —il·lic'it·ly, *adv.*

ĭl·lĭt'ĕr·āte, *adj.* 1. unable to read. —*n.* 2. illiterate person. —il·lit'er·a·cy, *n.*

ĭll'nĕss, *n.* sickness.

ĭl·lŏg'ĭ·căl, *adj.* opposed to logic.

ĭl·lŭ'mĭ·nāte'', *v.t.*, -nated, -nating. 1. Also, il·lu'mine, light up. 2. elucidate.

3. decorate with gold and color. —il·lu''mi·na'tion, *n.*

ĭll-ūse', *v.t.*, -used, -using. abuse. —ill'use', ill'-us'age, *n.*

ĭl·lū'sion, *n.* 1. deceptive impression. 2. false conception. —il·lu'sive, —il·lu'so·ry, *adj.*

ĭl'lŭs·trāte'', *v.t.*, -trated, -trating. 1. explain with examples. 2. add pictures to, as a narrative. —il''lus·tra'tion, *n.* —il''lus·tra''tor, *n.* —il·lus'tra·tive, *adj.*

ĭl·lŭs'trĭ·oŭs, *adj.* distinguished; famous.

ĭll wĭll, hostility.

ĭm'āge, *n.* 1. picture. 2. popular conception. —im'age·ry, *n.*

ĭ·măg'ĭne, *v.t.*, -ined, -ining. 1. create in the mind. 2. suppose to exist. 3. believe wrongly to exist. —i·mag'in·a·ble, *adj.* —i·mag'in·a·bly, *adv.* —i·mag'in·a''ry, *adj.* —i·mag''i·na'tion, *n.* —i·mag'i·na·tive, *adj.*

ĭm·băl'ănce, *n.* lack of balance.

ĭm'bė·cīle, *n.* idiot. —im''be·cil'ic, *adj.* —im'be·cil'i·ty, *n.*

ĭm·bībe', *v.*, -bibed, -bibing. *v.t.*, *v.i.* drink.

im·bro·gli·o (ĭm brōl'yō), *n.*, *pl.* -os. confused situation.

ĭm·būe', *v.t.*, -bued, -buing. permeate.

ĭm'ĭ·tāte'', *v.t.*, -tated, -tating. have the same characteristics as. —im''i·ta'tion, *n.* —im'i·ta''tor, *n.* —im'i·ta''tive, *adj.*

ĭm·măc'ū·lāte, *adj.* without dirt or sin. —im·mac'u·late·ly, *adv.*

ĭm'mă·nĕnt, *adj.* inherent. —im'ma·nent·ly, *adv.* —im'ma·nence, *n.*

ĭm''mȧ·tē'rĭ·ăl, *adj.* 1. irrelevant. 2. not composed of matter.

ĭm'mȧ·tūre, *n.* with an undeveloped character. —im''ma·tu'ri·ty, *n.*

ĭm·mĕas'ūr·ȧ·ble, *adj.* not to be measured. —im·meas'ur·a·bly, *adv.*

ĭm·mē'dĭ·āte, *adj.* 1. unseparated by anything else. 2. direct. —im·me'di·a·cy, *n.* —im·me'di·ate·ly, *adv.*

ĭm''mė·mō'rĭ·ăl, *adj.* from before memory.

ĭm·mĕnse', *adj.* huge. —im·men'si·ty, *n.* —im·mense'ly, *adv.*

ĭm·mĕrse', *v.t.*, -mersed, -mersing. bury

completely, as in a liquid. —**im·mer′ sion**, *n.*

ĭm′mĭ·grāte″, *v.i.*, **-grated**, **-grating**. enter a country to settle. —**im′mi grant**, *n.*, *adj.* —**im′′mi·gra′tion**, *n.*

ĭm′mĭ·nĕnt, *adj.* soon to happen. —**im′ mi·nence**, **im′mi·nen·cy**, *n.*

ĭm·mō′bĭle, *adj.* fixed in place. —**im′ mo·bil′i·ty**, *n.* —**im·mo′bi·lize″**, *v.t.*

ĭm·mŏd′e·rāte, *adj.* lacking moderation. —**im·mod′e·rate·ly**, *adv.*

ĭm·mŏd′ĕst, *adj.* lacking modesty. —**im· mod′es·ty**, *n.*

ĭm′mŏ·lāte″, *v.t.*, **-lated**, **-lating**. kill as a sacrifice. —**im′′mo·la′tion**, *n.*

ĭm·môr′al, *adj.* not moral. —**im′′mo·ral′i·ty**, *n.*

ĭm·môr′tal, *adj.* 1. never to die. 2. never to be forgotten. —*n.* 3. immortal being. —**im′′mor·tal′i·ty**, *n.* —**im·mor′tal·ize″**, *v.t.*

ĭm·mov′a·ble, *adj.* fixed in place.

ĭm·mūne′, *adj.* proof against disease, etc. —**im·mun′i·ty**, *n.* —**im′mu·nize″**, *v.t.* —**im′′mu·ni·za′tion**, *n.*

ĭm·mū′ta·ble, *adj.* unchangeable. —**im· mu′′ta·bil′i·ty**, *n.*

ĭmp, *n.* small demon. —**imp′ish**, *adj.*

ĭm′păct, *n.* 1. violent shock. —*v.t.* (im pact′) 2. force against something else.

ĭm·pāir′, *v.t.* put out of order. —**im·pair′ ment**, *n.*

ĭm·pāle′, *v.t.*, **-paled**, **-paling**. pierce and support with a sharpened pole, etc.

ĭm·păl′pa·ble, *adj.* 1. imperceptible to the touch. 2. subtle.

ĭm·păn′el, *v.t.*, **-eled**, **-eling**. enroll for or as a jury.

ĭm·pärt′, *v.t.* reveal, as news.

ĭm·pâr′tial, *adj.* unbiased. —**im·par′ tial·ly**, *adv.* —**im·par′ti·al′i·ty**, *n.*

ĭm·păs′sa·ble, *adj.* impossible to pass along or over.

ĭm′păsse, *n.* deadlock.

ĭm·păs′sioned, *adj.* passionate.

ĭm·păs′sĭve, *adj.* revealing no emotion. —**im′′pas·siv′i·ty**, *n.*

ĭm·pā′tĭent, *adj.* without patience. —**im· pa′tience**, *n.*

ĭm·pēach′, *n.* try for wrongdoing in office. —**im·peach′ment**, *n.*

ĭm·pĕc′ca·ble, *adj.* flawless.

ĭm′′pe·cū′nĭ·oŭs, *adj.* penniless.

ĭm·pēde′, *v.t.*, **-peded**, **-peding**. hinder. —**im·ped′ance**, **im·ped′i·ment**, *n.*

ĭm·pĕd′′ĭ·mĕn′ta, *n. pl.* things to be carried along.

ĭm·pĕl′, *v.t.*, **-pelled**, **-pelling**. 1. drive forward. 2. urge.

ĭm·pĕnd′, *v.i.* be about to happen.

ĭm·pĕn′e·trà·ble, *adj.* impossible to penetrate.

ĭm·pĕn′i·tĕnt, *adj.* not repentant.

ĭm·pĕr′a·tĭve, *adj.* 1. vitally necessary. 2. pertaining to command.

ĭm·pĕr·cĕp′tĭ·ble, *adj.* impossible or difficult to perceive. —**im′′per·cep′ti·bly**, *adv.*

ĭm·pĕr′fĕct, *adj.* 1. flawed; deficient. 2. pertaining to uncompleted or continuing action. —**im·per′fect·ly**, *adv.* —**im′′ per·fec′tion**, *n.*

ĭm·pē′rĭ·al, *adj.* pertaining to empires or emperors.

ĭm·pē′rĭ·al·ĭsm, *n.* policy of creating or holding an empire. —**im·pe′ri·al·ist**, *n.*, *adj.* —**im·pe′′ri·al·is′tic**, *adj.*

ĭm·pĕr′ĭl, *v.t.*, **-iled**, **-iling**. endanger.

ĭm·pē′rĭ·oŭs, *adj.* imposing one's will on others. —**im·pe′ri·ous·ly**, *adv.*

ĭm·pĕr′ĭsh·à·ble, *adj.* not perishable.

ĭm·pĕr′ma·nĕnt, *adj.* not permanent.

ĭm·pĕr′mē·à·ble, *adj.* impossible to seep through.

ĭm·pĕr′sŏn·àl, *adj.* pertaining to no individuals —**im·per′son·al·ly**, *adv.*

ĭm·pĕr′sŏn·āte″, *v.t.*, **-ated**, **-ating**. pretend to be, as in acting. —**im·per′′son·a′tion**, *n.* —**im·per′son·a′′tor**, *n.*

ĭm·pĕr′tĭ·nĕnt, *adj.* insolent. —**im·per′ ti·nence**, *n.*

ĭm′′pĕr·tûrb′à·ble, *adj.* impossible to disturb visibly. —**im′′per·turb′a·bly**, *adv.*

ĭm·pĕr′vĭ·oŭs, *adj.* impenetrable, esp. by moisture.

ĭm·pĕt′ū·oŭs, *adj.* hasty; rash. —**im· pet′′u·os′i·ty**, *n.*

ĭm′pe·tŭs, *n.* 1. force in motion. 2. motivation.

ĭm·pī′e·tў, *n.* disrespect, esp. for God. —**im′pi·ous**, *adj.*

ĭm·pĭnge′, *v.i.*, **-pinged**, **-pinging**. encroach. —**im·pinge′ment**, *n.*

ĭm·plăc′a·ble, *adj.* impossible to appease. —**im·plac′a·bly**, *adv.*

im·plănt', *v.t.* fix or plant firmly.

im·plăus'ĭ·ble, *adj.* not plausible.

im'plĕ·mĕnt, *n.* **1.** piece of equipment.
—*v.t.* **2.** put in effect. —**im''ple·men·**
ta'tion, *n.*

im·plĭ·cāte'', *v.t.*, **-cated, -cating.** reveal
as party to a crime.

im''plĭ·cā'tion, *n.* act or instance of implying or implicating.

im·plĭc'ĭt, *adj.* **1.** implied. **2.** absolute, as
trust. —**im·plĭc'it·ly**, *adv.*

im·plōre', *v.t.*, **-plored, -ploring.** plead
earnestly with or for. —**im·plor'ing·ly,**
adv.

im·plȳ', *v.t.*, **-plied, -plying.** suggest as
existing or being so.

im''pŏ·līte', *adj.* rude.

im·pŏl'ĭ·tĭc, *adj.* unwise as giving offense.

im·pŏn'dĕr·ȧ·ble, *adj.* **1.** immeasurable.
—*n.* **2.** something imponderable.

im·pôrt', *v.t.* **1.** bring into a country, esp.
for sale. **2.** signify. —*n.* (im'port). **3.**
something imported. **4.** significance.
—**im·port'er**, *n.* —**im''por·ta'tion,**
n.

im·pôrt'ant, *adj.* **1.** of great significance.
2. of great power. —**im·por'tance,** *n.*

im''pôr·tūne', *v.t.*, **-tuned, -tuning.** urge
insistently. —**im''por·tun'i·ty**, *n.*
—**im·por'tu·nate**, *adj.*

im·pōse', *v.*, **-posed, -posing.** *v.t.* **1.** force
to accept. —*v.i.* **2.** take advantage.
—**im''po·si'tion**, *n.*

im·pōs'ĭng, *adj.* impressive. —**im·pos'**
ing·ly, *adv.*

im·pŏs'sĭ·ble, *adj.* **1.** not possible. **2.** totally unsuitable or disagreeable. —**im·**
pos''si·bil'i·ty, *n.*

im'pŏst, *n.* tax on imports.

im·pŏs'tŏr, *n.* person pretending to an
identity, competence, etc. he does not
have. —**im·pos'ture**, *n.*

im'po·tĕnt, *adj.* **1.** helpless. **2.** without
strength. **3.** incapable of sexual intercourse. —**im'po·tence, im'po·ten·cy,**
n.

im·poŭnd', *v.t.* **1.** seize and hold legally.
2. dam.

im·pŏv'ĕr·ĭsh, *v.t.* make poor. —**im·pov'**
er·ish·ment, *n.*

im·prăc'tĭ·cȧ·ble, *adj.* impossible to do.

im·prăc'tĭ·cȧl, *adj.* not practical.

im''prĕ·cā'tion, *n.* curse.

im''prĕ·cīse', *n.* not precise; vague.
—**im''pre·ci'sion**, *n.*

im·prĕg'nȧ·ble, *adj.* proof against attack.

im·prĕg'nāte'', *v.t.*, **-nated, -nating. 1.**
saturate. **2.** make pregnant. —**im''**
preg·na'tion, *n.*

im·prĕss', *v.t.* **1.** command respectful attention. **2.** print. **3.** force into military
service.

im·prĕs'sion, *n.* **1.** mental effect. **2.**
vague idea. **3.** pressed mark.

im·prĕs'sion·ȧ·ble, *adj.* easily influenced.

im·prĕs'sĭve, *adj.* commanding respect.
—**im·pres'sive·ly**, *adv.*

im·prĭnt', *v.t.* **1.** affix or print as a mark.
—*n.* (im'print). **2.** imprinted mark. **3.**
effect.

im·prĭs'on, *v.t.* confine in prison. —**im·**
pris'on·ment, *n.*

im·prŏb'ȧ·ble, *adj.* unlikely. —**im·**
prob''a·bil'i·ty, *n.*

im·prŏmp'tū, *adj.*, *adv.* without preparation.

im·prŏp'ĕr, *adj.* not proper. —**im''pro·**
pri'e·ty, *n.*

im·prove', *v.*, **-proved, -proving.** make or
become better. —**im·prove'ment**, *n.*

im·prŏv'ĭ·dĕnt, *adj.* not thrifty. —**im·**
prov'i·dence, *n.*

im'prō·vīse'', *v.*, **-vised, -vising.** *v.t.* **1.**
create at short notice or with what is
available. —*v.i.* **2.** perform extempora-
neously. —**im·prov''i·sa'tion**, *n.*

im·prŭd'ĕnt, *adj.* not prudent. —**im·**
prud'ence, *n.*

im·pūgn', *v.t.* oppose as false.

im·pŭlse', *n.* **1.** surge of force. **2.** sudden
decision to act. —**im·pul'sive**, *adj.*

im·pū'nĭ·tȳ, *n.* freedom from punishment.

im·pūre', *adj.* **1.** adulterated. **2.** immoral.
—**im·pur'i·ty**, *n.*

im·pūte', *v.t.*, **-puted, -puting.** attribute.
—**im''pu·ta'tion** *n.*

ĭn, *prep.* **1.** surrounded or contained by. **2.**
during. **3.** into. **4.** subjected to. —*adv.*
5. to the inside.

ĭn-, prefix meaning "not" or "lack
of." **inaccurate, inadequate, inap-**
plicable, inappropriate, inarticulate,
incertitude, inclement, incoher-

ent, incompetent, incongruous, inconsequential, inconsistent, inconspicuous, incontinent, incredible, incredulous, incurable, indecent, indecision, indefinite, indelicate, indigestible, indiscreet, indispensable, indistinct, indivisible, inedible, ineligible, inequitable, inexact, infallible, infertile, informal, infrequent, inhumane, inhumanity, inoffensive, insane, insatiable, insecure, insincere, insufficient, intemperate, intolerable, intransitive, invisible, involuntary, invulnerable.

ĭn ăb·sĕn′tĭ·á, in his, her, or their absence.

ĭn′′ăd·vĕrt′ĕnt, *adj.* **1.** unobservant. **2.** due to unawareness or oversight. —**in′′ad·vert′ent·ly**, *adv.* —**in′′ad·vert′ence**, *n.*

ĭn·ăl′ĭ·ĕn·á·ble, *adj.* not to be taken away.

ĭn·āne′, *adj.* pointless; silly. —**in·an′i·ty**, *n.*

ĭn′′ăs·mŭch′ăs **1.** considering that. **2.** to the extent that.

ĭn·ău′gŭ·rāte′′, *v.t.*, **-rated, -rating.** begin formally in a term of office, service, etc. —**in·aug′′u·ra′tion**, *n.* —**in·aug′u·ral**, *adj.*, *n.*

ĭn′bôard′′, *adj.*, *adv.* within a ship or aircraft.

ĭn′bôrn′′, *adj.* present at birth; innate.

ĭn′brĕd′, *adj.* **1.** inborn. **2.** resulting from inbreeding.

ĭn′brēed′, *v.*, **-bred, -breeding.** *v.t.*, *v.i.* breed from closely related stocks.

ĭn′′cán·dĕs′cent, *adj.* glowing from heat. —**in′′can·des′cence**, *n.*

ĭn′′căn·tā′tion, *n.* formula producing a magic spell.

ĭn′′cá·pác′ĭ·tāte′′, *v.t.*, **-tated, -tating.** make unable or incompetent. —**in′′ca·pac′i·ty**, *n.*

ĭn·cär′cer·āte′′, *v.t.*, **-ated, -ating.** imprison.

ĭn·cär′nāte, *adj.*, *v.t.*, **-nated, -nating.** *adj.* **1.** in fleshly, mortal form. —*v.t.* (in kahr′nāt) **2.** create in incarnate form. —**in′′car·na′tion**, *n.*

ĭn′cĕn·dĭ·ār′′ÿ, *adj.*, *n.*, *pl.* **-ies.** *adj.* **1.** causing fires. —*n.* **2.** incendiary bomb. **3.** deliberate setter of fires.

ĭn′cĕnse, *n.*, *v.t.*, **-censed, -censing.** *n.* **1.** gum or resin giving off perfumed smoke. —*v.t.* (in cense′) **2.** enrage.

ĭn·cĕn′tĭve, *n.* motive.

ĭn·cĕp′tion, *n.* beginning.

ĭn·cĕs′sánt, *adj.* never ceasing. —**in·ces′sant·ly**, *adv.*

ĭn′cĕst, *n.* sexual relations between very close relatives. —**in·ces′tu·ous**, *adj.*

ĭnch, *n.* **1.** twelfth part of a foot, as in linear measure. —*v.i.*, *v.t.* **2.** move very slowly.

ĭn·chō′ate (in kō it), *adj.* new and formless.

ĭn′cĭ·dĕnce, *n.* frequency of occurrence.

ĭn′cĭ·dĕnt, *n.* **1.** something that happens. **2.** minor fight, etc. —*adj.* **3.** probably consequent.

ĭn′′cĭ·dĕn′tál, *adj.* **1.** happening in connection with something important. —*n.* **2.** something incidental. **3.** miscellaneous item.

ĭn′′cĭ·dĕn′tál·lÿ, *adv.* **1.** while we are on the subject. **2.** in an incidental manner.

ĭn·cĭn′êr·āte′′, *v.*, **-ated, -ating.** *v.t.*, *v.i.* burn to ashes. —**in·cin′er·at′′or**, *n.*

ĭn·cĭp′ĭ·ent, *adj.* beginning to develop. —**in·cip′i·ence**, *n.*

ĭn·cīse′, *v.t.*, **-cised, -cising.** cut into. —**in·ci′sion**, *n.*

ĭn·cīs′ĭve, *adj.* penetrating in perception.

ĭn·cīs′ôr, *n.* human front tooth.

ĭn·cīte′, *v.t.*, **-cited, -citing.** urged to act. —**in·cite′ment**, *n.*

ĭn·clīne′, *v.*, **-clined, -clining.** *v.i.* **1.** slope or slant. **2.** have a tendency or liking. —*v.t.* **3.** cause to incline. —*n.* (in′cline) **4.** slope. —**in·cli·na′tion**, *n.*

ĭn·clōse′, *v.t.*, **-closed, -closing.** enclose.

ĭn·clūde′, *v.t.*, **-cluded, -cluding.** have or consider among other things. —**in·clu′sion**, *n.*

ĭn·clū′sĭve, *adj.* **1.** including the limiting items mentioned. **2.** considering everything.

ĭn·cŏg·nĭ′tō, *adj.* under an assumed name.

ĭn′cŏme′′, *n.* money received.

ĭn′′cŏm·mū′′nĭ·cá′dō, *adj.* without being allowed to communicate.

ĭn′cŏm′pár·á·ble, *adj.* not to be compared to others, esp. as an equal. —**in·com′par·a·bly**, *adv.*

in·côr′pó·räte″, *v.*, **-rated, -rating.** *v.t.*, *v.i.* **1.** form into a corporation. —*v.t.* **2.** embody. —**in·cor″po·ra′tion**, *n.*

in·côr′rĭ·gĭ·ble, *adj.* incapable of correction.

in·crease′, *v.*, **-creased, -creasing**, *n.* *v.t.* **1.** add to. —*v.i.* **2.** become larger or more numerous. —*n.* (in′crease) **3.** act, instance or amount of increasing. —**in·creas′ing·ly**, *adv.*

in′cre·mĕnt, *n.* increase.

in·crĭm′ĭ·nāte″, *v.t.*, **-nating, -nating. 1.** accuse of crime. **2.** subject to such accusation.

in·crŭst′, *v.t.* cover thickly. —**in″crus·ta′tion**, *n.*

in·cü·bāte″, *v.t.*, **-bated, -bating. 1.** hatch. **2.** encourage the development of. —**in″cu·ba′tion**, *n.* —**in′cu·ba″tor**, *n.*

in′cu·bus, *n.* **1.** annoying burden. **2.** evil spirit.

in·cŭl′cāte, *v.t.*, **-cated, -cating.** impress on the mind.

in·cŭl′pāte, *v.t.*, **-pated, -pating.** incriminate.

in·cŭm′bĕnt, *adj.* **1.** obligatory. **2.** in office. —*n.* **3.** present office holder. —**in·cum′ben·cy**, *n.*

in·cûr′, *v.t.*, **-curred, -curring.** bring on oneself.

in·cûr′sion, *n.* invasion.

in·dĕbt′ĕd, *adj.* owing a debt of money or gratitude. —**in·debt′ed·ness**, *n.*

in·deed′, *adv.* **1.** truly. —*interj.* **2.** exclamation of surprise.

in″de·făt′ï·gà·ble, *adj.* tireless.

in·dĕf′ĭ·nïte·lÿ, *adj.* **1.** in an indefinite way. **2.** with no known termination.

in·dĕl′ĭ·ble, *adj.* impossible to erase.

in·dĕm′nï·fÿ″, *v.t.*, **-fied, -fying.** compensate for. —**in·dem′ni·ty**, *n.*

in·dĕnt′, *v.t.* **1.** notch. **2.** begin to the right of the normal margin. —**in·den′tion, in″den·ta′tion**, *n.*

in·dĕn′tūre, *n.*, *v.t.*, **-tured, -turing.** *n.* **1.** contract, esp. for work. —*v.t.* **2.** bind with an indenture.

in″de·pĕn′dĕnt, *adj.* free of or needing no outside control. —**in″de·pen′dent·ly**, *adv.* —**in″de·pen′dence**, *n.*

in′dĕx, *n.*, *pl.* **-dexes, -dices**, *v.t.* *n.* **1.** orderly list of subjects. **2.** something that

indicates. **3.** forefinger. —*v.t.* **4.** make an index for.

in′dĭ·cāte″, *v.t.*, **-cated, -cating. 1.** call attention to. **2.** imply. —**in″di·ca′tion**, *n.* —**in·dic′a′tive**, *adj.* —**in′di·ca″tor**, *n.*

in·dict (in dīt′), *v.t.* charge formally with crime. —**in·dict′ment**, *n.*

in·dĭf′fĕr·ĕnt, *adj.* **1.** not caring. **2.** mediocre. **3.** neutral. —**in·dif′fer·ence**, *n.*

in·dĭg′en·oŭs, *adj.* native.

in′dĭ·gĕnt, *adj.* needy. —**in′di·gence**, *n.*

in·dĭ·gĕs′tion, *n.* difficulty in digesting food; discomfort caused by this.

in·dĭg′nànt, *adj.* righteously angry. —**in·dig′nant·ly**, *adv.* —**in″dig·na′tion**, *n.*

in·dĭg′nï·tÿ, *n.*, *pl.* **-ties.** offense to dignity.

in′dĭ·gō″, *n.* deep blue dye.

in″dĭs·pōsed′, *adj.* **1.** disinclined. **2.** slightly ill. —**in·dis″po·si′tion**, *n.*

in″dĭ·vĭd′ū·àl, *adj.* **1.** separate or distinct. **2.** pertaining to one person or thing. *n.* **3.** single or unique person or thing. —**in″di·vid′u·al·ly**, *adv.* —**in″di·vid′u·al′i·ty**, *n.*

in″dĭ·vĭd′ū·àl·ĭsm, *n.* use of personal judgment alone. —**in″di·vid′u·al·ist**, *n.*

in·dŏc′trī·nāte″, *v.t.*, **-nated, -nating.** instill doctrine into. —**in·doc″tri·na′tion**, *n.*

in′dō·lĕnt, *adj.* making little effort. —**in′do·lence**, *n.*

in·dŏm′ï·tà·ble, *adj.* impossible to defeat or dishearten.

in′dôor″, *adj.* for use, etc. inside.

in′dôors′, *adv.* within a building.

in·dū′bï·tà·ble, *adj.* impossible to doubt. —**in·du′bi·ta·bly**, *adv.*

in·dūce′, *v.t.*, **-duced, -ducing. 1.** persuade. **2.** cause. **3.** infer. —**in·duce′ment**, *n.*

in·dŭct′, *v.t.* enter formally, as in a military organization. —**in·duc·tee′**, *n.*

in·dŭc′tion, *n.* **1.** act or instance of inducing or inducting. **2.** reasoning from the particular to the general. —**in·duc′tive**, *adj.*

in·dŭlge′, *v.*, **-dulged, -dulging.** satisfy.

in·dŭl′gĕnce, *n.* **1.** act or instance of indulging. **2.** indulgent manner.

in·dŭl′gĕnt, *adj.* leniently kind.

ĭn′dŭs·trȳ, *n., pl.* **-tries. 1.** manufacture and commerce. **2.** type of manufacture or commerce. **3.** diligent work. —**in·dus′tri·al**, *adj.* —**in·dus′tri·al·ist**, *n.* —**in·dus′tri·al·ize′**, *v.t.* —**in·dus′tri·ous**, *adj.*

ĭn·ē′brĭ·āte′′, *v.t.*, **-ated, -ating,** *n. v.t.* **1.** make drunk. —*n.* (in e′bri·ate) **2.** drunkard. —**in·e′′bri·a′tion**, *n.*

ĭn·ĕf′fa·ble, *adj.* indescribable in words.

in′′e·luc′ta·ble, *adj.* inescapable.

ĭn·ĕpt′, *adj.* **1.** unsuitable. **2.** foolish or awkward. —**in·ept′i·tude′′**, **in·ept′ness**, *n.*

ĭn·êrt′, *adj.* **1.** powerless to move. **2.** without active properties. —**in·er′tia**, *n.* —**in·er′tial**, *adj.*

ĭn·ĕv′ĭ·tá·ble, *adj.* impossible to avoid. —**in·ev′i·ta·bly**, *adv.* —**in·ev′′i·ta·bil′i·ty**, *n.*

ĭn·ĕx′ö′rá·ble, *adj.* **1.** impossible to persuade. **2.** impossible to halt or change. —**in·ex′o·ra·bly**, *adv.*

ĭn·ĕx′plĭ·cá·ble, *adj.* impossible to explain.

ĭn·ĕx·trē′mĭs, at the point of death.

ĭn′fá·moŭs, *adj.* of evil reputation.

ĭn′fá·mȳ, *n., pl.* **-mies.** infamous state or act.

ĭn′fânt, *n.* very young child. —**in′fan·cy**, *n.* —**in′fan·tile′′**, *adj.*

ĭn′fan·trȳ, *n., pl.* **-tries.** corps of foot soldiers. —**in′fan·try·man**, *n.*

ĭn·făt′ū·āte′′, *v.t.*, **-ated, -ating.** make foolish with love. —**in·fat′′u·a′tion**, *n.*

ĭn·fĕct′, *v.t.* **1.** afflict with germs or a virus. **2.** influence with one's feelings. —**in·fec′tion**, *n.* —**in·fec′tious**, *adj.*

ĭn·fêr′, *v.t.*, **-ferred, -ferring.** conclude from evidence. —**in′fer·ence**, *n.* —**in′′fer·en′tial**, *adj.*

ĭn·fē′rĭ·ôr, *adj.* **1.** of lesser worth. **2.** inadequate. **3.** of lesser rank. —*n.* **4.** inferior person. —**in·fe′′ri·or′i·ty**, *n.*

ĭn·fêr′nál, *adj.* hellish.

ĭn·fêr′nō, *n.* hell, esp. as a fiery place.

ĭn·fĕst′, *v.t.* penetrate harmfully in large numbers. —**in′′fes·ta′tion**, *n.*

ĭn′fǐ·dĕl, *n.* unbeliever.

ĭn′fīght′′ing, *n.* combat at close range.

ĭn′fĭl·trāte′′, *v.t.*, **-trated, -trating.** penetrate in many places. —**in′′fil·tra′tion**, *n.*

ĭn′fī·nīte, *adj.* without bounds or end. —**in′fin·ite·ly**, *adv.* —**in·fin′i·tude′′**, *n.* —**in·fin′i·ty**, *n.*

ĭn′′fĭn·ĭ·tĕs′ĭ·mál, *adj.* extremely small.

ĭn·fĭn′ĭ·tĭve, *n.* form of a verb without person, number, or tense.

ĭn·fĭrm′, *adj.* not in good health. —**in·firm′i·ty**, *n.*

ĭn·fĭr′má·rȳ, *n., pl.* **-ries.** place for treating the sick.

ĭn·flăme′, *v.t.*, **-flamed, -flaming. 1.** cause to become red, sore, swollen, etc. **2.** rouse to anger, etc. —**in′′flam·ma′tion**, *n.* —**in·flam′ma·to′′ry**, *adj.*

ĭn·flăm′má·ble, *adj.* **1.** readily burned. **2.** readily aroused to anger, etc.

ĭn·flāte′, *v.*, **-flated, -flating.** *v.t.* **1.** cause inflation in or to. —*v.i.* **2.** be filled with air or gas. —**in·flat′a·ble**, *adj.*

ĭn·flā′tion, *n.* **1.** filling with air or gas. **2.** fall in the value of money. —**in·fla′tion·ar′′y**, *adj.*

ĭn·flĕct′, *v.t.* vary in tone, form, etc. —**in·flec′tion**, *n.* —**in·flec′tion·al**, *adj.*

ĭn·flĭct′, *v.t.* harm or punish someone with. —**in·flic′tion**, *n.*

ĭn′flŭ·ĕnce, *n., v.t.*, **-enced, -encing. 1.** ability to determine events or decisions. **2.** person or thing that influences. —*v.t.* **3.** use influence on.

ĭn′′flŭ·ĕn′tiál, *adj.* having much influence.

ĭn′′flŭ·ĕn′zà, *n.* contagious virus infection.

ĭn′flŭx′′, *n.* inward flow.

ĭn·fôrm′, *v.t.* give knowledge to. —**in·form′ant**, **in·form′er**, *n.* —**in′′for·ma′tion**, *n.* —**in·form′a·tive**, *adj.*

ĭn·fôrmed′, *adj.* **1.** in possession of essential facts. **2.** learned; erudite.

ĭn·frăc′tion, *n.* violation, as of a law.

ĭn′′frá·rĕd′, *adj.* pertaining to invisible rays beyond the red end of the spectrum.

ĭn·frĭnge′, *v.*, **-fringed, -fringing.** *v.t.* **1.** violate —*v.i.* **2.** encroach. —**in·fringe′ment**, *n.*

ĭn·fū′rĭ·āte′′, *v.t.*, **-ated, -ating.** make furious.

ĭn·fūse′, *v.t.*, **-fused, -fusing. 1.** instill. **2.** steep. —**in′′fu′sion**, *n.*

ĭn·gēn'ioŭs, *adj.* clever. **—in·gen'ious·
ly,** *adv.* **—in''gen·u'i·ty,** *n.*

ĭn·gĕn'ū·oŭs, *adj.* **1.** naive. **2.** candid.
—in·gen'u·ous·ness, *n.*

ĭn·gĕst', *v.t.* eat. **—in·ges'tion,** *n.*

ĭn'gŏt, *n.* cast piece of metal.

ĭn·grāined', *adj.* deeply imbedded.

ĭn·grāte, *n.* ungrateful person.

ĭn·grā'tĭ·āte'', *v.t.*, **-ated, -ating.** to gain
favor of another. **—in·gra''ti·a'tion,**
n.

ĭn·grē'dĭ·ent, *n.* component.

ĭn·grĕss, *n.* entry.

ĭn'grŏwn'', *adj.* grown into the flesh.

ĭn·hăb'ĭt, *v.t.* live in. **—in·hab'it·ant,** *n.*

ĭn·hāle', *v.t.*, *v.i.*, **-haled, -haling.**
breathe in. **—in''ha·la'tion,** *n.*

ĭn·hēre', *v.i.* **-hered, -hering.** be naturally part of something. **—in·her'ent,**
adj.

ĭn·hĕr'ĭt, *v.t.* be an heir to. **—in·her'i·
tance,** *n.*

ĭn·hĭb'ĭt, *v.t.* check; restrain. **—in''hi·bi'
tion,** *n.*

ĭn·hū'măn, *adj.* emotionally cold; callous. **—in''hu·man'i·ty,** *n.*

ĭn·ĭm'ĭ·căl, *adj.* hostile.

ĭn·ĭq'uĭ·tў, *n.*, *pl.* **-ties.** wickedness or
wicked act. **—in·iq'ui·tous,** *adj.*

ĭn·ĭ'tĭal, *adj.*, *n.*, *v.t.*, **-tialed, -tialing.**
adj. **1.** beginning. **—n. 2.** beginning letter of a word. **—v.t. 3.** mark with initials. **—in·i'tial·ly,** *adv.*

ĭn·ĭ'tĭ·āte'', *v.t.*, **-ated, -ating. 1.** begin.
2. acquaint with basics. **3.** accept as a
member with ceremony. **—in·i''ti·a'
tion,** *n.*

ĭn·ĭ'tĭ·a·tĭve, *n.* **1.** readiness to initiate
actions. **2.** personal decision to act.

ĭn·jĕct', *v.t.* force beneath the skin. **—in·
jec'tion,** *n.*

ĭn·jŭnc'tion, *n.* order, as from a court.

ĭn·jūre, *v.t.*, **-jured, -juring.** harm.
—in''ju'ri·ous, *adj.* **—in'ju·ry,** *n.*

ĭnk, *n.* **1.** pigmented liquid for printing,
writing, or drawing. **—v.t. 2.** apply ink
to. **—ink'y,** *adj.*

ĭnk'lĭng, *n.* vague perception.

ĭn'lănd'', *adj.*, *adv.* **1.** away from the
shore, etc. **—n. 2.** inland region.

ĭn'-lāw'', *n.* relative by marriage.

ĭn'lāy'', *v.t.*, **-laid, -laying,** *n.* *v.t.* **1.** set

into another piece. **—n. 2.** something
inlaid.

ĭn'lĕt, *n.* small extension of a body of water.

ĭn'māte'', *n.* person under confinement.

ĭnn, *n.* small hotel or restaurant.

ĭn'nāte'', *adj.* present from birth. **—in·
nate'ly,** *adv.*

ĭn'nêr, *adj.* farther inside. **—in'ner·
most'',** *adj.*

ĭn'nĭng, *adj.* turn at bat.

ĭn'nŏ·cent, *adj.* **1.** free of guilt. **2.** unso-
phisticated. **—n. 3.** innocent person.
—in'no·cent·ly, *adv.* **—in'no·cence,**
n.

ĭn·nŏc'ū·oŭs, *adj.* harmless.

ĭn''nŏ·vā'tion, *n.* new discovery or development. **—in'no·vat''or,** *n.* **—in'
no·vat''ive,** *adj.*

ĭn''nū·ĕn'dō, *n.*, *pl.* **-does, -dos.** sly implication.

ĭn·nū'mêr·a·ble, *adj.* too many to count.

ĭn·ŏc'ū·lāte'', *v.t.*, **-lated, -lating.** im-
munize with an injection. **—in·oc''u·
la'tion,** *n.*

ĭn·ôr'dĭ·nāte, *adj.* excessive. **—in·or'di·
nate·ly,** *adv.*

ĭn'pŭt, *n.* **1.** something supplied. **2.** (computers) data entered into a computer.

ĭn'quĕst'', *n.* coroner's investigation.

ĭn·quīre', *v.i.*, **-quired, -quiring. 1.** ask.
2. investigate. **—in'quir·y,** *n.*

ĭn·quĭs'ĭ·tĭve, *adj.* desiring to know many
things.

ĭn'rōad'', *n.* encroachment.

ĭn·scrībe', *v.t.*, **-scribed, -scribing.** write
or letter. **—in·scrip'tion,** *n.*

ĭn·scrū'ta·ble, *adj.* hard to understand.
—in·scru'ta·bly, *adv.*

ĭn'sĕct, *n.* six-legged invertebrate.

ĭn·sĕc'tĭ·cīde'', *n.* insect-killing preparation.

ĭn·sĕm'ĭ·nāte'', *v.t.*, **-nated, -nating.** in-
ject semen into. **—in·sem''i·na'tion,**
n.

ĭn·sĕn'sāte, *adj.* insensitive.

ĭn·sĕn'sĭ·ble, *adj.* **1.** unconscious. **2.** impossible to sense. **—in·sen''si·bil'i·ty,**
n.

ĭn·sêrt', *v.t.* **1.** place into something. **—n.**
(in'sert) **2.** something inserted. **—in·
ser'tion,** *n.*

ĭn·sīde', *adv.*, *prep.* **1.** within. **—adj. 2.**

inner. —*n.* **3.** inner part. —**in·sid′er**, *n.*

in·sid′i·oŭs, *adj.* slyly dangerous.

in′sĭght″, *n.* deep understanding.

in·sig′ni·à, *n.*, *pl.* distinguishing badges, etc.

in·sin′ū·āte″, *v.t.*, -ated, -ating. **1.** imply slyly. **2.** introduce imperceptibly. —**in·sin″u·a′tion**, *n.*

in·sĭp′ĭd, *adj.* flavorless; dull. —**in″si·pid′i·ty**, *n.*

in·sĭst′, *v.t.* make repeated demands or assertions. —**in·sis′tent**, *adj.* —**in·sis′tence**, *n.*

in″sō·fär′, *adv.* to such an extent.

in′sō·lent, *adj.* disrespectful. —**in′so·lence**, *n.*

in·sŏm′ni·à, *n.* inability to sleep. —**in·som′ni·ac″**, *n.*

in·spĕct′, *v.t.* examine carefully. —**in·spec′tion**, *n.* —**in·spec′tor**, *n.*

in·spīre′, *v.*, -spired, -spiring. *v.t.*, *v.i.* **1.** breathe in. —*v.t.* **2.** stimulate to mental activity. **3.** arouse in someone. —**in″spi·ra′tor**, *n.* —**in″spi·ra′tion·al**, *adj.*

in·stăll′, *v.t.* -stalled, -stalling. put in place. —**in″stal·la′tion**, *n.*

in·stăll′ment, *n.* item in a series.

in′stănce, *n.*, *v.t.*, -stanced, -stancing. *n.* **1.** example. **2.** occasion. —*v.t.* **3.** cite.

in′stănt, *n.* **1.** moment. —*adj.* **2.** happening or ready quickly. **3.** imminent. —**in″stan·ta′ne·ous**, *adj.* —**in′stant·ly**, *adv.*

in·stĕad′, *adv.* in the place.

in′stĭ·gāte″, *v.t.*, -gated, -gating. urge, as to action. —**in″sti·ga′tion**, *n.* —**in′sti·ga″tor.**

in·stĭll′, *v.t.*, -stilled, -stilling. implant. Also, **in·stil′.**

in·stĭnct′, *n.* inborn prompting or reaction. —**in·stinc′tive**, *adj.* —**in·stinc′tu·al**, *adj.*

in′stĭ·tūte″, *n.*, *v.t.*, -tuted, -tuting. *n.* **1.** professional organization or school. —*v.t.* **2.** establish. **3.** start.

in″stĭ·tū′tion, *n.* **1.** act or instance of instituting. **2.** institute. **3.** established law or custom. —**in′sti·tu′tion·al**, *adj.*

in·strŭct′, *v.t.*, **1.** inform or advise. **2.** command. —**in·struc′tion**, *n.* —**in·struc′tive**, *adj.* —**in·struc′tor**, *n.*

in′strŭ·ment, *n.* **1.** tool, etc. **2.** means. **3.** measuring device. **4.** musical device. **5.** legal document.

in″strŭ·měn′tàl, *adj.* **1.** pertaining to music by instruments. **2.** useful. —**in″stru·men′tal·ist**, *n.* —**in″stru·men′tal′i·ty**, *n.*

in′sŭ·làr, *adj.* **1.** pertaining to islands. **2.** narrow-minded; parochial.

in′sŭ·lāte″, *v.t.*, -lated, -lating. isolate, esp. from heat, sound, or electricity. —**in″su·la′tion**, *n.* —**in′su·la″tor**, *n.*

in′sŭ·lĭn, *n.* hormone secreted by the pancreas.

in·sŭlt′, *v.t.* **1.** treat so as to hurt the feelings. —*n.* (in′sult) **2.** epithet, etc. that insults. —**in·sult′ing**, *adj.*

in·su′per·a·ble, *adj.* impossible to overcome.

in″sŭp·pôrt′a·ble, *adj.* **1.** intolerable. **2.** impossible to prove.

in·sûre′, *v.t.*, -sured, -suring. **1.** guarantee against loss with money. **2.** make sure. —**in·sur′ance**, *n.*

in·sûr′gent, *n.*, *adj.* revolutionary. —**in·sur′gence**, *n.*

in″sûr·rĕc′tion, *n.* revolution.

in·tăct′, *adj.* undamaged.

in′tāke″, *n.* **1.** amount received, absorbed, etc. **2.** opening for receiving air, etc.

in·tăn′gĭ·ble, *adj.* **1.** non-material. **2.** non-monetary. **3.** indefinable.

in′te·gêr, *n.* whole number.

in′te·gral, *adj.* **1.** forming an essential part. **2.** complete.

in′te·grāte″, *v.t.*, -grated, -grating. **1.** make complete. **2.** bring together into a whole. **3.** end racial segregation in or among. —**in″te·gra′tion**, *n.*

in·tĕg′ri·ty, *n.* **1.** intactness. **2.** firmness of character, honesty, etc.

in·tĕg′u·ment, *n.* covering, e.g. skin.

in·tĕl′lĕct″, *n.* ability to comprehend or reason. —**in″tel·lec′tu·al**, *adj.*, *n.*

in·tĕl′li·gence, *n.* **1.** ability to comprehend, reason, and think creatively. **2.** news. —**in·tel′li·gent**, *adj.*

in·tĕl″li·gĕnt′si·à, *n. pl.* intellectuals as a group.

in·tĕl′li·gĭ·ble, *adj.* able to be understood.

in·tĕnd′, *v.t.* have as a purpose.

in·tĕnd′ĕd, *n.* fiancé or fiancée.

ĭn·těnse′, *adj.* **1.** very strong. **2.** with much emotion. —**ĭn·těn′sĭ·ty**, *n.* —**ĭn·těn′sĭ·fy**, *v.t.*, *v.i.*

ĭn·těn′sĭve, *adj.* **1.** thorough. **2.** *Grammar.* giving emphasis.

ĭn·těnt′, *adj.* **1.** earnest. **2.** firmly intending. —*n.* **3.** purpose. —**ĭn·těnt′ly**, *adv.*

ĭn·těn′tion, *n.* purpose. —**ĭn·těn′tion·al**, *adj.*

ĭn·těr′, *v.t.*, **-terred, -terring.** bury.

ĭn″tĕr·cēde′, *v.i.*, **-ceded, -ceding.** mediate. —**ĭn″tĕr·ces′sion**, *n.*

ĭn″tĕr·cĕpt′, *v.t.* halt or attack along the way. —**ĭn″tĕr·cep′tion**, *n.*

ĭn″tĕr·chānge′, *v.*, **-changed, -changing,** *n. v.i., v.t.* **1.** exchange. **2.** alternate. —*n.* (ĭn′tĕr chānge″) **3.** access to an express highway. —**ĭn″tĕr·change′a·ble**, *adj.*

ĭn″tĕr·con·nĕct′, *v.i.* connect with one another. —**ĭn″tĕr·con·nec′tion**, *n.*

ĭn″tĕr·côurse″, *n.* **1.** communication. **2.** copulation.

ĭn″tĕr·dē·pĕn′dĕnt, *adj.* dependent on one another. —**ĭn″tĕr·de·pen′dence**, *n.*

ĭn″tĕr·dĭct′, *v.t.* **1.** prohibit. —*n.* (ĭn′tĕr dĭct″) **2.** prohibition. —**ĭn″tĕr·dic′tion**, *n.*

ĭn″tĕr·dĭs′cĭ·plĭ·nâr″y, *adj.* involving varied disciplines.

ĭn′tĕr·ĕst, *n.* **1.** willing attention. **2.** share in a business. **3.** profit on a loan. —*v.t.* **4.** obtain willing attention from.

ĭn″tĕr·fēre′, *v.i.*, **-fered, -fering. 1.** meddle. **2.** intervene. —**ĭn′tĕr·fer′ence,** *n.*

ĭn″tĕr·ĭm, *n.* intervening time.

ĭn·tē′rĭ·ör, *n.* **1.** inside. **2.** room. —*adj.* **3.** inside. **4.** personal.

ĭn″tĕr·jĕct′, *v.t.* insert as an interruption or addition.

ĭn″tĕr·jĕc′tion, *n.* **1.** exclamation. **2.** act or instance of interjecting.

ĭn′tĕr·lāce″, *v.i.* be entwined or woven together.

ĭn′tĕr·lârd″, *v.t.* scatter throughout.

ĭn′tĕr·lŏck″, *v.i.* be connected or act together.

ĭn′tĕr·lŏp″ĕr, *n.* person who interferes.

ĭn′tĕr·lūde″, *n.* episode, musical piece, etc. between major events.

ĭn″tĕr·mär′ry, *v.i.*, **-ried, -rying. 1.** become associated by marriage. **2.** marry a close relation. —**ĭn″tĕr·mar′riage**, *n.*

ĭn″tĕr·mē′dĭ·âr″y, *adj., n., pl.* **-ies.** *adj.* **1.** coming between. —*n.* **2.** go-between.

ĭn″tĕr·mē′dĭ·āte, *adj.* coming between.

ĭn″tĕr′mĕnt, *n.* burial.

ĭn″tĕr′mĭn·á·ble, *adj.* seemingly endless. —**ĭn·ter′min·a·bly**, *adv.*

ĭn″tĕr·mĭn′gle, *v.i.*, **-gled, -gling.** be blended.

ĭn″tĕr·mĭs′sion, *n.* pause, as between acts of a play.

ĭn″tĕr·mĭt′tĕnt, *adj.* occurring at intervals. —**ĭn″tĕr·mit′tent·ly**, *adv.*

ĭn′tĕrn, *n.* **1.** Also, **ĭn′tĕrne.** assistant resident doctor. —*v.t.* (ĭn tern′) **2.** detain and confine. —**ĭn·tern′ment**, *n.*

ĭn·tĕr′nál, *adj.* **1.** interior. **2.** non-foreign. —**ĭn·ter′nal·ly**, *adv.*

ĭn″tĕr·nă′tion·ál, *adj.* **1.** among nations. **2.** regardless of nation.

ĭn″tĕr·nē′cĭne, *adj.* deadly to both sides.

ĭn′tĕr·nĭst, *n.* doctor using non-surgical treatment.

ĭn″tĕr·plăy″, *n.* mutual influence.

ĭn·tĕr′pò·lāte″, *v.t.*, **-lated, -lating.** alter with new material. —**ĭn·ter′po·la′tion**, *n.*

ĭn″tĕr·pōse″, *v.t.*, **-posed, -posing.** place between or among. —**ĭn″ter·po·si′tion**, *n.*

ĭn·tĕr′prĕt′, *v.t.* **1.** clarify. **2.** understand. **3.** translate. —**ĭn·ter′pret·er**, *n.* —**ĭn·ter″pre·ta′tion**, *n.* —**ĭn·ter′pre·tive**, *adj.*

ĭn″tĕr·rā′ciál, *adj.* among races.

ĭn″tĕr·rē·lāte″, *v.t.*, **-lated, -lating.** relate one to the other. —**ĭn″ter·re·la′tion**, *n.*

ĭn″tĕr·rŏ′gāte″, *v.t.*, **-gated, -gating.** question. —**ĭn·ter″ro·ga′tion**, *n.* —**ĭn·ter′ro·ga″tor**, *n.* —**ĭn·ter·rŏg′a·tive,** **ĭn″ter·rog′a·to·ry**, *adj.*

ĭn″tĕr·rŭpt″, *v.t.*, **1.** halt with an action, remark, etc. **2.** break the uniformity of. —**ĭn″ter·rup′tion**, *n.*

ĭn″tĕr·sĕct′, *v.t.*, *v.i.* cross. —**ĭn′ter·sec′tion**, *n.*

ĭn″tĕr·spêrse″, *v.t.*, **-spersed, -spersing. 1.** scatter. **2.** vary with scattered things.

ĭn·têr·stāte", *adj., adv.* from state to state.

ĭn·têr'stĭce, *n.* gap.

ĭn''têr·ûr'bǎn, *adj.* from city to city.

ĭn'têr·vǎl, *n.* intervening period or space.

ĭn''têr·vēne', *v.i.*, -vened, -vening. 1. come or occur between. 2. mediate. —ĭn''ter·ven'tion, *n.*

ĭn'têr·vīew", *n.* 1. person-to-person meeting. —*v.t.* 2. question at an interview. —ĭn''ter·view''er, *n.* —ĭn''ter·view''ee', *n.*

ĭn·tĕs'tāte", *adj.* without having made a will.

ĭn·tĕs'tĭne, *n.* either of two organs for converting food. Also, ĭn·tĕs'tines. —ĭn·tes'tin·al, *adj.*

ĭn'tĭ·māte, *adj., n., v.t.*, -mated, -mating. *adj.* 1. emotionally close. 2. personal. 3. thorough. —*n.* 4. intimate friend. —*v.t.* (ĭn''tĭ māte') 5. hint. —ĭn'tĭ·māte·ly, *adv.* —ĭn'tĭ·ma·cy, *n.* —ĭn''tĭ·ma'tion, *n.*

ĭn·tĭm'ĭ·dāte", *v.t.*, -dated, -dating. command through fear. —ĭn·tĭm''i·da'tion, *n.*

ĭn'to, *prep.* 1. to the interior or depths of. 2. up against. 3. to some material, number of parts, etc.

ĭn·tōne', *v.t.*, -toned, -toning. 1. utter in a songlike tone. 2. utter with a controlled or varied pitch. —ĭn''to·na'tion, *n.*

ĭn tō'tō, as a whole.

ĭn·tŏx'ĭ·cāte", *v.t.*, -cated, -cating. make drunk. —ĭn·tox''i·ca'tion, *n.* —ĭn·tox'i·cant, *n.*

ĭn·trăc'tà·ble, *adj.* unruly.

ĭn''trà·mū'ral, *adj.* within an institution.

ĭn·trăn'sĭ·gĕnt, *adj.* uncompromising. —ĭn·tran'si·gence, *n.*

ĭn''trà·vē'noŭs, *adj.* into a vein from outside the body.

ĭn·trĕp'ĭd, *adj.* fearless. —ĭn''tre·pid'i·ty, *n.*

ĭn'trĭ·cāte, *adj.* complicated; complex. —ĭn'tri·cate·ly, *adv.* —ĭn'tri·ca·cy, *n.*

ĭn·trĭgue', *v.*, -trigued, -triguing. *v.i.* 1. plot in stealth. —*v.t.* 2. make curious. —*n.* 3. stealthy plot or plotting.

ĭn·trĭn'sĭc, *adj.* essential; inherent. —ĭn·trin'si·cal·ly, *adv.*

ĭn''trŏ·dūce', *v.t.*, -duced, -ducing. 1. present for the first time. 2. bring into use. 3. insert. —ĭn''tro·duc'tion, *n.* —ĭn''tro·duc'to·ry, *adj.*

ĭn''trŏ·spĕc'tion, *n.* self-examination. —ĭn''tro·spec'tive, *adj.*

ĭn''trŏ·vêrt", *n.* withdrawn person. —ĭn''tro·ver'sion, *n.*

ĭn·trūde', *v.*, -truded, -truding. *v.i.* 1. come as an interruption or surprise. —*v.t.* 2. force upon others. —ĭn·trud'er, *n.* —ĭn·tru'sion, *n.* —ĭn·tru'sive, *adj.*

ĭn·tū·ĭ'tion, *n.* non-logical insight. —ĭn·tu'i·tive, *adj.*

ĭn·ŭn·dāte", *v.t.*, -dated, -dating. flood. —ĭn''un·da'tion, *n.*

ĭn·ūre', *v.t.*, -ured, -uring. to harden oneself to something disagreeable; accustom.

ĭn·vāde', *v.t.*, -vaded, -vading. enter with force. —ĭn·vad'er, *n.* —ĭn·va'sion, *n.*

ĭn·vǎl'ĭd, *n.* 1. sick person. —*adj.* (in val' id). 2. not valid. —ĭn·val'i·date", *v.t.*

ĭn·vǎl'ū·à·ble, *adj.* valuable beyond reckoning.

ĭn·vĕc'tĭve, *n.* verbal attack.

ĭn·veigh' (ĭn·vā'), *v.i.* make a verbal attack.

ĭn·vēi'gle, *v.t.*, -gled, -gling. trick into an action.

ĭn·vĕnt', *v.t.* discover, as a product or process. —ĭn·ven'tion, *n.* —ĭn·ven'tive, *adj.* —ĭn·ven'tor, *n.*

ĭn'vĕn·tô''rȳ, *n., pl.* -ries. *v.t.*, -ried, -rying. *n.* 1. precise list. 2. stock of goods. —*v.t.* 3. make an inventory of.

ĭn·vêrse', *adj.* 1. oppose in kind. —*n.* 2. something inverse. —ĭn·verse'ly, *adv.*

ĭn·vêrt', *v.t.* 1. turn upside down. 2. reverse in order or position. —ĭn·ver'sion, *n.*

ĭn·vêr'tè·brāte, *adj.* 1. having no backbone. —*n.* 2. invertebrate animal.

ĭn·vĕst', *v.t.* 1. put into something in the hope of profit. 2. give authority or office to. —*v.i.* 3. invest money. —ĭn·vest'or, *n.* —ĭn·vest'ment, *n.* —ĭn·vest'i·ture", *n.*

ĭn·vĕs'tĭ·gāte", *v.t.*, -gated, -gating. examine or explore. —ĭn·ves'ti·ga''tor, *n.* —ĭn·ves''ti·ga'tion, *n.*

ĭn·vĕt'êr·àte, *adj.* habitual. —ĭn·vet'er·a·cy, *n.*

ĭn·vĭd'ĭ·oŭs, *adj.* causing ill will.

in·vĭg′ŏr·āte″, *v.t.*, **-ated, -ating.** make vigorous. —**in·vĭg″or·a′tion**, *n.*

in·vĭnc′ĭ·ble, *adj.* impossible to conquer. —**in·vĭnc″i·bil′i·ty**, *n.*

in·vī′ŏl·à·ble, *adj.* not to be violated. —**in·vi″ol·a·bil′i·ty**, *n.*

in·vī′ó·lāte, *adj.* unviolated.

in·vīte′, *v.t.*, **-vited, -viting. 1.** ask to be present. **2.** give a pretext for. —**in″vi·ta′tion**, *n.*

in·vīt′ing, *adj.* enticing.

in′vŏ·cā′tion, *n.* prayerlike speech.

in′voĭce, *n.* list of goods supplied.

in·vōke′, *v.t.*, **-voked, -voking. 1.** call upon, as a god. **2.** cite as a justification.

in′vŏ·lū′tion, *n.* intricacy. —**in′vo·lut″ ed,** *adj.*

in·vŏlve′, *v.t.*, **-volved, -volving. 1.** include as relevant. **2.** affect or trouble. **3.** occupy. **4.** complicate. —**in·volve′ ment,** *n.*

in′ward, *adj.* **1.** inside. **2.** toward the inside. **3.** mental. —*adv.* **4.** Also, **in′ wards,** towards the inside. —**in·ward′ ly,** *adv.*

ī′ó·dīne″, *n.* nonmetallic chemical element. —**i′o·dize″**, *v.t.*

ī′ŏn, *n.* electrically charged atom or group of atoms.

ī·ō′tà, *n.* minute quantity.

ĭp′sŏ făc′tō, by the very fact.

IQ, intelligence quotient (measure of intelligence). Also **I.Q.**

ĭr-, prefix meaning "not" or "lack of." **irrational, irreconcilable, irredeemable, irregular, irrelevant, irreligious, irremediable, irreparable, irreplaceable, irresponsible, irreverent, irreversible, irrevocable.**

ĭ·răs′cĭ·ble, *adj.* easily angered.

īre, *n.* wrath. —**i·rate′**, *adj.*

ĭr″ĭ·dĕs′cĕnt, *adj.* with a play of rainbow-like colors. —**ir″i·des′cence**, *n.*

ī′rĭs, *n.*, *pl.* **irises.** *n.* **1.** pigmented part surrounding the eye pupil. **2.** plant with sword-shaped leaves.

îrk, *v.t.* annoy. —**irk′some**, *adj.*

ī′ron, *n.* **1.** metallic element attracting magnets. **2.** device made of iron. **3. irons,** shackles. —*v.t.* **4.** smooth with an iron.

Iron Curtain, *n.* former barrier to travel, information, etc. around the communist countries.

ī′ró·nў, *n.*, *pl.* **-nies.** figure of speech conveying meaning through words of opposite meaning. —**i·ron′i·cal**, **i·ron′ic**, *adj.*

ir″rā′dĭ·āte″, *v.t.*, **-ated, -ating.** expose to rays.

ir″rē·gârd′lĕss, *adj.*, *adv.* regardless.

ir″rē·sĭst′ĭ·ble, *adj.* **1.** impossible to resist. **2.** overwhelmingly tempting.

ir″rĭ·gāte′, *v.t.*, **-gated, -gating.** introduce water to, to raise crops. —**ir″ri·ga′tion**, *n.*

ir″rĭ·ta·ble, *adj.* readily irritated. —**ir′ri·ta·bly,** *adv.* —**ir″ri·ta·bil′i·ty**, *n.*

ir″rĭ·tāte′, *v.t.*, **-tated, -tating. 1.** annoy. **2.** make sore. —**ir″ri·ta′tion**, *n.* —**ir′ ri·tant,** *adj.*, *n.*

ir·rŭpt′, *v.i.* **1.** burst forth; expand. —**ir· rup′tion,** *n.*

ī′sĭn·glâss″, *n.* **1.** gelatin from fish bladders. **2.** mica.

Ĭs′lâm, *n.* religion of Muhammad.

īs·lănd (ī′lənd), *n.* **1.** body of land surrounded by water. **2.** isolated platform, etc.

īs·lĕt (ī′lət), *n.* small island.

ī′só·lāte″, *v.t.*, **-lated, -lating.** keep apart. —**i″so·la′tion**, *n.*

ī″só·lā′tion·ĭst, *n.* believer in no alliances with other countries. —**i″so·la′tion·ism**, *n.*

ī″só·mĕt′rĭc, *adj.* **1.** with all dimensions represented to the same scale. **2.** pertaining to isometrics. —*n.* **3. isometrics,** type of muscular exercise.

ī·sŏs′cĕl·ēs″, *adj.* pertaining to triangles with two equal sides.

ī′só·tōpe″, *n.* form of an element coinciding in atomic number but not in atomic weight with another.

īs′sūe, *v.*, **-sued, -suing,** *v.t.* **1.** give out. **2.** publish. —*v.i.* **3.** emerge. —*n.* **4.** something that issues. **5.** periodical of one date. **6.** thing in dispute. **7.** offspring. **8.** result. —**is′su·ance**, *n.*

ĭsth′mŭs, *n.*, *pl.* **-muses.** narrow neck of connecting land between bodies of water.

ĭt, *pron.*, *pl.* **they 1.** thing referred to. **2.** (subject of various impersonal verbs).

ĭ·tăl′ĭc, *adj.* **1.** pertaining to letters

printed thus: *Italics*. —*n*. **2. italics**,
italic letters. —**i·tal'i·cize''**, *v.t.*

ĭtch, *v.i.* **1.** feel a mild irritation tempting
one to scratch. **2.** desire restlessly. —*n*.
3. act or instance of itching. —**itch'y**,
adj.

ī'tĕm, *n*. **1.** listed thing. **2.** piece of news.
—**i'tem·ize''**, *v.t.* —**i''tem·i·za'tion**,
n.

ĭt'ĕr·āte'', *v.t.*, **-ated, -ating.** repeat.
—**it''er·a'tion**, *n*.

ī·tĭn'ĕr·ant, *adj.* **1.** traveling; migratory.
—*n*. **2.** itinerant person.

ī·tĭn'ĕr·ār''y̆, *n., pl.* **-ies.** plan of travel.

ĭts, *pron.* belonging or pertaining to it.

ĭt's, *pron.* contraction of *it is*.

ĭt·sĕlf', *pron.* **1.** (intensive or reflexive of
it). **2.** its true self.

ī'vŏ·rў, *n*. creamy-white substance of
tusks.

ī'vў, *n., pl.* **ivies.** climbing evergreen
vine. —**i'vied**, *adj.*

J

J, j, *n*. tenth letter of the English alphabet.

jăb, *v.*, **jabbed, jabbing.** *v.t., v.i., n.*
poke.

jăb'bĕr, *n*. **1.** fast, incoherent talk. —*v.i.*
2. talk in a jabber.

jăck, *n*. **1.** lifting machine. **2.** playing
card; knave. **3.** flag at a ship's stern. **4.**
point of connection; place where something is plugged in. —*v.t.* **5.** to raise
something with a jack.

jăck'ăl, *n*. wild African and Asian dog.

jăck'ăss', *n*. **1.** male donkey. **2.** fool.

jăck'ĕt, *n*. **1.** short coat. **2.** covering.

jăck'knife', *n., v.i.*, **-knifed, -knifing.**
n. **1.** folding knife. **2.** type of swimmer's
dive. —*v.i.* **3.** fold accidentally at a joint.

jăck'pŏt', *n*. accumulated stakes that are
won.

jăck'răb'bĭt, *n*. large North American
hare.

jāde, *n., v.t.*, **jaded, jading.** *n*. **1.** ornamental stone, usually green. —*v.t.* **2.**
satiate.

jăg, *n*. **1.** sharp point. **2.** *Informal.* orgy.

jăg'gĕd, *adj.* with a rough, sharp edge or
surface.

jăg'uâr, *n*. large cat of Latin America and
the U.S. Southwest.

jāil, *n*. **1.** prison for short confinements.
—*v.t.* **2.** put in jail. —**jail'er, jail'or**, *n*.

jȧ·lŏp'y̆, *n., pl.* **-ies.** old, ill-kept car.

jăl'ou·sie, *n*. louvered blind.

jăm, *v.*, **jammed, jamming.** *n. v.t., v.i.* **1.**
crowd. **2** stick tight. —*n*. **3.** act or instance of jamming. **4.** fruit boiled with
sugar. **5.** *Informal.* adverse situation.

jămb, *n*. upright of a doorway or window.

jăm''bō·rēe', *n*. *Informal.* noisy celebration.

jăm'păcked', *adj.* crowded to capacity.

jăn'gle, *v.* **-gled, -gling.** *v.i.* **1.** jingle
harshly. —*v.t.* **2.** irritate, as the nerves.

jăn'ĭ·tör, *n*. person who takes care of a
building.

Jăn'ū·âr''y̆, *n*. first month.

jär, *n., v.*, **jarred, jarring.** *n*. **1.** cylindrical container. **2.** jolt. —*v.t.* **3.** jolt. —*v.i.*
4. clash. **5.** have an irritating effect.

jär'gŏn, *n*. abstruse technical language.

jăs'mĭne, *n*. fragrant-flowered plant.

jăs'pêr, *n*. opaque, colored quartz.

jaūn'dĭce, *n., v.t.*, **-diced, -dicing.** *n*. **1.**
disease characterized by yellowing due
to bile in the blood. —*v.t.* **2.** predispose
against.

jaūnt, *n*. **1.** pleasure excursion. —*v.i.* **2.** go
on a jaunt.

jaūn'ty̆, *adj.*, **-tier, -tiest.** cheerful.
—**jaun'ti·ly**, *adv.*

jăv'e·lĭn, *n*. throwing spear.

jăw, *n*. **1.** bony framing member of the
mouth. **2.** gripping part of a vise, etc.

jāy, *n*. **1.** crowlike bird. **2.** bluejay.

jāy'wălk'', *v.i.* cross a street heedlessly.
—**jay'walk''er**, *n*.

jăzz, *n*. syncopated, rhythmic modern music.

jĕal'ous, *adj.* **1.** feeling jealousy. **2.**
watchful.

jeans, *n., pl.* trousers of strong cloth.

jēep, *n*. rugged, military-style car.

jēer, *v.i.* **1.** make scornful utterances. —*n*.
2. such an utterance.

Jē·hō'văh, *n*. God.

je·jūne', *adj.* **1.** unfulfilling. **2.** childish.

jĕll, *v.i.* **1.** harden, as gelatin. **2.** come to
fulfillment.

jĕl'lў, *n., pl.* **-lies,** *v.t.* **-lied, -lying.** *n.* **1.** gelatinous food. —*v.t.* **2.** make into jelly.

jĕo'pärd·īze'', *v.t.,* **-ized, -izing.** put in danger. —**jeo'pard·y,** *n.*

jĕr''ē·mī'ăd, *n.* tale of lamentation or anger.

jêrk, *n.* **1.** sharp pull. —*v.t.* **2.** pull sharply. —*v.i.* **3.** twitch. —**jerk'y,** *adj.*

jĕr'rў-bǔilt, *adj.* cheaply and flimsily built.

jĕr'sĕy, *n., pl.* **-sies.** closefitting knitted shirt.

jĕst, *n.* joke.

jĕt, *n., v.i.* **jetted, jetting.** *n.* **1.** forced stream. **2.** jet-propelled airplane. **3.** coal-like mineral used in jewelry. —*v.i.* **4.** emerge in a jet. **5.** travel by jet.

jĕt prŏpǔl'sion, propulsion by the reactive thrust of a jet. —**jet'pro·pelled',** *adj.*

jĕt'săm, *n.* material thrown overboard.

jĕt'tī·sòn, *v.t.* throw away or overboard.

jĕt'tў, *n., pl.* **-ties.** pier or wall into the water.

jĕw'ĕl, *n.* precious stone. —**jew'el·er, jew'el·ler,** *n.* —**jew'el·ry,** *n.*

jīb, *n.* triangular sail at the bow.

jībe, *v.i.,* **jibed, jibing,** *n.* gibe.

jĭf'fў, *n., pl.* **-fies.** *Informal.* short period.

jĭg, *n., v.i.,* **jigged, jigging.** *n.* **1.** fast dance. **2.** tool guide. **3.** fishing device. —*v.i.* **4.** dance a jig.

jĭg'gêr, *n.* one-and-a-half ounce glass.

jĭg'gle, *v.,* **-gled, -gling,** *n. v.i., v.t.* **1.** move in rapid jerks. —*n.* **2.** act or instance of jiggling.

jĭg'saw'', *n.* narrow-bladed saw.

jĭlt, *v.t.* reject.

jĭn'gle, *v.,* **-gled, -gling,** *n. v.i., v.t.* **1.** ring lightly and rapidly. —*n.* **2.** act or instance of jingling. **3.** simple verse.

jĭnx, *n.* **1.** bringer of ill-luck. —*v.t.* **2.** bring ill-luck to.

jĭt'têrs, *n. Informal.* nervousness. —**jit'ter·y,** *adj.*

jŏb, *n., v.t.,* **jobbed, jobbing.** *n.* **1.** task. **2.** occupation. **3.** duty. —*v.t., v.i.* **4.** buy in quantity for resale to dealers. —**job'less,** *adj.* —**job'ber,** *n.*

jŏck'ĕy, *n., pl.* **-eys,** *v.i.,* **-eyed, -eying.** *n.* **1.** rider of race horses. —*v.i.* **2.** maneuver for advantage.

jō·cōse', *adj.* playful. Also, **joc'und.** —**jo·cos'i·ty,** *n.*

jŏc'ū·lȧr, *adj.* joking; playful.

jŏg, *v.,* **jogged, jogging,** *n. v.t.* **1.** nudge. —*v.i.* **2.** run steadily. —*n.* **3.** act or instance of jogging. **4.** abrupt change of direction.

jŏin, *v.t.* **1.** put together. **2.** become a member of. —*v.i.* **3.** come or act together.

jŏin'êr, *n.* **1.** woodworker. **2.** *Informal.* person who likes to join groups. —**join'er·y,** *n.*

jŏint, *n.* **1.** connection. —*adj.* **2.** shared. **3.** sharing with others. —*v.t.* **4.** assemble with joints. —**joint'ly,** *adv.*

jŏist, *n.* floor beam.

jōke, *n., v.i.,* **joked, joking.** *n.* **1.** laugh-provoking story or remark. **2.** playful act. —*v.i.* **3.** make a joke.

jŏl'lў, *adj.,* **-lier, -liest,** *v.t.,* **-lied, -lying.** *adj.* **1.** full of high spirits. —*v.t.* **2.** *Informal.* **a.** cajole. **b.** tease. —**jol'li·ly,** *adv.* —**jol'lity,** *n.*

jŏlt, *v.t.* **1.** shake or bump. —*v.i.* **2.** move bumpily. —*n.* **3.** act or instance of jolting.

jŏsh, *v.t.* banter.

jŏs'tle, *v.,* **-tled, -tling.** *v.t., v.i.* shove, as in a crowd.

jŏt, *n., v.t.,* **jotted, jotting.** *n.* **1.** minimal amount. —*v.t.* **2.** make a note of.

jŏunce, *v.i.,* **jounced, jouncing.** jolt and bounce. —**jounc'y,** *adj.*

jour'năl, *n.* **1.** periodical. **2.** diary. **3.** section of an axle in a bearing.

jour'nal·ĭsm, *n.* work for a periodical. —**jour'nal·ist,** *n.* —**jour''nal·is'tic,** *adj.*

jour'nĕy, *n., pl.* **-neys,** *v.i.,* **-neyed, -neying.** *n.* **1.** long trip. —*v.i.* **2.** go on a journey.

jour'nĕy·mȧn, *n.* skilled worker.

jō'vī·ȧl, *adj.* merry. —**jo''vi·al'i·ty,** *n.*

jŏwl, *n.* lower cheek.

jŏy, *n.* **1.** intense happiness. **2.** source of this. —**joy'ful, joy'ous,** *adj.*

jŏy'stĭck, *n.* (computers) grippable device for data manipulation, used mostly for graphics and games.

jū'bǐ·lȧnt, *adj.* rejoicing. —**ju''bi·la'tion,** *n.*

jū'bǐ·lēe'', *n.* **1.** major anniversary. **2.** time of rejoicing.

Jū′dà·ĭsm, *n*. Jewish religion. —**Ju·da′ic**, *adj*.

jŭdge, *n*., *v.t.*, **judged, judging**. *n*. **1**. preside over a trial, contest, etc. **2**. qualified evaluator. —*v.t.* **3**. evaluate. —**judg′ment**, *n*. —**judge′ship′′**, *n*.

ju·dĭ′cĭàl, *adj*. **1**. pertaining to judges or courts. **2**. impartial.

ju·dĭ′cĭ·âr′′ÿ, *adj*., *n*., *pl*. **-ies**. *adj*. **1**. judicial. —*n*. **2**. judges.

ju·dĭ′cĭoŭs, *adj*. with sound judgment. —**ju·di′cious·ly**, *adv*.

jū′dō, *n*. Japanese system of wrestling.

jŭg, *n*. broad vessel with a narrow neck.

jŭg′gêr·nâut′′, *n*. crushing force.

jŭg′gle, *v*., **-gled, -gling**. *v.t.* toss, balance with skill. —*v.i.* **2**. perform such activities for a living. —**jug′gler**, *n*.

jŭg′u·làr, *adj*. **1**. pertaining to the neck. —*n*. **2**. neck vein.

jūice, *n*., *v.t.*, **juiced, juicing**. *n*. **1**. liquid from a fruit, etc. —*v.t.* **2**. extract juice from. —**juic′y**, *adj*.

ju·jĭt′sū, *n*. Japanese system of wrestling. Also, **ju·jut′su**.

jūke′bŏx′′, *n*. coin-operated record player.

Jū·lÿ′, *n*. seventh month.

jŭm′ble, *v.t.*, **-bled, -bling**, *n*. *v.t.* **1**. mix in disorder. —*n*. **2**. disorderly mixture.

jŭm′bō, *adj*. very large.

jŭmp, *v.i.* **1**. leave the ground with a muscular effort. **2**. move abruptly. —*v.t.* **3**. jump over. —*n*. **4**. act or instance of jumping.

jŭmp′êr, *n*. sleeveless dress.

jŭm′pÿ, *adj*., **-pier, -piest**. very nervous.

jŭnc′tion, *n*. place of joining.

jŭnc′tûre, *n*. **1**. junction. **2**. moment. **3**. crisis.

Jūne, *n*. sixth month.

jŭn′gle, *n*. densely grown tropical area.

jŭn′ior, *adj*. **1**. being the son of a father with the same name. **2**. lesser in rank, size, etc. —*n*. **3**. junior person. **4**. third-year student.

jū′nĭ·pér, *n*. evergreen with berry-like cones.

jŭnk, *n*. **1**. rejected or worthless material. **2**. Chinese sailing boat. —*v.t.* **3**. scrap.

jŭnk′ĕt, *n*. **1**. curdled milk dish. **2**. excursion. —*v.i.* **3**. go on a junket.

jŭnk′ĭē, *n*. *Informal*. narcotics addict. Also, **junk′y**.

jun·ta (hŏŏn tà), *n*. military in power after a coup d'etat.

jū′′rĭs·dĭc′tion, *n*. **1**. administration of justice. **2**. area of authority. —**ju′′ris·dic′tion·al**, *adj*.

jū′′rĭs·prū′dénce, *n*. philosophy of law.

jū′rĭst, *n*. expert in law.

jū′rÿ, *n*., *pl*. **-ries**. group deciding the outcome of a trial, hearing, or contest. —**ju′ry·man, ju′ror**, *n*.

jŭst, *adj*. **1**. fair. **2**. righteous. **3**. accurate. —*adv*. **4**. exactly. **5**. only. **6**. by a short margin. —**just′ly**, *adv*. —**just′ness**, *n*.

jŭs′tĭce, *n*. **1**. fairness. **2**. righteousness. **3**. administration of law. **4**. judge.

jŭs′tĭ·fÿ′′, *v.t.*, **-fied, -fying**. give valid reasons for. —**jus′′ti·fi′a·ble**, *adj*. —**jus′′ti·fi·ca′tion**, *n*.

jŭt, *v.i.*, **jutted, jutting**. project.

jūte, *n*. coarse plant fiber.

jū′vén·ĭle, *adj*. **1**. pertaining to children. **2**. childish. —*n*. **3**. child.

jŭx′tà·pōse′′, *v.t.*, **-posed, -posing**. place close or in contrast. —**jux′′ta·po·si′tion**, *n*.

K

K, k, *n*. eleventh letter of the English alphabet.

kaī′sêr, *n*. Germanic emperor.

kāle, *n*. type of cabbage. Also, **kail**.

kà·leī′dò·scōpe′′, *n*. device creating symmetrical patterns for viewing. —**ka·lei′′do·scop′ic**, *adj*.

kăn′′gà·rōō′, *n*. leaping Australian marsupial.

kà·pŭt′, *adj*. destroyed or out of order.

kăr′àt, *n*. twenty-fourth part pure gold.

kà·rä′tē, *n*. Japanese technique of fighting with hands and feet.

kâr′mà, *n*. one's acts as a determinant of one's fate.

kā′tÿ·dĭd′′, *n*. shrill, green insect.

kaÿ′ăk, *n*. Eskimo canoe.

kēel, *n*. central structural member of a ship.

keen, *adj.* **1.** sharp. **2.** eager. **3.** shrewd.

keep, *v.*, **kept, keeping**, *n. v.t.* **1.** retain. **2.** look after. **3.** protect or support. **4.** be observant of. —*v.i.* **5.** be preserved. **6.** abstain. **7.** remain or continue. —*n.* **8.** support; custody.

keep'ing, **1.** care; custody. **2.** conformity.

keep'sake'', *n.* souvenir.

keg, *n.* small barrel.

ken, *n.* range of awareness or knowledge.

ken'nel, *n.*, *v.t.*, **-neled, -neling**. *n.* doghouse. —*v.t.* **2.** put in a kennel.

ker'chief, *n.* cloth for covering the head.

ker'nel, *n.* **1.** seed. **2.** inner nut.

ker'o·sene'', *n.* petroleum derivative.

ketch'up, *n.* sauce, often made with tomatoes.

ket'tle, *n.* pot for boiling water.

ket'tle-drum'', *n.* large, potlike drum.

key, *n.*, *adj.*, *v.t.*, **keyed, keying**. *n.* **1.** metal instrument operating a lock. **2.** device on a piano, etc. pressed to produce a tone. **3.** thing that explains. **4.** system of musical tones. —*adj.* **5.** decisive. —*v.t.* **6.** *Music*. put into a key. —**key'hole''**, *n.*

key'board, *n.* (computers). **1.** device resembling a typewriter keyboard used for data input. —*v.* **2.** to input data with a keyboard.

key'note'', *n.* **1.** lowest note of a scale. **2.** basic theme.

key'stone'', *n.* top stone of an arch.

kha'ki, *n.*, *pl.* **-kis**. **1.** dull yellowish brown. **2.** **khakis**, clothing made of cloth this color.

kib'bitz, *v.t.* give unwanted advice.

kib·butz', *n.*, *pl.* **-butzim**. Israeli collective settlement.

kick, *v.t.*, *v.i.* **1.** strike with the foot. —*v.i.* **2.** recoil. **3.** *Informal*. complain. —*n.* **4.** act or instance of kicking. **5.** *Informal*. **a.** grievance. **b.** thrill.

kick'back'', *n.* *Informal*. rebate, usually illicit.

kid, *n.*, *v.*, **kidded, kidding**. *n.* **1.** young goat. **2.** *Informal*. child. —*v.t.* **3.** *Informal*. tease. —*v.i.* **4.** *Informal*. joke.

kid'nap'', *v.t.*, **-napped** or **-naped**, **-napping** or **-naping**. abduct and hold prisoner. —**kid'nap''er**, *n.*

kid'ney, *n.* **1.** organ that forms urine. **2.** sort or kind.

kill, *v.t.* **1.** cause to die. **2.** end abruptly. —*n.* **3.** act or instance of killing. **4.** game killed. —**kill'er**, *n.*

kiln (kil, kiln), *n.* furnace for processing materials.

ki'lo, *n.*, *pl.* **-los**. **1.** kilogram. **2.** kilometer.

ki'lo·gram'', *n.* one thousand grams or 2.2046 pounds.

ki'lo·hertz'', *n.* one thousand hertz. Also, **ki'lo·cy''cle**.

ki'lo·me''ter, *n.* one thousand meters or 3,281 feet.

ki'lo·watt'', *n.* one thousand watts.

kilt, *n.* knee-length Scottish skirt for men.

kil'ter, *n.* *Informal*. good condition.

ki·mo'no, *n.*, *pl.* **-nos**. *n.* full-length Japanese dress.

kin, *n.* relatives.

kind, *n.* **1.** sort. —*adj.* **2.** benevolent; compassionate. —**kind'ness**, *n.*

kin'der·gar''ten, *n.* pre-elementary school.

kin'dle, *v.*, **-dled, -dling**. *v.t.* **1.** set on fire. **2.** arouse. —*v.i.* **3.** be kindled. —**kind'ling**, *n.*

kind'ly, *adj.* **1.** kind. —*adv.* **2.** in a kind way. **3.** graciously; favorably. —**kind'li·ness**, *n.*

kin'dred, *n.*, *pl.* **1.** relatives. —*adj.* **2.** of the same kind.

ki·net'ic, *adj.* pertaining to motion.

kin'folk'', *n.*, *pl.* relatives. Also, **kin'folks''**.

king, *n.* **1.** male national ruler. **2.** playing card. —**king'ly**, *adj.*

king'dom, *n.* **1.** state ruled by a king. **2.** major category.

king'fish''er, *n.* diving bird that eats fish.

king'-size'', *adj.* *Informal*. extra-large.

kink, *n.* short loop or coil. —**kink'y**, *adj.*

kin'ship'', *n.* family relationship.

ki'osk, *n.* small open shelter.

kip'per, *n.* salted, smoked herring.

kiss, *n.* **1.** touching with the lips as a sign of affection, etc. —*v.t.* **2.** give a kiss to. —*v.i.* **3.** exchange kisses.

kitch'en, *n.* place for preparing meals.

kite, *n.* flying toy on a string.

kith and kin, friends and relatives.

kitsch, *n.* vulgar, affected art. —**kitsch'y**, *adj.*

kit'ten, *n.* young cat. —**kit'ten·ish**, *adj.*

kĭt'tÿ, *n., pl.* **-ties.** *n. Informal.* **1.** cat. **2.** accumulated stakes.

kĭ'wĭ, *n.* **1.** any flightless bird of genus Apteryx. *n.* **2.** fuzzy fruit of Asian climbing plant, the Chinese gooseberry.

klĕp''tó·mā'nĭ·á, *n.* compulsion to steal. **—klĕp''to·ma'ni·ac**, *n.*

knăck, *n.* talent.

knăp'săck'', *n.* sack worn on the back.

knāve, *n.* **1.** *Archaic.* deceitful person. **2.** playing card; jack. **—knav'ish**, *adj.* **—knav'er·y**, *n.*

knēad, *v.t.* press and work with the fingers.

knēe, *n.* joint of the leg.

knēel, *v.i.,* **knelt** or **kneeled, kneeling.** be upright on the knees.

knĕll, *n.* slow tolling of a bell.

knĭck' êrs, *n. pl.* trousers ending at the knees. Also **knick'er·bock''ers.**

knĭck'knăck'', *n.* small decorative object.

knïfe, *n., pl.* **knives**, *v.t.,* **knifed, knifing.** *n.* **1.** small cutting tool. **—***v.t.* **2.** stab with a knife.

knïght, *n.* **1.** possessor of an honorable rank, formerly military. **2.** chesspiece. **—***v.t.* **3.** declare to be a knight. **—knight'hood**, *n.* **—knight'ly**, *adj.*

knïght''-ĕr'rȧnt, *n., pl.* **knights-errant.** knight seeking adventure.

knish (kė nish'), *n.* filled, baked dish of thin dough.

knĭt, *v.,* **knitted** or **knit, knitting.** *v.t.* **1.** assemble from yarn with two needles. **2.** draw together in wrinkles, as the brows. **—***v.i.* **3.** join again after a fracture.

knŏb, *n.* rounded projection or handle. **—knob'by**, *adj.*

knŏck, *v.t.* **1.** hit, as with the fist. **2.** *Informal.* disparage. **—***v.i.* **3.** strike blows. **—***n.* **4.** act or instance of knocking. **5.** adverse happening. **—knock'er**, *n.*

knŏck'ōut'', *n.* victory in boxing, esp. by knocking an opponent unconscious.

knŏll, *n.* small, round hill.

knŏt, *n., v.t.,* **knotted, knotting.** *n.* **1.** fastening of intertwined cord. **2.** small cluster. **3.** hard lump in wood. **4.** one nautical mile per hour. **—***v.t.* **5.** make into a knot. **—knot'ty**, *adj.*

knōw, *v.t.,* **knew, known, knowing.** **1.** have full evidence. **2.** be fully informed

or skilled. **3.** have as an acquaintance. **4.** recognize. **—know'ing·ly**, *adv.*

knōw-hōw'', *n.* technical ability.

knōw'ĭng, *n.* **1.** ability to know. **—***adj.* **2.** shrewd.

knōw'-ĭt-äll'', *n.* pretender to omniscience.

knōwl'ĕdge, *n.* **1.** state of knowing. **2.** what is known.

knōwl'ĕdge·a·ble, *adj.* well-informed.

knŭck'le, *n.* central finger joint.

Kò·răn', *n.* Muslim holy scriptures.

kō'shêr, *adj. Judaism.* fit to eat under religious law.

kōw'tōw', *v.t.* show servility or deference.

kū'dōs, *n. Informal.* praise; fame.

kŭm'quăt'', *n.* small, tart citrus fruit.

L

L, l, *n.* twelfth letter of the English alphabet.

lā'bĕl, *n., v.t.,* **-beled, -beling.** *n.* **1.** attached paper with information. **—***v.t.* **2.** designate with a label.

lā'bĭ·al, *adj.* pertaining to lips.

lā'bȯr, *n.* **1.** hard work. **2.** workers collectively. **3.** process of giving birth. **—***v.i.* **4.** work hard. **—la'bor·er**, *n.*

lăb'ȯ·rá·tō''rÿ, *n., pl.* **-ries.** place for scientific research.

lȧ·bō'rĭ·oŭs, *adj.* difficult; tedious.

lăb'ÿ·rĭnth'', *n.* **1.** maze. **2.** intricate problem. **—lab''y·rin'thine**, *adj.*

lāce, *n., v.t.,* **laced, lacing.** *n.* **1.** binding string, as on a shoe. **2.** openwork cloth. **—***v.t.* **3.** fasten or furnish with a lace. **—lace'work''**, *n.*

lăc'ĕr·āte'', *v.t.,* **-ated, -ating.** tear jaggedly. **—lac''er·a'tion**, *n.*

lăch'rÿ·mōse'', *adj.* tearful.

lăck, *n.* **1.** absence or shortage. **—***v.t.* **2.** be without. **—***v.i.* **3.** be deficient.

lăck''ä·dāi'sĭ·cal, *adj.* without spirit or drive.

lăck'lŭs''têr, *adj.* dull.

lȧ·cŏn'ĭc, *adj.* short-spoken; terse. **—la·con'i·cal·ly**, *adv.*

lăc′quêr, *n.* **1.** transparent varnish-like coating. —*v.t.* **2.** coat with lacquer.

là·crŏsse′, *n.* game with netlike racquets.

là·cū′nà, *n., pl.* **-nas, -nae.** gap.

lăc′ў, *adj.*, **-ier, -iest.** open and intricate.

lăd, *n.* boy.

lăd′dêr, *n.* steep set of steps.

lă′děn, *adj.* burdened; loaded.

lăd′ĭng, *n.* freight.

lā′dle, *n., v.t.*, **-dled, -dling.** *n.* **1.** long-handled bowl for dipping. —*v.t.* **2.** dip with a ladle.

lā′dў, *n.*, **-dies.** **1.** respectable woman. **2.** title of certain British women. —**la′dy·like′**, *adj.* —**la′dy·ship′′**, *n.*

lā′dў·bŭg′′, *n.* small, spotted red beetle. Also, **la′dy·bird′′.**

lăg, *v.i.*, **lagged, lagging**, *n. v.i.* **1.** fall behind. —*n.* **2.** act or instance of lagging. —**lag′gard**, *n., adj.*

lā′gêr, *n.* type of beer.

là·gōōn′, *n.* enclosed body of water near a larger one.

lāid′′băck′′, *adj.* relaxed; serene.

lâir, *n.* den, as of an animal.

lais′′sez faire′ (lä′′zā·fâr′), noninterference, esp. in economic activity.

lā′ĭ·tў, *n., pl.* **-ties.** laymen collectively.

lāke, *n.* inland body of water.

lâ′mà, *n.* Tibetan Buddhist monk. —**la′ma·ser′′y**, *n.*

lămb, *n.* young sheep.

lăm·băste′, *v.t.*, **-basted, -basting.** *Informal.* punish with blows or words.

lăm′bĕnt, *adj.* gently glowing. —**lam′ben·cy**, *n.*

lāme, *adj., v.t.*, **lamed, laming.** *adj.* **1.** unable to walk properly. **2.** ineffectual. —*v.t.* **3.** make lame. —**lame′ly**, *adv.*

là·mĕnt′, *v.t., v.i.* **1.** mourn. —*n.* **2.** speech, poem, or song of mourning. —**la′′men·ta′tion**, *n.* —**lam·en·ta·ble**, *adj.*

lăm′ĭ·nāte′′, *v.t.*, **-nated, -nating.** **1.** build up in layers. **2.** cover with a layer of material. —**lam′′i·na′tion**, *n.*

lămp, *n.* device for emitting rays of light, etc. —**lamp′post′′**, *n.*

lămp′blăck′′, *n.* pigment of fine soot.

lăm·pōōn′, *n.* **1.** satirical writing. —*v.t.* **2.** satirize in a lampoon.

là·naī′, *n.* Hawaiian open-air living area.

lănce, *n., v.t.*, **lanced, lancing.** *n.* **1.** spear carried by a horseman. —*v.t.* **2.** prick, as to discharge pus.

lănd, *n.* **1.** earth's surface above water. **2.** nation; country. **3.** real estate. —*v.t.* **4.** bring to shore or earth. **5.** secure; obtain. —*v.i.* **6.** come to shore or earth. **7.** fall.

lănd′ĕd, *adj.* land-owning.

lănd′fäll′′, *n.* **1.** land sighted from a ship. **2.** sighting of such land.

lănd′ĭng, *n.* **1.** act of coming to shore or earth. **2.** place to land. **3.** unstepped area on a stair.

lănd′lŏcked′′, *adj.* with little or no access to the sea.

lănd′lôrd′′, *n.* **1.** man from whom one rents. **2.** innkeeper. Also, *fem.*, **land′la′′dy.**

lănd′mârk′′, *n.* visible aid to finding one's way.

lănd′măss′′, *n.* major land area.

lănd′scāpe′′, *n., v.t.*, **-scaped, -scaping.** *n.* **1.** large visible area of land. —*v.t.* **2.** create a landscape from.

lănd′slīde′′, *n.* fall of earth down a slope.

lāne, *n.* **1.** path or narrow road. **2.** path of highway travel.

lăn′guáge, *n.* system of communication.

lăn′guĭd, *adj.* without energy. —**lan′guid·ly**, *adv.*

lăn′guĭsh, *v.i.* **1.** long wistfully. **2.** weaken.

lăn′gŭor, *n.* lack of vitality. —**lan′guor·ous**, *adj.*

lănk, *adj.* **1.** lean. **2.** long and straight, as hair.

lăn′kў, *adj.* **-ier, -iest.** awkwardly tall and lean.

lăn′ŏ·lĭn, *n.* oil from wool used in ointments and cosmetics.

lăn′têrn, *n.* **1.** transparent lamp casing. **2.** cupola.

lăp, *n., v.*, **lapped, lapping.** *n.* **1.** area between waist and knees when seated. **2.** overlap. **3.** once around a racetrack. —*v.t.* **4.** wrap. **5.** overlap. —*v.i.* **6.** drink by licking. **7.** splash gently. —**lap′dog′′.**

là·pĕl′, *n.* continuation of a coat collar folded back.

lăp′ĭ·där′′ў, *n., pl.* **-ies**, *adj. n.* **1.** worker in gems. —*adj.* **2.** fine; meticulous.

lăpse, *v.i.*, **lapsed, lapsing**, *n. v.i.* **1.** go passively. **2.** elapse. **3.** become void.

—*n.* **4.** act or instance of lapsing. **5.** minor error.

lâr′ce·nỹ, *n., pl.* **-nies.** theft. —**lar′ce·nous,** *adj.*

lârd, *n.* rendered animal fat.

lârd′ẽr, *n.* place for storing food.

lârge, *adj., adv.,* **larger, largest,** *n. adj.* **1.** big. **2.** large-scale. —*adv.* **3.** in a large way. —*n.* **4. at large,** unconfined. —**large′ly,** *adv.*

lär·gĕss′, *n.* **1.** generous gift. **2.** generosity. Also, **lar·gesse′.**

lär′gō, *adj., adv. Music.* slow.

lär′ĭ·ăt, *n.* tether or lasso.

lârk, *n.* **1.** songbird. **2.** frolic. —*v.i.* **3.** frolic.

lâr·vá, *n., pl.* **-vae.** early form of an animal. —**lar′val,** *adj.*

lăr′′ỹn·gī′tis, *n.* inflammation of the larynx.

lâr′ỹnx, *n., pl.* **-ynxes, -ynges.** container of the vocal cords.

lăs·cĭv′ĭ·oŭs, *adj.* lustful.

lä′sêr, *n.* device for amplifying and concentrating light waves.

lăsh, *v.t.* **1.** tie. **2.** whip. —*v.i.* **3.** strike. —*n.* **4.** whip. **5.** blow from a whip. **6.** eyelash.

lăss, *Dialect.* young woman.

lăs′sĭ·tūde′′, *n.* lack of vigor.

lăs′sō, *n., pl.* **-sos, -soes,** *v.t.,* **-soed, -soing.** *n.* **1.** rope for capturing cattle, etc. —*v.t.* **2.** capture with a lasso.

lăst, *adj., adv.* **1.** after all others. —*n.* **2.** last one. —*v.i.* **3.** remain. —*v.t.* **4.** be enough for. —**last′ly,** *adv.*

lătch, *n.* **1.** device to hold a door, etc. shut. —*v.t.* **2.** fasten with a latch.

lāte, *adj., adv.,* **later** or (for adj.) **latter, latest** or **last.** *adj., adv.* **1.** after the right time. **2.** near the end. **3.** in recent times. —*adj.* **4.** recently alive.

lāte′ly, *adv.* recently.

lā′tĕnt, *n.* unmanifested or undeveloped. —**la′ten·cy,** *n.*

lă′tĕr·ăl, *adj.* pertaining to a side. —**la′ter·al·ly,** *adv.*

lăth, *n., pl.* **laths. 1.** wood strip for holding plaster. **2.** any material for this.

lāthe, *n.* machine for cutting a rotating object.

lăth′ẽr, *n.* **1.** foam. —*v.t.* **2.** cover with foam.

lăt′ĭ·tūde′′, *n.* **1.** north-south measurement. **2.** scope.

lä·trĭne′, *n.* military bathroom.

lăt′têr, *adj.* **1.** more recently mentioned. **2.** more recent. —**lat′ter·ly,** *adv.*

lăt′tĭce, *n.* screen of crisscrossed strips. —**lat′tice·work′′,** *n.*

laŭd, *v.t.* praise. —**laud′a·ble,** *adj.* —**laud′a·to′′ry,** *adj.*

laū′dàn·ŭm, *n.* opium-alcohol solution.

laūgh, *n.* **1.** rhythmic sound indicating amusement, scorn, etc. —*v.i.* **2.** make such a sound. —**laugh′a·ble,** *adj.* —**laugh′ter,** *n.*

laūnch, *v.t.* **1.** send from land. **2.** put into effect, use, etc. —*n.* **3.** open boat.

laŭn′dẽr, *v.t.* wash, as clothes. —**laun′der·er,** *fem.,* **laun′dress,** *n.*

laŭn′drỹ, *n., pl.* **-dries.** place for laundering. —**laun′dry·man,** *n.*

lâu′rĕl, *n.* **1.** shrub with glossy leaves. **2.** **laurels,** honors.

lä′vá, *n.* molten volcanic rock.

lăv′á·tô′′rỹ, *n., pl.* **-ries.** washing place.

lăv′ĕn·dẽr, *n.* **1.** pale purple. **2.** European mint with pale purple flowers.

lăv′ĭsh, *adj.* **1.** very ample. **2.** generous. —*v.t.* **3.** give generously. —**lav′ish·ly,** *adv.* —**lav′ish·ness,** *n.*

lăw, *n.* **1.** rule established by government. **2.** legal profession. **3.** police. **4.** rule of natural phenomena. —**law′-a·bid′′ing,** *adj.* —**law′break′′er,** *n. adj.* —**law′giv′′er,** *n.* —**law′less,** *adj.* —**law′mak′′er,** *n.* —**law′suit′′,** *n.*

lăwn, *n.* **1.** expanse of grass. **2.** sheer cotton or linen.

lăw′yẽr, *n.* professional legal adviser and representative.

lăx, *adj.* negligent. —**lax′i·ty,** *n.*

lăx′á·tĭve, *adj.* **1.** easing constipation. —*n.* **2.** laxative medicine.

lāy, *v.t.,* **laid, laying,** *n., adj. v.t.* **1.** set down gently. **2.** set in place. **3.** place, as emphasis or a claim. —*n.* **4.** situation. **5.** ballad. —*adj.* **6.** not professional or clerical. —**lay′man,** *n.*

lāy′ẽr, *n.* level or thickness of material.

lāy′ŏff′′, *n.* dismissal due to lack of work.

lā′zỹ, *adj.,* **-zier, -ziest.** unwilling to work. —**la′zi·ly,** *adv.* —**la′zi·ness,** *n.*

lēach, *v.t., v.i.,* dissolve with a filtering liquid.

lead (lēd for 1 to 6; lĕd for 7), v., **led, lead-ing,** n. v.t. **1.** direct or guide. **2.** be ahead of. **3.** conduct. —v.i. **4.** tend or result. —n. **5.** leading role or place. **6.** guidance. **7.** heavy metallic chemical element. —**lead′er,** n. —**lead′er·ship′′,** n. —**lead·en,** adj.

leaf, n., pl. **leaves,** v.i. n. **1.** flat thin termination of a plant stem. **2.** thin sheet. —v.i. **3.** turn over pages. —**leaf′y,** adj.

leaf′let, n. small printed sheet.

league, n., v., **leaguing.** n. **1.** alliance. **2.** unit of about 3 miles. —v.t., v.i. **3.** form into a league.

leak, n. **1.** accidental release or admission. —v.i. **2.** have or pass through a leak. —v.t. **3.** pass through a leak. —**leak′age,** n. —**leak′y,** adj.

lean, v., **leaned** or **leant, leaning,** adj. v.t., v.i. **1.** stand against something supporting the upper end. —v.i. **2.** bend; incline. **3.** be predisposed. **4.** rely. —adj. **5.** with little fat.

leap, v., **leaped** or **leapt, leaping,** n. jump.

leap year, year with 29 days in February.

learn, v., **learned** or **learnt, learning.** v.t. **1.** come to know or know how. —v.i. **2.** get information. —**learn′er,** n. —**learn′ing,** n. —**learn′ed,** adj.

lease, n., v.t., **leased, leasing.** n. **1.** rental contract. —v.t. **2.** rent by lease.

leash, n. tether, as for a dog.

least, adj. **1.** smallest in size, importance, etc. —adv. **2.** to the smallest extent.

leath′ĕr, n. tanned hide.

leave, v., **left, leaving,** n. v.i. **1.** go away. —v.t. **2.** go away from. **3.** abandon. **4.** to cause to remain behind one. **5.** bequeath. —n. **6.** departure. **7.** permission. —**leave′tak′′ing,** n.

lĕav′en, n. **1.** substance making dough rise —v.t. **2.** cause to rise.

lĕav′ings, n. pl. leftovers.

lĕch′ĕr, n. lustful person. —**lech′er·ous,** adj. —**lech′er·y,** n.

lĕc′tŭre, n., v., **-tured, -turing.** n. **1.** informative speech. —v.t. **2.** give a lecture to. —v.i. **3.** give a lecture.

lĕdge, n. narrow shelf or platform.

lĕd′gĕr, n. accountant's book.

lĕe, adj. **1.** away from the wind. —n. **2.** lee side, etc. **3.** lees, dregs.

lĕech, n. blood-sucking worm.

lĕek, n. onionlike vegetable.

lĕer, n. **1.** sly, malicious or lustful look. —v.i. **2.** give a leer.

lĕe′wăy′′, n. **1.** Informal. scope for action. **2.** Nautical. leeward drift.

lĕft, n. **1.** west when facing north. **2.** liberal or socialistic position. —adv. **3.** toward the left. **4.** at or in the left. —**left′ist,** n., adj. —**left′-hand′,** adj.

lĕft′ō′′vĕr, n. remnant for later use.

lĕft wĭng, political left. —**left′-wing′′,** adj. —**left′-wing′er,** n.

lĕg, n. **1.** supporting and walking limb. **2.** vertical support.

lĕg′a·cў, n., pl. **-cies.** something left to posterity.

lē′găl, adj. **1.** permitted by law. **2.** pertaining to law. —**le′gal·ly,** adv. —**le·gal′i·ty,** n. —**le′gal·ize′′,** v.t.

lĕg′ate, n. papal envoy.

lĕg′′a·tĕe′, n. recipient of a legacy.

lĕ·gā′tion, n. office of a diplomat.

lĕ·gä′tō, adj. Music. smooth and even.

lĕg′end, n. **1.** folk tale. **2.** inscription. —**leg′end·ar′′y,** adj.

lĕg′′ĕr·de·māin′, n. cunning of the hand.

lĕg′gĭng, n. outer leg covering.

lĕg′i·ble, adj. possible to read. —**leg′′i·bil′i·ty,** n.

lē′gĭon, n. large band, esp. of soldiers. —**le′gion·ar′′y,** adj., n. —**le′′gion·naire′,** n.

lĕg′ĭs·lāte′, v., **-lated, -lating.** v.t. **1.** determine by law. —v.i. **2.** enact laws. —**leg′′is·la′tion,** n. —**leg′is·la′′tive,** adj. —**leg′is·la′′tor,** n.

lĕg′ĭs·lā′′tŭre, n. lawmaking body.

lĕ·gĭt′ĭ·măte, adj. **1.** right; proper. **2.** of married parents. —**le·git′i·ma·cy,** n. —**le·git′i·mize′,** v.t.

lĕg′ūme, n. vegetable with seed pods. —**le·gu′mi·nous,** adj.

lei (lā), n., pl. **leis.** Hawaiian flower garland.

lĕi′sŭre, n. **1.** time for rest or recreation. **2.** at one's leisure, when convenient.

lĕi′sŭre·lў, adj., adv. without haste or hurry.

lĕm′ŏn, n. yellow citrus fruit. —**lem′′on·ade′,** n.

lĕnd, v.t., **lent, lending. 1.** give for later return. **2.** impart.

lĕngth, *n.* **1.** end-to-end extent. **2.** piece measured by length. —**length'en,** *v.t., v.i* —**length'wise'', length'ways'', adj., adv.** —**length'y, adj.**

lē'ni·ent, *adj.* not strict or harsh. —**le'ni·en·cy, le'ni·ence,** *n.*

lĕns, *n., pl.* **lenses.** transparent object concentrating or dispersing rays of light.

Lĕnt, *n.* Christian time of penance from Ash Wednesday to Easter. —**Lent'en,** *adj.*

lĕn'til, *n.* small legume seed used as food.

lē'o·nīne, *adj.* lion-like.

lĕop'ărd, *n.* spotted cat of the panther family.

lĕp'er, *n.* person with leprosy.

lĕ'pre·chäun'', *n.* Irish fairy.

lĕp'ro·sў, *n.* deforming chronic disease. —**lep'rous,** *adj.*

lĕs'bi·àn, *n.* **1.** homosexual woman. —*adj.* **2.** pertaining to such women. —**les'bi·an·ism,** *n.*

lē·sion, *n.* bodily injury resulting in impairment of function.

lĕss, *adj.* **1.** smaller or fewer. —*adv.* **2.** to a smaller extent. —*prep.* **3.** minus. —**les'sen,** *v.t., v.i.*

lĕs·sēe', *n.* tenant on a lease.

lĕs'sêr, *adj.* smaller; less important.

lĕs'sòn, *n.* something learned at one time.

lĕs'sör, *n.* landlord on a lease.

lĕst, *conj.* for fear that.

lĕt, *v.t.,* **let, letting,** *n. v.t.* **1.** allow. **2.** rent. **3.** allow to issue. —*n.* **4.** obstacle.

lĕt'dŏwn'', *n.* **1.** disappointment. **2.** slackening.

lē'thal, *adj.* deadly.

lĕth'ăr·gў, *n., pl.* **-gies.** sluggishness. —**le·thar'gic,** *adj.*

lĕt'têr, *n.* **1.** alphabetic character. **2.** message in an envelope. **3.** literal meaning. **4.** letters, literature. —*v.t.* **5.** write letter by letter. —**let'ter·ing,** *n.*

lĕt'têred, *adj.* educated.

lĕt'tŭce, *n.* green, leafy vegetable.

leū·kē'mi·à, *n.* blood disease.

lĕv'ēe, *n.* embankment against rising water.

lĕv'ĕl, *n., v.t.,* **-eled, -eling.** *n.* **1.** point or plane between top and bottom. **2.** device for finding horizontals or verticals. **3.** point on a scale of values. —*adj.* **4.** flat. **5.** horizontal. **6.** even. —*v.t.* **7.** make level.

lĕv'ĕl-hĕad'ĕd, *adj.* of calm, sound judgment.

lĕv'êr, *n.* pivoted raising device lifted at one end. —**lev'er·age,** *n.*

lĕ·vī'à·thàn, *n.* sea monster.

lĕv''ī·tā'tion, *n.* raising or rising without physical support.

lĕv'ī·tў, *n.* mirth, often unseemly.

lĕv'ў, *v.t.,* **-ied, -ying,** *n., pl.* **-ies.** *v.t.* **1.** impose for payment. **2.** enlist. —*n.* **3.** something levied.

lēwd, *adj.* obscene. —**lewd'ly,** *adv.* —**lewd'ness,** *n.*

lĕx'ī·cŏn, *n.* dictionary.

lī''à·bĭl'ī·tў, *n., pl.* **-ties.** **1.** loss or payment of money. **2.** state of being liable. **3.** disadvantage.

lī'à·ble, *adj.* **1.** responsible. **2.** subject to something. **3.** likely.

lī'ăi·sŏn'', *n.* **1.** connection, as for communication. **2.** love affair.

lī'ăr, *n.* teller of lies.

lī·bā'tion, *n.* outpouring of liquid.

lī'bĕl, *n., v.t.,* **-beled, -beling.** *n.* **1.** defamation in writing or print. —*v.t.* **2.** defame by this means. —**li'bel·ous, li'bel·lous,** *adj.*

līb'êr·àl, *adj.* **1.** generous. **2.** not literal. **3.** favoring more civil liberty. —*n.* **4.** person favoring more civil liberty. —**lib''er·al'i·ty,** *n.* —**lib'er·al·ism,** *n.* —**lib'er·al·ize'',** *v.t.*

līb'êr·āte', *v.t.,* **-ated, -ating.** free. —**lib''er·a'tion,** *n.* —**lib'er·a''tor,** *n.*

līb''êr·tär'ī·àn, *n.* believer in personal liberties.

līb'êr·tīne'', *n.* licentious person.

līb'êr·tў, *n., pl.* **-ties.** **1.** freedom. **2.** privilege. **3.** liberties, impertinences.

lī·bī'dō, *n.* **1.** sexual urge. **2.** psychic energy.

lī'brär''ў, *n., pl.* **-ies.** **1.** collection of books. **2.** place for books. —**li·brar'i·an,** *n.*

lī·brĕt'tō, *n., pl.* **-tos, -ti.** text of an opera, etc. —**li·bret'tist,** *n.*

lī'cĕnse, *n., v.t.,* **-censed, -censing.** *n.* **1.** privilege of doing. **2.** abuse of liberty. —*v.t.* **3.** grant a license to. —**li''cen·see',** *n.* —**li·cen'tious,** *adj.*

lī·chĕn, *n.* mosslike growth.

lĭc´ĭt, *adj.* permitted.

lĭck, *v.t.* **1.** rub with the tongue. **2.** *Informal.* **a.** defeat. **b.** beat. —*v.i.* **3.** lap. —*n.* **4.** act or instance of licking.

lĭc´ó·rĭce, *n.* European root used for flavoring.

lĭd, *n.* cover.

lie, *v.i.,* **lay** (for 1, 2) or **lied** (for 3), **lain** (for 1, 2), **lying,** *n. v.i.* **1.** rest on something horizontal. **2.** be situated. **3.** make statements intended to deceive. —*n.* **4.** situation. **5.** lying statement.

lĭef, *adv. Archaic.* willingly.

lĭen, *n.* legal claim on property.

lĭeu, *n.* **in lieu of,** in place of.

lĭeu·tĕn´ant, *n.* commissioned military or naval officer below a captain or lieutenant commander. —**lĭeu·ten´an·cy,** *n.*

lĭfe, *n., pl.* **lĭves. 1.** period of existence. **2.** living things collectively. **3.** human experience. **4.** way of living. **5.** animation. **6.** biography. —**life´less,** *adj.* —**life´long´´,** *adj.* —**life´time´´,** *n.*

life´bōat´´, *n.* emergency boat.

life´guârd´´, *n.* one employed to protect swimmers, esp. from drowning, etc.

life´līke´, *adj.* resembling a living being.

life´-sīze´´, *adj.* as large as the living model. Also, **life´-sized´´.**

lĭft, *v.t.* **1.** raise. —*v.i.* **2.** attempt to raise something. **3.** rise. —*n.* **4.** act or instance of lifting. **5.** hoist.

lĭg´a·mĕnt, *n.* body connective tissue.

lĭg´a·tûre, *n.* tie.

lĭght, *n., adj., v.,* **lĭghted** or **lĭt, lĭghting.** *n.* **1.** visible radiant energy. **2.** lamp. **3.** flame. **4.** truth. **5.** public awareness. —*adj.* **6.** not dark or serious. **7.** not heavy. **8.** not serious. —*v.t.* **9.** set fire to. **10.** cause to give off light. **11.** show in light. —*v.i.* **12.** be lighted. **13.** alight. **14.** happen; venture. —**lĭght´en,** *v.t., v.i.* —**lĭght´weĭght´,** *adj.*

lĭght´ĕr, *n.* **1.** lighting device. **2.** freight barge.

lĭght´-hĕad´ĕd, *adj.* dizzy.

lĭght´-heârt´ĕd, *adj.* cheerful.

lĭght´hōuse´´, *n.* tower with a navigational beacon.

lĭght´nĭng, *n.* flash of electricity in the sky.

lĭght´-yēar´, *n.* distance light travels in a year, about 6 trillion miles.

lĭg´nīte, *n.* soft brown coal.

līke, *prep., adj., n., v.t.,* **līked, līking.** *prep.* **1.** similar or similarly to. **2.** characteristic or suggestive of. **3.** inclined to. —*adj.* **4.** similar. —*n.* **5.** similar person or thing. **6.** preference. —*v.t.* **7.** be pleased with. **8.** wish. —**līke´a´ble, līk´a·ble,** *adj.* —**līke´ness,** *n.*

līke´lў, *adj.,* **-lier, -liest,** *adv. adj.* **1.** probable. **2.** suitable. —*adv.* **3.** probably.

lĭk´en, *v.t.* compare.

līke´wīse´´, *adv.* similarly, also.

lī´lăc, *n.* pale purple flower.

lĭlt, *n.* light, bouncy rhythm.

lĭl´ў, *n., pl.* **-ies.** flower with trumpet-shaped blossoms.

lī´má bēan, broad, pale green bean.

lĭmb, *n.* **1.** large tree branch. **2.** arm or leg.

lĭm´bêr, *adj.* **1.** flexible. —*v.t.* **2.** make limber. —*v.i.* **3.** become limber.

lĭm´bō, *n.* **1.** abode of the unbaptized, innocent dead. **2.** oblivion.

līme, *n., v.t.,* **līmed, līming.** *n.* **1.** calcium oxide. **2.** tart green citrus fruit. —*v.t.* **3.** treat with lime. —**līme´ade´,** *n.*

līme´lĭght´´, *n.* state of much publicity.

lĭm´êr·ĭck, *n.* amusing five-lined verse.

līme´stōne´´, *n.* stone containing much calcium carbonate.

lĭm´ĭt, *n.* **1.** edge or boundary. **2.** permissible extent. —*v.t.* **3.** set a limit to. —**lĭm´´i·ta´tion,** *n.* —**lĭm´it·ed,** *adj.* —**lĭm´it·less,** *adj.*

lĭm´ōu·sīne´´, *n.* long, chauffeured automobile.

lĭmp, *v.i.* **1.** walk lamely. —*n.* **2.** lame gait. —*adj.* **3.** not rigid or firm.

lĭm´pĭd, *adj.* perfectly clear. —**lĭm·pĭd´i·ty,** *n.*

lĭn´dĕn, *n.* tree with heart-shaped leaves.

līne, *n., v.,* **līned, līning.** *n.* **1.** long, narrow mark. **2.** row. **3.** boundary. **4.** course. **5.** transit system. **6.** rope, pipe, etc. **7.** occupation. —*v.t.* **8.** put a lining in. **9.** mark with lines. —*v.i.* **10.** assemble in a line.

lĭn´e·âge, *n.* ancestry.

lĭn´e·ăl, *adj.* **1.** pertaining to direct ancestry. **2.** linear.

lĭn´e·a·mĕnts, *n. pl.* features of the face.

lĭn´e·âr, *adj.* pertaining to lines or length.

lĭn´en, *n.* **1.** cloth made of flax. **2.** linens, bedsheets, etc.

lin′êr, *n.* **1.** ship or airplane on scheduled service. **2.** something that lines.

line′ŭp′′, *n.* arrangement or muster in a row.

lin′gêr, *v.i.* remain; stay.

lin·ger·ie (län′′zē rā′), *n.* women's underwear.

lin′gō, *n.*, *pl.* **-goes.** *Informal.* strange language.

lin′guist, *n.* **1.** speaker of many languages. **2.** student of languages. **—lin·guis′tics,** *n.* **—lin·guis′tic,** *adj.*

lin′ĭ·mènt, *n.* soothing liquid for external use.

lin′ĭng, *n.* material applied to an interior.

lĭnk, *n.* **1.** unit of a chain or series. **2.** connection. **—v.t., v.i. 3.** connect. **—link′age,** *n.*

lĭnks, *n. pl.* golf course.

lĭ·nō′lē·ŭm, *n.* smooth sheeting for floors.

lĭn′sēed′′, *n.* flax seed.

lĭnt, *n.* fibrous waste.

lĭn′tel, *n.* beam over a doorway, etc.

lī′òn, *n.* **1.** large catlike animal of Africa and southwest Asia. **2.** celebrity. Also, *fem.*, **lī′on·ess.**

lī′òn·īze′′, *v.t.*, **-ized, -izing.** treat as a celebrity.

lĭp, *n.* **1.** feature at top and bottom of the mouth. **2.** surface for pouring.

lĭp′stĭck′′, *n.* coloring for the lips.

lĭq′ue·fŷ′′, *v.*, **-fied, -fying.** *v.t., v.i.* change to liquid. **—lĭq′′ue·fac′tion,** *n.*

lĭ′queûr, *n.* sweet strong alcoholic drink.

lĭq′uĭd, *n.* **1.** fluid incapable of indefinite expansion. **—adj. 2.** in the form of a liquid. **3.** readily turned into cash. **—lĭ·quid′i·ty,** *n.*

lĭq′ui·dāte′′, *v.t.*, **-dated, -dating. 1.** terminate, as a business. **2.** convert into cash. **3.** kill. **—lĭq′′ui·da′tion,** *n.*

lĭq′uör, *n.* alcoholic liquid.

lisle (līl), *n.* fine cotton.

lĭsp, *n.* **1.** mispronunciation of *s* and *z.* **—v.i. 2.** make such mispronunciations.

lĭs′sóme, *adj.* agile and supple.

lĭst, *n.* **1.** series of related items. **2.** tilt, as of a ship. **—v.t. 3.** put on a list. **—v.i. 4.** tilt.

lĭs′tèn, *v.i.* **1.** hear attentively. **2.** pay heed. **—lĭs′ten·er,** *n.*

lĭst′lèss, *adj.* indifferent from fatigue, etc. **—list′less·ly,** *adv.* **—list′less·ness,** *n.*

lĭt′à·nӳ, *n.*, *pl.* **-nies.** uttered prayer with responses.

lĭ′têr, *n.* metric unit equal to 1.0567 liquid quarts or 0.908 dry quart. Also, **lĭ′tre.**

lĭt′êr·ál, *adj.* according to the exact wording. **—lĭt′er·al·ly,** *adv.*

lĭt′êr·ār′′ӳ, *adj.* pertaining to literature.

lĭt′êr·āte, *adj.* **1.** able to read. **2.** well-read. **—lĭt′er·a·cy,** *n.*

lĭt′′e·rā′tĭ, *n. pl.* well-read persons.

lĭt′êr·à·tûre, *n.* fiction, poetry, etc. of lasting value.

lithe, *adj.* supple.

lĭth′ó·grăph′′, *n.* print from a flat surface with special ink. **—lĭth′′o·graph′ic,** *adj.* **—li·thog′ra·phy,** *n.* **—li·thog′ra·pher,** *n.*

lĭt′ĭ·gāte′′, *v.*, **-gated, -gating.** *v.t., v.i.* contest in a lawsuit. **—lĭt′′i·ga′tion,** *n.* **—lit′i·gant, lit′i·ga′′tor,** *n.*

lĭt′têr, *n.* **1.** trash. **2.** newly-born animals. **3.** animal bedding. **4.** frame for carrying a person. **—v.t. 5.** scatter carelessly.

lĭt′tle, *adj.* littler or less or lesser, littlest or least, *adv.*, less, least, *n. adj.* **1.** small. **2.** petty. **—adv. 3.** not much. **—n. 4.** short while. **5.** small amount.

lĭt′ûr·gӳ, *n.*, *pl.* **-gies.** ritual of worship. **—li·tur′gi·cal,** *adj.*

lĭv′à·ble, *adj.* pleasant to inhabit. Also, **live′a·ble.**

live′li·hōōd′′, *n.* means of sustenance.

lïve (liv for 1-5; līv for 6-8). *v.i.* **1.** be alive. **2.** dwell. **3.** spend one's life. **4.** depend for existence. **—v.t. 5.** experience or spend. **—adj. 6.** alive. **7.** vital. **8.** electrically charged.

līve′lӳ, *adj.*, **-lier, -liest,** *adv. adj.* **1.** full of vitality. **—adv. 2.** in a lively way. **—live′li·ness,** *n.*

lĭv′èn, *v.t.* **1.** make lively. **—v.i. 2.** become lively.

lĭv′êr, *n.* organ secreting bile.

lĭv′êr·wûrst′′, *n.* sausage made with ground liver.

live′stŏck′′, *n.* cattle, sheep, etc.

lĭv′ĭd, *adj.* **1.** discolored, as flesh. **2.** enraged.

lĭv′ĭng, *adj.* **1.** alive. **2.** pertaining to being alive. **—n. 3.** livelihood.

lĭz′àrd, *n.* scaly, four-legged reptile.

llä´má, *n.* South American beast of burden.

lōad, *n.* **1.** something carried. —*v.t.* **2.** put a load on or in. **3.** supply in large amounts. **4.** make ready for firing. —*v.i.* **5.** take on a load.

lōaf, *n., pl.* **loaves,** *v.i., n.* **1.** regularly shaped piece of bread. —*v.i.* **2.** be idle. —**loaf´er,** *n.*

lōam, *n.* rich soil. —**loam´y,** *adj.*

lōan, *n.* **1.** act or instance of lending. **2.** something lent. —*v.t., v.i.* **3.** lend.

lōath, *adj.* reluctant.

lōathe, *v.t.,* **loathed, loathing.** dislike intensely. —**loath´some,** *adj.*

lŏb, *v.t.,* **lobbed, lobbing.** hurl with a high curve.

lŏb´bÿ, *n., pl.* **-bies.** *v.i.,* **-bied, -bying.** *n.* **1.** entrance room. **2.** group seeking favorable legislation. —*v.i.* **3.** seek favorable legislation. —**lob´by·ist,** *n.*

lōbe, *n.* rounded projection. —**lo´bar, lo´bate,** *adj.*

lŏb´stēr, *n.* sea crustacean with pincers.

lō´cál, *adj.* **1.** pertaining or limited to a place. **2.** making most or all stops. —*n.* **3.** local train or bus. **4.** local branch of a labor union. —**lo´cal·ly,** *adv.*

lō·cále´, *n.* scene of an event.

lō·cál´i·tÿ, *n., pl.* **-ties. 1.** location. **2.** district.

lō´cal·īze´´, *v.t.,* **-ized, -izing.** trace or confine to one place. —**lo´´cal·i·za´tion,** *n.*

lō´cāte, *v.t.,* **-cated, -cating.** establish the place of. —**lo·ca´tion,** *n.*

lŏck, *n.* **1.** device for securing doors, etc. **2.** canal chamber between levels. **3.** firing mechanism. **4.** curl of hair. —*v.t.* **5.** fasten with a lock. **6.** shut in or out. —*v.i.* **7.** be jammed. —**lock´smith´´,** *n.*

lŏck´ēr, *n.* compartment that can be locked.

lŏck´ét, *n.* round case worn as a pendant to a necklace.

lŏck´jaw´´, *n.* form of tetanus.

lŏck´ōut´´, *n.* exclusion of workers from a workplace.

lō´cō, *adj. Informal.* crazy.

lō´´cò·mō´tion, *n.* movement from place to place.

lō´´cò·mō´tĭve, *n.* **1.** railroad traction engine. —*adj.* **2.** pertaining to locomotion.

lō´cŭst, *n.* **1.** crop-eating insect. **2.** flowering tree.

lō·cū´tion, *n.* spoken expression.

lōde, *n.* deposit of metallic ore.

lōde´stōne´´, *n.* magnetic iron ore.

lōdge, *n., v.,* **lodged, lodging.** *n.* **1.** forest house. **2.** fraternity chapter. —*v.t.* **3.** house. **4.** push into a fixed position. —*v.i.* **5.** become fixed. **6.** dwell.

lōdg´ing, *n.* **1.** temporary home. **2.** **lodgings,** rented rooms.

lŏft, *n.* open upper floor.

lŏft´ÿ, *adj.,* **-ier, -iest.** very high. —**loft´i·ly,** *adv.*

lŏg, *n., v.t.,* **logged, logging.** *n.* **1.** cut tree trunk or limb. **2.** record of events. —*v.t.* **3.** take logs from. **4.** record in a log.

lō´gan·bĕr´´rÿ, *n.* hybrid of blackberry and red raspberry.

lŏg´á·rĭthm, *n. Math.* power of one number if multiplied to equal another. —**log´´a·rith´mic,** *adj.*

lōge, *n.* theater mezaanine.

lŏg´gĕr·hĕad´´, *n.* **at loggerheads,** in sharp dispute.

lŏg´ic, *n.* **1.** correct reasoning. **2.** predictable sequence. —**log´i·cal,** *adj.* —**log´i·cal·ly,** or **lo·gi´cian,** *n.*

lō·gĭs´tĭcs, *n.* science of military housing, supply, etc. —**lo·gis´tic, lo·gis´ti·cal,** *adj.*

lō´´gō, *n.* symbol or trademark of an enterprise.

lō´gÿ, *adj.* **-gier, -giest.** sluggish.

lōĭn, *n.* **1.** Also, **loins,** lower human back. **2.** front hindquarter as a cut of meat.

lōĭ´tĕr, *n.* linger in one place. —**loi´ter·er,** *n.*

lŏll, *v.i.* **1.** remain idle. **2.** hang loosely.

lŏl´li·pop´´, *n.* candy on a stick for sucking.

lōne, *adj.* single; solitary.

lōne´lÿ, *adj.* **-lier, -liest. 1.** sad because alone. **2.** isolated. Also, **lone´some.** —**lone´li·ness,** *n.*

lŏng, *adj., adv.,* **longer, longest,** *v.i. adj.* **1.** of great distance between ends. **2.** in length. **3.** occupying much time. —*adv.* **4.** for a long time. **5.** from start to finish. **6.** at a long time. —*v.i.* **7.** wish passionately. —**long´ing,** *n., adj.*

lŏn·gĕv'ĭ·tỳ, *n.* long life.

lŏng'hănd'', *n.* ordinary handwriting.

lŏn''gĭ·tūde'', *n.* east-west measurement.

lŏn''gĭ·tū'dĭ·nål, *adj.* pertaining to length or longitude.

lŏng'shōre''mån, *n.* loader and unloader of ships.

lŏng'-stănd'ĭng, *adj.* long-continued.

lŏng'-sŭf'fĕr·ĭng, *adj.* patient.

lŏng tòn, ton of 2,240 pounds.

lŏŏk, *v.i.* **1.** direct one's gaze. **2.** search. **3.** appear to be. —*v.t.* **4.** stare at. —*n.* **5.** act or instance of looking. **6.** appearance. —*interj.* **7.** pay heed!

lŏŏk'ŏut'', *n.* **1.** vigilance. **2.** spy or sentinel. **3.** place for observing.

lŏŏm, *n.* **1.** weaving frame. —*v.i.* **2.** appear indistinctly as huge.

lŏŏn, *n.* diving bird.

lŏŏn'ỳ, *adj.,* **-ier, -iest.** *Informal.* crazy.

lŏŏp, *n.* **1.** closed curve of rope, etc. —*v.t.* **2.** make into a loop. —*v.i.* **3.** form a loop.

lŏŏp'hōle'', *n.* **1.** slit for shooting. **2.** means of evasion.

lŏŏse, *adj.,* **looser, loosest,** *v.t.,* **loosed, loosing.** *adj.* **1.** not tight. **2.** not confined. **3.** not strict or precise. **4.** immoral. —*v.t.* **5.** make loose. —**loose'lỳ,** *adv.* —**loos'en,** *v.t., v.i.*

lŏŏt, *n.* **1.** things stolen. —*v.t.* **2.** steal the contents of.

lŏp, *v.t.,* **lopped, lopping.** chop.

lŏp'sīd''ĕd, *adj.* out of balance.

lŏ·quā'ciŏŭs, *adj.* talkative. —**lŏ·quac'ĭ·tỳ,** *n.*

lôrd, *n.* **1.** landed noble. **2. the Lord, a.** God. **b.** Christ. —**lord'lỳ,** *adj., adv.* —**lord'ship'',** *n.*

lôre, *n.* traditional learning.

lose, *v.,* **lost, losing.** *v.t.* **1.** fail to keep. **2.** misplace. **3.** fail to win. —*v.i.* **4.** have a loss. —**los'er,** *n.* —**lost,** *adj.*

lŏss, *n.* act or instance of losing. **2.** something lost.

lŏt, *n.* **1.** chance. **2.** personal fate. **3.** area of ground. **4.** Also, **lots.** *Informal.* many or much.

lō'tiŏn, *n.* skin preparation.

lŏt'tĕr·ỳ, *n.,* *pl.* **-ies.** choice by chance, esp. of a winner.

lō'tŭs, *n.* **1.** tropical waterlily. **2.** legendary plant causing forgetfulness.

lŏŭd, *adj.* **1.** with much noise. **2.** *Informal.* flashy. —*adv.* **3.** loudly. —**loud'lỳ,** *adv.* —**loud'ness,** *n.*

lŏŭnge, *v.i.,* **lounged, lounging,** *n. v.i.* **1.** be idle or relaxed. —*n.* **2.** couch. **3.** place for lounging.

lŏŭse, *n., pl.* **lice.** parasitic insect.

lŏŭs'ỳ, *adj.,* **-ier, -iest.** *Informal.* bad.

lŏŭt, *n.* stupid, offensive person. —**lout'ish,** *adj.*

lŏŭ'vĕr, *n.* opening screened with inclined slats.

lŏve, *n., v.t.,* **loved, loving.** *n.* **1.** powerful attraction to another. **2.** warm concern. **3.** loved person. —*v.t.* **4.** feel love for. —**lov'a·ble, love'a·ble,** *adj.* —**love'less,** *adj.* —**lov'er,** *n.* —**lov'ing,** *adj.* —**lov'ing·lỳ,** *adv.*

lŏve'lôrn'', *adj.* pining with love.

lŏve'lỳ, *adj.,* **-lier, -liest.** beautiful.

lŏw, *adj.* **1.** of less than average height. **2.** of less than average quantity, etc. **3.** depressed. **4.** vulgar. **5.** meanly wicked. —*adv.* **6.** in a low way. —*n.* **7.** something low. —*v.i.* **8.** moo.

lŏw'brŏw'', *n., adj.* non-intellectual.

lŏw'ĕr, *adj.* **1.** more low. —*v.t.* **2.** cause to be low or lower. —*v.i.* **3.** become low or lower. **4.** (lōō'ĕr) frown.

lŏw'lỳ, *adj.,* **-lier, -liest.** humble.

lŏy'ål, *adj.* faithful. —**loy'al·ly,** *adv.* —**loy'al·tỳ,** *n.*

lŏz'enge, *n.* cough drop, etc..

lu·au', *n.* (lōō'ow) Hawaiian feast.

lŭb'bĕr, *n.* clumsy person. —**lub'ber·lỳ,** *adj.*

lū'brĭ·cāte'', *v.t.,* **-cated, -cating. 1.** make slippery. **2.** cause the wearing parts of to slide easily. —**lu''bri·ca'tion,** *n.* —**lu'bri·cant,** *n.*

lū'cĭd, *adj.* **1.** clear, as to understand. **2.** mentally competent. —**lu'cid·ly,** *adv.* —**lu·cid'i·ty,** *n.*

lŭck, *n.* **1.** chance. **2.** favorable chance. —**luck'less,** *adj.*

lŭck'ỳ, *adj.,* **-ier, -iest.** having or marked by good luck. —**luck'i·lỳ,** *adv.*

lūc'rå·tĭve, *adj.* profitable.

lū'crê, *n.* riches.

lū'dĭ·croŭs, *adj.* laughable.

lŭg, *v.t.,* **lugged, lugging,** *n. v.t.* **1.** haul with effort. —*n.* **2.** projection for lifting, etc.

lŭg′gåge, *n.* baggage.

lu·gū′bri·oŭs, *adj.* foolishly mournful.

lūke′wårm′′, *adj.* **1.** slightly warm. **2.** unenthusiastic.

lŭll, *v.t., v.i., n.* calm.

lŭll′a·bȳ′′, *n., pl.* **-bies.** soothing song for children.

lŭm·bā′gō, *n.* pain in the lower back.

lŭm′bår, *adj.* pertaining to the loins.

lŭm′bĕr, *n.* **1.** building wood. —*v.i.* **2.** move ponderously. —**lum′ber·man,** *n.*

lŭm′bĕr·jăck′′, *n.* feller of trees.

lū′mĭ·når′′ȳ, *n., pl.* **-ies. 1.** light source. **2.** brilliant person.

lū′mĭ·nĕs′cĕnce, *n.* light without heat. —**lu′′min·nes′cent,** *adj.*

lū′mĭ·noŭs, *adj.* light-giving. —**lu′′mi·nos′i·ty,** *n.*

lŭmp, *n.* **1.** shapeless mass. **2.** swelling. —*adj.* **3.** collective. —*v.t.* **4.** assemble or treat in a lump. **5.** tolerate despite oneself. —*v.i.* **6.** form in lumps. —**lump′y,** *adj.*

lū′når, *adj.* pertaining to the moon.

lū′na·tĭc, *n.* **1.** insane person. —*adj.* **2.** insane. —**lu′na·cy,** *n.*

lŭnch, *n.* **1.** midday meal. —*v.i.* **2.** eat lunch.

lŭnch′eŏn, *n.* formal lunch.

lŭng, *n.* breathing organ.

lŭnge, *n., v.,* **lunged, lunging. n. 1.** sudden move forward. —*v.t., v.i.* **2.** move with a lunge.

lŭrch, *n.* **1.** sudden sideways movement. **2. leave in the lurch,** desert in time of need. —*v.i.* **3.** make a lurch.

lūre, *v.t.,* **lured, luring,** *n. v.t.* **1.** entice —*n.* **2.** enticement; bait.

lūr′ĭd, *adj.* **1.** glowing through haze. **2.** violently sensational.

lŭrk, *v.i.* be in hiding.

lŭs′cioŭs, *adj.* appealing to the senses.

lŭsh, *adj.* **1.** rich; abundant. —*n.* **2.** *Informal.* alcoholic.

lŭst, *n.* **1.** strong appetite. **2.** strong sexual appetite. —*v.i.* **3.** feel lust. —**lust′ful,** *adj.*

lŭs′têr, *n.* **1.** sheen. **2.** brightness. —**lus′trous,** *adj.*

lŭst′ȳ, *adj.,* **-ier, -iest.** vigorous. —**lust′i·ly,** *adv.*

lŭx·ū′rĭ·ånt, *adj.* lavishly growing. —**lux·u′ri·ance,** *n.*

lŭx·ū′rĭ·āte′′, *v.i.,* **-ated, -ating.** live luxuriously.

lŭx′ū·rȳ, *n., pl.* **-ries. 1.** great comfort or pleasure. **2.** something superfluous. —**lux·u′ri·ous,** *adj.*

lȳ·cē′ŭm, *n.* institute for lectures.

lȳe, *n.* strong alkaline substance.

lȳ′ĭng-ĭn′, *n.* confinement in childbirth.

lȳmph, *n.* clear, watery body liquid. —**lym·phat′ic,** *adj.*

lynch, *v.t.* kill as a mob.

lynx, *n., pl.* **lynxes, lynx.** wildcat of the northern hemisphere.

lyr′ĭc, *adj.* **1.** pertaining to emotion expressed in poetry. —*n.* **2.** lyric poem. **3.** Usually **lyrics,** words to music. —**lyr′i·cal,** *adj.* —**lyr′i·cist,** *n.*

M

M, m, *n.* thirteenth letter of the English alphabet.

măch·i·nā′tion, *n.* plot, scheme.

ma·chĭne′, *n., v.t.,* **-chined, -chining.** *n.* **1.** device for doing work. **2.** political organization. —*v.t.* **3.** shape by machine. —**ma·chin′er·y,** *n.*

ma·chĭn′ĭst, *n.* worker with machine-operated tools.

mă·chĭs′mō, *n.* assertion of masculinity.

măck′êr·ĕl, *n., pl.* **-el, -els.** North Atlantic fish.

măck′ĭ·năw′′, *n.* heavy jacketlike coat.

măck′ĭn·tŏsh′′, *n.* rubberized cloth coat.

mac′ra·me′′ (măk′rĕ·mā′′), *n.* lace or string tied in patterns.

măc′′rō·bī·ŏt′ics, *n.* art of lengthening life. —**mac′′ro·bi·ot′ic,** *adj.*

măc′rō·cŏsm, *n.* **1.** universe. **2.** complex of microcosms.

măd, *adj.,* **madder, maddest. 1.** insane. **2.** infatuated. **3.** angry. —**mad′ly,** *adv.* —**mad′ness,** *n.* —**mad′den,** *v.t.* —**mad′house,** *n.* —**mad′man′′,** **mad′wom′′an,** *n.*

măd′åm, *n.* **1.** polite form of address to a woman. **2.** woman running a brothel.

măd′åme, *n., pl.* **mesdames.** *French.* madam or Mrs.

măd′căp″, *adj*. **1.** reckless. —*n*. **2.** reckless person.

mă″dé·mói·sĕlle′, *n*., *pl*. **mesdemoiselles**. *French*. Miss.

Má·dŏn′nà, *n*. Virgin Mary.

măd′rĭ·gal, *n*. **1.** a part song for several voices sung a capella. **2.** a short lyric poem.

mäel′strŏm, *n*. whirlpool.

măg′à·zĭne, *n*. **1.** periodical with covers. **2.** storage chamber, esp. for ammunition.

mà·gĕn′tà, *n*. purplish red.

măg′gŏt, *n*. wormlike larva. —**mag′got·y**, *adj*.

măg′ĭc, *n*. **1.** use of supernatural methods. **2.** illusions using sleight of hand. —*adj*. **3.** existing or operated by magic. —**mag′i·cal**, *adj*. —**ma·gi′cian**, *n*.

măg′′ĭs·tě′ri·al, *adj*. authoritative.

măg′ĭs·trāte, *n*. minor judge. —**mag′is·tra·cy**, *n*.

măg·năn′ĭ·moŭs, *adj*. above pettiness. —**mag·nan′i·mous·ly**, *adv*. —**mag′′na·nim′i·ty**, *n*.

măg′nāte, *n*. man of wealth or power.

măg·nē′sĭum, *n*. light metallic element.

măg′nét, *n*. object attracting ferrous metal. —**mag·net′ic**, *adj*. —**mag′net·ism**, *n*. —**mag′net·ize″**, *v.t.*

măg·nē′tō, *n*., *pl*. **-toes**. generator with permanent magnets.

măg·nĭf′ĭ·cént, *adj*. splendid in form, accomplishments, etc. —**mag·nif′i·cence**, *n*. —**mag·nif′i·cent·ly**, *adv*.

măg′nĭ·fÿ″, *v.t.*, **-fied**, **-fying**. increase the apparent or real size of. —**mag′′ni·fi·ca′tion**, *n*. —**mag′ni·fi′′er**, *n*.

măg′nĭ·tūde″, *n*. size.

măg′nō′lĭ·à, *n*. flowering tree.

măg′pīe″, *n*. black-and-white bird.

mà′′há·rá′jàh, *n*. major Indian ruler. Also, **ma′′ha·ra′ja**, *fem.*, **ma′′ha·ra′ni**, **ma′′ha·ra′nee**.

mà·hŏg′à·nÿ, *n*. reddish-brown tropical wood.

mäid, *n*. **1.** Also, **maid′ser′vant**, woman servant. **2.** *Archaic*. young woman.

mäid′én, *n*. **1.** *Archaic*. young woman. —*adj*. **2.** very first. —**maid′en·hood″**, *n*. —**maid′en·ly**, *adj*.

mäid′én·hĕad″, *n*. hymen.

mäil, *n*. **1.** material shipped by post offices. **2.** flexible armor. —*v.t.* **3.** give to a post office for shipping. —**mail′box″**, *n*. —**mail′man″**, *n*.

mäil′grăm, *n*. message teletyped between post offices and finally delivered by mail.

mäim, *v.t.* mutilate.

mäin, *adj*. **1.** principal. —*n*. **2.** major utility line. **3.** *Archaic*. sea. —**main′ly**, *adv.* —**main′spring″**, *n*.

mäin′frāme, *n*., *adj*. (computers) large-scale, high-speed computing system.

mäin′länd″, *n*. continental land, as opposed to islands.

mäin′stāy″, *n*. main support.

mäin′strēam″, *n*. main way of thinking, acting, etc.

mäin·tāin′, *v.t.* **1.** keep in good order. **2.** house, feed, etc. **3.** assert persistently. —**main′ten·ance**, *n*.

mâî·tre d′ho·tel′ (mě′′trä dô tĕl′), *n*. headwaiter. Also, *Informal*. **mai·tre d′** (mät′ êr dē′).

măj′és·tÿ, *n.*, *pl*. **-ies**. **1. Majesty**, title of respect for a sovereign. **2.** grandeur. —**ma·jes′tic**, *adj*.

mà′jör, *adj*. **1.** greater. **2.** *Music*. in a scale a half tone above the minor. —*v.i.* **3.** *Education*. specialize. —*n*. **4.** army officer. **5.** specialty in school.

mà·jör′ĭ·tÿ, *n.*, *pl*. **-ties**. **1.** greater number. **2.** legal adulthood.

mäke, *v.t.*, **made**, **making**. **1.** cause to be or occur. **2.** force. **3.** constitute. **4.** earn. **5.** interpret.

mäke′-bé·lĭeve″, *n*. **1.** pretense to oneself. —*adj*. **2.** imaginary.

mäke′shĭft″, *adj*. improvised; temporary.

mäke′ŭp″, *n*. **1.** constitution; contents. **2.** cosmetics, etc.

măl′′ád·jŭst′éd, *adj*. badly adjusted, esp. to life. —**mal′′ad·just′ment**, *n*.

măl′′à·droĭt″, *adj*. clumsy.

măl′à·dÿ, *n.*, *pl*. **-dies**. illness.

mà·läise′, *n*. uneasiness.

măl′à·prŏp″ĭsm″, *n*. ludicrous misuse of a word.

mà·lār′ĭ·à, *n*. mosquito-transmitted disease. —**ma·lar′i·al**, *adj*.

măl′cŏn·tĕnt″, *n*. person discontented, esp. with society.

māle, *adj.* **1.** of the sex that inseminates. —*n.* **2.** male being.

mäl′e·dīc′tion, *n.* curse.

mäl′e·fäc′′tör, *n.* doer of evil.

mà·lĕv′o·lĕnt, *adj.* wishing harm. —**ma·lev′o·lence**, *n.*

mäl·fēa′sànce, *n.* wrongdoing in office.

mäl′′för·mā′tion, *n.* bad formation, esp. of a body part. —**mal·formed′**, *adj.*

mäl′ĭce, *n.* ill will. —**ma·li′cious**, *adj.*

mà·līgn′, *adj.* **1.** intending or doing harm. —*v.t.* **2.** slander.

mà·lĭg′nànt, *adj.* harmful or dangerous. —**ma·lig′nan·cy**, *n.*

mà·lĭn′gēr, *v.i.* pretend sickness or weakness.

mäll, *n.* **1.** tree-lined walk or lawn. **2.** shopping area.

mäl′lard, *n.* wild duck.

mäl′le·à·ble, *adj.* readily shaped by hammering. —**mal′′le·a·bil′i·ty**, *n.*

mäl′lĕt, *n.* short, heavy hammer.

mäl′′nū·trĭ′tion, *n.* inadequate nutrition. —**mal·nour′ished**, *adj.*

mäl·ō′dör·oŭs, *adj.* bad-smelling.

mäl·prăc′tĭce, *n.* improper professional practice.

mält, *n.* soaked and dried grain.

mäl′trēat′′, *v.t.* treat badly. —**mal·treat′ment**, *n.*

mäm′′bō, *n.* dance of Latin American origin.

mäm′mà, *n.* mother. Also, **ma′ma.**

mäm′măl, *n.* **1.** animal giving milk. —*adj.* **2.** being such an animal. —**mam·mal′i·an**, *adj.*, *n.*

mäm′mà·rў, *adj.* pertaining to breasts.

Măm′mòn, *n.* riches or their pursuit, personified.

mäm′mŏth, *adj.* **1.** very large. —*n.* **2.** extinct, long-tusked elephant.

măn, *n.*, *pl.* **men**, *v.t.*, **manned, manning. 1.** human being. **2.** adult male human. **3.** humanity. —*v.t.* **4.** furnish with persons.

măn′à·cles, *n. pl.* shackles.

măn′age, *v.*, **-aged, -aging.** *v.t.* **1.** supervise. **2.** control. —*v.i.* **3.** contrive to succeed. —**man′age·a·ble**, *adj.* —**man′age·ment**, *n.* —**man′ag·er**, *n.* —**man′a·ge′ri·al**, *adj.*

mà·ñā′nà, *adv. Spanish.* tomorrow; some time later.

măn′dà·rĭn, *n.* imperial Chinese official.

măn′dāte, *n.* command.

măn′dà·tō′′rў, *adj.* required.

măn′′dĭ·ble, *n.* lower jaw bone.

măn′dò·lĭn, *n.* plucked musical instrument.

măn′drĕl, *n.* support for work being shaped. Also, **man′dril.**

māne, *n.* long hair on an animal's neck.

mà·neū′vēr, *n.* **1.** military exercise. **2.** controlled movement. —*v.t.*, *v.i.* **3.** move under control.

măn′fŭl, *adj.* courageous.

măn′gà·nēse′′, *n.* grayish chemical element.

mänge, *n.* animal skin disease. —**man′gy**, *adj.*

măn′gēr, *n.* feeding trough.

măn′gle, *v.t.*, **-gled, -gling**, *n.* *v.t.* **1.** crush out of shape. —*n.* **2.** ironing machine.

măn′gō, *n.*, *pl.* **-goes.** fruit-bearing tropical tree.

măn′grōve, *n.* tropical tree.

măn′hăn′′dle, *v.t.*, **-dled, -dling.** handle roughly.

măn′hōle′′, *n.* small access hole.

măn′hōōd′′, *n.* **1.** virility. **2.** majority.

mā′nĭ·à, *n.* **1.** violent insanity. **2.** excitement.

mā′nĭ·ăc′′, *n.* violently insane person. —**ma·ni′a·cal**, *adj.*

măn′ĭc, *adj.* displaying unstable, frenzied behavior.

măn′ĭ·cūre, *n.* care of the hands. —**man′i·cur′′ist**, *n.*

măn′ĭ·fĕst′′, *v.t.* **1.** make apparent. —*adj.* **2.** obvious. —*n.* **3.** list of cargo or passengers.

măn′′ĭ·fĕs′tō, *n.*, *pl.* **-toes.** public declaration.

măn′′ĭ·fōld′′, *adj.* in many forms.

măn′ĭ·kĭn, *n.* professional model. Also, **man′ne·quin.**

măn·ĭl′′à, *n.* strong, light brown paper.

mà·nĭp′′ū·lāte′′, *v.t.*, **-lated, -lating.** handle cunningly. —**ma·nip′u·la′′tor**, *n.*

măn′kĭnd′, *n.* humanity.

măn′lў, *adj.* **-lier, -liest.** virile; brave. —**man′li·ness**, *n.*

măn·nà, *n.* miraculous food.

măn′nêr, *n.* **1.** way of doing. **2.** sort. **3. manners,** personal conduct.

măn′nêr·ĭsm, *n.* personal pecularity.

măn′nêr·lў, *adj.* well-mannered.

măn′nĭsh, *adj.* man-like.

mà·noeū′vrê, *n., v., -vred, -vring. n., v.t., v.i.* maneuver.

măn′-ôf-wâr′, *n.* warship.

măn′ör, *n.* large estate. **—ma·no′ri·al,** *adj.*

măn′pōw′′êr, *n.* available labor force.

măn′sârd, *n.* hip roof with two pitches.

mănse, *n.* home of a clergyman.

măn′siŏn, *n.* impressive house.

măn′slaūgh′′têr, *n.* unintentional homicide.

măn′těl, *n.* fireplace surround. Also, **man′tel·piece′′.**

man·til′la, *n.* lace shawl.

măn′tle, *n., v.t., -tled, -tling.* cloak.

măn′ū·àl, *adj.* **1.** pertaining to or operated by hands. **—n. 2.** handbook. **—man′u·al·lў,** *adv.*

măn′′ū·făc′tūre, *v.t., -tured, -turing. n. v.t.* **1.** make industrially. **—n. 2.** act or instance of manufacturing. **—man′′u·fac′tur·er,** *n.*

mà·nūre′, *n., v.t., -nured, -nuring. n.* **1.** animal feces. **—v.t. 2.** spread with manure as fertilizer.

măn′ū·scrĭpt, *n.* **1.** unprinted writing. **—adj. 2.** written or typed.

măn′ў, *adj.* **more, most.** in a large number.

măp, *n., v.t.,* **mapped, mapping.** *n.* **1.** measured representation of an area of land, etc. **—v.t. 2.** measure for a map. **3.** plan.

mā′ple, *n.* broad-leafed deciduous tree.

măr, *v.t.,* **marred, marring.** make imperfect.

măr′à·thŏn′′, *n.* **1.** foot race of 26 miles, 385 yards. **2.** endurance contest.

mà·raūd′êr, *n.* raider and plunderer.

măr′ble, *n.* **1.** hard, fine-grained limestone. **2.** colored glass ball. **3. marbles,** game played with such balls.

mârch, *v.i.* **1.** walk with measured steps to a cadence. **—v.t. 2.** cause to march. **—n. 3.** marching walk or journey. **4.** piece of music accompanying such a walk. **5. March,** third month.

măr′chiŏn·ĕss, *n.* wife of a marquess, or woman equal to one in rank.

māre, *n.* female horse.

mâr′gà·rĭne, butter-like vegetable oil compound.

mâr′gĭn, *n.* **1.** border or border area. **2.** difference in amounts. **—mar′gin·al,** *adj.*

mâr′′ĭ·gōld′′, *n.* orange-flowered plant.

mă′′rĭ·juà′nà, *n.* dried hemp leaves and blossoms, sometimes smoked. Also, **ma′′ri·hua′na.**

mà·rĭm′bà, *n.* xylophone with tubelike resonators.

mà·rĭ′nà, *n.* yacht landing.

mă′′rĭ·nāde′, *n.* pickling solution.

măr′ĭ·nāte′′, *v.t., -nated, -nating.* steep in a marinade.

mà·rĭne′, *adj.* **1.** pertaining to the sea. **—n. 2.** soldier performing sea duty.

măr′ĭ·nêr, *n.* sailor.

măr′′ĭ·ŏ·nĕtte′, *n.* puppet hung from strings.

măr′ĭ·tàl, *adj.* pertaining to marriage. **—mar′i·tal·lў,** *adv.*

măr′ĭ·tĭme′, *adj.* pertaining to shipping.

mâr′jŏ·ràm, *n.* fragrant herb.

mârk, *n.* **1.** something visible on a surface. **2.** target. **—v.t. 3.** make a mark on. **4.** indicate. **5.** note. **6.** review and grade. **—mark′er,** *n.* **—mark′ing,** *n.*

mârked, *adj.* noticeable; emphatic. **—mark′ed·lў,** *adv.*

mârk′ĕt, *n.* **1.** place for selling. **—v.t. 2.** offer for sale. **—v.i. 3.** shop. **—mark′et·a·ble,** *adj.*

mârks′màn, *n.* shooter at targets. **—marks′man·ship′′,** *n.*

mâr′lĭn, *n., pl.* **-lins, -lin.** large deep-sea fish.

mâr′mà·lāde′′, *n.* fruit preserve.

mà·rōōn′, *v.t.* **1.** abandon on a deserted island. **—n. 2.** dark brownish red.

mâr′quee′, *n.* open projecting shelter.

mâr′quĕss, *n.* nobleman superior to an earl or count. Also, **mar′quis,** *fem.,* **mar·quise′.**

măr′rōw, *n.* inner bone tissue.

măr′rў, *v., -ried, -rying. v.t.* **1.** take as spouse. **2.** unite as spouses. **—v.i. 3.** be married. **—mar′riage,** *n.* **—mar′riage·a·ble,** *adj.*

mârsh, *n.* swamp. **—marsh′y,** *adj.*

mâr′shál, *n.*, *v.t.*, **-shaled, -shaling.** *n.* **1.** sheriff-like U.S. officer. —*v.t.* **2.** put in order. **3.** guide; escort.

mârsh′mál″low, *n.* sweet, spongy confection.

mâr·sū′pĭ·ál, *n.* animal carrying its young in a pouch.

mârt, *n.* salesplace.

mâr′tén, *n.* soft-furred weasel-like animal.

mâr′tiál, *adj.* pertaining to war or the military.

mâr′tĭn, *n.* bird of the swallow family.

mâr″tĭ′nĕt′, *n.* rigid disciplinarian.

mâr·tĭ′nĭ, *n.* cocktail of gin or vodka and dry vermouth.

mâr′týr, *n.* **1.** person who dies or suffers for beliefs. —*v.t.* **2.** kill as a martyr. —**mar′tyr·dom**, *n.*

mâr′vĕl, *n.*, *v.i.*, **-veled, -veling.** wonder. —**mar′vel·ous**, *adj.*

măs·că′rà, *n.* cosmetic for darkening eyelashes.

măs′cŏt, *n.* **1.** thing kept for luck. **2.** group pet.

măs′cū·line, *adj.* pertaining to or characteristic of males. —**mas″cu·lin′i·ty**, *n.*

măsh, *v.t.* **1.** crush to pulp. —*n.* **2.** pulped and watered grain.

măsk, *n.* **1.** face covering. **2.** concealment. —*v.t.* **3.** cover with a mask.

măs′och·ism, *n.* abnormal pleasure obtained from suffering pain. —**mas′och·ist**, *n.* —**mas″och·is′tic**, *adj.*

mā′sòn, *n.* **1.** builder with stones, bricks, etc. **2.** **Mason**, Freemason. —**Ma·son′ic**, *adj.* —**ma′son·ry**, *n.*

măs″quér·äde″, *n.*, *v.i.*, **-aded, -ading.** *n.* **1.** ball of masked and costumed persons. **2.** something falsified. —*v.i.* **3.** appear falsely.

măss, *n.* **1.** large, shapeless quantity. **2.** *Physics.* matter as related to inertia. **3.** Often **Mass**, Eucharistic service. —*v.t.*, *v.i.* **4.** gather in a mass.

măs′sà·crĕ, *n.*, *v.t.*, **-cred, -cring.** *n.* **1.** killing of many. —*v.t.* **2.** kill in a massacre.

măs′säge, *n.*, *v.t.*, **-saged, -saging.** *n.* **1.** manipulation of muscles, as to stimulate circulation. —*v.t.* **2.** give a massage to. —**mas·seur′**, *fem.*, **mas·seuse′**, *n.*

măs′sĭve, *adj.* in large mass.

măst, *n.* tall spar used as a support.

măs′tér, *n.* **1.** person in control. **2.** accomplished craftsman. —*adj.* **3.** principal; controlling. —*v.t.* **4.** make submissive. **5.** become expert in. —**mas′ter·y**, *n.*

măs′tér·fŭl, *adj.* imposing one's will.

măs′tér·lў, *adj.* accomplished.

măs′tér·piēce″, *n.* **1.** greatest accomplishment. **2.** proof of masterly skill. Also, **mas′ter·work″**.

măstér sergéant, army sergeant of high rank.

măs′tĭ·cāte″, *v.t.*, **-cated, -cating.** chew.

măs′tĭff, *n.* large, strong-jawed dog.

măs′tó·dŏn, *n.* extinct elephantlike animal.

măs′tûr·băte″, *v.t.*, **-bated, -bating.** manipulate one's genitals.

măt, *n.*, *v.t.*, **matted, matting,** *adj.* *n.* **1.** thick, flat, flexible object. **2.** tangled mass. —*v.t.* **3.** cover with mats. **4.** make into a mat. —*adj.* **5.** without gloss.

măt′á·dŏr″, *n.* bullfighter who kills.

mătch, *n.* **1.** fire-making friction device. **2.** equal or counterpart. **3.** marriage. **4.** game. —*v.t.* **5.** compare. **6.** equal. —*v.i.* **7.** be a match or matches. —**match·mak″er**, *n.*

mătch′lèss, *adj.* incomparable.

māte, *n.*, *v.*, **mated, mating.** *n.* **1.** spouse. **2.** companion. **3.** co-worker. **4.** one of a pair. **5.** ship's officer. —*v.t.*, *v.i.* **6.** join as mates.

mà·tē′rĭ·ál, *n.* **1.** that which an object is made of. —*adj.* **2.** composed of material. **3.** non-spiritual. **4.** relevant.

mà·tē′rĭ·ál·ism, *n.* **1.** doctrine that all is matter. **2.** concern with wealth, goods, etc. —**ma·te′ri·al·ist**, *n.*, *adj.* —**ma·te″ri·al·is′tic**, *adj.*

mà·tē″rĭ·ĕl′, *n.* military supplies.

mà·tér′nál, *adj.* **1.** pertaining to mothers. **2.** motherlike. —**ma·ter′ni·ty**, *n.*

măth″è·măt′ics, *n.* study of the relations of quantities or forms. Also, *Informal*, **math.** —**math″e·mat′i·cal**, *adj.* —**math″e·ma·ti′cian**, *n.*

măt″ĭ·nee′, *n.* afternoon performance.

măt′ĭns, *n.* morning prayer service.

mā′trĭ·ârch″, *n.* woman acting as master or ruler. —**ma″tri·ar′chal**, *adj.* —**ma·tri·ar″chy**, *n.*

ma·tric′u·late″, *v.*, **-lated, -lating.** *v.i.*, *v.t.* enroll as a student.

mat′ri·mo″nȳ, *n., pl.* **-nies.** marriage. **—mat″ri·mo′ni·al**, *adj.*

ma′trix, *n.* environment in which one comes to be.

ma′tron, *n.* **1.** mature woman. **2.** woman supervisor or guard. **—ma′tron·ly**, *adj.*

matte, *n.* not glossy; flat.

mat′ter, *n.* **1.** solid, liquid, or gas. **2.** affair. **3.** importance. **—**v.i.** **4.** be important.

mat′tock, *n.* digging tool.

mat′tress, *n.* pad for a bed.

ma·ture′, *adj., v.*, **-tured, -turing.** *adj.* **1.** fully ripe or grown. **2.** due for payment. **—**v.t.** **3.** make mature. **—**v.i.** **4.** become mature. **—mat″u·ri′tion**, *n.* **—ma·tu′ri·ty**, *n.*

mat·zo′, *n., pl.* **-zos, -zot, -zoth.** unleavened wafer.

maud′lin, *adj.* foolishly sentimental.

maul, *v.t.* handle or beat severely.

mau″so·le′um, *n., pl.* **-leums, -lea.** large and magnificent tomb.

mauve, *n.* light bluish purple.

mav′er·ick, *n.* nonconformist.

maw, *n.* mouth and throat.

mawk′ish, *adj.* weakly sentimental.

max′im, *n.* rule of conduct.

max′i·mum, *n., pl.* **-mums, -ma**, *adj. n.* **1.** greatest amount. **—**adj.** **2.** Also, **max′i·mal**, greatest.

may, *v.*, *v.t.* **1.** am, are, or is permitted to. **2.** will possibly. **3.** can. **—**n.** **4.** May, fifth month.

may′be, *adv.* possibly.

may′day, *n.* distress call used by aircraft and ships.

may′hem″, *n.* criminal maiming.

may′on·naise″, *n.* salad dressing made with egg yolks.

may′or, *n.* chief city official. **—may′or·al·ty**, *n.*

maze, *n.* intricate system of corridors, lines, etc.

ma·zur′ka, *n.* fast Polish dance.

mead′ow, *n.* area of grassy land.

mea′ger, *adj.* scanty; inadequate. Also, **mea′gre. —mea′ger·ly**, *adv.* **—mea′ger·ness**, *n.*

meal, *n.* **1.** food at one sitting. **2.** coarsely ground grain. **—meal′y**, *adj.*

meal′y-mouthed″, *adj.* not frank.

mean, *v.t.*, **meant, meaning,** *adj., n. v.t.* **1.** intend. **2.** wish to say. **3.** signify. **—**adj.** **4.** ill-tempered. **5.** shabby. **6.** average. **—**n.** **7.** part between extremes. **8. means, a.** something serving a purpose. **b.** personal resources. **—mean′ly**, *adv.* **—mean′ness**, *n.*

me·an′der, *v.i.* wander aimlessly.

mean′ing, *n.* **1.** intended message. **—**adj.** **2.** intended as expressive. **—mean′ing·ful**, *adj.* **—mean′ing·less**, *adj.*

mean′time″, *n.* **1.** time in between. **—**adv.** **2.** during the meantime. **3.** at the same time. Also, **mean′while″.**

mea′sles, *n.* virus disease producing a rash.

mea′sly, *adj.*, **-lier, -liest.** *Informal.* contemptibly small.

meas′ure, *v.*, **-ured, -uring**, *n. v.t.* **1.** find the size or amount of. **—**v.i.** **2.** amount to. **—**n.** **3.** measurement. **4.** means of measuring. **5.** course of action. **—meas′ur·a·ble**, *adj.* **—meas′ure·less**, *adj.* **—meas′ure·ment**, *n.*

meas′ured, *adj.* deliberate.

meat, *n.* **1.** animal flesh. **2.** edible part of a nut. **3.** essential part. **—meat′y**, *adj.*

me·chan′ic, *n.* **1.** worker with machinery. **2. mechanics,** study of the action of forces.

me·chan′i·cal, *adj.* **1.** working by machinery. **2.** unthinkingly automatic.

mech′a·nism, *n.* piece of machinery.

mech′a·nize″, *v.t.*, **-nized, -nizing.** equip with machinery.

med′al, *n.* metal disk indicating distinction, religious affiliation, etc.

me·dal′lion, *n.* round design.

med′al·ist, *n.* winner of a medal.

med′dle, *v.i.*, **-dled, -dling.** interfere mischievously. **—med′dler**, *n.* **—med′dle·some**, *adj.*

me′di·an, *n.* **1.** *Math.* central in a series of numbers. **—**adj.** **2.** *Math.* pertaining to a median. **3.** middle.

me′di·ate″, *v.*, **-ated, -ating.** v.i. **1.** act as an intermediary. **—**v.t.** **2.** resolve as an intermediary. **—me′di·a″tor**, *n.*

med′i·cal, *adj.* pertaining to medicine.

med′i·cate″, *v.t.*, **-cated, -cating. 1.** treat with medicine. **2.** put medicine in. **—med″i·ca′tion**, *n.*

mé·dĭc'ĭ·nȧl, *adj.* serving as medicine.

mĕd'ĭ·cĭne, *n.* **1.** science of healing. **2.** healing substance.

mē''dĭ·ē·ē'vȧl, *adj.* pertaining to the Middle Ages.

mē''dĭ·ō'crē, *adj.* of indifferent value. —me''dĭ·oc'rĭ·ty, *n.*

mĕd'ĭ·tāte'', *v.i.*, -tated, -tating. think deeply. —med''i·ta'tion, *n.* —med''i·ta'tive, *adj.*

mē'dĭ·ŭm, *n.*, *pl.* -ums, -a, *adj. n.* **1.** something in the middle. **2.** means. **3.** *pl.*, media, means of communication. **4.** *pl.*, mediums, communicators with the dead. *Informal,* mem'o. **5.** intermediate.

mĕd'lĕy, *n.*, *pl.* -leys. mixture of tunes.

mēek, *adj.* mild; submissive. —meek'ly, *adv.* —meek'ness, *n.*

mēer'schäum, *n.* white, claylike mineral.

mēet, *v.*, met, meeting, *n.*, *adj. v.t.* **1.** come into contact with. **2.** be introduced to. —*v.i.* **3.** be mutually met. —*n.* **4.** sports meeting. —*adj.* **5.** *Archaic.* suitable. —meet'ing, *n.*

mĕg'ȧ·hērtz'', *n.*, *pl.* -hertz. one million hertz.

mĕg''ȧ·lō·mā'nĭ·ȧ, *n.* delusions of or appetite for grandeur.

mĕg''ȧ·lŏp''ō·lĭs, *n.* huge urban area.

mĕg'ȧ·phōne'', *n.* horn magnifying the voice.

mĕg'ȧ·tŏn'', *n.* explosive force equal to one million tons of TNT.

mĕl''ȧn·chŏ'lĭ·ȧ, *n.* pathological melancholy.

mĕl'ȧn·chŏl'' y̆, *n.* **1.** sadness. —*adj.* **2.** sad.

mê'lee, *n.* confused combat.

mĕl'lĭ·flŭ·oŭs, *n.* smooth and sweet-sounding. Also, mel·lif'flu·ent.

mĕl'lōw, *adj.* **1.** rich-flavored. **2.** gentle. —*v.t.* **3.** make mellow. —*v.i.* **4.** become mellow.

mé·lō'dĭ·oŭs, *adj.* tuneful.

mĕl'ō·drä''mä, *n.* drama of suspense and extravagant emotion. —mel''o·dra·mat'ic, *adj.* —mel''o·dra·mat'ics, *n.*, *pl.*

mĕl'ó·dy̆, *n.*, *pl.* -dies. tune. —me·lod'ic, *adj.*

mĕl'ón, *n.* large, juicy fruit.

mĕlt, *v.*, melted, melted or molten, melting. *v.t.*, *v.i.* liquefy by applying heat.

mĕm'bêr, *n.* **1.** person in an organization. **2.** component part. —mem'ber·ship'', *n.*

mĕm'brāne, *n.* thin organic tissue.

mé·mĕn'tō, *n.*, *pl.* -tos, -toes. souvenir.

mĕm'ŏirs, *n.*, *pl.* written personal recollections.

mĕm'ó·rá·ble, *adj.* compelling remembrance. —mem'o·ra·bly, *adv.*

mĕm''ó·răn'dŭm, *n.*, *pl.* -dums, -da. note of something to be remembered. Also, *Informal,* mem'o.

mé·mô'rĭ·ȧl, *adj.* **1.** in remembrance. —*n.* **2.** something made or done in remembrance.

Mémôriȧl Dāy, legal holiday in May, in memory of dead servicemen.

mĕm'ó·rīze'', *v.t.*, -rized, -rizing. act so as to remember. —mem''o·ri·za'tion, *n.*

mĕm'ó·ry̆, *n.*, *pl.* -ries. **1.** ability to recall past experience. **2.** something remembered. **3.** thing of the past. **4.** (computers) electronic data storage through circuitry or a recording medium.

mĕn'ȧce, *n.*, *v.t.*, -aced, -acing. *n.* **1.** visible threat. —*v.t.* **2.** threaten. —men'ac·ing·ly, *adv.*

mé·năg'êr·iē, *n.* collection of captive wild animals.

mĕnd, *v.t.* **1.** repair. —*v.i.* **2.** improve in condition. —*n.* **3.** mended place.

mĕn·dā'cioŭs, *adj.* lying. —men·dac'i·ty, *n.*

mĕn'dĭ·cȧnt, *adj.* **1.** begging. —*n.* **2.** mendicant person.

mē'nĭ·ȧl, *adj.* **1.** servile. —*n.* **2.** menial person.

mĕn'o·pause'', *n.* permanent end of menstruation.

mĕn·ō'rȧh, *n. Judiasm.* branched candlestick.

mĕn'sēs, *n. pl.* periodic discharge of blood from the uterus.

mĕn'strū·āte'', *v.i.*, -ated, -ating. experience menses. —men'stru·al, *adj.* —men''stru·a'tion, *n.*

mĕn''sū·rā'tion, *n.* measurement.

mĕn'tȧl, *adj.* pertaining to the mind. —men'tal·ly, *adv.*

mĕn·tăl'ĭ·ty̆, *n.*, *pl.* -ties. mental power.

mĕn'thŏl, *n.* alcohol from oil of peppermint. —men'tho·lat''ed, *adj.*

měn'tion, *n.* **1.** brief allusion. —*v.t.* **2.** make a mention of.

měn'tôr, *n.* teacher or advisor.

měn'ū, *n.* list of dishes offered.

mē·ōw', *n.* sound of a cat.

měr'căn·tĭle, *adj.* pertaining to trade.

měr'ce·năr'ÿ, *adj., n., pl.* **-ies.** *adj.* **1.** devoted to money-making. **2.** done for pay. —*n.* **3.** hired soldier.

měr'cêr·īze'', *v.t.*, **-ized, -izing.** impart gloss and strength to, chemically.

měr'chăn·dīse'', *n., v.t.*, **-dised, -dising.** *n.* **1.** goods for sale. —*v.t.* **2.** Also, **mer'chan·dize''**, promote the sale of.

měr'chănt, *n.* seller of goods.

měrchànt marïne, commercial ships of a country.

měr·cū'rǐ·ăl, *adj.* quick to change, esp. in emotion.

měr·cū'rÿ, *n.* heavy metallic chemical element.

měr'cÿ, *n., pl.* **-cies. 1.** kindness toward the helpless. **2.** lucky thing. —**mer'ci·ful**, *adj.* —**mer'ci·less**, *adj.*

mēre, *adj.* no more than. —**mere'ly**, *adv.*

měr'e·trī'cioŭs, *adj.* showy and specious.

mêrge, *v.*, **merged, merging.** *v.t., v.i.* combine.

mêrg'êr, *n.* unification of business organizations.

mé·rĭd'ĭ·ăn, *n.* north-south line.

me·ringue' (mé·răng'), *n.* stiff-beaten egg white.

měr'ĭt, *n.* **1.** worth. **2.** merits, aspects right or wrong. —*v.t.* **3.** deserve. —**mer''i·to'ri·ous**, *adj.*

měr'mäid'', *n.* legendary sea creature, half-woman, half-fish. Also, *masc.*, **mer'man''**.

měr'rÿ, *adj.*, **-rier, -riest.** cheerful. —**mer'ri·ly**, *adv.* —**mer'ri·ment**, *n.*

měr'rÿ-gō-roûnd'', *n.* rotating structure giving a pleasure ride.

měr'rÿ·māk''ĭng, *n.* festivity. —**mer'ry·mak''er**, *n.*

mē'sà, *n.* high, steep-sided plateau.

měsh, *n.* **1.** open space in a net. **2.** net-like material. **3.** engagement of gears. *v.t., v.i.* **4.** entangle. —*v.i.* **5.** become engaged.

měs'mêr·īze'', *v.t.*, **-ized, -izing.** hypnotize. —**mes'mer·ism**, *n.* —**mes'mer·ist**, *n.*

měs·quǐte, *n.* southwestern U.S. tree.

měss, *n.* **1.** disorder or disorderly scene. **2.** difficult situation. **3.** military meal. —*v.t.* **4.** make untidy. **5.** do badly. —*v.i.* **6.** eat mess. —**mes'sy**, *adj.* —**mes'si·ly**, *adv.* —**mes'si·ness**, *n.*

měs'sàge, *n.* **1.** communication. **2.** idea, etc. to communicate.

měs'sèn·gêr, *n.* carrier of messages.

Měs·sī'·àh, *n.* deliverer of mankind.

měs·tī'zō, *n., pl.* **-zos, -zoes.** Hispano-Indian.

me·tăb'o·lĭsm, *n.* breakdown of an organism's nourishment into protoplasm, energy, and waste. —**met''a·bol'ic**, *adj.*

mět'ăl, *n.* iron, gold, brass, etc. —**me·tal'lic**, *adj.*

mět'al·lûr''gÿ, *n.* separation and refining of metals. —**met''al·lur'gi·cal**, *adj.* —**met'al·lur''gist**, *n.*

mět''á·môr'phô·sĭs, *n.* transformation. —**met''a·mor'phic**, *adj.* —**met''a·mor'phose**, *v.t., v.i.*

mět'á·phôr'', *n.* use of an analogous idea. —**met''a·phor'i·cal**, *adj.*

mět''á·phys'ĭcs, *n.* study of the nature of being and reality. —**met''a·phys'i·cal**, *adj.* —**met''a·phy·si'cian**, *n.*

mét''ĕm·psÿ·chō'sĭs, *n., pl.* **-ses.** transfer of souls from body to body.

mē'tē·ôr, *n.* meteoroid in the earth's atmosphere.

mē''tē·ôr'ĭc, *adj.* temporarily brilliant.

mē'tē·ôr·īte'', *n.* meteoroid surviving a fall to earth.

mē''tē·ôr·oĭd'', *n.* solid body traveling through outer space.

mē''tē·ôr·ŏl'ô·gÿ, *n.* study of climate and weather. —**me''te·or·o·log'i·cal**, *adj.* —**me''te·or·ol'o·gist**, *n.*

mē'têr, *n.* **1.** unit of 100 centimeters or 39.37 inches. **2.** rhythmic pattern. **3.** measuring device for fluids, etc. —*v.t.* **4.** measure with a meter.

měth'ŏd, *n.* process or system of doing.

mē·thŏd'ĭ·căl, *adj.* orderly; deliberate. —**me·thod'i·cal·ly**, *adv.*

měth''ŏd·ŏl'ô·gÿ, *n., pl.* **-gies.** system of methods.

me·tĭc'ū·loŭs, *adj.* attentive to details.

mĕt'rĭc, *adj.* **1.** pertaining to the metric system. **2.** metrical. **—met'ri·cal·ly**, *adv.*

mĕt'rĭ·cal, *adj.* **1.** pertaining to poetic meter. **2.** pertaining to measurement.

mĕt'ri·cīze'', *v.t.*, **-cized**, **-cizing.** express in the metric system.

mĕtric sỹstém, decimal system of measurement based on the meter, gram, and liter.

mĕt'ró·nōme'', *n.* time-beating machine.

mé·trŏp'ó·lĭs, *n.* **1.** principal or major city. **2.** city and surrounding built-up area. **—met''ro·pol'i·tan**, *adj.*

mĕt'tle, *n.* spirit; courage. **—met'tle·some**, *adj.*

mĕz'zá·nĭne'', *n.* balcony-like floor.

mĕz'zō·só·prä'nō, *n.*, *pl.* **-nos**, **-ni.** singer with a range between soprano and contralto.

mī·ăs'mà, *n.* marsh vapor.

mī'cá, *n.* crystallized transparent laminated mineral.

mī'crōbe, *n.* microorganism, esp. harmful.

mī'crō chĭp, *n.* small wafer of silicon, etc., containing electronic circuits.

mĭc''rō·cóm·pū'tér, *n.* a complete computing system of compact size, sometimes portable.

mī'cró·cŏsm, *n.* little world.

mī'cró·fĭche'', *n.* card on microfilm images.

mī'cró·fĭlm'', *n.* **1.** film with images at greatly reduced size. **—***v.t.* **2.** record on microfilm.

mī'crŏm'é·tér, *n.* instrument for fine measurements.

mī''crō·ŏr'gàn·ĭsm, *n.* organism visible only through a microscope.

mī'cró·phōne'', *n.* instrument transforming sound into electrical impulses.

mī'cró·scōpe'', *n.* instrument for very high magnification. **—mī''cro·scop'ic**, *adj.*

mĭc'ró·wāve, *n.* electromagnetic radiation of extremely high frequency.

mĭd'āir'', *n.* area away from the ground.

mĭd'dāy'', *n.* noon.

mĭd'dle, *n.* **1.** place with ends equally far away. **—***adj.* **2.** intermediate.

mĭd'dle-āged', *adj.* neither young nor old.

mĭd'dle·măn'', *n.* intermediary between producer and consumer.

mĭd'dlĭng, *adj.* **1.** intermediate. **—***adv.* **2.** *Informal.* moderately.

mĭd'lănd, *n.* middle region.

mĭd'nīght'', *n.* twelve o'clock at night.

mĭd'pōint'', *n.* center point.

mĭd'rĭff, *n.* middle part of the torso.

mĭd'shĭp''man, *n.* naval cadet.

mĭdst, *n.* middle part.

mĭd'wāy'', *n.* **1.** thoroughfare of sideshows. **—***adj.*, *adv.* **2.** halfway.

mĭd'wīfe'', *n.* deliverer of babies. **—mid'wife''ry**, *n.*

mĭd'yēar'', *n.* middle of the year.

mĭen, *n.* manner; bearing.

mĭff, *v.t.* offend.

mĭght, *n.* **1.** strength. **—***v.* **2.** (past tense of *may*). **3.** will possibly. **—might'y**, *adj.* **—might'i·ly**, *adv.*

mī'grāine, *n.* intense headache.

mī'grāte, *v.i.*, **-grated**, **-grating.** move in a group. **—mi·gra'tion**, *n.* **—mi'grant**, *adj.*, *n.* **—mi'gra·to''ry**, *adj.*

mĭld, *adj.* not severe or harsh. **—mĭld'ly**, *adv.* **—mĭld'ness**, *n.*

mĭl'dēw'', *n.* fungus of damp cloth, etc.

mīle, *n.* unit equal to 5,280 feet on land, 6,076 feet on water.

mīle'áge, *n.* **1.** rate per mile. **2.** number of miles per unit.

mī·lĭeū', *n.* social or working environment.

mĭl'i·tànt, *adj.* **1.** fighting for a cause. **—***n.* **2.** militant person. **—mil'i·tan·cy**, *n.*

mĭl'i·tàr·ĭsm, *n.* emphasis on military affairs. **—mil'i·tar·ist**, *n.* **—mil''i·ta·ris'tic**, *adj.*

mĭl'i·tàr·īze'', *v.t.*, **-ized**, **-izing.** invest or equip with military force.

mĭl'i·tār''ў, *adj.* **1.** pertaining to armed forces. **—***n.* **2. the military**, armed forces.

mĭl'i·tāte'', *v.i.*, **-tated**, **-tating.** be an influence.

mi·lĭ'tià, *n.* emergency citizen army. **—mi·li'tia·man**, *n.*

mĭlk, *n.* **1.** white fluid secreted by female mammals for nourishing their young. **—***v.t.* **2.** get milk from. **—milk'maid''**, *n.* **—milk'man''**, *n.* **—milk'y**, *adj.*

milk′shāke″, *n.* shaken drink of milk, ice cream, and flavoring.

mill, *n.* **1.** place for processing or manufacturing; factory. **2.** tenth of a cent. —*v.t.* **3.** process in a mill. —*v.i.* **4.** move about confusedly. —**mill′er,** *n.*

mil·lĕn′i·ŭm, *n., pl.* **-ums, -a.** **1.** period of a thousand years. **2.** time of perfection.

mil′li·grăm″, *n.* thousandth of a gram.

mil′li·mē″tẽr, *n.* thousandth of a meter.

mil′li·nẽr, *n.* dealer in women's hats. —**mil′lin·er·y,** *n.*

mil′lion, *n.* a thousand thousand. —**mil′lionth,** *adj.*

mil′lion·âire′, *n.* owner of at least a million dollars.

mill′stōne″, *n.* stone for grinding flour.

mīme, *n., v.t.,* **mimed, miming.** *n.* **1.** acting without words. —*v.t.* **2.** imitate in mime. —**mi·met′ic,** *adj.*

mĭm′ic, *n., v.t.,* **-icked, -icking.** *n.* **1.** person who imitates mannerisms of others. —*v.t.* **2.** imitate as a mimic. —**mim′ic·ry,** *n.*

mi·mō′sà, *n.* flowering plant of warm regions.

min″à·rĕt′, *Islam.* tower for summoning to prayer.

mince, *v.,* **minced, mincing.** *v.t.* **1.** chop finely. **2.** mitigate the meaning of. —*v.i.* **3.** be affectedly dainty. —**minc′ing,** *adj.*

mince′mēat″, *n.* finely chopped fruit mixture, with or without meat.

mind, *n.* **1.** that which thinks. **2.** personality. **3.** sanity. —*v.t.* **4.** heed. **5.** be troubled or annoyed by.

mind′ful, *adj.* heedful.

mind′less, *adj.* **1.** heedless. **2.** stupid.

mīne, *pron., n., v.,* **mined, mining.** *pron.* **1.** my own. —*n.* **2.** excavation for coal or minerals. **3.** buried or floated bomb. —*v.t.* **4.** dig for a mine. **5.** put mines in. —*v.i.* **6.** work a mine. —**min′er,** *n.*

min′ĕr·ăl, *n.* **1.** something neither vegetable nor animal. **2.** inorganic earth material.

min″ẽr·ăl′o·gy̆, *n.* study of minerals. —**min″er·al·og′i·cal,** *adj.* —**min″er·al′o·gist,** *n.*

min′gle, *v.,* **-gled, -gling.** *v.t., v.i.* mix together.

min′i·à·tūre″, *n.* **1.** small copy. **2.** small painting. —*adj.* **3.** smaller than standard. —**min′i·a·tur·ize″,** *v.t.*

mi″ni·cŏm·pū′tẽr, *n.* a computing system that is larger than a microcomputer but smaller than a mainframe computer.

min′im, *n.* **1.** *Pharmacy.* liquid measure equalling a drop. **2.** *Music.* half note.

min′i·mīze″, *v.t.,* **-mized, -mizing.** **1.** reduce to a minimum. **2.** treat as of minimum importance.

min′i·mŭm, *n., pl.* **-mums, -ma,** *adj. n.* **1.** least amount. —*adj.* **2.** Also, **min′i·mal,** least.

min′ion, *n.* minor official.

min′is·tẽr, *n.* **1.** clergyman. **2.** diplomat. **3.** cabinet member. —*v.i.* **4.** give help. —**min″is·te′ri·al,** *adj.* —**min″is·tra′tion,** *n.* —**min′is·trant,** *n., adj.*

min′is·try̆, *n., pl.* **-tries.** **1.** profession of a minister. **2.** government department. **3.** act of ministering.

mĭnk, *n.* weasel-like mammal.

min′nōw, *n.* tiny fresh-water fish.

mī′nŏr, *adj.* **1.** lesser in size or importance. **2.** *Music.* in a scale a half tone below the major. —*n.* **3.** person not of age.

mi·nôr′i·ty̆, *n., pl.* **-ities.** **1.** lesser part. **2.** social group too small to have control. **3.** state of being a minor.

min′strel, *n.* **1.** medieval strolling singer. **2.** blackface singer.

mint, *n.* **1.** place for coining money. **2.** plant with aromatic leaves. —*adj.* **3.** absolutely fresh. —*v.t.* **4.** coin.

min′u·ĕnd″, *n.* *Math.* number subtracted from.

min′u·ĕt″, *n.* slow dance.

mī′nŭs, *prep.* **1.** from which is subtracted. **2.** without.

mi·nŭs′cūle, *adj.* tiny.

min′ūte, *n.* **1.** one sixtieth of an hour. **2.** one sixtieth of a degree of arc. **3. minutes,** record of a meeting. —*adj.* (mī nyōōt′) **4.** tiny. **5.** precise.

min′ūte·măn″, *n.* volunteer soldier of the American Revolution.

mi·nū′ti·àe, *n. pl.* minor details.

mir′à·cle, *n.* supernatural event. —**mi·rac′u·lous,** *adj.*

mi·râge′, *n.* optical illusion caused by the atmosphere.

mīre, *n., v.t.,* **mired, miring.** *n.* **1.** sticky

mud. —*v.t.* **2.** stick fast, as with mud. —**mir′y,** *adj.*

mir′ror, *n.* **1.** reflecting object. —*v.t.* **2.** reflect.

mirth, *n.* gaiety. —**mirth′ful,** *adj.* —**mirth′less,** *adj.*

mis- prefix meaning "wrong" or "wrongly." misapply, misbehave, miscalculate, misconceive, misconduct, misconstrue, miscount, misdeed, misdirect, misdoing, misgovern, misguide, mishandle, misinform, misinterpret, misjudge, mismanage, mismatch, misprint, mispronounce, misquote, misread, misrule, misshapen, misspell, misspend, misstate, mistime, mistreat, misunderstand.

mis′′ad·ven′ture, *n.* bad luck.

mis′an·thrope′′, *n.* hater of mankind. Also, **mis·an′thro·pist.** —**mis′′an·throp′ic,** *adj.* —**mis·an′thro·py,** *n.*

mis′ap′′pre·hend′, *v.t.* understand wrongly. —**mis·ap′′pre·hen′sion,** *n.*

mis′′ap·pro′pri·āte′′, *v.t.,* **-ated, -ating.** take and use wrongly.

mis′′be·got′ten, *adj.* begotten wrongly; illegitimate.

mis·car′ry, *v.t.,* **-ried, -rying. 1.** give birth to a fetus that cannot live. **2.** go wrong. —**mis·car′riage,** *n.*

mis′′ce·′′ge·nā′tion, *n.* interbreeding of races.

mis′′cel·lā′ne·ous, *adj.* various. —**mis′cel·la·ny,** *n.*

mis·chánce′, *n.* bad luck.

mis′chief, *n.* **1.** damage. **2.** malice. **3.** gentle malice. —**mis′chie·vous,** *adj.*

mis′′con·strúc′tion, *n.* wrong interpretation.

mis′crē·ant, *n.* villain.

mis′′de·mēa′nor, *n.* offense less serious than a felony.

mi′sēr, *n.* morbid saver of money. —**mi′ser·ly,** *adj.*

mis′er·a·ble, *adj.* **1.** very unhappy. **2.** causing misery. **3.** contemptibly meager or poor. —**mis′er·a·bly,** *adv.*

mis′er·ȳ, *n., pl.* **-ies. 1.** suffering. **2.** source of suffering.

mis·fire′, *v.i.,* **-fired, -firing. 1.** fail to fire. **2.** fail to be effective.

mis′fit′, *n., v.i.,* **-fitted, -fitting. 1.**

person unhappy in society. —*v.t., v.i.* **2.** fit badly.

mis·for′tūne, *n.* **1.** bad luck. **2.** piece of bad luck.

mis·giv′ing, *n.* apprehension; doubt.

mis′hăp, *n.* unfortunate incident.

mis·lāy, *v.t.,* **-laid, -laying.** put somewhere later forgotten.

mis·lēad′, *v.t.,* **-led, -leading. 1.** advise or urge wrongly. **2.** deceive.

mis·nō′mêr, *n.* wrong name.

mi·sŏg′y·nÿ, *n.* hatred of women. —**mi·sog′y·nist,** *n.*

mis·plāce′, *v.t.,* **-placed, -placing. 1.** mislay. **2.** put in a wrong place.

mis·prí′sion, *n.* deviation from duty.

mis′′rep·re·sĕnt′, *v.t.* give a wrong idea of. —**mis′′rep·re·sen·ta′tion,** *n.*

miss, *v.t., n., pl.* **misses.** *v.t.* **1.** fail to hit, seize, meet, etc. **2.** be lonely without. —*n.* **3.** act or instance of missing. **4. Miss,** title for an unmarried woman.

mis′sal, *n.* book of prayers for Mass.

mis′sīle, *n.* something thrown or shot to hit a target.

mis′sĭng, *adj.* lost or absent.

mis′sion, *n.* **1.** commanded or requested journey. **2.** group of missionaries. **3.** group sent to a place. **4.** duty or purpose.

mis′sion·ār′′ÿ, *n., pl.* **-ies.** person sent to make religious conversions.

mis′sīve, *n.* written message.

mis·stĕp′, *n.* **1.** wrong step. **2.** wrong act.

mist, *n.* **1.** thin fog. —*v.t.* **2.** fog. —*v.i.* **3.** become misty. —**mist′y,** *adj.*

mis·tāke′, *n., v.t.,* **-took, -taken, -taking.** *n.* **1.** wrong act or opinion. —*v.t.* **2.** understand wrongly. —**mis·tak′a·ble,** *adj.*

mis′tle·tōe′′, *n.* semi-parasitic evergreen.

mis′trĕss, *n.* **1.** female master. **2.** unmarried female sexual partner.

mis·trī′al, *n.* trial invalidated for technical reasons.

mis·trŭst′, *v.t.* **1.** have no trust in. —*n.* **2.** lack of trust. —**mis·trust′ful,** *adj.*

mis·use, *v.t.* **-used, -using,** *n., v.t.* (mis yōōz′) **1.** use wrongly. **2.** mistreat. —*n.* (mis yōōs′) **3.** wrong use or treatment.

mīte, *n.* **1.** tiny arachnid. **2.** tiny sum of money.

mī'têr, *n.* **1.** bishop's headpiece. **2.** diagonal joint. —*v.t.* **3.** join in a miter.

mĭt'ĭ·gāte'', *v.*, **-gated, -gating.** *v.t., v.i.* lessen in severity. —**mĭt''ĭ·ga'tion**, *n.*

mĭtt, *n.* padded glove.

mĭt'tĕn, *n.* glove with only the thumb separate.

mĭx, *v.*, **mĭxed, mixing**, *n. v.t.* **1.** assemble and make uniform. **2.** have together. —*v.i.* **3.** be on social terms. —*n.* **4.** mixture. —**mix'ture**, *n.*

mĭxed, *adj.* **1.** blended. **2.** imperfect or impure.

mĭx'ŭp'', *n.* confusion.

mne·mon'ic (nĭ·mŏn'ĭk), *adj.* helping memory.

mōan, *n.* **1.** low, sad sound. —*v.i.* **2.** make such a sound.

mōat, *n.* defensive, water-filled ditch.

mŏb, *n., v.t.*, **mobbed, mobbing.** *n.* **1.** disorderly or hostile crowd. —*v.t.* **2.** attack in a mob.

mō'bĭle, *adj.* movable. —**mo·bil'i·ty**, *n.*

mō'bĭ·līze'', *v.*, **-lized, -lizing.** *v.t., v.i.* make ready for war.

mŏc'ca·sĭn, *n.* soft heelless slipper.

mō'chà, *n.* **1.** type of coffee. —*adj.* **2.** coffee-flavored.

mŏck, *n.* **1.** ridicule. **2.** imitate; mimic. —*adj.* **3.** imitation. —**mock'er·y**, *n.*

mŏck'ĭng·bĭrd'', *n.* bird imitating calls of other birds.

mŏck'ŭp'', *n.* full-scale model.

mōde, *n.* **1.** manner of doing. **2.** fashion. —**mod'ish**, *adj.*

mŏd'el, *n.* **1.** small-scale three-dimensional copy. **2.** something to imitate. **3.** poser for pictures. —*adj.* **4.** exemplary. —*v.t.* **5.** copy in three dimensions. **6.** mold as in making a model. **7.** make as a copy.

mō'dĕm, *n.* (computers) device for linking computers via telephone lines.

mod·er·ate, *adj., n., v.*, **-ated, -ating.** *adj.* (mod'∂r ∂t). **1.** avoiding extremes, —*n.* **2.** moderate person.—*v.t.* (mod'∂r āt) **3.** make moderate. **4.** preside over. —*v.i.* **5.** become moderate. —**mod'er·ate·ly**, *adv.* —**mod'er·a''tor**, *n.*

mŏd'êrn, *adj.* **1.** pertaining to the present. **2.** reflecting advanced taste, thought, technology, etc. —*n.* **3.** mod-

ern person. —**mo·dern'i·ty**, *n.* —**mod'ern·ize''**, *v.t., v.i.*

mŏd'êrn·ism, *n.* advocacy of something deemed modern.

mŏd''êrn·ĭs'tĭc, *adj.* self-consciously modern in style.

mŏd'ĕst, *adj.* **1.** disliking praise, publicity, etc. **2.** avoiding self-exposure. **3.** not outstanding. —**mod'est·ly**, *adv.* —**mod·es'ty**, *n.*

mŏd'ĭ·cŭm, *n.* small amount.

mŏd'ĭ·fy'', *v.*, **-fied, -fying.** *v.t., v.i.* **1.** alter in nature. —*v.t.* **2.** limit slightly. —**mod''i·fi·ca'tion**, *n.* —**mod'i·fi''er**, *n.*

mŏd'ŭ·lāte'', *v.t.*, **-lated, -lating.** vary or adjust. —**mod''u·la'tion**, *n.*

mŏd'ūle, *n.* **1.** unit of measurement. **2.** part scaled to the dimensions of such a unit.

mō'hāir, *n.* fabric of Angora goat hair.

Mō·hăm'mĕd·án, *n., adj.* Muslim. —**Mo·ham'med·an·ism**, *n.*

mŏĭst, *adj.* slightly wet. —**moist'en**, *v.t., v.i.* —**mois'ture**, *n.*

mō'lär, *n.* grinding tooth.

mo·lăs'sĕs, *n.* syrup from sugar refining.

mōld, *n.* **1.** device for forming a casting. **2.** model. **3.** destructive fungus. —*v.t.* **4.** model. **5.** cast in a mold. —*v.i.* **6.** become moldy. —**mold'y**, *adj.*

mōld'êr, *v.i.* crumble to dust.

mōld'ĭng, *n.* shaped strip or band.

mōle, *n.* **1.** spot on the skin. **2.** burrowing animal. **3.** breakwater. —**mole'hill''**, *n.* —**mole'skin''**, *n.*

mŏl'e·cūle'', *n.* smallest characteristic particle of an element or compound. —**mo·lec'u·lar**, *adj.*

mó·lĕst'', *v.t.* trouble or interfere with. —**mo''les·ta'tion**, *n.*

mŏl'lĭ·fy'', *v.t.*, **-fied, -fying. 1.** appease. **2.** mitigate.

mŏl'lŭsk, *n.* soft-bodied invertebrate, often in a shell. Also, **mol'lusc.**

mōlt, *v.i.* shed hair, feathers, etc. for replacement.

mōl'tĕn, *adj.* melted.

mō'mĕnt, *n.* **1.** very brief period. **2.** present time. **3.** importance. —**mo'men·tar''y**, *adj.* —**mo''men·tar·i·ly**, *adv.*

mō·mĕn'toŭs, *adj.* of great importance.

mō·měn'tŭm, *n.*, *pl.* **-tums, -ta.** force of a moving object.

mŏm'mў̆, *n.*, *pl.* **-mies.** mother: child's word.

mŏn'ärch, *n.* king, queen, etc. **—mon'arch·y,** *n.* **—mo·nar'chi·cal,** *adj.*

mŏn'ärch·ĭst, *n.* person in favor of a monarchy. **—mon'ar·chism''**, *n.*

mŏn'ás·tĕr''ў̆, *n.*, *pl.* **-ies.** *n.* home of monks or nuns.

mó·năs'tĭc, *adj.* pertaining to monks or nuns. Also, **mo·nas'ti·cal,** *adj.*

mŏn·äu'răl, *adj.* reproducing sound on one channel.

Mŏn'dăy, *n.* second day.

mŏn'ĕў̆, *n.*, *pl.* **-eys, -ies.** paper or metal accepted everywhere in payment of debts. **—mon'eyed,** *adj.* **—mon'e·tar'y,** *adj.*

mŏn'grĕl, *adj.* **1.** of mixed breed. **—n. 2.** animal with mixed bloodlines.

mŏn'ĭ·tŏr, *n.* **1.** device for checking or supervising. **—v.t. 2.** check or supervise.

mŏnk, *n.* member of a religious order.

mŏn'kĕў̆, *n.*, *pl.* **-keys. 1.** primate other than a human or ape. **2.** small, long-tailed primate.

mŏn'ó·chrōme'', *n.* color with shading varied but not hue.

mŏn'ó·cle, *n.* corrective lens for one eye.

mó·nŏg'á·mў̆, *n.* marriage to one spouse at a time. **—mo·nog'a·mous,** *n.*

mŏn'ó·grăph'', *n.* scholarly work on one subject.

mŏn'ó·lĭth'', *n.* object made from one stone. **—mon''o·lith'ic,** *adj.*

mŏn'ó·lŏgue'', *n.* uninterrupted speech of one person. Also, **mon'o·log''. —mon'o·log''ist,** *n.*

mŏn''ó·mā'nĭ·à, *n.* obsession with one thing. **—mon''o·ma'ni·ac'',** *n.*

mó·nŏp'ó·lў̆, *n.*, *pl.* **-lies.** exclusive use, control, or possession. **—mo·nop'o·list,** *n.* **—mo·nop''o·lis'tic,** *adj.* **—mo·nop'o·lize'',** *v.t.*

mŏn'ó·räil'', *n.* one-rail railway.

mŏn'ó·syl''lá·ble, *n.* one-syllable word. **—mon''o·syl·lab'ic,** *adj.*

mŏn''ó·thē'ĭsm, *n.* belief in one god. **—mon''o·the'ist,** *n.* **—mon''o·the·is'tic,** *adj.*

mŏn'ó·tōne'', *n.* sound with unvarying pitch.

mó·nŏt'ó·noŭs, *adj.* tediously unvaried. **—mo·not'o·ny,** *n.*

mon·sieur (mẹ sŷur'), *n.*, *pl.* **messieurs.** *French.* **1.** gentleman. **2. Monsieur. a.** Sir. **b.** Mister.

Mon·si·gnor (mŏn sēn'yẹr), *n.*, *pl.* **-gnors, -gnori.** high-ranking Roman Catholic priest.

mŏn·sōon', *n.* season of wind and rain in south Asia.

mŏn'stĕr, *n.* **1.** frightening legendary creature. **2.** grotesque or disgusting person. **—mon'strous,** *adj.* **—mon·stros'i·ty,** *n.*

mon·tage (mahn tahzh'), *n.* composite photograph, etc.

mŏnth, *n.* one of the twelve divisions of the year. **—month'ly,** *adj., adv., n.*

mŏn'ü·mĕnt, *n.* **1.** something built or put up in remembrance. **2.** formal, impressive construction. **—mon''u·men'tal,** *adj.*

mōō, *n.*, *v.i.*, **mooed, mooing.** *n.* **1.** sound of a cow. **—v.i. 2.** make this sound.

mōōch, *Informal. v.i.* **1.** beg; cadge. **—v.t. 2.** obtain by begging.

mōōd, *n.* state of mind.

mōōd'ў̆, *adj.*, **-ier, -iest. 1.** gloomy. **2.** changing mood quickly. **—mood'i·ly,** *adv.* **—mood'i·ness,** *n.*

mōōn, *n.* **1.** satellite of the earth. **2.** lighted portion of this satellite as seen from the earth. **—v.i. 3.** be abstracted or sentimental. **—moon'beam'',** *n.* **—moon'light'',** *n.* **—moon'lit'',** *adj.* **—moon'scape'',** *n.*

mōōn'light''ĭng, *n.* holding of a second job.

mōōn'shīne'', *n.* **1.** illicit whiskey. **2.** moonlight. **—moon'shin''er,** *n.*

mōōn'shŏt'', *n.* start of a trip to the moon.

mōōn'strŭck'', *adj.* **1.** crazy. **2.** dreamy.

mōōn'wälk'', *n.* walk on the moon.

môor, *v.t.* tie or anchor.

môor'ĭngs, *n. pl.* **1.** tackle for mooring. **2.** place to moor.

mōōse, *n.*, *pl.* **moose.** large animal of the deer family.

mōōt, *adj.* **1.** hypothetical. **2.** open to question.

mŏp, *n.*, *v.t.*, **mopped, mopping.** *n.* **1.** long-handled device for washing or dusting. **—v.t. 2.** clean with a mop.

mōpe, *v.i.*, **moped, moping.** brood. —**mop′ey, mop′y,** *adj.*

mò·rāine′, *n.* mass of rock, etc. left by a glacier.

mŏr′ăl, *adj.* **1.** pertaining to morality. **2.** in accord with morality. **3.** pertaining to morale. —*n.* **4.** lesson of an experience. **5. morals,** moral principles. —**mor′al·ist,** *n.* —**mo·ral′i·ty,** *n.*

mò·răle′, *n.* confidence in oneself, a situation, etc.

mŏr′′ăl·ĭs′tĭc, *adj.* **1.** pertaining to morals. **2.** overconcerned with morals.

mŏr′ăl·īze′′, *v.i.,* **-ized, -izing.** discuss morality.

mò·răss′, *n.* swamp.

mŏr′′à·tō′rĭ·ŭm, *n., pl.* **-ums, -a.** authorized delay.

mŏr′bĭd, *adj.* **1.** pertaining to disease. **2.** mentally unhealthy. —**mor·bid′i·ty,** *n.* —**mor′bid·ly,** *adv.*

mŏr′dănt, *adj.* biting. —**mor′dan·cy,** *n.*

mōre, *adj.* **1.** greater in number, amount, etc. **2.** additional. —*adv.* **3.** additionally. —*n.* **4.** greater number, amount, etc. **5.** something additional.

mōre·ō′vêr, *adj.* besides.

mō′rēs, *n. pl.* prevailing social customs.

mȯrgue, *n.* place for keeping the unidentified dead.

mŏr′ĭ·bŭnd, *adj.* about to die.

mȯrn′ĭng, *n.* early part of the day.

mȯrning glȯrÿ, vine with trumpet-shaped flowers.

mò·rŏc′cō, *n.* goat leather.

mō′rŏn, *n.* feeble-minded person. —**mo·ron′ic,** *adj.*

mó·rōse′, *adj.* downhearted or surly. —**mo·rose′ly,** *adv.* —**mo·rose′ness,** *n.*

mȯr′phĭne, *n.* analgesic opiate.

mȯrse, *n.* code of dots and dashes. Also, **Morse.**

mȯr′sĕl, *n.* small portion of food.

mŏr′tăl, *adj.* **1.** having eventually to die. **2.** human. **3.** fatal. **4.** threatening the soul. —*n.* **5.** human being. —**mor′tal·ly,** *adv.* —**mor·tal′i·ty,** *n.*

mȯr′tàr, *n.* **1.** adhesive for masonry. **2.** bowl for grinding. **3.** short cannon.

mȯr′tàr·bȯärd′′, *n.* academic cap.

mȯrt′gàge, *n., v.i.,* **-gaged, -gaging.** *n.* **1.** pledge of property as security for a loan. —*v.t.* **2.** pledge in this way.

—**mȯrt′′ga·gee′,** *n.* —**mȯrt′ga·gor,** *n.*

mȯr·tĭ′cĭàn, *n.* undertaker.

mȯr′tĭ·fȳ′′, *v.t.,* **-fied, -fying. 1.** humiliate. **2.** suppress with austerities. —**mȯr′′ti·fi·ca′tion,** *n.*

mȯr′tĭse, *n., v.t.* **-tised, -tising.** *n.* **1.** socket forming part of a joint. —*v.t.* **2.** join with a mortise.

mȯr′tū·ār′′ÿ, *adj., n., pl.* **-ies.** *adj.* **1.** pertaining to death or funerals. —*n.* **2.** place for receiving the dead.

mō·sā′ĭc, *n.* picture of inlaid pieces.

mō′sēÿ, *v.i. Informal.* amble.

Mŏs′lĕm, *n.* Muslim.

mȯsque, *n.* Muslim house of prayer.

mós·quī′tō, *n., pl.* **-toes, -tos.** small blood-sucking insect.

mŏss, *n.* green, velvety plant. —**mos′sy,** *adj.*

mŏst, *adj.* **1.** greatest in number, amount, etc. **2.** in the majority. —*adv.* **3.** to the greatest extent. —*n.* **4.** greatest number, extent, etc.

mōst′lÿ, *adv.* in most cases.

mō·tĕl′, *n.* hotel for motorists.

mŏth, *n., pl.* **moths.** nocturnal flying insect.

mŏth′băll′, *n.* ball of moth repellent.

mŭth′êr, *n.* **1.** female parent. —*v.t.* **2.** act as a mother to. —**moth′er·hood′′,** *n.* —**moth′er·less,** *adj.* —**moth′er·ly,** *adj.*

mŭth′êr-ĭn-lāw′, *n., pl.* **mothers-in-law.** mother of a spouse.

mŭth′êr-ȯf-pêärl′, *n.* inner shell of the pearl oyster.

mō·tĭf′, *n.* basic theme or subject.

mō′tĭon, *n.* **1.** movement. **2.** formal proposal. —*v.i.* **3.** gesture. —*v.t.* **4.** direct with a gesture. —**mo′tion·less,** *adj.*

mōtion pĭctûre, series of photographs projected at high speed.

mō′tĭ·vāte′, *v.t.,* **-vated, -vating.** give desire or incentive. —**mo′′ti·va′tion,** *n.*

mō′tĭve, *n.* **1.** desire for action. **2.** motif. —*adj.* **3.** pertaining to motion.

mŏt′lĕÿ, *adj.* of many colors or kinds.

mō′tȯr, *n.* **1.** machine providing motive force. —*adj.* **2.** causing motion. —**mo′tor·bike′′,** *n.* —**mo′tor·boat′′,** *n.* —**mo′tor·car′′,** *n.* —**mo′tor·ize′′,** *v.t.*

mō′tŏr·cāde″, *n*. procession of automobiles.

mō′tŏr·cȳ″cle, *n*. two-wheeled motorized vehicle.

mō′tŏr·ĭst, *n*. automobile driver.

mō′tŏr·mǎn, *n*. driver of a streetcar.

mŏt′tle, *v.t.*, **-tled, -tling.** mark with spots, etc.

mŏt′tō, *n*., *pl*. **-toes, -tos.** formal statement of aims or ideals.

mōuld, *n*., *v.t.* mold.

mōund, *n*., *v.t.* heap.

mōunt, *v.t.* **1.** climb onto or up. **2.** set in place. —*v.i.* **3.** climb. —*n*. **4.** steed. **5.** setting or support. —**mount′ing**, *n*.

mōun′tain, *n*. very high feature of the earth. —**moun′tain·ous**, *adj*.

mōun″tàin·ēer′, *n*. **1.** mountain dweller. **2.** mountain climber. —**moun″tain·eer′ing**, *n*.

mōun′tè·bǎnk″, *n*. charlatan.

mōurn, *v.t.*, *v.i.* lament. —**mourn′ful**, *adj*. —**mourn′ing**, *n*.

mōuse, *n*., *pl*. **mice. 1.** small, timid rodent. **2.** (computers) compact device for convenient data manipulation on a monitor.

mōus·tăche′, *n*. mustache.

mōus′ÿ, *adj*., **-ier, -iest.** mouselike, esp. in timidity.

mōuth, *n*. **1.** orifice for eating and breathing. **2.** opening of a river, etc. —**mouth′ful**, *n*.

mōuth′piēce″, *n*. **1.** part of a horn, etc. blown through. **2.** spokesman or apologist.

move (mōŏv), *v.*, **moved, moving**, *n. v.t.* **1.** change the place of. **2.** inspire or motivate. **3.** propose formally. —*v.i.* **4.** change place. **5.** change residence or workplace. **6.** become in motion. —*n*. **7.** act or instance of moving. **8.** purposeful action. —**mov′a·ble, move′a·ble**, *adj*.

move′mént (mōŏv′mént), *n*. **1.** motion. **2.** action in a cause. **3.** assembly of clockwork. **4.** division of a musical composition.

mov′ïē (moo′vē), *n*. motion picture. Also, **moving picture.**

mōw, *v.t.*, **mowed, mowed** or **mown, mowing. 1.** cut down, as grass. **2.** cut down the plants on.

Mr. (mis′tèr), title for a man. Also, **Mis′ter.**

Mrs. (mis′iz), title for a married woman.

Ms. (miz, em′es′), *n*. title for a woman disregarding marital status.

mŭch, *adj*., *adv.*, *n. adj.* **1.** in great quantity. —*adv.* **2.** to a great extent. **3.** about. —*n*. **4.** something considerable. **5.** a great amount.

mū′cĭ·làge, *n*. liquid glue.

mŭck, *n*. sticky filth. —**muck′y**, *adj*.

mŭck′rǎk″ĭng, *n*. searching for scandalous information. —**muck′rak″er**, *n*.

mū′cŏŭs, *adj*. **1.** having mucus. **2.** slimy.

mū′cŭs, *n*. slimy body secretion, esp. from the nose.

mŭd, *n*. sticky earth. —**mud′dy**, *adj*., *v.t.*

mŭd′dle, *v.t.*, **-dled, -dling**, *n. v.t.* **1.** bungle or confuse. —*n*. **2.** act or instance of muddling. —**mud′dle·head′ed**, *adj*.

mŭd′slīng″ĭng, *n*. defamation, esp. of a political opponent. —**mud′sling″er**, *n*.

mū·ĕz′zĭn, *n*. Muslim caller to prayer.

mŭff, *n*. **1.** cylinder made esp. of fur for keeping the hands warm. —*v.t.* **2.** bungle.

mŭf′fĭn, *n*. small round bread or cake.

mŭf′fle, *v.t.*, **-fled, -fling. 1.** wrap closely. **2.** deaden, as sound.

mŭf′flèr, *n*. **1.** heavy scarf. **2.** sound deadener.

mŭf′tĭ, *n*. dress other than a uniform.

mŭg, *n*., *v.t.*, **mugged, mugging.** *n.* **1.** cylindrical cup. —*v.t.* **2.** attack from behind, esp. in order to rob.

mŭg′gÿ, *adj*., **-gier, -giest.** hot and humid.

Mu·hăm′mà·dàn, *n*., *adj*. Muslim.

mŭl′bĕr″rÿ, *n*., *pl*. **-ries.** tree with purplish-red fruit.

mŭlch, *n*. plant matter spread to keep the ground from freezing.

mŭlct, *v.t.* **1.** fine. **2.** obtain by fraud.

mūle, *n*. **1.** offspring of a donkey and a mare. **2.** heelless slipper. —**mu·le·teer′**, *n*.

mŭl′ĭsh, *adj*. stubborn.

mŭll, *v.t.* **1.** to warm and spice, as wine. —*v.i.* **2.** *Informal*. ponder.

mŭl″tĭ·făr′ĭ·oŭs, *adj*. with many components.

mŭl″tĭ·mĭl″lìon·āire′, *n*. one who has many millions of dollars.

mŭl'tĭ·ple, *adj*. 1. in a large number. —*n*. 2. number evenly divisible by another.

mŭl''tĭ·plĭ·cănd', *n*. *Math*. number to be multiplied.

mŭl''tĭ·plĭc'ĭ·tỹ, *n*. large number or variety.

mŭl'tĭ·plỹ', *v*., **-plied, -plying**. *v.t*. 1. repeat a specified number of times for a final sum. —*v.i*. 2. increase in size or number. —**mul'ti·pli'er**, *n*. —**mul''ti·pli·ca'tion**, *n*.

mŭl'tĭ·stãge'', *adj*. in many stages.

mŭl'tĭ·tūde'', *n*. large number. —**mul''ti·tu'di·nous**, *adj*.

mŭm, *adj*. 1. unspeaking. 2. short for chrysanthemum.

mŭm'ble, *v.i*., **-bled, -bling**, *n*. *v.i*. 1. say something quietly and indistinctly. —*n*. 2. mumbling speech or remark.

mŭm'bō jŭm'bō, pretentious or meaningless ceremony.

mŭm'mêr, *n*. wearer of a mask or costume. —**mum'mer·y**, *n*.

mŭm'mỹ, *n*., *pl*. **-mies**. preserved dead body. —**mum'mi·fy''**, *v.t*., *v.i*.

mŭmps, *n*. communicable disease characterized by swollen glands.

mŭnch, *v.t*., *v.i*. chew crunchingly.

mŭn·dāne', *adj*. 1. worldly. 2. commonplace.

mū·nĭc'ĭ·pál, *adj*. pertaining to city government.

mū·nĭc''ĭ·pǎl'ĭ·tỹ, *n*., *pl*. **-ties**. incorporated community.

mū·nĭf'ĭ·cĕnt, *adj*. lavish; generous. —**mu·nif'i·cence**, *n*.

mū·nĭ'tions, *n*. *pl*. military supplies, esp. guns and ammunition.

mū'rǎl, *n*. wall painting. —**mu'ral·ist**, *n*.

mûr'dêr, *n*. 1. willful unlawful killing. —*v.t*. 2. commit murder against. —**mur'der·er**, *fem*., **mur'der·ess**, *n*. —**mur'der·ous**, *adj*.

mûrk, *n*. gloom; darkness. —**murk'y**, *adj*.

mûr'mûr, *n*. 1. low, indistinct speech or sound. —*v.i*. 2. make a murmur.

mŭs''cà·těl', *n*. sweet wine.

mŭs'cle, *n*. body tissue which contracts to cause movement. —**mus'cu·lar**, *adj*. —**mus'cu·la·ture**, *n*.

mūse, *v.i*. 1. be meditative. —*n*. 2. Muse, goddess presiding over an art.

mū·sē'ŭm, *n*. public institution for displaying things of interest.

mŭsh, *n*. 1. porridge of boiled meat. 2. *Informal*. foolish sentiment. —**mush'y**, *adj*.

mŭsh'rōōm'', *n*. 1. edible fungus. —*v.i*. 2. grow rapidly.

mū'sĭc, *n*. art of composing series of tones, etc. —**mu·si'cian**, *n*. —**mu''si·col'o·gy**, *n*.

mū'sĭ·cál, *adj*. 1. pertaining to music. 2. sweet-sounding. —*n*. 3. Also, **musical comedy**, play with frequent musical numbers.

mū''sĭ·cǎle', *n*. party with music.

mŭsk, *n*. animal secretion used in perfumes. —**musk'y**, *adj*.

mŭs'kĕt, *n*. antique smooth-bored gun. —**mus''ket·eer'**, *n*.

mŭsk'mĕl''ŏn, *n*. type of sweet melon.

Mūs'lĭm, *n*. 1. follower of the teachings of Muhammad. —*adj*. 2. pertaining to Islam or the Muslims.

mŭs'lĭn, *n*. cotton cloth.

mŭss, *n*. 1. disorderly state. —*v.t*. 2. put in a muss. —**mus'sy**, *adj*.

mŭs'sĕl, *n*. type of bivalve.

mŭst, *v*. 1. have or has to. 2. compelled to do as stated.

mŭs·tăche', *n*. hair on the upper lip.

mŭs'tăng, *n*. wild horse of the Southwest.

mŭs'tàrd, *n*. condiment made from ground yellow seeds.

mŭs'têr, *v.t*. 1. summon; rally. 2. enlist or discharge from military service. —*n*. 3. gathering, as for inspection.

mŭs'tỹ, *adj*., **-ier, -iest**. moldy in smell or taste.

mū''tà·ble, *adj*. changeable. —**mu''ta·bil'i·ty**, *n*.

mū·tā'tion, *n*. 1. living things with characteristics not inherited; sport. 2. change. —**mu'tate**, *v.i*., *v.t*. —**mu'tant**, *adj*., *n*.

mūte, *adj*., *n*., *v.t*., **muted, muting**. *adj*. 1. unable to speak. 2. not speaking. —*n*. 3. mute person. —*v.t*. 4. soften the effect of. —**mute'ly**, *adv*. —**mute'ness**, *n*.

mū'tĭ·lāte'', *v.t*., **-lated, -lating**. injure severely and conspicuously. —**mu''ti·la'tion**, *n*.

mū'tĭ·nỹ, *n*., *pl*. **-nies**, *v.i*., **-nied, -nying**.

revolt against superiors. —**mu′′ti·
neer′**, *n.* —**mu′ti·nous**, *adj.*

mŭt′tẽr, *v.i.* **1.** speak in a low, indistinct
voice. —*n.* **2.** muttering voice.

mŭt′tŏn, *n.* sheep meat.

mū′tū·ȧl, *adj.* affecting one another.
—**mu′tu·al·ly**, *adj.*

mŭz′zle, *n., v.t.*, **-zled, -zling.** *n.* **1.** nose
and jaws of an animal. **2.** device to pre-
vent biting. **3.** end of a gun facing the target. —*v.t.* **4.** put a muzzle on. **5.** keep
from talking.

mȳ, *pron.* pertaining or belonging to me.

mȳ·ō′pi·ȧ, *n.* nearsightedness. —**my·op′
ic**, *adj.*

mȳr′ï·ȧd, *adj.* **1.** very many. —*n.* **2.** great
number.

mȳr′mi·dŏn, *n.* follower.

mȳrrh, *n.* fragrant resin.

mȳr′tle, *n.* flowering evergreen shrub.

mȳ·sẽlf′, *pron., pl.* **ourselves. 1.** (intensive and reflexive of *me*). **2.** my true self.

mȳs′tẽr·ȳ, *n., pl.* **-ies. 1.** something not
readily explained. **2.** secrecy. **3.** story
based on the solution of a criminal case.
—**mys·te′ri·ous**, *adj.*

mȳs′tic, *adj.* **1.** pertaining to secret rites
and teachings. **2.** Also, **mys′ti·cal**, of
spiritual significance. —*n.* **3.** person
having deep spiritual experiences.
—**mys′ti·cism**, *n.*

mȳs′ti·fȳ′′, *v.t.*, **-fied, -fying.** puzzle.
—**mys′′ti·fi·ca′tion**, *n.*

mȳs·tïque, *n.* air of mysticism surrounding a person, profession, etc.

mȳth, *n.* **1.** religious legend. **2.** false belief. —**myth′i·cal**, *adj.* —**my·thol′o·
gy**, *n.* —**myth′′o·log′i·cal**, *adj.*—**my·
thol′o·gist**, *n.*

N

N, n, *n.* fourteenth letter of the English alphabet.

năb, *v.t.*, **nabbed, nabbing.** *Informal.*
seize.

nā′dïr, *n.* lowest point.

năg, *v.t.*, **nagged, nagging.** *n. v.t.* **1.** pester. —*n.* **2.** poor horse.

năil, *n.* **1.** pointed, driven fastening. **2.**
horny growth on fingers or toes. —*v.t.* **3.**
fasten with nails.

na·ive (nah ēv′), *adj.* simple; unsophisti-
cated. —**na·ive·té′**, *n.*

nā′kĕd, *adj.* **1.** unclothed; unconcealed.
2. unassisted by lenses.

năm′bȳ-păm′bȳ, *adj.* insipid; character-
less.

nāme, *n., v.t.*, **named, naming.** *n.* **1.**
word or words by which a person or
thing is recognized. **2.** reputation. **3.** insulting epithet. —*v.t.* **4.** give a name to.
5. appoint. —**name′less**, *adj.*

nāme′lȳ, *adv.* that is to say.

nāme′sāke′′, *n.* person or thing having the
same name as another.

năp, *n., v.i.*, **napped, napping.** *n.* **1.** brief
sleep. **2.** fuzzy surface. —*v.i.* **3.** have a
brief sleep.

nāpe, *n.* back of the neck.

năph′thȧ, *n.* inflammable fluid.

năp′kĭn, *n.* cloth covering the lap at
meals.

när′cĭs·sĭsm, *n.* love of oneself. —**nar′
cis·sist**, *n.* —**nar′′cis·sis′tic**, *adj.*

när·cĭs′sŭs, *n.* flowering bulb plant.

när·cō′sĭs, *n.* unconsciousness from a
narcotic.

när·cŏt′ĭc, *n.* **1.** pain-relieving drug, often addictive. —*adj.* **2.** pertaining to
narcotics.

năr′rāte, *v.t.*, **-rated, -rating.** tell the
story of. —**nar′ra·tor**, *n.*

năr′ra·tïve, *adj.* **1.** story-telling. —*n.* **2.**
story; account.

năr′rŏw, *n.* **1.** not wide. **2.** not ample. **3.**
illiberal. —*v.t.* **4.** make narrow. —*v.i.* **5.**
become narrow.

năr′rŏw-mīnd′ĕd, *adj.* lacking a broad,
liberal outlook.

när′whăl, *n.* small, tusked whale.

năr′ȳ, *adj. Dialect.* not any.

nā′sȧl, *adj.* spoken through the nose.

nās′cĕnt, *adj.* coming into being.

nȧs·tûr′tiŭm, *n.* pungent-smelling flowering herb.

năs′tȳ, *adj.*, **-tier, -tiest. 1.** revolting as
from filth. **2.** unpleasant.

nā′tȧl, *adj.* pertaining to birth.

nā′tion, *n.* **1.** group with common ances-
tral and traditional associations. **2.** po-

litically independent state. —**na′tion·al**, adj. —**na′tion·wide″**, adj., adv.

nă′tion·al·ĭsm, n. assertion of the rights, cultural values, etc. of a nation. —**na′tion·al·ist**, n. adj. —**na″tion·al·is′tic**, adj.

na′tion·al·īze″, v.t., -ized, -izing. put under government ownership. —**na″tion·al·i·za′tion**, n.

na′tĭve, adj. **1.** born in or characteristic of a certain place. **2.** inborn. —n. **3.** native person.

na·tĭv′ĭ·tỹ, n., pl. -ties. **1.** birth. **2.** the **Nativity**, birth of Jesus.

năt′tỹ, adj., -tier, -tiest. neat and stylish.

năt′ū·răl, adj. **1.** pertaining to nature. **2.** inborn. **3.** unaffected; easy. **4.** to be expected. **5.** Music. not sharped or flatted.

năt′ū·răl·ist, n. student of nature.

năt′ū·răl·īze″, v.t., -ized, -izing. admit to citizenship.

năt′ū·răl·lỹ, adv. **1.** by nature. **2.** of course. **3.** in a natural way.

na′tŭre, n. **1.** everything not man-made. **2.** essential quality or composition.

naught, n. **1.** nothing. **2.** zero.

naugh′tỹ, adj., -tier, -tiest. ill-behaved. —**naugh′ti·lỹ**, adv.

nau′sē·á, n. sickness at the stomach. —**nau′se·ate″**, v.t. —**nau′se·ous**, adj.

nau′tĭ·căl, adj. pertaining to ships and navigation.

nau′tĭ·lŭs, n. mollusk with a spiral shell.

na′văl, adj. **1.** pertaining to navies. **2.** pertaining to ships.

na′vĕl, n. mark where the umbilical cord was attached.

năv′ĭ·gà·ble, adj. able to be sailed over.

năv′ĭ·gāte″, v., -gated, -gating. v.t. **1.** cross or pass through in a ship or aircraft. **2.** determine the position and course of. —v.i. **3.** direct a ship or aircraft. —**nav′i·ga″tor**, n.

nă′vỹ, n., pl. -ies. seagoing fighting force.

nāy, n. vote of no.

nēap tĭde, lowest of high tides.

nĕar, adj. **1.** short in distance. **2.** closely related. —adv. **3.** at a short distance. —prep. **4.** close to. —v.t. **5.** approach.

nĕar′bỹ′, adj., adv. near.

nĕar′lỹ, adv. almost.

nĕar′sĭght′ĕd, adj. seeing distant objects poorly.

nēat, adj. **1.** free of dirt and clutter. **2.** finely done.

nĕb′ū·là, n., pl. -lae, -las. cloudlike cluster of stars, etc. —**neb′u·lar**, adj.

nĕb′ū·loŭs, adj. vague.

nĕc′es·săr″ỹ, adj. **1.** not to be dispensed with. **2.** inevitable. —**nec″es·sar′i·ly**, adv.

ne·cĕs′sĭ·tāte″, v.t., -tated, -tating. require.

ne·cĕs′sĭ·toŭs, adj. needy.

ne·cĕs′sĭ·tỹ, n., pl. -ties. **1.** state of needing. **2.** something needed.

nĕck, n. **1.** part of the body which supports the head. **2.** narrow feature. —**neck′wear″**, n.

nĕck′êr·chief, n. broad covering for the neck.

nĕck′làce, n. ornamental chain, string of beads, etc. worn around the neck.

nĕck′tĭe″, n. decorative band of cloth tied around the neck.

ne·crŏl′ō·gỹ, n., pl. -gies. list of the dead.

nĕc′rō·măn″cỹ, n. **1.** divination by communication with the dead. **2.** sorcery. —**nec′ro·man″cer**, n.

nĕc′tár, n. **1.** drink of the classical gods. **2.** sweetish liquid of flowers.

nĕc′tár·īne″, n. small, smooth peach.

nēe, adj. born as: said of the maiden name of a married woman. Also, **née**.

nēed, v.t. **1.** be obligated to have or do. —n. **2.** state of needing. **3.** thing needed. **4.** poverty or trouble. —**need′ful**, adj. —**need·less**, adj.

nēe′dle, n., v.t., -dled, -dling. n. **1.** sharp object used for passing thread through cloth. **2.** any of various sharp or pointed objects. —v.t. **3.** Informal. goad; annoy. —**nee′dle·work″**, n.

nēe′dle·pŏint″, n. **1.** embroidery on canvas. **2.** lace made on a paper pattern.

nēeds, adv. of necessity.

nēed′ỹ, adj., -ier, -iest. in need. —**need′i·ness**, n.

nĕ′er·do·wĕll″, n. shiftless person.

ne·fâr′ĭ·oŭs, adj. wicked.

ne·gāte′, v.t., -gated, -gating. **1.** deny. **2.** render ineffective.

nĕg′à·tĭve, adj. **1.** saying or meaning no. **2.** opposite to positive. **3.** less than zero. —n. **4.** negative statement or attitude. **5.**

photographic film, etc. that reverses light and shade. —**neg′a·tive·ly,** *adv.*

něg·lěct′, *v.t.* **1.** deny proper care to. **2.** disregard. —*n.* **3.** state of being neglected. **4.** state of neglecting. —**neg′lect′ful,** *adj.*

neg·li·gee (něg″lĕ zhā′), *n.* loosely fitting woman's gown.

něg′li·gĕnt, *adj.* neglecting responsibilities. —**neg′li·gence,** *n.*

něg′li·gi·ble, *adj.* too unimportant to matter.

ne·gō′ti·a·ble, *adj.* **1.** transferable. **2.** capable of being dealt with.

ne·gō′ti·āte′, *v.,* -ated, -ating. *v.i.* **1.** bargain. —*v.t.* **2.** establish by bargaining. **3.** succeed in passing through or across. —**ne·go′ti·a″tor,** *n.*

Nē′grō, *n., pl.* -groes. dark-skinned person of African origin. —**Neg′roid,** *adj.*

neigh (nā), *n.* **1.** sound of a horse. —*v.i.* **2.** emit such a sound.

neigh′bŏr (na′ber), *n.* **1.** person living near by. **2.** fellow human. —*v.i.* **3.** be situated near by. —**neigh′bor·ing,** *adj.* —**neigh′bor·ly,** *adj.*

neigh′bŏr·hood″, *n.* **1.** area within a town. **2.** approximate area or range.

nēither, *adj., pron., conj.* not either.

něm′e·sĭs, *n., pl.* -ses. **1.** just fate or vengeance. **2.** bringer of this.

Nē′ŏ·lĭth′ic, *adj.* pertaining to the later Stone Age.

nē·ŏl′ó·gĭsm, *n.* newly invented word or expression.

nē′ŏn, *n.* gaseous element used in lighting tubes.

nē′ó·phyte″, *n.* beginner.

něph′ew, *n.* son of a brother, sister, brother-in-law, or sister-in-law.

něp′ó·tĭsm, *n.* favoritism toward relatives in giving employment.

nerve, *n.* **1.** fiber carrying signals through the body. **2.** courage. **3.** insolent boldness. **4. nerves,** nervousness.

nêrve′lĕss, *adj.* **1.** without strength. **2.** not nervous.

nêrve′-răck″ĭng, *adj.* emotionally upsetting. Also, **nerve′wrack″ing.**

nêrv′oŭs, *adj.* **1.** full of apprehension or restlessness. **2.** pertaining to nerves.

nêrv′ȳ, *adj.* -ier, -iest. *Informal.* impudent.

něst, *n.* **1.** place for bearing and sheltering young. —*v.i.* **2.** settle in a nest.

n′est-ce pas? (něs päh′), *French.* isn't it so?

něs′tle, *v.i.,* -tled, -tling. settle down.

nět, *n., adj., v.t.,* **netted, netting.** *n.* **1.** open cloth for capturing or supporting. **2.** amount after deductions. —*adj.* **3.** after deductions. —*v.t.* **4.** capture, as in a net.

něth′êr, *adj.* lower. —**neth′er·most″,** *adj.*

nět′tle, *n., v.t.,* -tled, -tling. *n.* **1.** prickly weed. —*v.t.* **2.** irritate; annoy.

nět′wôrk″, *n.* **1.** net-like arrangement. **2.** system of isolated entities working in coordination.

neū′răl, *adj.* pertaining to nerves.

neū·răl′gìà, *n.* pain along a nerve.

neū″răs·thē′nĭ·à, *n.* neurosis with lassitude, anxiety, etc. —**neu″ras·the′nic,** *adj., n.*

neū·rī′tĭs, *n.* inflammation of a nerve.

neū·rŏl′ó·gȳ, *n.* study of nerves. —**neu″ro·log′i·cal,** *adj.* —**neu·rol′o·gist,** *n.*

neū·rō′sĭs, *n., pl.* -ses. compulsive mental disorder. —**neu·rot′ic,** *adj., n.*

neū′têr, *adj.* **1.** without sex. **2.** without gender. —*v.t.* **3.** remove the sex organs of.

neū′trăl, *adj.* **1.** taking no sides. **2.** having no pronounced character. —*n.* **3.** neutral person or country. —**neu′tral·ism,** *n.* —**neu·tral′i·ty,** *n.* —**neu′tra·lize,** *v.t.*

neū′trŏn, *n.* uncharged atomic particle.

něv′êr, *adv.* at no time.

něv″êr·môre′, *adv.* never again.

něvêr-něvêr lănd, purely imaginary place.

něv″êr·the·lĕss′, *adv.* despite this.

něw, *adj.* **1.** never existing before. **2.** unfamiliar. **3.** fresh. **4.** additional. —**new′born″,** *adj.* —**new′com″er,** *n.*

něw′el, *n.* support for a winding stair.

něws, *n. sing.* **1.** information of public interest, esp. as published. **2.** recent information. —**news′boy″,** *n.* —**news′deal″er,** *n.* —**news′let″ter,** *n.* —**news′man″,** *n.* —**news′pa″per,** *n.* —**news′stand″,** *n.* —**news′wor″thy,** *adj.*

něws′căst″, *n.* broadcast of news.

něwt, *n.* amphibious salamander.

next, *adj.* **1.** directly alongside another. —*adv.* **2.** directly afterward.

next'-door', *adj.* in the next building.

nib, *n.* **1.** bird's beak. **2.** pen point.

nib'ble, *v.*, **-bled**, **-bling**, *n.* *v.t.*, *v.i.* **1.** eat with small bites. —*n.* **2.** small bite.

nice, *adj.*, **nicer**, **nicest.** **1.** agreeable. **2.** delicate; subtle.

ni'ce·ty, *n.*, *pl.* **-ties.** **1.** precision. **2.** fine detail or distinction.

niche, *n.* recessed area in a wall, as for a statue.

nick, *n.* **1.** small notch. —*v.t.* **2.** cut such a notch.

nick'el, *n.* **1.** white metallic element. **2.** five-cent piece.

nick'el·o'de·on, *n.* coin-operated automatic piano.

nick'name'', *n.*, *v.t.*, **-named**, **-naming.** *n.* **1.** informal name. —*v.t.* **2.** give a nickname to.

nic'o·tine'', *n.* poisonous extract from tobacco leaves.

niece, *n.* daughter of a brother, sister, brother-in-law, or sister-in-law.

nif'ty, *adj.*, **-tier**, **-tiest.** *Informal.* smart; handsome.

nig'gard·ly, *adj.* stingy.

nigh, *adj.*, *adv.* *Archaic.* near.

night, *n.* period when the sun is absent. —**night'clothes''**, *n.* *pl.* —**night'dress''**, *n.* —**night'fall''**, *n.* —**night'gown''**, *n.* —**night'ly**, *adv.*, *adj.* —**night'time''**, *n.* —**night'wear''**, *n.*

night'cap'', *n.* **1.** cap for sleeping in. **2.** *Informal.* drink just before bed.

night'mare'', *n.* bad dream. —**night'mar''ish**, *adj.*

night'shade'', *n.* plants related to potatoes, tomatoes, etc., some being poisonous.

ni'hil·ism, *n.* rejection of all social institutions. —**ni'hil·ist**, *n.* —**ni''hil·is'tic**, *adj.*

nim'ble, *adj.*, **-bler**, **-blest.** quick and deft.

nim'bus, *n.*, *pl.* **-bi**, **-buses.** halo.

nin'com·poop'', *n.* fool.

nine, *n.* eight plus one. —**ninth'**, *adj.*

nine·teen', *n.* ten plus nine. —**nine'teenth'**, *adj.*

nine'ty, *adj.*, *n.* nine times ten. —**nine'ti·eth**, *adj.*

nip, *v.t.*, **nipped**, **nipping**, *n.* *v.t.* **1.** bite or pinch lightly. **2.** freeze injuriously. —*n.* **3.** act or instance of nipping. **4.** sharp chill. **5.** tiny drink. —**nip'per**, *n.* —**nip'pers**, *n.*

nip'ple, *n.* **1.** small projection from the breast from which milk is sucked. **2.** anything resembling this.

nir·vâ'na, *n.* *Buddhism.* loss of self in ultimate bliss.

nit'-pick''ing, *n.* quibbling. —**nit'-pick''er**, *n.*

ni'tro·gen, *n.* gaseous element. —**ni·trog'e·nous**, *adj.*

ni''tro·glyc'er·in, *n.* explosive oil used in dynamite.

nit'ty-grit'ty, *n.* *Informal.* fundamentals.

nit'wit'', *n.* stupid person.

nix, *adv.* *Informal.* no.

no, *adv.*, *adj.*, *n.*, *pl.* **noes.** *adv.* **1.** it is not so. **2.** I will not. **3.** do not. **4.** not at all. —*adj.* **5.** not any. —*n.* **6.** vote of no.

no'ble, *adj.*, **-bler**, **-blest.** *adj.* **1.** of high and titled rank. **2.** having or revealing a fine character. **3.** of high quality. —*n.* **4.** person of noble rank. —**no'bly**, *adv.* —**no·bil'i·ty**, *n.* —**no'ble·man**, *n.*

no'bod·y, *pron.*, *n.*, *pl.* **-ies.** *pron.* **1.** no person. —*n.* **2.** unimportant person.

noc·tur'nal, *adj.* pertaining to night.

noc'turne, *n.* musical composition to be heard at night.

nod, *v.i.*, **nodded**, **nodding**, *n.* *v.i.* **1.** give a quick forward motion of the head, esp. meaning affirmation. —*n.* **2.** act or instance of nodding.

node, *n.* **1.** swelling. **2.** focal point. —**nod'al**, *adj.*

nog'gin, *n.* **1.** small cup. **2.** a person's head.

noise, *n.* loud sound. —**noise'less**, *adj.* —**nois'y**, *adj.* —**nois'i·ly**, *adv.*

noi'some, *adj.* smelly.

no'mad, *n.* wanderer. —**no·mad'ic**, *adj.*

nom de plume, author's assumed name.

no''men·cla''ture, *n.* system of names, terms, or symbols.

nom'in·al, *adj.* **1.** in name only. **2.** trifling in amount.

nom'i·nate'', *v.t.*, **-nated**, **-nating.** **1.** appoint. **2.** propose for election. —**nom''i·nee'**, *n.*

nŏm′ĭ·nā·tĭve, n. Grammar. case of a verb subject.

nŏn-, prefix meaning "not." nonalcoholic, nonassignable, nonattendance, nonbeliever, nonbreakable, nonburnable, noncombatant, noncombustible, noncommunicable, noncompetitive, noncompliance, nonconducting, nonconductor, nonconforming, nonconformist, nonconformity, nondeductible, nonessential, nonexclusive, nonexempt, nonexistence, nonexistent, nonfactual, nonfiction, nonflammable, nonhazardous, nonhereditary, nonhuman, noninclusive, noninterference, nonintervention, nonintoxicating, nonirritating, nonliterary, nonmilitary, nonobjective, nonobligatory, nonobservance, nonpartisan, nonpayment, nonperishable, nonpolitical, nonproductive, nonprofessional, nonracial, nonreciprocal, nonreligious, nonresident, nonresidential, nonresistant, nonreturnable, nonscientific, nonseasonal, nonsectarian, nonsmoker, nonspiritual, nonstandard, nonstop, nonstructural, nonsupport, nontaxable, nontoxic, nontransferable, nonuser, nonviolent, nonvoter, nonvoting.

nŏn′àge, n. minority; non-adulthood.

nŏn′′à·gè·nār′ĭ·àn, n. person in his or her nineties.

nŏnce, n. time being.

nŏn′′chà·lànt′, adj. casual in manner. —non′′cha·lance′, n.

nŏn′′com·mĭs′sioned ŏfficêr, military or naval officer with no commission, e.g. a sergeant or petty officer.

nŏn′′com·mĭt′tàl, adj. not committing oneself.

nŏn′cŏm′pòs mĕn′tĭs, of unsound mind.

nŏn′′dè·scrĭpt′, adj. not to be described precisely.

nóne, pron. 1. not one or any. —n. 2. not any amount. —adv. 3. by no means.

nŏn·ĕn′tĭ·tў, n., pl. -ties. very unimportant person or thing.

nóne′′the·lĕss′, adv. nevertheless.

nŏn′plŭs′, v.t., -plused, -plusing. baffle into inaction.

nŏn·prŏf′ĭt, adj. not established for profit.

nŏn′sĕnse, n. meaningless talk or action. —non·sen′si·cal, adj.

nŏn·sĕ′quĭ·tûr, illogical continuation of something previously said.

nōō′dle, n. strip of dough.

nŏŏk, n. semi-enclosed place.

nōōn, n. twelve o'clock in the daytime.

nō one, nobody.

nōōse, n. loop made with a knot.

nôr, conj. and not; and yet not.

nôrm, n. something generally expected.

nôr′mál, adj. 1. conforming to a norm. 2. average. —nor′mal′i·ty, n. —nor′mal·ize′′, v.t.

nôrm′à·tĭve, adj. establishing a norm.

nôrth, n. 1. direction of the north pole. 2. region lying northward. —adv. 3. toward or in the north. —north′ern, adj. —north′ern·er, n. —north′er·ly, adj. —north′ward, adj., adv. —north′wards, adv.

nôrth′′ēast′, n. 1. direction halfway between north and east. 2. region lying northeastward. —adj., adv. 3. toward or in the northeast. —north′′east′ern, adj. —north′′east·ern·er, n.

nôrth′′wĕst′, n. 1. direction halfway between north and west. 2. region lying northwestward. —adj., adv. 3. toward or in the northwest. —north′′west′ern, adj. —north′′west′ern·er, n.

nōse, n., v., nosed, nosing. n. 1. part of the head with nostrils. 2. noselike features. —v.t. 3. nuzzle. —v.i. 4. sniff. 5. advance. —nose′bleed′′, n.

nōse dīve, n. headlong plunge. —nose′dive′′, v.i.

nōse′gāy′′, n. small bouquet.

nŏs·tăl′gìà, n. sentiment over the bygone or remote. —nos·tal′gic, adj.

nŏs′trĭl, n. one of the openings in the nose for breathing.

nŏs′trŭm, proprietary medicine.

nōs′ў, adj., -ier, -iest. Informal. inquisitive. Also, nos′ey.

nŏt, adv. in no way.

nō′tà·ble, adj. remarkable.

nō′tà·rў, n., pl. -ries. official who certifies documents. Also, notary public. —no′ta·rize′′, v.t.

nō·tā′tion, *n.* **1.** symbol or system of symbols. **2.** brief note.

nŏtch, *n.* **1.** shallow knife cut. —*v.t.* **2.** make such cuts in.

nōte, *n., v.t.,* **noted, noting.** *n.* **1.** short message. **2.** reminder of something. **3.** sound. **4.** notice. **5.** distinction. **6.** feeling; air. —*v.t.* **7.** observe. **8.** make a note of. —**note′book′′,** *n.* —**note′wor′′thy,** *adj.*

nŏt′ĕd, *adj.* well-known.

nŏth′ĭng, *n.* **1.** not any thing. **2.** something non-existent. **3.** something insignificant. —*adv.* **4.** in no way. —**noth′ing·ness,** *n.*

nō′tĭce, *v.t.,* -ticed, -ticing. *n. v.t.* **1.** be aware of. —*n.* **2.** awareness. **3.** announcement or warning. —**no′tice·a·ble,** *adj.*

nō′tĭ·fy′′, *v.t.,* -fied, -fying. give notice to.

nō′tĭon, *n.* **1.** idea. **2.** vague opinion. **3.** whim. **4. notions,** minor but useful merchandise. —**no′tion·al,** *adj.*

nō·tō′rĭ·oŭs, *adj.* unfavorably well-known. —**no′′to·ri·e·ty,** *n.*

nŏt′′wĭth·stănd′ĭng, *adv.* **1.** nevertheless. —*prep.* **2.** in spite of. —*conj.* **3.** although.

noū′găt, *n.* soft candy with nuts.

noŭn, *n.* name of a person, place, or thing.

noûr′ĭsh, *v.t.* feed. —**nour′ish·ment,** *n.*

nou′veau riche (nū′ vō rēsh), *n.* *French.* person recently acquiring large sums of money.

nŏv′ĕl, *adj.* **1.** new; unprecedented. —*n.* **2.** long written story. —**nov′el·ty,** *n.* —**nov′′el·ette′,** *n.* —**nov′el·ist,** *n.*

Nō·vĕm′bĕr, *n.* eleventh month.

nŏv′īce, *n.* **1.** monk or nun in a religious house who has not yet taken the vow. **2.** beginner. —**no·vi′ti·ate,** *n.*

nŏw, *adj.* **1.** at present. **2.** at some past or future moment. **3.** as matters are. —*conj.* **4.** inasmuch. —*n.* **5.** present moment.

nŏw′′a·dāys′′, *adv.* at present.

nō′whēre′, *adv.* not in any place.

nŏx′ioŭs, *adj.* harmful.

nŏz′zle, *n.* pouring end of a pipe, etc.

nth, *adj.* concluding an unspecified number or amount.

nū′ánce, *n.* slight variation in meaning, etc.

nū′bĭle, *adj.* mature enough to take a spouse.

nū′clē·ár, *adj.* **1.** forming a nucleus. **2.** pertaining to atomic nuclei.

nū′clē·ŭs, *n., pl.* -clei, -cleuses. **1.** core. **2.** center of growth or development. **3.** center of an atom.

nūde, *adj.* **1.** naked. —*n.* **2.** state of nakedness. —**nu′di·ty,** *n.*

nŭdge, *v.t.,* nudged, nudging. *n. v.t.* **1.** jab with the elbow. **2.** hint to sharply. —*n.* **3.** act or instance of nudging.

nūd′ĭsm, *n.* practice of nudity. —**nud′ist,** *n., adj.*

nū′gá·tô′′rў, *adj.* **1.** worthless. **2.** invalid.

nŭg′gĕt, *n.* lump of natural gold.

nŭi′sánce, *n.* source of annoyance.

nŭll, *adj.* null and void, invalid; without force.

nŭl′lĭ·fy′′, *v.t.,* -fied, -fying. invalidate.

nŭmb, *adj.* **1.** without feeling. —*v.t.* **2.** make numb.

nŭm′bĕr, *n.* **1.** expression of quantity or order. **2.** quantity or order. **3.** item on a program of entertainment. —*v.t.* **4.** establish the number of. **5.** include in a group. —**num′ber·less,** *adj.*

nŭmb′skŭll′′, *n.* *Informal.* stupid person. Also, **num′skull′′.**

nū′mĕr·ál, *n.* symbol for a number.

nū·mĕr·ā′′tŏr, *n.* expression of the number of parts in a fraction.

nū·mĕr′ĭ·cál, *adj.* pertaining to or expressed in numbers.

nū′′mĕr·ŏl′ó′gў, *n.* study of occult meanings in numbers.

nū′mĕr·oŭs, *adj.* in large numbers.

nū′′mĭs·măt′ĭcs, *n.* study of money and medals. —**nu·mis′ma·tist,** *n.*

nŭn, *n.* female member of a religious order. —**nun′ner·y,** *n.*

nŭp′tiăl, *adj.* **1.** pertaining to marriage. —*n.* **2.** nuptials, wedding.

nûrse, *n., v.t.,* nursed, nursing. *n.* **1.** attendant of the sick. **2.** attendant of children. —*v.t.* **3.** suckle. **4.** tend in illness. **5.** conserve or foster.

nûrse′māid′′, *n.* children's nurse.

nûrs′ĕr·ў, *n., pl.* -ies. **1.** day room for children. **2.** place for the care of children. **3.** place for raising plants. —**nurs′er·y·man**, n.

nûr′tûre, v.t., **-tured, -turing.** n. v.t. **1.** nourish. **2.** raise, as a child. —n. **3.** food. **4.** upbringing.

nŭt, n. **1.** dry seed in a woody husk. **2.** threaded block used with a bolt. **3.** Informal. insane person. —adj. **4. nuts,** Informal. crazy. —interj. **5. nuts,** bah! —**nut′crack″er**, n. —**nut′meat″**, n. —**nut′shell″**, n. —**nut′ty**, adj.

nŭt′mĕg″, n. East Indian spice.

nū′tri·ent, adj. **1.** nourishing. —n. **2.** Also, **nu′tri·ment**, nourishment.

nū·trī′tion, n. **1.** assimilation of food. **2.** food. —**nu·tri′tion·al**, adj. —**nu′tri·tive**, adv. —**nu·tri′tious**, adj.

nŭz′zle, v., **-zled, -zling.** v.t., v.i. rub with the nose.

nȳ′lŏn, n. synthetic material.

nymph, n. classical nature goddess.

nȳm″phō·mā′nĭ·à, n. uncontrollable sexual desire in women. —**nym″pho·ma′ni·ac″**, n., adj.

O

Ō, o, n. fifteenth letter of the English alphabet.

ōaf, n. clumsy person. —**oaf′ish**, adj.

ōak, n. acorn-bearing hardwood tree. —**oak′en**, adj.

ōar, n. bladed lever for rowing. —**oars′man**, n. —**oar′lock″**, n.

ō·ā′sĭs, n., pl. **-ses. 1.** place in the desert with water. **2.** refuge.

ōat, n. cereal grass. —**oat′meal″**, n.

ōath, n., pl. **oaths. 1.** vow in the name of a god. **2.** blasphemous remark.

ŏb·dū′râte, adj. stubborn. —**ob′du·ra·cy**, n.

ō·bēi′sánce, n. bow.

ŏb′e·lĭsk, n. tapered monument.

ō·bēse′, adj. very fat. —**o·bes′i·ty**, n.

ō·bey′, v.i. **1.** do as told. —v.t. **2.** perform as told. **3.** perform the orders of. —**o·be′di·ent**, adj. —**o·be′di·ence**, n.

ŏb′fŭs·cāte″, v.t., **-cated, -cating.** obscure or confuse.

ō·bĭt′ū·ār″ỹ, n., pl. **-ies.** death notice.

ŏb′jĕct, n. **1.** something tangible. **2.** something acted toward or aimed for. **3.** matter for consideration. —v.i. (ob jekt′) **4.** protest. —**ob·jec′tion**, n. —**ob·jec′tion·a·ble**, adj. —**ob·jec′tion·a·bly**, adv. —**ob·jec′tor**, n.

ŏb·jĕc′tĭve, adj. **1.** in the world outside the mind. **2.** concerned with reality, rather than thought or emotion. —**ob″jec·tiv′i·ty**, n.

ŏb′jûr·gāte″, v.t., **-gated, -gating.** rebuke. —**ob·jur′ga·to″ry**, adj.

ŏb′li·gāte″, v.t., **-gated, -gating.** bind with a duty. —**ob·lig′a·to″ry**, adj.

ō·blīge′, v.t., **-bliged, -bliging. 1.** force. **2.** put in one's debt.

ō·blīg′ing, adj. ready to do favors. —**o·blig′ing·ly**, adv.

ob·līque′, adj. **1.** slanting. **2.** indirect. —**ob·liq′ui·ty**, n. **ob·lique′ness**, n.

ŏb·lĭt′ēr·āte″, v.t., **-ated, -ating.** efface.

ŏb·lĭv′ĭ·ŏn, n. **1.** forgetfulness. **2.** unremembered past. —**ob·liv′i·ous**, adj.

ŏb′lŏng, adj. **1.** longer than broad. —n. **2.** oblong figure, esp. a rectangle.

ŏb′lō·quỹ, n., pl. **-quies. 1.** censure. **2.** infamy.

ŏb·nŏx′ioŭs, adj. offensive.

ō′bōe, n. low-pitched musical reed instrument. —**o′bo·ist**, n.

ŏb·scēne′, adj. offensive to decency. —**ob·scen′i·ty**, n.

ŏb·scūre′, adj., v.t., **-scured, -scuring.** adj. **1.** indefinite. **2.** dark. **3.** little-known. —v.t. **4.** make obscure. —**ob·scur′i·ty**, n. —**ob″scu·ra′tion**, n.

ŏb′sé·quĭes, n. pl. funeral ceremonies.

ŏb·sē′quĭ·oŭs, adj. fawningly servile.

ŏb·sêrv′á·tô″rỹ, n., pl. **-ries.** place for observing heavenly bodies.

ŏb·sêrve′, v.t., **-served, -serving. 1.** study with the eye. **2.** notice. **3.** remark. **4.** obey or respect. —**ob·serv′ance**, n. —**ob·serv′ant**, adj. —**ob″ser·va′tion**, n. —**ob·serv′er**, n.

ŏb·sĕss′, v.t. preoccupy constantly. —**ob·ses′sive**, adj. —**ob″ses′sion**, n.

ŏb″sō·lĕs′cent, adj. going out of date. —**ob″so·les′cence**, n. —**ob·so·lesce′**, v.i.

ŏb″sō·lēte′, adj. out of date.

ŏb·stá·cle, *n.* something hindering advance.

ŏb·stĕt′rĭcs, *n.* branch of medicine for pregnancy and childbirth. —**ob·stet′ric, ob·stet′ri·cal,** *adj.* —**ob′′ste·tri′cian,** *n.*

ŏb·stĭ·nåte, *adj.* stubborn. —**ob′sti·na·cy,** *n.*

ŏb·strĕp′ĕr·oŭs, *adj.* rowdy.

ŏb·strŭct′, *v.t.* 1. hinder; thwart. 2. block. —**ob·struc′tion,** *n.* —**ob·struc′tion·ism,** *n.* —**ob·struc′tion·ist,** *n., adj.* —**ob·struc′tive,** *adj.*

ŏb·tāin′, *v.t.* 1. get. —*v.i.* 2. be in effect. —**ob·tain′ment,** *n.*

ŏb·trūde′, *v.,* **-truded, -truding.** *v.t.* 1. force on others. —*v.i.* 2. obtrude oneself. —**ob·tru′sion,** *n.* —**ob·tru′sive,** *adj.*

ŏb·tūse′, *adj.* 1. blunt, as an angle. 2. slow to understand.

ŏb·vêrse′, *adj.* 1. toward an observer. 2. being a counterpart. —*n.* 3. counterpart.

ŏb′vĭ·āte′′, *v.t.* **-ated, -ating.** avoid by alternatives.

ŏb′vĭ·oŭs, *adj.* perceived or understood without effort.

óc·cā′sion, *n.* 1. specific time or event. 2. opportunity. 3. reason; pretext. —*v.t.* 4. bring about.

óc·cā′sion·ǎl, *adj.* occurring now and then.

Ŏc′cĭ·dĕnt, *n.* Europe and the Americas. —**Oc′′ci·den′tal,** *adj.*

óc·cŭlt′, *adj.* 1. hidden from ordinary persons. 2. mystical. —**oc·cult′ism,** *n.*

ŏc′′cū·pā′tion, *n.* 1. type of work. 2. act or instance of occupying.

ŏc′cū·pў′′, *v.t.,* **-pied, -pying.** 1. be in. 2. be engaged in or concerned with. 3. take possession of, as by capture. —**oc′cu·pan·cy,** *n.* —**oc′cu·pant,** *n.*

óc·cûr′, *v.i.,* **-curred, -curring.** 1. happen. 2. come to mind. —**oc·cur′rence,** *n.*

ō′cĕan, *n.* vast body of salt water. —**o·ce·an′ic,** *adj.*

ō′′cĕan·ŏg′rå·phў, *n.* study of the ocean.

ŏ′cĕ·lŏt′′, *n.* American wildcat.

ō′chêr, *n.* yellow or reddish-brown clay used as pigment. Also, **o′chre.**

o′clŏck′, *adv.* by the clock.

ŏc′tá·gŏn, *n.* eight-sided plane figure. —**oc·tag′o·nal,** *adj.*

ŏc′′tá·hē′drŏn, *n.* eight-sided solid.

ŏc′tåve, *n.* 1. *Music.* group including eight full tones. 2. *Poetry.* unit of eight lines.

ŏc·tĕt′, *n.* group of eight musicians. Also, **oc·tette′.**

Ŏc·tō′bêr, *n.* tenth month.

ŏc′′tó·gè·nâr′ĭ·ǎn, *n.* person in his or her eighties.

ŏc′tó·pŭs, *n., pl.* **-puses, -pi.** soft mollusk with eight arms.

ŏc′ū·lår, *adj.* pertaining to the eyes.

ŏc′ū·lĭst, *n.* ophthalmologist.

ŏdd, *adj.* 1. not evenly divisible by two. 2. peculiar. 3. occasional. 4. remaining. —*n.* 5. **odds,** factors for or against. —**odd′i·ty,** *n.*

ŏdds ånd ĕnds, miscellaneous things.

ōde, *n.* poem of praise.

ō′dĭ·oŭs, *adj.* hateful.

ō′dĭ·ŭm, *n.* hatred or disgrace.

ō′dôr, *n.* smell. —**o′dor·ous,** *adj.* —**o′dor·less,** *adj.*

ō′′dôr·ĭf′ĕr·oŭs, *adj.* giving off an odor.

ŏf, *prep.* 1. coming from or produced by. 2. belonging to. 3. owning. 4. regarding. 5. specified as.

ŏff, *prep.* 1. away or up from. 2. with sustenance from. —*adv.* 3. away or up. 4. so as not to work or be in effect. —*adj.* 5. not working or in effect. 6. on one's way. 7. not right.

ŏf′fǎl, *n.* garbage.

ŏff′-cŏl′ôr, *adj.* risqué.

ŏf·fĕnd′, *v.i.* 1. commit an offense. —*v.t.* 2. annoy or wound. 3. displease.

ŏf·fĕnse′, *adj.* 1. unlawful act. 2. resentment or hurt. 3. cause of this. 4. attack. Also, **of·fence′.**

ŏf·fĕn′sĭve, *adj.* 1. tending to offend. 2. attacking. —*n.* 3. attacker's status.

ŏf′fêr, *v.t.* 1. present, as for acceptance or consideration. 2. shown signs of. —*v.i.* 3. present itself. —*n.* 4. act or instance of offering. —**of′fer·ing,** *n.*

ŏff′hånd′, *adv.* 1. unprepared. —*adj.* 2. Also, **off′hand′ed,** casual.

ŏf′fĭce, *n.* 1. position of authority. 2. Often **offices,** work done for another. 3. place for commercial or government work.

ȯf′fĭ·cêr, *n*. **1.** holder of a position of authority. **2.** policeman.

ȯf·fĭ′cĭǎl, *adj*. **1.** pertaining to or coming from supreme authority. —*n*. **2.** person in public office. —**ȯf·fĭ′cĭǎl·dom**, *n*.

ȯf·fĭ′cĭ·āte″, *v.i*., **-ated, -ating.** perform official or ceremonial duties.

ȯf·fĭ′cĭoŭs, *adj*. giving unwanted help or orders.

ȯf′fĭng, *n*. distance.

ȯff′-lĭm′ĭts, *adj. Military*. not to be entered.

ȯff′-līne′, *n*. not connected to a network or system.

ȯff′-rōad′, *adj*. designed to be used in rough terrain, as in *off-road vehicle*.

ȯff′sĕt″, *v.t*., **-set, -setting.** compensate for.

ȯff′shŏōt″, *n*. thing derived from a major source.

ȯff′shōre′, *adj., adv*. away from the shore.

ȯff′spring″, *n., pl*. **-spring, -springs.** young of a human or animal.

ȯff′-whīte′, *n*. white tinted with grey or yellow.

ȯf′tĕn, *adv*. many times.

ō′grĕ, *n*. man-eating giant. Also, *fem*., o′gress. —**o′gre·ish**, *adj*.

ŏh, *interj*. exclamation of surprise, etc.

ŏhm, *n. Electricity*. unit of resistance.

ō·hō′, *interj*. (exclamation of surprise or triumph)

ȯil, *n*. **1.** any of various combustible liquids. **2.** paint with an oil vehicle. —*v.t.* **3.** lubricate with oil. —**ȯil′y**, *adj*. —**ȯil′i·ness**, *n*.

ȯil′clŏth″, *n*. cloth treated to be waterproof.

ȯint′mĕnt, *n*. fatty salve.

O.K. or **ōkăy**, *interj., adj., adv., v.t.,* **O.K.′d, O.K.′ing.** *interj., adj., adv.* **1.** all right. —*v.t.* **2.** approve.

ō′krà, *n*. plant with edible pods.

ōld, *adj., older* or *elder, oldest* or *eldest*. **1.** long in existence. **2.** experienced. **3.** longer in existence than another. **4.** former.

ōld′-făsh′ĭoned, *adj*. obsolete. **1.** favoring older manners, etc. —*n*. **3.** whiskey cocktail.

ōld māid, mature, virginal woman.

ōld schōōl, *n*. conservatives collectively. —**old′-school′**, *adj*.

ōld′-tīm′êr, *n. Informal*. **1.** old man. **2.** long-time incumbent.

Ōld Wŏrld, Europe, Asia, and Africa. —**Old′-World′, old′-world′**, *adj*.

ō″lē·ō·mâr′gà·rĭne, *n*. margarine. Also, **o″le·o·mar′ga·rin**.

ŏl·făc′tŏ·rў, *adj*. pertaining to smell.

ŏl′ĭ·gärch″ў, *n., pl*. **-ies.** government by a few. —**ol″i·garch′ic**, *adj*. —**oli·garch**, *n*.

ŏl′īve, *n*. fruit of a Mediterranean tree.

ŏm·bŭds′mán, *n., pl*. **-men.** investigator of citizen's complaints.

ŏm′elĕt, *n*. fried pancake of beaten eggs. Also, **om′elette**.

ō′mĕn, *n*. sign of the future.

ŏm′ĭ·noŭs, *adj*. threatening.

ō·mĭt′, *v.t*., **-mitted, -mitting. 1.** leave out. **2.** forget; neglect. —**o·mis′sion**, *n*.

ŏm′nĭ·bŭs, *n*. **1.** bus. **2.** complete anthology.

ŏm·nĭp′ō·tĕnt, *adj*. all-powerful. —**om·nip′o·tence**, *n*.

ŏm″nĭ·prĕs′ĕnt, *adj*. present everywhere at once. —**om″ni·pres′ence**, *n*.

ŏm·nĭs′cĭĕnt, *adj*. knowing everything. —**om·nis′cience**, *n*.

ŏm·nĭv′ȯ·roŭs, *adj*. consuming anything.

ŏn, *prep*. **1.** supported by. **2.** down against. **3.** regarding. **4.** with the help or sustenance of. **5.** at the time of. **6.** engaged in. **7.** being part of. —*adv*. **8.** onto oneself or something else. **9.** further; forward. **10.** into operation. —*adj*. **11.** in operation or effect.

once (wuns), *adv*. **1.** one time. **2.** formerly. **3.** at any time. —*conj*. **4.** when.

ŏn′cŏm″ĭng, *adj*. approaching.

one (wun), *n*. **1.** lowest whole cardinal number. **2.** person. —*adj*. **3.** being one in number. **4.** identical. **5.** united. —*pron*. **6.** one person or thing.

ŏn′êr·oŭs, *adj*. burdensome.

one·sĕlf′, *pron*. **1.** person's own self. **2.** person's true self. Also, **one's self.**

one′-sīd′ĕd, *adj*. **1.** involving only one side. **2.** with all advantages on one side. **3.** prejudiced.

ŏn′gō″ĭng, *adj*. in progress.

ŏn′ĭŏn, *n*. edible bulb of the lily family.

ŏn'-līne', *n.* connected to a network or system.

ŏn'lŏŏk''ẽr, *n.* spectator.

ŏn'lӯ, *adj.* **1.** single; sole. —*adv.* **2.** solely. **3.** at last, however. **4.** as lately as.

on·o·mat·o·poe·ia (ahn''ə mat''ə pē'ə), *n.* coining of a word imitating a sound.

ŏn'sĕt'', *n.* attack.

ŏn'slăught'', *n.* vigorous attack.

ŏn'to, *prep.* into a position on.

ō'nŭs, *n.* **1.** burden. **2.** blame.

ŏn'wạrd, *adv.* **1.** Also, **on'wards**, **forward.** —*adj.* **2.** forward.

ŏn'ӯx, *n.* striped agate.

ōō'dles, *n. pl. Informal.* vast amounts.

ōōze, *v.* oozed, oozing, *n. v.i.* **1.** flow slowly. —*v.t.* **2.** emit slowly. —*n.* **3.** slime. —**ooz'y**, *adj.*

ō'pạl, *n.* gem of multicolored silica. —**o''pal·es'cent**, *adj.*

ō·pâque', *adj.* **1.** passing no light. **2.** obscure. —**o·paque'ness, o·pac'i·ty**, *n.*

ō'pĕn, *adj.* **1.** able to be entered, seen through, etc. **2.** with the inside revealed. **3.** available or accessible. **4.** candid. —*v.t.* **5.** make open. —*v.i.* **6.** become open. —*v.t., v.i.* **7.** start. —*n.* **8.** open or unconcealed place or state.

ō'pĕn-âir', *adj.* outdoor.

ō'pĕn-ĕnd'ĕd, *adj.* unrestricted.

ō'pĕn-hănd'ĕd, *adj.* generous.

ō'pĕn·ing, *n.* **1.** perforation. **2.** beginning. **3.** opportunity.

ŏp'ẽr·ȧ, *n.* musical drama. —**op''ẽr·at'ic**, *adj.*

ŏp'ẽr·ȧ·ble, *adj.* **1.** treatable by surgery. **2.** able to be operated.

ŏp'ẽr·āte', *v.*, -ated, -ating. *v.t.* **1.** cause to function. **2.** control; manage. —*v.i.* **3.** function; act. **4.** perform surgery. —**op''er·a'tion**, *n.* —**op''er·a'tion·al**, *adj.* —**op'er·a''tor**, *n.*

ŏp'ẽr·ȧ·tĭve, *adj.* **1.** pertaining to operations. **2.** able to operate. —*n.* **3.** detective.

ŏp'ẽr·ä''tŏr, *n.* **1.** person who operates something, as telephone equipment. **2.** *Informal.* person living by his wits.

ŏp''ẽr·ĕt'tȧ, *n.* light opera.

ŏphth''ăl·mŏl'ȯ·gӯ, *n.* branch of medicine concerning the eye. —**ophth''al·mo·log'i·cal**, *adj.* —**ophth''al·mol'o·gist**, *n.*

ō'pĭ·ȧte, *n.* opium-based drug.

ȯ·pĭn'ȯn, *n.* **1.** personal belief. **2.** personal evaluation.

ȯ·pĭn'iȯn·ȧt''ĕd, *adj.* stubborn in one's opinions.

ō'pĭ·ŭm, *n.* drug derived from poppies.

ȯ·pŏs'sŭm, *n.* small tree-dwelling marsupial.

ȯp·pō'nĕnt, *n.* adversary.

ŏp''pȯr·tūne', *adj.* occurring when useful.

ŏp''pȯr·tūn'ĭsm, *n.* unprincipled advantage-taking.

ŏp''pȯr·tūn'ĭ·tӯ, *n., pl.* -ties. favorable occasion.

ȯp·pōse', *v.t.*, -posed, -posing. **1.** resist; fight. **2.** be in contrast with. —**op''po·si'tion**, *n.*

ŏp'pȯ·sĭte, *adj.* **1.** in the other direction from somewhere between. **2.** totally different in nature. —*n.* **3.** something opposite.

ȯp·prĕss', *v.t.* **1.** bully or exploit. **2.** worry or make uncomfortable. —**op·pres'sion**, *n.* —**op·pres'sor**, *n.* —**op·pres'sive**, *adj.*

ȯp·prō'brĭ·ŭm, *n.* scorn; shame. —**op·pro'bri·ous**, *adj.*

ŏpt, *v.i.* make a choice.

ŏp'tĭc, *adj.* pertaining to sight.

ŏp'tĭ·cȧl, *adj.* **1.** visual. **2.** pertaining to optics.

ŏp·tĭ'ciȧn, *n.* dealer in aids to eyesight.

ŏp'tĭcs, *n.* study of light and vision.

ŏp'tĭ·mĭsm, *n.* readiness to see or predict the best. —**op'ti·mist**, *n.* —**op''ti·mis'tic**, *adj.*

ŏp'tĭ·mŭm, *adj.* **1.** best, esp. in amount, etc. —*n.* **2.** optimum amount, etc.

ŏp'tiȯn, *n.* **1.** choice. **2.** right to buy or not to buy something. —**op'tion·al**, *adj.*

ŏp·tŏm'ē·trӯ, *n.* profession of testing and prescribing for eye conditions. —**op·tom'e·trist**, *n.*

ŏp'ū·lĕnt, *adj.* **1.** rich. **2.** lavish. —**op'u·lence**, *n.*

ō'pŭs, *n., pl.* -pera, -puses. work of an artist, musician, etc., esp. when numbered.

ôr, *conj.* **1.** (indicating alternatives). **2.** (indicating synonyms).

ôr'ȧ·cle, *n.* **1.** medium for consulting a

god. **2.** great authority. **—o·rac′u·lar,** *adj.*

ô·ral, *adj.* **1.** pertaining to the mouth. **2.** spoken.

ôr·ange, *n.* **1.** mixture of red and yellow. **2.** fruit of this color. **—or′ange·ade′,** *n.*

o·rång′u·tån′, *n.* manlike ape of Indonesia. Also, **o·rang′u·tang′.**

o·rā′tion, *n.* formal speech. **—o·rate′,** *v.i.* **—o′ra·tor,** *n.*

ôr′á·tô′rĭ·ō′′, *n.*, *pl.* **-os.** play sung but not acted.

ôr′á·tô′rÿ, *n.*, *pl.* **-ies.** **1.** public speaking. **2.** small chapel. **—or′′a·tor′i·cal,** *adj.*

ôrb, *n.* **1.** heavenly body. **2.** spherical object.

ôr′bĭt, *n.* **1.** path of a heavenly body. **—v.i. 2.** be in orbit. **—or′bĭt·al,** *adj.*

ôr′chård, *n.* grove of fruit trees.

ôr′chĕs·trå, *n.* **1.** large, varied musical group. **2.** main floor in an auditorium. **—or·ches′tral,** *adj.*

ôr′chĕs·trāte′′, *v.t.*, **-trated, -trating.** arrange for orchestra.

ôr′chĭd, *n.* tropical flowering plant.

ôr·dāin′, *v.t.* **1.** decree; establish. **2.** grant the office of clergyman to. **—or·dain′ment, or′′di·na′tion,** *n.*

ôr·dēal′, *n.* severe trial.

ôr′dêr, *n.* **1.** proper or meaningful condition. **2.** command. **3.** request to purchase. **4.** religious group. **—v.t. 5.** make an order for. **6.** put in order.

ôr′dêr·lÿ, *adj.*, *n.*, *pl.* **-lies.** *adj.* **1.** in order. **2.** quiet in behavior. **—n. 3.** attendant.

ôr′dĭ·nål, *adj.* **1.** pertaining to a meaningful series. **—n. 2.** ordinal number.

ôr′dĭ·nånce, *n.* law.

ôr′dĭ·när′′ÿ, *adj.* **1.** usual, customary. **—n. 2.** customary experience.

ôrd′nånce, *n.* military weapons.

ôre, *n.* metal-bearing mineral.

ô·rĕg′á·nō, *n.* fragrant-leafed plant.

ôr′gån, *n.* **1.** body part performing a specific function. **2.** keyboard, wind, or electronic instrument. **3.** institutional periodical. **—or′gan·ist,** *n.*

ôr·găn′ĭc, *adj.* **1.** pertaining to or suggesting organisms. **2.** pertaining to bodily organs. **3.** containing carbon.

ôr′gån·ĭsm, *n.* living thing.

ôr′gán·īze′′, *v.*, **-ized, -izing.** *v.t.*, *v.i.* **1.** join in a coordinated group. **—v.t. 2.** coordinate the functioning of. **3.** arrange for. **4.** cause to join a group. **—or′′gan·i·za′tion,** *n.* **—or′′gan·i·za′tion·al,** *adj.*

ôr′găsm, *n.* climax of a sex act.

or·gy (or′jē), *n.*, *pl.* **-gies.** wild revelry.

ô′rĭ·ĕnt, *v.i.* **1.** establish one's location or course. **—v.t. 2.** establish the location or course of. **3.** initiate in fundamentals. **4.** face in a certain direction. **—n. 5. the Orient,** Asia. **—o′′ri·en·ta′tion,** *n.* **—O′′ri·en′tal,** *adj.*, *n.*

ôr′ĭ·fĭce, *n.* opening.

ôr′ĭ·gĭn, *n.* **1.** commencement. **2.** source.

o·rĭg′ĭ·nål, *adj.* **1.** earliest. **2.** copied to make others. **3.** never before seen. **4.** creative. **—n. 5.** authentic. **—o·rig′′i·nal′i·ty,** *n.* **—o·rig′i·nate′′,** *v.t.*, *v.i.* **—o·rig′i·na′′tor,** *n.*

ô′rĭ·ōle′′, *n.* black and orange bird.

or·na·ment, *n.* (or′nə ment) **1.** decoration. **—v.t.** (or′nə ment′′) **2.** decorate. **—or′′na·men′tal,** *adj.* **—or′′na·men·ta′tion,** *n.*

ôr·nāte′, *adj.* greatly ornamented.

ôr′nêr·ÿ, *adj.* *Dialect.* mean or stubborn. **—or′ner·i·ness,** *n.*

ôr′′ni·thŏl′o·gÿ, *n.* study of birds. **—or′′ni·thol′o·gist,** *n.* **—or′′ni·tho·log′i·cal,** *adj.*

ô′rō·tŭnd′′, *adj.* with resonant, often pompous, speech.

ôr′phán, *n.* **1.** child of dead parents. **—v.t. 2.** kill the parents of.

ôr′phán·åge, *n.* home for orphans.

ôr′′thô·dŏn′tĭcs, *n.* branch of dentistry that corrects irregular teeth. **—or′′thodon′tist,** *n.*

ôr′thô·dŏx′′, *adj.* **1.** conforming to standard doctrine. **2. Orthodox,** pertaining to an east European or Near Eastern church. **—or′′tho·dox′′y,** *n.*

ôr′thŏg′rá·phÿ, *n.*, *pl.* **-phies.** spelling. **—or′′tho·graph′ic,** *adj.*

ôr′′thô·pē′dĭcs, *n.* surgery of bones and joints. **—or′′tho·pe′dic,** *adj.* **—or′′tho·pe′dist,** *n.*

ŏs′cĭl·lāte′′, *v.* **-lated, -lating.** *v.t.*, *v.i.* swing back and forth.

ŏs′cŭ·lāte′′, *v.*, **-lated, -lating.** *v.i.*, *v.t.* kiss.

ŏs·mō'sĭs, *n.* passage of fluids through membranes. —os'mot'ic, *adj.*

ŏs'sē·oŭs, *adj.* bony.

ŏs'sĭ·fy'', *v.*, -fied, -fying. *v.t.*, *v.i.* 1. turn to bone. 2. turn inadaptable, as a custom.

ŏs·tĕn'sĭ·ble, *adj.* seeming.

ŏs''tĕn·tā'tion, *n.* great and deliberate display. —os''ten·ta'tious, *adj.*

ŏs''tē·ŏp'a·thÿ, *n.* school of medicine emphasizing bones and muscles. —os''te·o·path'ic, *adj.* —os'te·o·path'', *n.*

ŏs'trá·cīze'', *v.t.*, -cized, -cizing. expel; exclude. —os'tra·cism, *n.*

ŏs'trĭch, *n.* running, flightless bird of Africa and the Near East.

ŏth'ĕr, *adj.* 1. not yet mentioned. 2. additional; remaining. —*pron.* 3. other one. —*adv.* 4. otherwise.

ŏth'ĕr·wīse'', *adv.* 1. in a different way. 2. in other respects. 3. under other conditions.

ō'tĭ·ōse'', *adj.* idle; useless.

ŏt'tĕr, *n.* furred swimming mammal.

ŏt'tō·man, *n.* upholstered footstool.

oŭch, *interj.* exclamation of pain.

oŭght, *aux. v.* 1. am, is, or are obligated. 2. will very probably.

oŭī, *adv. French.* yes.

oŭnce, *n.* 1. sixteenth of an avoirdupois pound or twelfth of a troy pound. 2. thirty-second of a liquid quart.

oŭr, *adj.* pertaining to us.

oŭrs, *pron.* our own.

oŭr·sĕlves', *pron.* 1. (intensive or reflexive of *we*). 2. our true selves.

oŭst, *v.t.* expel.

oŭst'ĕr, *n.* act or instance of ousting.

oŭt, *adv.* 1. away from inside. 2. away from existence, action, etc. 3. away from a group. 4. away from consciousness. —*adj.* 5. away from one's usual place. 6. out of existence, action, etc. 7. inaccurate. 8. unconsciousness. 9. **out of,** with no supply of. —*n.* 10. *Informal.* means of evasion.

oŭt'·ånd-oŭt', *adj.* utter.

oŭt'bôard', *adj.*, *adv.* outside the hull of a boat.

oŭt'break'', *n.* sudden manifestation.

oŭt'build''ing, *n.* separate, subsidiary building.

oŭt'bûrst'', *n.* vigorous outbreak.

oŭt'căst'', *adj.* 1. rejected by all. —*n.* 2. outcast person.

oŭt'cóme'', *n.* result.

oŭt'cróp'', *n.* rock rising above the soil.

oŭt'crÿ'', *n.*, *pl.* -cries. strong protest.

oŭt'dāt'ĕd, *adj.* obsolete.

oŭt''dĭs'tánce, *v.t.*, -tanced, -tancing. get ahead of in a race or pursuit.

oŭt''dō', *v.t.*, -did, -done, -doing. act more effectively than.

oŭt'dōōr'', *adj.* pertaining to the outdoors.

oŭt'dōōrs', *adv.* 1. away from the insides of buildings. —*n.* 2. nature.

oŭt'ĕr, *adj.* further out. —out'er·most'', *adj.*

oŭt'fĭt'', *n.*, *v.t.*, -fitted, -fitting. *n.* 1. equipment. 2. ensemble of clothes. —*v.t.* 3. supply with an outfit.

oŭt''fŏx'', *v.t.* outwit.

oŭt'gō''ing, *adj.* 1. departing. 2. affable.

oŭt'grow'', *v.t.*, -grew, -grown, -growing. become too large or mature for.

oŭt'growth'', *n.* 1. something that grows out. 2. development; consequence.

oŭt'guĕss'', *v.t.* guess better than.

oŭt'ing, *n.* pleasure trip.

oŭt'länd''ĭsh, *adj.* strange.

oŭt'lăst'', *v.t.* last longer than.

oŭt'lāw'', *n.* 1. criminal. —*v.t.* 2. forbid by law.

oŭt'lāy'', *n.* expenditure.

oŭt'lĕt'', *n.* 1. means of emergence. 2. sales market.

oŭt'līne'', *n.*, *v.t.*, -lined, -lining. *n.* 1. outer edge; silhouette. 2. summary of essentials. —*v.t.* 3. make an outline of.

oŭt''līve'', *v.t.*, -lived, -living. live longer than.

oŭt'lōōk'', *n.* 1. view. 2. viewing place. 3. prospect.

oŭt'lÿ''ing, *adj.* situated at a distance.

oŭt·mŏd'ĕd, *adj.* no longer in use.

oŭt''nŭm'bĕr, *v.t.* be more than.

oŭt'-of-dāte', *adj.* obsolete.

oŭt'-of-the-wāy', *adj.* not often encountered.

oŭt'pā''tiĕnt, *n.* non-resident hospital patient.

oŭt'pŏst'', *n.* remote fort, settlement, etc.

oŭt'pŭt, *n.* 1. production. 2. (computers) data sent from a computer after processing.

ōut′răge, *n., v.t.,* **-raged, -raging.** *n.* **1.** indignation. **2.** act causing indignation. —*v.t.* **3.** make indignant. —**out·ra′ geous,** *adj.*

ōut′rĭg′′gêr, *n.* **1.** floating spar giving a narrow boat stability. **2.** boat with such a spar.

ōut′rīght′′, *adj.* **1.** pure and unambiguous. —*adv.* **2.** entirely. **3.** candidly.

ōut′sĕt′′, *n.* beginning.

ōut′sīde′, *n.* **1.** exterior. —*adj.* **2.** pertaining to an exterior. **3.** extreme. **4.** remotely possible. —*adv.* **5.** to the exterior. —*prep.* **6.** away from the interior of.

ōut′sīd′êr, *n.* non-member.

ōut′sīze′′, *adj.* over normal size.

ōut′skĭrts′′, *n. pl.* border areas.

ōut′smärt′, *v.t.* be more cunning than.

ōut′′spō′kĕn, *adj.* frank.

ōut′′sprĕad′, *adj.* extended.

ōut′′stănd′ĭng, *adj.* **1.** prominent. **2.** unpaid.

ōut′strĕtch′, *v.t.* extend.

ōut′strĭp′, *v.t.,* **-stripped, -stripping. 1.** go faster than. **2.** surpass.

ōut′wârd, *adj.* **1.** outer; exterior. —*adv.* **2.** Also, **out′wards,** toward the outside.

ōut′′weigh′, *v.t.* **1.** matter more than. **2.** be heavier than.

ōut′′wĭt′, *v.t.,* **-witted, -witting.** outsmart.

ō′vāl, *n.* **1.** racetrack in an oval shape. —*adj.* **2.** shaped like an egg.

ō′vá·rȳ, *n., pl.* **-ries.** female reproductive gland. —**o·var′i·an,** *adj.*

ō·vä′tion, *n.* act of enthusiastic applause.

ŏv′ĕn, *n.* heating chamber.

ō′vêr, *prep.* **1.** above or on. **2.** to or on the far side of. **3.** superior to. **4.** more than. **5.** concerning. —*adj.* **6.** above. **7.** across. **8.** more. **9.** again. **10.** upside down. **11.** to a new attitude or belief. **12.** to completion. —*adj.* **13.** upper. **14.** finished.

ō′vêr-, prefix indicating "to excess." **overabundant, overactive, overanxious, overburden, overcautious, overcharge, overconfident, overcrowd, overdo, overdose, overeat, overemphasize, overestimate, overexert, overexpose, overheat, overindulge, overload, overmuch, over-populate, overprice, overproduce, overreact, overripe, oversexed, overspend, overstock, overstrict, oversupply, overwork.**

ō′′vêr·ăll′, *adj., adv.* **1.** end-to-end. —*adj.* **2.** total. —*n.* **3. overalls,** protective covering for other clothes.

ō′′vêr·āwe′, *v.t.,* **-awed, -awing.** subdue with awe.

ō′′vêr·beār′ĭng, *adj.* domineering.

ō′′vêr·bōard′, *adv.* into the water from a vessel.

ō′′vêr·căst′′, *adj.* cloudy, as the sky.

ō′′vêr·cōat′′, *n.* heavy outer coat.

ō′′vêr·cŏme′, *v.t.,* **-came, -come, -coming.** get the better of.

ō′′vêr·dōse′, *v.* to ingest, with harmful effect, too much of a drug.

ō′′vêr·drăw′, *v.t.,* **-draw, -drawn, -drawing.** draw on in excess of one's balance. —**o′′ver·draft′′,** *n.*

ō′′vêr·dūe′, *adj.* past the time when due.

ō′′vêr·ĕs′tĭ·māte′′, *v.t.,* **-mated, -mating.** esteem too highly or as too much. —**o′′ver·es′ti·mate, o′′ver·es′′ti·ma′tion,** *n.*

o·ver·flow′, *v.t.* (o′′vər flō′) **1.** spill over the rim of. —*v.i.* **2.** be filled beyond capacity. —*n.* (o′vər flō′′) **3.** act or instance of overflowing. **4.** amount that overflows.

ō′′vêr·grōw′, *v.t.* **-grew, -grown, -growing.** cover with growth.

ō′′vêr·hănd′′, *adv., adj.* with the hand raised.

ō′′vêr·haul′, *v.t.* **1.** inspect thoroughly. **2.** repair. —*n.* **3.** act or instance of overhauling.

ō′′vêr·hĕad′′, *adj., adv.* **1.** above one's head. —*n.* **2.** continuing business costs.

ō′′vêr·hēar′, *v.t.,* **-heard, -hearing.** hear without being spoken to.

ō′′vêr·jōyed′, *adj.* filled with joy.

ō′′vêr·lănd′, *adj., adv.* across the land.

ō·vêr·lăp′, *v.,* **-lapped, -lapping.** *n. v.t.* (ō′′vər lap′) **1.** extend within the edge of. —*v.i.* **2.** extend within each other's edges. —*n.* (ō′vər lap′′) **3.** act or instance of overlapping.

ō′′vêr·lāy′, *v.t.,* **-laid, -laying.** cover or lay over.

ō′′vêr·lōōk′, *v.t.* **1.** omit by mistake. **2.** look out over.

ō′vêr·lȳ, *adv.* excessively.

ō′′vêr·nīght′, *adv.* 1. during the night. —*adj.* (ō′vər nīt′′) 2. from beginning to end of one night. 3. for one night.

ō′vêr·păss′, *n.* roadway passing over another, etc.

ō′′vêr·pŏw′êr, *v.t.* reduce to helplessness.

ō′′vêr·rāte′, *v.t.*, -rated, -rating. rate too highly.

ō′′vêr·rēach′, *v.t.* reach beyond.

ō′′vêr·rīde′, *v.t.*, -rode, -ridden, -riding. prevail against or nullify.

ō′′vêr·rūle′, *v.t.*, -ruled, -ruling. nullify with superior authority.

ō′′vêr·rŭn′, *v.t.*, -ran, -run, -running. 1. overflow. 2. infest.

ō′vêr·sēas′, *adv., adj.* 1. beyond the sea. —*adj.* Also, o′vêr·sea′′. 2. foreign.

ō′′vêr·sēe′, *v.t.* -saw, -seen, -seeing. supervise.

ō′vêr·shoe′′, *n.* waterproof shoe covering.

ō′′vêr·sīght′′, *n.* mistaken omission.

ō′′vêr·sĭm′pli·fȳ′′, *v.t.*, -fied, -fying. distort by simplification.

ō′′vêr·sīze′′, *adj.* 1. too large. 2. larger than usual. Also, o′ver·sized′′.

ō′′vêr·slēep′, *v.i.* -slept, -sleeping. sleep too long.

ō′′vêr·stāte′, *v.t.*, -stated, -stating. exaggerate.

ō′′vêr·stĕp′, *v.t.*, -stepped, -stepping. exceed.

ō′′vêr·stŭff′, *v.t.* 1. upholster with stuffing all over. 2. stuff to excess.

ō·vêrt′, *adj.* 1. unhidden. 2. open and deliberate.

ō′′vêr·tāke′, *v.t.*, -took, -taken, -taking. catch up with.

ō′′vêr·thé·cōŭn′′têr, *adj.* (drugs) available without a prescription.

ō·vêr·thrŏw′, *v.t.*, -threw, -thrown, -throwing, *n. v.t.* (ō′′vər thrō′) 1. cause to fall over. 2. banish from power. —*n.* (ō′vər thrō′′). 3. act or instance of overthrowing.

ō′′vêr·tīme′, *adj., adv.* 1. beyond regular hours. —*n.* 2. time beyond regular hours. 3. overtime pay.

ō′′vêr·tōne′, *n.* 1. tone modifying a pure tone. 2. subtle implication.

ō′′vêr·tûre′, *n.* 1. musical composition

beginning an opera, etc. 2. friendly advance.

ō′′vêr·tûrn′, *v.t., v.i.* upset.

ō′′vêr·wēen′ing, *adj.* arrogant.

ō′vêr·weight′, *adj.* too heavy.

ō′′vêr·whĕlm′′, *v.t.* render powerless.

ō′vêr·wrôught′′, *adj.* very nervous.

ō′vŏid, *adj.* egg-shaped.

ō′vŭm, *n., pl.* -va. female germ cell.

ōwe, *v.t.* owed, owing. 1. be obligated to give or pay. 2. be obligated to. 3. have someone to thank for.

ōwl, *n.* nocturnal bird of prey.

ōwn, *v.t.* 1. be the rightful possessor of. —*v.t., v.i.* 2. admit or confess. —*adj.* 3. personally or individually possessed. —own′er·ship, *n.*

ŏx, *n., pl.* oxen. domesticated bovine.

ŏx′īde, *n.* compound containing oxygen.

ŏx′y·gĕn, *n.* gaseous element needed for breathing and burning.

ŏx·y·môr′ŏn, *n.* figure of speech in which two ideas of opposite meaning are combined to form an expressive phrase.

ōys′têr, *n.* edible mollusk.

ō′zōne, *n.* a form of oxygen created by electric spark.

P

P, p, *n.* sixteenth letter of the English alphabet.

păb′ū·lŭm. *n.* soft food, esp. for babies.

pāce, *n., v.,* paced, pacing. *n.* 1. rate of movement, esp. in walking or running. 2. linear measure roughly equivalent to a footstep. 3. an individual step. —*v.t.* 4. establish the pace for, esp. in a race. 5. measure by pacing off. —*v.i.* 6. take slow, measured steps.

pāce′māk′′êr, *n.* artificial device to regulate the heartbeat.

păch′y·dêrm, *n.* thick-skinned mammal, e.g. an elephant.

pá·cĭf′ĭc, *adj.* 1. peaceful; calm. 2. peace-making; conciliatory.

păc′i·fĭsm, *n.* opposition to violence and war. —pac′i·fist, *n.* —pac′′i·fis′tic, *adj.*

păc′i·fy″, *v.t.*, **-fied, -fying. 1.** quiet or calm. **2.** appease. **—pac′i·fi·ca′tion**, *n.* **—pac′i·fi″er**, *n.*

păck, *n.* **1.** bundle or package. **2.** group of people, animals, or things. **3.** complete set of. **—v.t. 4.** make into a bundle. **5.** fill, as with things for a journey. **6.** cram. **7.** carry, as a gun.

păck′age, *n.*, *v.t.*, **-aged, -aging.** *n.* **1.** bundle; parcel. **2.** container. **—v.t. 3.** enclose or wrap in a package.

păck′ĕt, *n.* **1.** small package or bundle. **2.** passenger boat on a regular schedule.

păct, *n.* agreement; treaty.

păd, *n.*, *v.t.*, **padded, padding.** *n.* **1.** soft cushion. **2.** tablet of writing paper. **3.** cushioned part of an animal foot. **—v.t. 4.** furnish with pads. **5.** lengthen or falsify with extraneous matter.

păd′dle, *n.*, *v.*, **-dled, -dling.** *n.* **1.** oarlike implement, esp. for a canoe. **2.** Ping-Pong racket. **—v.t. 3.** move with paddles. **4.** spank. **—v.i. 5.** move in water using the hands.

păd′dŏck, *n.* enclosed area for horses.

păd′lŏck, *n.* **1.** portable lock with a shackle. **—v.t. 2.** fasten with a padlock.

paē′an, *n.* song of praise, joy, or thanksgiving.

pā′gàn, *n.* **1.** heathen; **—***adj.* **2.** heathen: barbaric. **—pa′gan·ism**, *n.*

pāge, *n.*, *v.t.* **paged, paging.** *n.* **1.** single side of a leaf, as in a book. **2.** young servant. **—v.t. 3.** number the pages of. **4.** hail by naming loudly.

păg′eant, *n.* elaborate spectacle. **—pag′eant·ry**, *n.*

păg′êr, *n.* electronic device for remote alerting and communication with a person.

pà·gō′dà, *n.* tall Oriental building, usually a Buddhist temple.

pāil, *n.* bucket.

pāin, *n.* **1.** physical or mental suffering. **2.** effort; struggle. **3.** punishment. **—v.t. 4.** hurt; distress. **—pain′ful**, *adj.* **—pain′less**, *adj.*

pāins′tāk″ĭng, *adj.* careful.

pāint, *n.* **1.** pigmented liquid used to coat surfaces. **—v.i. 2.** engage in the art of painting. **—v.t. 3.** cover with paint. **—paint′er**, *n.* **—paint′ing**, *n.*

pāir, *n.*, *pl.* **pairs, pair**, *v. n.* **1.** set of two, esp. when matching. **—v.t. 2.** arrange in pairs. **—v.i. 3. pair off**, separate in couples.

pāis′lēy, *n.* soft fabric with colorful, intricate design.

pà·jä′más, *n. pl.* loose, two-piece sleeping clothes.

păl, *n. Informal.* friend or acquaintance.

păl′ace, *n.* official residence of a sovereign, etc. **—pa·la′tial**, *adj.*

păl′at·a·ble, *adj.* tasty.

păl′ate, *n.* roof of the mouth. **—pal′a·tal**, *adj.*

pà·lăv′êr, *n.* long parley.

pāle, *adj.*, **paler, palest**, *v.*, **paled, paling**, *n. adj.* **1.** lacking intensity of color; whitish. **2.** lacking vividness. **—v.i. 3.** become pale. **—n. 4.** stake. **5.** limits; bounds. **6.** enclosed area.

pā″lē·ō·lĭth′ĭc, *adj.* pertaining to the earlier part of the Stone Age.

păl′ĕtte, *n.* board on which a painter spreads colors.

păl′ĭd, *adj.* pale, drawn. **—pal′lor**, *n.*

păl′ĭng, *n.* board or picket.

păl′ī·sāde″, *n.* **1.** high fence of palings. **2.** line of high cliffs.

pȧll′beār″êr, *n.* person who attends or carries the coffin at a funeral.

păl′lĕt, *n.* **1.** straw mattress. **2.** platform used to support freight.

păl′li·āte″, *v.t.* **1.** ease without curing. **2.** mitigate with excuses. **—pal′li·a″tive**, *adj.*

păll, *n.* **1.** cloth draped over a coffin. **—v.i. 2.** become tiresome or distasteful.

pȧlm, *n.* **1.** soft inner surface of the hand. **2.** tall unbranched tropical tree or shrub topped with large leaves. **—v.i. 3.** conceal in the hand.

pȧlm′ĭs·trȳ, *n.* fortune-telling from the lines of a person's palm.

păl″ȯ·mī′nō, *n.*, *pl.* **-nos**. *n.* light tan horse.

păl′pà·ble, *adj.* **1.** tangible. **2.** obvious, clear. **—pal′pa·bly**, *adv.*

păl′pi·tāte″, *v.i.*, **-tated, -tating.** pulsate with unnatural rapidity. **—pal″pi·ta′tion**, *n.*

păl′sȳ, *n.*, *pl.* **-sies**, *v.t.*, **-sied, -sying. 1.** paralysis. **2.** condition characterized by tremors. **—v.t. 3.** paralyze.

päl′trÿ, *adj.*, **-trier, -triest**. *adj.* trifling, trivial.

păm′pêr, *v.t.* treat with excessive indulgence; coddle.

păm·phlĕt, *n.* unbound booklet with a paper cover.

păn, *n.*, *v.*, **panned, panning**. *n.* **1.** broad, shallow metal container. —*v.t.* **2.** separate from sand by washing. **3.** *Informal.* criticize severely, in a review. **4.** to rotate, esp. a camera.

păn′′á·cē′á, *n.* cure-all.

păn′cāke′′, *n.* flat batter cake fried on both sides.

păn′crē·ás, *n.* gland that secretes digestive fluid. —**pan′′cre·at′ic**, *adj.*

păn′dà, *n.* bearlike, black and white Asiatic mammal.

păn′′dé·mō′nī·ŭm, *n.* wild uproar, chaos.

păn′dêr, *n.* **1.** pimp. —*v.i.* **2.** cater to another's passions or weaknesses. —**pan′der·er**, *n.*

pāne, *n.* sheet of glass, esp. for doors and windows.

păn′′é·gyr′ĭc, *n.* eulogy.

păn′ĕl, *n.* **1.** list of persons called for a special task, e.g. jury duty. **2.** wood filling for a wall or door. **3.** mounting for controls or instruments. —**pan′el·ing**, *n.* —**pan′el·ist**, *n.*

păng, *n.* sudden feeling of distress or guilt.

păn′hăn′′dle, *v.i.* **-dled, -dling**. *Informal.* beg for money on the street. —**pan′han′′dler**, *n.*

păn′ĭc, *n.* **1.** sudden, overpowering fear. —*v.i.* **2.** be affected by panic. —**pan′ick·y**, *adj.* —**pan′ic-strick′′en**, *adj.*

păn′o·plÿ, *n.*, *pl.* **-plies**. *n.* **1.** impressive array. **2.** suit of armor.

păn′′o·răm′á, *n.* **1.** wide view of a large area. **2.** continuously changing scene or unfolding of events. —**pan′′o·ram′ic**, *adj.*

păn′sÿ, *n.* colorful outdoor flower related to the violet.

pănt, *v.i.* **1.** breathe hard and quickly, as after exercise. **2.** long or yearn for.

păn′thē′′ĭsm, *n.* doctrine that equates God with nature and natural forces.

păn′thêr, *n.* large wild cat, e.g. leopard, cougar, puma.

păn′to·mīme′′, *n.*, *v.t.*, **-mimed, mim-** ing. *n.* **1.** expression through movement and gesture only. **2.** drama using movement and no speech. —*v.t.* **3.** express in pantomime; mime.

păn′trÿ, *n.*, *pl.* **-tries**. small supply room or closet off a kitchen.

pănts, *n. pl.* trousers.

păp, *n.* soft food for babies or the infirm.

pä′pà, *n.* father.

pā′pá·cÿ, *n.* office of the pope. —**pa′pal**, *adj.*

pá·pá′yà, *n.* tropical tree with yellow-black edible fruit.

pä′pêr, *n.* **1.** fibrous compound made in sheets to receive writing, etc. **2.** scholarly essay. **3.** newspaper. **4. papers**, documents. —*v.t.* **5.** decorate with wallpaper.

pä′pêr·băck′′, *n.* inexpensive book with paper cover.

pä′′piêr-ma·che′, *n.* molding material made of wet paper pulp and glue.

pá·pĭl′là, *n.*, *pl.* **-pillaē**. small protuberance concerned with the senses, e.g. taste buds.

pā′pĭst, *n. Disparaging*. Roman Catholic. —**pa′pism**, *n.* —**pa·pis′ti·cal, pa·pis′tic**, *adj.*

pă′pōose′, *n.* Native American baby.

păp′rĭ′kà, *n.* red spice made from sweet peppers.

pá·pÿ′rŭs, *n.* plant from the Nile from which the Egyptians prepared paperlike material.

pâr, *n.* **1.** equality in level or value. **2.** accepted standard; average.

păr′á·ble, *n.* story conveying a moral.

păr′á·chūte′, *n.*, *v.*, **-chuted, -chuting**, *n.* **1.** umbrellalike device used for descents from aircraft. —*v.i.* **2.** jump with a parachute. —*v.t.* **3.** send by parachute.

pá·rāde′, *n.*, *v.*, **-raded, -rading**. *n.* **1.** ostentatious display. **2.** ceremonial procession or march. —*v.t.* **3.** display ostentatiously. —*v.i.* **4.** march in a parade.

păr′á·dĭgm, *n.* ideal; model.

păr′á·dīse′′, *n.* **1.** heaven. **2.** Garden of Eden.

păr′á·dŏx′′, *n.* true statement that seems to contradict itself. —**par′′a·dox′i·cal**, *adj.*

păr′áf·fĭn, *n.* waxy substance used in candles and to seal jars.

păr′à·gŏn′′, *n.* model of perfection.

păr′á·grăph′′, *n.* **1.** subdivision of a writing that contains one or more sentences. —*v.t.* **2.** divide into paragraphs.

păr′à·kēet′′, *n.* any of numerous slender, small parrots.

păr′ăl·lăx′′, *n.* apparent displacement of an object seen from different positions.

păr′ăl·lĕl′′, *adj., n., v.t.* **-leled, -leling.** *adj.* **1.** lying or moving in the same direction but equidistant at all points. **2.** essentially similar or comparable. —*n.* **3.** anything parallel. **4.** counterpart. **5.** similarity. —*v.t.* **6.** compare. **7.** be parallel to.

păr′ăl·lĕl′ō·grăm′′, *n.* quadrilateral with parallel opposite sides.

pá·răl′ÿ·sĭs, *n., pl.* **-ses,** loss of voluntary muscular control. —**par′a·lyt′ic**, *n., adj.* —**par′a·lyze′′**, *v.t.*

păr′à·mŏunt′′, *adj.* superior; predominant.

păr′à·môur′′, *n.* extra-marital lover.

păr′à·noī′à, *n.* mental disorder characterized by delusions. —**par′a·noid′′**, *n., adj.* —**par′′a·noi′ac**, *n., adj.*

păr′à·pĕt, *n.* protecting wall or railing.

păr′à·phêr·năl′ĭà, *n. pl.* **1.** personal belongings. **2.** equipment.

păr′à·phrāse′′, *v.t.* **-phrased, -phrasing,** *n. v.t.* **1.** restate in other words. —*n.* **2.** restatement in different words.

păr′à·plē′gĭ·à, *n.* paralysis of the lower half of the body. —**par′′a·pleg′ic**, *n.*

păr′à·sīte′′, *n.* **1.** organism which lives in or on another. **2.** person who depends on or exploits another. —**par′′a·sit′ic**, *adj.*

păr′à·sŏl′′, *n.* sun umbrella.

păr′à·trŏops′′, *n. pl.* soldiers who parachute from planes. —**par′a·trooper**, *n.*

pâr′bŏil′′, *v.t.* boil partly.

pâr′cĕl, *n., v.t.,* **-celed, -celing.** *n.* **1.** wrapped package, esp. for mailing. **2.** lot, esp. for sale. **3.** tract of land. —*v.t.* **4.** divide.

pârch, *v.t.* **1.** dry by heat. —*v.i.* **2.** suffer from heat or thirst.

pârch′mĕnt, *n.* skin of sheep or goat prepared for writing on.

pâr′dŏn, *n.* **1.** official release from penalty or punishment. **2.** indulgence, for-

giveness. —*v.t.* **3.** grant pardon to. —**par′don·a·ble,** *adj.*

pāre, *v.t.* **pared, paring. 1.** trim off the outside part or skin of. **2.** reduce.

păr′′ė·gôr′ĭc, *n.* soothing medicine, esp. to control diarrhea.

păr′ĕnt, *n.* mother or father. —**pa·ren′tal,** *adj.* —**par′ent hood′′.** *n.*

păr′ĕnt·āge, *n.* descent, origin, or lineage.

pá·rĕn′thė·sĭs, *n., pl.* **-ses. 1.** punctuation marks, (or), used to enclose parenthetic material. **2.** matter interpolated in writing to modify or explain the idea. —**par′′en·thet′ic, par′′en·thet′i·cal,** *adj.*

pâr·fāit′, *n.* frozen, layered dessert.

pâ·rī′àh, *n.* outcast.

păr′ĭ·mū′tū·ĕl, *n.* system of betting in which winners share the winnings and the management takes a percentage.

păr′ĭsh, *n.* **1.** ecclesiastical district under one pastor. **2.** local church community. —**pa·rish′ion·er,** *n.*

pâr′ĭ·tÿ, *n.* equality; equivalence.

pârk, *n.* **1.** land set aside as a recreation area or game preserve. **2.** site for athletic events. —*v.t., v.i.* **3.** halt for an extended period.

pâr′kà, *n.* hooded, cold-weather coat.

pârk′wäy′′, *n.* highway with landscaped median strip.

pâr′lănce, *n.* manner of speaking; idiom.

pâr′lāy, *n.* **1.** bet of previous winnings along with the original sum betted. —*v.t.* **2.** bet as a parlay.

pâr′lēy, *n., pl.* **-leys,** *v.i.,* **-leyed, -leying.** *n.* **1.** informal conference, esp. to settle differences. —*v.i.* **2.** hold a parley.

pâr′liá·mĕnt, *n.* national legislative body. —**par′′lia·men·tar′i·an,** *n.* —**par′′lia·men′ta·ry,** *adj.*

pâr′lŏr, *n.* room for entertaining.

pá·rō′chĭ·àl, *adj.* **1.** pertaining to a parish. **2.** narrow or limited in scope. —**pa·ro′chi·al·ism,** *n.*

păr′ō·dÿ, *n., pl.* **-dies,** *v.t.,* **-died, -dying.** *n.* **1.** satiric or humorous imitation. —*v.t.* **2.** ridicule, travesty. —**par′o·dist,** *n.* —**pa·rod′ic,** *adj.*

pá·rōle′, *n., v.t.,* **-roled, -roling.** *n.* **1.** conditional early release from prison. —*v.t.* **2.** put on parole.

pär·ŏx·ỵsm (par'ok siz"im), *n.* sudden, sharp attack; convulsion, fit.

par·quet (par kā'), *n.* floor with an inlaid design, esp. in wood.

păr'rĭ·cĭde, *n.* killing of a parent or close relative.

păr'rŏt, *n.* **1.** hook-billed tropical bird capable of talking. —*v.t.* **2.** repeat or imitate unthinkingly.

păr'rỹ, *v.t.*, **-ried, -rying**, *n.*, *pl.* **-ries.** *v.t.* **1.** evade, avoid. —*n.* **2.** act or instance of parrying.

pär'sĭ·mō''nỹ, *n.* extreme frugality or cheapness. —**par''si·mo'ni·ous**, *adj.*

pärs'lẽy, *n.* garden herb used as garnish or seasoning.

pärs'nĭp, *n.* plant with long, white edible root.

pär'sŏn, *n.* clergyman, esp. Protestant.

pär'sŏn·ăge, *n.* house for a parson.

pärt, *n.* **1.** portion or division. **2.** spare or replacement piece for a machine. **3.** function, duty, job. **4.** role in drama, etc. —*v.t.* **5.** divide. —*v.i.* **6.** dissolve a relationship.

pär·tāke', *v.i.*, **-took -taken, -taking**. *v.i.* **1.** participate. **2.** receive or take a portion.

pär'tiăl, *adj.* **1.** favoring one over another; biased. **2.** especially fond. **3.** affecting a part only. —**par'tial'i·ty**, *n.* —**par'tial·ly**, *adv.*

pär·tĭc'ĭ·pāte'', *v.i.*, **-pated, -pating.** take part; share. —**par·tic'i·pant**, *n.* —**par·tic''i·pa'tion**, *n.*

pär'tĭ·cĭ·ple, *n.* adjective based on a verb. —**par''ti·cip'i·al**, *adj.*

pär'tĭ·cle, *n.* **1.** very small piece or amount. **2.** small, functional word, e.g. a preposition, etc.

pär·tĭc'ū·lăr, *adj.* **1.** pertaining to a specific person or thing. **2.** distinctive, special. **3.** attentive to details; fastidious. —*n.* **4.** detail. —**par·tic'u·lar·ly**, *adv.*

pär'tĭng, *n.* **1.** separation, division. **2.** departure. —*adj.* **3.** done, etc. in farewell.

pär'tĭ·săn, *n.* **1.** person who takes a side in a controversy. **2.** guerrilla.

pär·tĭ'tion, *n.* **1.** division into parts. **2.** divider. —*v.t.* **3.** divide into parts.

pärt'lỹ, *adv.* in some measure; not fully.

pärt'nẽr, *n.* **1.** associate; colleague. **2.** spouse. **3.** joint owner. —**part'ner·ship''**, *n.*

pär'trĭdge, *n.* any of various game birds.

pär'tỹ, *n.*, *pl.* **-ties.** *n.* **1.** social gathering. **2.** group of people with common political interests and opinions. **3.** person or group concerned in a specific action; participant. **4.** group engaged in a special task.

păss, *v.t.* **1.** go past. **2.** hand over; serve. **3.** spend, as time. **4.** approve or ratify. **5.** succeed at, as a test. —*v.i.* **6.** go past. **7.** come to an end. **8.** go from place to place. **9.** be approved or ratified. —*n.* **10.** situation. **11.** paper granting admission, leave, etc. **12.** route, as between mountains. **13.** motion of the hands.

păss'á·ble, *adj.* **1.** able to be passed or crossed. **2.** good enough; tolerable. —**pass'ab·ly**, *adv.*

păs'săge, *n.* **1.** right or freedom to pass. **2.** means of passing. **3.** transportation, esp. ship passage. **4.** act or instance of passing. **5.** enactment. —**pas'sage·way''**, *n.*

păss'bŏŏk'', *n.* bankbook, esp. for savings account.

păs'sĕn·gẽr, *n.* traveler, esp. on a vehicle.

păs·sé', *adj.* out of date; old fashioned.

păs'sĭng, *adj.* **1.** transitory; fleeting. —*n.* **2.** act of a person who passes, esp. in death.

păs'sion, *n.* **1.** strong feeling or emotion. **2.** love, esp. sexual desire. **3.** anger; rage. **4. the Passion**, sufferings of Christ. —**pas'sion·ate, pas'sion·less**, *adj.* —**pas'sion·ate·ly**, *adv.*

păs'sĭve, *n.* **1.** inactive; not in action. **2.** acted upon. **3.** submissive, meek; patient. —**pas·siv'i·ty, pas'sive·ness**, *n.* —**pas'sive·ly**, *adv.*

Păss'ō''vẽr, *n.* Jewish holiday celebrating the Hebrews' liberation from slavery in Egypt.

păss'pôrt'', *n.* official document carried by a foreign traveler.

păst, *adj.* **1.** gone by or elapsed. **2.** pertaining to an earlier time or age. **3.** *Grammar.* pertaining to a verb tense expressing time gone by. —*n.* **4.** time gone by. **5.** past tense. **6.** secret past life. —*prep.*, *adv.* **7.** beyond.

pâs'tä, *n.* food, esp. Italian, prepared from flour and egg dough.

pāste, *n., v.t.,* **pasted, pasting.** *n.* **1.** soft mixture, esp. for sticking things together. **2.** shiny glass used in imitation gems. *—v.t.* **3.** fasten with paste. **—pas′ty,** *adj.*

pāste′bôard′′, *n.* board made of sheets of paper pasted together.

păs′tĕl′, *n.* **1.** light or pale color. **2.** drawing or painting in pastel.

păs′tĕrn, *n.* part of a horse's foot between the fetlock and the hoof joint.

păs′tĕur·ize′′, *v.t.,* **-ized, -izing.** heat to destroy harmful bacteria. **—pas′teur·i·za′tion,** *n.*

păs′tiche (pas tēsh′), *n.* artistic composition composed of selections or motifs from other works.

păs′time′′, *n.* diversion; hobby.

păs′tŏr, *n.* clergyman serving a local parish or church.

păs′tŏ·ral, *adj.* **1.** pertaining to shepherds or the rural life. **2.** pertaining to a golden age. **3.** pertaining to pastors.

păs′trÿ, *n.* sweet baked goods.

păs′tūre, *n., v.t.,* **-tured, -turing.** *n.* **1.** grassy land used for grazing animals. *—v.t.* **2.** feed by allowing to graze.

păt, *n., adj., v.i.,* **patted, patting.** *n.* **1.** light stroke with the flat of the hand. **2.** flat piece of butter, etc. *—adj.* **3.** glib. **4.** perfectly learned. *—v.i.* **5.** place the flat of the hand on lightly.

pătch, *n.* **1.** piece used to cover or repair a worn spot. **2.** a small area distinct from that around it. *—v.t.* **3.** mend or cover with a patch. **4.** repair hastily. **—patch′work′′,** *n., adj.* **—patch′y,** *adj.*

pāte, *n.* head, esp. the crown.

pá·tĕl′là, *n., pl.* **-tellae.** kneecap.

pát′ĕn, *n.* plate, esp. one used in the Eucharist.

păt′ĕnt, *n.* **1.** certificate of exclusive rights to an invention. *—v.t.* **2.** secure a patent on. *—adj.* **3.** something protected by a patent. **4.** evident; obvious.

pá·tĕr′nal, *adj.* **1.** fatherly. **2.** related through or derived from a father.

pà·tĕr′nal·ĭsm, *n.* benevolent or fatherly administration. **—pa·ter′′nal·is′tic,** *adj.*

pá·tĕr′nĭ·tÿ, *n.* fatherhood.

păth, *n.* **1.** narrow road. **2.** course of action. **—path′way′′,** *n.*

pá·thĕt′ĭc, *adj.* **1.** evoking pity. **2.** miserably inadequate. **—pa·thet′i·cal·ly,** *adv.*

pă·thŏl′ŏ·gÿ, *n.* **1.** study of the nature of a disease. **2.** characteristics of disease. **—path′′o·log′i·cal,** *adj.* **—pa·thol′o·gist,** *n.*

pā′thŏs, *n.* element evoking pity or compassion.

pā′tiĕnt, *n.* **1.** person under the care of a doctor. *—adj.* **2.** enduring without complaint. **—pa′tience,** *n.* **—pa′tient·ly,** *adv.*

pá′tĭ·nà, *n.* green film formed on copper and bronze.

pă′tĭ·ō′′, *n., pl.* **patios.** open courtyard.

pā′tri·ärch′′, *n.* **1.** father or founder, e.g. of a tribe or institution. **2.** venerable old man; father. **3.** ecclesiastical dignitary. **—pa′tri·ar′′chal,** *adj.* **—pa′tri·ar′′chy,** *n.*

pá·trī′ciàn, *adj.* **1.** aristocratic; of high birth. *n.* **2.** aristocrat.

păt′rĭ·mō′nÿ, *n.* inherited estate.

pā′trĭ·ŏt, *n.* person who loves and supports his country. **—pa′′tri·ot′ic,** *adj.* **—pa′tri·ot′′ism,** *n.*

pá·trōl, *n., v.t., v.i.,* **-trolled, -trolling.** *n.* **1.** guard making a round. *—v.t.* **2.** guard with a patrol. **3.** pass along regularly. **—pa·trol′man,** *n.*

pā′trŏn, *n.* **1.** influential or wealthy supporter. **2.** customer or client.

pā′trŏn·àge, *n.* **1.** support by a patron. **2.** support of a business by customers. **3.** personal control of appointments to government jobs.

pā′trŏn·īze′′, *v.t.,* **-ized, -izing. 1.** be a customer of. **2.** treat with condescension.

păt′tĕr, *v.i.* **1.** make a succession of light tapping sounds. **2.** talk glibly or nonsensically. **3.** walk quickly and lightly. *—n.* **4.** glib, rapid speech. **5.** quick pattering sound.

păt′tĕrn, *n.* **1.** decorative design. **2.** ideal model. **3.** model for making or copying. *—v.t.* **4.** make after a pattern.

păt′tÿ, *n., pl.* **-ties. 1.** little pie. **2.** flat, round cake of chopped food, e.g. hamburger.

pau′ci·tÿ, *n.* scarcity.

pāunch, *n.* belly, esp. when large. **—paunch′y,** *adj.*

pau´pêr, n. poor person.

pause, n. **1.** temporary stop. —v.i. **2.** stop temporarily.

pave, v.t., **paved, paving.** cover with hard material, as a road. —**pave´ment,** n.

pa·vil´ion, n. **1.** light, open structure for entertainment or shelter. **2.** large tent.

paw, n. **1.** animal foot with nails or claws. —v.t., v.i. **2.** scrape or strike as if with paws.

pawn, v.t. **1.** pledge or stake. **2.** deposit as security for a loan. —n. **3.** state of being pawned. **4.** chess piece of the lowest value.

pawn´brö´´kêr, n. person who lends money on pledged goods.

pay, v., **paid, paying,** n. v.t. **1.** give money to in return for goods or services. **2.** satisfy, as a debt. —v.i. **3.** give money in exchange. **4.** yield a profit. **5.** undergo punishment. —n. **6.** wages or salary. **7.** paid employment. **8.** profit. —**pay·ee´,** n. —**pay´er,** n. —**pay´ment,** n.

pay´a·ble, adj. **1.** to be paid. **2.** able to be paid.

pay´-ôff, n. **1.** final payment. **2.** final consequence.

pea, n. round, edible vegetable seed.

peace, n. **1.** calm and quiet. **2.** state of accord. **3.** freedom from troubling emotions or thoughts. —**peace´a·ble, peace´ful,** adj. —**peace´time´´,** n.

peach, n. sweet juicy fruit.

pea´cŏck´´, n. male peafowl with long, brilliant tail feathers.

pea´fŏwl´´, n. large domesticated Asiatic pheasant.

pea´hĕn´´, n. female peafowl.

peak, n. **1.** pointed top. **2.** top of a mountain or hill.

peaked, adj. **1.** pointed. **2.** (pē´kid) pale, sickly.

peal, n. **1.** loud, prolonged ringing of bells. **2.** set of tuned bells. **3.** any loud, prolonged series of sounds. —v.i. **4.** sound in a peal.

pea´nŭt´´, n. pod or edible seed of an annual herb.

peâr, n. fleshy fruit related to the apple.

pêarl, n. hard, lustrous gem formed within the shell of an oyster. —**pearl´y,** adj.

pĕas´ant, n. poor farm worker.

pēat, n. highly organic soil dried for use as fuel.

pĕb´ble, n. small stone. —**peb´bly,** adj.

pē·căn´, n. smooth-shelled nut from the hickory tree.

pĕc´´ca·dĭl´lō, n., pl. **-loes, -los,** slight or minor offense.

pĕc´ca·rÿ, n. small piglike animal.

pĕck, v.t., v.i. **1.** jab repeatedly with a beak. —v.t. **3.** dig with such jabs. —n. **3.** dry measure of eight quarts.

pĕc´tĭn, n. plant substance used to thicken jellies, etc.

pĕc´´u·lāte´´, v.t., **-lated, -lating,** embezzle. —**pec´´u·la´tion,** n.

pé·cū´li·ar, adj. **1.** strange, odd. **2.** unique. **3.** distinctive, characteristic. —**pe·cu´´li·ar´i·ty,** n. —**pe·cul´iar·ly,** adv.

pé·cū´nĭ·âr´´ÿ, adj. pertaining to money; monetary.

pĕd´á·gŏgue´´, n. teacher; scholar. Also, **ped´a·gog´´,** —**ped´a·go´´gy,** n. —**ped´´a·gog´ic, ped´´a·gog´i·cal,** adj.

pĕd´ál, n. **1.** lever worked by the foot. —v.t., v.i. **2.** move by means of pedals.

pĕd´ânt, n. **1.** person who makes a display of his learning. **2.** unimaginative adherent to the letter of a doctrine. —**pe·dan´tic,** adj. —**ped´an´try,** n.

pĕd´dle, v.t., v.i., **-dled, -dling.** sell on the street or road. —**ped´dler,** n.

pĕd´és·tál, n. base for a statue, etc.

pĕ·dĕs´trī·an, n. **1.** walker. —adj. **2.** prosaic; commonplace.

pē´´dĭ·ăt´rĭcs, n. study of care and diseases of children. —**pe´di·a·tri´´cian,** n. —**pe´´di·at´ric,** adj.

pĕd´ĭ·gree´´, n. **1.** certificate of ancestry. **2.** ancestry, esp. when distinguished. —**ped´´i·greed´´,** adj.

pĕd´ĭ·ment, n. decorative triangular gable.

pēek, v.i. **1.** glance furtively. —n. **2.** brief or furtive glance.

peel, v.t. **1.** strip or remove. —n. **2.** skin of fruit or vegetable. —**peel´ing,** n.

pēen, n. wedge or ball-shaped end of a hammer.

pēep, v.i. **1.** peek. **2.** utter a faint, shrill cry. —n. **3.** quick look or glance. **4.** faint sound.

peer, *v.i.* **1.** look intently or searchingly.
—*n.* **2.** equal in rank or abilities. **3.** nobleman. —**peer'age,** *n.*

peer'less, *adj.* without equal, supreme.

peeve, *n., v.t.,* **peeved, peeving,** *v.t.* **1.** annoy, irritate. —*n.* **2.** source of annoyance. **3.** complaint. —**peev'ish,** *adj.*

peg, *n., v.t.,* **pegged, pegging.** *n.* **1.** small hook, pin or fastener, esp. one fitting into a hole. —*v.t.* **2.** fasten with pegs.

pe·jo'ra·tive, *adj.* disparaging, negative.

pe'koe, *n.* black Oriental tea.

pelf, *n.* money; riches.

pel'i·can, *n.* large bird with a pouched lower bill.

pel·la'gra, *n.* chronic disease caused by inadequate diet.

pel'let, *n.* small ball.

pell'-mell', *adv.* in a disorderly or hasty manner.

pel·lu'cid, *adj.* clear or limpid; transparent.

pelt, *n.* **1.** animal hide, esp. with fur. —*v.t.* **2.** attack with blows or missiles. —*v.i.* **3.** beat relentlessly, as rain.

pel'vis, *n.* basinlike bone in the lower part of the trunk. —**pel'vic,** *adj.*

pen, *n., v.t.,* **penned, penning.** *n.* **1.** instrument for writing with ink. **2.** small enclosure for animals or storage. —*v.t.* **3.** write. **4.** enclose.

pe'nal, *adj.* pertaining to punishment. —**pe'nal·ize'',** *v.t.*

pen·al'ty, *n., pl.* **-ties.** **1.** punishment. **2.** disadvantage; hardship.

pen'ance, *n.* **1.** self-imposed punishment for sin. **2.** sacrament of confession of sin.

pen'chant, *n.* strong inclination; liking.

pen'cil, *n.* **1.** cylindrical implement containing graphite for writing, etc. —*v.t.* **2.** paint, draw, or write.

pend'ant, *n.* **1.** hanging ornament, e.g. an earring. **2.** duplicate or balancing feature.

pend'ent, *adj.* hanging; overhanging.

pend'ing, *adj.* **1.** undecided; imminent. —*prep.* **2.** while awaiting; until.

pen'du·lum, *n.* freely swinging suspended weight.

pen'e·trate'', *v.t.* **-trated, -trating.** **1.** enter. **2.** permeate. **3.** understand. **4.** affect

deeply. —**pen'e·tra·ble,** *adj.* —**pen''e·tra'tion,** *n.*

pen'guin, *n.* short-legged, flightless aquatic bird.

pen''i·cil'lin, *n.* antibiotic produced by certain molds.

pen·in'su·la, *n.* land body surrounded by water on three sides.

pe'nis, *n.* male organ of copulation and urination.

pen'i·tent, *adj.* **1.** feeling repentance. —*n.* **2.** repentant person. —**pen'i·tence,** *n.* —**pen''i·ten'tial,** *adj.*

pen''i·ten'tia·ry, *n.* prison.

pen'knife'', *n.* small pocketknife; jack-knife.

pen'man, *n., pl.* **-men.** person skilled in using a pen. —**pen'man·ship'',** *n.*

pen'nant, *n.* **1.** small flag for signaling. **2.** flag of championship.

pen'ny, *n., pl.* **-nies.** smallest denomination of U.S. currency. —**pen'ni·less,** *adj.*

pe·nol'o·gy, *n.* study of criminal punishment. —**pe·nol'o·gist,** *n.* —**pe''no·log'i·cal,** *adj.*

pen'sion, *n.* **1.** fixed, periodic payment to a retiree. —*v.t.* **2.** give a pension to. **pen'sion·er,** *n.*

pen'sive, *adj.* sadly or dreamily thought-ful; quiet.

pent, *adj.* confined; shut up.

pen'ta·gon'', *n.* polygon of five sides.

pen·tam'e·ter, *n.* verse line of five metrical feet.

Pen'ta·teuch'', *n.* first five books of the Old Testament.

pent'house'', *n.* habitable structure on the roof of a building.

pent'-up', *adj.* confined, as emotions.

pen·ul'ti·mate, *adj.* next to the last.

pe·num'bra, *n.* partial shadow. —**pe·num'bral,** *adj.*

pe·nu'ri·ous, *adj.* **1.** miserly; stingy. **2.** impoverished. —**pen'u·ry,** *n.*

pe'on, *n.* unskilled worker, esp. one in bondage. —**pe'on·age,** *n.*

pe'o·ny, *n., pl.* **-nies.** perennial garden plant with large colorful flowers.

peo'ple, *n., v.t.,* **-pled, -pling.** *n.* **1.** humanity generally. **2.** random group of persons. **3.** peoples, national, cultural, or racial group. —*v.t.* **4.** populate.

pĕp, *Informal. n.* **1.** energy, vigor. —*v.t.* **2. pep up,** make lively; energize. —**pep'py,** *adj.*

pĕp'pêr, *n.* **1.** pungent condiment from an East Indian plant. **2.** hot or mild fruit used as a condiment vegetable. —*v.t.* **3.** season with pepper. **4.** pelt with missiles. **5.** sprinkle as with pepper. —**pep'per·y,** *adj.*

pĕp'pêr·mĭnt'', *n.* aromatic herb used as a flavoring.

pĕp'sĭn, *n.* stomach enzyme which digests proteins.

pĕp'tĭc, *adj.* pertaining to digestion; digestive.

pêr, *prep.* thought; by means of; according to.

pêr·ăm'bū·lāte'', *v.i.,* **-ated, -ating.** walk about; stroll. —**per·am''bu·la'tion,** *n.*

pêr·cāle', *n.* smooth, closely woven cotton.

pêr·cēive', *v.t.* **1.** become aware of. **2.** apprehend or understand. —**per·ceiv'a·ble, per·cep'ti·ble,** *adj.* —**per·cep'tion,** *n.*

pêr·cĕnt', *n.* part in a hundred.

pêr·cĕnt'age, *n.* **1.** proportion per hundred. **2.** allowance, commission, or rate of interest.

pêr·cĕp'tĭve, *adj.* **1.** pertaining to perception. **2.** understanding; discerning.

pêrch, *n.* **1.** roost for birds. **2.** high spot. **3.** freshwater food fish. —*v.t., v.i.* **4.** set or rest as on a perch.

pêr·chánce', *adv.* perhaps.

pêr'co·lāte'', *v.t., v.i.* **-lated, -lating.** filter. —**per''co·la'tion,** *n.*

pêr·cŭs'sion, *n.* **1.** hard, sharp impact. **2.** musical instruments plucked or struck. —**per·cus'sive,** *adj.*

pêr dī'ĕm, by the day.

pêr·dĭ'tion, *n.* damnation.

pêr''ē·grĭ·nā'tion, *n.* travel from one place to another. —**per'e·gri·nate'',** *v.i.*

pêr·ĕmp'tö·rȳ, *adj.* **1.** giving no opportunity to refuse or deny. **2.** imperative. —**per·emp'to·ri·ly,** *adv.*

pê·rĕn'nĭ·al, *adj.* **1.** enduring. **2.** lasting more than two years. —*n.* **3.** plant growing every year. —**per·en·ni'al·ly,** *adv.*

pêr'fĕct, *adj.* **1.** flawless and complete. **2.** unmodified. **3.** *Grammar.* denoting completed action. —*v.t.* (pər fekt'). **4.** make perfect. —**per'fect·ly,** *adj.* —**per·fec'tion,** *n.*

pêr·fĕc'tion·ĭst, *n.* person who demands perfection.

pêr'fĭ·dȳ, *n., pl.* **-dies,** treachery; faithlessness. —**per·fid'i·ous,** *adj.*

pêr'fō·rāte'', *v.t.* **-rated, -rating.** pierce through.

pêr·fôrce', *adv.* necessarily.

pêr·fôrm', *v.t.* **1.** carry out; execute. **2.** enact, play, etc. for an audience. —*v.i.* **3.** appear in a play, concert, etc. —**perform'ance,** *n.* —**per·form'er,** *n.*

pêr·fūme', *n., v.t.* **-fumed, -fuming,** *n.* **1.** sweet odor; fragrance. **2.** sweet-smelling liquid for scenting. —*v.t.* **3.** scent.

pêr·fūnc'tö·rȳ, *adj.* routine and unenthusiastic. —**per·func'to·ri·ly,** *adv.* —**per·func'to·ri·ness,** *n.*

pêr·hăps', *adv.* maybe, possibly.

pêr'ĭ·gēe, *n.* nearest point of an orbit to the earth.

pêr'ĭ·hē'lĭ·ŏn, *n.* nearest point of an orbit to the sun.

pêr'ĭl, *n.* **1.** danger. **2.** source of danger. —**per'il·ous,** *adj.*

pé·rĭm'ē·têr, *n.* outer boundary.

pē'rĭ·ŏd, *n.* **1.** division or extent of time. **2.** end; stop. **3.** punctuation point at the end of a declarative sentence.

pē''rĭ·ŏd'ĭc, *adj.* intermittently or regularly recurring.

pē''rĭ·ŏd'ĭ·căl, *n.* publication appearing at regular intervals. —**pe''ri·od'i·cal·ly,** *adv.*

pê·rĭph'êr·ȳ, *n., pl.* **-eries.** **1.** boundary of a rounded figure. **2.** outer limits; border. —**pe·riph'er·al,** *adj.*

pêr'ĭ·scōpe, *n.* optical instrument for viewing around an obstruction with prisms or mirrors.

pêr'ĭsh, *v.i.* **1.** die, esp. from privation or violence. **2.** decay. —**per'ish·a·ble,** *adj.*

pêr''ĭ·tö·nī'tĭs, *n.* inflammation of the abdominal lining.

pêr'ĭ·wĭn''kle, *n.* **1.** edible snail. **2.** trailing evergreen plant.

pêr·jûre, *v.t.* **-jured, -juring.** make

guilty of perjury. —**per'jur·er**, *n.*
—**per'jured**, *adj.*

pêr'ju·rŷ, *n., pl.* **-ries. 1.** lying under
oath. **2.** lie so uttered. —**per·ju'ri·ous**,
adj.

pêrk, *v.i.* **1.** become lively or vigorous.
—*v.t.* **2.** raise jauntily, as the head.
—**perk'y**, *adj.*

pêr'ma·nent, *adj.* existing always.
—**per'ma·nence, per'ma·nen·cy**, *n.*
—**per'ma·nent·ly**, *adv.*

pêr'mē·āte'', *v.*, **-ated, -ating**. *v.t.* **1.**
penetrate. **2.** be diffused through. —*v.i.*
3. become diffused. —**per''me·a'tion**,
n. —**per'me·a·ble**, *adj.*

pêr·mis'sĭve, *adj.* **1.** granting permission.
2. indulgent; lenient.

pêr·mĭt *v.t.*, **-mitted, -mitting**, *n. v.t.* (pər
mit'). **1.** allow. **2.** tolerate. **3.** give opportunity for. —*n.* (pər'mit) **4.** written
permission; license. —**per·mis'sion**,
n. —**per·mis'si·ble**, *adj.*

pêr''mū·tā'tion, *n.* change; alteration.

pêr''nĭ·cioŭs, *adj.* injurious; hurtful.

pêr''ō·rā'tion, *n.* concluding part of a
speech.

pêr·ŏx'ĭde, *n.* **1.** oxide containing a large
proportion of oxygen. —*v.t.* **2.** bleach
with a peroxide, esp. the hair.

pêr''pén·dĭc'ū·lảr, *adj.* **1.** vertical. **2.**
meeting another line at a right angle.
—*n.* **3.** perpendicular plane or line.

pêr''pe·trāte'', *v.t.*, **-trated, -trating**,
commit; be guilty of. —**per''pe·tra'
tion**, *n.* —**per'pe·tra''tor**, *n.*

pêr·pĕt'ū·ăl, *adj.* **1.** permanent. **2.** un-
ceasing; constant. —**per·pet'u·al·ly**,
adv. —**per·pet'u·ate''** *v.t.* —**per·pet''
u·a'tion**, *n.*

pêr''pe·tū'ĭ·tŷ, *n.* endless duration.

pêr·plĕx', *v.t.* bewilder. —**per·plex'i·ty**,
n.

pêr'quĭs·ĭte, *n.* benefit added to regular
salary.

pêr se', by, of, or in itself.

pêr'se·cūte, *v.t.*, **-cuted, -cuting**. continually harass or oppress. —**per''se·cu'
tion**, *n.* —**per'se·cu''tor**, *n.*

pêr''se·vēre', *v.t.*, **-vered, -vering**. persist in spite of obstacles. —**per''se·ver'
ance**, *n.*

pêr·sĭm'mŏn, *n.* astringent, edible North
American fruit.

pêr·sĭst', *v.i.* **1.** continue resolutely. **2.**
last; endure. —**per·sist'ence**, *n.* —**per·
sist'ent**, *adj.* —**per·sist'ent·ly**, *adv.*

pêr'sŏn, *n.* **1.** human being; individual. **2.**
personality. **3.** one's body.

pêr'sŏn·à·ble, *adj.* **1.** pleasing in appearance. **2.** sociable.

pêr'sŏn·àge, *n.* person of distinction or
note.

pêr'sŏn·àl, *adj.* **1.** pertaining to one individual. **2.** pertaining to the body and its
care, clothing, etc. —**per'son·al·ly**,
adv. —**per'son·al·ize''**, *v.t.*

pêr''sŏn·ăl'ĭ·tŷ, *n., pl.* **-ties. 1.** distinctive personal character. **2.** personally
disparaging remark. **3.** notable person.

pêr·sō'nà nŏn grā'tà, unwelcome or unacceptable person.

pêr·sŏn'ĭ·fŷ, *v.t.*, **-fied, -fying**. **1.** attribute personal character to. **2.** embody;
typify. —**per·son''i·fi·ca'tion**, *n.*

pêr''sŏn·nĕl', *n.* employees of an organization.

pêr·spĕc'tĭve, *n.* **1.** technique of three-
dimensional representation. **2.** extended
view. **3.** basis for interpretation.

pêr''spĭ·cā'cioŭs, *adj.* acutely perceptive; discerning. —**per''spi·cac'i·ty**,
n.

pêr·spīre', *v.i.* sweat. —**per''spi·ra'
tion**, *n.*

pêr·suāde', *v.t.*, **-suaded, -suading**. **1.**
prevail on by argument. **2.** induce belief
in; convince. —**per·sua'sĭve**, *adj.*

pêr·suā'sion, *n.* **1.** process or act of per-
suading. **2.** conviction or belief, opinion.

pêrt, *adj.* **1.** bold; saucy; impudent. **2.**
lively, sprightly.

pêr·tāin', *v.t.* have reference to; relate.

pêr''tĭ·nā'cioŭs, *adj.* holding firmly to
an opinion or purpose. —**per'ti·nac'i·
ty**, *n.*

pêr'tĭ·nént, *adj.* relevant; applicable.
—**per'ti·nence, per'ti·nen·cy**, *n.*

pêr·tûrb', *v.t.* greatly disturb in mind; upset. —**per·tur·ba'tion**, *n.*

pé·rūse', *v.t.* read or survey, esp. with
thoroughness. —**pe·ru'sal**, *n.*

pêr·vāde', *v.t.* **-vaded, -vading**. extend or
spread throughout; permeate. —**per·
va'sĭve**, *adj.*

pêr·vêrse', *adj.* **1.** abnormal; corrupt. **2.**

stubbornly contrary; obstinate. —**per·verse′ly**, *adv.* —**per·ver′si·ty**, *n.*

pêr·vêrt′, *n.* **1.** perverted person, esp. sexually. —*v.t.* **2.** deviate from the proper or right course of action. **3.** misapply; misconstrue; distort. —**per·ver′sion**, *n.*

pe′sō, *n.* monetary unit of Mexico, etc.

pĕs′sĭ·mĭsm′′, *n.* disposition toward the least favorable interpretation or expectation. —**pes′si·mist**, *n.* —**pes′si·mis′tic**, *adj.*

pĕst, *n.* troublesome person or thing; nuisance.

pĕs′tēr, *v.t.* annoy.

pĕs′tĭ·cīde′′, *n.* insecticide.

pĕs′tĭ·lĕnce, *n.* deadly epidemic or disease; plague. —**pes′ti·lent**, *adj.*

pĕs′tle, *n.* implement for grinding or crushing (with a mortar).

pĕt, *n., adj., v.t.*, **petted, petting.** *n.* **1.** tamed animal kept for pleasure. **2.** darling; favorite. —*v.t.* **3.** indulge; pamper. **4.** stroke or fondle affectionately. —*adj.* **5.** treated lovingly.

pĕt′al, *n.* colored leaf of a flower.

pĕ·tīte′, *adj.* small or tiny: used in reference to women.

pĕ·tĭ′tion, *n.* **1.** request or entreaty, esp. when written. —*v.i.* **2.** present a petition; ask for. —**pe·ti′tion·er**, *n.*

pĕt′rel, *n.* small sea bird.

pĕt′rĭ·fŷ′′, *v.*, **-fied, -fying.** *v.t.* **1.** turn into stone; stiffen. **2.** paralyze or stupefy with horror, wonder, etc. —*v.i.* **3.** become petrified.

pĕt′′rō·chĕm′ĭ·cal, *n.* chemical derived from petroleum.

pé·trō′lē·ŭm, *n.* natural oily liquid found underground.

pé·trŏl′o·gŷ, *n.* study of rocks.

pĕt′tĭ·cōat′′, *n.* skirt worn under a dress.

pĕt′tĭsh, *adj.* peevish; petulant.

pĕt′tŷ, *adj.* **-tier, -tiest. 1.** of little importance; trivial. **2.** narrow-minded; mean. —**pet′ti·ness**, *n.*

pĕt′ū·lànt, *adj.* marked by impatient irritation; irritable, peevish.

pe·tū′nĭa, *n.* annual garden plant with bright funnel-shaped flowers.

pēw, *n.* enclosed church bench.

pē′wēe, *n.* any of various small birds.

pēw′tēr, *n.* alloy composed primarily of tin.

pey·ō′tē, *n.* hallucinogenic drug derived from the mescal cactus.

phā′lănx, *n., pl.* **-lanxes, -langes, 1.** body or group in formation, e.g. troops. **2.** any of the bones of the fingers or toes of mammals.

phăl′lŭs, *n., pl.* **phalli. 1.** penis. **2.** symbolic representation of the penis. —**phal′lic**, *adj.*

phăn′tăsm, *n.* apparition; illusion.

phăn·tăs′′mà·gō′rĭà, *n.* succession of imagined things.

phăn′tŏm, *n.* insubstantial image; dreamlike apparition.

Phăr·aōh (fa′ro), *n.* ancient Egyptian ruler.

phăr′ĭ·sēe′′, *n.* **1.** self-righteous person. **2.** member of early Jewish sect.

phăr′′mà·ceū′tĭ·cal, *adj.* of or pertaining to pharmacy. Also, **phar′′ma·ceu′tic.**

phăr′′mà·cŏl′o·gŷ, *n.* study of drugs, esp. for medicinal use. —**phar′′ma·col′o·gist**, *n.*

phăr′mà·cŷ, *n., pl.* **-cies. 1.** practice of preparing medicines. **2.** drug store. —**phar′ma·cist**, *n.*

phăr′ynx, *n., pl.* **-ynges, -rynxes.** cavity that connects mouth and nasal passages with the esophagus. —**pha·ryn′ge·al**, *adj.*

phāse, *n.* **1.** stage of a process. **2.** aspect. —*v.t.* **3.** introduce or withdraw in stages.

phēas′ànt, *n.* large, long-tailed, brightly colored game bird.

phē′′nó·bâr′bĭ·tŏl, *n.* white powder used as sedative and hypnotic.

phé·nŏm′é·nàl, *n.* **1.** amazing. **2.** pertaining to phenomena.

phé·nŏm′é·nŏn, *n., pl.* **-na, -nons. 1.** apparent occurrence, circumstance, or fact. **2.** extraordinary person or thing.

phī′àl, *n.* vial.

phī·lăn′dēr, *v.i.* (of a man) make love with no serious intentions. —**phi·lan′der·er**, *n.*

phī·lăn′thrò·pŷ, *n., pl.* **-pies. 1.** love of mankind. **2.** charitable act, work, or organization. —**phil′′an·throp′ic, phil′′an·throp′i·cal**, *adj.* —**phi·lan′thro·pist**, *n.*

phi·lat'e·ly, *n.* collection and study of postage stamps. **—phi·lat'e·list,** *n.*

phil''har·mon'ic, *adj.* music-loving.

phi·lis'tine, *n.* person indifferent to cultural matters.

phi·lol'o·gy, *n.* linguistics. **—phi·lol'o·gist,** *n.*

phi·los'o·pher, *n.* **1.** reflective thinker. **2.** scholar trained in philosophy. **3.** person who meets difficulties calmly.

phi·los'o·phy, *n., pl.* **-phies. 1.** study of the fundamental truths of life and the universe. **2.** system of philosophical concepts. **—phil''o·soph'i·cal, phil'o·soph'ic,** *adj.* **—phi·los'o·phize'',** *v.i.*

phleg·mat'ic, *adj.* stolid, impassive; apathetic.

phlegm, *n.* thick mucus secreted in the nose and throat.

phlox, *n.* garden plant with colorful flowers.

pho'bi·a, *n.* persistent and irrational morbid fear.

phoe'be, *n.* small eastern American bird.

phoe'nix, *n.* mythical bird said to rise from its own ashes.

phone, *n., v.t.,* **phoned, phoning. 1.** telephone. **—v.t. 2.** make a phone call to.

pho·net'ics, *n.* study of speech sounds. **—pho·net'ic,** *adj.*

pho'no·graph'', *n.* machine for playing records.

pho'ny, *n., adj.,* **-nier, -niest,** *Informal.* *n.* **1.** fake person or thing. **—adj. 2.** fake; counterfeit.

phos'phate, *n.* chemical salt often used in fertilizers.

phos''pho·res'cence, *n.* luminescence without sensible heat. **—phos'pho·res'cent,** *adj.*

phos'pho·rus, *n.* solid nonmetallic element found in bones, nerves, etc. **—phos·phor'ic, phos'pho·rous,** *adj.*

pho'to, *n., pl.* **-tos.** photograph.

pho''to·e·lec'tric, *adj.* pertaining to electric effects resulting from light.

pho'to·en·grav''ing, *n.* process of producing an etched printing plate from a photograph or drawing. **—pho'to·en·grave'',** *v.t.*

pho''to·gen'ic, *adj.* suitable for being photographed.

pho'to·graph'', *n.* **1.** picture taken by photography. **—v.i. 2.** take a photograph. **—pho·tog'ra·pher,** *n.*

pho·tog'ra·phy, *n.* process of producing images on treated surfaces by the action of light. **—pho''to·graph'ic,** *adj.*

pho''to·sen'si·tive, *adj.* sensitive or sensitized to light.

pho''to·syn'the·sis, *n.* process by which chlorophyll-containing plants exposed to sunlight produce carbohydrates.

phrase, *n., v.t.,* **phrased, phrasing.** *n.* **1.** sequence of words conveying a thought. **2.** brief expression or remark. **3.** unit of musical composition. **—v.t. 4.** express in a certain way.

phra''se·ol'o·gy, *n.* **1.** manner of speaking. **2.** collective expressions or phrases.

phre·net'ic, *adj.* delirious.

phre·nol'o·gy, *n.* study that infers personal characteristics from the shape of the skull. **—phre·nol'o·gist,** *n.*

phy'lum, *n., pl.* **-la.** major division of plant and animal classes.

phys'ic, *n.* medicine, esp. a purgative.

phys'i·cal, *adj.* **1.** pertaining to the body. **2.** pertaining to matter or the material world. **3.** pertaining to physics. **—n. 4.** medical examination. **—phys'i·cal·ly,** *adv.*

phy·si'cian, *n.* medical doctor.

phys'ics, *n.* science dealing with motion, matter, energy, and force. **—phys'i·cist,** *n.*

phys''i·og'no·my, *n., pl.* **-mies.** facial appearance.

phys''i·og'ra·phy, *n.* science of the earth's surface.

phys''i·ol'o·gy, *n.* science of the functioning of living matter and beings. **—phys''i·o·log'i·cal,** *adj.* **—phys''i·ol'o·gist,** *n.*

phys''i·o·ther'a·py, *n.* treatment of disease by physical means, e.g. exercise, massage, etc.

phy·sique', *n.* physical constitution of the body; build.

pi, *n.* Greek letter π, symbol for the value 3.1416, ratio of circumference to diameter.

pi''á·nĭs'sĭ·mō, *adj., adv. Music.* very soft.

pĭ'ăn'ō, *n., pl.* **-anos,** *adj., adv. n.* **1.** Also, **pi·an''o for'te,** percussive, musical keyboard instrument with steel strings struck by hammers. —*adj.* **2.** soft. —*adv.* **3.** softly. —**pi·an'ist,** *n.*

pĭ'ăz'zȧ, *n.* veranda or porch.

pĭ'cȧ, *n.* measure of printing type equal to about a sixth of an inch.

pĭc''á·yūne', *adj.* insignificant; trivial; petty.

pĭc'cȧ·lĭl''lĭ, *n.* spicy vegetable relish.

pĭc'cō·lō'', *n., pl.* **-los,** small shrill flute.

pick, *v.t.* **1.** choose or select. **2.** gather, e.g. flowers. **3.** separate or pull apart. **4.** pierce with a pointed instrument. **5.** provoke, e.g. pick a fight. —*n.* **6.** choice; selection. **7.** Also, **pick'ax, pick'axe,** sharp tool for breaking rock. —**pick'er,** *n.*

pĭck'êr·ĕl, *n.* small pike.

pĭck'ĕt, *n.* **1.** protestor stationed by a striking labor union. **2.** body or group of soldiers on lookout. **3.** pointed fence with pickets. —*v.i.* **4.** serve as a picket.

pĭck'ĭngs, *n.* **1.** gleanings. **2.** rewards; spoils.

pick'le, *n., v.t.,* **-led, -ling.** *n.* **1.** cucumber cured in spiced vinegar. **2.** any food preserved in a pickling solution. **3.** *Informal.* difficult predicament; bind. —*v.t.* **4.** preserve in brine or vinegar.

pick'pŏck''ĕt, *n.* thief who steals from pockets.

pĭck'ŭp, *n.* **1.** acceleration; energy. **2.** revival of action. **3.** small open-body truck for hauling.

pĭck'ÿ, *adj.* fussy, finicky.

pĭc'nĭc, *n., v.i.,* **-nicked, -nicking.** *n.* **1.** outing with an outdoor meal. —*v.t.* go on a picnic. —**pic'nick·er,** *n.*

pĭc'tûre, *n., v.t.,* **-tured, -turing.** *n.* **1.** painting, drawing, photograph, etc. **2.** motion picture. —*v.t.* **3.** represent in a picture. **4.** conceive; visualize. —**pic'tor'i·al,** *adj.*

pĭc''tûr·ĕsque', *adj.* **1.** charming; quaint. **2.** striking; vivid.

pie, *n.* baked dish of pastry crust and filling, e.g. meat, fruit, etc.

pie'bȧld'', *adj.* marked by patches of different colors.

piece, *n., v.t.,* **pieced, piecing.** *n.* **1.** part or single portion. **2.** artistic creation. **3.** firearm. —*v.t.* **4.** join or repair from pieces.

piece'meal'', *adv.* **1.** piece by piece. **2.** into fragments.

pied, *adj.* many-colored; variegated.

pier, *n.* **1.** massive support. **2.** structure loading and unloading vessels.

pierce, *v.t.,* **pierced, piercing, 1.** penetrate into or through. **2.** make a hole into.

pī'é·tÿ, *n.* religious dutifulness; devoutness.

pĭg, *n.* **1.** swine, esp. young. **2.** oblong metal casting.

pĭ'gĕon, *n.* short-legged, stout-bodied bird.

pĭ'gĕon·hōle'', *n., v.t.,* **-holed, -holing.** *n.* **1.** small compartment, e.g. in a desk. —*v.t.* **2.** place in a pigeonhole; classify.

pĭg'mĕnt, *n.* coloring matter. —**pig''men·ta'tion,** *n.*

pĭg'tȧil, *n.* tight braid of hair.

pīke, *n.* **1.** large, slender freshwater fish. **2.** long wooden spear. **3.** highway.

pīk'êr, *n. Informal.* person who does things in a small or cheap way.

pĭ'lȧf'', *n.* seasoned rice dish.

pĭ·lăs'têr, *n.* column that projects slightly from a wall.

pile, *n., v.t.,* **piled, piling.** *n.* **1.** heap. **2.** support driven into the ground. **3.** short standing fibers, as in a rug. **4.** nuclear reactor. **5. piles,** hemorrhoids. —*v.t.* **6.** put in a pile. —*v.t., v.i.* **7.** accumulate.

pil'fêr, *v.i., v.t.* steal.

pĭl'grĭm, *n.* traveler in foreign lands, esp. to a holy place. —**pil'grim·age,** *n.*

pĭll, *n.* medicine in tablet or capsule form.

pĭl'lȧge, *v.t.,* **-laged, -laging.** loot; plunder.

pĭl'lȧr, *n.* masonry column.

pĭll'bŏx'', *n.* **1.** low shelter against gunfire. **2.** small container for pills.

pĭl'lō·rÿ, *n., pl.* **-ries.** wooden frame with head and arm holes for public punishment.

pĭl'lōw, *n.* cushion filled with feathers, etc. for support, esp. of the head. —**pil'low·case'',** *n.*

pī'lŏt, *n.* **1.** person who guides a ship or

airplane. —*v.t.* **2.** steer; guide. —*adj.* **3.** experimental.

pi·mĕn'tō, *n., pl.* **-tos. 1.** dried fruit of a tropical tree; allspice. **2.** pimiento.

pĭ·miĕn'tō, *n., pl.* **-tos.** sweet, red, garden pepper.

pĭmp, *n.* person who finds clients for a prostitute.

pĭm'ple, *n.* small, inflamed swelling on the skin. —**pim'ply,** *adj.*

pĭn, *n., v.t.,* **pinned, pinning.** *n.* **1.** slender, pointed fastener. **2.** piece of jewelry fastened to a garment. **3.** wooden target piece in bowling. —*v.t.* **4.** fasten with a pin. **5.** hold tight; bind.

pĭn'a·fōre'', *n.* sleeveless dress or apron, esp. for a child.

pince'-nez'', *n.* eyeglasses held on the nose by a pinching spring.

pĭn'cĕrs, *n.* gripping tool with two handles.

pĭnch, *v.t.* **1.** squeeze, e.g. with the thumb and forefinger. **2.** economize''. **3.** steal. **4.** arrest. —*n.* **5.** act or instance of pinching. **6.** tiny amount.

pĭnch'hĭt'', *v.i.,* **-hit, -hitting.** substitute for someone else. —**pinch''hit'ter,** *n.*

pīne, *v.i.,* **pined, pining.** *n.v.i.* **1.** yearn, esp. painfully. **2.** gradually fail in health from grief. —*n.* **3.** cone-bearing evergreen tree with needle-like leaves.

pīne'ăp''ple, *n.* tropical plant with a juicy, edible fruit.

pĭn'fĕath''ĕr, *n.* feather just beginning to develop.

pĭn'iŏn, *n.* **1.** end of a bird's wing. **2.** small gear wheel. —*v.t.* **3.** restrain; bind.

pĭnk, *n.* **1.** light red. **2.** colorful, showy garden flower. **3.** highest condition of health. —*adj.* **4.** of the color pink.

pĭn'na·cle, *n.* highest part or position.

pĭ·nŏch'le'', *n.* game played with forty-eight cards.

pĭnt, *n.* **1.** unit of liquid measure equal to 16 fluid ounces or half a quart. **2.** unit of dry measure equal to half a quart.

pĭn'tō, *n., pl.* **-tos. 1.** horse with white and brown patches. **2.** mottled.

pĭn'ŭp'', *n.* picture of a beautiful man or woman, esp. unclothed.

pĭn'whēel'', *n.* toy with a wheel that spins on the end of a stick.

pī''ò·nēer', *n.* **1.** early settler or adventurer. **2.** first person to do something. —*v.i.* **3.** prepare a way for others.

pī'ŏŭs, *adj.* **1.** devout. **2.** sacred. —**pi'ous·ly,** *adv.* —**pi'ous·ness,** *n.*

pīpe, *n., v.t.,* **piped, piping.** *n.* **1.** tube for carrying gas, water, etc. **2.** tube with a bowl at one end for smoking tobacco. **3.** tube used in a musical instrument. —*v.t.* **4.** carry by pipe. —**pi'per,** *n.* —**pipe'line'',** *n.*

pīp'ĭng, *n.* **1.** pipes; plumbing. **2.** music of pipes. **3.** material to trim edges.

pĭp'pĭn, *n.* kind of yellowish apple.

pī'quànt, *adj.* **1.** pleasantly sharp; pungent. **2.** provocative; charming. —**pi'quan·cy,** *n.*

pĭque, *n., v.t.,* **-piqued, piquing.** *n.* **1.** irritation; resentment. —*v.t.* **2.** arouse resentment in, esp. by wounding pride. **3.** provoke or incite.

pī'ra·cÿ, *n., pl.* **-cies. 1.** robbery at sea or in the air. **2.** unauthorized use of copyrighted or patented material. —**pi'rate,** *n., v.t.*

pĭr''oŭ·ĕtte', *v.i.,* **-etted, -etting.** *n. v.i.* **1.** whirl about on one foot or on the toes, esp. in ballet. —*n.* **2.** such a movement.

pĭs''cà'tô·rĭ·àl, *adj.* pertaining to fishing.

pĭs·tă'chĭ·ō'', *n., pl.* **-os.** nut with an edible greenish seed.

pĭs'tĭl, *n.* seed-bearing organ in a flower.

pĭs'tŏl, *n.* small hand-carried firearm.

pĭs'tŏn, *n.* reciprocating disk moved by the pressure of steam, combustion gas, etc. in a cylinder.

pĭt, *n., v.t.,* **pitted, pitting.** *n.* **1.** hole in the ground. **2.** cavity or hollow in the body. **3.** front part of the main floor in a theater. **4.** stone or seed of a fruit. —*v.t.* **5.** set against another. **6.** remove the pit from.

pĭtch, *v.t.* **1.** set up, as a tent. **2.** throw or toss. **3.** set at a certain level or point. —*v.i.* **4.** fall or plunge. —*n.* **5.** height. **6.** slope. **7.** musical tone. **8.** sticky substance from coal tar or pine bark. **9.** act or instance of pitching.

pĭtch'blĕnde'', *n.* mineral that is the principal source of radium and uranium.

pĭtch'ĕr, *n.* **1.** spouted container for liquids. **2.** one who pitches.

pĭtch′fŏrk′′, *n.* large, sharp-pointed fork for pitching hay.

pĭt′ē·oŭs, *adj.* pitiful; pathetic.

pĭt′făll′′, *n.* snare; hidden difficulty.

pĭth, *n.* **1.** loose spongy tissue. **2.** essence; gist. —**pith′y**, *adj.*

pĭt′ĭ·a·ble, *adj.* **1.** deserving pity. **2.** contemptible. —**pĭt′i·a·bly**, *adv.*

pĭt′ĭ·fŭl, *adj.* **1.** deserving pity. **2.** feeling pity. —**pit′i·ful·ly**, *adv.* —**pĭt′i·ful·ness**, *n.*

pĭt′tănce, *n.* small portion or amount.

pĭ·tū′ĭ·tār′′ÿ, *n.* pertaining to a gland at the base of the brain.

pĭtÿ, *n.*, *pl.* **pities**, *v.t.*, **pitied, pitying.** *n.* **1.** sympathy for wretchedness. **2.** cause for regret. —*v.t.* **3.** feel pity for. —**pĭt′i·less**, *adj.* —**pĭt′i·less·ly**, *adv.*

pĭv′ŏt, *n.* **1.** point or object for turning. —*v.i.* **2.** turn around a point.

pĭx′ÿ, *n.*, *pl.* **pixies.** fairy; mischievous sprite. Also, **pix′ie.**

pĭz′za, *n.* flat pie covered with a spiced mixture of tomato sauce, cheese, etc.

plăc′ărd, *n.* posted public notice.

plă′cāte, *v.t.*, **-cated, -cating.** appease; pacify. —**pla′ca·ble**, *adj.* —**pla·ca′tion**, *n.*

plăce, *n.*, *v.t.*, **placed, placing.** *n.* **1.** particular point in space. **2.** function. **3.** social position. **4.** stead; lieu. —*v.t.* **5.** put in a place. **6.** identify; recognize. —**place′ment**, *n.*

plă·cĕn′tă, *n.* uterine organ which nourishes the fetus.

plăc′ĕr, *n.* gravel containing gold particles.

plăc′ĭd, *adj.* serene; peaceful. —**plac′id·ly**, *adv.* —**pla·cid′i·ty**, *n.*

plăck′ĕt, *n.* slit in a garment.

plā′gĭ·a·rīze′′, *v.t.*, **-rized, -rizing.** appropriate wrongfully, as another's writings. —**pla′gi·a·rism′′**, *n.* —**pla′gi·a·rist**, *n.*

plāgue, *n.*, *v.t.*, **plagued, plaguing.** *n.* **1.** pestilence. **2.** affliction; vexation; irritation. —*v.t.* **3.** trouble; annoy.

plăid, *n.* **1.** woolen garment with a pattern of multi-colored crossbars. —*adj.* **2.** such a pattern.

plāin, *adj.* **1.** evident; obvious. **2.** candid. **3.** unpretentious. **4.** simple, uncompli-

cated. **5.** homely. —*n.* **6.** flat, open area or space of ground. —**plain′ly**, *adv.*

plāin′tĭff, *n.* complaining party in a civil case.

plāin′tĭve, *n.* melancholy, sad.

plāit, *n.*, *v.t.* **1.** braid. **2.** pleat.

plăn, *n.*, *v.t.*, **planned, planning.** *n.* **1.** drawing or diagram. **2.** intended scheme or method. —*v.t.* **3.** make a plan of. —**plan′ner**, *n.*

plāne, *n.*, *adj.*, *v.*, **planed, planing.** *n.* **1.** flat surface. **2.** level, e.g. of experience, attainment, etc. **3.** airplane. **4.** bladed tool for smoothing wood. —*adj.* **5.** flat, level. **6.** smooth or shape with a plane. —*v.i.* **7.** glide.

plăn′ĕt, *n.* solid celestial body that revolves around the sun. —**plan′e·tar′′ÿ**, *n.*

plăn′′e·tār′ĭ·ŭm, *n.* optical device which projects images of celestial bodies on a dome.

plănk, *n.* long slab of lumber.

plănt, *n.* **1.** any of the vegetable group of organisms. **2.** buildings and equipment of a business. —*v.t.* **3.** put in the ground to grow. **4.** put plants in. —**plant′er**, *n.*

plăn·tā′tion, *n.* estate esp. for farming, etc.

plăque, *n.* decorative or commemorative tablet.

plăs′mä, *n.* liquid element of blood or lymph.

plăs′tĕr, *n.* **1.** composition applied to walls, etc. **2.** medicinal dressing. —*v.t.* **3.** treat or cover with plaster.

plăs′tĭc, *n.* **1.** molded synthetic material. —*adj.* **2.** capable of being molded. **3.** characterized or produced by molding. —**plas·tic′i·ty**, *n.*

plāte, *n.*, *v.t.*, **plated, plating.** *n.* **1.** thin, flat piece of material. **2.** shallow dish from which food is served and eaten. **3.** silver or gold ware. **4.** denture. —*v.t.* **5.** coat with metal.

pla·teau (plă·tō′), *n.* large, raised plain.

plăt′fŏrm, *n.* **1.** raised floor area. **2.** declaration of political principles.

plăt′ĭ·nŭm, *n.* valuable, silver-white metallic element.

plăt′ĭ·tūde′′, *n.* trite, pompous, or self-righteous remark. —**plat′′i·tu′di·nous**, *adj.*

plá·tŏn´ĭc, *adj.* **1.** spiritual; idealistic. **2.** pertaining to close, non-sexual love.

plá·tŏon´, *n.* small military unit.

plăt´tēr, *n.* large, shallow serving dish.

plăt´y·pŭs, *n.* small Australian aquatic mammal.

plaū´dĭt, *n.* burst of applause.

plaū´sĭ·ble, *adj.* seemingly true or believable. **—plau´si·bil´i·ty**, *n.* **plau´si·bly**, *adv.*

plăy, *n.* **1.** dramatic composition. **2.** recreational activity. **3.** fun; pleasure. **4.** maneuver, as in sports. **5.** free motion. **—v.t. 6.** participate in a play or game. **7.** perform on a musical instrument. **—v.i. 8.** amuse oneself. **9.** move freely. **—play´er**, *n.* **—play´ful**, *adj.*

plăy´pĕn, *n.* portable enclosed play area for a baby.

plăy´thing, *n.* toy.

plăy´wright, *n.* writer of plays.

plá´zà, *n.* **1.** public square. **2.** shopping center.

plēa, *n.* **1.** appeal. **2.** acknowledgment or denial of guilt.

plēad, *v.*, **pleaded** or **pled**, **pleading.** *v.i.* **1.** appeal earnestly. **2.** make allegations in court. **3.** argue a case in court. **—v.t. 4.** allege in excuse or justification.

plĕas´ănt, *adj.* agreeable; pleasing. **—pleas´ant·ly**, *adv.*

plĕas´ăn·trў, *n.*, *pl.* **-tries.** humorous or agreeable remark.

plēase, *v.*, **pleased**, **pleasing.** *v.t.* **1.** give satisfaction or pleasure to. **—v.i. 2.** give pleasure. **—interj. 3.** will you kindly? **—pleas´ing·ly**, *adv.*

plĕas´ûre, *n.* **1.** enjoyment. **2.** will or desire. **—pleas´ur·a·ble**, *adj.*

plēat, *n.* **1.** double fold in cloth. **—v.t. 2.** fold in pleats.

plē·bē·iàn, *adj.* **1.** of or pertaining to the common people. **2.** common; vulgar. **—n. 3.** plebeian person.

plĕb´´ĭ·scīte´, *n.* direct vote by the people.

plĕc´trŭm, *n.* pick for a guitar, etc.

plĕdge, *n.*, *v.*, **pledged**, **pledging.** *n.* **1.** solemn promise or oath. **2.** property given in security for a loan. **—v.t. 3.** bind or vow by a pledge. **4.** stake.

plē´nà·rў, *adj.* full; complete.

plĕn´´ĭ·pŏ·tĕn´tĭ·ăr´´ў, *n.*, *pl.* **-aries.** diplomat having full authority.

plĕn´ĭ·tūde´´, *n.* fullness.

plĕn´tў, *n.* abundant supply. **—plen´te·ous, plen´ti·ful**, *adj.*

plĕth´o·rà, *n.* profuseness.

pleu´rĭ·sў, *n.* inflammation of chest and lung membranes.

plĕx´ŭs, *n.* **1.** network of nerves or blood vessels. **2.** intricate network of component parts.

pli´a·ble, *adj.* **1.** flexible or easily bent. **2.** easily influenced; adaptable. **—pli´´a·bil´i·ty**, *n.*

plī´ănt, *adj.* pliable. **—pli´an·cy**, *n.*

plī´ĕrs, *n. pl.* small pincers for grabbing, bending, etc.

plĭght, *n.* **1.** predicament. **—v.t. 2.** promise in marriage.

plŏd, *v.i.*, **plodded**, **plodding**, **1.** walk slowly or heavily. **2.** work laboriously; drudge. **—plod´der**, *n.*

plŏt, *n.*, *v.*, **plotted**, **plotting.** *n.* **1.** secret scheme. **2.** outline of a novel, etc. **3.** piece of land. **—v.t. 4.** plan secretly. **5.** mark on a map, esp. position or course. **—v.i. 6.** make secret plans; conspire. **—plot´ter**, *n.*

plŏv´ĕr, *n.* shore bird related to the sandpiper.

plŏw, *n.* **1.** implement for dividing soil. **2.** scraping implement for removing snow. **—v.t. 3.** turn or furrow with or as with a plow. **—v.i. 4.** move slowly or forcefully. Also, **plough. —plow´man**, *n.*

plŏw´shàre´´, *n.* blade of a plow.

plŏў, *n.* trick intended to trap or embarrass; tactic.

plŭck, *v.t.* **1.** pull things from. **2.** pull suddenly or forcefully. **—n. 3.** courage.

plŭg, *n.*, *v.*, **plugged**, **plugging.** *n.* **1.** object for stopping a hole. **2.** device on an electrical cord which makes the connection in the socket. **3.** *Informal.* endorsement or advertisement. **—v.t. 4.** stop or close with a plug; insert.

plŭm, *n.* sweet, juicy fruit.

plŭm´age, *n.* feathers of a bird; finery, esp. in dress.

plŭmb, *n.* **1.** heavy weight on a measuring line. **—adv. 2.** vertically. **3.** fully. **—adj. 4.** vertical. **—v.t. 5.** measure the depth of.

plŭmb´ĭng, *n.* system of water pipes. **—plumb´er**, *n.*

plüme, *n.* **1.** feather, esp. a large, conspicuous one. **2.** ornamental tuft.

plüm′mĕt, *n.* **1.** plumb on a line. —*v.i.* **2.** plunge.

plŭmp, *adj.* **1.** fat; chubby. —*v.i.* **2.** drop or fall heavily. **3.** favor something strongly.

plŭn′dĕr, *v.t.* **1.** rob or pillage. —*n.* **2.** act or instance of plundering. **3.** loot; spoils.

plŭnge, *v.,* **plunged, plunging.** *n. v.t.* **1.** thrust, as into liquid. **2.** thrust into a condition or predicament. —*v.i.* **3.** rush; dash. **4.** pitch forward. —*n.* **5.** dive or fall.

plü′răl, *adj.* denoting more than one.

plü·răl′ĭ·tў, *n.* **1.** majority. **2.** number of votes for a leading candidate over the number for a rival.

plŭs, *prep.* **1.** increased by. —*n.* **2.** mathematical sign for addition or for a positive number. **3.** something additional. —*adj.* **4.** pertaining to addition. **5.** positive.

plŭsh, *n.* **1.** long-piled fabric. —*adj.* **2.** fancy. —**plush′y**, *adj.*

plü·tŏc′rȧ·cў, *n., pl.* **-cies. 1.** rule by or power of the wealthy. **2.** controlling wealthy group. —**plu′to·crat′′i**, *n.*

plü·tō′nĭ·ŭm, *n.* radioactive element.

plȳ, *v.,* **plied, plying.** *n., pl.* **plies.** *v.t.* **1.** work at or with. **2.** attempt to persuade. —*v.t., v.i.* **3.** travel regularly. —*n.* **4.** thickness or layer.

plȳ′wŏŏd, *n.* sheeting of thin plies of wood glued together.

pneu·măt′ĭc, *adj.* pertaining to, or using air or wind.

pneŭ·mō′nĭȧ, *n.* inflamed lung disease.

pōach, *v.i.* **1.** trespass to hunt or fish illegally. —*v.t.* **2.** cook in hot but not boiling water. —**poach′er**, *n.*

pŏck, *n.* mark on the skin; scar, esp. from smallpox.

pŏck′ĕt, *n.* **1.** pouch in a garment. **2.** cavity. **3.** isolated group or area. —*v.t.* **4.** put in one's pocket. **5.** take possession of.

pŏck′ĕt·bŏŏk′′, *n.* purse; handbag.

pŏd, *n.* vegetable seed covering.

pō·dī′a′trĭst, *n.* medical treatment of the foot. —**po·di′a′trist**, *n.*

pō′dĭ·ŭm, *n.* small platform.

pō′ĕm, *n.* composition in verse.

pō′ĕt·rў, *n.* rhythmical verse composition. —**po′et**, *fem.,* **po′et·ess**, *n.* —**po·et′ic**, **po·et′i·cal**, *adj.*

pō′grŏm, *n.* organized massacre.

poign′ant (poin′yȧnt), *adj.* deeply moving. —**poign′an·cy**, *n.*

pōĭn·sĕt′tĭ·ȧ, *n.* tropical plant with scarlet flowers.

pōĭnt, *n.* **1.** sharp end. **2.** dot. **3.** specific time or position. **4.** individual detail or idea. **5.** reason or meaning. —*v.i.* **6.** indicate a direction. —*v.i.* **7.** direct or turn. —**point′less**, *adj.*

pōĭnt′-blänk′, *adj.* **1.** direct; plain. —*adv.* **2.** directly.

pōĭnt′ēr, *n.* **1.** something that points or indicates. **2.** breed of hunting dog.

pōĭse, *n., v.,* **poised, poising.** *n.* **1.** balance; composure. —*v.i.* **2.** be balanced. **3.** hover, e.g. a bird in the air. —*v.t.* **4.** balance.

pōĭ′sȯn, *n.* **1.** substance that kills or harms. —*v.t.* **2.** administer poison to. **3.** corrupt. —**poi′son·ous**, *adj.*

pōke, *v.,* **poked, poking.** *n. v.i., v.t.,* **1.** thrust.

pōk′ēr, *n.* **1.** metal rod for poking fires. **2.** card game.

pō′lȧr, *adj.* pertaining to a pole of the earth, a magnet, etc.

pōle, *n.* **1.** long, slender, round object. **2.** end of an axis. **3.** terminal of a battery. **4.** area where magnetism is concentrated.

pōle′căt′′, *n.* skunk.

pó·lĕm′ĭcs, *n.* art of argument. —**po·lem′ic**, *adj.*

pó·lĭce′, *n., v.t.,* **-liced, -licing.** *n.* **1.** governmental organization for enforcing the law. —*v.t.* **2.** control or regulate. —**po·lice′man**, *fem.,* **po·lice′wom′′an**, *n.*

pŏl′ĭ·cў, *n., pl.* **-cies. 1.** course of principle action. **2.** insurance contract.

pŏl′′ĭ·ō·mȳ′′ĕ·lī′tĭs, *n.* infantile spinal paralysis. Also, **po′li·o.**

pŏl′ish, *v.t.* **1.** make smooth and glossy. **2.** refine in behavior. **3.** bring to a perfected state. —*n.* **4.** polishing material. **5.** gloss. **6.** refinement.

pō′lĭt·bū′′rō, *n.* primary governing body of a Communist country.

pó·līte′, *adj.* **1.** marked by good manners.

2. cultivated. **—po·lite'ly,** *adv.* **—po·lite'ness,** *n.*

pol'i·tĭc, *adj.* **1.** expedient. **2.** political.

pol'i·tics, *n.* **1.** theory and conduct of government. **2.** political affairs and methods. **—po·lit'i·cal,** *adj.* **—pol''i·ti'cian,** *n.*

pol'kȧ, *n.* lively dance, eastern European in origin.

pŏll, *n.* **1.** casting of votes. **2.** total of votes. **3.** place of voting. **4.** solicitation of opinion. **—v.t. 5.** receive votes. **6.** question regarding opinions.

pŏl'lĕn, *n.* spores of a seed plant. **—pol'li·nate'',** *v.t.* **—pol''li·na'tion,** *n.*

pol·lūte', *v.t.,* **-luted, -luting.** make impure; contaminate. **—pol·lu'tion,** *n.*

pō'lō, *n.* ball game played on horseback.

pŏl''o·nāise', *n.* slow dance from Poland.

po·lō'nĭ·ŭm, *n.* radioactive metallic element.

pŏl'tẽr·geīst'', *n.* mischievous ghost or spirit.

pŏl·trōōn', *n.* coward.

pŏl'y·ăn''drȳ, *n.* marriage to more than one husband at a time.

po·lȳg'a·mȳ, *n.* marriage to more than one spouse at a time. **—po·lyg'a·mist,** *n.* **—po·lyg'a·mous,** *adj.*

pŏl'y·glŏt'', *adj.* **1.** knowing a number of languages. **2.** made up of several languages.

pŏl'y·gŏn'', *n.* closed plane figures with three or more sides. **—po·lyg'o·nal,** *adj.*

pŏl'y·grăph, *n.* a lie detector.

pŏl''y·hē'dron, *n., pl.* **-drons, -dra.** closed solid figure.

pŏl'y·mẽr, *n.* chemical compound of large molecules formed by smaller but similar molecules.

pŏl'yp, *n.* **1.** projecting growth from a mucous membrane surface. **2.** small aquatic organism.

po·lȳ'phó'nȳ, *n.* musical composition with independent melodic lines. **—pol''y·phon'ic,** *adj.*

pŏl''y·sȳl·lăb'ĭc, *adj.* having many syllables.

pŏl'y·thē''ĭsm, *n.* belief in more than one god. **—pol'y·the''ist,** *n.* **—pol''y·the'is·tic,** *adj.*

pŏmé'grăn''ăte, *n.* tropical red fruit with edible seeds.

pŏm'mĕl, *n., v.t.* **-eled, -eling.** *n.* **1.** knob, e.g. on a sword hilt. **—v.t. 2.** beat or strike repeatedly.

pŏmp, *n.* stately display.

pŏm'pȧ·dôur'', *n.* hair style with hair brushed high over the forehead.

pŏm'pŏn, *n.* ornamental ball or tuft.

pŏmp'oŭs, *adj.* **1.** pretentiously self-important; ostentatious. **2.** excessively dignified. **—pom·pos'i·ty,** *n.* **—pomp'ous·ly,** *adv.*

pŏn'chō, *n., pl.* **-chos.** *n.* blanket-like cloak with an opening for the head.

pŏnd, *n.* small body of water.

pŏn'dêr, *v.i., v.t.* consider deeply.

pŏn'dêr'oŭs, *adj.* **1.** heavy. **2.** lacking grace.

pōne, *n.* oval-shaped cornmeal biscuit.

pŏn'iàrd, *n.* dagger.

pŏn'tĭff, *n.* bishop or head priest, esp. a pope. **—pon·tif'i·cal,** *adj.*

pŏn·tif'i·căte, *v.i.,* **-cated, -cating.** speak dogmatically.

pŏn·tōōn', *n.* flat-bottomed boat used esp. in construction.

pō'nȳ, *n., pl.* **-nies.** young horse.

pōō'dle, *n.* curly-haired breed of dog.

pōōl, *n.* **1.** small, still body of fresh water. **2.** group of available workers, automobiles, etc. **3.** game similar to billiards. **—v.t. 4.** put into a common fund or effort.

pōōp, *n.* upper deck at the stern of a ship.

pôor, *adj.* **1.** having little money. **2.** lacking. **3.** inferior. **—n. 4.** poor people. **—poor'ly,** *adv.*

pŏp, *v.,* **popped, popping,** *n. v.i., v.t.* **1.** burst with a quick, explosive sound. **—v.i. 2.** bulge, as of the eyes. **—n. 3.** sound of popping. **4.** carbonated soft drink.

pŏp'côrn'', *n.* Indian corn whose kernels open in a soft, starchy mass when heated.

pōpe, *n. Often cap.* head of the Roman Catholic Church.

pŏp'làr, *n.* any of various quick-growing trees.

pŏp'lĭn, *n.* ribbed, plain-woven fabric.

pŏp'ō''vêr, *n.* very light biscuit.

pŏp'pȳ, *n., pl.* **-pies.** herb with a showy

flower, one type of which yields opium.

pŏp'u·lăce, *n.* people; general public.

pŏp'u·lăr, *adj.* **1.** pertaining to the general public. **2.** widely liked or approved. —**pop'u·lar·ly**, *adv.* —**pop''u·lar'i·ty**, *n.* —**pop'u·lar·ize**, *v.t.*

pŏp'u·lăte'', *v.t.*, **-lated, -lating. 1.** inhabit. **2.** furnish with inhabitants.

pŏp''u·lā'tion, *n.* **1.** number of people. **2.** body of inhabitants.

pŏp'u·lŏus, *adj.* having many people.

pôr'cě·lăin, *n.* shiny ceramic ware.

pôrch, *n.* open, often roofed, appendage to a building; veranda.

pôr'cĭne, *adj.* of or suggesting swine.

pôr'cū·pĭne'', *n.* rodent covered with stiff, sharp quills.

pôre, *v.i.*, pored, poring, *n. v.i.* **1.** meditate or read attentively. —*n.* **2.** minute opening in the skin.

pôr'gў, *n.* salt-water food fish.

pôrk, *n.* flesh of swine used as food.

pôr·nŏg'rå·phў, *n.* erotic writing or art intended for sexual excitement. —**por''no·graph'ic**, *adj.*

pô'rŏŭs, *adj.* permeable to liquids and air.

pôr'pŏise, *n.* any of several aquatic mammals including the common dolphin.

pôr'rĭdge, *n.* cereal boiled in milk or water.

pôr'rĭn·gêr, *n.* low dish, often with a handle.

pôrt, n. **1.** loading and unloading place for ships and aircraft. **2.** when facing the bow, the left side of a ship. **3.** a sweet, red wine. **4.** (computers) point at which peripheral components can be connected.

pôrt''a·ble, *adj.* easily carried; small. —**port''a·bil'i·ty**, *n.*

pôr'tăge, *n.* carrying of goods and boats overland.

pôr'tăl, *n.* gate or door.

pôr·tĕnd', *v.t.* **1.** indicate in advance. **2.** indicate; signify.

pôr'tĕnt, *n.* **1.** omen. **2.** ominous significance. —**por·ten'tous**, *adj.*

pôr'têr, *n.* **1.** doorman. **2.** baggage carrier.

pôr'têr·hŏŭse'', *n.* choice cut of beefsteak with a large tenderloin.

pôrt·fō'lĭ·ō'', *n.* **1.** portable case for documents. **2.** office and duties of a government minister. **3.** securities and stocks held by an investor. **4.** samples of work, esp. art.

pôrt'hōle'', *n.* window, esp. round, in the side of a plane or ship.

pôr'tĭ·cō'', *n., pl.* **-coes** or **-cos.** roof supported by a colonnade; porch.

pôr'tĭon, *n.* **1.** part or share. **2.** personal fate. —*v.t.* **3.** divide into portions.

pôrt'lў, *adj.* fat; chubby.

pôr'trait, *n.* picture or description of a person. —**por'trai·ture**, *n.*

pôr·trāy', *v.t.* **1.** depict or represent in a portrait. **2.** represent dramatically. —**por·tray'al**, *n.*

pôr·tū·lăc'å, *n.* tropical herb with showy flowers.

pōse, *v.*, posed, posing. *n. v.i.* **1.** hold a position. **2.** assume a character or attitude. —*v.t.* **3.** propound or state. —*n.* **4.** fixed position. **5.** assumed character. —**po'ser**, *n.*

pŏ·sĭ'tion, *n.* **1.** location. **2.** posture. **3.** opinion on an issue. **4.** job. —*v.t.* **5.** place.

pŏs'ĭ·tĭve, *adj.* **1.** affirmative. **2.** certain. **3.** with light and shade as in the original. **4.** numerically greater than zero. **5.** electrical charge with more protons than electrons. **6.** showing the presence of something tested for. —*n.* **7.** something positive. —**pos'i·tive·ly**, *adv.* —**pos'i·tive·ness**, *n.*

pŏs'sē, *n.* group or persons assisting a law enforcement officer.

pŏs·sĕss', *v.t.* **1.** have or own. **2.** dominate. —**pos·ses'sive**, *adj.* —**pos·ses'sion**, *n.* —**pos·ses'sor**, *n.*

pŏs'sĭ·ble, *adj.* capable of existing or happening. —**pos'sibly**, *adv.* —**pos''si·bil'i·ty**, *n.*

pŏs'sŭm, *n.* oppossum.

pōst, *n.* **1.** upright column or pole. **2.** appointed job, station, or task. **3.** permanent military station. —*v.t.* **4.** put up, as a public announcement. **5.** assign to a place. **6.** enter in a ledger. **7.** mail.

pōst'ăge, *n.* **1.** charge for mailing. **2.** stamps, etc. for mailing.

pōst'ăl, *adj.* pertaining to mail.

pōst'cârd'', *n.* message card mailed without an envelope.

pōst'êr, *n.* public advertisement.

pos·tē′rĭ·ör, *adj.* **1.** situated behind. **2.** later in time. —*n.* **3.** buttocks, rump.

pos·tĕr′ĭ·tȳ, *n.* **1.** descendants. **2.** succeeding or future generations.

pos′tĕrn, *n.* **1.** back door or gate. **2.** private entrance.

post′hāste′, *adv.* as quickly as possible.

post′hŭ·mŏus, *adj.* **1.** published after the death of the author. **2.** born after the death of the father. —**post′hu·mous·ly,** *adv.*

post′măn, *n.* mailman.

post′märk″, *n.* **1.** postal mark indicating a time and place of reception by a post office. —*v.t.* **2.** put a postmark on.

post′măs″tĕr, *n.* manager of a post office.

post·môr′tĕm, *adj.* **1.** following death. —*n.* **2.** examination of a corpse.

post′ôf″fice, *n.* government agency that handles mail.

post·ŏp′ĕr·ă·tĭve, *adj.* following a surgical operation.

post′pāid′, *adj., adv.* with postage prepaid.

post·pōne′, *v.t.,* **-poned, -poning.** delay, as action. —**post·pone′ment,** *n.*

post′scrĭpt″, *n.* note added to a finished letter.

pŏs·tū·lāte, *v.t.,* **-lated, -lating.** *n.* *v.t.* (pos′tyoo lāt) **1.** assume as true. —*n.* (pos′tyoo let) **2.** postulated proposition.

pŏs′tūre, *n., v.,* **-tured, -turing.** *n.* **1.** position of the body. **2.** attitude on a given subject. —*v.i.* **3.** affect an attitude. —*v.t.* **4.** place in a specific position.

post′war′, *adj.* after a war.

pō′sȳ, *n., pl.* **-sies.** small bouquet.

pŏt, *n., v.t.,* **potted, potting.** *n.* **1.** deep, round container. —*v.t.* **2.** put or plant in a pot.

pō′tà·ble, *adj.* drinkable.

pŏt′ăsh″, *n.* potassium carbonate, esp. from wood ashes.

pò·tăs′sĭ·ŭm, *n.* silver, metallic, chemical element used in glass, fertilizer, etc.

pō·tā′tion, *n.* drink, esp. alcoholic.

pò·tā′tō, *n., pl.* **-toes.** edible tuber of a common vegetable plant.

pō′tĕnt, *adj.* **1.** powerful. **2.** sexually capable. —**po′tence, po′ten·cy,** *n.*

pō′tĕn·tāte′, *n.* sovereign; ruler.

pò·tĕn′tiàl, *adj.* **1.** possible; capable of being realized. —*n.* **2.** possible ability. —**po·ten″ti·al′i·ty,** *n.* —**po·ten′tial·ly,** *adv.*

pō′tion, *n.* drink, esp. a medicinal one.

pot′pour·ri (pō″pə rē′), *n.* **1.** miscellaneous collection. **2.** flower petals and spices used for scent.

pŏt′tĕr, *n.* maker of earthenware.

pŏt′tĕr·ȳ, *n.* **1.** dishes, pots, mugs, etc. made of baked clay. **2.** place where earthenware is made.

pŏuch, *n.* **1.** sack or bag. **2.** baglike part of a marsupial.

pŏul′trȳ, *n.* domestic fowl, e.g. chicken.

pŏunce, *v.i.* **pounced, pouncing.** swoop down suddenly.

pŏund, *n.* **1.** unit of avoirdupois weight equal to 16 ounces or troy weight equal to 12 ounces. **2.** British monetary unit. **3.** enclosure for stray dogs, etc. —*v.t.* **4.** strike forcefully and repeatedly. **5.** crush or compact by pounding. —*v.i.* **6.** throb or beat violently, as the heart.

pŏund′cāke″, *n.* rich, sweet cake.

pŏur, *v.t.* **1.** cause to flow. —*v.i.* **2.** rain heavily. —*n.* **3.** act or instance of pouring.

pŏut, *v.i.* **1.** look sullen; act hurt. —*n.* **2.** sullen mood, look or behavior.

pŏv′ĕr·tȳ, *n.* **1.** lack of money. **2.** deficiency.

pŏw′dĕr, *n.* **1.** dry substance of very fine particles. —*v.t.* **2.** reduce to powder. **3.** apply powder to. —**pow′der·y,** *adj.*

pŏw′ĕr, *n.* **1.** ability to act. **2.** personal ability. **3.** authority. **4.** influential person, nation, etc. **5.** physical force. **6.** magnifying capacity of a lens. —**pow′er·ful,** *adj.* —**pow′er·ful·ly,** *adv.* —**pow′er·less,** *adj.*

pŏw′wŏw″, *n.* **1.** Native American conference. **2.** a meeting.

pŏx, *n.* any disease marked by skin pustules.

prăc′tĭ·cà·ble, *adj.* feasible.

prăc′tĭ·càl, *adj.* **1.** pertaining to practice. **2.** useful. **3.** aware of realities. **4.** virtual. —**prac″ti·cal′i·ty,** *n.* —**prac′ti·cal·ly,** *adv.*

prăc′tice, *n., v.,* **-ticed, -ticing.** *n.* **1.** custom. **2.** actual performance. **3.** repeated exercise. **4.** professional activity. —*v.i.,* *v.t.* **5.** Also, **prac'tise,** perform habitually or repeatedly. —**prac'ticed,** *adj.*

prăc·tī'tion·êr, *n.* person who practices a profession.

prăg·mă'tĭc, *adj.* concerned with practical values and consequences. —**prag'ma·tist,** *n.* —**prag'ma·tism,** *n.*

prāi'riē, *n.* flat, treeless, rolling grassland.

prāise, *n., v.t.,* **praised, praising.** *n.* **1.** expressed approval. **2.** homage. —*v.t.* **3.** express approval of. **4.** worship. —**praise'wor''thy,** *adj.*

prănce, *v.i.,* **pranced, prancing. 1.** spring on the hind legs. **2.** swagger.

prănk, *n.* mischievous trick. —**prank'ster,** *n.*

prāte, *v.,* **prated, prating.** *v.i., v.t.* talk excessively and foolishly.

prăt'tle, *v.i.,* **-tled, -tling.** *n. v.i.* **1.** chatter childishly or foolishly. —*n.* **2.** chatter. —**prat'tler,** *n.*

prăwn, *n.* large, edible, shrimplike shellfish.

prāy, *v.i.* **1.** petition or worship a divinity. **2.** implore. **3.** ask earnestly for.

prāyêr, *n.* **1.** act of addressing a divinity. —*v.t.* **2.** earnest request. —**prayer'ful,** *adj.*

prēach, *v.t.* **1.** advocate. —*v.i.* **2.** give a sermon. —**preach'er,** *n.*

prē'ăm''ble, *n.* introductory section.

prė·cār'ĭ·oŭs, *adj.* risky. —**pre·car'i·ous·ly,** *adv.*

prė·caū'tion, *n.* caution beforehand. —**pre·cau'tion·ar''y,** *adj.*

prė·cēde', *v.,* **-ceded, -ceding.** *v.i., v.t.* go before. —**pre·ced'ence,** *n.*

prĕc'ė·dĕnt, *n.* past occurrence or principle used as an example or justification.

prē'cĕpt, *n.* principle or rule of conduct.

prē·cĕp'tôr, *n.* teacher or tutor.

prē'cĭnct, *n.* administrative district.

prē'cioŭs, *adj.* **1.** valuable. **2.** cherished. **3.** overly refined. —**pre'cious·ly,** *adv.*

prĕc'ĭ·pĭce, *n.* steep cliff.

prė·cĭp'ĭ·tāte'', *v.t.,* **-tated, -tating.** *adj., n. v.t.* **1.** throw down violently. **2.** hasten in occurring. **3.** separate from a solution. **4.** condense. —*adj.* **5.** hasty; rash; headlong. —*n.* **6.** condensed moisture. —**pre·cip''i·ta'tion,** *n.*

prė·cĭp'ĭ·toŭs, *adj.* **1.** steep. **2.** precipitate.

prė·cīse', *adj.* **1.** specific. **2.** scrupulous; strict. —**pre·ci'sion, pre·cise'ness,** *n.* —**pre·cise'ly,** *adv.*

pre·cis (prā sē'), *n.* concise summary.

prė·clūde', *v.t.,* **-cluded, -cluding.** exclude the possibility of. —**pre·clu'sion,** *n.* —**pre·clu'sive,** *adj.*

prė·cō'cioŭs, *adj.* advanced in development, esp. of the mind. —**pre·coc'i·ty,** *n.*

prē''con·cēive', *v.t.* form an idea or opinion of in advance. —**pre''con·cep'tion,** *n.*

prē''cûr'sôr, *n.* **1.** forerunner. **2.** harbinger.

prĕd'ė·cĕs''sôr, *n.* person or thing that precedes another.

prē·dĕs''tĭ·nā'tion, *n.* determination in advance of actions and consequences; fate. —**pre·des'tine,** *v.t.*

prė·dĭc'ă·mĕnt, *n.* difficult or dangerous situation.

prĕd'ĭ·cāte'', *v.t.,* **-cated, -cating.** *n. v.t.* **1.** declare; assume. **2.** base on an assumption. —*n.* (pred'ək ət) **3.** *Grammar.* part of a sentence or clause expressing what is said of its subject. —**pred''i·ca'tion,** *n.*

prė·dĭct', *v.t.,* tell in advance. —**pre·dic'tion,** *n.* —**pre·dict'a·ble,** *adj.*

prē''dĭ·lĕc'tion, *n.* preference; inclination.

prė·dŏm'ĭ·nāte'', *v.,* **-nated, -nating.** *v.i.* **1.** be stronger or more numerous. —*v.i.* **2.** master. —**pre·dom'i·nance,** *n.* —**pre·dom'i·nant,** *adj.* —**pre·dom'i·nant·ly,** *adv.*

prē·ĕm'ĭ·nĕnt, *adj.* outstanding; superior. —**pre·em'i·nent·ly,** *adv.* —**pre·em'i·nence,** *n.*

prē''ĕmpt', *v.t.* **1.** acquire before others do. **2.** settle on to establish the right of purchase.

prēen, *v.t.* **1.** trim with the beak, as a bird. —*v.i.* **2.** fuss over one's appearance.

prē·făb'rĭ·cāte'', *v.t.,* **-cated, -cating.** assemble from large, previously finished, components.

prĕf'ăce, *n., v.t.,* **-aced, -acing.** *n.* **1.** introductory text. —*v.t.* **2.** serve as a preface to. —**pref'a·to''ry,** *adj.*

pre′fěct, *n.* magistrate; high official.

pre·fěr′, *v.t.,* **-ferred, -ferring. 1.** like better or favor more than others. **2.** present, as an accusation. **—pref′er·a·ble,** *adj.* **—pref′er·a·bly,** *adv.* **—pref′er·ence,** *n.* **—pref′′er·en′tial,** *adj.*

pre·fěr′mênt, *n.* promotion; advancement.

pre′fǐx, *n.* **1.** qualifying beginning of a word. *—v.t.* **2.** put before.

prěg′nánt, *adj.* **1.** being with child. **2.** significant; meaningful. **—preg′nan·cy,** *n.*

pre·hěn′sǐle, *adj.* able to grasp.

pre′′hǐs·tǒr′ǐc, *adj.* pertaining to the time before recorded history.

prěj′u·dǐce, *n., v.t.,* **-diced, -dicing.** *n.* **1.** opinion without adequate basis. **2.** disadvantage or injury. *—v.t.* **3.** influence or affect with prejudice. **—prej′′u·di′cial,** *adj.*

prěl′ate, *n.* high church official.

pre·lǐm′ǐ·nǎr′′y, *adj., pl.* **-naries.** *adj.* **1.** introductory. *—n.* **2.** introductory feature.

pre′lūde, *n.* preliminary to a larger work.

pre′má·tūre′′, *adj.* **1.** born or happening too early. **2.** overly hasty. **—pre′′ma·ture′ly,** *adv.* **—pre′′ma·tur′i·ty,** *n.*

pre·měd′ǐ′′tāte, *v.,* **-tated, -tating.** *v.i., v.t.* plan or consider beforehand. **—pre′′med·i·ta′tion,** *n.*

pre·mǐer′, *n.* **1.** chief officer, esp. a prime minister. *—adj.* **2.** first in rank.

pre·mǐere′, *n.* first public performance.

prěm′ǐse, *n.* **1.** basis of an argument or conclusion. **2. premises,** building and grounds; property.

pre′mǐ·ŭm, *n.* **1.** prize. **2.** high evaluation. **3.** bonus. **4.** cost of an insurance policy.

pre′′mò·nǐ′tion, *n.* foreboding; presentiment. **—pre·mon′i·to′′ry,** *adv.*

pre·nā′tál, *adj.* prior to birth.

pre·ŏc′cū·pǐed′′, *adj.* completely engrossed. **—pre·oc′cu·py′′,** *v.t.* **—pre·oc′′cu·pa′tion,** *n.*

pre·pāre′, *v.,* **-pared, -paring.** *v.t.* **1.** put in readiness. **2.** manufacture. **—v.i. 3.** get or put oneself in readiness. **—prep′′a·ra′tion,** *n.* **—pre·par′a·to′′ry,** *adj.* **—pre·par′ed·ness,** *n.*

pre·pŏn′děr·ánt, *adj.* superior in numbers, strength, etc. **—pre·pon′der·ance,** *n.*

prěp′′o·sǐ′tion, *n.* word or words placed before a noun or adjective to form a modifying phrase. **—prep′′o·si′tion·al,** *adj.*

pre′′pòs·sěss′ǐng, *adj.* impressing favorably.

pre·pŏs′těr·oŭs, *adj.* absurd.

pre·rěq′uǐ·sǐte, *n.* something required beforehand; condition.

pre·rǒg′á·tǐve, *n.* special power, right, or privilege.

prěs′age, *v.t.,* **-aged, -aging. 1.** foreshadow. **2.** predict.

prěs′′by·tē′rǐ·án, *adj.* **1.** of or pertaining to the principle of church government by a presbytery. **2.** pertaining to a Protestant church with this form of government. *—n.* **3.** member of a Presbyterian church.

prěs′by·těr′′y, *n., pl.* **-teries,** group of church elders and ministers.

pre·sci·ence (pre′shē əns, prĕsh′əns), *n.* foreknowledge; foresight. **—pre′sci·ent,** *adj.*

pre·scrǐbe′, *v.t.,* **-scribed, -scribing.** order for use, or adoption. **—pre·scrip′tion,** *n.* **—pre·scrip′tive,** *adj.*

prěs′ênce, *n.* **1.** state of being present. **2.** vicinity or view. **3.** figure or bearing of a person.

prěs′ênt, *adj.* **1.** being or happening now. **2.** being in a specific place. **3.** *Grammar.* denoting state or action now taking place. *—n.* **4.** present time. **5.** present tense. **6.** gift. *—v.t.* (prǐ zent′) **7.** give, bring, or offer. **8.** furnish or allow. **9.** introduce or make public. **—pres′′en·ta′tion,** *n.*

pre·sěnt′a·ble, *adj.* suitable in appearance, manners, etc. **—pre·sent′ab′ly,** *adv.*

pre′·sěn′tǐ·mênt, *n.* premonition.

prěs′ênt·lў, *adv.* **1.** soon. **2.** at present; now.

pre·sěrve′, *v.t.,* **-served, -serving.** *n. v.t.* **1.** keep safe. **2.** keep in good condition. **3.** prepare for storage, as food. *—n.* **4. preserves,** preserved fruit. **5.** sanctuary for game animals. **—pres′′er·va′tion,** *n.* **—pre·serv′a·tive,** *n., adj.*

pré·sīde′, *v.i.*, **-sided, -siding.** act as chairman; be at the head of.

prĕs′ĭ·dĕnt, *n.* **1.** chief officer of a corporation. **2.** highest elected official. —**pres′i·den·cy**, *n.* —**pres′i·den′tial**, *adj.*

pré·sĭd′ĭ·ŭm, *n.* major administrative committee of a communist state.

prĕss, *v.t.* **1.** act against with weight or force. **2.** urge forcefully. **3.** oppress. **4.** iron, as clothing. —*v.i.* **5.** move or push forcefully. —*n.* **6.** journalism. **7.** machine for printing. **8.** urgency.

prĕss′ĭng, *adj.* urgent.

prĕs′sûre, *n.* **1.** exertion of force. **2.** compulsion toward a certain action or decision. **3.** urgency.

prĕs″tĭ·dĭg″ĭ·tā′tion, *n.* sleight of hand. —**pres″ti·dig′i·ta″tor**, *n.*

prĕs·tĭge (pres tēzh′), *n.* respected standing or reputation. —**pres·tig′ious**, *adj.*

prĕs′tō, *adv.* quickly.

pré·sūme′, *v.*, **-sumed, -suming.** *v.t.* **1.** take for granted. —*v.i.* **2.** act with unwarranted boldness. —**pre·sum′a·ble**, *adj.* —**pre·sum′a·bly**, *adv.*

pré·sŭmp′tion, *n.* **1.** assumption. **2.** unwarranted boldness. —**pre·sump′tive**, *adj.* —**pre·sump′tu·ous**, *adj.*

prē″sŭp·pōse′, *v.t.* **-posed, -posing. 1.** suppose beforehand. **2.** require beforehand as a condition.

pré·tĕnd′, *v.t.* **1.** imagine as a fantasy. **2.** profess or appear falsely. —*v.i.* **3.** make believe. **4.** make a claim. —**pre·ten′der**, *n.* —**pre·tense′**, *n.*

pré·tĕn′sion, *n.* **1.** ostentation; self-importance. **2.** act or instance of alleging or pretending. —**pre·ten′tious**, *adj.* —**pre·ten′tious·ly**, *adv.*

prē″tĕr·năt′ŭ·răl, *adj.* **1.** supernatural. **2.** abnormal or exceptional.

prē′tĕxt, *n.* ostensible or false reason; excuse.

prĕt′tў, *adj.*, **-tier, -tiest**, *adv.* *adj.* **1.** pleasingly attractive. —*adv.* **2.** moderately. —**pret′ti·fy″**, *v.t.* —**pret′ti·ly**, *adv.* —**pret′ti·ness**, *n.*

prĕt′zĕl, *n.* brittle, salted cracker, usually twisted.

prē·vāil′, *v.i.* **1.** be widespread. **2.** prove superior in force, etc. **3.** succeed in persuasion. —**prev′a·lent**, *adj.* —**prev′a·lence**, *n.*

pré·văr′ĭ·cāte″, *v.i.*, **-cated, -cating.** speak falsely; lie. —**pre·var″i·ca′tion**, *n.*

pré·vĕnt′, *v.t.* stop; hinder. —**pre·vent′a·ble, pre·vent′i·ble**, *adj.* —**pre·ven′tion**, *n.* —**pre·ven′tive, pre·vent′a·tive**, *adj.*

prē′vieŵ″, *n.* **1.** advance showing, as of a motion picture. —*v.t.* **2.** show or view in advance.

prē′vĭ·oŭs, *adj.* happening or going earlier. —**pre′vi·ous·ly**, *adj.*

prey, *n.* **1.** animal hunted for food. **2.** victim. —*v.i.* **3.** search for prey. **4.** have an oppressive effect.

prīce, *n.*, *v.t.*, **priced, pricing.** *n.* **1.** amount for which something is sold. **2.** value. —*v.t.* **3.** set a price on. **4.** check or ask the price of.

prīce′less, *adj.* invaluable; beyond any price.

prick, *n.* **1.** puncture or cut from a thorn, needle, etc. —*v.t.* **2.** pierce or stab lightly.

prick′lў, *adj.* sharp; scratchy.

prīde, *n.*, *v.t.*, **prided, priding.** *n.* **1.** high opinion of one's worth. **2.** self-respect. **3.** person or object one is proud of. **4.** a group of lions. —*v.t.* **5.** give pride to.

prīĕst, *n.* **1.** clergyman; person authorized to perform religious ceremonies. **2.** Also, *fem.*, **priest′ess**, one who performs religious rites. —**priest′hood**, *n.* —**priest′ly**, *adj.*

prĭg, *n.* self-righteous person. —**prig′gish**, *adj.*

prĭm, *adj.* rigidly proper. —**prim′ly**, *adv.*

prī″mă·dŏn′nà, *n.* **1.** principal female opera singer. **2.** *Informal.* temperamental or vain person.

prī′măl, *adj.* **1.** primitive; original. **2.** most important; basic.

prī″mā′rў, *adj.*, *n.*, *pl.* **-ries.** *adj.* **1.** first in rank or importance. **2.** first in time. —*n.* **3.** preliminary election. —**pri′mar′i·ly**, *adv.*

prī′māte, *n.* **1.** any of the order of mammals that includes man. **2.** high church official.

prīme, *adj.*, *n.*, *v.t.*, **primed, priming.** *adj.* **1.** first in rank, value, etc. **2.** original. —*n.* **3.** best part or period. —*v.t.* **4.** prepare.

prim'ĕr, *n.* **1.** elementary or basic book. **2.** (prī'mər) material for preparing a surface.

prī·mē'vàl, *adj.* pertaining to the earliest ages.

prĭm'ĭ·tĭve, *adj.* **1.** earliest. **2.** simple; crude. —*n.* **3.** naive work of art. —**prim'i·tive·ly,** *adv.* —**prim'i·tive·ness,** *n.*

prĭmp, *v.t., v.i.* dress or adorn oneself fastidiously.

prĭm'rōse'', *n.* colorful perennial garden flower.

prĭnce, *n.* **1.** son of royalty. **2.** ruler. Also, *fem.,* **prin'cess.**

prĭnce'lȳ, *adj.* lavish.

prĭn'cĭ·pàl, *adj.* **1.** most important. —*n.* **2.** leader. **3.** head of a school. **4.** capital sum. —**prin'ci·pal·ly,** *adv.*

prĭn''cĭ·pǎl'ĭ·tȳ, *n., pl.* **-ties.** state governed by a prince.

prĭn'cĭ·ple, *n.* **1.** rule of action, conduct, or belief. **2.** adherence to rules of conduct. **3.** scientific law.

prĭnt, *v.t.* **1.** reproduce from inked type. **2.** produce a photographic positive from. —*v.i.* **3.** draw letters or characters. —*n.* **4.** state of being printed. **5.** printed lettering. **6.** printed picture. —**print'er,** *n.*

prĭnt'ĕr, *n.* **1.** one who prints. **2.** (computers) device for transcribing data to paper.

prĭnt'ōut, *n., v.* (computers) data transcribed onto paper.

prī'ör, *adj.* **1.** earlier. —*adv.* **2.** previously. —*n.* **3.** Also, *fem.,* **pri'or·ess,** head of a religious house. —**pri'o·ry,** *n.*

prī·ôr'ĭ·tȳ, *n., pl.* **-ties.** **1.** state of being earlier in time. **2.** precedence in order, privilege, etc.

prĭsm, *n.* three-sided glass object that breaks light into its spectrum. —**pris'ma'tic,** *adj.*

prĭs'ŏn, *n.* jail; building for confining criminals. —**pris'on·er,** *n.*

prĭs'tĭne, *adj.* unspoiled; pure.

prī'vàte, *adj.* **1.** belonging to a specific person or group. **2.** confidential.—*n.* **3.** lowest soldier. —**pri'vate·ly,** *adv.* —**pri'va·cy,** *n.*

prī''và·tēer', *n.* private ship commissioned for warfare.

prī·vā'tion, *n.* **1.** deprivation. **2.** lack; want; need.

prĭv'ĭ·lĕge, *n.* special advantage. —**priv'i·leged,** *adj.*

prĭv'ȳ, *adj., n., pl.* **privies.** *adj.* **1.** admitted to a secret. **2.** private; personal. —*n.* **3.** outhouse; outdoor toilet.

prīze, *n., v.t.,* **prized, prizing.** *n.* **1.** reward for victory. **2.** something desirable. —*v.t.* **3.** value or esteem highly.

prō, *n., pl.* **pros,** *adv., adj. n.* **1.** *Informal.* professional. —*adv., adj.* **2.** in favor.

prŏb'à·ble, *adj.* **1.** likely to happen, etc. **2.** giving ground for belief. —**prob'a·bly,** *adv.* —**prob''a·bil'i·ty,** *n.*

prō'bāte, *n., adj., v.t.,* **-bated, -bating.** *n.* **1.** certification of a will. —*adj.* **2.** of or pertaining to probate. —*v.t.* **3.** establish the validity of.

prō·bā'tion, *n.* act or instance of testing. —**pro·ba'tion·ar''y,** *adj.*

prōbe, *v.t.,* **probed, probing,** *n.* *v.t.* **1.** search into thoroughly. —*n.* **2.** surgical instrument for examining wounds, etc.

prŏb'lĕm, *n.* question or situation involving difficulty. —**prob''lem·at'i·cal,** *adj.*

prō·bŏs'cĭs, *n., pl.* **-ces.** flexible snout, e.g. an elephant's trunk.

prō·cēed', *v.i.* **1.** go onward. **2.** continue an action. **3.** issue forth. —*n.* **4.** **proceeds,** revenue from selling. —**pro·ce'dure,** *n.* —**pro·ce'du·ral,** *adj.*

prō·cēed'ĭng, *n.* **1.** action or conduct. **2.** **proceedings, a.** records of a meeting, etc. **b.** legal action.

prō'cĕss, *n.* **1.** series of actions ending in a result. **2.** continuous action. **3.** legal summons. —*v.t.* **4.** treat or prepare by a specific process.

prō·cĕs'sion, *n.* parade.

prō·cĕs'sion·àl, *n.* **1.** hymn for a procession. **2.** hymnbook.

prō-choīce, *adj.* supporting legalized abortion.

prō·clāim', *v.t.* **1.** announce publicly. **2.** reveal conspicuously. —**proc''la·ma'tion,** *n.*

prō·clĭv'ĭ·tȳ, *n., pl.* **-ties.** natural tendency or inclination.

prō·crǎs'tĭ·nāte'', *v.,* **-nated, -nating.**

v.i., v.t. put off to another time. —**pro·cras′′ti·na′tion**, *n.* —**pro·cras′ti·na′′tor**, *n.*

pro·cure′, *v. t.,* **-cured, -curing. 1.** obtain. **2.** bring about. —**pro·cure′ment**, *n.*

prod, *v.t.,* **prodded, prodding,** *n. v.t.* **1.** poke; jab. **2.** goad; incite. —*n.* **3.** poke. **4.** pointed instrument.

prod′i·gal, *adj.* **1.** recklessly extravagant. **2.** lavish. —**prod′′i·gal′i·ty**, *n.*

pro·di′gious, *adj.* **1.** wonderful. **2.** huge. —**pro·di′gious·ly**, *adv.*

prod′i·gy, *n., pl.* **-gies.** very talented young person.

pro·duce′, *v.,* **-duced, -ducing**, *v.t.* **1.** bring into existence. **2.** give birth to or bear. **3.** exhibit. —*n.* (prō′dōōs) **4.** product. **5.** fresh fruit and vegetables. —**pro·duc′er**, *n.* —**pro·duc′tion**, *n.* —**pro·duc′tive**, *adj.* —**pro′′duc·tiv′i·ty, pro·duc′tive·ness**, *adj.* —**pro′′duc·tiv′i·ty, pro·duc′tive·ness**, *n.*

pro·fam′i·ly, *adj.* anti-abortion; pro-life.

pro·fane′, *adj., v.t.,* **-faned, -faning.** *adj.* **1.** secular. **2.** impure; foul. **3.** irreverent; disrespectful. —*v.t.* **4.** treat with irreverence.

pro·fan′i·ty, *n.* **1.** sacrilege. **2.** cursing.

pro·fess′, *v.t.* **1.** claim of oneself. **2.** affirm allegiance to or faith in.

pro·fes′sion, *n.* **1.** learned occupation. **2.** act or instance of professing.

pro·fes′sion·al, *adj.* **1.** pursuing a profession. **2.** pertaining to a profession. **3.** meeting the standards of a profession. —*n.* **4.** professional person. —**pro·fes′sion·al·ly**, *adv.* —**pro·fes′sion·al′′ism**, *n.*

pro·fes′sor, *n.* college teacher of the highest rank. —**pro′′fes·sor′i·al**, *adj.*

prof′fer, *v.t., n.* offer.

pro·fi′cient, *adj.* skillful; learned. —**pro·fi′cient·ly**, *adv.* —**pro·fi′cien·cy**, *n.*

pro·file, *n.* **1.** side view. **2.** succinct sketch of a person. —*v.t.* **3.** do a biographical profile of.

prof′it, *n.* **1.** gain from a business deal. **2.** net gain from business. **3.** benefit. —*v.i.* **4.** gain a profit. **5.** take advantage. —**prof′it·a·ble**, *adj.* —**prof′it·a·bly**, *adv.*

prof′′it·eer′, *n.* **1.** person who takes an unreasonably large profit. —*v.i.* **2.** act as a profiteer.

prof′li·gate, *adj.* **1.** licentious. **2.** extravagant. —*n.* **3.** profligate person. —**prof′li·ga·cy**, *n.*

pro·found′, *adj.* **1.** characterized by deep thought. **2.** deeply felt. **3.** deep. —**pro·found′ly**, *adv.* —**pro·fun′di·ty**, *n.*

pro·fuse′, *adj.* **1.** plentiful. **2.** lavish. —**pro·fuse′ly**, *adv.* —**pro·fus′ion, pro·fuse′ness**, *n.*

pro·gen′i·tor, *n.* forefather; precursor.

prog′e·ny, *n., pl.* **-nies.** children; descendants.

prog·no′sis, *n., pl.* **-noses.** forecast of the course of a disease.

prog·nos′ti·cate′, *v.,* **-cated, -cating.** *v.t.* **1.** predict; presage. —*v.i.* **2.** prophesy. —**prog·nos′′ti·ca′tion**, *n.*

pro′gram, *n.* **1.** plan; method. **2.** list of subjects or events. **3.** (computers) a set of instructions to perform specific operations to data. —*v.* **4.** create a computer program. —**pro′′gram·ming**, *n.*

prog′ress, *n.* (prog′res) **1.** advancement. **2.** improvement. —*v.i.* (pro gres′) **3.** advance. **4.** improve. —**pro·gres′sion**, *n.* —**pro·gres′sive**, *adj.* —**pro·gres′sive·ly**, *adv.*

pro·hib′it, *v.t.* **1.** forbid. **2.** prevent. —**pro·hib′i·tive**, *adj.* —**pro′′hi·bi′tion**, *n.* —**pro′′hi·bi′tion·ist**, *n.*

proj·ect′, *n.* **1.** plan; scheme. —*v.t.* (prō jekt′) **2.** plan or intend. **3.** throw or impel forward. **4.** cast on a surface, as an image. —*v.i.* **5.** protrude. —**pro·jec′tion**, *n.* —**pro·jec′tor**, *n.*

pro·jec′tile, *n.* missile from a gun.

pro′′le·tar′i·at, *n.* working class. —**pro′′le·tar′i·an**, *n., adj.*

pro·lif′er·ate′, *v.,* **-ated, ating.** *v.i., v.t.* **1.** grow rapidly by multiplication. **2.** spread rapidly. —**pro·lif′′er·a′tion**, *n.*

pro·lif′ic, *adj.* productive.

pro′logue, *n.* introduction to a play, novel, etc. Also, **pro′log.**

pro·long′, *v.t.* lengthen, esp. in duration.

prom′′e·nade′, *n., v.,* **-naded, -nading.** *n.* **1.** leisurely walk. **2.** place for strolling. —*v.i.* **3.** take a promenade. —*v.t.* **4.** promenade on or through.

prom′i·nent, *adj.* **1.** conspicuous. **2.**

distinguished. —**prom'i·nence**, *n.*
—**prom'i·nent·ly**, *adv.*

pró·mis'cu·oŭs, *adj.* indiscriminate.
—**pro''mis·cu'i·ty**, *n.* —**pro·mis'cu·ous·ly**, *adv.*

prŏm'ise, *n., v.t.,* **-ised, -ising.** *n.* 1. assurance to do or not to do something. 2. indication of future improvement or success. —*v.t.* 3. make a promise. —*v.i.* 4. give grounds for hope. —**prom'is·ing**, *adj.*

prŏm'is·sô''rў, *adj.* containing a promise.

prŏm'ŏn·tô''rў, *n., pl.* **-ries.** high land mass jutting into the sea.

pró·môte', *v.t.* 1. advance in rank or position. 2. further the growth or progress of. —**pro·mo'ter**, *n.* —**pro·mo'tion**, *n.*

prŏmpt, *adj.* 1. ready to act. 2. quick or punctual. —*v.t.* 3. induce to action. —**prompt'ly**, *adv.*

prô·mŭl'gāte, *v.t.,* **-gated, -gating.** proclaim publicly. —**pro''mul·ga'tion**, *n.*

prōne, *adj.* 1. inclined; liable. 2. lying face downward.

prŏng, *n.* pointed projection.

prō'noŭn'', *n.* word used as a substitute for a noun.

pró·noŭnce', *v.,* **-nounced, -nouncing.** *v.t.* 1. utter; deliver. 2. declare to be. —*v.i.* 3. articulate words or phrases. —**pro·nounce'ment**, *n.*

prō·noŭnced', *adj.* strongly marked or apparent.

prō·nŭn''cī·ā'tion, *n.* act or manner of speaking.

proof, *n.* 1. evidence demonstrating a fact. 2. standardized strength for liquor. 3. preliminary printing, for inspection. —*adj.* 4. impervious; invulnerable.

proof'read'', *v.t.,* **-read, -reading.** read to check for errors. —**proof'read''er**, *n.*

prŏp, *n., v.t.,* **propped, propping.** *n.* 1. rigid support. 2. emotional support. 3. any object used in a stage play. —*v.t.* 4. support; strengthen.

prŏp''à·găn'dà, *n.* assertions, etc. intended to help or oppose a cause. —**prop''a·gan'dist**, *n.* —**prop''a·gan·dis'tic**, *adj.* —**prop''a·gan'dize**, *v.t., v.i.*

prŏp'à·gāte'', *v.,* **-gated, -gating.** *v.t., v.i.* 1. reproduce; breed. —*v.t.* 2. transmit, as ideas. —**prop''a·ga'tion**, *n.*

pró·pĕl'lêr, *n.* screwlike propelling device.

pró·pĕn'sĭ·tў, *n.* inclination; tendency.

prŏp'êr, *adj.* 1. suitable. 2. correct. 3. *Grammar.* indicating a specific person, place, or thing. —**prop'er·ly**, *adv.*

prŏp'êr·tў, *n., pl.* **-ties.** 1. possessions. 2. attribute.

prŏph·e·sў (pro'fə sī), *v.,* **-sied, -sying.** *v.t.* 1. foretell; predict. —*v.i.* 2. speak by divine inspiration. —**proph'e·cy**, *n.*

prŏph'êt, *n.* 1. utterer of divine revelations. 2. person who prophesies the future. Also, *fem.,* **proph'et·ess.** —**pro·phet'ic**, *adj.* —**pro·phet'i·cal·ly**, *adv.*

prō''phў·lăx'ĭs, *n.* prevention of or protection from disease. —**pro''phy·lac'tic**, *adj.*

prō·pĭn'quĭ'tў, *n.* kinship; nearness.

prō·pī'tī·āte', *v.t.,* **-ated, -ating.** make favorable; appease.

prō·pī'tioŭs, *adj.* favorable; auspicious. —**pro·pi'tious·ly**, *adv.*

pró·pō'nent, *n.* advocate; backer.

pró·pôr'tion, *n.* 1. quantitative relation. 2. due relationship. 3. **proportions**, dimensions. —*v.t.* 4. put in due proportion. —**pro·por'tion·al**, **pro·por'tion·ate**, *adj.*

pró·pōse', *v.,* **-posed, -posing.** *v.t.* 1. suggest or offer. 2. intend. —*v.i.* 3. suggest marriage. —**prop''o·si'tion**, *n.* —**pro·pos'al**, *n.*

pró·poŭnd', *v.t.* offer for consideration.

pró·prī'e·tôr, *n.* manager or owner. —**pro·pri'e·tor·ship''**, *n.* —**pro·pri'e·tar''y**, *adj.*

pró·prī'e·tў, *n., pl.* **-ties.** 1. respectability. 2. suitability.

pró·pŭl'sion, *n.* propelling force.

prō·rāte', *v.,* **-rated, -rating.** *v.i., v.t.* distribute or divide proportionately.

prō·sā'ĭc, *adj.* commonplace; dull.

prōse, *n.* ordinary language of speech and writing.

prŏs'e·cūte'', *v.t.,* **-cuted, -cuting.** 1. begin legal proceedings against. 2. continue to completion. —**pros''e·cu'tion**, *n.* —**pros''e·cu'tor**, *n.*

prŏs'e·lўte'', *n.* convert.

prŏs'pĕct, *n.* **1.** likelihood, esp. of success. **2.** view. **3.** potential customer or buyer. —*v.i.* **4.** search or explore, e.g. for gold. —**pros·pec'tive,** *adj.* —**pros'pec·tor,** *n.*

prŏ·spĕc'tŭs, *n.* description of a new venture, etc. for prospective buyers.

prŏs'pĕr, *v.i.* be successful. —**pros·per'i·ty,** *n.* —**pros'per·ous,** *adj.* —**pros'per·ous·ly,** *adv.*

prŏs'tāte, *n.* gland at the base of the male bladder.

prŏs'tī·tūte'', *n., v.t.,* **-tuted, -tuting.** *n.* **1.** person who engages in sexual intercourse for pay. —*v.t.* **2.** misuse, as talent. —**pros''ti·tu'tion,** *n.*

prŏs'trāte, *v.t.,* **-trated, -trating,** *adj. v.t.* **1.** lay flat. **2.** exhaust of strength. —*adj.* **3.** lying. **4.** without strength. —**pros·tra'tion,** *n.*

prŏs'ў, *adj.,* **prosier, prosiest.** dull; uninteresting.

prŏ·tĕct', *v.t.* defend or preserve. —**pro·tec'tion,** *n.* —**pro·tec'tive,** *adj.* —**pro·tec'tive·ly,** *adv.* —**pro·tec'tor,** *n.*

prŏ·tĕc'tor·āte, *n.* protection and partial control of one state by another.

prŏ·tĕ·gé (prō'tə zhā''), *n.* person under patronage. Also, *fem.,* **pro'té·gée''.**

prŏ·tē·in, *n.* nitrogenous compound essential for life processes present in living matter.

prŏ'tĕst, *n.* **1.** objection. —*v.i., v.t.* **2.** make an objection. —*v.t.* **3.** declare solemnly. —**pro''tes·ta'tion,** *n.* —**pro·tes'ter,** *n.*

Prŏt'ĕs·tànt, *n.* western Christian not belonging to the Roman Catholic Church. —**Prot'es·tant·ism'',** *n.*

prŏ'tò·cŏl, *n.* code of etiquette, esp. diplomatic.

prŏ'tŏn, *n.* elementary atomic particle carrying a positive charge.

prŏ'tò·plăsm'', *n.* basic protein substance of living matter.

prŏ'tò·type'', *n.* model; first specimen.

prŏ·trăct', *v.t.* lengthen; prolong. —**pro·trac'tion,** *n.*

prŏ·trăc'tŏr, *n.* instrument for measuring angles.

prŏ·trūde', *v.i.,* **-truded, -truding.** pro-

ject. —**pro·tru'sion,** *n.* —**pro·tru'sive,** *adj.*

prŏ·tū''bĕr·ànt, *adj.* bulging out. —**pro·tu'ber·ance,** *n.*

prōud, *adj.* **1.** having self-respect. **2.** feeling honored. **3.** arrogant. **4.** glorious. —**proud'ly,** *adv.*

prove (prōōv), *v.,* **proved, proving,** *v.t.* **1.** establish the truth of. **2.** test. —*v.i.* **3.** turn out. —**prov'a·ble,** *adj.*

prŏv'ĕn·dĕr, *n.* food.

prŏv'ĕrb, *n.* wise popular saying. —**pro·ver'bi·al,** *adj.*

prŏ·vīde', *v.,* **-vided, -viding.** *v.t.* **1.** supply; equip. **2.** yield. —*v.i.* **3.** prepare beforehand. —**pro·vi'der,** *n.*

prŏ·vī'dĕd, *conj.* if; on condition that.

prŏv'ĭ·dĕnce, *n.* **1.** divine care or guidance. **2.** economy. —**prov''i·den'tial,** *adj.* —**prov'i·dent,** *adj.*

prŏv'ince, *n.* **1.** administrative district. **2.** personal area of operations or expertise.

prŏ·vīn'cĭàl, *adj.* **1.** of a province. **2.** narrow-mindedly local.

prŏ·vī'sion, *n.* **1.** stipulation. **2.** act or instance of providing. **3.** prearrangement. **4. provisions,** food supply; goods. —*v.t.* **5.** supply with provisions.

prŏ·vī'sion·àl, *adj.* temporary; conditional.

prŏ·vī'sō, *n., pl.* **-sos, -soes.** stipulation.

prŏ·vōke', *v.t.,* **-voked, -voking. 1.** exasperate. **2.** call into being or effect. —**prov''o·ca'tion,** *n.* —**pro·voc'a·tive,** *adj.* —**pro·voc'a·tive·ly,** *adv.*

prŏ'vōst, *n.* high official, esp. of a university.

prōw, *n.* bow of a ship or airplane.

prōw'ĕss, *n.* **1.** bravery; strength, esp. military. **2.** extraordinary ability.

prōwl, *v.i.* roam about or search stealthily. —**prowl'er,** *n.*

prŏx·ĭm'ĭ·tў, *n.* nearness.

prŏx'ў, *n., pl.* **proxies. 1.** agent. **2.** authority to act or vote for another.

prūde, *n.* extremely modest person. —**prud'ish,** *adj.*

prū'dĕnce, *n.* **1.** caution. **2.** practical wisdom. —**pru'dent,** *adj.*

prūne, *v.t.,* **pruned, pruning.** *n. v.t.* **1.** cut off; trim. —*n.* **2.** dried plum.

prū'rĭ·ĕnt, *adj.* having lewd thoughts. —**pru'ri·ence,** *n.*

prȳ, v., **pried, prying.** n. v.i. **1.** inquire unjustifiably into another's affairs. —v.i. **2.** move by leverage. —n. **3.** act or instance of prying. **4.** lever.

psalm (sahm), n. sacred song or poem.

pseü·dō·ným, n. assumed or false name.

pseü·dō (soō'dō), adj. false; spurious.

psy·chè·dĕl·ĭc (sī''kə del'ik), adj. **1.** pertaining to intense hallucinatory effects. —n. **2.** hallucination-producing drug.

psy·che (sī'kē), n. human self or soul.

psy·chī'a·trȳ, n. science of healing mental disorders. —**psy·chi'a·trist**, n. —**psy''chi'at·ric**, adj.

psy'chĭc, n. **1.** medium or clairvoyant. —adj. Also, **psy'chi·cal. 2.** pertaining to the psyche. **3.** supernatural.

psy''chō·a·nǎl'ỹ·sĭs, n. detailed study and treatment of neuroses. —**psy''cho·an'a·lyst**, n. —**psy''cho·an'a·lyze**, v.t. —**psy''cho·an''a·lyt'ic**, adj.

psy·chŏl'ō·gỹ, n. **1.** study of the mind and behavior. **2.** mental and behavioral constitution. —**psy''cho·log'i·cal**, adj. —**psy·chol'o·gist**, n.

psy''chō·neu·rō'sĭs, n., pl. **-ses.** emotional disorder or disease. —**psy''cho·neu·rot'ic**, adj.

psy'chŏ·păth'', n. mentally ill person. —**psy''cho·path'ic**, adj. —**psy·chop'a·thy**, n.

psy·chō'sĭs, n., pl. **-ses.** mental disease marked by loss of contact with reality. —**psy·chot'ic**, n., adj.

psy''chō·sō·mǎt'ĭc, adj. pertaining to physical effects caused by mental states.

psy''chō·thèr'a·pȳ, n. treatment of mental and emotional disorders. —**psy''cho·ther'a·pist**, n.

ptō·mǎine (tō'mān), n. substance produced by bacteria in decaying matter.

pŭb, n. British. bar; tavern.

pū·bêr·tȳ (pyoō'bər tē), n. sexual maturity.

pŭb'lĭc, adj. **1.** of or for all people. **2.** known by or knowable to all. —n. **3.** people generally. —**pub'lic·ly**, adv.

pŭb''lĭ·cā'tion, n. **1.** act or instance of publishing. **2.** published work.

pŭb·lĭc'ĭ·tȳ, n. **1.** public attention or notice. **2.** material claiming public attention.

pŭb'lĭ·cīze'', v.t., **-cized, -cizing.** bring to public attention or notice.

pŭb'lĭsh, v.t. **1.** print or issue for distribution. **2.** announce publicly. —**pub'lish·er**, n.

pŭck'êr, v.t., v.i., n. curl; wrinkle.

pŭd'dĭng, n. soft, sweet dessert.

pŭd'dle, n. small pool of water.

pŭdg'ỹ, adj., **pudgier, pudgiest.** short and fat; chubby. —**pudg'i·ness**, n.

pueb·lo (pweb'lō), n. **1.** adobe Indian village of U.S. Southwest. **2. Pueblo,** Southwestern U.S. Indian people.

pu·er·ile (poō'ər il), adj. silly; childish. —**pu''er·il'i·ty**, n.

pu·er·per·al (poō ur'pər əl), adj. pertaining to childbirth.

pŭff, n. **1.** short quick gust, e.g. of wind. **2.** anything soft and light. **3.** light piece of pastry. —v.i. **4.** blow or breathe in puffs. **5.** become inflated or swollen. —v.t. **6.** blow or puff on.

pŭf'fĭn, n. sea bird.

pŭg, n. small short-haired dog.

pū'gĭl·ĭsm'', n. boxing. —**pu'gil·ist**, n.

pŭg·nā'cioŭs, adj. fond of fighting; belligerent. —**pug·nac'i·ty**, n.

pūke, v., **puked, puking.** v.i., v.t. vomit.

pŭl'chri·tūde'', n. beauty.

pŭll, v.t. **1.** move toward or after one. **2.** strain by pulling. **3.** select from a group. —v.i. **4.** attempt to move toward one. **5.** move oneself. —n. **6.** act or instance of pulling. **7.** something to pull on. **8.** Informal. influence.

pŭl'lĕt, n. young hen.

pŭl'lĕy, n., pl. **-leys.** wheel with a rim grooved for a rope.

pŭl'mò·nǎr''ỹ, adj. of the lungs.

pŭlp, n. **1.** soft, fleshy material. —v.t. **2.** crush or grind to pulp. —v.i. **3.** become pulp. —**pulp'y**, adj.

pŭl'pĭt, n. raised platform or lectern used by a clergyman.

pŭl'sāte'', v.i., **-sated, -sating.** throb; quiver. —**pul·sa'tion**, n.

pŭlse, n. **1.** regular throb of the arteries produced by the heart. —v.i. **2.** throb regularly.

pŭl'vêr·ize'', v., **-ized, -izing.** v.t. **1.** reduce to powder or dust. **2.** completely crush. —v.i. **3.** become reduced to dust. —**pul''ver·i·za'tion**, n.

pū′mȧ, *n.* cougar.

pŭm′ĭce, *n.* porous volcanic glass.

pŭm′mĕl, *v.t.* beat; thrash.

pŭmp, *n.* **1.** device for applying force to liquids and gases. **2.** low shoe. —*v.t.* **3.** move with a pump. **4.** inflate. **5.** attempt to wheedle information from.

pŭm″pĕr·nĭck′ĕl, *n.* hard rye bread.

pŭmp′kĭn, *n.* large orange fruit that grows on a vine.

pŭn, *n., v.i.,* **punned, punning,** *n.* **1.** play with similar-sounding words with different meanings. —*v.i.* **2.** make a pun.

pŭnch, *n.* **1.** quick blow, esp. with the fist. **2.** piercing or sinking implement. **3.** sweet mixed beverage. —*v.t.* **4.** hit. **5.** perforate. —**punch′er,** *n.*

pŭnc·tĭl′ĭ·oŭs, *adj.* adhering to correct procedure.

pŭnc′tū·ȧl, *adj.* on time; prompt. —**punc″tu·al′i·ty,** *n.* —**punc′tu·al·ly,** *adv.*

pŭnc′tū·āte″, *v.t.,* **-ated, -ating. 1.** mark with commas, periods, etc. **2.** mark or interrupt periodically. **3.** give emphasis to. —**punc″tu·a′tion,** *n.*

pŭnc′tūre, *v.t.,* **-tured, -turing,** *n. v.t.* **1.** pierce with a pointed object. —*n.* **2.** act or instance of puncturing.

pŭn′dĭt, *n.* expert.

pŭn′gĕnt, *v.t.* **1.** sharp of taste. **2.** biting. —**pun′gen·cy,** *n.* —**pun′gent·ly,** *adv.*

pŭn′ĭsh, *v.t.* **1.** subject to penalty or revenge. **2.** inflict a penalty for. —**pun′ish·a·ble,** *adj.* —**pun′ish·ment,** *n.*

pū′nĭ·tĭve, *adj.* punishing.

pŭnt, *n.* **1.** flat-bottomed shallow boat. **2.** kick in football. —*v.i.* **3.** kick in mid-air.

pū′nў, *adj.* **-nier, -niest.** small; slight; weak.

pŭp, *n.* young dog. Also, **pup′py.**

pū′pȧ, *n., pl.* **-pae, -pas.** insect halfway between larva and adult.

pū′pĭl, *n.* **1.** student. **2.** dark opening in the iris of the eye.

pŭp′pĕt, *n.* **1.** small figure moved by hand or by wires. **2.** supposedly autonomous party obeying another. —**pup″pe·teer′,** *n.*

pûr′chȧse, *v.t.,* **-chased, -chasing,** *n. v.t.* **1.** buy. —*n.* **2.** act or instance of pur-

chasing. **3.** thing purchased. **4.** leverage. —**pur′chas·er,** *n.*

pūre, *adj.,* **purer, purest. 1.** unmixed or unpolluted. **2.** absolute. **3.** abstract. **4.** innocent. —**pure′ly,** *adv.*

pu·ree (pyo͞o rā′), *n.* cooked and sieved food.

pûr′gȧ·tô″rў, *n., pl.* **-ries. 1.** temporary punishment. **2.** place for purification from sin after death.

pûrge, *v.t.,* **purged, purging.** *n. v.t.* **1.** cleanse; purify. **2.** rid; remove. **3.** eliminate or kill for political reasons. —*n.* **4.** act or instance of purging. —**pur′ga′tion,** *n.* —**pur′ga·tive,** *adj., n.*

pū′rĭ·fў, *v.,* **-fied, -fying.** *v.t.* **1.** make pure. **2.** free from sin or guilt. —*v.i.* **3.** become pure. —**pu″ri·fi·ca′tion,** *n.*

pū′rĭ·tȧn, *n.* **1.** member of a strict religious group. **2.** adherent to an unusually strict moral code. —**pu′ri·tan′i·cal,** *adj.*

pū′rĭ·tў, *n.* quality or condition of being pure.

pûrl, *v.t., v.i.* knit with an inverted stitch.

pur·lieu (par′lo͞o), *n.* bordering or outlying district.

pûr·loin′, *v.t.* steal.

pûr′ple, *n.* **1.** bluish-red color. —*adj.* **2.** of the color purple.

pur·port, *v.t.* (pər′′port′). **1.** claim or profess. **2.** express; imply. —*n.* **3.** (pər′port) significance.

pûr′pōse, *n., v.t.,* **-posed, -posing.** *n.* **1.** intention; object. —*v.t.* **2.** intend. —**pur′pose·ful,** *adj.* —**pur′pose·less,** *adj.*

pûr′pōse·lў, *adv.* intentionally.

pûrr, *n.* **1.** soft continuous sound made by a cat. —*v.i.* **2.** make this sound.

pûrse, *n., v.t.,* **pursed, pursing.** *n.* **1.** small bag for money. **2.** sum of money offered as a prize. —*v.t.* **3.** pucker.

pûrs′er, *n.* financial officer of a ship.

pûr·sū′ȧnt, *adv.* according.

pûr·sūe′, *v.t.,* **-sued, -suing. 1.** chase. **2.** proceed with. —**pur·su′ance,** *n.* —**pur·su′er,** *n.*

pûr·sūit′, *n.* **1.** act or instance of pursuing. **2.** occupation; calling.

pū·rū·lĕnt (pyo͞or′ə lənt), *adj.* containing pus. —**pu′ru·lence,** *n.*

pûr·vey, *v.t.* furnish; supply. —pur·vey'·ance, *n.* —pur·vey'·or, *n.*

pûs, *n.* yellowish fluid found in sores.

push, *v.t.* **1.** press against to move. **2.** urge; press. —*v.i.* **3.** move with force. —*n.* **4.** act or instance of pushing. —push'·er, *n.*

push'·ÿ, *adj.*, -ier, -iest. aggressive.

pū·sĭl·lăn''i·moŭs, *adj.* cowardly.

pŭss'·ÿ, *n.*, *pl.* -sies. cat. Also, puss.

pŭss'·ÿ-foŏt, *v.i.* act stealthily.

pŭssÿ wĭllŏw, *n.* small American willow tree.

pŭs'·tūle, *n.* pus-filled pimple.

pŭt, *v.*, put, putting. *v.t.* **1.** carry to a specified place. **2.** cause to be in a specified condition. **3.** present for consideration. **4.** hurl overhand. **5.** put off, postpone. **6.** put out, **a.** extinguish. **b.** trouble. —*v.i.* **7.** put up with, tolerate.

pū·tā·tive, *adj.* reputed; supposed.

pū'·trĕ·fÿ'', *v.*, -fied, -fying. *v.i.*, *v.t.* decay; rot. —pu''tre·fac'tion, *n.*

pū'·trĭd, *adj.* **1.** rotten; decayed. **2.** corrupt; vile.

pŭtt, *v.t.* Golf. **1.** hit gently. —*n.* **2.** act or instance of putting.

pŭt'·tĕr, *v.i.* **1.** be active without effect. —*n.* **2.** golf club for putting.

pŭt'·tÿ, *n.*, *v.t.*, -tied, -tying. *n.* **1.** cement of linseed oil and whiting. —*v.t.* **2.** secure with putty.

pŭz'·zle, *n.*, *v.*, -zled, -zling. *n.* **1.** device or problem posing difficulties. —*v.t.* **2.** mystify; perplex. —*v.i.* **3.** attempt to study or figure out a problem.

pÿg'·mÿ, *n.*, *pl.* -mies. dwarf.

pÿ'·lŏn, *n.* **1.** support tower. **2.** cone-shaped road marker.

pÿ''or·rhē'ȧ, *n.* disease of the gums.

pÿr'·ȧ·mĭd, *n.* **1.** structure or form with triangular sides. —*v.t.* **2.** increase gradually. —py·ram'i·dal, *adj.*

pÿre, *n.* heap of material for burning a corpse.

pÿ'·rīte, *n.* yellow sulfur and iron.

pÿ''ró·mā'nĭ·ȧ, *n.* mania for starting fires. —py''ro·ma'ni·ac'', *n.*

pÿ''rō·tĕch'nĭcs, *n.* **1.** fireworks. **2.** display of virtuosity. —pyro·tech'nic, *adj.*

pÿ'·thŏn, *n.* large constricting snake.

Q

Q, q, *n.* seventeenth letter of the English alphabet.

quăck, *n.* **1.** fraudulent doctor. **2.** sound of a duck. —*v.i.* **3.** utter a quack. —quack'·er·y, *n.*

quăd'·răn''gle, *n.* **1.** closed figure with four angles. **2.** enclosed four-sided yard. —quad·ran'gu·lar, *adj.*

quăd'·rȧnt, *n.* **1.** arc of 90°. **2.** instrument for measuring altitudes.

quăd·rȧ·phŏn'ĭc, *adj.* of a sound system using four independent speakers.

quăd''rĭ·lăt'ĕr·ȧl, *adj.* **1.** four-sided. —*n.* **2.** plane figure with four sides.

quȧ·drōōn'', *n.* a person of one-quarter black ancestry.

quăd'rū·pĕd'', *n.* animal with four feet.

quăd'rū·ple, *adj.*, *v.*, -pled, -pling. *adj.* **1.** fourfold. **2.** having four parts. —*v.t.*, *v.i.* **3.** multiply by four.

quăd·rū'plĕt, *n.* one of four children born together.

quăd·rū'plĭ·căte, *n.* any of four copies.

quaff (kwof), *v.t.* drink with gusto.

quăg'mīre'', *n.* boggy area.

qua·hog (quo'hog), *n.* edible American clam.

quăil, *n.*, *pl.* quails, quail, *v.i.* *n.* **1.** game bird. —*v.i.* **2.** lose heart or courage.

quăint, *adj.* pleasingly odd or old-fashioned. —quaint'ness, *n.* —quaint'ly, *adv.*

quăke, *v.i.*, quaked, quaking, *n.* *v.i.* **1.** tremble or shake. —*n.* **2.** earthquake.

Quăk'ĕr, *n.* member of the Society of Friends.

quăl'ĭ·fÿ'', *v.*, -fied, -fying. *v.t.* **1.** make eligible or capable. **2.** modify. —*v.i.* **3.** be qualified. —qual''i·fi·ca'tion, *n.* —qual'i·fied'', *adj.*

quăl'ĭ·tÿ, *n.*, *pl.* -ties. **1.** essential characteristic. **2.** degree of merit. **3.** excellence. —qual'i·ta''tive, *adj.*

qualm (kwahlm), *n.* **1.** misgiving. **2.** sick feeling.

quăn'dȧ·rÿ, *n.*, *pl.* -ries. perplexed state.

quăn'tĭ·tÿ, *n.*, *pl.* -ties. **1.** amount or number. **2.** large or considerable amount. —quan'ti·ta''tive, *adj.*

quâr'ȧn·tīne'', *n.*, *v.t.*, -tined, -tining.

n. **1.** isolation of suspected disease bearers. —*v.t.* **2.** put in quarantine.

quar′rel, *n.* **1.** angry argument; fight. —*v.i.* **2.** have a quarrel. —**quar′rel·some,** *adj.*

quar′rỹ, *n., pl.* **-ries,** *v.t.,* **-ried, -rying.** *n.* **1.** place from which stone is extracted. **2.** object of pursuit; prey. —*v.t.* **3.** get or take from a quarry.

quart, *n.* unit of measure equal to one fourth of a gallon.

quar′ter, *n.* **1.** fourth part. **2.** coin with the value of 25 cents. **3. quarters,** lodgings. **4.** mercy. —*v.t.* **5.** divide into quarters. **6.** lodge. —*adj.* **7.** being a quarter.

quar′ter·băck′, *n.* position in football.

quar′ter·lỹ, *adj., n., pl.* **-lies.** *adj.* **1.** occurring every three months. —*n.* **2.** periodical published four times a year.

quar′ter·măs″ter, *n.* **1.** army officer who oversees supplies, etc. **2.** petty officer in charge of a ship's signals, steering, etc.

quar·tĕt′, *n.* **1.** group of four, esp. musicians. **2.** composition for four instruments. Also, **quar·tette′.**

quar′tō, *n.* book printed on sheets folded into quarters.

quârtz, *n.* common shiny crystalline mineral.

quäsh, *v.t.* **1.** put down completely. **2.** invalidate.

quä·sī (kwah′sī), *adj.* **1.** resembling. —*adv.* **2.** seemingly.

quät′răin, *n.* four-line verse unit.

quä′věr, *v.i.* **1.** tremble. **2.** speak or sing tremulously. —*n.* **3.** quavering tone.

quay (kē), *n.* pier; wharf.

quēa′sỹ, *adj.,* **-sier, -siest. 1.** nauseous. **2.** uneasy.

quēen, *n.* **1.** female sovereign. **2.** spouse of a king. **3.** fertile female of bees.

quēer, *adj.* peculiar. —**queer′ly,** *adv.* —**queer′ness,** *n.*

quĕll, *v.t.* **1.** subdue. **2.** pacify.

quĕnch, *v.t.* **1.** slake, as thirst. **2.** extinguish. **3.** cool by immersion.

quĕr′u·loŭs, *adj.* peevish.

quĕ′rỹ, *n., pl.* **-ries,** *v.t.,* **-ried, -rying.** *n.* **1.** question; inquiry. —*v.t.* **2.** inquire regarding.

quĕst, *n., v.i.* search.

quĕs′tion, *n.* **1.** interrogative sentence. **2.**

problem or issue. —*v.t.* **3.** ask questions of. **4.** challenge; doubt. —**ques′tion·a·ble,** *adj.* —**ques′tion·er,** *n.*

ques″tion·nāire′, *n.* set or list of questions.

queue (kyōō), *n., v.,* **queued, queuing.** *n.* **1.** line of waiting persons. **2.** braid of hair at the back of the head. —*v.t., v.i.* **3.** form in a line.

quĭb′ble, *v.i.,* **-bled, -bling,** *n. v.i.* **1.** speak evasively. **2.** cavil; carp. —*n.* **3.** act or instance of quibbling.

quiche (kēsh), *n.* French tart filled with egg, cheese, etc.

quick, *adj.* **1.** prompt. **2.** intelligent. **3.** speedy. —*n.* **4.** living persons. **5.** vital part. —**quick′ly,** *adv.* —**quick′ness,** *n.*

quick′en, *v.t.* **1.** hasten. —*v.i.* **2.** become alive or sensitive.

quick′sănd″, *n.* watery, soft mass of sand that yields under weight.

quick′sĭl″věr, *n.* mercury.

quĭd, *n.* cut something chewable, esp. tobacco.

qui·es·cent (kwē·es′ent), *adj.* inactive. —**qui·es′cence,** *n.*

quī′ĕt, *adj.* **1.** at rest. **2.** silent. **3.** restrained. —*v.t.* **4.** make quiet. —*v.i.* **5.** become quiet. —*n.* **6.** silence; tranquillity. —**qui′et·ly,** *adv.* —**qui′et·ness,** *n.* —**qui′e·tude″,** *n.*

qui·e·tus (kwī ēt′əs), *n.* **1.** final settlement. **2.** death.

quĭll, *n.* **1.** large stiff feather. **2.** bristle or spine.

quĭlt, *n.* lined and padded bedcovering.

quĭnce, *n.* hard yellowish fruit.

quī′nīne, *n.* bitter saltlike substance used medically.

quĭn·tĕs′sĕnce, *n.* **1.** purest essence. **2.** completely typical example. —**quin″tes·sen′tial,** *adj.*

quĭn·tĕt′, *n.* **1.** group of five, esp. musicians. **2.** composition for five instruments. Also, **quin·tette′.**

quĭn·tŭ′ple, *adj., v.,* **-pled, -pling.** *adj.* **1.** fivefold. **2.** having five parts. —*v.t., v.i.* **3.** multiply by five.

quĭn′tŭ·plĕt, *n.* **1.** one of five children born together. **2.** group of five.

quĭp, *n., v.i.,* **quipped, quipping.** *n.* **1.** sarcastic or clever remark. —*v.i.* **2.** make a quip.

quire, *n.* set of 24 sheets of paper.

quirk, *n.* peculiarity.

quis'ling, *n.* traitor.

quit, *v.,* **quitted, quitting.** *v.t., v.i.* **1.** discontinue. —*v.t.* **2.** leave. **3.** abandon. —**quit'ter,** *n.*

quite, *adv.* **1.** completely. **2.** positively.

quits, *adj.* on equal terms.

quit'tance, *n.* **1.** recompense. **2.** discharge from obligation or debt.

quiv'êr, *v.t., v.i.* **1.** tremble; shake. —*n.* **2.** case for arrows.

quix·ôt'ĭc, *adj.* foolishly idealistic.

quiz, *v.,* **quizzed, quizzing** *n. v.t.* **1.** give a brief test to. **2.** question closely. —*n.* **3.** test or questioning.

quiz'zĭ·cál, *adj.* **1.** comically odd. **2.** questioning. **3.** chaffing. —**quiz'zĭ·cal·ly,** *adv.*

quoĭt, *n.* flat ring used in throwing games.

quŏn'dăm, *adj.* former.

quŏ'rŭm, *n.* sufficient number of attending members.

quo'tá, *n.* assigned share or number.

quo·tā'tion, *n.* **1.** word-for-word citation. **2.** specified price.

quo·tā'tion mârks, *n.* pair of punctuation marks, " ", used to mark the beginning and end of a direct quotation.

quōte, *v.t.,* **quoted, quoting,** *n. v.t.* **1.** repeat verbatim. **2.** cite as evidence. **3.** state, as a price. —*n.* **4.** quotation. —**quot'a·ble,** *adj.*

quŏth, *v.t. Archaic.* said.

quō'tiėnt, *n. Math.* number of times one number contains another.

R

R, r, *n.* eighteenth letter of the English alphabet.

răb'bĕt, *n., v.t.,* **-beted, -beting.** *n.* **1.** L-shaped notch on the end of timber, etc. —*v.t.* **2.** cut a rabbet on. **3.** join with rabbets.

răb'bī, *n., pl.* **-bis.** Jewish preacher. —**rab·bin'ic, rab·bin'i·cal,** *adj.*

răb'bĭt, *n.* small long-eared mammal.

răb'ble, *n.* mob.

răb'ĭd, *adj.* **1.** irrationally extreme. **2.** having rabies.

rā'bĭēs, *n.* infectious disease transmitted by animal bites.

răc·cōōn', *n.* small nocturnal mammal.

rāce, *n., v.,* **raced, racing.** *n.* **1.** contest of speed. **2.** group of persons with a common origin. —*v.i.* **3.** participate in a race. **4.** move quickly. —*v.t.* **5.** cause to move quickly.

rā'cĭăl, *adj.* concerning race or the differences between races. —**rac'ism,** *n.*

răck, *n.* **1.** framework for storage. **2.** bar-like gear engaging a pinion. —*v.t.* **3.** torture. **4.** strain.

răck''ĕt, *n.* **1.** noise; commotion. **2.** dishonest or illegal activity. **3.** cross-stringed light bat, used esp. in tennis.

răck''ĕ·tēer', *n.* gangster.

rac·on·teur (rak"on·tur') *n.* story-teller.

răc'ў, *adj.,* **-ier, -iest. 1.** lively. **2.** risqué.

rā'dâr, *n.* device using radio waves to locate objects.

rā'dĭ·ál, *adj.* pertaining to rays or a radius.

rā'dĭ·ant, *adj.* **1.** bright; shiny. **2.** emitting light. —**ra'di·ance,** *n.*

rā'dĭ·āte'', *v.,* **-ated, -ating.** *v.i.* **1.** move or spread like rays from a center. —*v.t.* **2.** emit, as rays.

rā'dĭ·ā''tŏr, *n.* convection heater.

răd'ĭ·cál, *adj.* **1.** fundamental. **2.** favoring drastic or extreme change. —*n.* **3.** person with radical ideas. —**rad'i·cal·ism'',** *n.*

rā'dĭ·ō'', *n.* **1.** wireless transmission of sound by electromagnetic waves. **2.** device for receiving radio transmissions.

rā''dĭ·ō·ăc'tĭve, *adj.* emitting nuclear radiation.

răd'ĭsh, *n.* edible root of a garden plant.

rā'dĭ·ŭm, *n.* radioactive metallic element.

rā'dĭ·ŭs, *n., pl.* **-dii, -diuses. 1.** straight line to an arc from its center. **2.** forearm bone.

răf'fle, *n., v.t.,* **-fled, -fling.** *n.* **1.** lottery for which chances are sold. —*v.t.* **2.** dispose of by raffle.

răft, *n.* floating platform.

răf'tėr, *n.* roof beam.

răg, *n.* torn or waste piece of cloth. —**rag'ged,** *adj.*

răg′a·mŭf′fĭn, n. scruffy child.

răge, n., v.i., **raged, raging.** n. **1.** violent anger. **2.** popular vogue. —v.i. **3.** be violently angry. **4.** proceed or prevail with violence.

răg′lăn, n. loose overcoat with shoulders continuing from the sleeves.

ra·gout (ra gōō′), n. stew.

răg′tīme″, n. syncopated American popular music.

răg′wēed″, n. weed whose pollen causes hay fever.

răid, n. **1.** sudden attack. —v.t. **2.** attack suddenly.

răil, n. **1.** horizontal bar or beam. **2.** guide for a wheel of a railroad car. **3.** railroad. **4.** wading bird. —v.i. **5.** complain bitterly.

răil′ĭng, n. barrier of uprights and rails.

răil′lĕr·ў, n. banter; ridicule.

răil′rōad″, n. **1.** road of rails on which trains run. —v.t. **2.** transport by railroad. **3.** Informal. convict wrongly an innocent person.

răin, n. **1.** condensed water falling in drops from the clouds. **2.** rainstorm. —v.i. **3.** fall as rain. —v.t. **4.** give abundantly; shower. —**rain′y,** adj. —**rain′ fall″,** n.

răin′bōw″, n. colored arc of sunlight refracted through raindrops.

răin′cōat″, n. water-repellent overcoat.

răise, v.t., **raised, raising.** n. v.t. **1.** lift. **2.** set upright. **3.** solicit and collect. **4.** grow. **5.** bring up. **6.** call to attention. —n. **7.** increase in salary.

răi′sĭn, n. sweet dried grape.

râ′jäh, n. oriental prince or king. Also, **ra′ja.**

răke, n., v.t., **raked, raking.** n. **1.** pronged implement for collecting leaves, etc. **2.** libertine. **3.** slope. —v.t. **4.** smooth, collect, etc. with a rake.

răk′ĭsh, adj. jaunty.

răl′lў, v., **-lied, -lying,** n., pl. **-lies.** v.t., v.i. **1.** gather. —v.t. **2.** reorganize. **3.** tease. —v.i. **4.** recover strength. —n. **5.** gathering. **6.** recovery of strength.

răm, n., v.t., **rammed, ramming.** n. **1.** male sheep. **2.** device for battering, crushing, etc. —v.t. **3.** run into forcibly.

răm′ble, v.i., **-bled, -bling,** n. v.i. **1.**

wander leisurely. **2.** talk discursively. —n. **3.** leisurely stroll.

răm′ĭ·fў″, v., **-fied, -fying.** v.t., v.i. branch out.

rămp, n. sloping road or walk.

răm′pāge, n., v.i., **-paged, -paging.** n. **1.** violent behavior. —v.i. **2.** rush about furiously.

răm′pănt, adj. **1.** unchecked; raging. **2.** standing on the hind legs.

răm′pârt, n. mound of earth erected as a defense; parapet.

răm′shăck″le, adj. shaky; rickety.

rănch, n. large stock farm.

răn·cĭd (ran′sid), adj. stale; spoiled. —**ran·cid′i·ty,** n.

răn′cör, n. resentment. —**ran′cor·ous,** adj.

răn′dŏm, adj. without pattern or aim.

rānge, n., v., **ranged, ranging.** n. **1.** extent. **2.** row. **3.** mountain chain. **4.** grazing area. **5.** distance of gunfire, reach, etc. **6.** shooting ground. **7.** stove. —v.t. **8.** put in a row. **9.** pass over. —v.i. **10.** have a range.

rāng′êr, n. warden or trooper policing a rural area.

rănk, n. **1.** group, class, or standing. **2.** high position. **3.** row. **4.** ranks, ordinary troops. —v.t. **5.** arrange in formation. —v.i. **6.** have a specified standing. —adj. **7.** excessively grown. **8.** offensively strong in taste or smell. **9.** utter.

răn′kle, v., **-kled, -kling.** v.t. **1.** cause long-lasting resentment in. —v.i. **2.** cause long-lasting resentment.

răn′săck, v.t. **1.** search thoroughly. **2.** plunder; pillage.

răn′sòm, n. **1.** price deemed for return of a prisoner. —v.t. **2.** redeem for money.

rănt, v.i. **1.** speak violently or wildly. —n. **2.** violent or extravagant speech.

răp, v.t., **rapped, rapping,** n. v.t. **1.** strike sharply. —n. **2.** quick, sharp blow. **3.** Informal. blame; responsibility. **4.** musical talk or patter.

ra·pā′cious, adj. predatory.

răpe, n., v.t., **raped, raping.** n. **1.** forced sexual violation. —v.t. **2.** commit rape on. **3.** seize and carry off by force. —**ra′ pist,** n.

răp′ĭd, adj. **1.** speedy. —n. **2. rapids,**

fast-moving sections of a river. —**ra·pid'i·ty**, *n.*

ra·pi·er (rā'pē ər), *n.* small narrow sword.

rap·ine (rap'in), *n.* plunder.

răpt, *adj.* engrossed.

răp'tûre, *n.* ecstatic or beatific joy. —**rap'tur·ous**, *adj.*

râre, *adj., rarer, rarest.* 1. unusual. 2. thin. 3. not completely cooked. —**rar'i·ty**, *n.*

rär'e·fȳ'', *v.,* **-fied, -fying.** *v.t., v.i.* thin. —**rar''e·fac'tion**, *n.*

răs'căl, *n.* unscrupulous person. —**ras·cal'i·ty**, *n.*

răsh, *adj.* 1. unreasonably hasty. —*n.* 2. skin irritation.

răsh'êr, *n.* thin slice of ham or bacon.

răsp, *v.t.* 1. scrape or grate. 2. talk with a grating sound. —*n.* 3. rasping sound. 4. coarse file.

răsp'bĕr''rȳ, *n., pl.* **-ries.** juicy small red or black fruit.

răt, *n.* long-tailed rodent larger than a mouse.

rătch'ĕt, *n.* gear controlled by a pawl.

rāte, *n., v.,* **rated, rating.** *n.* 1. fixed relation between variables. —*v.t.* 2. establish a rate for. 3. judge to be as specified. —*v.i.* 4. have a specified value.

răth'êr, *adv.* 1. to a certain extent. 2. on the contrary. 3. in preference.

răt'i·fȳ'', *v.t.,* **-fied, -fying.** approve formally.

rā'tion, *n.* 1. limited allotment. —*v.t.* 2. put on a ration.

rā'tion·al, *adj.* 1. reasonable. 2. sane. —**ra''tion·al'i·ty**, *n.*

ră·tion·āle, *n.* rational basis.

rā'tion·al·īze'', *v.t.,* **-ized, -izing.** 1. attempt to justify with reasons. 2. make methodical. —**ra''tion·al·i·za'tion**, *n.*

ra·tio (rā'shō), *n.* relation of quantities.

răt'tăn', *n.* hollow stem of a climbing palm.

răt'tle, *v.,* **-tled, -tling.** *n. v.i.* 1. make successive short sharp noises. 2. chatter. —*v.t.* 3. confuse; disconcert. —*n.* 4. rattling sounds. 5. child's toy that rattles.

răt'tle·snāke'', *n.* poisonous American snake.

rău'coŭs, *adj.* harsh; hoarse.

răv'åge, *n., v.t., v.i.,* **-aged, -aging.** ruin; pillage.

răve, *v.i.,* **raved, raving.** *n. v.i.* 1. talk wildly. —*n.* 2. *Informal.* unequivocally favorable review.

răv'ĕl, *v.t.* 1. disengage the threads of. 2. solve; make clear. —*v.i.* 3. fray. 4. become tangled.

rä'vĕn, *n.* large glossy black bird.

răv'ĕn·oŭs, *adj.* exceedingly hungry.

rá·vïne', *n.* narrow valley.

răv'ĭsh, *v.t.* 1. transport or fill with joy. 2. rape.

răw, *adj.* 1. in a natural state; naked. 2. uncooked. 3. untrained; young.

răw'hīde'', *n.* untanned hide.

rāy, *n.* 1. narrow beam of light. 2. glimpse. 3. radiating line. 4. flat ocean fish.

rāy'ŏn, *n.* synthetic silk-like fabric.

rāze, *v.t.,* **razed, razing.** demolish.

rä'zŏr, *n.* sharp instrument for shaving.

rē-, prefix meaning "again." **reaccustom, reacquaint, reacquire, readapt, reaffirm, realign, reappear, reapply, reappoint, reappraisal, rearrange, reassemble, reassert, reassess, reassign, rebind, rebutton, recheck, recommence, reconnect, reconquer, recopy, rededicate, redefine, redevelop, rediscover, redo, reelect, reemerge, reemphasize, reerect, reestablish, reevaluate, reexperience, refill, reformulate, refurnish, regrow, reheat, reignite, reinsert, reinterpret, rekindle, remarry, rename, renumber, reoccur, reorient, replant, replay, reread, resell, resupply, retake, retell, retest, retrain, retransmit, retype, reusable, reuse, reunion, reunite, reverify, rewarm, rewin, rework, rewrap.**

rē, *prep.* in the affair of.

rēach, *v.t.* 1. arrive at. 2. extend. 3. be able to touch. 4. communicate with. —*v.i.* 5. extend the hand. —*n.* 6. act, instance, or extent of reaching.

rē·ăct', *v.i.* 1. act in response. 2. interact.

rē·ăc'tion, *n.* 1. action in response. 2. extreme political conservatism. —**re·ac'tion·ar''y**, *adj., n.*

rēad'ĭng, *n.* interpretation of a play or musical composition.

rĕad'ÿ, *adj.*, *v.t.*, **readied, readying,** *n.* *adj.* **1.** prepared. **2.** willing. **3.** imminent. —*v.t.* **4.** make ready. —*n.* **5.** state of readiness. —**read'i·ly,** *adv.* —**read' i·ness,** *n.*

rē'al, *adj.* **1.** not false; genuine. **2.** not imaginary or ideal. —**re·al'i·ty,** *n.* —**re·al'ly,** *adv.*

real éstate, *n.* property, esp. land with buildings. Also, **re'al·ty.**

rē'al·ism, *n.* **1.** close imitation of reality. **2.** acceptance of actual conditions. —**re' al·ist,** *n.* —**re''al·is'tic,** *adj.*

rē'al·īze'', *v.t.* **1.** understand completely. **2.** bring into actuality. **3.** obtain as a profit. —**re''al·i·za'tion,** *n.*

rĕalm, *n.* **1.** special field of expertise. **2.** kingdom.

rē'al·tör, *n.* agent selling real estate.

rēam, *n.* **1.** twenty quires of paper. —*v.t.* **2.** make or enlarge by a rotary tool.

rēap, *v.t.* **1.** harvest. **2.** get as a reward. —**reap'er,** *n.*

rēar, *n.* **1.** back part. **2.** backside. —*adj.* **3.** pertaining to the rear. —*v.t.* **4.** raise; erect. **5.** bring up to maturity. —*v.i.* **6.** rise on the rear legs.

rēa'són, *n.* **1.** cause or justification. **2.** objectivity; logic. **3.** sanity. —*v.i.* **4.** think or argue logically. —*v.t.* **5.** infer or conclude. —**rea'son·a·ble,** *adj.* —**rea' son·a·bly,** *adv.*

rē''às·sūre', *v.t.*, **-sured, -suring.** restore the confidence of. —**re''as·sur'ance,** *n.*

rē'bāte, *v.t.*, **-bated, -bating.** *n.* *v.t.* **1.** refund after payment. —*n.* **2.** amount rebated.

re·bel, *v.i.*, **-belled, -belling.** *n.*, *v.* (rē bel'). **1.** arise against authority. —*n.* (reb'əl). **2.** person who rebels. —**re· bel'lion,** *n.* —**re·bel'lious,** *adj.*

rē·bōund, *v.i.* (rē bownd') **1.** bounce back after impact. —*n.* (rē'bownd). **2.** act or instance of rebounding.

rē·būff', *n.* **1.** blunt rejection or refusal. —*v.t.* **2.** reject curtly.

rē·būke', *v.t.*, **-buked, -buking.** *n.* reprimand.

rē'būs, *n.* combination of pictures whose names combine to form a word or phrase.

rē·būt', *v.t.*, **-butted, -butting.** refute. —**re·but'tal,** *n.*

rē·căl'cǐ·tránt (rē kal'sə trənt), *adj.* stubborn; refractory. —**re·cal'ci·trance,** *n.*

rē·căll', *v.t.* **1.** remember. **2.** withdraw. **3.** call or summon back. —*n.* **4.** act or instance of recalling. **5.** memory.

rē·cănt', *v.t.*, *v.i.* retract; renounce. —**re'' can·ta'tion,** *n.*

rē''cà·pǐt'ū·lāte, *v.* **-lated, -lating.** *v.t.*, *v.i.* restate briefly; sum up. —**re''ca· pit''u·la'tion,** *n.*

rē·cēde', *v.i.*, **-ceded, -ceding. 1.** move back. **2.** diminish.

rē·cēipt', *n.* **1.** act or instance of receiving. **2.** document acknowledging payment or delivery. **3. receipts,** income.

rē·cēive', *v.t.*, **-ceived, -ceiving. 1.** take when offered or sent. **2.** sustain; experience. **3.** welcome. —**re·ceiv'a·ble,** *adj.*

rē·cēiv'ēr, *n.* **1.** person or thing that receives. **2.** apparatus receiving radio signals. **3.** administrator of property in litigation. —**re·ceiv'er·ship,** *n.*

rē'cĕnt, *adj.* not long past. —**re'cen·cy,** *n.*

rē·cĕp'tà·cle, *n.* container.

rē·cĕp'tion, *n.* **1.** act or instance of receiving. **2.** formal social function. **3.** quality of radio signals, etc. as received.

rē·cĕp'tive, *adj.* **1.** ready to consider new ideas. **2.** amenable.

rē·cĕss', *n.* **1.** pause in work. **2.** hollowed-out space. **3. recesses,** inner areas. —*v.i.* **4.** pause in work.

rē·cĕs'sion, *n.* **1.** withdrawal. **2.** economic decline.

rē·cĕs'sion·àl, *n.* hymn sung during the withdrawal of clergy.

rĕc'ǐ·pē'', *n.* method or formula, esp. in cooking.

rē·cǐp'ǐ·ént, *n.* receiver.

rē·cǐp'rō·cál, *adj.* **1.** mutual. —*n.* **2.** counterpart.

rē·cǐp'rō·cāte'', *v.*, **-cated, -cating.** *v.t.*, *v.i.* **1.** give, receive, etc. in return. **2.** move back and forth. —**rec''i·proc'i· ty,** *n.*

rē·cǐ'tál, *n.* **1.** account or narration. **2.** performance of music.

rē·cīte', *v.t.*, **-cited, -citing. 1.** repeat from memory. **2.** narrate; read aloud. —**rec''i·ta'tion,** *n.*

rĕck´less, *adj.* foolhardy, careless.

rĕck´on, *v.t.* **1.** calculate. **2.** esteem. **3.** *Dialect.* believe; suppose. —*v.i.* **4.** deal; cope.

rĕck´on·ing, *n.* **1.** computation. **2.** settling of accounts. **3.** accounting.

re·claim´, *v.t.* **1.** make usable. **2.** make usable. **3.** redeem from vice, etc. —**rec´´la·ma´tion**, *n.*

re·cline´, *v.*, **-clined, -clining.** *v.i., v.t.* lie or lay back.

re·cluse´, *n.* person who lives in seclusion. —**re·clu´sive**, *adj.*

re·cog´ni·zance, *n.* formal pledge of action.

rĕc´og·nīze´´, *v.t.*, **-nized, -nizing. 1.** identify from memory. **2.** be aware of. **3.** acknowledge formally. —**rec´´og·ni´ tion**, *n.*

re·coil´, *v.i.* **1.** draw or shrink back. **2.** spring back. —*n.* **3.** act or instance of recoiling.

rĕc´´ol·lect´, *v.t., v.i.* remember. —**rec´´ ol·lec´tion**, *n.*

rĕc´´om·mĕnd´, *v.t.* **1.** speak favorably of. **2.** advise. —**rec´´om·men·da´tion**, *n.*

rĕc´om·pĕnse´´, *v.t.*, **-pensed, -pensing.** *n. v.t.* **1.** reward or compensate. —*n.* **2.** reward or compensation.

rĕc´´on·cīle´, *v.t.*, **-ciled, -ciling. 1.** return to harmony. **2.** make compatible. **3.** settle amicably. **4.** make acquiescent. —**rec´´on·cil´a·ble**, *adj.* —**rec´´on· cil´´i·a´tion**, *n.*

rĕ´´con·noī´ter, *v.t., v.i.* search or scout. —**re·con´nais·sance**, *n.*

re·cord, *v.t.* (rĕ kord´) **1.** make a written account of. **2.** put in reproducible form. —*n.* (rĕk´ərd) **3.** written account. **4.** disk for sound reproduction. **5.** best performance. —*adj.* **6.** being the best to date.

re·count, *v.t.* **1.** narrate. **2.** count again. —*n.* **3.** (rĕ´kownt). second count.

re·coup´ (ri kōōp´), *v.t.* recover; make up.

re·cŏurse´, *n.* **1.** appeal for help. **2.** possible source of help.

re·cŏv´er, *v.t.* **1.** get back. **2.** salvage. —*v.i.* **3.** regain health. **4.** regain composure. —**re·cov´er·a·ble**, *adj.* —**re·cov´ er·y**, *n.*

rĕc´´rē·ā´tion, *n.* refreshing occupation. —**rec´´re·a´tion·al**, *adj.*

re·crim´´i·nāte´´, *v.i.*, **-nated, -nating.** make an accusation in return.

re·crūit´, *n.* **1.** newly enlisted person. —*v.t.* **2.** enlist. —**re·cruit´ment**, *n.*

rĕc´tăn·gle, *n.* parallelogram with four right angles. —**rec·tan´gu·lar**, *adj.*

rĕc´ti·fy´´, *v.t.*, **-fied, -fying.** correct. —**rec´´ti·fi´a·ble**, *adj.* —**rec´´ti·fi·ca´ tion**, *n.*

rĕc´´ti·lin´e·ăr, *adj.* **1.** forming a straight line. **2.** bounded by straight lines.

rĕc´ti·tūde´´, *n.* moral uprightness.

rĕc´tŏr, *n.* **1.** clergyman in charge of a parish. **2.** head of certain universities and colleges.

rĕc´tŏ·rў, *n.* parsonage.

rĕc´tŭm, *n.* terminal part of the large intestine. —**rec´tal**, *adj.*

re·cŭm´bĕnt, *adj.* lying down. —**re· cum´ben·cy**, *n.*

re·cū´pêr·āte´´, *v.i.*, **-ated, -ating.** regain health. —**re·cu´per·a·tive**, *adj.*

re·cûr´, *v.i.*, **-curred, -curring. 1.** occur again or repeatedly. **2.** return to one's thoughts. —**re·cur´rence**, *n.* —**re·cur´ rent**, *adj.* —**re·cur´rent·ly**, *adv.*

re·cý´cle, *v.t.* convert into reusable material.

rĕd, *n., adj.*, **redder, reddest.** *n.* **1.** color of blood. **2.** Red, *Informal.* Communist. —*adj.* **3.** of or pertaining to red. —**red´ den**, *v.t., v.i.*

re·dēem´, *v.t.* **1.** recover. **2.** pay off. **3.** exchange for premiums. **4.** deliver from sin. **5.** fulfill, as a promise. —**re·demp´ tion**, *n.*

Re·dēem´êr, *n.* Jesus Christ.

rĕd´-lĕt´têr, *adj.* memorable.

rĕd´o·lĕnt, *adj.* **1.** odorous. **2.** suggestive. —**red´o·lence**, *n.*

re·dŏubt´a·ble, *adj.* formidable.

re·dŏund´, *v.i.* occur as a consequence.

re·dress´, *v.t.* (rĕ dres´) **1.** right, as a wrong. —*n.* (rĕ´dres) **2.** act or instance of redressing.

rĕd tāpe, bureaucratic procedures.

re·dūce´, *v.*, **-duced, -ducing.** *v.t.* **1.** lessen. **2.** alter. **3.** lower in rank, etc. **4.** subdue. —*v.i.* **5.** act so as to lose weight. —**re·duc´i·ble**, *adj.* —**re·duc´tion**, *n.*

re·dŭn´dănt, *adj.* **1.** excess; surplus. **2.** repetitive. —**re·dun´dance, re·dun´ dan·cy**, *n.*

rĕd´wŏŏd´´, *n.* huge California evergreen tree.

rēed, *n.* **1.** tall marsh grass. **2.** vibrating part of the mouthpiece on certain wind instruments. —**reed´y,** *adj.*

rēef, *n.* **1.** ridge near the surface of a body of water. **2.** part of a sail. —*v.t.* **3.** shorten, as a sail.

rēef´ĕr, *n.* **1.** short jacket or coat. **2.** *Informal.* marijuana cigarette.

rēek, *v.i.* **1.** smell strongly. —*n.* **2.** strong or foul smell.

rēel, *n.* **1.** revolving drum for winding. **2.** lively dance. —*v.t.* **3.** wind on a reel. —*v.i.* **4.** stagger or sway. **5.** whirl.

re·fĕc´to·rŷ, *n.* dining hall.

re·fĕr´, *v.*, **-ferred, -ferring.** *v.i.* **1.** allude. **2.** look for information. —*v.t.* **3.** direct for help or information. **4.** submit for arbitration. —**re·fer´a·ble,** *adj.* —**re·fer´ral,** *n.*

rĕf·ĕr·ēe´, *n.* **1.** arbiter. *v.t.*, *v.i.* **2.** arbitrate.

rĕf´ĕr·ence, *n.* **1.** act or instance of referring. **2.** something referred to. **3.** recommendation. **4.** person giving a recommendation.

rĕf´´ĕr·ĕn´dŭm, *n.* submission of a proposed law for citizen approval.

re·fīne´, *v.t.,* **-fined, -fining. 1.** free from impurities. **2.** make cultured. —**re·fine´ment,** *n.*

re·fīn´ĕr·ŷ, *n.*, *pl.* **-eries.** factory for refining, esp. petroleum.

re·flĕct´, *v.t.* **1.** return, as images, light, etc. **2.** think about. —**re·flec´tion,** *n.* —**re·flec´tive,** *adj.* —**re·flec´tor,** *n.*

rē·flĕx, *adj.* **1.** denoting involuntary reaction. —*n.* **2.** involuntary reaction.

re·flĕx´ive, *adj.* **1.** having the same subject and object as a verb. **2.** used as the object of a reflexive verb, as a pronoun.

re·fŏrm´, *n.* **1.** correction of wrongs. —*v.t.* **2.** correct the wrongs of. —*v.i.* **3.** correct one's wrongdoing. —**ref´´or·ma´tion,** *n.*

re·fŏrm´a·tō´´ry, *n.*, *pl.* **-ries.** penal institution for minors.

re·frăc´tion, *n.* bending of light or heat rays in passing from one medium to another. —**re·fract´,** *v.t.* —**re·frac´tive,** *adj.* —**re·frac´tor,** *n.*

re·frāin´, *v.i.* **1.** hold back; forbear. —*n.*

2. recurring passage in a song or poem.

re·frĕsh´, *v.t.* **1.** revive after stress. **2.** quicken; stimulate. —**re·fresh´ment,** *n.*

re·frĭg´ĕr·āte´´, *v.t.,* **-ated, -ating.** keep or make cold. —**re·frig´er·ant,** *n.* —**re·frig´er·a´´tor,** *n.*

rĕf´ūge, *n.* shelter from danger.

rĕf´´ū·gēe´, *n.* seeker of refuge.

re·fŭnd´, *v.t.* (re fund´) **1.** repay. —*n.* **2.** (rē´fund). repayment.

rē·fŭr´bĭsh, *v.t.* renovate.

re·fūse´, *v.t.,* **-fused, -fusing,** *n.* *v.t.* (rē fyōoz) **1.** decline. **2.** decline to accept. **3.** deny, as a request. —*n.* (ref´yōoz). **4.** rubbish. —**re·fus´al,** *n.*

re·fūte´, *v.t.,* **-futed, -futing.** prove wrong or false. —**re·fu´ta·ble,** *adj.* —**ref´´u·ta´tion,** *n.*

rē·gāin´, *v.t.* **1.** get again. **2.** return to again.

rē´găl, *adj.* royal.

re·gāle´, *v.t.,* **-galed, -galing.** entertain lavishly.

re·gā´li·a, *n. pl.* royal or official insignia.

re·gärd´, *v.t.* **1.** look on. **2.** consider. **3.** concern; relate to. **4.** hold in respect. —*n.* **5.** look; gaze. **6.** relation. **7.** affection and respect. **8.** particular point. **9.** **regards,** good wishes.

re·gärd´less, *adj.* **1.** careless. —*adv.* **2.** anyway.

re·găt´ta, *n.* boat race.

re·gĕn´ĕr·āte´´, *v.t.,* *adj.* **-ated, -ating.** *v.t.* **1.** produce anew. **2.** reform. **3.** *Biol.* regrow. —*adj.* **4.** renewed; reformed. —**re·gen´er·a·tive,** *adj.*

rē´gĕnt, *n.* **1.** appointed substitute for a monarch. **2.** member of a governing board. —**re´gen·cy,** *n.*

re·gīme´, *n.* **1.** system of government, etc. **2.** period of rule. Also, **ré·gime´.**

rĕg´i·men, *n.* **1.** government; rule. **2.** *Medicine.* system of diet, etc.

rĕg´i·ment, *n.* (rĕj´ə mənt). **1.** army unit of two or more battalions. —*v.t.* (rĕj´ə ment´´) **2.** subject to strict discipline. —**reg´´i·men´tal,** *adj.* —**reg´´i·men´ta·tion,** *n.*

rē´giŏn, *n.* part of the earth's surface. —**re´gion·al,** *adj.*

rē´giŏn·ăl·ĭsm, *n.* **1.** sponsorship of or adherence to regional culture. **2.** regional peculiarity.

reg′is·ter, *n.* **1.** written record, list, etc. **2.** cash register. **3.** device for regulating the passage of air. **4.** *Music.* range. —*v.t., v.i.* **5.** enroll. —*v.t.* **6.** show, as on the face. —*v.i.* **7.** make an impression. —**reg′is·trant,** *n.* —**reg′′is·tra′tion,** *n.* —**reg′is·try,** *n.*

reg′is·trar′′, *n.* official record keeper.

re·gress′, *v.i.* **1.** go back. **2.** revert. —*n.* **3.** going back. —**re·gres′sion,** *n.* —**re·gres′sive,** *adj.*

re·gret′, *v.t.,* **-gretted, -gretting,** *n. v.t.* **1.** feel sorry about. —*n.* **2.** sorrow or remorse. —**re·gret′ful,** *adj.* —**re·gret′ta·ble,** *adj.*

reg′u·lar, *adj.* **1.** customary. **2.** consistent. **3.** symmetrical. **4.** permanent, as an army. **5.** *Informal.* **a.** complete. **b.** likeable. —*n.* **6.** someone regularly seen. **7.** regular soldier. —**reg′′u·lar′i·ty,** *n.* —**reg′u·lar·ize′′,** *v.t.*

reg′u·late′′, *v.t.,* **-lated, -lating. 1.** control by rule. **2.** make regular. —**reg′u·la′′tor,** *n.* —**reg′′u·la·to′′ry,** *adj.* —**reg′u·la′′tive,** *adj.*

re·gur′gi·tate′′, *v.,* **-tated, -tating.** *v.i., v.t.* belch or vomit.

re′′ha·bil′i·tate′′, *v.t.,* **-tated, -tating.** restore to a former good condition. —**re′′ha·bil′i·ta′′tion,** *adj.*

re·hash′, *v.t.* work over again. —*n.* **2.** rehashing.

re·hearse′, *v.,* **-hearsed, -hearsing.** *v.t., v.i.* practice for a performance. —**re·hears′al,** *n.*

reign (rān), *n.* **1.** royal power. **2.** period of rule. —*v.i.* **3.** rule as a monarch. **4.** prevail.

re′′im·burse′, *v.t.,* **-bursed, -bursing.** pay back. —**re′′im·burse′ment,** *n.*

rein (rān), strap for controlling a horse.

re′′in·car·na′tion, *n.* rebirth in a new body.

rein·deer′′, *n., pl.* **-deer.** large northern deer.

re′′in·force′, *v.t.,* **-forced, -forcing.** strengthen. —**re′′in·force′ment,** *n.*

re′′in·state′, *v.t.,* **-stated, -stating.** restore to a former state. —**re′′in·state′ment,** *n.*

re·it′er·ate′′, *v.t.,* **-ated, -ating.** say or do again. —**re·it′er·a′′tive,** *adj.*

re·ject′, *v.t.* **1.** refuse to accept. **2.** discard. —*n.* (rē′ jekt). **3.** rejected person or thing. —**re·jec′tion,** *n.*

re·joice′, *v.,* **-joiced, -joicing.** *v.t.* **1.** gladden. —*v.i.* **2.** feel joy. —**re·joic′ing,** *n.*

re·join′, *v.t., v.i.* **1.** join again. **2.** answer.

re·join′der, *n.* **1.** reply. **2.** *Law.* defendant's response.

re·ju′ve·nate′′, *v.t.,* **-nated, -nating.** make young again.

re·lapse′, *v.i.,* **-lapsed, -lapsing,** *n. v.i.* **1.** fall into a former state. —*n.* **2.** act or instance of relapsing.

re·late′, *v.,* **-lated, -lating.** *v.t.* **1.** tell; narrate. **2.** connect; associate. —*v.i.* **3.** have a relation.

re·la′tion, *n.* **1.** narrative. **2.** connection; association. **3.** connection by blood or marriage. —**re·la′tion·ship′′,** *n.*

rel′a·tive, *adj.* **1.** comparative. **2.** related to each other. —*n.* **3.** person related by blood or marriage.

rel′′a·tiv′i·ty, *n.* **1.** interdependence. **2.** *Physics.* theory of the relative character of position, motion, etc. and the interdependence of time and space.

re·lax′, *v.t., v.i.* rest, as from work or tension. —**re′′lax·a′tion,** *n.*

re·lay *n.* (rē′ lā) **1.** relief crew or team. **2.** race in which team members run individual portions. —*v.t.* (rē′ lā; also ri lā′) **3.** send by relay or relays. **4.** lay away.

re·lease′, *v.t.,* **-leased, -leasing,** *n. v.t.* **1.** free. **2.** let go of. **3.** license for publication. —*n.* **4.** act or instance of releasing. **5.** communication, etc. **6.** *Law.* surrender, as of a claim.

rel′e·gate′′, *v.t.,* **-gated, -gating. 1.** consign to a lesser place or position. **2.** refer for decision.

re·lent′, *v.i.* become less severe, cruel, etc. —**re·lent′less,** *adj.*

rel′e·vant, *adj.* relating to the matter at hand. —**rel′e·vance, rel′e·van·cy,** *n.*

re·li′a·ble, *adj.* dependable. —**re·li′′a·bil′i·ty,** *n.*

re·li′ance, *n.* **1.** trust; confidence. **2.** something relied on. —**re·li′ant,** *adj.*

rel′ic, *n.* **1.** survival from the past. **2.** souvenir.

re·lief′, *n.* **1.** release from pain, discomfort, etc. **2.** means of such relief. **3.** sculptured surface. **4.** projection from a background.

rē·liēve′, *v.t.*, **-lieved, -lieving. 1.** ease, as from pain or discomfort. **2.** vary. **3.** release from duty.

rē·lī′giòn, *n.* **1.** belief in a divine being or beings. **2.** specific form of belief and practice. **—re·li′gious**, *adj.*

rē·lin′quish, *v.t.* **1.** give up. **2.** renounce, as a right. **—re·lin′quish·ment**, *n.*

rĕl′ĭsh, *n.* **1.** zest. **2.** condiment. **3.** appetizing flavor. **—v.t. 4.** take pleasure in.

rē·līve′, *v.t.*, **-lived, -living.** experience again in the imagination.

rē·lō′cāte, *v.*, **-cated, -cating.** *v.t., v.i.* settle in a new location.

rē·lŭc′tànt, *adj.* unwilling. **—re·luc′tance**, *n.*

rē·lȳ′, *v.i.*, **-lied, -lying.** depend; trust.

rē·māin′, *v.i.* **1.** stay behind. **2.** endure; persist. **3.** continue as before. **—n. 4. re·mains, a.** remainder. **b.** corpse. **—re·main′der**, *n.*

rē·mănd′, *v.t.* send back or consign again.

rē·märk′, *v.t., v.i., n.* **1.** comment. **—v.t., n. 2.** notice.

rē·märk′a·ble, *adj.* worthy of notice or comment.

rĕm′ē·dy̆, *n.*, *v.t.*, **-died, -dying.** *n.* **1.** medicine or treatment. **2.** something that corrects wrong. **—v.t. 3.** cure; correct. **—re·me′di·al**, *adj.*

rē·mĕm′bêr, *v.t.* **1.** recall to mind. **2.** not forget. **3.** carry greetings from. **—re·mem′brance**, *n.*

rē·mīnd′, *v.t.* cause to remember. **—re·mind′er**, *n.*

rĕm′′i·nĭsce′′, *v.i.*, **-nisced, -niscing.** discuss or think about the past. **—rem′′i·nis′cence**, *n.* **—rem′′i·nis′cent**, *adj.*

rē·mĭss′, *adj.* careless; slack.

rē·mĭs′sion, *n.* **1.** forgiveness. **2.** diminution, as of disease.

rē·mĭt′, *v.t.*, **-mitted, -mitting. 1.** forgive. **2.** refrain from imposing. **3.** relax; abate. **4.** send in payment. **—re·mit′tance**, *n.*

rĕm′nànt, *n.* something left over.

rē·mŏd′él, *v.t.*, **-eled, -eling.** make over; rebuild.

rē·mŏn′strāte, *v.*, **-strated, -strating.**

v.t., v.i. protest; object. **—re·mon′strance**, *n.*

rē·môrse′, *n.* mental anguish from guilt. **—re·morse′ful**, *adj.* **—re·morse′less**, *adj.*

rē·mōte′, *adj.*, **-moter, -motest. 1.** distant. **2.** slight.

rē·mōve′, *v.*, **-moved, -moving.** *n.* *v.t.* **1.** move from a place. **2.** dismiss, as from office. **—v.i. 3.** change residence. **—n. 4.** interval; step. **—re·mov′a·ble**, *adj.* **—re·mov′al**, *n.*

rē·mū′nêr·āte′′, *v.t.*, **-ated, -ating.** pay; recompense. **—re·mu′ner·a′′tive**, *adj.*

rĕn′ais·sänce′′, *n.* **1.** rebirth. **2. Renaissance,** revival of classical learning in Europe.

rē′nàl, *adj.* pertaining to the kidneys.

rē·năs′cénce, *n.* rebirth; revival.

rĕnd, *v.*, **rent, rending.** *v.t., v.i.* split apart by force.

rĕn′dêr, *v.t.* **1.** give in return. **2.** submit. **3.** state, as a decision. **4.** furnish. **5.** express or interpret. **6.** translate.

ren·dez·vous (ran′dā voo′′), *n.*, *pl.* **-vous. 1.** meeting place. **2.** appointment to meet.

rĕn·dī′tion, *n.* rendering; performance.

rĕn′e·gāde′′, *n.* deserter of a cause.

rē·nēge′, *v.i.*, **-neged, -neging.** *Informal.* go back on one's word.

rē·nēw′, *v.t.* **1.** make new. **2.** revive. **—re·new′al**, *n.*

rē·nōunce′, *v.t.*, **-nounced, -nouncing.** give up formally. **—re·nun′′ci·a′tion, re·nounce′ment**, *n.*

rĕn′ō·vāte′′, *v.t.* **-vated, -vating.** make as if new.

rē·nōwn′, *n.* great reputation. **—re·nowned′**, *adj.*

rĕnt, *n.* **1.** Also, **rent′al,** payment for temporary use. **2.** tear; rip. **—v.t. 3.** use by paying. **4.** grant temporarily for payment.

rē·pāir′, *v.t.* **1.** return to good condition. **2.** set right. **—v.i. 3.** go. **—n. 4.** act or instance of repairing. **5.** good condition. **—rep′a·ra·ble, re·pair′a·ble**, *adj.*

rĕp′′à·rā′tion, *n.* **1.** amends for injury. **2. reparations,** compensation for war damage.

rĕp′′ár·tēe′, *n.* clever, quick-witted talk.

repast 226

re·past', *n.* meal.

re·pa·tri·ate'', *v.,* -ated, -ating. *v.t., v.i.* return to one's country.

re·pay', *v.t.* -paid, -paying. pay back. —re·pay'ment, *n.*

re·peal', *v.t.* 1. revoke. —*n.* 2. revocation.

re·peat', *v.t., v.i.* 1. say or do again. —*n.* 2. act or instance of repeating. —rep'e·ti'tion, *n.* —rep''e·ti'tious, *adj.*

re·pel', *v.t.,* -pelled, -pelling. 1. drive back. 2. disgust. —re·pel'lent, *adj., n.*

re·pent', *v.t., v.i.* regret as wrong or mistaken. —re·pent'ance, *n.* —re·pent'ant, *adj.*

re''per·cus'sion, *n.* 1. indirect result. 2. reverberation. —re''per·cus'sive, *adj.*

rep'er·toire (rĕp'ẽr·twär''), *n.* stock of songs, plays, etc. performed. Also, rep'er·to''ry, *n.*

re·place', *v.t.,* -placed, -placing. 1. put back in place. 2. substitute for. —re·place'a·ble, *adj.* —re·place'ment, *n.*

re·plen'ish, *v.t.* make full again. —re·plen'ish·ment, *n.*

re·plete', *adj.* plentifully filled. —re·ple'tion, *n.*

rep'li·ca, *n.* copy. —rep'li·cate. *v.t.*

re·ply', *v.* -plied, -plying, *n., pl.* -plies. *v.t., v.i., n.* answer.

re·port', *n.* 1. statement. 2. rumor. 3. explosive noise. —*v.t.* 4. give an account of. 5. inform against. —*v.i.* 6. make a report. 7. present oneself.

re·pose', *v.t., v.i.* -posed, -posing, *n. v.t.* 1. rest or sleep. 2. place. 3. depend. —*n.* 4. rest or sleep. 5. tranquillity.

re·pos'i·tor''y, *n., pl.* -tories. place of storage.

rep''re·hend', *v.t.* rebuke. —rep''re·hen'si·ble, *adj.* —rep''re·hen'sion, *n.*

rep''re·sent', *v.t.* 1. exemplify. 2. portray. 3. act or speak for. —rep''re·sen'ta'tion, *n.*

rep''re·sen'ta·tive, *adj.* 1. serving as an example. 2. acting or speaking for others. —*n.* 3. person who represents. 4. elected legislator.

re·press', *v.t.* restrain; check. —re·pres'sive, *adj.* —re·pres'sion, *n.*

re·prieve', *v.t.,* -prieved, -prieving. *n. v.t.* 1. relieve temporarily. —*n.* 2. temporary delay; respite.

rep'ri·mand'', *n.* 1. severe or formal rebuke. —*v.t.* 2. rebuke; censure.

re·pris'al, *n.* retaliation.

re·proach', *v.t.* 1. scold for a fault; blame. —*n.* 2. discredit. —re·proach'ful, *adj.*

rep'ro·bate, *n., adj., v.t.,* -bated, -bating. *n.* 1. depraved person. —*adj.* 2. depraved. —*v.t.* 3. condemn.

re''pro·duce', *v.t.,* -duced, -ducing. 1. copy; duplicate. 2. produce by propagation. —re''pro·duc'tion, *n.* —re''pro·duc'tive, *adj.*

re·proof', *n.* rebuke; censure.

re·prove', *v.t.,* -proved, -proving. rebuke; censure. —re·prov'al, *n.*

rep'tile, *n.* cold-blooded vertebrate. —rep·til'i·an, *adj.*

re·pub'lic, *n.* state governed by elected legislators.

re·pub'li·can, *adj.* 1. pertaining to or favoring a republic. —*n.* 2. **Republican,** member of the Republican party. 3. partisan of a republican form of government. —re·pub'li·can·ism, *n.*

re·pu'di·ate'', *v.t.,* -ated, -ating. disown; disavow.

re·pug'nant, *adj.* distasteful. —re·pug'nance, *n.*

re·pulse', *v.t.,* -pulsed, -pulsing, *n. v.t.* 1. drive back, as an attack. 2. reject; rebuff. —*n.* 3. act or instance of repulsing. —re·pul'sion, *n.*

re·pul'sive, *adj.* disgusting.

rep'u·ta·ble, *adj.* of good reputation.

rep''u·ta'tion, *n.* 1. estimation of a person or thing. 2. fame.

re·pute', *n. v.t.,* -puted, -puting. *n.* 1. reputation. —*v.t.* 2. consider or regard.

re·quest', *v.t.* 1. ask for. —*n.* 2. act or instance of requesting. 3. something requested.

re''qui·em, *n.* service for the dead.

re·quire', *v.t.,* -quired, -quiring. 1. need. 2. demand. —re·quire'ment, *n.*

req'ui·site, *n.* 1. something necessary. —*adj.* 2. required; necessary.

req''ui·si'tion, *n.* 1. act or instance of requiring. 2. formal order for goods, etc. —*v.t.* 3. take by authority.

re·quite', *v.t.,* -quited, -quiting. repay; return. —re·quit'al, *n.*

re·scind', *v.t.* revoke; annul.

res'cue, *v.t.,* -cued, -cuing. *n. v.t.* 1. free

or save. —*n.* **2.** act or instance of rescuing.

re·search', *n.* **1.** careful investigation. —*v.t.* **2.** do research on or in.

re·sem'ble, *v.t.*, -bled, -bling. be like or similar to. —re·sem'blance, *n.*

re·sent', *v.t.* feel indignant at. —re·sent'ful, *adj.* —re·sent'ment, *n.*

res''er·va'tion, *n.* **1.** act or instance of reserving. **2.** advance request for accommodation. **3.** public land for Native Americans.

re·serve', *v.t.,* -served, -serving, *n. v.t.* **1.** keep back; set aside. —*n.* **2.** something reserved. **3.** reticence, as about feelings. **4.** inactive troops subject to call. **5.** reserved district.

re·serv'ist, *n.* member of a military reserve.

res'er·voir'' (rĕz'er vwar''), *n.* storage place for water.

re·side', *v.i.,* -sided, -siding. **1.** dwell. **2.** be present.

res'i·dence, *n.* **1.** dwelling place. **2.** act or instance of residing. —res'i·dent, *n., adj.* —res''i·den'tial, *adj.*

res'i·due'', *n.* remainder. —re·sid'u·al, *adj.*

re·sign', *v.i.* **1.** give up a job or duty. —*v.t.* **2.** give up. **3.** yield or submit.

res''ig·na'tion, *n.* **1.** act or instance of resigning. **2.** submission, as to the inevitable.

re·signed', *adj.* reluctantly submissive.

re·sil'i·ent, *adj.* elastic; buoyant. —re·sil'i·ence, *n.*

res'in, *n.* substance exuded by certain plants. —res'in·ous, *adj.*

re·sist', *v.t., v.i.* withstand; oppose. —re·sist'ance, *n.*

res'o·lute'', *adj.* firm in purpose; determined.

res''o·lu'tion, *n.* **1.** formal expression of opinion. **2.** decision. **3.** firmness of purpose.

re·solve', *v.,* -solved, -solving, *n. v.t., v.i.* **1.** decide; determine. —*v.t.* **2.** analyze. **3.** solve. **4.** dispel, as fear. —*n.* **5.** determination.

res'o·nant, *adj.* **1.** resounding. **2.** vibrant; sonorous. —res'o·nance, *n.* —res'o·nate'', *v.t., v.i.* —res'o·na''tor, *n.*

re·sort', *v.i.* **1.** have recourse. —*n.* **2.** public place, as for recreation. **3.** recourse.

re·sound', *v.i.* reverberate; ring out. —re·sound'ing, *adj.*

re·source'', *n.* **1.** source of help or support. **2.** resources, money; means.

re·source'ful, *adj.* clever; able.

re·spect', *n.* **1.** esteem; honor. **2.** consideration. **3.** detail. **4.** deference; regard. —*v.t.* **5.** show consideration for. **6.** hold in honor. —re·spect'a·ble, *adj.* —re·spect'ful, *adj.*

re·spect'ing, *prep.* concerning.

re·spec'tive, *adj.* relating to each of several.

res'pi·ra''tor, *n.* apparatus for artificial breathing.

re·spire', *v.,* -spired, -spiring. *v.t., v.i.* breathe. —res''pi·ra'tion, *n.* —re·spir'a·to''ry, *adj.*

res'pite, *n.* temporary relief.

re·splend'ent, *adj.* shining brightly. —re·splend'ence, *n.*

re·spond', *v.i.* **1.** answer. **2.** react.

re·spond'ent, *n. Law.* defendant.

re·sponse'', *n.* reply. —re·spon'sive, *adj.*

re·spon''si·bil'i·ty, *n., pl.* -ties. **1.** state of being responsible. **2.** obligation.

re·spon'si·ble, *adj.* **1.** accountable. **2.** reliable. **3.** distinguishing between right and wrong. —re·spon'si·bly, *adv.*

rest, *n.* **1.** sleep; repose. **2.** inactivity after work. **3.** support; base. **4.** *Music.* silent interval. —*v.i.* **5.** be at rest. **6.** lay. **7.** lie. —*v.t.* **8.** cause to rest. **9.** base. —rest'ful, *adj.* —rest'less, *adj.*

res'tau·rant, *n.* public eating place.

res''tau·ra·teur', *n.* proprietor of a restaurant.

res''ti·tu'tion, *n.* **1.** return of something taken away. **2.** reparation.

res'tive, *adj.* **1.** balky; stubborn. **2.** restless.

re·store', *v.t., -stored, -storing.* **1.** return to a former state. **2.** give back. —res''to·ra'tion, *n.* —re·stor'a·tive, *adj.*

re·strain', *v.t.* hold back; check. **2.** confine.

re·straint', *n.* **1.** control of emotions, etc. **2.** confinement. **3.** something that restrains.

re·strict', *v.t.* limit; confine. —re·stric'

tion, *n.* —re·stric'tive, *adj.* —re·strict'ed, *adj.*

re·sult', *n.* 1. consequence; outcome. —*v.i.* 2. follow as a consequence. —re·sult'ant, *adj.*, *n.*

re·sume', *v.t.*, -sumed, -suming. 1. continue. 2. take again. —re·sump'tion, *n.*

ré·su·mé', *n.* summary, as of work experience.

re·sur'gent, *adj.* tending to rise again. —re·sur'gence, *n.*

res''ûr·rêct', *v.t.* raise from the dead. —res''ur·rec'tion, *n.*

re·sus'ci·tâte', *v.*, -tated, -tating. *v.t.*, *v.i.* revive from unconsciousness. —re·sus''ci·ta'tion, *n.* —re·sus'ci·ta'tor, *n.*

re'tail, *n.* 1. sale of consumer goods. —*v.t.*, *v.i.* 2. sell at retail.

re·tain', *v.t.* 1. keep; hold. 2. hire by a retainer.

re·tain'er, *n.* 1. fee for continuing services. 2. servant.

re·tal'i·ate', *v.i.*, -ated, -ating. give like for like, esp. in revenge. —re·tal'i·a·to''ry, *adj.*

re·târd', *v.t.* hinder; slow. —re·tar·da'tion, *n.* —re·tard'ant, *n.*

re·târd'ed, *adj.* limited or slow in mental development.

rětch, *v.i.* try to vomit.

re·těn'tion, *n.* 1. act or instance of retaining. 2. power of remembering. —re·ten'tive, *adj.*

rět'i·cênt, *adj.* disposed to silence; taciturn. —ret'i·cence, *n.*

rět'i·nà, *n.* coating of the posterior interior of the eyeball.

rět'i·nūe', *n.* group of attendants.

re·tīre', *v.*, -tired, -tiring. *v.i.*, *v.t.* 1. withdraw. 2. withdraw from working life. —*v.i.* 3. go to bed. —*v.t.* 4. pay off, as bonds. —re·tir'ee', *n.* —re·tire'ment, *n.*

re·tīr'ing, *adj.* shy; reserved.

re·tôrt', *v.t.*, *v.i.* 1. answer smartly or wittily. —*n.* 2. quick, witty answer.

re·touch', *v.t.* touch up or improve, as a photograph.

re·trăct', *v.t.*, *v.i.* withdraw. —re·tract'a·ble, *adj.* —re·trac'tion, *n.*

re·trēat', *n.* 1. withdrawal, as from dan-

ger. 2. secluded place. —*v.i.* 3. withdraw.

re·trěnch', *v.t.*, *v.i.* cut down as an economy. —re·trench'ment, *n.*

rět''rī·bū'tion, *n.* retaliation; punishment. —re·trib'u·tive, *adj.*

re·triève', *v.t.*, -trieved, -trieving. 1. regain. 2. recover. 3. make good, as a mistake. —re·triev'al, *n.*

rět''rō·ăc'tĭve, *adj.* valid for some past period.

rět'rō·grāde'', *adj.*, *v.i.*, -graded, -grading. *adj.* 1. directed backward; reversed. —*v.i.* 2. go backward. 3. degenerate. —ret''ro·gres'sion, *n.* —ret''ro·gres'sive, *adj.*

rět'rō·spêct', *n.* look to the past. —ret''ro·spec'tive, *adj.* —ret''ro·spec'tion, *n.*

re·tûrn', *v.i.* 1. go back. 2. reply. —*v.t.* 3. put back. 4. repay. 5. elect or reelect. 6. yield, as a profit. —*n.* 7. act or instance of returning. 8. recurrence. 9. repayment; yield. 10. report; response. —re·turn'a·ble, *adj.*

rěv, *v.t.*, revved, revving, *n. Informal. v.t.* 1. increase the speed of, as a motor. —*n.* 2. revolution, as of a machine.

re·vămp', *v.t.* redo; revise.

re·vēal', *v.t.* 1. disclose. 2. manifest.

rěv·eil·lē (rev'ə lē), *n. Military.* signal for awakening.

rěv'êl, *v.i.*, -eled, -eling, *n. v.i.* 1. take great delight. 2. make merry. —*n.* 3. merrymaking. —rev'el·ry, *n.*

rěv''e·lā'tion, *n.* 1. act or instance of revealing. 2. **Revelation,** last book of the New Testament.

re·věnge', *n.*, *v.t.*, -venged, -venging. *n.* 1. retaliation. 2. vindictiveness. —*v.t.* 3. take revenge for. —re·venge'ful, *adj.*

rěv'e·nūe'', *n.* income, as from taxes.

rě·vêr'bêr·āte'', *v.*, -ated, -ating. *v.t.*, *v.i.* reecho; resound.

re·vēre', *v.t.*, -vered, -vering. regard with deep respect, love, etc.

rěv'êr·ence, *n.*, *v.t.*, -enced, -encing. 1. deep respect. —*v.t.* 2. revere; honor. —rev'er·ent, rev''er·en'tial, *adj.*

rěv'êr·end, *adj.* 1. worthy of reverence. 2. **Reverend,** title of respect for a clergyman.

rĕv′ĕr·iĕ, *n., pl.* **-ies.** daydreaming; deep musings. Also, **rev′er·y.**

re·vêrse′, *adj., n., v.,* **-versed, -versing.** *adj.* **1.** turned backward. **2.** making an opposite motion. —*n.* **3.** opposite; contrary. **4.** misfortune. —*v.t.* **5.** turn back or in an opposite direction. **6.** exchange; transpose. —*v.i.* **7.** move in an opposite direction. —**re·vers′i·ble,** *adj.*

re·vêrt′, *v.i.* return as to a former way or state, etc. —**re·ver′sion,** *n.*

re·view′, *n.* **1.** reexamination. **2.** general survey or report. **3.** critical writing. —*v.t.* **4.** reexamine. **5.** look back on. **6.** write a review of. **7.** inspect formally.

re·vile′, *v.t.,* **-viled, -viling.** speak abusively. —**re·vile′ment,** *n.*

re·vîse′, *v.t.,* **-vised, -vising.** amend. —**re·vi′sion,** *n.*

re·vîv′al, *n.* **1.** return to life, use, etc. **2.** emotional religious meeting. —**re·viv′al·ist,** *n.*

re·vîve′, *v.,* **-vived, -viving.** *v.i., v.t.* return to consciousness or effectiveness.

re·vōke′, *v.t.,* **-voked, -voking.** repeal or nullify. —**rev′o·ca·ble,** *adj.* —**rev′o·ca′tion,** *n.*

re·vōlt′, *n.* **1.** uprising; rebellion. —*v.i.* **2.** rebel. —*v.t.* **3.** disgust.

rĕv′′o·lū′tion, *n.* **1.** war against one's government. **2.** complete change. **3.** rotation. —**rev′′o·lu′tion·ar′′y,** *adj., n.* —**rev′′o·lu′tion·ist,** *n.*

rĕv′′o·lū′tion·ize′, *v.t.,* **-ized, -izing.** change completely or radically.

re·vōlve′, *v.,* **-volved, -volving.** *v.t.* **1.** cause to rotate. —*v.i.* **2.** rotate.

re·vōlv′er, *n.* pistol with a revolving magazine.

re·vūe′, *n.* light musical show.

re·vŭl′sion, *n.* **1.** violent change of feeling. **2.** disgust.

re·ward′, *n.* **1.** grateful gift or payment. —*v.t.* **2.** give a reward to.

rhăp′sò·dy̆, *n., pl.* **-dies. 1.** free, irregular musical composition. **2.** emotional ecstasy. —**rhap·sod′ic,** *adj.*

rhē′ō·stăt′, *n.* device for varying an electric current.

rhē′sŭs, *n.* monkey of India.

rhĕt′o·rĭc, *n.* **1.** art of using language effectively. **2.** exaggerated speech. —**rhe·tor′i·cal,** *adj.*

rheū′mà·tĭsm′′, *n.* painful condition of the muscles and joints. —**rheu·mat′ic,** *adj.*

rhīne′stōne′′, *n.* imitation diamond.

rhi·nŏc′êr·òs, *n.* massive, thick-skinned mammal with a horned snout.

rhŏ′′dò·dĕn′dròn, *n.* evergreen shrub with pink, white, or purple flowers.

rhŏm′bŭs, *n., pl.* **-buses, -bi.** equilateral parallelogram with oblique angles.

rhū′bârb, *n.* edible plant with long, thick stalks.

rhȳme, *n., v.,* **rhymed, rhyming.** *n.* **1.** similarity of sound at verse ends. **2.** poetry with such similarity. —*v.i., v.t.* **3.** compose in rhyme.

rhȳthm, *n.* regular recurrence of stress, as in poetry or music. —**rhyth′mic,** *adj.*

rĭb, *n., v.t.,* **ribbed, ribbing.** *n.* **1.** one of the curved bones around the chest cavity. **2.** rib-like structure. —*v.t.* **3.** reinforce with ribs. **4.** *Informal.* tease.

rĭb′ăld, *adj.* indecent or vulgar in language. —**rib′ald·ry,** *n.*

rĭb′bòn, *n.* narrow strip of fabric.

rī′bò·flā′′vĭn, *n.* component of the vitamin B complex found in milk, eggs, meat, etc.

rīce, *n.* edible cereal of warm climates.

rĭch, *adj.* **1.** having much wealth. **2.** abundant; abounding. **3.** full of desirable qualities or resources. **4.** appetizing but hard to digest. **5.** mellow. —*n.* **6. the rich,** people of wealth. **7. riches,** wealth. —**rich′ly,** *adv.* —**rich′ness,** *n.*

rĭck, *n.* stack of hay, straw, etc.

rĭck′ĕts, *n.* nutritional deficiency disease of childhood characterized by bone deformities.

rĭck′ĕt·y̆, *adj.* shaky; feeble.

rĭck′shaw, *n.* carriage pulled by a man. Also, **rick′sha.**

ric·o·chet (rik′ə sha′′), *n., v.i.,* **-cheted, -cheting.** *n.* **1.** rebound of an object from a hard surface. —*v.i.* **2.** rebound.

rĭd, *v.t.,* **rid** or **ridded, ridding.** free; clear. —**rid′dance,** *n.*

rĭd′dle, *n., v.,* **-dled, -dling.** *n.* **1.** puzzle; enigma. **2.** coarse sieve. —*v.t.* **3.** pierce with holes. **4.** sift through a riddle. **5.** permeate.

rīde, *v.,* **rode, ridden, riding.** *n. v.t.* **1.** be carried on or within. **2.** be carried over or through. —*v.i.* **3.** be carried. **4.** depend (on). **5.** be at anchor. —*n.* **6.** act or instance of riding.

rĭd′êr, *n.* **1.** person who rides. **2.** addition to a document.

ridge, *n.*, *v.*, **ridged, ridging.** *n.* **1.** narrow, raised edge. **2.** sharp crest or elevation of land. —*v.t.*, *v.i.* **3.** form into a ridge.

rĭd′ĭ·cūle′′, *n.*, *v.t.*, **-culed, -culing.** *n.* **1.** derision. —*v.t.* **2.** make fun of; mock. —**ri·dic′u·lous**, *adj.*

rife, *adj.* **1.** widespread. **2.** abundant.

riff′räff′′, *n. pl.* worthless people.

rĭ′fle, *n.*, *v.t.*, **-fled, -fling.** *n.* **1.** shoulder gun with a rifled barrel. —*v.t.* **2.** ransack and rob. **3.** cut spiral grooves in, as a gun barrel. —**ri′fle·man**, *n.*

rift, *n.*, *v.t.*, *v.i.* split.

rĭg, *v.t.*, **rigged, rigging**, *n.* *v.t.* **1.** equip, as for sailing. **2.** manipulate. —*n.* **3.** arrangement of the sails, etc. on a ship. **4.** equipment. **5.** tractor-trailer.

rĭg′a·mä·rōle′′, *n.* complicated, often meaningless, procedure or talk. Also, **rig′ma·role′′.**

rig′ging, *n.* ropes and other tackle for a ship, crane, etc.

right, *adj.* **1.** good; virtuous. **2.** correct. **3.** suitable. **4.** opposite to left. **5.** straight. —*n.* **6.** what is right, just, etc. **7.** lawful power or privilege. **8.** *Politics.* conserva tive. —*adv.* **9.** properly. —*v.t.* **10.** correct; put in order. **11.** set upright.

right ängle, 90-degree angle.

rĭgh′teous, *adj.* **1.** virtuous; blameless. **2.** just; worthy.

right′ful, *adj.* just; legitimate.

right′ĭst, *n.*, *adj.* conservative in politics.

right′-wĭng′, *adj.* politically conservative.

rĭg′ĭd, *adj.* **1.** stiff; unyielding. **2.** strict. —**rig′id·ness, ri·gid′i·ty**, *n.*

rĭg′ör, *n.* **1.** strictness. **2.** hardship. —**rig′or·ous**, *adj.*

rĭ′gör môr′tĭs, stiffening of the muscles after death.

rīle, *v.t.*, **riled, riling.** *Informal.* anger; irritate.

rĭll, *n.* small stream.

rĭm, *n.*, *v.t.*, **rimmed, rimming.** *n.* **1.** edge; border; margin. —*v.t.* **2.** furnish with a rim.

rīme, *n.*, *v.*, **rimed, riming.** *n.* **1.** rhyme. **2.** hoarfrost —*v.t.*, *v.i.* **3.** form a rhyme.

rīnd, *n.* hard outer coating, as of cheese or fruit.

ring, *n.*, *v.*, **rang, rung, ringing.** *n.* **1.** sound of a bell. **2.** finger band. **3.** circular object or area. **4.** group of conspirators. **5.** telephone call. —*v.t.* **6.** sound, as a bell. **7.** call by telephone. **8.** encircle. —*v.i.* **9.** resound. **10.** sound clearly. **11.** seem to be true or false.

ring′êr, *n.* **1.** person who rings bells. **2.** *Informal.* **a.** fraudulent substitute. **b.** identical-seeming person or thing.

ring′lēad′êr, *n.* person who leads others in mischief.

ring′lĕt, *n.* **1.** little ring. **2.** curl of hair.

ring′wôrm′′, *n.* contagious fungous skin disease.

rĭnk, *n.* area for skating.

rĭnse, *v.t.*, **rinsed, rinsing**, *n.* *v.t.* **1.** wash lightly, as to remove soap. —*n.* **2.** act or instance of rinsing. **3.** solution for rinsing.

rī′ŏt, *n.* **1.** act of mob violence. —*v.i.* **2.** take part in a riot. —**ri′ot·ous**, *adj.*

rĭp, *v.t.*, *v.i.*, **ripped, ripping**, *n.* tear.

rīpe, *adj.*, **riper, ripest.** fully aged or developed. —**rip′en**, *v.i.*, *v.t.*

rĭp′ple, *v.*, **-pled, -pling**, *n.* *v.i.*, *v.t.* **1.** form in little waves. —*n.* **2.** little wave.

rĭp′-rôar′ĭng, *adj.* *Informal.* lively and boisterous.

rĭp′sâw′′, *n.* saw for cutting wood along the grain.

rīse, *v.i.*, **rose, risen, rising**, *n.* *v.i.* **1.** get up. **2.** rebel. **3.** ascend. **4.** begin. **5.** increase in amount, degree, etc. **6.** originate. —*n.* **7.** act or instance of rising. **8.** small hill. **9.** increase. **10.** advance in rank, power, etc.

rĭs′′ĭ·bĭl′ĭ·tȳ, *n.*, *pl.* **-ties.** ability to laugh.

rĭs′ĭ·ble, *adj.* causing laughter; ridiculous.

rĭsk, *n.* **1.** chance of defeat, injury, loss, etc. —*v.t.* **2.** expose to risk. **3.** incur the risk of. —**risk′y**, *adj.*

rĭs·qué′, *adj.* suggestive of indecency.

rīte, *n.* ceremonial act.

rĭt′ū·al, *n.* **1.** set form for rites. —*adj.* **2.** according to a ritual. —**rit′u·al·ism′′**, *n.* —**rit′u·al·ist**, *n.* —**rit″u·al·is′tic**, *adj.*

ri′val, *n., adj., v.t.,* **-valed, -valing.** *n.* **1.** competitor. **2.** equal. *adj.* **3.** competing. —*v.t.* **4.** compete with. **5.** equal. —**ri′val·ry**, *n.*

rive, *v.t., v.i.,* **rived, rived** or **riven, riving. 1.** tear apart. **2.** split.

riv′er, *n.* large natural stream of water.

riv′et, *n.* **1.** metal bolt forged tight after insertion. —*v.t.* **2.** fasten with rivets.

riv′u·let, *n.* small brook.

roach, *n.* cockroach.

road, *n.* way for travel. —**road′side″**, *n., adj.* —**road′way″**, *n.*

roam, *v.i.* wander.

roan, *n.* horse with white or gray spots.

roar, *v.i.* **1.** emit a bellow. —*n.* **2.** act or instance of roaring.

roast, *v.t.* **1.** cook with dry heat. —*n.* **2.** roasted piece of meat.

rob, *v.t.,* **robbed, robbing.** take from without right. —**rob′ber·y**, *n.*

robe, *n., v.t.,* **robed, robing.** *n.* **1.** long, loose piece of clothing. —*v.t.* **2.** clothe in a robe.

rob′in, *n.* bird with a red breast.

ro′bot, *n.* man-like machine.

ro·bust′, *adj.* vigorous.

rock, *n.* **1.** piece of stone. —*v.i., v.t.* **2.** swing back and forth. —**rock′y**, *adj.*

rock′er, *n.* curved base for rocking objects.

rock′et, *n.* object propelled by reactive thrust. —**rock′et·ry**, *n.*

rock ′n′ roll, *n., adj.* a form of popular music originating in the U.S. and characterized by a distinct beat. Also, **rock.**

rod, *n.* **1.** round, slender object. **2.** five-and-a-half linear yards.

ro′dent, *n.* gnawing mammal.

ro′de·o′, *n., pl.* **-os.** cowboy show.

roe, *n.* fish eggs.

rogue, *n.* rascal. —**ro′guish**, *adj.* —**ro′guer·y**, *n.*

roil, *v.t.* soil. —**roil′y**, *adj.*

rois′ter, *v.i.* carouse.

role, *n.* character assumed. Also, **rôle.**

roll, *v.i.* **1.** move like a ball, or as if on wheels. **2.** revolve; turn over and over. **3.** move like waves; billow. —*v.t.* **4.** cause to roll. **5.** move on wheels. **6.** shape into a round or cylindrical form.

7. smooth or flatten with a cylinder, as metal. —*n.* **8.** act or instance of rolling. **9.** a cylinder, as of paper, wire, etc. **10.** list of names. **11.** small loaf of bread.

rol′lick·ing, *adj.* jolly; boisterous.

ro·maine′, *n.* type of lettuce.

ro·man′ à clef″, *n.* novel that disguises real people and events.

ro·mance′, *n.* **1.** love affair. **2.** fanciful story. **3.** realm of fantasy. —**ro·man′tic**, *adj.* —**ro·man′ti·cal·ly**, *adv.*

Roman numerals, I for 1, V for 5, X for 10, L for 50, C for 100, D for 500, M for 1,000.

ro·man′ti·cism, *n.* romantic artistic movement. —**ro·man′ti·cist**, *n., adj.*

romp, *v.i.* **1.** play boisterously. —*n.* **2.** act or instance of romping.

romp′ers, *n. pl.* loose overall for a child.

roof, *n., pl.* **roofs,** *v.t. n.* **1.** covering for a building. —*v.t.* **2.** furnish with a roof. —**roof′ing**, *n.* —**roof′less**, *adj.* —**roof′top″**, *n.*

rook, *n.* **1.** castle-like chesspiece. —*v.t.* **2.** *Informal.* cheat.

rook′ie, *n. Informal.* raw recruit.

room, *n.* **1.** space. **2.** fully enclosed space in a building. —*v.i.* **3.** lodge. —**room′ful″**, *n.* —**room′mate″**, *n.* —**room′y**, *adj.*

roost, *n., v.i.* perch.

roost′er, *n.* male chicken.

root, *n.* **1.** buried part of a plant. **2.** similar part of a tooth, hair, etc. **3.** basic cause. —*v.t.* **4.** plant. **5.** dig. —*v.i.* **6.** grow roots. **7.** cheer.

rope, *n., v.t.,* **roped, roping.** *n.* **1.** length composed of strands used for pulling or binding. —*v.t.* **2.** tie with rope.

ro′sa·ry, *n., pl.* **-ries. 1.** chain of beads used by Roman Catholics to count prayers said. **2.** series of prayers.

rose, *n.* flowers with thorns and scented petals. —**rose′bud″**, *n.* —**rose′bush″**, *n.*

ro·sé, *n.* pink light wine.

ro′se·ate, *adj.* **1.** rose-colored. **2.** brightly promising.

rose′mar″y, *n.* leaves of an evergreen shrub, used in cooking.

ro·sette′, *n.* round ornament.

rose′wood″, *n.* reddish wood used in cabinetmaking.

rŏs′ĭn, *n.* solid substance remaining after distilling turpentine, used esp. for treating bows of violins, etc.

rŏs′têr, *n.* list.

rŏs′trŭm, *n.*, *pl.* **-trums**, **-tra.** speaker's platform.

rŏs′ỹ, *adj.* **-ier**, **-iest.** 1. pink. 2. optimistic; promising. **—ros′i·ly**, *adv.*

rŏt, *v.*, **rotted**, **rotting**, *n.* decay. **—rot′ ten**, *adj.*

rō′tà·rỹ, *adj.* rotating as a whole or in part.

rō′tāte″, *v.*, **-tated**, **-tating.** *v.t.*, *v.i.* 1. turn around a point. —*v.t.* 2. assign regular turns to. **—ro′ta·to″rỹ**, *adj.*

rōte, *n.* memorization.

rō′tŏr, *n.* rotating part of a machine.

rō·tŭnd′, *adj.* plump. **—ro·tun′di·ty**, *n.*

rō·tŭn′dà, *n.* round hall.

roü·é′, *n.* dissipated man.

roŭge, *n.* red cosmetic or polishing powder.

roŭgh, *adj.* 1. unfinished. 2. violent. 3. *Informal.* troublesome. **—rough′en**, *v.t.*, *v.i.*

roŭgh′àge, *n.* coarse food.

roŭgh′hoŭse″, *n.* *Informal.* violent amusement or fight.

roŭgh′něck″, *n.* *Informal.* boisterous or violent person.

roü·lètte′, *n.* gambling wheel.

rōund, *adj.* 1. curved, or with a curved exterior. 2. approximate. —*n.* 3. repeated series. 4. single shot. —*adv.*, *prep.* 5. around. —*v.t.* 6. make round. 7. go around.

rŏund′·à·bŏut″, *adj.* indirect.

rŏund′lỹ, *adv.* 1. in a round way. 2. thoroughly.

rŏund′ŭp″, *n.* 1. gathering of cattle. 2. summary.

roŭse, *v.*, **roused**, **rousing**. *v.t.*, *v.i.* 1. awaken. —*v.t.* 2. excite.

roŭt, *v.t.* 1. put to flight. 2. gouge. —*n.* 3. disorderly flight.

roŭte, *n.*, *v.t.*, **routed**, **routing**. *n.* 1. course of travel. —*v.t.* 2. assign a route to.

roü·tine′, *n.* 1. standard course of action. —*adj.* 2. ordinary; customary.

rōve, *v.i.*, **roved**, **roving**. wander.

rŏw, *v.*, **rowed**, **rowing**, *n.* *v.t.*, *v.i.* 1. move with oars. —*n.* 2. group in a line.

3. rŏw, fight; quarrel. **—row′boat″**, *n.*

rŏw′dỹ, *adj.*, **-dier**, **-diest**, *n.*, *pl.* **-dies.** *adj.* 1. boisterous or violent. —*n.* 2. rowdy person.

rŏy′àl, *adj.* 1. pertaining to kings or queens. —*n.* 2. sail above a top gallant. **—roy′al·ist**, *n.*

rŏy′àl·tỹ, *n.*, *pl.* **-ties.** 1. kings and queens. 2. fee to an author, patentee, etc.

R.S.V.P., *French.* Abbr. for *répondez s'il vous plaît:* please send an answer.

rŭb, *v.*, **rubbed**, **rubbing**, *n.* *v.t.* 1. apply friction to. 2. apply with friction. —*v.i.* 3. apply friction. —*n.* 4. act or instance of rubbing. 5. source of difficulty.

rŭb′bêr, *n.* 1. resilient substance. 2. decisive game. **—rub′ber·ize″**, *v.t.* **—rub′ ber·y**, *adj.*

rŭb′bĭsh, *n.* 1. cast-off material. 2. worthless speech, etc.

rŭb′ble, *n.* broken stone or masonry.

rŭb′ĭ·cŭnd, *adj.* ruddy.

rŭb′rĭc, *n.* note to a text.

rū′bỹ, *n.*, *pl.* **-bies.** deep red precious stone.

rŭck′ŭs, *n.* *Informal.* disturbance.

rŭd′dêr, *n.* steering device.

rŭd′dỹ, *adj.*, **-dier**, **-diest**. reddish. **—rud′di·ness**, *n.*

rŭde, *adj.* **ruder**, **rudest**. 1. offensive in manner. 2. rough; rugged.

rū′dĭ·mėnt, *n.* basic principle, etc. **—ru″ di·men′ta·ry**, *adj.*

rŭe, *v.t.*, **rued**, **ruing**, *n.* *v.t.* 1. feel remorse or regret for. —*n.* 2. remorse or regret. **—rue′ful**, *adj.*

rŭf′fĭ·àn, *n.* hoodlum.

rŭf′fle, *v.t.*, **-fled**, **-fling**. 1. disturb the surface of. 2. disturb the calm of.

rŭg, *n.* floor cloth.

rŭg′gėd, *adj.* 1. rough in surface or outline. 2. harsh.

rŭin, *n.* 1. Also, **ruins**, remains of something destroyed or injured. 2. downfall. 3. source of one's downfall. —*v.t.* 4. bring to ruin. **—ru″in·a′tion**, *n.* **—ru′ in·ous**, *adj.*

rŭle, *n.*, *v.*, **ruled**, **ruling**. *n.* 1. principle or law. 2. government; dominion. 3. measuring stick. —*v.t.*, *v.i.* 4. govern. —*v.t.* 5. make a formal authoritative decision. **—rul′ing**, *n.*, *adj.*

rul'êr, *n.* **1.** sovereign. **2.** measuring stick.

rŭm, *n.* alcoholic liquor made from sugar.

rŭm'bá, *n.* Cuban dance.

rŭm'ble, *v.i., v.,* **-bled, -bling,** *n. v.i.* **1.** dull continuous noise. —*n.* **2.** act or instance of rumbling.

rŭ'mĭ·nāte'', *v.i.,* **-nated, -nating. 1.** chew the cud. **2.** muse; meditate. —**ru' mi·nant,** *adj., n.*

rŭm'máge, *v.,* **-maged, -maging.** *v.t., v.i.* search thoroughly.

rŭ'mŏr, *n.* **1.** unconfirmed popular report. —*v.t.* **2.** tell in a rumor.

rŭmp, *n.* hindquarters.

rŭm'ple, *v.t.,* **-pled, -pling.** muss.

rŭm'pŭs, *n.* disorderly or noisy activity.

rŭn, *v.,* **ran, run, running,** *n.; v.i.* **1.** move quickly on the feet. **2.** be in motion; operate. **3.** flow. —*v.t.* **4.** operate or manage. **5.** drive. —*n.* **6.** act or instance of running. **7.** route or journey. **8.** series. **9.** brook.

rŭn'á·rŏund'', *n. Informal.* evasive treatment.

rŭn'á·wăy'', *n., adj.* fugitive.

rŭn'-dŏwn'', *adj.* **1.** without energy. **2.** out of repair. **3.** (of a clock, etc.) needing to be wound up.

rŭn'dŏwn'', *n.* summary.

rŭng, *n.* rodlike crosspiece.

rŭn'lĕt, *n.* small stream. Also, **run'nel.**

rŭn'nêr, *n.* **1.** person who runs. **2.** long foot or slide, as on a sled, etc. **3.** long rug.

rŭn'nêr-ŭp, *n., pl.* **-ners-up.** second-best racer or performer.

rŭn'nĭng, *n.* **1.** competitive condition. —*adj.* **2.** operating. **3.** (of measurement) linear. **4.** continuous.

rŭn'-ŏf-thē-mĭll'', *adj.* not special.

rŭnt, *n.* stunted creature. —**runt'y,** *adj.*

rŭn'wăy'', *n.* strip, pavement, etc. for running, esp. by airplanes landing or taking-off.

rŭp'tūre, *n., v.,* **-tured, -turing.** *n.* **1.** hernia. **2.** break. —*v.t.* **3.** cause a rupture. —*v.i.* **4.** undergo a rupture.

rûr'ál, *adj.* pertaining to the country.

rŭse, *n.* trick.

rŭsh, *v.i.* **1.** hurry. —*v.t.* **2.** charge; attack with speed. —*n.* **3.** hurry. **4.** grasslike marsh plant.

rŭs'sĕt, *n.* reddish brown.

rŭst, *n.* **1.** coating of oxydized iron or steel. **2.** plant fungus disease. —*v.i.* **3.** have rust. —*v.t.* **4.** cause to rust. —**rust' y,** *adj.*

rŭs'tĭc, *adj.* **1.** rural. —*n.* **2.** rural person.

rŭs'tle, *v.,* **-tled, -tling,** *n. v.i.* **1.** make a soft, whispering sound. —*v.t.* **2.** steal, as cattle. —*n.* **3.** rustling sound.

rŭt, *n., v.t.,* **rutted, rutting.** *n.* **1.** worn track. **2.** fixed routine. —*v.t.* **3.** make ruts in. —**rut'ty,** *adj.*

rŭ''tá·bā'gá, *n.* type of turnip.

rŭth'lĕss, *adj.* without compunction or compassion.

rȳe, *n.* **1.** edible grain. **2.** whiskey distilled from this.

S

S, s, *n.* nineteenth letter of the English alphabet.

Săb'báth, *n.* day of worship and rest.

sā'bêr, *n.* singled-edged curved sword. Also, **sa'bre.**

sā'ble, *n.* weasellike mammal with dark-brown fur.

săb'o·tâge'', *n., v.t.* **-taged, -taging.** *n.* **1.** intentional damage to equipment. —*v.t.* **2.** damage intentionally. —**sab'o· teur''.**

săc, *n.* baglike part of the body.

săc·chá·rĭne, *adj.* **1.** too sweet, as in manner. —*n.* **2.** saccharin.

săc·chá·rĭn, *n.* sugar substitute.

sac·er·do·tal (sas''ər dō'təl, sak''ər dō' təl), *adj.* pertaining to or suggesting priests.

sa·chet (sa chā'), *n.* bag of scented powder.

săck, *n.* **1.** bag, esp. a large, strong one. **2.** plunder. —*v.t.* **3.** put into a sack or sacks. **4.** plunder.

săck'clŏth, *n.* coarse cloth worn by penitents.

săc'rá·mĕnt, *n.* **1.** ceremony or act regarded as sacred. **2. Sacrament,** Eucharist. —**sac''ra·men'tal,** *adj.*

sā'crĕd, *adj.* **1.** holy. **2.** safe from attack,

ridicule, etc. **3.** binding, as a promise. —**să·cred·ly**, *adv.* —**să·cred·ness**, *n.*

săc´rĭ·fice, *n.*, *v.*, **-ficed, -ficing.** *n.* **1.** offer of something valuable to a deity. **2.** intentional loss of one thing to gain another. —*v.t.* **3.** offer or lose in a sacrifice. —*v.i.* **4.** make a sacrifice. —**sac´´ri·fi´cial**, *adj.*

săc´rĭ·lège, *n.* violation or mockery of something sacred. —**sac´´ri·le´gious**, *adj.*

săc´rĭs·tàn, *n.* person in charge of a sacristy.

săc´rĭs·tў, *n.*, *pl.* **-ties.** place for keeping the sacred vessels, etc. of a church.

săc´rō·sănct, *adj.* sacred.

săd, *adj.*, **sadder, saddest.** low in spirits; melancholy. —**sad´ly**, *adv.* —**sad´ness**, *n.* —**sad´den**, *v.t.*, *v.i.*

săd´dle, *n.*, *v.t.*, **-dled, -dling.** *n.* **1.** seat for the rider of a horse, bicycle, etc. —*v.t.* **2.** put a saddle on. **3.** impose a burden on. —**sad´dle·bag**, *n.*

săd´ĭsm, *n.* practice of cruelty for pleasure. —**sad´ist**, *n.* —**sa·dis´tic**, *adj.*

sa·fa·ri (sə fah´rē), *n.* journey, esp. in Central Africa, for hunting or exploration.

săfe, *adj.*, **safer, safest**, *n.* *adj.* **1.** free from danger or risk. —*n.* **2.** container protecting against theft, fire, etc. —**safe´ly**, *adv.* —**safe´ty**, *n.*

săfe´guârd, *v.t.* **1.** protect from danger. —*n.* **2.** something protective.

săg, *v.i.*, **sagged, sagging**, *n.* *v.i.* **1.** bend or hang downwards where not supported; droop. —*n.* **2.** distortion caused by sagging.

sä´gà, *n.* Nordic heroic legend.

sà·gă´cĭ·tў, *n.* wisdom. —**sa·ga´cious**, *adj.* —**sa·ga´cious·ly**, *adv.*

săge, *n.*, *adj.*, **sager, sagest**. *n.* **1.** wise and learned person. **2.** seasoning herb. —*adj.* **3.** wise. —**sage´ly**, *adv.* —**sage´ness**, *n.*

sa·hib (sah´ēb), *n.* respectful term for a European, used in the Indian subcontinent.

said, *adj.* previously mentioned.

săil, *n.* **1.** area of cloth used to drive a ship or boat by the force of moving air. **2.** excursion in a ship or boat so driven. —*v.i.*

3. make such an excursion or excursions. **4.** depart in a ship.

săil´bōat´´, *n.* boat moved by sails.

săil´fĭsh, *n.* large fish with saillike dorsal fin.

săil´ör, *n.* **1.** member of a ship's crew. **2.** enlisted man in a navy.

sâint, *n.* **1.** person officially venerated by a church. **2.** person leading a religious or upright life. —**saint´hood**, *n.* —**saint´ly**, *adj.*

săke, *n.* **1.** benefit. **2.** purpose. **3.** (sak´ē) Japanese rice wine.

săl´à·ble, *adj.* able to be sold. Also, **sale´a·ble.**

sà·lā·ciŏus, *adj.* obscene; lewd.

săl´ăd, *n.* dish mainly of raw vegetables or fruits.

săl´à·măn´´dêr, *n.* small, tailed amphibian.

sà·lā´mĭ, *n.* spiced sausage.

săl´à·rў, *n.*, *pl.* **-ries.** regular payment for a permanent employee. —**sal´a·ried**, *adj.*

săle, *n.* **1.** act or occasion of selling. **2.** demands for something sold. **3.** offer of goods at reduced prices. —**sales´clerk´´**, *n.* —**sale´room´´**, **sales´room´´**, *n.*

sâles´măn, *n.* man who sells merchandise, etc. Also, *fem.*, **sales´wom´´an**, **sales´la´´dy**, **sales´girl´´**.

sā´lĭ·ent, *adj.* **1.** outstanding. **2.** projecting. —*n.* **3.** area that projects. —**sa´li·ent·ly**, *adv.* —**sa´li·ence**, *n.*

sā·lĭne (sā´lĭn), *adj.* salty. —**sa·lin´i·ty**, *n.*

sà·lī´và, *n.* fluid secreted in mouth by glands to aid digestion. —**sa´li·va´´ry**, *adj.*

săl´lōw, *adj.* with a sickly, yellowish complexion.

săl´lў, *n.*, *pl.* **-lies**, *v.i.*, **-lied, -lying**. *n.* **1.** counterattack from a fortified position. **2.** witticism. —*v.i.* **3.** emerge briskly.

săl´mŏn, *n.* edible fish with pink flesh.

sà·lŏn´, *n.* **1.** room for conversation. **2.** art gallery.

sà·lŏŏn´, *n.* **1.** place where liquor is served. **2.** public room, esp. on a ship.

sălt, *n.* **1.** sodium chloride. **2.** *Chemistry.* compound derived from an acid. **3.** wit;

piquancy. —*v.t.* **4.** treat with salt. —**salt′ y,** *adj.* —**salt′shak′′er,** *n.*

sält′ïne′, *n.* salted cracker.

sält′′pē′têr, *n.* potassium nitrate. Also, **salt′′pe′tre.**

sá·lū′brï·oŭs, *adj.* promoting health. —**sa·lu′brï·ous·ly,** *adv.*

sál′ū·târ′′y, *adj.* beneficial.

sál′′ū·tā′tion, *n.* **1.** greeting. **2.** opening phrase of a letter, naming the addressee.

sá·lūte′, *n.*, *v.* **-luted, -luting.** *n.* **1.** act expressing respect or attention in military etiquette. **2.** greeting. **3.** firing of cannons, etc. as a sign of welcome. —*v.t.* **4.** recognize with a salute. —*v.i.* **5.** perform a salute.

sál′vàge, *v.t.*, **-vaged, -vaging,** *n.* *v.t.* **1.** rescue from loss, as a ship. **2.** gather for reuse, as discarded material. —*n.* **3.** salvaged material.

sál′′vā′tion, *n.* act of saving or state of being saved, as from damnation or destruction.

sálve, *n.*, *v.t.*, **salved, salving,** *n.* **1.** soothing or healing ointment. —*v.t.* **2.** cover with salve.

sál′vö, *n.*, *pl.* **-vos, -voes.** discharge of many guns, etc. in rapid succession.

sãme, *adj.* **1.** identical. **2.** without change. **3.** previously mentioned. —*n.* **4.** same thing or person. —**same′ness,** *n.*

säm′ö·vâr, *n.* metal tea urn.

säm′pän, *n.* sculled Chinese or Japanese boat.

säm′ple, *n.*, *adj.*, *v.t.*, **-pled, -pling,** *n.* **1.** something representing more or others of its kind. —*adj.* **2.** serving as a sample. —*v.t.* **3.** take a sample of.

säm′plêr, *n.* piece of needlework demonstrating skill.

sän′′á·tô′rï′ŭm, *n.* sanitarium.

sänc′tï·fÿ, *v.t.*, **-fied, -fying. 1.** make sacred. **2.** free of sin. —**sanc′′ti·fi·ca′ tion,** *n.*

sänc′tï·mō′′nÿ, *n.* showy or false piety. —**sanc′′ti·mo′ni·ous,** *adj.*

sänc′tion, *n.* **1.** permission or support. **2.** non-belligerent measure against a nation by other nations. —*v.t.* **3.** authorize.

sänc′tï·tÿ, *n.* holiness or sacredness.

sänc′tū·âr′′ÿ, *n.*, *pl.* **-aries. 1.** consecrated place. **2.** place of refuge.

sänc′tŭm, *n.* consecrated place.

sänd, *n.* **1.** fine pieces of rock. **2. sands,** sandy area. —*v.t.* **3.** rub with sandpaper. —**sand′er,** *n.* —**sand′storm′′,** *n.*

sän′dàl, *n.* open shoe secured by straps.

sän′dàl·wŏŏd, *n.* aromatic Asiatic wood.

sänd′bâr′′, *n.* low island of sand.

sänd′pā′′pêr, *n.* **1.** sand-coated paper for smoothing or reducing surfaces. —*v.t.* **2.** rub with sandpaper.

sänd′pïp′′êr, *n.* small shore bird.

sänd′stöne, *n.* stone made of sand naturally cemented together.

sänd′wïch, *n.* **1.** bread, roll, etc. in two slices with meat, etc. between them. —*v.t.* **2.** insert.

sänd′ÿ, *adj.*, **ier, -iest. 1.** abounding in sand. **2.** colored like sand.

säne, *adj.*, **saner, sanest.** mentally sound. —**sane′ly,** *adv.*

sang-froid (säh′′frwah′), *n.* control of one's emotions.

sän′guï·när′′ÿ, *adj.* **1.** bloody. **2.** bloodthirsty.

sän′guine, *adj.* optimistic.

sän′′ï·târ′′ï·ŭm, *n.* place for the recovery of health.

sän′ï·tär′ÿ, *adj.* **1.** free of harmful bacteria, etc. **2.** pertaining to health.

sän′′ï·tā′tion, *n.* provisions against disease.

sän′ï·tÿ, *n.* mental soundness.

säp, *n.*, *v.t.*, **sapped, sapping,** *n.* **1.** juice of a tree, etc. **2.** *Informal.* fool. —*v.t.* **3.** weaken.

sä′pï·ent, *adj.* wise; knowing. —**sa′pi· ence,** *n.*

säp′lïng, *n.* young tree.

säp′phïre, *n.* blue gemstone.

säp′sŭck′′êr, *n.* variety of woodpecker.

sâr′cäsm, *n.* **1.** making of agreeably worded but harshly intended remarks. **2.** such a remark. —**sar·cas′tic,** *adj.* —**sar·cas′ti·cal·ly,** *adv.*

sâr·cŏph′à·gŭs, *n.*, *pl.* **-gi.** stone coffin.

sâr·dïne′, *n.* trade name for a small canned ocean fish.

sâr·dŏn′ïc, *adj.* bitterly sarcastic. —**sar· don′i·cal·ly,** *adv.*

sar·sa·pa·ril·la (sas′′pə ril′ə, sahrs′′pə ril′ə), *n.* tropical vine with fragrant roots.

sâr·tô′rï·ál, *adj.* pertaining to tailors or tailoring.

sǎsh, *n.* **1.** cloth band worn over the upper part of the body or around the waist. **2.** frame for window glass.

sǎs'sǎ·frǎs, *n.* American tree with aromatic bark at the roots.

Sā'tàn, *n.* the Devil. —**sa·tan'ic**, *adj.*

sǎtch'ĕl, *n.* small cloth suitcase or bag.

sāte, *v.t.*, **sated**, **sating**. satisfy fully or to excess, as an appetite.

sä·tēen', *n.* satinlike cotton fabric.

sǎt'ĕl·līte, *n.* **1.** heavenly body moving around a planet. **2.** organization, etc. dominated or controlled by another.

sa·ti·ate (sā'shē āt), *v.t.*, **-ated**, **-ating**. glut. —**sa''ti·a'tion**, **sa·ti'e·ty**, *n.*

sǎt'ĭn, *n.* glossy fabric or silk or a silk substitute. —**sat'in·y**, *adj.*

sǎt'īre, *n.* **1.** sarcasm or ridicule in the exposure of wrongful actions or attitudes. **2.** story, etc. using these means. —**sa·tir'i·cal**, **sa·tir'ic**, *adj.* —**sa·tir'i·cal·ly**, *adv.* —**sat'ir·ist**, *n.*

sǎt'īr·īze, *v.t.*, **-ized**, **-izing**. portray satirically.

sǎt'ĭs·fȳ, *v.t.*, **-fied**, **-fying**. **1.** fulfill the wishes or needs of. **2.** convince. **3.** pay, as a debt. —**sat''is·fac'tion**, *n.* —**sat''is·fac'to·ry**, *adj.*

sǎt'ū·rāte, *v.t.*, **-rated**, **-rating**. cause complete absorption by. —**sat''u·ra'tion**, *n.*

Sǎt'ûr·dây, *n.* seventh day of the week.

Sǎt'ûrn, *n.* second-largest planet in the solar system.

sat·ur·nine (sat'ǝr nīn''), *adj.* gloomy.

sä'tyr, *n.* **1.** classical forest deity. **2.** lecherous man.

sǎuce, *n.* **1.** liquid for flavoring or cooking. **2.** semiliquid stewed fruit.

sǎuce'pǎn'', *n.* small, handled cooking pot.

sǎu'cĕr, *n.* small dish.

sǎu'cȳ, *adj.*, **-cier**, **-ciest**. impudent. —**sau'ci·ness**, *n.* —**sau'ci·ly**, *adv.*

sǎuer'krǎut'', *n.* chopped fermented cabbage.

sǎu'nà, *n.* Finnish hot-air bath.

sǎun'tĕr, *v.i.*, *n.* stroll.

sǎu'sàge, *n.* minced and seasoned meat, often in a casing.

sǎu·têrne, *n.* sweet white wine.

sǎu·té', *v.t.*, **-téed**, **-téeing**. fry quickly in a little fat.

sǎv'àge, *adj.* **1.** uncivilized. **2.** fierce or harsh. —*n.* **3.** uncivilized person. —**sav'age·ly**, *adv.* —**sav'age·ry**, *n.*

sä·vǎnt (sa vahnt'), *n.* learned person.

sāve, *v.t.*, **saved**, **saving**, *prep.*, *conj. v.t.* **1.** keep from harm. **2.** keep for future use. **3.** keep from being wasted. **4.** keep from sin or its consequences. —*prep.*, *conj.* **5.** except.

sāv'ĭng, *adj.* **1.** redeeming. **2.** thrifty. —*n.* **3.** economy. **4. savings**, money saved. —*prep.* **5.** with the exception of.

sāv'iôr, **1.** rescuer. **2. the Savior**, Christ. Also, **sav'iour.**

sa·voir-faire (sav''wahr fār'), *n.* skill in human relations.

sā'vör, *n.*, *v.t.* taste or smell. Also, **sa'vour.**

sā'vör·ȳ, *adj.* pleasant-tasting or smelling.

sǎw, *n.*, *v.t.*, **sawed**, **sawing**. *n.* **1.** cutting tool with a row of teeth. **2.** saying or proverb. —*v.i.* **3.** cut with a saw. —**saw'mill''**, *n.* —**saw'yer**, *n.*

sǎx'ö·phöne, *n.* keyed metal reed instrument. —**sax'o·phon''ist**, *n.*

sǎy, *v.t.*, **said**, **saying**, *n. v.t.* **1.** speak. **2.** declare to be true. —*n.* **3.** chance to speak.

sǎy'ĭng, *n.* proverb.

scǎb, *n.*, *v.i.*, **scabbed**, **scabbing**. *n.* **1.** crust over a healing wound or sore. **2.** worker who replaces a striking worker. —*v.i.* **3.** form a scab. —**scab'by**, *adj.*

scǎb'bàrd, *n.* sword sheath.

scǎ'bĭes, *n.* itching skin disease.

scǎf'fold, *n.* **1.** Also, **scaf'fold·ing**, temporary platform. **2.** platform for execution of condemned persons.

scǎl'à·wǎg'', *n.* scoundrel.

scǎld, *v.t.* **1.** burn with hot fluid. **2.** heat almost to boiling. —*n.* **3.** burn made by hot fluid.

scǎle, *n.*, *v.t.*, **scaled**, **scaling**. *n.* **1.** platelike portion of the covering of a fish, snake, etc. **2.** flake or layer of material. **3.** Also, **scales**, weighing device. **4.** range of musical tones. **5.** system of relations, as of actual size to represented size or of different degrees of a thing. —*v.t.* **6.** remove scales from. **7.** climb. **8.** determine the relative size of. —**scal'y**, *adj.*

scăl'lión, *n.* any of several varieties of small onion.

scăl·lŏp, *n.* **1.** bivalve mollusk. **2.** any of the curves forming part of a decorative border. —*v.t.* **3.** decorate with scallops.

scălp, *n.* **1.** hair and skin covering the top of the head. —*v.t.* **2.** take a scalp from, esp. as a trophy.

scăl'pĕl, *n.* surgical knife.

scăm, *n.* con game; deception practiced to defraud.

scămp, *n.* rascal; imp.

scăm'pêr, *v.i.* **1.** run quickly. —*n.* **2.** fast run.

scăn, *v.t.,* **scanned, scanning. 1.** examine in detail. **2.** examine quickly. **3.** analyze the rhythmic pattern of.

scăn'dăl, *n.* **1.** malicious gossip. **2.** disgraceful occurrence or situation. —**scan'dal·ous,** *adj.*

scăn'dăl·ize, *v.t.,* **-ized, -izing.** shock with a scandal.

scănt, *adj.* scarcely sufficient. Also, **scant'y.** —**scant'i·ly,** *adv.* —**scant'i·ness,** *n.*

scăpe'goăt, *n.* person blamed for the misdeeds of others.

scăpe'grăce, *n.* rascal.

scăp'u·lă, *n., pl.* **-lae, -las.** shoulder blade. —**scap'u·lar,** *adj.*

scăr, *n., v.t.,* **scarred, scarring.** *n.* **1.** mark left by a cut. —*v.t.* **2.** cut so as to make a scar.

scăr'ăb, *n.* carved image of a beetle.

scărce, *adj.,* **scarcer, scarcest.** not plentiful or common. —**scarc'i·ty, scarce'ness,** *n.*

scărce'ly̆, *adv.* **1.** only just; barely. **2.** hardly.

scăre, *n., v.t.,* **scared, scaring,** *v.t.* **1.** frighten. —*v.i.* **2.** become frightened. —*n.* **3.** frightening occurrence.

scăre'crŏw'', *n.* device to frighten birds from a planted field.

scărf, *n., pl.* **scarfs, scarves.** length of cloth for warming the neck and chest.

scăr'ĭ·fy̆, *v.t.,* **-fied, -fying.** scratch or cut.

scăr'lĕt, *adj., n.* bright red.

scăr'lĕt fĕvêr, contagious disease marked by fever and scarlet rash.

scăt, *v.i.,* **scatted, scatting.** *Informal.* run away.

scăth'ĭng, *adj.* bitterly harsh, as something said or written. —**scath'ing·ly,** *adv.*

scăt'têr, *v.t.* **1.** throw in all directions. —*v.i.* **2.** move away rapidly in all directions.

scăv'ĕnge, *v.,* **-enged, -enging.** *v.t.* **1.** clean out. —*v.i.* **2.** search for refuse that can be eaten or reused. —**scav'en·ger,** *n.*

scé·năr'ĭ·ō, *n.* story outline, esp. in the motion pictures.

scēne, *n.* **1.** what is seen from a certain place. **2.** location of an action. **3.** subdivision of a dramatic act. **4.** emotional display in public. —**scen'ic,** *adj.*

scēn'êr·y̆, *n.* **1.** pleasant outdoor scene. **2.** painted canvases, etc. representing the scene of a dramatic action.

scĕnt, *n.* **1.** distinctive smell. **2.** trail left by something with such a smell. **3.** perfume. **4.** sense of smell. —*v.t.* **5.** smell. **6.** perfume.

scĕp'têr, *n.* short staff symbolizing royal power. Also, **scep'tre.**

scĕp'tĭc, *n.* skeptic.

schĕd'ūle, *n., v.t.,* **-uled, -uling.** *n.* **1.** list of the times of planned actions or events. **2.** any orderly list. —*v.t.* **3.** put on a schedule.

schēme, *n., v.i.,* **schemed, scheming.** *n.* **1.** plan or design. **2.** plot; intrigue. —*v.i.* **3.** plot to do or attain something. —**schem'er,** *n.*

schism (siz'əm), *n.* division, as between factions in an organization. —**schis·mat'ic,** *adj., n.*

schist (shist), *n.* layered crystalline rock.

schiz·o·phre·ni·a (skit''zə frē'nē ə), *n.* mental disorder. —**schiz''o·phre'nic schiz'oid,** *adj.*

schlé·miĕl', *n.* *Yiddish.* a person who is a habitual failure.

schlŏck, *Yiddish. n.* **1.** inferior goods or materials. —*adj.* **2.** inferior in material or workmanship.

schmăltz, *n.* *Informal.* sentimental art.

schŏl'ăr, *n.* **1.** person who studies to acquire knowledge. **2.** school pupil.

schŏl'ăr·ly̆, *adj.* pertaining to or in the manner of scholars.

schŏl'ăr·shĭp, *n.* **1.** activities and accomplishments of scholars. **2.** grant of money to make school attendance possible.

scho·lăs'tĭc, *adj.* pertaining to education.

school, *n.* 1. place or institution for education or training. 2. educational activity. 3. group with a common set of beliefs or practices. 4. group of fish, etc. —*v.t.* 5. educate or train. —**school'book,** *n.* —**school'boy,** *n.* —**school'girl,** *n.* —**school'mate,** *n.* —**school'house,** *n.* —**school'room,** *n.* —**school'teach·er,** *n.*

schoon'er, *n.* fore-and-aft rigged sailing vessel with two or more masts, including a foremast.

schwa (shwah), *n.* unstressed vowel sound, e.g. the *o* in *factor,* represented by the symbol ə.

sci·ăt'i·ca (sī at'ik ə), *n.* neuralgia of the hip and thigh. —**sci·ăt'ic,** *adj.*

sci'ence, *n.* 1. systematic acquisition of knowledge, esp. knowledge that can be measured precisely. 2. precise method or skill. —**sci''en·tif'ic,** *adj.* —**sci''en·tif'i·cal·ly,** *adv.* —**sci'en·tist,** *n.*

scĭn·tĭl'la, *n.* glimmering; trace.

scĭn''til·late, *v.i.* **-lated, -lating.** sparkle. —**scin''til·la'tion,** *n.*

sci·on (sī'ən), *n.* 1. descendant. 2. plant shoot or bud, esp. for grafting.

scĭs'sŏrs, *n.* instrument for cutting by means of two moving blades.

sclĕ·rō'sĭs, *n.* hardening of body tissue. —**scle·rot'ic,** *adj.*

scŏff, *n., v.i.* jeer. —**scof'fer,** *n.*

scold, *v.t.* 1. reproach at length. —*n.* 2. person who scolds.

scŏnce, *n.* wall bracket for lights.

scōne, *n.* flat biscuit.

scoop, *n.* 1. device for digging deeply. 2. act or instance of scooping. 3. amount held by a scoop. 4. *Informal.* prior publication of news. —*v.t.* 5. remove or empty with a scoop. 6. *Informal.* get the better of by publishing news first.

scoot, *v.i.* go quickly.

scoot'er, *n.* small, low-built two-wheeled vehicle.

scōpe, *n.* range of responsibility or possibility for action.

scŏrch, *v.t.* 1. burn on the surface. —*n.* 2. surface burn.

score, *n., v.,* **scored, scoring.** *n.* 1. total,

as of points in a game. 2. *Informal.* **know the score,** know the actual situation. 3. long, shallow cut. 4. group of twenty. 5. musical arrangement. —*v.t.* 6. add, as points in a game. 7. mark with a long, shallow cut. —*v.t.* 8. gain points, as in a game.

scŏrn, *n.* 1. contempt. 2. derision. —*v.t.* 3. treat with scorn. —**scorn'ful,** *adj.* —**scorn'ful·ly,** *adv.*

scŏr'pĭ·ŏn, *n.* poisonous, long-tailed, eight-legged animal.

Scŏtch, *n.* malted-barley whisky made in Scotland.

scŏtch, *v.t.* make ineffective.

scoun'drel, *n.* rascal.

scour, *v.t.* 1. clean with a steady rubbing action. 2. go over repeatedly, as during a search.

scourge (skərj), *n., v.t.,* **scourged, scourging.** *n.* 1. whip. 2. major affliction. —*v.t.* 3. beat with a whip. 4. punish or harass severely.

scout, *n.* 1. person sent to explore or search. —*v.t.* 2. reject as absurd. —*v.i.* 3. act as a scout.

scow, *n.* flat-bottomed barge or boat.

scowl, *v.t.,* 1. frown angrily. —*n.* 2. angry frown.

scrăb'ble, *v.i.,* **-bled, -bling.** 1. scratch or scrape with the hands. 2. struggle without dignity.

scrăg'glў, *adj.,* **-glier, -gliest.** ragged.

scrăg·gў, *adj.* **-gier, -giest.** scrawny.

scrăm'ble, *v.,* **-bled, -bling,** *n.* *v.t.* 1. mix up; confuse. —*v.i.* 2. move in short, rapid steps. —*n.* 3. scrambling motion or gait. 4. undignified struggle, as for something of value.

scrăp, *n., adj., v.t.,* **scrapped, scrapping.** *n.* 1. small piece. 2. refuse material, esp. when reclaimable. 3. *Informal.* fight. —*adj.* 4. in the form of scrap. —*v.t.* 5. make into scrap. 6. discard. —**scrap'heap,** *n.*

scrăp'book, *n.* album for printed and written material, etc.

scrāpe, *v.,* **scraped, scraping,** *n.* *v.t.* 1. rub against roughly. 2. remove by rough rubbing. 3. get by tedious labor. —*v.i.* 4. rub roughly against something. —*n.* 5. act of scraping. 6. area scraped. 7. dangerous situation. —**scrap'er,** *n.*

scrăp′ple, *n.* fried dish of meal and meat scraps.

scratch, *v.t.* **1.** make a long, shallow cut in. **2.** cross out; eliminate. —*n.* **3.** long, shallow cut. **4. from scratch**, from the beginning. **5. up to scratch**, up to standard.

scratch′y̆, *adj.*, **-ier**, **-iest.** suggesting scratching, esp. in sound.

scrawl, *v.t.*, *v.i.* **1.** write with a bad hand. —*n.* **2.** writing in a bad hand.

scrawn′y̆, *adj.*, **-nier**, **-niest.** disagreeably thin.

scream, *n.* **1.** loud, high-pitched cry. —*v.i.* **2.** utter such a cry.

screech, *n.* **1.** harsh screamlike sound. —*v.i.* **2.** utter such sounds.

screen, *n.* **1.** flat object or surface for division, protection, or concealment. **2.** surface on which motion pictures, television programs, etc. are projected. **3. the screen**, motion-picture industry. —*v.t.* **4.** enclose or protect with or as if with a screen. **5.** sift through a screen. **6.** investigate for suitability.

screw, *n.* **1.** simple machine for fastening, moving, etc., in the form of an inclined plane wound around an axis. **2.** propeller. —*v.t.* **3.** fasten with screws. **4.** turn as one does a screw. —**screw′driv′′er**, *n.*

scrib′ble, *v.*, **-bled**, **-bling** *n. v.t.*, *v.i.* **1.** write hastily and carelessly. —*n.* **2.** hasty or careless writing.

scribe, *n. Archaic.* writer or clerk.

scrim′mage, *n.*, *v.i.* **-maged**, **-maging**. *n.* **1.** play in football. —*v.i.* **2.** take part in a scrimmage.

scrimp, *v.i.* save; economize.

scrip, *n.* certificate used in place of money.

script, *n.* **1.** handwriting. **2.** manuscript, esp. of a play, etc.

Scrip′ture, *n.* **1.** portion or portions of the Bible. **2. the Scriptures**, the Bible. —**scrip′tur·al**, *adj.*

scrŏf′ŭ·là, *n.* tuberculosis of the lymph glands.

scroll, *n.* **1.** roll of paper, etc. bearing writing or print. **2.** spiral ornamental motif. —*v.* **3.** (computers) to move the display on a monitor so that other data can be read.

scro′tŭm, *n.* baglike skin enclosure for testicles.

scrounge, *v.*, **scrounged**, **scrounging**. *v.t.* **1.** *Informal.* beg or steal in a minor way. —*v.i.* **2.** *Informal.* look for something desired.

scrub, *v.t.*, **scrubbed**, **scrubbing**, *n.*, *adj.*, *v.t.* **1.** wash with a vigorous rubbing action. **2.** *Informal.* eliminate; cross off. —*n.* **3.** stunted trees or shrubbery. —*adj.* **4.** inferior.

scruff, *n.* nape of the neck.

scru′ple, *n.* prompting of the conscience.

scru′pu·lous, *adj.* **1.** conscientious. **2.** careful. —**scru′pu·lous·ly** *adv.*

scru′ti·nize, *v.t.*, **-nized**, **-nizing.** examine carefully. —**scru′ti·ny**, *n.*

scŭd, *v.i.*, **scudded**, **scudding.** move rapidly.

scŭff, *v.t.* **1.** wear by rubbing or scraping. —*v.i.*, *v.i.* **2.** shuffle, as the feet.

scŭf′fle, *v.i.*, **-fled**, **-fling**, *n.*, *v.i.* **1.** fight confusedly at close quarters. —*n.* **2.** confused fight at close quarters.

scull, *n.* **1.** oar used at a boat's stern. **2.** racing rowboat. —*v.t.*, *v.i.* **3.** move with a scull.

scul′lêr·y̆, *n.* room for cleaning dishes, kitchen utensils, etc.

sculp′tûre, *n.* **1.** art of composing in three dimensions. **2.** example of this art. —**sculp′tur·al**, *adj.* —**sculp′tor**, *n.*, *fem.*, **sculp′tress**.

scŭm, *n.* **1.** film on a liquid surface. **2.** rabble. —**scum′my**, *adj.*

scŭp′pêr, *n.* drainage opening in a deck or flat roof.

scûrf, *n.* flecks of dead skin.

scûr′ril·oŭs, *adj.* grossly insulting. —**scur′ril·ous·ly**, *adv.* —**scur′ril·i·ty**, **scur′ril·lous·ness**, *n.*

scûr′ry̆, *v.i.*, **-ried**, **-rying**, *n.*, *pl.* **-ries**. *v.i.* **1.** move hastily. —*n.* **2.** hasty movement.

scûr′vy̆, *n.* disease due to vitamin deficiency.

scŭt′tle, *n.*, *v.*, **-tled**, **-tling**. *n.* **1.** hatchlike opening in a deck or roof. **2.** coal bucket. —*v.t.* **3.** sink intentionally. —*v.i.* **4.** scurry.

scythe, *n.* mowing instrument with curved blade and long handle.

sea, *n.* **1.** part of an ocean, esp. one partly

bounded by land. **2. the sea,** the oceans. **3.** large inland body of water. **4.** relative turbulence of ocean water at a given time. —**sea′board″, sea′coast″,** *n.*

sea′far′ing, *n.* activity of one who travels on or works at sea. —**sea′far″er,** *n.*

sea′gō″ing, *adj.* pertaining to or suitable for travel on the sea.

sea hôrse, semitropical fish with head of horselike form.

seal, *n.* **1.** device for giving official character to or preventing tampering with a document, locked space, etc. **2.** stamp used to shape such a device. **3.** device to prevent passage of air, etc. **4.** four-flippered sea mammal. —*v.t.* **5.** put seal on. **6.** enclose with a seal.

sea′lïon, large seal.

seam, *n.* **1.** line of junction. **2.** mineral stratum. —*v.t.* **3.** join at or with a seam. —**seam′less,** *adj.*

sea′mán, *n., pl.* -**men.** sailor. —**sea′man·ship″,** *n.*

seam′stress, *n.* sewing woman.

seam′ÿ, *adj.* **seamier, seamiest. 1.** having seams. **2.** less attractive; sordid.

se·ance′, (sā′ahns), *n.* meeting for communication with the dead.

sea′plāne, *n.* airplane able to land on water.

sea′pôrt″, *n.* port fronting on an ocean.

sear, *v.t.* **1.** burn the surface of. **2.** wither.

search, *n.* **1.** methodical attempt to find something. —*v.t.* **2.** examine in making a search. —*v.i.* **3.** hunt. —**search′er,** *n.*

search′ïng, *adj.* deep and perceptive, as an investigation.

search′light, *n.* directed light for distinguishing objects in the dark.

sea′shell″, *n.* shell of saltwater mollusk.

sea′shôre″, *n.* shore of an ocean. Also, **sea′side″.**

sea′sïck″, *adj.* sick from the motion of a ship. —**sea′sick″ness,** *n.*

sea′són, *n.* **1.** quarter of the year beginning at a solstice or equinox. **2.** appropriate time. —*v.t.* **3.** flavor with salt, spices, herbs, etc. **4.** prepare for use by aging or exposure to weather. —**sea′son·al,** *adj.*

sea′són·a·ble, *adj.* coming at the appropriate time.

sea′són·ing, *n.* flavoring of salt, spices, herbs, etc.

seat, *n.* **1.** place for sitting. **2.** place of governmental activities, residence, etc. **3.** location. **4.** place in a legislature, etc. —*v.t.* **5.** put onto a seat. **6.** install in a seat.

sea′wäy″, *n.* **1.** inland waterway to the sea. **2.** area of open sea.

sea′weed″, *n.* ocean plant.

sea′wôr″thÿ, *adj.* suitable for navigation at sea.

se·ba·ceous (si bā′shəs), *adj.* fatty.

se·cēde′, *v.i.,* -**ceded, -ceding.** withdraw from a political state, etc. —**se·ces′sion,** *n.*

se·clūde′, *v.t.,* -**cluded, -cluding.** isolate, esp. from society or activity. —**se·clu′sion,** *n.*

sec′ónd, *adj.* **1.** next after the first. —*n.* **2.** sixtieth of a minute. **3.** person serving as an assistant or witness. **4. seconds,** goods rejected for ordinary sale. —*v.t.* **5.** approve. —*adv.* **6.** as a second point. —**sec′ond·ly,** *adv.*

sec′ónd·ār·ÿ, *adv.* **1.** forming a second stage or phase. **2.** of a second level of importance. —**sec′on·dar″i·ly,** *adv.*

sec′ónd-hănd′, *adj.* **1.** belonging to or offered to a new owner. **2.** not original.

se′crèt, *n.* **1.** something not to be known by everyone. **2.** hidden cause or reason. —*adj.* **3.** hidden or not to be known by everyone. —**se′cret·ly,** *adv.* —**se′cre·cy,** *n.*

sec″rė·tär′ï·át, *n.* group of administrative officials.

sec′rė·tār″ÿ, *n., pl.* -**taries. 1.** assistant to a businessman, official, etc. **2.** head of a government department. **3.** writing desk. —**sec″rė·tar′i·al,** *adj.*

se·crēte′, *v.t.,* -**creted, -creting. 1.** produce and release substances, as a gland. **2.** hide. —**se·cre′tion,** *n.* —**se·cre′to·ry,** *adj.*

se′crė·tïve, *adj.* **1.** reluctant to reveal information. **2.** pertaining to secretion. —**se′cre·tive·ly,** *adv.* —**se′cre·tive·ness,** *n.*

sèct, *n.* religious group.

sèc·tär′ï·àn, *adj.* **1.** pertaining to separate sects. —*n.* **2.** member of a sect.

sec′tion, *n.* **1.** separate part. **2.** act or instance of dividing. **3.** view of a thing as if divided. —*v.t.* **4.** divide. —**sec′tion·al,** *adj.*

sec′tor, *n.* **1.** *Geometry.* plane figure formed of a segment of a circle and two of its radii. **2.** area, esp. of military operation.

sec′u·lar, *adj.* not religious. —**sec′u·lar·ize,** *v.t.*

se·cure′, *adj., v.t.,* **-cured, -curing.** *adj.* **1.** safe or certain. **2.** firmly in place. —*v.t.* **3.** make secure. **4.** obtain. —**se·cure′ly,** *adv.*

se·cur′i·ty, *n., pl.* **-ties. 1.** state of being secure. **2.** protection or precaution. **3.** pledge on a loan, etc. **4. securities,** bonds, stocks, etc.

se·dan′, *n.* closed automobile with front and rear seats.

se·date′, *n.* quiet in manner. *v.* apply (or administer) a sedative.

sed′a·tive, *n.* **1.** medicine to relieve pain or nervousness. —*adj.* **2.** relieving pain or nervousness. —**se·da′tion,** *n.*

sed′en·tar′′y, *adj.* not physically active.

Se·der (sā′dər′′), *n.* Jewish home ceremony at Passover.

sed′i·ment, *n.* matter falling to the bottom of a body of liquid.

se·di′tion, *n.* incitement to rebellion. —**se·di′tious,** *adj.*

se·duce′, *v.t.,* **-duced, -ducing. 1.** tempt or induce to commit a wrong. **2.** induce to perform a sexual act. —**se·duc′er,** *fem.,* **se·duc′tress,** *n.* —**se·duc′tion,** *n.*

se·duc′tive, *adj.* tempting; attractive.

sed′u·lous, *adj.* diligent.

see, *v.,* **saw, seen, seeing,** *n. v.t.* **1.** sense with the eyes. **2.** realize or understand. **3.** make sure. **4.** escort. —*v.i.* **5.** have use of the eyes. **6.** find out or understand. **7.** attend, as to a task. **8.** bishopric.

seed, *n., pl.* **seeds, seed,** *v.t. n.* **1.** thing from which a plant grows. **2.** offspring. —*v.t.* **3.** sow seed in. **4.** remove seeds from. —**seed′less,** *adj.*

seed′ling, *n.* new growth from a seed.

seed′y, *adj.* **seedier, seediest. 1.** having seeds. **2.** shabby.

see′ing, *conj.* in view of the fact.

seek, *v.t.,* **sought, seeking. 1.** look for. **2.** intend and attempt. —**seek′er,** *n.*

seem, *v.t., v.i.* give the effect of being or acting in some specified way.

seem′ing, *adj.* apparent. —**seem′ing·ly,** *adv.*

seem′ly, *adj.,* **-lier, -liest.** proper in appearance or effect. —**seem′li·ness,** *n.*

seep, *v.i.* ooze. —**seep′age,** *n.*

seer, *n.* person who professes to foresee the future. Also, *fem.,* **seer′ess.**

seer′suck′′er, *n.* crinkled striped fabric.

see′saw′′, *n.* recreation of swinging up and down on a balanced plank.

seethe, *v.,* **seethed, seething.** *v.t., v.i.* boil.

seg′ment, *n.* **1.** portion. —*v.t.* **2.** divide into portions. —**seg′′men′tal,** *adj.* —**seg′′men·ta′tion,** *n.*

seg′re·gate, *v.t.,* **-gated, -gating.** keep apart from others. —**seg′′re·ga′tion,** *n.*

seine (sān), *n.* **1.** weighted fishing net. —*v.t., v.i.* **2.** fish with such a net.

seis·mic (sīz′mik), *adj.* pertaining to or affected by earth tremors.

seis′mo·graph, *n.* device for measuring earth tremors.

seize, *v.t.,* **seized, seizing. 1.** take by authority or force. **2.** grasp, as an idea.

seiz′ure, *n.* **1.** taking by authority or force. **2.** attack of illness.

sel′dom, *adv.* rarely.

se·lect′, *v.t.* **1.** choose. —*adj.* **2.** selected; choice. —**se·lec′tion,** *n.*

se·lec′tive, *adj.* **1.** pertaining to selection. **2.** careful in selecting.

se·lect′man, *n.* New England town officer.

self, *n.* **1.** one's own person. **2.** one's own well-being. —*adj.* **3.** of the same kind.

self′′-as·sur′ance, *n.* self-confidence. —**self′′-as·sured′,** *adj.*

self′-cen′tered, *adj.* seeing all things in reference to one's self or self-interest.

self′-con·ceit′, *n.* excessively good opinion of oneself.

self′′-con·fi′dence, *n.* confidence in one's own ability, rightness, etc. —**self′′-con′fi·dent,** *adj.*

self′′-con·scious, *adj.* excessively aware of the impression one may be making.

self''·còn·tāined', *adj.* **1.** complete in itself. **2.** reserved in manner.

self''·còn·tról', *n.* ability to restrain one's impulses or expressions of emotion.

self''·dè·ni'al, *n.* readiness to forgo gratifications to further a cause, help another, etc. —**self''·de·ny'ing**, *adj.*

self'·ès·tēem', *n.* good opinion of one's self.

self'·èv'ĭdènt, *adj.* evident without further proof or explanation.

self'·èx·plăn'á·tô''rў, *adj.* needing no explanation; obvious.

self''·ĭm·pôrt'ant, *adj.* seeming to have an excessive idea of one's own importance.

self''·ĭn'tèr·èst, *n.* concern for one's own well-being.

self'ĭsh, *adj.* acting for or thinking of one's own well-being alone. —**self'ish·ly**, *adv.* —**self'ish·ness**, *n.*

self'lèss, *n.* self-sacrificing.

self'·māde', *n.* prosperous, famous, or powerful through one's own efforts.

self''·pós·sès'sion, *n.* self-control. —**self''·pos·sessed'**, *adj.*

self'·rē·lï'ánce, *n.* reliance on one's own resources. —**self''·re·li'ant**, *adj.*

self'·rè·spèct', *n.* respect for one's own dignity, rights, etc. —**self'·re·spect'ing**, *adj.*

self''·rïgh'teoùs, *adj.* conceitedly sure of one's righteousness.

self'sāme', *adj.* identical.

self''·săt'ĭs·fïed, *adj.* satisfied with one's own personality, accomplishments, etc. —**self'·sat'is·fac'tion**, *n.*

self-sēek'ĭng, *adj.* motivated by self-interest.

self'·stýled', *adj.* called by oneself.

self''·süf·fï'cìent, *adj.* able to depend on one's own resources. —**self''·suf·fi'cien·cy**, *n.*

sèll, *v.t.,* **sold, selling. 1.** exchange for money. **2.** offer for sale. —*v.i.* **3.** attract the buying public. —**sel'ler**, *n.*

sèlt'zèr, *n.* carbonated water.

sèl'văge, *n.* woven edge on a length of cloth. Also, **sel'vedge.**

se·măn'tĭcs, *n.* study of word meanings. —**se·man'tic**, *adj.*

sĕm'á·phôre'', *n.* signal using different positions of arms or flags.

sĕm'blànce, *n.* **1.** seeming state. **2.** resemblance.

sē'mèn, *n.* fluid containing sperm.

sè·mĕs'têr, *n.* unit consisting of half a school year.

sè'mĭ·cîr''cle, *n.* half a circle. —**se''mi·cir'cu·lar**, *adj.*

sĕm'ĭ·cöl'òn, *n.* punctuation mark of the form ; that is used to divide clauses of a sentence.

sĕm''ĭ·còn·dŭc'tòr, *n.* a material used to modify electrical current, used in solid-state circuitry.

sĕm'ĭ·nâr'', *n.* academic class with a format of discussion or research.

sĕm'ĭ·nâr''ў, *n., pl.* **-naries. 1.** school for divinity students. **2.** school for young women. —**sem'i·nar'i·an**, *n.*

sĕm''ĭ·prē'cioùs, *adj.* not considered precious, as certain decorative stones used as gems.

sèn'áte, *n.* **1.** senior legislative body. **2. the senate,** upper legislative house in the United States or Canada. —**sen'a·tor**, *n.* —**sen''a·tor'i·al**, *adj.*

sĕnd, *v.,* **sent, sending.** *v.t.* **1.** cause to go. —*v.i.* **2.** send for, cause to come. —**send'er**, *n.*

sē'nïle, *adj.* decrepit, esp. mentally, in old age. —**se·nil'i·ty**, *n.*

sēn'ĭor, *adj.* **1.** older. **2.** higher in authority. **3.** having more years of employment or service. **4.** in the last year of school. —*n.* **5.** senior person. —**sen·ior'i·ty**, *n.*

se·ñôr', *n., pl.* **-nores.** *Spanish.* Mr. or Sir.

se·ñō'rà, *n., pl.* **-noras.** *Spanish.* Mrs. or Madam.

se·ñō·rī'tà, *n., pl.* **-ritas.** *Spanish.* Miss.

sèn·sā'tion, *n.* **1.** use of the senses. **2.** experience obtained through the senses. **3.** intuition or feeling. **4.** something causing excited public interest.

sèn·sā'tion·al, *adj.* causing or intended to cause excited public interest. —**sen·sa'tion·al·ly**, *adv.* —**sen·sa'tion·al·ism**, *n.*

sĕnse, *n., v.t.,* **sensed, sensing.** *n.* **1.** sight, hearing, touch, taste, or smell. **2.** impression obtained through one of these. **3.** intuition regarding a situation. **4.** Often, **senses,** reason. **5.** meaning.

—v.t. **6.** perceive by or as if by one of the senses.

sense′less, adj. **1.** unreasonable. **2.** unconscious.

sen″si·bíl′i·ty, n., pl. **-ties. 1.** ability to sense or be aware of things. **2.** Often, **sensibilities**, emotional sensitivity.

sen′si·ble, n. **1.** reasonable. **2.** perceptible through the senses. **3.** aware. **—sen′si·bly**, adv.

sen′si·tive, n. **1.** able to sense or register objects, data, etc. in small amounts. **2.** easily disturbed. **—sen″si·tiv′i·ty**, n.

sen′si·tize, v.t. **-tized, -tizing.** make sensitive.

sen′so·rý, adj. pertaining to the senses.

sen′su·al, adj. **1.** given to the pleasures of the senses. **2.** pertaining to such pleasure. **—sen′su·al·ism**, n. **—sen′su·al·ist**, n.

sen′su·oùs, n. **1.** pertaining to the senses. **2.** pleasing to the senses or emotions. **—sen′su·ous·ly**, adv. **—sen′su·ous·ness**, n.

sen′tence, n., v.t., **-tenced, -tencing.** n. **1.** unit of prose writing expressing one thought. **2.** legal decision, esp. regarding a punishment. **3.** punishment, esp. a term of imprisonment. —v.t. **4.** determine the punishment of.

sen″ten′tious, adj. tiresomely opinionated or voluble on matters of right and wrong.

sen′tient, adj. having feeling or perception. **—sen′tience**, n.

sen′ti·ment, n. **1.** personal feeling. **2.** statement of such feeling. **3.** opinion.

sen″ti·men′tal, adj. characterized by love, pity, etc., esp. to an unreasonable extent. **—sen″ti·men″tal′i·ty**, n. **—sen′ti·men′tal·ism**, n. **—sen″ti·men′tal·ist**, n.

sen′ti·nel, n. guard.

sen′trý, n., pl. **-tries.** soldier on guard duty.

sep·a·rate, v., **-rated, -rating,** adj. v.t., v.i. **1.** part. —adj. (sep′ərət) **2.** unconnected; individual. **—sep′a·rate·ly**, adv. **—sep″a·ra′tion**, n. **—sep′a·ra·ble**, adj. **—sep′a·ra″tor**, n.

se′pi·a, n. dark brown.

sep′sis, n. infection of the blood. **—sep′tic**, adj.

Sep·tem′ber, n. ninth month.

sep′tic, adj. **1.** pertaining to putrefaction. **2.** pertaining to sepsis.

sep″tu·a·ge·när′i·an, n. person in his or her seventies.

sep′ul·cher, n. tomb. Also, **sep′ul·chre**.

se·pul′chral, adj. **1.** lugubrious or gloomy. **2.** pertaining to sepulchers.

se′quel, n. **1.** event that follows. **2.** story continuing the subject of a previous one.

se′quence, n. **1.** succession or series. **2.** consequence. **3.** episode in a motion picture or television program.

se·ques′ter, v.t. **1.** set apart. **2.** seize or impound. **—se″ques·tra′tion**, n.

se′quin, n. small glittering disk sewn to a costume.

ser′aph, n., pl. **-aphs, -aphim.** angel of the highest order. **—se·raph′ic**, adj.

sere, adj. withered.

ser′e·nade″, n., v.t., **-naded, -nading.** n. **1.** musical composition for outdoor evening performance. —v.t. **2.** perform a serenade for.

se·rene′, adj. **1.** calm. **2.** fair, as the weather. **—se·ren′i·ty**, n. **—se·rene′ly**, adv.

serf, n. person in bondage to a landlord. **—serf′dom**, n.

serge, n. twilled fabric.

ser′geant (sar′gent), n. highest noncommissioned army officer.

se′ri·al, adj. **1.** forming part of a series. —n. **2.** story appearing in installments. **—se′ri·al·ly**, adv.

se′ries, n., pl. **-ries.** group of things coming one after the other.

se′ri·oùs, adj. **1.** solemn. **2.** earnest, sincere. **3.** important. **—se′ri·ous·ly**, adv. **—se′ri·ous·ness**, n.

ser′mon, n. speech to a religious congregation.

ser′pent, n. any large snake.

ser·pen′tine, adj. winding in snakelike loops.

ser′rat·ed, adj. resembling sawteeth in outline. **—ser·ra′tion**, n.

se′rum, n. liquid part of the blood, sometimes used in inoculation.

ser′vant, n. person hired to work in a household.

serve, v., **served, serving.** v.t. **1.** act in the service of. **2.** be of use to. **3.** present for consumption, as food or drink. **4.** undergo, as a prison sentence. —*v.i.* **5.** act in the service of a person, organization, or cause. **6.** suffice.

sêr'vĭce, *n., v.t.*, **-viced, -vicing**. *n.* **1.** activity on behalf of a person, organization, or cause. **2.** employment as a domestic worker. **3.** military organization or the military. **4.** favor. **5.** session of public worship. **6.** set of matched dishes, eating implements, etc. —*v.t.* **7.** supply, maintain, or repair.

sêr'vĭce·a·ble, *adj.* useful.

sêr'vĭce·măn'', *n.* **1.** member of an armed force. **2.** person who maintains, repairs, or fuels machinery.

sêr'vĭle, *adj.* slavelike; obsequious. —**ser·vil'i·ty**, *n.*

sêr'vĭ·tŭde, *n.* bondage.

sĕs'a·mē, *n.* East Indian plant yielding oil and edible seeds.

sĕs''qui·cĕn·tĕn'ni·ăl, *n.* **1.** one hundred fiftieth anniversary. —*adj.* **2.** pertaining to such an anniversary.

sĕs'sion, *n.* **1.** occasion of the gathering of members of a group. **2. in session,** formally convened.

sĕt, *v.*, **set, setting**, *n., adj. v.t.* **1.** place or put. **2.** put in proper or specified order or condition. **3.** place before others, as an example, problem, etc. —*v.i.* **4.** become fixed or firm. **5.** go below the horizon, as a star or planet. **6. set out** or **off,** begin to travel. —*n.* **7.** apparatus. **8.** complete group or collection. **9.** television or radio receiver. **10.** arrangement of theatrical scenery. —*adj.* **11.** firm or fixed. **12.** determined. **13.** prearranged.

sĕt'băck'', *n.* temporary defeat or hindrance.

sĕt'tēe', *n.* sofa or bench with a back.

sĕt'tĕr, *n.* hunting dog.

sĕt'tĭng, *n.* **1.** locale of a story. **2.** environment. **3.** music of a song.

sĕt'tle, *v.*, **-tled, -tling**. *v.t.* **1.** resolve, as a dispute. **2.** free from disturbance. **3.** pay, as a debt. **4.** set in a position of rest. **5.** colonize. —*v.i.* **6.** fall gently into a position of rest. **7.** reach an agreement or compromise. **8.** take up residence. —**set'tler**, *n.* —**set'tle·ment**, *n.*

sĕv'ĕn, *n., adj.* one plus six.

sĕv''ĕn·tēen', *n., adj.* seven plus ten. —**sev''en·teenth'**, *adj.*

sĕv''ĕn·tў, *n., adj.* seven times ten. —**sev'en·ti'eth**, *adj.*

sĕv'ĕr, *v.t.* cut off or separate. —**sev'er·ance**, *n.*

sĕv'êr·ăl, *adj.* **1.** a few. **2.** individual. **3.** respective. —**sev'er·al·ly**, *adv.*

sé·vēre', *adj.* **1.** sternly demanding. **2.** harsh or violent. **3.** seriously bad. **4.** austerely simple. —**se·vere'ly**, *adv.* —**se·ver'i·ty**, *n.*

sew (sō), *v.t.*, **sewed, sewed** or **sewn, sewing.** join with thread. —**sew'er**, *n.*

sēw'âge, *n.* waste material in sewers. Also, **sew'er·age.**

sēw'êr, *n.* covered channel for waste.

sĕx, *n.* **1.** individual nature as determined by the reproductive system. **2.** either of two divisions of a species as so determined. **3.** activities, thoughts, etc. as influenced by the reproductive system. —**sex'u·al**, *adj.* —**sex'u·al·ly**, *adv.*

sĕx'ĭs·m, *n.* discrimination on the basis of sex.

sĕx'tănt, *n.* navigational instrument using the elevation of the sun.

sĕx·tĕt, *n.* **1.** group of six, esp. musicians. **2.** musical composition for six instruments. Also, **sex·tette'.**

sĕx'tŏn, *n.* caretaker of a church.

sĕx'tŭ·ple, *adj.* occurring six times.

shăb'bў, *adj.*, **-bier, -biest. 1.** worn and untidy-looking. **2.** mean. —**shab'bi·ness**, *n.* —**shab'bi·ly**, *adv.*

shăck, *n.* shanty.

shăck'le, *n., v.t.*, **-led, -ling**. *n.* **1.** Usually, **shackles,** chains for binding prisoners. **2.** binding part of a padlock. —*v.t.* **3.** bind with or as with shackles.

shăd, *n., pl.* **shads, shad.** herringlike fish spawning in rivers.

shāde, *n., v.t.*, **shaded, shading**. *n.* **1.** area sheltered from direct light. **2.** device for cutting off direct light. **3.** variety of color or tone. **4.** slight degree. **5.** soul of a dead person. —*v.t.* **6.** shelter from direct light. **7.** vary, as a color or tone.

shăd'ŏw, *n.* **1.** darkness of a shaded area. **2.** slight remnant or trace. —*v.t.* **3.** shade. **4.** follow secretly. —**shad'ow·y**, *adj.*

shād′ÿ, *adj.* **1.** in the shade. **2.** *Informal.* to be suspected.

shǎft, *n.* **1.** long, cylindrical object for support, rotation, etc. **2.** beam of light. **3.** narrow vertical space.

shǎg, *n.* long, rough hair, fur, or nap. —**shag′gy,** *adj.*

shǎh, *n.* former sovereign of Iran.

shāke, *v.,* **shook, shaken, shaking,** *n.* *v.t.,* **1.** cause to move rapidly back and forth. **2.** upset emotionally. —*v.i.* **3.** move rapidly back and forth. —*n.* **4.** act or instance of shaking. **5.** wood shingle.

shāk′ẽr, *n.* **1.** device for sprinkling seasoning. **2. Shaker,** member of an American celibate religious sect.

shāk′ÿ, *adj.,* **-kier, -kiest. 1.** unstable. **2.** tending to shake. **3.** of doubtful validity. —**shak′i·ly,** *adv.* —**shak′i·ness,** *n.*

shāle, *n.* layered rock of hardened clay.

shǎll, *v.* am, is, or are going to.

shǎl′lŏt, *n.* onionlike plant used in cooking.

shǎl′lōw, *adj.* **1.** not deep. **2.** without depth of thought or feeling.

shǎm, *adj., n., v.t.,* **shammed, shamming.** *adj.* **1.** false; imitation. —*n.* **2.** something false or imitative. —*v.t.* **3.** pretend; feign.

shǎm′ble, *v.i.,* **-bled, -bling.** *n.* *v.i.* **1.** walk draggingly or awkwardly. —*n.* **2. shambles, a.** scene of disorder. **b.** slaughterhouse. **3.** shambling gait.

shāme, *n., v.t.,* **shamed, shaming.** *n.* **1.** painful sense of guilt or inadequacy. **2.** disgrace. **3.** deplorable situation. —*v.t.* **4.** put to shame. —**shame′ful,** *adj.* —**shame′less,** *adj.*

shāme′fāced, *adj.* showing embarrassment. —**shame′fac′ed·ly,** *adv.*

shǎm·pōō′, *v.t.,* **-pooed, -pooing.** *n.* *v.t.* **1.** wash with soap, as the hair or a carpet. —*n.* **2.** soap, etc. used for shampooing.

shǎm′rŏck, *n.* cloverlike plant with a triple leaf: symbol of Ireland.

shǎng′haī′, *v.t.,* **-haied, -haiing.** abduct for work on a ship.

shǎnk, *n.* **1.** lower leg above the ankle. **2.** shaft of a hand tool between the handle and working end.

shǎn′tǔng, *n.* textured silk.

shǎn′tÿ, *n., pl.* **-ties.** roughly built wooden house.

shāpe, *n., v.t.,* **shaped, shaping.** *n.* **1.** form. **2.** *Informal.* condition. —*v.t.* **3.** give form to. —**shape′less,** *adj.*

shāpe′lÿ, *adj.* handsome in form. —**shape′li·ness,** *n.*

shāre, *n., v.t.,* **shared, sharing.** *n.* **1.** rightful or predetermined portion. —*v.t.* **2.** divide into such portions. **3.** use or experience together.

shärk, *n.* **1.** large predatory fish. **2.** person who preys on others.

shärp, *adj.* **1.** having or as if having a cutting point or edge. **2.** clearly defined. **3.** shrewd. **4.** alert. **5.** abrupt. **6.** *Music.* raised in pitch. —*adv.* **7.** punctually. —*n.* **8.** a semitone higher than a stated tone. —**sharp′en·er,** *n.* —**sharp′ly,** *adv.* —**sharp′ness,** *n.* —**sharp′en,** *v.t.*

shärp′ẽr, *n.* swindler.

shärp′shōōt′′ẽr, *n.* good marksman.

shǎt′tẽr, *v.t., v.i.* break in small pieces.

shāve, *v.t.,* **shaved, shaved or shaven, shaving,** *n.* *v.t.* **1.** cut the hair off with a razor. **2.** remove with a plane. **3.** cut in thin layers with a tool. —*n.* **4.** act or instance of being shaved.

shāv′ing, *n.* thin layer of material shaved from a larger piece.

shāwl, *n.* cloth covering head and shoulders.

shē, *pron.* woman or female previously mentioned.

shēaf, *n., pl.* **sheaves.** bundle.

shēar, *v.t.,* **sheared, sheared or shorn, shearing,** *n.* *v.t.* **1.** divide as with the motion of one blade across another. —*n.* **2.** device for shearing.

shēars, *n. pl.* large scissors.

shēath, *n., pl.* **sheaths.** closely fitting case or cover.

shēathe, *v.t.,* **sheathed, sheathing.** put into a sheath.

shĕd, *v.t.,* **shed, shedding,** *n.* *v.t.* leave or cast off. **2.** pour forth, as light. —*n.* **3.** rough shelter.

shēen, *n.* dull reflection.

shēep, *n., pl.* **sheep.** mammal yielding fleece and mutton.

shēep′ish, *adj.* bashful or embarrassed.

shēer, *adj.* **1.** absolute; utter. **2.** very steep

or perpendicular. **3.** transparent, as a fabric. —*v.i.* **4.** swerve.

sheet, *n.* **1.** broad, thin piece of material. **2.** cloth used to cover a mattress or a sleeper. **3.** rope for controlling the position of a sail.

shĕik, *n.* Arab chief.

shĕk'el, *n.* ancient Hebrew coin.

shĕlf, *n., pl.* **shelves. 1.** horizontal ledge or slab of supporting objects. **2.** ledge, as of rock.

shĕll, *n.* **1.** hard outer covering. **2.** shotgun cartridge. **3.** explosive artillery missile. **4.** racing rowboat. —*v.t.* **5.** separate from its shell. **6.** bombard with shells.

shĕl·lăc', *n.* **1.** varnish containing a certain resin. **2.** the resin itself. —*v.t.* **3.** varnish with shellac.

shĕll'fĭsh'', *n.* any aquatic animal with a shell.

shĕl'tẽr, *n.* **1.** something serving as a protection, as against the weather. —*v.t.* **2.** protect. —*v.i.* **3.** take shelter.

shĕlve, *v.,* **shelved, shelving. 1.** put on a shelf. **2.** postpone action or decision on. **3.** provide with shelves. —*v.i.* **4.** slope.

shĕp'hẽrd, *n.* **1.** Also, *fem.,* **shep'herd·ess,** person who leads and guards sheep. —*v.t.* **2.** escort with close vigilance.

shẽr'bĕt, *n.* frozen dessert of water, gelatin, flavoring, and sometimes milk.

shẽr'ĭff, *n.* county police officer.

shĕr'rÿ, *n., pl.* **-ries.** Spanish fortified wine.

shiĕld, *n.* **1.** piece of armor worn on the arm. **2.** any defensive device. —*v.t.* **3.** protect or hide.

shift, *v.t., v.i.* **1.** move from place to place. **2.** change, as one's place. **3.** change, as the gears of a motor vehicle. —*n.* **4.** act or instance of shifting. **5.** lever for changing gears in a motor vehicle. **6.** daily period of labor.

shift'lĕss, *n.* lazy or feeble.

shift'ÿ, *adj.,* **shiftier, shiftiest.** tricky; unreliable. —**shift'i·ly,** *adv.* —**shift'i·ness,** *n.*

shĭl'lĭng, *n.* former British coin, one-twentieth of a pound.

shĭl'lÿ-shăl'lÿ, *v.i.,* **-lied, -lying.** hesitate or quarrel over trifles.

shĭm, *n.* thin piece for raising an object or filling a gap.

shĭm'mẽr, *v.i.* **1.** glow or appear in a flickering, unsteady way. —*n.* **2.** effect given in so doing. —**shim'mer·y,** *adj.*

shĭn, *n.* front of the shank of the leg.

shĭne, *v.,* **shone** or, for *v.t.,* **shined, shining,** *n. v.i.* **1.** emit or reflect strong light. **2.** gain distinction. —*v.t.* **3.** polish to a high gloss. —*n.* **4.** shining light. —**shin'y,** *adj.*

shĭn'gle, *n.* **1.** thin plate of wood or other material used on houses as a roof covering or siding. **2. shingles.** virus disease with blisters as a symptom. —*v.t.* **3.** cover with shingles.

shĭn'nÿ, *n.* street hockey.

shĭp, *n., v.,* **shipped, shipping.** *n.* **1.** large ocean-going vessel. **2.** sailing vessel square-rigged on all of at least three masts. —*v.t.* **3.** send by a foreign carrier. —*v.i.* **4.** engage to work on a voyage. —**ship'mate'',** *n.* —**ship'ment,** *n.* —**ship'per,** *n.*

shĭp'pĭng, *n.* vessels, esp. merchant ships.

shĭp'shāpe'', *adj., adv.* in good order.

shĭp'wrĕck'', *n.* destruction of a ship from running aground.

shĭp'yârd'', *n.* place for building or repairing ships.

shĭre, *n.* British county.

shĭrk, *v.t.* **1.** evade, as an obligation. —*n.* **2.** person who shirks something. —**shirk'er,** *n.*

shĭrr, *v.t.* gather on parallel strands for decorative effect, as curtain material.

shĭrt, *n.* a long- or short-sleeved upper garment usually having a front opening, collar and cuffs, worn esp. by men.

shĭv'ẽr, *v.i.* **1.** tremble. —*v.t.* **2.** smash to pieces. —*n.* **3.** trembling movement. **4.** broken fragment. —**shiv'er·y,** *adj.*

shōal, *n.* **1.** area of shallow water. **2.** large number of fish.

shōat, *n.* young pig.

shŏck, *n.* **1.** violent impact. **2.** violent emotional disturbance. **3.** bodily disturbance caused by loss of blood circulation, a current of electricity passing through the body, etc. **4.** stack of sheaves of grain. **5.** tangled mass, as of hair. —*v.t.* **6.** disturb with a shock. —**shock'ing,** *adj.*

shŏd′dy̆, *adj.* poor in quality. —**shod′di**-**ness**, *n.*

shoe (shoō), *n., v.t.,* **shod, shoeing.** *n.* **1.** protective covering for the foot. **2.** something suggesting this. —*v.t.* **3.** provide with shoes. —**shoe′lace′′, shoe′ string′′,** *n.* —**shoe′mak′′er,** *n.*

shoe′hôrn′′, *n.* device to assist slipping the foot into a shoe.

shoot, *v.t.* **1.** send a missile from. **2.** hit with a missile. **3.** emit rapidly, as a missile. —*v.i.* **4.** use a gun, bow, etc. **5.** grow or sprout. —*n.* **6.** sporting event with shooting. **7.** young plant growth. —**shoot′er,** *n.*

shŏp, *n., v.i.,* **shopped, shopping.** *n.* **1.** store, esp. a small specialized one. **2.** industrial workroom. —*v.i.* **3.** look for or make purchases. —**shop′per,** *n.* —**shop′keep′′er,** *n.*

shŏp′lĭft′′êr, *n.* person who steals from shops.

shôre, *n., v.t.,* **shored, shoring.** *n.* **1.** land bordering a body of water. **2.** seacoast. **3.** prop. —*v.t.* **4.** prop.

shôrt, *n.* **1.** not tall or long. **2.** abrupt in manner. **3.** scanty, as a supply. **4.** below the required amount. **5.** flaky, as pastry. —*adv.* **6.** abruptly. —*n.* **7.** short circuit. **8. shorts,** short-legged pants or underpants. —*v.t.* **9.** create a short circuit in. —**short′ly,** *adv.* —**short′ness,** *n.* **short′en,** *v.t.*

shôrt′âge, *n.* short supply.

shôrt cĭrcuĭt, deviation of current in an electrical circuit rendering it useless.

shôrt′cŏm′′ing, *n.* fault or inadequacy.

shôrt′cŭt′′, *n.* shorter way than the usual.

shôrt′ĕn·ĭng, *n.* greasy substance for making pastry short.

shôrt′hănd′′, *n.* system of writing for fast note-taking.

shôrt′-lĭved′′, *adj.* not living or existing long.

shôrt′-sĭght′′ĕd, *adj.* without foresight.

shŏt, *n., pl.* **shots** or (for 3) **shot. 1.** discharge of a missile. **2.** range of a gun, bow, etc. **3.** *Often pl.* missiles, esp. shotgun pellets or cannonballs. **4.** iron ball for hurling in athletic contests. **5.** marksman.

shŏt′gŭn, *n.* gun firing shells filled with metal pellets.

should (shŏod), *v.* **1.** ought to. **2.** were to. **3.** past tense of *shall.*

shŏul′der, *n.* **1.** part of the human body between the upper arms and neck. **2.** corresponding area in animals. **3.** unpaved strip alongside a road. —*v.t.* **4.** push with the shoulder. **5.** take up and carry.

shŏut, *n.* **1.** very loud call or voice. —*v.i.* **2.** give such a call. —*v.t.* **3.** utter in such a voice.

shŏve, *v.,* **shoved, shoving.** *n. v.t., v.i.* **1.** push vigorously. —*n.* **2.** vigorous push.

shŏv′ĕl, *n.* **1.** hand tool or machine for scooping up material. —*v.t.* **2.** raise or move with a shovel. **3.** clear with a shovel.

shŏw, *v.,* **showed, shown** or **showed, showing.** *n. v.t.* **1.** display. **2.** guide. **3.** prove or demonstrate. —*v.i.* **4.** be visible or apparent. —*n.* **5.** entertainment. **6.** exhibit. **7.** ostentation. —**show′boat′′,** *n.* —**show′case′′,** *n.* —**show′man,** *n.* —**show′piece,** *n.* —**show′room,** *n.*

show′down′′, *n.* **1.** confrontation, as between enemies. **2.** climactic event.

show′êr, *n.* **1.** brief rainstorm. **2.** bath in which water is sprayed from above. **3.** large number of small objects dropped or hurled. —*v.t.* **4.** bestow liberally. —*v.i.* **5.** rain briefly.

show′ŏff′′, *n.* vain, ostentatious person.

show′y̆, *adj.,* **-ier, -iest.** attracting attention, esp. through gaudiness.

shrăp′nĕl, *n.* small fragments hurled by the bursting of an artillery shell.

shrĕd, *n., v.t.,* **shredded, shredding.** *n.* **1.** torn strip. **2.** bit, as of doubt or evidence. —*v.t.* **3.** tear into shreds.

shrĕw, *n.* **1.** small mouselike mammal. **2.** quarrelsome woman. —**shrew′ish,** *adj.*

shrĕwd, *adj.* clever in dealing with or understanding others. —**shrewd′ly,** *adv.* —**shrewd′ness,** *n.*

shriĕk, *n.* **1.** loud, shrill cry. —*v.i.* **2.** utter such a cry.

shrike, *n.* bird of prey.

shrĭll, *adj.* high-pitched. —**shril′ly,** *adv.* **shrill′ness,** *n.*

shrĭmp, *n.* small, long-tailed shellfish.

shrĭne, *n.* sacred place.

shrĭnk, *v.,* **shrank** or **shrunk, shrunk** or **shrunken, shrinking.** *v.i.* **1.** become smaller. **2.** draw back, as in fear. —*v.t.* **3.** cause to shrink. —**shrink'age,** *n.*

shriv'el, *v.i.* shrink and become wrinkled.

shroud, *n.* **1.** wrapping for a corpse. **2.** line steadying a ship's mast. —*v.t.* **3.** wrap or conceal.

shrub, *n.* small, treelike plant. —**shrub'ber·y,** *n.*

shrug, *n., v.,* **shrugged, shrugging.** *n.* **1.** movement of raising both shoulders. —*v.i.* **2.** make such a movement. —*v.t.* **3.** move in shrugging.

shuck, *n., v.t.* husk or shell.

shud'der, *v.i.* **1.** tremble violently and briefly. —*n.* **2.** act or instance of shuddering.

shuf'fle, *v.i.,* **-fled, -fling,** *n. v.i.* **1.** walk with feet scraping the ground. **2.** mix, as playing cards. —*n.* **3.** shuffling gait.

shuf'fle·board'', *n.* game played by shoving wooden disks along a marked surface.

shun, *v.t.,* **shunned, shunning.** avoid.

shunt, *v.t.* **1.** divert. **2.** move, as cars in a railroad yard.

shut, *v.,* **shut, shutting,** *adj. v.t.* **1.** close. **2.** keep in or out. —*v.i.* **3.** be closed. —*adj.* **4.** closed.

shut'ter, *n.* **1.** cover for a window opening. **2.** device for timed exposure of film in a camera.

shut'tle, *v.i.,* **-tled, -tling,** *n. v.i.* **1.** go short distances back and forth. —*n.* **2.** device on a loom for moving warp thread back and forth. **3.** public transit vehicle that runs between two closely spaced terminals.

shy, *adj.,* **shier, shiest,** *v.,* **shied, shying,** *n., pl.* **shies.** *adj.* **1.** timid in the presence of others. **2.** lacking by a specified number. —*v.t.* **3.** toss, esp. with a sideways motion. —*v.i.* **4.** start with surprise, as a horse. —*n.* **5.** act or instance of shying. —**shy'ly,** *adv.* —**shy'ness,** *n.*

sib'ling, *n.* brother or sister.

sic, *v.t.,* **sicked, sicking,** *adv. v.t.* **1.** urge to an attack. —*adv.* **2.** *Latin.* thus; (it is written).

sick, *adj.* **1.** not in health. **2.** suffering nausea. **3.** disgusted or upset. **4.** *Informal.* mentally warped. —*n.* **5.** sick people. —**sick'ness,** *n.* —**sick'en,** *v.t., v.i.*

sick'le, *n.* crescent-shaped tool for mowing.

sick'ly, *adj.,* **-lier, -liest.** not healthy or robust.

side, *n., adj., v.i.,* **sided, siding.** *n.* **1.** area of someone or something to the right or left of the face or front. **2.** direction or location to the right or left. **3.** any direction or location from a central point. **4.** line or surface defining a form. **5.** aspect. **6.** person or group in a dispute or conflict. **7.** opinion or cause of such a person or group. —*adj.* **8.** pertaining to a side direction or location. **9.** of secondary importance. —*v.i.* **10.** ally oneself.

side'board'', *n.* article of furniture for dishes, silver, and napkins.

side'burns'', *n. pl.* whiskers down the sides of the face.

side'line'', *n.* secondary source of income.

side'long'', *adj., adv.* to the side.

si·de're·al, *adj.* pertaining to stars.

side'show'', *n.* minor entertainment at a circus.

side'step'', *v.t.,* **-stepped, -stepping.** evade by or as if by stepping sideways.

side'swipe'', *v.t.,* **-swiped, -swiping.** brush the side of in passing.

side'track'', *v.t.* divert or distract from accomplishing a purpose.

side'walk'', *n.* walk beside a roadway.

side'ways'', *adv., adj.* **1.** with a side foremost. **2.** to or from one side. Also, **side'wise''.**

sid'ing, *n.* short track for trains halted beside a through track.

sidle, *v.i.,* **-dled, -dling.** move sideways.

SIDS, sudden infant death syndrome, unexplained death of baby while asleep.

siege, *n.* prolonged attack on a fortified place.

si·en'na, *n.* reddish- or yellowish-brown.

si·es'ta, *n.* brief daytime nap.

sieve, *n., v.t.,* **sieved, sieving.** *n.* **1.** strainer of wire mesh. —*v.t.* **2.** run through or separate with a sieve.

sift, *v.t.* separate with a sieve. —**sift'er,** *n.*

sigh, *v.i.* **1.** release pent-up breath in reaction to grief, annoyance, etc. —*n.* **2.** such a release of breath.

sight, *n.* **1.** sense perceived by the eyes. **2.** something seen. **3.** something remarkable to see. **4.** range of distances one's eyes can see clearly. **5.** aiming device for shooting or bombing. —*v.t.* **6.** discover with the eye. **7.** aim with a sight. —**sight′less,** *adj.*

sight′ly, *adj.,* **-lier, -liest.** pleasing to see.

sign, *n.* **1.** indication. **2.** written, printed, or hand-given symbol. **3.** display surface containing such symbols or writing. —*v.t.* **4.** put a signature on. —**sign′er,** *n.*

sig′nal, *n., adj., v.t.,* **-naled, -naling.** *n.* **1.** device presenting a message in symbols. **2.** message so presented. —*adj.* **3.** acting as a signal. **4.** marked. —*v.t.* **5.** indicate through a signal. **6.** communicate through a signal. —**sig′nal·er,** *n.* —**sig′nal·man,** *n.* —**sig′nal·ly,** *adv.*

sig′nal·ize″, *v.t.,* **-ized, -izing.** call attention to or make noteworthy.

sig′na·to″ry, *n., pl.* **-ries.** signer, esp. of a document.

sig′na·ture, *n.* **1.** one's name in one's handwriting. **2.** *Music.* sign indicating key and tempo.

sig′net, *n.* letter seal, often mounted on a ring.

sig·nif′i·cance, *n.* **1.** meaning. **2.** importance. —**sig·nif′i·cant,** *adj.*

sig·ni·fy″, *v.t.* **-fied, -fying. 1.** mean. **2.** indicate. —**sig″ni·fi·ca′tion,** *n.*

si′lence, *n., v.t.,* **-lenced, lencing.** *n.* **1.** absence of noise, conversation, or sound. **2.** absence of information or communication. —*v.t.* **3.** make silent. **4.** put out of action, as enemy guns. —**si′lent,** *adj.* —**si′lent·ly,** *adv.*

sil·hou·ette (sil″ōō et′), *n., v.t.,* **-etted, -etting** *n.* **1.** outline figure, usually filled in with black. —*v.t.* **2.** cause to appear in outline against a lighter background.

sil′i·ca, *n.* hard, glassy substance appearing in sand, quartz, etc.

sil′i·con, *n.* nonmetallic element appearing in various compounds.

silk, *n.* cloth made of fiber spun by silkworms.

silk′en, *adj.* **1.** made of silk. **2.** suggesting silk in smoothness. Also, **silk′y.**

silk′worm″, *n.* moth caterpillar whose cocoons provide silk fiber.

sill, *n.* horizontal structural member, esp. below a wall or opening.

sil′ly, *adj.,* **-lier, -liest. 1.** foolish or stupid. **2.** unreasonable. —**sil′li·ness,** *n.*

si′lo, *n.* airtight place for storing fodder.

silt, *n.* **1.** fine earth, etc. deposited by running water. —*v.t.* **2.** fill or clog with silt.

sil′ver, *n.* **1.** white noble metallic element. **2.** coins, utensils, etc. customarily made of silver. **3.** lustrous whitish gray. —*adj.* **4.** made of or colored silver. **5.** pertaining to a twenty-fifth wedding anniversary. **6.** eloquent, as the tongue. —**sil′ver·y,** *adj.* —**sil′ver·smith″,** *n.*

sil′ver·ware″, *n.* tableware traditionally made of silver.

sim′i·an, *adj.* **1.** pertaining to or suggesting apes and monkeys. —*n.* **2.** ape or monkey.

sim′i·lar, *adj.* of the same sort. —**sim′i·lar·ly,** *adv.* —**sim″i·lar′i·ty,** *n.*

sim′i·le″, *n.* expression comparing one thing to another.

si·mil′i·tude″, *n.* likeness.

sim′mer, *v.t., v.i.* almost boil.

si″mul·ta′ne·ous, *adj.* at the very same time. —**si″mul·ta′ne·ous·ly,** *adv.*

si′mo·ny, *n.* profiting financially from religion.

sim′per, *v.i.* **1.** smile foolishly or affectedly. —*n.* **2.** foolish or affected smile.

sim′ple, *adj.,* **-pler, -plest. 1.** of the most basic kind. **2.** readily understood or mastered. **3.** low in intelligence. —**sim′ply,** *adv.* —**sim·plic′i·ty,** *n.*

sim′ple-mind″ed, *adj.* foolish; low in intelligence.

sim′ple·ton, *n.* foolish or naive person.

sim′pli·fy″, *v.t.,* **-fied, -fying.** make easier to understand or master. —**sim″pli·fi·ca′tion,** *n.*

sim·plis′tic, *adj.* unrealistically oversimplified.

sim′u·late″, *v.t.,* **-lated, -lating. 1.** pretend; feign. **2.** imitate closely. —**sim″u·la′tion,** *n.*

sin, *n., v.i.,* **sinned, sinning.** *n.* **1.** violation of religious law. —*v.i.* **2.** commit such a violation. —**sin′ful,** *adj.* **sin′ful·ly,** *adv.* —**sin′ful·ness,** *n.*

since, *conj.* **1.** during the time after. **2.** because or inasmuch as. —*adv.* **3.** from that time on. **4.** at some time afterwards.

sin·cere′, *adj.,* **-cerer, -cerest.** genuine;

honest and unaffected. **—sin·cere′ly,** *adv.* **—sin·cer′i·ty,** *n.*

si·ne·cure (sī′ne kyŏŏr′′), *n.* salaried job requiring no serious work.

sin′ĕw, *n.* **1.** tendon. **2.** muscular strength. **—sin′ew·y,** *adj.*

sing, *v.,* **sang** or **sung, sung, singing.** *v.i.* **1.** make musical sounds with the voice. **—***v.t.* **2.** render by singing. **—sing′er,** *n.*

singe, *v.t.,* **singed, singeing.** burn on the surface.

sin′gle, *adj., v.t.,* **-gled, -gling,** *n.* *adj.* **1.** alone or unique. **2.** unmarried. **—***v.t.* **3. single out,** select. **—***n.* **4.** something single. **—sin′gly,** *adv.*

sing′sŏng′′, *adj.* monotonously rhythmical.

sin′gŭ·lăr, *adj.* **1.** peculiar or extraordinary. **2.** unique. **3.** *Grammar.* pertaining to one person or thing. **—***n.* **4.** *Grammar.* singular number of a word. **—sin′gu·lar·ly,** *adv.* **—sin′′gu·lar′i·ty,** *n.*

sin′is·têr, *adj.* evilly threatening.

sink, *v.,* **sank** or **sunk, sunk** or **sunken, sinking,** *n.* *v.i.* **1.** descend beneath a surface. **2.** pass into a depressed state. **—***v.t.* **3.** cause to descend or penetrate beneath a surface. **—***n.* **4.** basin with a drain. **—sink′er,** *n.*

sin′nêr, *n.* person who sins.

sin′ŭ·oŭs, *adj.* meandering; serpentine.

sī′nŭs, *n.* cavity, esp. one in the skull opening into the nasal passages.

sip, *v.,* **sipped, sipping,** *n.* *v.t.* **1.** drink in tiny amounts. **—***n.* **2.** act or instance of sipping. **3.** amount sipped at a time.

sī′phŏn, *n.* **1.** curved tube for sucking liquids automatically from place to place. **—***v.t.* **2.** pass through a siphon.

sîr, *n.* **1.** formal term used in addressing a man. **2.** title given a British knight or baronet.

sīre, *n.,* *v.t.,* **sired, siring,** *n.* **1.** male parent, esp. of an animal. **2.** formal term used in addressing a king. **—***v.t.* **3.** beget.

sī′rĕn, *n.* **1.** mythical sea nymph luring sailors with singing to shipwreck. **2.** horn with a wavering tone used on emergency vehicles.

sîr′lŏīn, *n.* cut of beef at the loin end by the rump.

sîr′ŭp, *n.* syrup.

sī′săl, *n.* plant fiber used for ropes, etc.

sĭs′sŷ, *n.* *Informal.* **1.** timid or unmanly male. **2.** nickname for a sister.

sĭs′têr, *n.* **1.** daughter of one's own parents. **2.** nun. **—sĭs′ter·ly,** *adj.*

sĭs′têr·hŏŏd′′, *n.* **1.** organization of nuns. **2.** condition of being a sister.

sĭs′têr·ĭn-lâw′′, *n.,* *pl.* **sisters-in-law. 1.** sister of a spouse. **2.** wife of a brother.

sĭt, *v.,* **sat, sitting.** *v.i.* **1.** rest on the behind. **2.** be located. **3.** pose, as for a portrait. **4.** be in session, as a court. **—***v.t.* **5.** seat. **—sit′ter,** *n.*

sīte, *n.* location, as of a building.

sĭt′tĭng, *n.* session.

sĭt′ū·āte′′, *v.t.,* **-ated, -ating.** place or locate.

sĭt′′ū·ā′tion, *n.* **1.** location. **2.** condition or predicament. **3.** job.

sĭx, *n., adj.* one plus five. **—sixth,** *adj.*

sĭx′′tēen′, *n., adj.* six plus ten. **—six·teenth′,** *adj.*

sĭx′tŷ, *n., adj.* six times ten. **—six′ti·eth,** *adj.*

sĭz′à·ble, *adj.* fairly large. Also, **size′a·ble.**

sīze, *n.,* *v.t.,* **sized, sizing.** *n.* **1.** area, volume, number, etc. by which something is measured or graded. **2.** Also, **siz′ing,** pasty substance used to coat or fill cloth, paper, etc. **—***v.t.* **3. size up,** measure or appraise intuitively. **4.** treat with sizing.

sĭz′zle, *v.i.,* **-zled, -zling,** *n.* *v.i.* **1.** hiss or crackle, as from being fried. **—***n.* **2.** hissing or crackling, as from being fried.

skāte, *n.,* *v.i.,* **skated, skating.** *n.* **1.** piece of footwear for gliding across ice. **2.** roller skate. **3.** flat-bodied fish of the ray family. **—***v.i.* **4.** go on skates. **—skat′er,** *n.*

skein (skān), *n.* coil of yarn or thread.

skĕl′ĕ·tŏn, *n.* **1.** bone structure of an animal. **2.** structural frame. **—skel′e·tal,** *adj.*

skĕp′tĭc, *n.* doubter. **—skep′ti·cal,** *adj.* **—skep′ti·cal·ly,** *adv.* **—skep′ti·cism′′,** *n.*

skĕtch, *n.* **1.** rough drawing. **2.** brief outline. **—***v.t.* **3.** make a sketch of.

skĕtch′ŷ, *adj.* vague or without detail. **—sketch′i·ly,** *adv.*

skĕw, *v.t.*, *v.i.* **1.** slant. —*adj.* **2.** aslant.

skĕw´ĕr, *n.* **1.** needle for holding pieces of meat together. —*v.t.* **2.** pierce with or as if with a skewer.

skĭ, *n.*, *pl.* **skis**, *vi.*, **skied, skiing.** *n.* **1.** long flat runner for gliding or walking on snow. —*v.i.* **2.** glide on skis. —**ski´er**, *n.*

skĭd, *v.*, **skidded, skidding**, *n. v.i.*, *v.t.* **1.** slide, by accident or intention. —*n.* **2.** object or surface on which objects are skidded. **3.** skidding motion.

skiff, *n.* rowboat.

skĭll, *n.* practiced ability. —**skilled**, *adj.* —**skill´ful**, *adj.* —**skill´ful·ly**, *adv.*

skĭl´lĕt, *n.* frying pan.

skĭm, *v.*, **skimmed, skimming.** *v.t.* **1.** remove from a liquid surface. —*v.i.* **2.** move lightly across a surface.

skĭmp, *v.i.* economize; scrimp.

skĭmp´ў, *adj.*, **skimpier, skimpiest.** scant.

skĭn, *n.*, *v.t.*, **skinned, skinning.** *n.* **1.** outer covering of an animal body. —*v.t.* **2.** remove skin or hide from. —**skin´ner**, *n.* —**skin´´less**, *adj.*

skĭn´flĭnt´´, *n.* miserly person.

skĭn´nў, *adj.* thin of body.

skĭp, *v.*, **skipped, skipping**, *n. v.i.* **1.** jump lightly. —*v.t.* **2.** omit. —*n.* **3.** light jump.

skĭp´pêr, *n.* ship or boat captain.

skĭr´mĭsh, *n.* **1.** brief, minor battle. —*v.i.* **2.** have a skirmish.

skĭrt, *n.* **1.** open-bottomed garment fastened around the waist. **2.** Often, **skirts**, portion of a coat, dress, etc. that falls below the waist. —*v.t.* **3.** pass around the border of. **4.** evade, as subject of controversy.

skĭt, *n.* brief comic play.

skĭt´tĭsh, *adj.* readily excited or frightened.

skŭl´´dŭg´gêr·ў, *n.* treacherous intrigue.

skŭlk, *v.i.* lurk.

skŭll, *n.* bony shell of a head.

skŭnk, *n.* small mammal defending itself with foul-smelling liquid.

skў, *n.*, *pl.* **skies.** **1.** part of the atmosphere visible from the earth. **2.** condition of this at a certain place and time.

skў´light´´, *n.* window in the surface of a roof or ceiling.

skў´līne´´, *n.* silhouette of a city against the horizon.

skў´rŏck´´ĕt, *n.* **1.** firework rising high before exploding. —*v.i.* **2.** rise rapidly.

skў´scräp´´êr, *n.* very tall building, esp. one for offices.

slăb, *n.* flat, fairly thick piece of material.

slăck, *adj.* **1.** loose. **2.** inactive. **3.** lazy or indifferent. —*n.* **4.** slack part. **5.** period of inactivity. —*v.t.*, *v.i.* **6.** slacken. —**slack´ly**, *adv.* —**slack´ness**, *n.*

slăck´ĕn, *v.t.*, *v.i.* **1.** make or become slack. **2.** lessen in intensity or vigor.

slăcks, *n. pl.* loosely fitting trousers.

slăg, *n.* molten waste from smelting.

slāke, *v.t.*, **slaked, slaking.** **1.** quench with a drink. **2.** pour water on, as quicklime.

slăm, *v.t.*, **slammed, slamming**, *n. v.t.* **1.** push violently and noisily into place. —*n.* **2.** act of pushing thus.

slăn´dêr, *n.* **1.** maliciously untrue statement or statements about someone. —*v.t.* **2.** utter such statements about. —**slan´der·ous**, *adj.*

slăng, *n.* highly informal speech. —**slang´y**, *adj.*

slănt, *v.t.*, *v.i.* **1.** move or head diagonally. —*n.* **2.** diagonal movement or heading. **3.** attitude or opinion.

slăp, *v.t.*, **slapped, slapping**, *n. v.t.* **1.** hit with a flat object, esp. the hand. **2.** put together, etc. in haste. —*n.* **3.** act or instance of slapping.

slăsh, *v.t.* **1.** cut deeply with a long, sweeping motion. —*n.* **2.** long, deep cut.

slăt, *n.* thin board.

slāte, *n.*, *v.t.*, **slated, slating.** *n.* **1.** stone that can be cleaved into thin pieces. **2.** list of candidates. —*v.t.* **3.** cover with slate. **4.** intend for nomination, promotion, dismissal, etc.

slăt´têrn, *n.* slovenly woman.

slăugh´têr, *n.* **1.** mass killing; massacre. **2.** killing of animals for meat. —*v.t.* **3.** submit to slaughter. —**slaugh´ter·house´´**, *n.*

slāve, *n.*, *v.i.*, **slaved, slaving.** *n.* **1.** person treated as the property of another. —*v.i.* **2.** drudge. —**slav´ery**, *n.*

slav·er (slăhv´ər), *v.i.* drool.

slăv´ĭsh, *adj.* in the manner of a slave, esp. in lacking originality or initiative.

slăw, *n.* coleslaw.

slăy, *v.t.,* **slew, slain, slaying.** kill. —**slay´ er,** *n.*

slēa´zy, *adj.,* **-zier, -ziest.** shoddy.

slĕd, *n., v.i.,* **sledded, sledding.** *n.* **1.** vehicle for gliding across snow or ice. —*v.i.* **2.** travel by sled.

slĕdge, *n., v.t.,* **sledged, sledging.** *n.* **1.** sledlike vehicle. **2.** Also, **sledge´ham· mer,** heavy hammer. —*v.t.* **3.** transport by sledge.

slēek, *adj.* **1.** smooth or glossy. —*v.t.* **2.** make smooth. —**sleek´ly,** *adv.* —**sleek´ ness,** *n.*

slēep, *n., v.i.,* **slept, sleeping.** *n.* **1.** periodic state of unconsciousness rest. —*v.i.* **2.** be in such a state. —**sleep´y,** *adj.* —**sleep´less,** *adj.*

slēep´ẽr, *n.* **1.** sleeping person. **2.** sill-like timber. **3.** railroad car with berths.

slēet, *n.* rain frozen in fine particles.

slēeve, *n.* part of a shirt or coat covering an arm.

sleigh (slā), *n.* horse-drawn light sled.

sleight of hănd, rapid, secret hand movements for creating illusions.

slĕn´dẽr, *adj.* **1.** attractively thin. **2.** meager, as means of livelihood. —**slen´der· ness,** *n.*

slēuth, *n. Informal.* detective.

slice, *n., v.t.,* **sliced, slicing.** *n.* **1.** thin piece cut from a larger one. —*v.t.* **2.** cut as a slice. **3.** cut slices from. —**slic´er,** *n.*

slĭck, *adj.* **1.** smooth or slippery. **2.** cunning. —*n.* **3.** area of floating oil. —*v.t.* **4.** make smooth.

slĭck´ẽr, *n.* raincoat with a slick outer surface.

slīde, *v.,* **slid, sliding.** *n. v.t., v.i.* **1.** move with surface contact between the object moving and something else. —*n.* **2.** act or instance of sliding. **3.** object or surface used in sliding. **4.** fall of earth, rock, etc. down a slope. **5.** transparent plate used with a microscope, magic lantern, etc.

slĭght, *adj.* **1.** unimportantly little. **2.** slender. —*v.t., n.* **3.** snub. —**slight´ly,** *adv.* —**slight´ness,** *n.* —**slight´ing·ly,** *adv.*

slī´lỹ, *adv.* slyly.

slĭm, *adj.,* **slimmer, slimmest. 1.** slender.

2. small in amount or size. —**slim´ness,** *n.*

slīme, *n.* semi-liquid, sticky matter.

slĭm´ỹ, *adj.,* **slimier, slimiest. 1.** of the nature of slime. **2.** disgustingly wheedling.

slĭng, *n., v.t.,* **slung, slinging.** *n.* **1.** flexible device for hurling missiles. **2.** suspended cloth support. —*v.t.* **3.** hurl or throw. **4.** put in a sling.

slĭnk, *v.i.,* **slunk, slinking.** walk furtively.

slĭp, *v.,* **slipped, slipping,** *n. v.t., v.i.* **1.** slide smoothly. **2.** escape. —*v.i.* **3.** loose grip or footing. **4.** make a mistake. —*n.* **5.** act or instance of slipping. **6.** underskirt. **7.** space between piers for a ship.

slĭp´pẽr, *n.* soft unlaced shoe for household wear.

slĭp´pẽr·ỹ, *adj.,* **-ier, -iest. 1.** allowing slipping. **2.** cunning and unreliable.

slĭp´shŏd´´, *adj.* careless.

slĭt, *n., v.t.,* **slitted, slitting.** *n.* **1.** long, deep opening. —*v.t.* **2.** cut with slits.

slĭth´ẽr, *v.i.* slide with a side-to-side motion.

slĭv´ẽr, *n., v.t.* splinter.

slŏb, *n. Informal.* uncouth or clumsy person.

slŏb´bẽr, *v.i., n.* drool.

slŏg, *v.i.,* **slogged, slogging.** advance heavily or with difficulty; plod.

slō´găn, *n.* motto.

slŏop, *n.* one-masted sailing vessel.

slŏp, *v.,* **slopped, slopping,** *n. v.t., v.i.* **1.** spill or toss carelessly, as a liquid. —*n.* **2.** something slopped. **3.** swill.

slōpe, *n., v.,* **sloped, sloping.** *n.* **1.** angled rise or descent. —*v.t.* **2.** cause to rise or descend in a slope. —*v.i.* **3.** form a slope.

slŏp´pỹ, *adj.* **1.** untidy. **2.** carelessly done. —**slop´pi·ly,** *adv.* —**slop´pi·ness,** *n.*

slŏsh, *v.t.* splash or slop.

slŏt, *n.* narrow opening.

slŏth, *n.* **1.** South American arboreal mammal. **2.** laziness. —**sloth´ful,** *adj.*

slŏuch, *v.i.* **1.** have a drooping posture. —*n.* **2.** drooping posture. **3.** incompetent or lazy person. —**slouch´y,** *adj.*

slough, *n.* **1.** (slōō or slō) muddy or marshy area. **2.** (sluf) dead, cast-off skin. —*v.t.* **3.** cast off. —*v.i.* **4.** be cast off, as dead skin.

slov·en (sluv′ən), *n.* untidy or careless person. **—slov′en·ly,** *adj.*

slow, *adj.* **1.** moving or acting without speed. **2.** not learning or understanding readily. **3.** behind the correct or appointed time. **4.** lacking in activity or vigor. *—adv.* **5.** slowly. *—v.t.* **6.** cause to move or act slowly. *—v.i.* **7.** move or act slowly. **—slow′ly,** *adv.* **—slow′ness,** *n.*

sludge, *n.* semi-liquid sediment.

slue, *v.,* **slued, sluing.** *v.t., v.i.* turn or swerve.

slug, *v.t.,* **slugged, slugging,** *n. v.t.* **1.** hit, esp. with the fists. *—n.* **2.** crawling mollusk leaving a slimy trail. **3.** bullet. **4.** false coin.

slug′gard, *n.* lazy person.

slug′gish, *adj.* abnormally slow or lacking in vigor. **—slug′gish·ly,** *adv.* **—slug′gish·ness,** *n.*

sluice, *n.* **1.** artificial channel controlled by a gate. **2.** Also, **sluice gate,** gate controlling this channel.

slum, *n.* squalid home or residential area.

slum′ber, *v.i.* **1.** sleep deeply. *—n.* **2.** deep sleep.

slump, *v.i.* **1.** drop or sag heavily. *—n.* **2.** act or instance of slumping.

slur, *v.t.,* **slurred, slurring,** *n. v.t.* **1.** say indistinctly. **2.** disparage. *—n.* **3.** indistinct speech. **4.** disparaging remark.

slush, *n.* melting snow. **—slush′y,** *adj.*

slut, *n.* immoral or slatternly woman.

sly, *adj.,* **slyer** or **slier, slyest** or **sliest. 1.** cunning; tricky. **2.** gently mischievous. **—sly′ly, sli′ly,** *adv.* **—sly′ness,** *n.*

smack, *v.t.* **1.** separate noisily, as the lips. **2.** slap. *—v.i.* **3.** have a taste or suggestion. *—n.* **4.** act or instance of smacking. **5.** taste or suggestion. **6.** fishing boat.

small, *adj.* **1.** little. **2.** of no great importance, value, etc. **3.** petty or mean. *—adv.* **4.** into small pieces. *—n.* **5.** narrow part, esp. of the back. **—small′ness,** *n.*

small′pox′′, *n.* contagious disease with fever and pustules as symptoms.

smart, *adj.* **1.** severe, as a blow. **2.** intelligent or clever. **3.** briskly efficient. **4.** in style. *—n.* **5.** sharp, stinging pain. *—v.i.* **6.** feel such a pain. **—smart′ly,** *adv.* **—smart′ness,** *n.* **—smart′en,** *v.t.*

smash, *v.t.* **1.** break into fragments. *—n.*

2. act or instance of smashing. **3.** serious automobile accident.

smat′ter·ing, *n.* slight knowledge.

smear, *v.t.* **1.** rub with greasy clinging material. **2.** slander. *—n.* **3.** smeared area. **4.** slander.

smell, *n.* **1.** sense perceived by the nose and olfactory organs. **2.** odor. *—v.t.* **3.** sense with the nose and olfactory organs. *—v.i.* **4.** have an odor.

smelt, *n., pl.* **smelts, smelt,** *v.t. n.* **1.** small northern salt-water fish. *—v.t.* **2.** melt or fuse so as to extract metal. **3.** extract from ore by melting or fusing. **—smelt′er,** *n.*

smile, *v.i.,* **smiled, smiling,** *n. v.i.* **1.** assume a look of pleasure, etc. by upturning the corners of the mouth. **2.** look favorably. *—n.* **3.** smiling appearance.

smirch, *v.t.* **1.** stain or soil. *—n.* **2.** stain.

smirk, *v.i.* **1.** have an affected or self-satisfied smile. *—n.* **2.** such a smile.

smite, *v.t.,* **smote, smitten** or **smiting.** *Archaic.* **1.** hit; strike. **2.** overcome with charm.

smith, *n.* metalworker.

smith′y, *n., pl.* **smithies.** blacksmith's shop.

smock, *n.* loose garment covering the whole body.

smog, *n.* fog with smoke.

smoke, *n., v.,* **smoked, smoking,** *n.* **1.** unconsumed material emitted by a fire. *—v.i.* **2.** inhale and exhale smoke from smoldering tobacco, etc. *—v.t.* **3.** burn in order to inhale and exhale the smoke. **4.** treat with smoke. **—smok′y,** *adj.* **—smoke′stack′′,** *n.*

smok′er, *n.* **1.** person who smokes. **2.** railroad car or compartment where smoking is permitted.

smol′der, *v.i.* **1.** burn flamelessly. **2.** exist partly suppressed. Also, **smoul′der.**

smooth, *adj.* **1.** without unevenness. **2.** without difficulty. **3.** without harsh or disturbing qualities. **4.** ingratiating. *—v.t.* **5.** make smooth. **—smooth′ly,** *adv.* **—smooth′ness,** *n.*

smoth′er, *v.t.* **1.** suffocate. **2.** cover completely.

smudge, *n., v.t.,* **smudged, smudging,** *n.* **1.** spot of smoke, dirt, ink, etc. *—v.t.* **2.** stain or treat with smoke, dirt, ink, etc.

smŭg, *adj.* excessively self-satisfied. —**smug′ly**, *adv.* —**smug′ness**, *n.*

smŭg′gle, *v.t.,* -**gled**, -**gling.** bring in or out secretly in violation of laws or regulations. —**smug′gler**, *n.*

smŭt, *n.* **1.** soot or smudge. **2.** obscenity. **3.** fungous plant disease. —**smut′ty**, *adj.*

snăck, *n.* small meal.

snăg, *n., v.,* **snagged, snagging**. *n.* **1.** projection that catches or tears. **2.** obstacle. —*v.t.* **3.** catch or damage, as with a snag.

snail, *n.* crawling mollusk with a shell.

snăke, *n., v.i.* **snaked, snaking**. *n.* **1.** scaly reptile without limbs. —*v.i.* **2.** move or lie sinuously.

snăp, *v.,* **snapped, snapping**, *n., adj. v.i.* **1.** make a sharp clicking sound. **2.** go into or out of a close-fitting socket. **3.** break abruptly. **4.** bite. **5.** speak crossly and abruptly. —*v.t.* **6.** cause to snap. **7.** photograph. —*n.* **8.** act or instance of snapping. **9.** fastener that snaps shut. —*adj.* **10.** hasty, as a judgment.

snăp′drăg′′on, *n.* plant with flowers in spikes.

snăp′pĭsh, *adj.* short-tempered.

snăp′pў, *adj.* quick.

snăp′shŏt′′, *n.* uncomposed photograph from a small, hand-held camera.

snâre, *n., v.t.,* **snared, snaring**. trap.

snârl, *v.i.* **1.** growl. —*v.t.* **2.** tangle.

snătch, *v.t.* **1.** grab. —*v.i.* **2.** reach suddenly or eagerly. —*n.* **3.** act or instance of snatching. **4.** fragment.

snēak, *v.i.* **1.** go furtively. —*v.t.* **2.** bring in or out furtively. —*n.* **3.** furtive, dishonest person. —**sneak′y**, *adj.*

snēak′ẽr, *n.* low, soft-soled shoe.

snēer, *v.i.* **1.** express contempt. —*n.* **2.** expression of contempt.

snēeze, *v.i.,* **sneezed, sneezing**, *n. v.i.* **1.** expel breath explosively and involuntarily. —*n.* **2.** act or instance of sneezing.

snick′ẽr, *n.* **1.** contemptuous, high-pitched laugh. —*v.i.* **2.** give such a laugh. Also, **snig′ger**.

snīde, *adj.* malicious, as a remark.

snĭff, *v.i.* **1.** inhale quickly through the nose. **2.** exhale loudly through the nose. —*n.* **3.** act or instance of sniffing.

snĭf′fle, *v.i.* **1.** inhale through the nose.

—*n.* **2. sniffles**, *Informal.* mild cold symptoms.

snĭp, *v.t.,* **snipped, snipping**, *n. v.t.* **1.** cut as with scissors. —*n.* **2.** snipped-off fragment. **3. snips**, shears.

snīpe, *n., v.i.,* **sniped, sniping**. *n.* **1.** wading bird. —*v.i.* **2.** shoot from a hidden position. —**snip′er**, *n.*

snĭp′pét, *n.* small piece, as of information.

snĭv′el, *v.i.* plead, complain, etc. in a whining tone.

snŏb, *n.* person with ostentatious likes and dislikes based on pretentious standards of excellence. —**snob′bish**, *adj.* —**snob′ber·y**, *n.*

snōod, *n.* net covering the back of a woman's hair.

snōop, *Informal. v.i.* **1.** seek information furtively. —*n.* **2.** Also, **snoop′er**, person who snoops.

snōoze, *v.i.,* **snoozed, snoozing**, *n.* nap.

snōre, *v.i.,* **snored, snoring**, *n. v.i.* **1.** breathe noisily while sleeping. —*n.* **2.** sound of such breathing.

snŏr′kel, *n.* ventilating tube for a submarine, etc. under water.

snôrt, *n.* **1.** loud exhalation through the nose. —*v.i.* **2.** give such an exhalation.

snŏt, *n. Informal.* mucus from the nose.

snout, *n.* protruding front of an animal head.

snōw, *n.* **1.** precipitation frozen in crystalline flakes. —*v.i.* **2.** precipitate snow. —**snow′drift′′**, *n.* —**snow′fall′′**, *n.* —**snow′flake′′**, *n.* —**snow′storm′′**, *n.* —**snow′y**, *adj.*

snōw′băll′′, *n.* **1.** ball of compacted snow. —*v.i.* **2.** increase with gathering speed.

snōw′shoe′′, *n.* webbed flat frame for supporting the foot on snow.

snŭb, *v.t.,* **snubbed, snubbing**, *n., adj. v.t.* **1.** refuse attention or respect to. —*n.* **2.** act or instance of snubbing. —*adj.* **3.** short and upturned, as a nose.

snŭff, *v.t.* **1.** trim, as a burned wick. **2.** extinguish or eliminate. —*n.* **3.** powdered tobacco.

snŭf′fle, *v.i.,* -**fled**, -**fling.** sniffle.

snŭg, *adj.,* **snugger, snuggest. 1.** cozy. **2.** neat. **3.** tight in fit. —**snug′ly**, *adv.*

snŭg′gle, *v.i.* -**gled**, -**gling.** cuddle or nestle.

solid

sō, *adv.* **1.** as stated or indicated. **2.** to such an extent. **3.** *Informal.* very; very much. **4.** in this way. —*conj.* **5.** therefore. **6.** in order that. —*adj.* **7.** true.

sōak, *v.t.* **1.** cover with a liquid. **2.** absorb. —*v.i.* **3.** become absorbed. —*n.* **4.** act or instance of soaking.

sōap, *n.* **1.** substance used in washing. —*v.t.* **2.** cover with soap. —**soap′y**, *adj.*

sōar, *v.i.* **1.** rise into the air. **2.** glide or hover in the air.

sōb, *v.i.*, **sobbed, sobbing**, *n. v.i.* **1.** weep convulsively. —*n.* **2.** sound of sobbing.

sō′bĕr, *adj.* **1.** not drunk. **2.** serious or quiet. —*v.t.* **3.** make sober. **4.** cause grave feelings in. —**so′ber·ly**, *adv.* —**so′′bri·e·ty, so′ber·ness**, *n.*

sō-cálled, *adj.* called thus; used esp. when so named without justification.

sŏc′cĕr, *n.* a variety of football played without using the hands and arms.

sō′cia·ble, *adj.* friendly; gregarious. —**so′cia·bly**, *adv.* —**so′′cia·bil′i·ty**, *n.*

sō′ciàl, *adj.* **1.** pertaining to society. **2.** sociable. —**so′cial·ly**, *adv.*

sō′ciàl·ism, *n.* theory advocating public ownership of means of production, with work and products shared. —**so′′cial·ist**, *n.* —**so′′cial·is′tic**, *adj.* —**so′′cial·ize′**, *v.t.*

sō′ciàl·īte′′, *n.* person in fashionable society.

sò·cī′e·tў, *n., pl.* **-ties. 1.** group sharing a common culture, location, etc. **2.** human beings, in their relations with one another. **3.** world of the upper class. **4.** organization, esp. a professional or public-service one.

sō′′cī·ŏl′ò·gў, *n.* study of society. —**so′′ci·o·log′i·cal**, *adj.* —**so′′ci·ol′o·gist**, *n.*

sŏck, *n.* **1.** short stocking. —*v.t.* **2.** *Informal.* hit.

sŏck′ĕt, *n.* a hollow part in which something is inserted and held.

sŏd, *n.* earth with growing grass.

sō′dà, *n.* **1.** drink with soda water. **2.** mixture of soda water, ice cream, and flavoring. **3.** chemical containing sodium.

sō·dǎl′i·tў, *n., pl.* **-ties.** Catholic religious or charitable society.

sōdà wâtĕr, *n.* water charged with carbon dioxide.

sŏd′dĕn, *n.* **1.** stupefied. **2.** soggy.

sō′dĭ′ŭm, *n.* alkaline chemical element.

sŏd·ò·mў *n.* abnormal sexual intercourse. —**sod′o·mite**, *n.*

sō′fà, *n.* wide, upholstered seat with a back and arms.

sŏft, *adj.* **1.** yielding readily to pressure. **2.** gentle. **3.** quiet. **4.** weak. **5.** non-alcoholic. **6.** permitting lathering, as water. —**soft′ly**, *adv.* —**soft′ness**, *n.* —**soft′en**, *v.t.*, *v.i.*

sŏft′bäll′′, *n.* baseball-like game using a softer ball.

sŏft′wāre, *n.* (computers) programming enabling a system to function.

sŏg′gў, *adj.* moist and heavy with absorbed liquid.

sŏĭl, *v.t.* **1.** dirty. —*n.* **2.** earth. **3.** sewage.

sō′joûrn, *v.i.* **1.** stay briefly. —*n.* **2.** brief stay.

sŏl′àce *n.* comfort in unhappiness.

sō′làr, *adj.* pertaining to the sun.

sŏl′dĕr, *n.* **1.** alloy with low melting point for joining or patching metal. —*v.t.* **2.** treat with solder.

sŏl′diêr, *n.* **1.** member of an army. —*v.i.* **2.** live as a soldier. —**sol′dier·ly**, *adj.* —**sol′dier·y**, *n.*

sōle, *n., v.t.*, **soled, soling**, *adj. n.* **1.** salt-water flatfish. **2.** wearing surface on the bottom of a shoe. —*v.t.* **3.** fit with soles. —*adj.* **4.** single; only. —**sole′ly**, *adv.*

sŏl′ĕmn, *adj.* **1.** serious; earnest. **2.** formal. **3.** sacred. —**sol′emn·ly**, *adv.* —**so·lem′ni·ty**, *n.*

sŏl′ĕm·nīze, *v.t.*, **-nized, -nizing.** observe or put into effect with a ceremony. —**sol′′em·ni·za′tion**, *n.*

sò·lĭc′ĭ·tŏr, *n.* **1.** person who solicits. **2.** English lawyer other than a barrister.

sò·lĭc′ĭ·toŭs, *adj.* showing friendly concern. —**so·lic′i·tous·ly**, *adv.* —**so·lic′i·tude′′**, *n.*

sò·lĭc′ĭt, *v.t.* **1.** request. **2.** canvass for. —**so·li′′ci·ta′tion**, *n.*

sŏl′ĭd, *adj.* **1.** pertaining to or existing in three dimensions. **2.** firm; substantial. **3.** not hollow. **4.** dense. **5.** reliable. **6.** entire. —*n.* **7.** three-dimensional object. **8.** non-fluid material. —**sol′id·ly**, *adv.* —**so·lid′i·ty**, *n.* —**so·lid′i·fy′′**, *v.t.*, *v.i.*

sŏl''ĭ·dăr'ĭ·tў, *n.* unity of purpose, resolve, etc.

sŏl''ĭd-stāte', *adj.* designating electronic circuitry that uses solid semiconductors, as transistors, to control current.

sò·lĭl'ò·quŷ, *n., pl.* **-quies.** speech made to or as if to oneself. —**so·lil'o·quize**, *v.i.*

sŏl'ĭ·tāire', *n.* **1.** card game for one. **2.** single gemstone in a setting.

sŏl'ĭ·tār''ў, *adj.* **1.** single. **2.** alone. **3.** isolated.

sŏl'ĭ·tūde, *n.* state of being alone or isolated.

sō'lō, *n.* performance by one person, esp. in music or aviation. —**so'lo·ist**, *n.*

sŏl'stĭce, *n.* point when the sun is furthest from the equator; beginning of summer or winter.

sŏl'ū·ble, *adj.* able to be dissolved. —**sol''u·bil'i·ty**, *n.*

sò·lū'tion, *n.* **1.** means of solving a problem. **2.** dispersal of one material in another. **3.** material, usually a liquid, that results from this.

sŏlve, *v.t.*, **solved, solving.** explain or find means to overcome, as a problem. —**solv'a·ble**, *adj.*

sŏl'vent, *n.* **1.** material that dissolves another. —*adj.* **2.** able to dissolve something. **3.** able to meet one's debts. —**sol'ven·cy**, *n.*

sŏm'bêr, *adj.* gloomy. Also, **som'bre.** —**som'ber·ly**, *adv.*

sŏm·brĕ'rō, *n.* broad-brimmed hat worn in Hispanic countries.

sŏme, *adj.* **1.** indefinite amount or number of. **2.** certain unknown or unspecified. —*pron.* **3.** unknown or unspecified number.

sòme'bŏdў'', *pron.* unspecified person. Also, **some'one''.**

sòme'hŏw'', *adv.* in some way. Also, **some'way''.**

sŏm'êr·sault'', *n.* **1.** overturn forward or backward of a crouched person. —*v.i.* **2.** execute a somersault.

sòme'thĭng'', *n.* thing not specified.

sòme'tĭme'', *adv.* **1.** at an indefinite time. —*adj.* **2.** *Archaic.* former.

sòme'tĭmes'', *adv.* now and then.

sòme'whăt'', *adv.* to some extent.

sòme'whĕre'', *adv.* at or to an unspecified place.

sŏm·năm'bū·lĭsm, *n.* sleepwalking. —**som·nam'bu·list**, *n.*

sŏm'nó·lĕnt, *adj.* drowsy. —**som'no·lence**, *n.*

sòn, *n.* male offspring.

sò·nä'tà, *n.* instrumental musical composition.

sŏng, *n.* vocal musical composition.

sŏn'ĭc, *adj.* pertaining to sound.

sòn'-ĭn-lăw, *n., pl.* **sons-in-law.** husband of one's daughter.

sŏn'nĕt, *n.* poem with fourteen lines.

sò·nō'roŭs, *adj.* deep or rich in sound. —**so'no·rous·ly**, *adv.* —**so·nor'i·ty**, *n.*

sōōn, *adv.* after a short time.

sōōt, *n.* black particles in smoke. —**soot'y**, *adj.*

sōōthe, *v.t.*, **soothed, soothing. 1.** free of agitation or annoyance. **2.** relieve, as pain.

sōōth'sāy''êr, *n.* person who claims to know the future.

sŏp, *n.* **1.** morsel dipped in liquid. **2.** something that appeases. —*v.t.*, *v.i.* **3.** soak. —*v.t.* **4.** absorb.

sò·phĭs'tĭ·cāte'', *v.t.* **1.** make sophisticated. —*n.* **2.** sophisticated person.

sò·phĭs'tĭ·cāt''ĕd, *adj.* **1.** acquainted with the ways of society. **2.** technologically advanced. —**so·phis''ti·ca'tion**, *n.*

sŏph'ĭs·trў, *n.* specious, unsound reasoning. —**soph'ist**, *n.*

sŏph'ò·mōre'', *n.* second-year secondary or college student.

sŏph'ò·mŏr'ĭc, *adj.* intellectually immature.

sò''pó·rĭf'ĭc, *adj.* **1.** sleep-inducing. —*n.* **2.** soporific drug.

sò·prăn'ō, *n.* singer in the highest vocal range.

sôr'cêr·êr, *n.* magician. Also, *fem.*, **sor'cer·ess.** —**sor'cer·y**, *n.*

sôr'dĭd, *adj.* **1.** disgustingly mean or ignoble. **2.** filthy.

sôre, *adj.*, **sorer, sorest**, *n. adj.* **1.** aching or tender. **2.** grieving. **3.** causing trouble or annoyance. **4.** *Informal.* angry. **5.** sore place on the body. —**sore'ly**, *adv.* —**sore'ness**, *n.*

sôr·ghum (sor'gəm), *n*. cereal grass made into syrup, etc.

so·rôr'ĭ·tў, *n*., *pl*. -ties. women's organization, esp. in a college.

sôr'rèl, *n*. **1.** reddish-brown. **2.** horse of this color. **3.** plant with sour-tasting leaves.

sôr'rŏw, *n*. **1.** great unhappiness or regret. —*v.i.* **2.** feel sorrow. **—sor'row·ful,** *adj*. **—sor'row·ful·ly,** *adv*.

sôr'rў, *adj*. **1.** feeling regret. **2.** feeling pity. **3.** miserable.

sôrt, *n*. **1.** type; classification. **2.** quality. —*v.t.* **3.** arrange by type.

sôr'tie, *n*. **1.** swift counterattack, as from a besieged place. **2.** aerial combat mission.

SOS, call for help.

sō'-sō'', *adj*. **1.** not especially good or bad. —*adv*. **2.** not especially well or badly.

sŏt, *n*. drunkard.

soûf·flé', *n*. light, puffy baked dish.

sough (sŏw, sŭf), *v.i.* rustle or sigh, as the wind.

soul, *n*. **1.** non-material aspect of a person. **2.** emotional or moral aspect of the personality. **3.** feeling or sensitivity. **4.** essence. **5.** human being. **—soul'ful,** *adj*. **—soul'less,** *adj*.

sŏund, *n*. **1.** air vibrations perceptible in part to the ear. **2.** tone or noise that is heard. **3.** inlet or channel of sea water. —*v.t.* **4.** cause to make a sound. **5.** measure the depth of. **6.** determine the attitude or opinion of. —*v.i.* **7.** make a sound. **8.** seem. **9.** sound like, imply. —*adj*. **10.** healthy. **11.** reasonable. reliable. **—sound'less,** *adj*. **—sound'proof'',** *adj*. **—sound'ly,** *adv*. **—sound'ness,** *n*.

soŭp, *n*. savory, mainly liquid food.

soûr, *adj*. **1.** acid-tasting. **2.** fermented beyond the normal state. **3.** ill-tempered. —*v.i.* **4.** become sour. **—sour'ly,** *adv*. **—sour'ness,** *n*.

sôurce, *n*. origin.

soûse, *v.t.*, **soused, sousing.** *n*. *v.t.* **1.** immerse or steep. **2.** pickle. —*n*. **3.** pickled food. **4.** act or instance of sousing.

soûth, *n*. **1.** direction of the South Pole. **2.** region located in this direction. —*adj*., *adv*. **3.** to or toward the south. **4.** from the south, as a wind. **—south'ward,** *adv*., *adj*. **south'ern,** *adj*. **—south'ern·er,** *n*. **—south'er·ly,** *adj*., *adv*.

soūth''ēast', *n*. direction halfway between south and east. **—south''east',** *adj*., *adv*.

soūth''wĕst', *n*. direction halfway between south and west. **—south''west',** *adj*., *adv*.

sou·ve·nir (sōō'və nēr), *n*. thing to remember a place, event, etc. by.

sov'er·eign (sov'rən), *n*. **1.** monarch. **2.** former British gold coin. —*adj*. **3.** having supreme political power. **4.** politically independent. **—sov'er·eign·ty,** *n*.

sō'vĭ·ét, *adj*. **1.** Soviet, pertaining to the Soviet Union. —*n*. **2.** former Russian governmental council.

sŏw, *v.t.* **1.** plant, as seed. —*n*. **2. sŏw,** female hog. **—sow'er,** *n*.

soy'bēan'', *n*. plant grown for its seeds.

spä, *n*. resort with mineral springs.

spăce, *n*., *v.t.*, **spaced, spacing.** *n*. **1.** limitless three-dimensional expanse. **2.** specific area within this. **3.** outer space. **4.** distance. —*v.t.* **5.** separate, esp. at regular intervals.

spāce'crăft'', *n*. vehicle for exploration of outer space.

spāce'flĭght'', *n*. flight through outer space.

spāce'shĭp'', *n*. vehicle for travel in outer space.

spāce'wălk'', *n*. personal movement away from a spacecraft in outer space.

spā'cioŭs, *adj*. amply extensive.

spāde, *n*., *v.t.*, **spaded, spading.** *n*. **1.** shovel with long shaftlike handle. **2. spades,** black suit of playing cards. —*v.t.* **3.** dig with a spade.

spä·ghĕt'tĭ, *n*. stringy pasta, usually served with a sauce.

spăn, *n*., *v.t.*, **spanned, spanning.** *n*. **1.** something between two supports. **2.** distance between the thumb and little finger, when extended. **3.** duration. **4.** pair of harnessed animals. —*v.t.* **5.** cross.

spăn'gle, *n*., *v.t.*, **-gled, -gling.** *n*. **1.** glittering decoration. —*v.t.* **2.** decorate with spangles.

spăn'iél, *n*. short-legged, long-eared dog.

spănk, *v.t.* slap on the behind.

spănk'ĭng, *adj*. brisk.

spär, *v.i.,* **sparred, sparring,** *n. v.i.* **1.** box with the fists. —*n.* **2.** pole. **3.** crystalline rock.

späre, *v.t.,* **spared, sparing,** *adj.,* **sparer, sparest.** *v.t.* **1.** use or spend with restraint. **2.** prevent from occurring, being known, etc., as something unpleasant. **3.** treat leniently. **4.** give without inconvenience. —*adj.* **5.** in reserve; extra. **6.** gaunt; lean.

späre'rĭb'', *n.* pork rib cut at the thin end.

spärk, *n.* **1.** glowing, burning piece of matter from a fire. **2.** electric flash. **3.** trace, as of life.

spär'kle, *v.i.,* **-kled, -kling,** *n. v.i.* **1.** emit or reflect small flashes of light. **2.** effervesce, as wine. **3.** glitter, as eyes. —*n.* **4.** act or instance of sparkling.

spär'röw, *n.* bird of the finch family.

spärse, *adj.,* **sparser, sparsest. 1.** scattered. **2.** scanty. —**sparse'ly,** *adv.* —**sparse'ness, spars'i·ty,** *n.*

Spär'tan, *adj.* austere; disciplined.

späsm, *n.* sudden and involuntary contraction of the muscles.

späs·mŏd'ĭc, *adj.* **1.** in spasms. **2.** at unpredictable intervals. —**spas·mod'i·cal·ly,** *adv.*

späs'tĭc, *adj.* characterized by spasms.

spăt, *n. Informal.* quarrel about a small matter.

spā'tiäl, *adj.* pertaining to space.

spăt'tĕr, *v.t.* splash, esp. in small amounts over a wide area.

spat·u·la (spach'ə lə), *n.* broad-bladed device for handling foods, etc.

spawn, *n.* **1.** eggs of some animals, esp. fish and mollusks. —*v.t.* **2.** originate in abundance. —*v.i.* **3.** lay spawn.

speak, *v.,* **spoke, spoken, speaking.** *v.i.* **1.** communicate with the voice. **2.** give a speech or lecture. —*v.t.* **3.** present by means of the voice. **4.** use in speaking, as a language.

speak'ĕr, *n.* **1.** person who speaks. **2.** president of a legislature. **3.** loudspeaker.

spear, *n.* **1.** long-handled, pointed weapon for hurling or thrusting. —*v.t.* **2.** wound with a spear. —**spear'head,** *n.*

spear'mĭnt'', *n.* fragrant mint used as flavoring.

spe'ciäl, *adj.* **1.** distinct from all others. **2.** remarkable. —**spe'cial·ly,** *adv.*

spe'ciäl·ĭze, *v.i.,* **-ized, -izing.** study, work, or trade in a special area. —**spe'cial·ist,** *n.*

spe'ciäl·tў, *n., pl.* **-ties.** area of specialization.

spe'cies, *n.* group of fundamentally identical plants or animals.

spe·cie (spe'she), *n.* coins.

spe·cĭf'ĭc, *adj.* **1.** detailed. **2.** exact. **3.** characteristic.

spe'cĭ·fў'', *v.t.,* **-fied, -fying.** state or demand specifically.

spĕc'ĭ·mĕn, *n.* typical example.

spe'cioŭs, *adj.* falsely seeming good or valid. —**spe'cious·ly,** *adv.* —**spe'cious·ness,** *n.*

spĕck, *n.* **1.** small particle or spot. —*v.t.* **2.** mark with specks.

spĕck'le, *n., v.t.,* **-led, -ling.** *n.* **1.** small spot. —*v.t.* **2.** mark with speckles.

spĕc'tä·cle, *n.* **1.** marvelous event or sight. **2.** grandiose public entertainment. **3. spectacles,** eyeglasses.

spĕc·tăc'ū·lär, *adj.* marvelous or grandiose in appearance, etc.

spĕc'tä·tŏr, *n.* person who sees an event or view.

spĕc'tĕr, *n.* ghost; apparition. Also, **spec'tre.** —**spec'tral,** *adj.*

spĕc'trō·scōpe, *n.* instrument for producing and analyzing spectra. —**spec''troscop'ic,** *adj.*

spĕc'trŭm, *n., pl.* **-tra, -trums.** group of color bands produced when light is dispersed by a prism.

spĕc'ū·lāte, *v.i.,* **-lated, -lating. 1.** think contemplatively. **2.** undertake a business risk in the hope of large profits. —**spec''u·la'tion,** *n.* —**spec''u·la'tive,** *adj.* —**spec''u·la'tor,** *n.*

speech, *n.* **1.** ability to speak. **2.** way of speaking. **3.** something spoken. **4.** talk to an audience. —**speech'less,** *adj.*

speed, *n., v.,* **sped** or **speeded, speeding.** *n.* **1.** swiftness of motion or action. **2.** rate of motion or action. —*v.t.* **3.** increase the speed of. —*v.i.* **4.** move swiftly. **5.** drive with excessive speed. —**speed'y,** *adj.* —**speed'i·ly,** *adv.* —**speed'er,** *n.*

spéed·ŏm′e·têr, n. speed-registering device.

spěll, v., **spelled** or **spelt, spelling,** n. v.t. **1.** name the letters of. **2.** comprise the letters of. **3.** take over from, as in a shared task. —v.i. **4.** name the letters forming ordinary words. —n. **5.** enchantment. **6.** period of time.

spěll′bŏund″, adj. entranced.

spěnd, v.t., **spent, spending. 1.** pay. **2.** pass, as a period of time. **3.** use up or exhaust. —**spend′er,** n.

spěnd′thrift″, n. spender to excess.

spěnt, adj. **1.** exhausted. **2.** used up or worn out.

spêrm, n. male germ cell carried by semen. —**sper′mat′ic,** adj.

spěw, v.t., v.i. vomit or pour with force.

sphêre, n. **1.** round solid with all radii equal; ball. **2.** area of influence, activity, knowledge, etc. —**spher′i·cal,** adj.

sphêr′ŏïd, n. approximately spherical solid.

sphĭnx, n. Classical mythology. creature with a human head and the body of a lion.

spïce, n., v.t., **spiced, spicing.** n. **1.** aromatic plant substance for seasoning, preservation, etc. —v.t. **2.** season or treat with spice. —**spic′y,** adj.

spi′dêr, n. eight-legged predatory arachnid that captures insects in a web. —**spi′der·y,** adj.

spĭg′ŏt, n. faucet.

spïke, n., v.t., **spiked, spiking.** n. **1.** large hammer-driven fastener. **2.** pointed feature. **3.** long stalk bearing grains or blossoms. —v.t. **4.** fasten with spikes. **5.** frustrate; thwart.

spĭll, v., **spilled** or **spilt, spilling.** v.t. **1.** lose, as from the tipping of a container. **2.** shed, as blood. —v.i. **3.** be lost, as over the rim of a container.

spĭll′wäy″, n. channel letting excess water escape.

spĭn, v., **spun, spinning,** n. v.t. **1.** make from twisted yarn. **2.** make into yarn or thread. **3.** make from secretions, as a spider web. —v.t., v.i. **4.** whirl. —n. **5.** whirling motion. **6.** Informal. brief ride. —**spin′ner,** n.

spĭn′ach, n. plant with dark-green edible leaves.

spĭn′dle, n. **1.** rod used in spinning thread. **2.** any slender round rod.

spĭn′dlĭng, adj. lanky. Also, **spin′dly.**

spĭn′drift″, n. spray from wave crests.

spĭne, n. **1.** Also called **spinal column.** backbone; vertebrae. **2.** thorn. —**spin′al,** adj. —**spin′y,** adj.

spïne′lĕss, adj. without courage.

spĭn′ĕt, n. small upright piano.

spĭn′stêr, n. unmarried woman past the normal marriageable age.

spï′rál, n. **1.** flat curve with steadily increasing radius. —adj. **2.** formed along such a curve. —v.i. **3.** move in such a curve. —**spi′ral·ly,** adj.

spïre, n. tall pyramidal structure forming the roof of a tower.

spĭr′ĭt, n. **1.** spiritual part of a person; soul. **2.** ghost. **3.** mood, sentiment, or intent. **4.** vigor or courage. **5.** spirits, a. state of mind. b. distilled alcoholic liquor. **6.** Holy Ghost. —v.t. **7.** smuggle. —**spir′it·ed,** adj. —**spir′it·less,** adj.

spĭr′ĭt·ū·ál, adj. **1.** pertaining to religion. **2.** pertaining to the soul. **3.** concerned with matters of the soul. —n. **4.** Negro religious song. —**spir′it·u·al·ly,** adv. —**spir″it·u·al′i·ty,** n.

spĭr′ĭt·ū·ál·ĭsm″, n. belief that the living and the dead can communicate. —**spir′it·u·al·ist,** n. —**spir″it·u·al·is′tic,** adj.

spĭr′ĭt·ū·oŭs, adj. alcoholic and distilled.

spĭt, v., **spat, spit,** or (for 2) **spitted, spitting,** n. v.t. **1.** eject from the mouth. **2.** skewer. —v.i. **3.** eject saliva from the mouth. —n. **4.** saliva. **5.** long skewer. **6.** small peninsula.

spïte, n., v.t., **spited, spiting.** n. **1.** small-minded hostility or vengefulness. **2. in spite of,** notwithstanding. —v.t. **3.** offend or hurt out of spite. —**spite′ful,** adj. —**spite′ful·ly,** adv. —**spite′ful·ness,** n.

spĭt′tle, n. saliva.

spĭt·tŏŏn′, n. receptacle for spit.

splăsh, v.t. **1.** cause to fly in various directions, as a liquid. —v.i. **2.** fly in various directions, as a liquid. —n. **3.** act, instance, or sound of splashing.

splăt′ter, v.i. be splashed.

splāy, v.t., v.i. **1.** spread apart. —adj. **2.** spreading apart.

spleen, *n.* **1.** organ for modifying the blood structure. **2.** anger or irritation. —**sple·net'ic,** *adj.*

splen'did, *adj.* **1.** magnificent. **2.** excellent. —**splen'did·ly,** *adv.* —**splen'dor,** *n.*

splice, *v.t.,* **spliced, splicing,** *n.* *v.t.* **1.** join into a single piece. —*n.* **2.** joint created by splicing.

splint, *n.* **1.** temporary reinforcement for a broken bone. **2.** thin slip of wood forming part of a basket.

splin'ter, *n.* **1.** sharp, broken fragment. —*v.t., v.i.* **2.** break into splinters.

split, *v.,* **split, splitting,** *n., adj. v.t., v.i.* **1.** break or pull in two. —*v.t.* **2.** share or divide. —*n.* **3.** act or instance of splitting. —*adj.* **4.** having been split.

splotch, *n., v.t.* spot or stain. —**splotch'y,** *adj.*

splurge, *v.i.,* **splurged, splurging,** *n. v.i.* **1.** spend money lavishly and showily. —*n.* **2.** act or instance of splurging.

splut'ter, *v.i.* **1.** babble, as with confusion or rage. —*n.* **2.** spluttering speech.

spoil, *v.,* **spoiled** or **spoilt, spoiling,** *n. v.t.* **1.** ruin. **2.** damage the character of with indulgence. —*v.i.* **3.** become unfit to eat, drink, or use. —*n.* **4. spoils,** loot. —**spoil'er,** *n.* —**spoil'age,** *n.*

spoke, *n.* shaft between the hub and rim of a wheel.

spokes'man, *n.* person who speaks for a group.

spo''li·a'tion, *n.* looting.

sponge, *n., v.,* **sponged, sponging.** *n.* a marine animal. **2.** skeleton of this animal or an imitation in plastic, used to absorb water. —*v.t.* **3.** wipe with a sponge. —*v.i.* **4.** *Informal.* live at the expense of others. —**spong'y,** *adj.*

spong'er, *n. Informal.* one who lives at the expense of others.

spon'sor, *n.* **1.** person who undertakes responsibility for another. **2.** godparent. **3.** advertiser who buys television or radio time. —*v.t.* **4.** act as sponsor for.

spon·ta'ne·ous, *adj.* **1.** occurring without an external cause. **2.** lively and natural in manner. —**spon·ta'ne·ous·ly,** *adv.* —**spon''ta·ne'i·ty, spon·ta'ne·ous ness,** *n.*

spook, *n. Informal.* ghost. —**spook'y,** *adj.*

spool, *n.* small drum on which thread, film, recording tape, etc. is wound.

spoon, *n.* **1.** utensil for handling or stirring liquids or food. —*v.t.* **2.** handle or serve with a spoon.

spoor, *n.* trail of animal scent.

spo·rad'ic, *adj.* occasional. —**spo·rad'i·cal·ly,** *adv.*

spore, *n.* seedlike body from which fungi, mosses, etc. grow.

sport, *n.* **1.** recreation involving bodily activity. **2.** amusement. **3.** plant or animal of abnormal form. —*v.i.* **4.** play vigorously. —**sports'man,** *n.* —**sports'man·ship'',** *n.* —**sports'man·ly,** *adj.*

spor'tive, *adj.* playful. —**spor'tive·ly,** *adv.* —**spor'tive·ness,** *n.*

spot, *n., v.t.,* **spotted, spotting,** *adj. n.* **1.** round mark. **2.** place. —*v.t.* **3.** mark with spots. **4.** notice. —*adj.* **5.** immediate. **6.** random, as a survey. —**spot'less,** *adj.* —**spot'ty,** *adj.* —**spot'ter,** *n.*

spouse, *n.* husband or wife.

spout, *n.* **1.** channel for discharging liquids, grain, etc. —*v.t.* **2.** emit with force. **3.** recite enthusiastically.

sprain, *v.t.* **1.** injure by wrenching muscles or ligaments. —*n.* **2.** injury so produced.

sprat, *n.* small fish of the herring family.

sprawl, *v.i.* **1.** stretch out in an ungraceful way. —*n.* **2.** act or instance of sprawling.

spray, *n.* **1.** liquid driven in fine particles. **2.** device for shooting such liquid. **3.** small branch with flowers or leaves. —*v.t.* **4.** drive as a spray. **5.** apply spray to. —**spray'er,** *n.*

spread, *v.,* **spread, spreading,** *n. v.t., v.i.* **1.** extend. **2.** scatter or disperse. —*v.t.* **3.** cover or apply thinly. —*n.* **4.** extent. **5.** distribution. **6.** cloth for covering a bed. **7.** soft food eaten with breadstuffs. —**spread'er,** *n.*

spree, *n.* occasion of uninhibited activity.

sprig, *n.* twig or spray.

spright'ly, *adj.,* **-lier, -liest.** lively. —**spright'li·ness,** *n.*

spring, *n., v.,* **sprang** or **sprung, sprung, springing,** *adj. n.* **1.** season between winter and summer, beginning at the vernal equinox. **2.** stream emerging from the earth. **3.** resilient elastic device, e.g. a wire coil. **4.** jump. —*v.i.* **5.** jump. **6.** arise or emerge. —*v.t.* **7.** cause to act suddenly. **8.** disclose suddenly. —**spring′time,** *n.* —**spring′y,** *adj.*

sprĭn′kle, *v.,* -**kled, -kling,** *n. v.t.* **1.** scatter thinly. —*v.i.* **2.** rain lightly. —*n.* **3.** act or instance of sprinkling. **4.** something sprinkled. —**sprink′ler,** *n.*

sprĭnt, *n.* **1.** short run. —*v.i.* **2.** make a short run. —**sprint′er,** *n.*

sprīte, *n.* elf or fairy.

sprŏck′ĕt, *n.* gear tooth engaging with a chain.

sprōut, *v.i.* **1.** begin to grow or send forth shoots. —*n.* **2.** shoot that has sprouted.

sprūce, *n., adj.,* **sprucer, spruciest,** *v.t., n.* **1.** coniferous evergreen. —*adj.* **2.** tidy; neat. —*v.t.* **3.** make tidy.

sprȳ, *adj.,* **sprier** or **spryer, spriest** or **spryest.** active; lively. —**spry′ly,** *adv.* —**spry′ness,** *n.*

spŭd, *n.* **1.** type of spade. **2.** *Informal.* potato.

spūme, *n.* foam.

spŭnk, *n. Informal.* courage. —**spunk′y,** *adj.*

spŭr, *n., v.t.,* **spurred, spurring.** *n.* **1.** sharp device for urging on a horse. **2.** short extension. —*v.t.* **3.** urge on.

spŭr·i·oŭs, *adj.* false; fraudulent. —**spur′i·ous·ly,** *adv.* —**spur′i·ous·ness,** *n.*

spŭrn, *v.t.* reject with scorn.

spŭrt, *v.t., v.i.* **1.** shoot forth, as a liquid. —*v.i.* **2.** have a sudden, short increase of energy or activity. —*n.* **3.** act or instance of spurting.

spŭt′nĭk, *n.* man-made satellite.

spŭt′tĕr, *v.t.* **1.** eject in drops or particles. —*v.i.* **2.** splutter. —*n.* **3.** act, instance, or sound of sputtering.

spū·tŭm *n.* saliva, etc. ejected from the mouth.

spȳ, *n., pl.* **spies,** *v.* **spied, spying.** *n.* **1.** person who attempts to obtain secret information. —*v.t.* **2.** notice, esp. at a distance. —*v.i.* **3.** act as a spy.

squăb, *n.* young pigeon.

squăb′ble, *n., v.i.,* -**bled, -bling.** quarrel over trifles.

squăd, *n.* small group, as of soldiers.

squăd′rŏn, *n.* military unit of airplanes, ships, or cavalry.

squăl′ĭd, *adj.* **1.** dirty or nasty. **2.** in miserable condition. —**squal′id·ly,** *adv.* —**squal′id·ness,** *n.* —**squal′or,** *n.*

squăll, *n.* **1.** strong, brief storm or gust of wind. —*v.i.* **2.** weep loudly. —**squal′ly,** *adj.*

squăn′dêr, *v.t.* spend or use up wastefully.

squâre, *n., adj.,* **squarer, squarest,** *v.t.,* **squared, squaring.** *n.* **1.** right-angled figure with four equal sides. **2.** paved public area. **3.** tool for laying out or checking angled lines. **4.** *Math.* product of a number multiplied by itself. —*adj.* **5.** formed like a square. **6.** of an area equal to linear measure squared. **7.** honest or substantial. —*adv.* **8.** fairly; straightforwardly. —*v.t.* **9.** make square. **10.** *Math.* multiply by itself. —*v.i.* **11.** be consistent. —**square′ly,** *adv.*

squâre′-rĭgged′, *adj.* with sails rigged athwart the vessel. —**square′-rig′ger,** *n.*

squăsh, *v.t.* **1.** crush. —*n.* **2.** game played with rackets. **3.** gourdlike fruit.

squăt, *v.i.,* **squatted** or **squat, squatting,** *n., adj. v.i.* **1.** crouch with the legs doubled under the body. **2.** settle without authority. —*n.* **3.** squatting position. —*adj.* **4.** Also, **squat′ty,** short and broad of figure. —**squat′ter,** *n.*

squăw, *n.* American Indian woman.

squăwk, *n.* **1.** loud, harsh cry. —*v.i.* **2.** utter a squawk.

squēak, *n.* **1.** shrill noise. —*v.i.* **2.** make squeaks. —**squeak′y,** *adj.*

squēal, *n.* **1.** shrill cry. —*v.i.* **2.** make squeals.

squēam′ĭsh, *adj.* **1.** easily disgusted. **2.** prudish. —**squeam′ish·ly,** *adv.* —**squeam′ish·ness,** *n.*

squēe′gēe, *n.* flat-bladed cleaner for plate glass.

squēeze, *v.t.,* **squeezed, squeezing,** *n. v.t.* **1.** press from both sides. **2.** cram. —*n.* **3.** act or instance of squeezing. **4.** hug.

squĕlch, *v.t.* **1.** silence with a crushing remark. —*n.* **2.** crushing remark.

squĭd, *n.* ten-armed sea mollusk.

squĭnt, *v.i.* **1.** see through partly-closed

eyes. **2.** be cross-eyed. —*n.* **3.** act or instance of squinting.

squire, *n.*, *v.t.*, **squired, squiring.** *n.* **1.** country gentleman. **2.** gentleman escorting a lady. —*v.t.* **3.** escort.

squirm, *v.i.*, *n.* wriggle.

squir′rel, *n.* bushy-tailed rodent living in trees.

squirt, *v.t.*, *v.i.* **1.** shoot, as a liquid. —*n.* **2.** jet of liquid. **3.** device for squirting.

stab, *v.t.*, **stabbed, stabbing,** *n.* *v.t.* **1.** wound with a knife, etc. —*n.* **2.** wound or thrust from such a weapon.

sta′bil·ize, *v.t.*, **-lized, -lizing.** cause to be or remain stable. —**sta′bi·liz″er,** *n.* —**sta″bi·li·za′tion,** *n.*

sta′ble, *n.*, *v.t.*, **-bled, -bling,** *adj.* *n.* **1.** Also, **stables,** accommodation for animals, esp. horses. —*v.t.* **2.** put into a stable, as a horse. —*adj.* **3.** resistant to displacement or change. —**sta·bil′i·ty,** *n.*

stac·ca′tō, *adj.* *Music.* separated by brief silences.

stack, *n.* **1.** orderly pile. **2.** Often, **stacks,** storage space for library books. **3.** chimney or funnel. —*v.t.* **4.** gather into stacks.

sta′di·um, *n.*, *pl.* **-diums, -dia.** outdoor arena for spectator sports.

staff, *n.*, *pl.* **staves** or **staffs** (for 1), **staffs** (for 1, 3), *v.t.* *n.* **1.** stick carried in the hand. **2.** group of employees, esp. in administrative jobs. **3.** *Music.* group of five horizontal lines used in musical notation. —*v.t.* **4.** provide or work as a staff for.

stag, *n.* **1.** adult male deer. —*adj.* **2.** for men only.

stage, *n.*, *v.t.*, **staged, staging,** *n.* **1.** distinct phase of a process, journey, etc. **2.** performers' platform. **3.** theatrical profession. —*v.t.* **4.** present on a stage. **5.** divide into phases.

stage′coach″, *n.* horse-drawn coach for long-distance travel.

stag′ger, *v.i.* **1.** walk or stand unsteadily. —*v.t.* **2.** cause to stagger or falter. **3.** schedule over a range of times. —*n.* **4.** staggering gait.

stag′ing, *n.* scaffolding.

stag′nant, *adj.* **1.** not flowing, as a body

of water. **2.** undesirably inactive. —**stag′nate,** *v.i.* —**stag″na′tion,** *n.*

staid, *adj.* sober and quiet; sedate. —**staid′ly,** *adv.* —**staid′ness,** *n.*

stain, *n.* **1.** discoloration. **2.** dye applied to wood or other materials. —*v.t.* **3.** discolor. **4.** apply dye to.

stair, *n.* tall flight of steps. Also, **stairs, stair′way″, —stair′well″,** *n.*

stair′case″, *n.* interior stair.

stake, *n.*, *v.t.*, **staked, staking,** *n.* **1.** upright post. **2.** something wagered. **3. stakes,** something to be gained through risk. **4. at stake,** in danger of loss. —*v.t.* **5.** mark or secure with a stake. **6.** wager.

sta·lac′tite, *n.* icicle-like deposit of lime on a cave roof.

sta·lag′mite, *n.* conical deposit of lime on a cave floor.

stale, *adj.*, **staler, stalest,** *v.i.* *adj.* **1.** no longer fresh. —*v.i.* **2.** become stale. —**stale′ness,** *n.*

stale′mate″, *n.* **1.** *Chess.* situation making a move impossible. **2.** deadlock. —*v.t.* **3.** halt through a stalemate.

stalk, *v.t.* **1.** pursue stealthily. —*v.i.* **2.** walk proudly or deliberately. —*n.* **3.** plant stem.

stall, *n.* **1.** compartment. **2.** stop because of malfunctioning. **3.** *Informal.* pretext for delay. —*v.t.* **4.** put or keep in a stall. **5.** *Informal.* delay or keep waiting. —*v.i.* **6.** stop because of malfunctioning.

stal′lion, *n.* ungelded male horse.

stal′wart, *adj.* **1.** reliable through bravery, vigor, or faithfulness. —*n.* **2.** stalwart person.

stam′i·na, *n.* enduring vigor.

stam′mer, *v.i.* **1.** speak with involuntary repetitions or pauses. —*n.* **2.** stammering way of speaking.

stamp, *v.t.* **1.** step on forcefully. **2.** form or print with a stamp. **3.** affix a stamp to. —*n.* **4.** act or instance of stamping. **5.** descending device for printing, embossing, cutting, etc. **6.** adhesive paper proving payment of postage, etc. **7.** type of personal character.

stam″pede′, *n.*, *v.*, **-peded, -peding.** *n.* **1.** mass flight, as of frightened cattle. —*v.i.* **2.** flee in a stampede. —*v.t.* **3.** cause to stampede.

stănce, *n.* **1.** position of a standing person. **2.** attitude or policy.

stănch, *adj.* **1.** (stonch) stalwart. —*v.t.* **2.** (stanch) stop from escaping, as blood. **3.** stop from bleeding. —**stanch'ly**, *adv.* —**stanch'ness**, *n.*

stăn'chiŏn, *n.* structural post.

stănd, *v.*, **stood, standing**, *n. v.i.* **1.** be or become upright on the feet. **2.** be located, as a tall object. **3.** halt or refrain from moving. **4.** take a position, as in a controversy. **5.** have toleration. —*v.t.* **6.** cause to be upright. **7.** endure or tolerate. —*n.* **8.** small platform or table. **9.** small sales booth. **10.** position, as in a controversy. **11.** halt. **12.** area of trees.

stăn'dărd, *n.* **1.** basis for evaluation or measurement. **2.** upright support. **3.** military or personal flag. —*adj.* **4.** of the normal or typical sort.

stăn'dărd·īze, *v.*, **-ized, -izing**, *v.t.*, *v.i.* conform to a standard. —**stan''dard·i·za'tion**, *n.*

stănd'-bȳ, *n.*, *pl.* **-bys**, *adj. n.* **1.** possible substitute. —*adj.* **2.** for emergency use.

stănd'ĭng, *n.* **1.** status. **2.** duration. —*adj.* **3.** upright. **4.** permanent. **5.** fixed in place. **6.** stagnant.

stănd'point'', *n.* viewpoint.

stăn'za, *n.* set of verses.

stā'ple, *n.*, *v.t.*, **-pled, -pling**, *adj. n.* **1.** fastener of bent wire or bar stock. **2.** main or standard commodity. **3.** textile fiber. —*v.t.* **4.** fasten with staples. —*adj.* **5.** main or standard. —**sta'pler**, *n.*

stăr, *n.*, *adj.*, *v.*, **starred, starring**, *n.* **1.** heavenly body of incandescent gas. **2.** figure with radiating points. **3.** prominent or leading performer or player. —*v.t.* **4.** have in a leading role. **5.** mark with a star. —*v.i.* **6.** have a leading role. —**star'ry**, *adj.*

stăr'board'', *Nautical. n.* **1.** right-hand side, facing forward. —*adj.* **2.** located on this side. —*adv.* **3.** toward this side.

stărch, *n.* **1.** tasteless vegetable substance found in potatoes, flour, etc. and used for stiffening. —*v.t.* **2.** treat with starch. —**starch'y**, *adj.*

stāre, *v.i.*, **stared, staring**, *n. v.i.* **1.** gaze with fixed, open eyes. —*n.* **2.** act or instance of staring.

stăr'fĭsh'', *n.* star-shaped sea animal.

stărk, *adj.* **1.** outright. **2.** bleak. **3.** stiff. —*adv.* **4.** utterly.

stăr'lĭng, *n.* small bird of European origin.

stărt, *v.t.*, *v.i.* **1.** begin. —*v.t.* **2.** knock loose. —*v.i.* **3.** jump with surprise. **4.** move or arise suddenly. —*n.* **5.** beginning. **6.** sudden movement from surprise. **7.** lead in a race or pursuit. —**start'er**, *n.*

stăr'tle, *v.t.*, **-tled, -tling**. disturb with sudden surprise.

stărve, *v.*, **starved, starving**. *v.t.* **1.** kill or trouble with hunger. —*v.i.* **2.** die or be troubled from hunger. —**star''va'tion**, *n.*

stāte, *n.*, *adj.*, *v.t.*, **stated, stating**. *n.* **1.** condition. **2.** politically autonomous or semi-autonomous region. **3.** civil government. **4.** pomp. —*adj.* **5.** formally conducted. —*v.t.* **7.** declare. —**state'hood''**, *n.*

stāte'hoūse'', *n.* U.S. state capitol.

stāte'lȳ, *adj.*, **-lier, -liest**. dignified. —**state'li·ness**, *n.*

stāte'mĕnt, *n.* **1.** declaration. **2.** financial account or bill.

stāte-ŏf-thē-ărt, *adj.* of or pertaining to the highest level of technological achievement to date.

stāte'roōm'', *n.* private cabin on a ship.

stātes'măn, *n.* person wise in government. —**states'man·ship**, *n.*

stăt'ĭc, *adj.* **1.** not moving. —*n.* **2.** unmoving electrical charges. **3.** radio interference caused by such charges.

stā'tiŏn, *n.* **1.** building where a train, bus, etc. stops or originates. **2.** place for sending broadcasts. **3.** place of duty. **4.** place where one stops. **5.** position, as in society. —*v.t.* **5.** assign to a place.

stā'tiŏn·ār''ȳ, *adj.* **1.** not in motion. **2.** not moving to another place.

stā'tiŏn·ĕr, *n.* seller of paper and writing materials. —**sta'tion·er''y**, *n.*

stā·tĭs'tĭcs, *n.* collection and analysis of numerical data. —**sta·tis'ti·cal**, *adj.* —**sta·tis'ti·cal·ly**, *adv.* —**sta''tis·ti'cian**, *n.*

stăt'ū·ār''ȳ, *n.* statues collectively.

stăt'ūe, *n.* three-dimensional sculpture of a human or animal.

stăt′ū·ĕsque′, *adj*. like a statue, esp. in posture.

stăt″ū·ĕtte′, *n*. small statue.

stăt′ūre, *n*. **1**. tallness. **2**. eminence or achievement.

stătŭs quō, *Latin*. present condition.

sta·tus (stā′tas, stă′tas), *n*. **1**. position, as in society. **2**. state or condition.

stăt′ūte, *n*. law; ordinance. **—stat′u·to″ry**, *adj*.

staûnch, *n*., *adj*. stanch.

stāve, *n*., *v.t.*, **staved** or (for 3) **stove, stav·ing**. *n*. **1**. curved board forming part of a barrel side. **2**. *Music*. staff. *—v.t.* **3**. break in or crush. **4**. repel.

stāy, *v.*, **stayed, staying**, *n*. *v.i.* **1**. remain or continue. *—v.t.* **2**. halt or delay. **3**. support or prop. *—n*. **4**. temporary residence. **5**. halt or delay. **6**. support or prop. **7**. fore-and-aft line supporting a mast.

stĕad, *n*. **1. in one's stead**, in place of one. **2. in good stead**, advantageously.

stĕad′fãst″, *adj*. **1**. unchanging. **2**. loyal or determined. **—stead′fast″ly**, *adv.* **—stead′fast″ness**, *n*.

stĕad′ỹ, *adj.*, **steadier, steadiest**, *v.*, **steadied, steadying**. *adj*. **1**. firm; unwavering. **2**. regular; unvarying. **3**. reliable. *—v.t.*, *v.i.* **4**. make or become steady. **—stead′i·ly**, *adv.*

steăk, *n*. slice of meat or fish for broiling or frying.

stēal, *v.*, **stole, stolen, stealing.** *v.t.* **1**. take without right. *—v.i.* **2**. move silently.

stĕalth, *n*. secret activity. **—stealth′y**, *adj*. **—stealth′i·ly**, *adv.*

stēam, *n*. **1**. gaseous or vaporized water. *—v.t.* **2**. treat with steam. *—v.i.* **3**. turn into or give off steam. *—adj*. **4**. working by steam. **5**. carrying steam. **—steam′y**, *adj.* **—steam′boat″**, *n.* **—steam′ship″**, *n.*

stēam′ĕr, *n*. **1**. vehicle operated by steam, esp. a ship or automobile. **2**. device for treating with steam.

stēed, *n*. riding horse.

stēel, *n*. **1**. iron alloyed with carbon. *—adj*. **2**. made of or resembling steel. *—v.t.* **3**. make resolute or courageous. **—steel′y**, *adj.*

stēel′yärd″, *n*. scale with a weighted arm.

stēep, *adj*. **1**. far from horizontal. *—v.t.* **2**. soak. **3**. absorb. **—steep′ly**, *adv.* **—steep′ness**, *n.*

stēe′ple, *n*. **1**. tall tower with a spire. **2**. spire.

stēe′ple·chāse″, *n*. horse race over obstacles.

stēer, *v.t.* **1**. direct or guide. *—n*. **2**. castrated bull.

stēer′ăge, *n*. cheap, cabinless passenger accommodations on a ship.

steïn, *n*. beer mug, esp. one of earthenware.

stĕl′lár, *adj*. pertaining to or suggesting stars.

stĕm, *n.*, *v.*, **stemmed, stemming**. *n*. **1**. support of a plant, leaf, or fruit. **2**. single support, as of a glass. **3**. uninflected part of a word. **4**. extreme forepart of a ship's bow. *—v.t.* **5**. take the stem from. **6**. check, as liquid. **7**. make headway against. *—v.i.* **8**. be derived or originate.

stĕnch, *n*. stink.

stĕn′cĭl, *n.*, *v.t.*, **-ciled, -ciling**. *n*. **1**. pierced sheet allowing paint or ink to mark an underlying surface. *—v.t.* **2**. paint or ink with a stencil.

ste·nŏg′ra·phÿ, *n*. shorthand writing. **—sten′o·graph′ic**, *adj*. **—ste·nog′ra·pher**, *n.*

stĕn·tô′ri·ăn, *adj*. very loud of voice.

stĕp, *n.*, *v.i.* **stepped, stepping**. *n*. **1**. movement of the walking foot. **2**. gait. **3**. raised surface on which one walks upwards. **4**. stage of a process. *—v.i.* **5**. walk. **6**. press down with the foot.

stĕp-, by the remarriage of a parent: a prefix.

stĕp′lăd″dĕr, *n*. ladder with steps.

stĕppe, *n*. plain, esp. in southeast Europe or Asia.

stĕr′ē·ō, *n*. device for playing recorded or broadcast music in stereophonic sound.

stĕr″′ē·ó·phŏn′ic, *adj*. pertaining to realistic sound reproduction through two or more loudspeakers.

stĕr′ē·ó·scōpe″, *n*. viewer using twin pictures and two eyepieces for a realistic effect.

stĕr′ē·ó·tÿpe″, *n.*, *v.t.*, **-typed, -typing**. *n*. **1**. process for casting printing plates. **2**. unimaginative or oversimplified conception. *—v.t.* **3**. reproduce by the stereotype process. **4.** conceive as a stereotype.

stĕr′īle, *adj.* **1.** free of microbes. **2.** barren. **3.** uncreative or unimaginative. —**ster·il′i·ty**, *n.*

stĕr′ĭ·līze′′, *v.t.*, **-lized, -lizing.** make sterile. —**ster′i·liz′′er**, *n.* —**ster′′i·li·za′tion**, *n.*

stĕr′lĭng, *adj.* **1.** composed of 92.5° silver. **2.** in British money. **3.** fine; noble.

stĕrn, *adj.* **1.** grimly strict. —*n.* **2.** after end of a ship. —**stern′ly**, *adv.* —**stern′ness**, *n.*

stĕr′nŭm, *n.* breastbone.

stĕth′o·scōpe′′, *n.* instrument for listening to body sounds.

stē′vė·dōre′′, *n.* handler of ship's cargoes.

stĕw, *n.* **1.** dish of simmered food. —*v.t.* **2.** simmer to cook.

stĕw′ărd, *n.* **1.** business manager, esp. on an estate. **2.** person in charge of food, supplies, and services. **3.** attendant. Also, *fem.*, **stew′ard·ess.**

stĭck, *v.*, **stuck, sticking**, *n.* *v.t.* **1.** pierce. **2.** thrust. **3.** cause to adhere. —*v.i.* **4.** fail to work properly. **5.** adhere. **6.** project. **7.** remain. —*n.* **8.** length of wood. **9.** short length. **10.** lever. **11.** walking cane.

stĭck′ĕr, *n.* **1.** person or thing that sticks. **2.** adhesive label.

stĭck′lĕr, *n.* person who insists on something.

stĭck′ў, *adj.*, **stickier, stickiest. 1.** adhesive. **2.** *Informal.* **a.** muggy. **b.** troublesome or difficult.

stiff, *adj.* **1.** unbending. **2.** not moving easily. **3.** formal or distant in manner. —**stiff′ly**, *adv.* —**stiff′ness**, *n.* —**stif′fen**, *v.t.*, *v.i.*

stĭ′fle, *v.*, **-fled, -fling.** *v.t.* **1.** smother. **2.** suppress. —*v.i.* **3.** suffer from lack of air.

stĭg′mȧ, *n.*, *pl.* **-mata, -mas.** mark or indication of disrepute. —**stig′ma·tize′′**, *v.t.*

stile, *n.* **1.** steps over a fence. **2.** upright framing member.

stĭ·lĕt′tō, *n.* Italian dagger.

stĭll, *adj.* **1.** motionless or silent. **2.** tranquil. **3.** not sparkling, as wine. —*adv.* **4.** up to an indicated time. **5.** even more or

even less. —*adv.*, *conj.* **6.** nevertheless. —*v.t.*, *v.i.* **7.** make or become still. —*n.* **8.** distillation apparatus. —**still′ness**, *n.*

stĭll′bôrn′′, *adj.* **1.** born dead. **2.** abortive.

stĭlt, *n.* pole serving as an extension of the legs.

stĭlt′ĕd, *adj.* affectedly dignified.

stĭm′ū·lāte, *v.t.*, **-lated, -lating. 1.** cause to be active or more active. **2.** inspire. —**stim′′u·la′tion**, *n.* —**stim′u·la·tive**, *adj.* —**stim′u·lant**, *n.*

stĭm′ū·lŭs, *n.*, *pl.* **-li.** something stimulating.

stĭng, *v.t.*, **stung, stinging.** *n.* *v.t.* **1.** inflict a small, painful wound or blow. **2.** annoy or goad severely. —*n.* **3.** wound from stinging. **4.** sharp part for stinging. **5.** undercover operation run by a law enforcement agency to catch suspected criminals.

stĭn′gỹ, *adj.* characteristic of or suggesting miserliness. —**stin′gi·ly**, *adv.* —**stin′gi·ness**, *n.*

stĭnk, *v.i.* **stănk** or **stŭnk, stunk, stinking,** *n.* *v.i.* **1.** have a bad smell. —*n.* **2.** bad smell.

stĭnt, *v.t.* **1.** limit. **2.** limit oneself. —*n.* **3.** limitation. **4.** task or work period.

stī′pĕnd, *n.* regular payment.

stĭp′ple, *v.t.*, **-pled, -pling,** *n.* *v.t.* **1.** paint in small dots. —*n.* **2.** texture of small dots.

stĭp′ū·lāte, *v.t.*, **-lated, -lating.** require as a condition. —**stip′′u·la′tion**, *n.*

stîr, *v.t.* **stirred, stirring,** *n.* *v.t.* **1.** mix by moving. **2.** move. **3.** rouse. —*n.* **4.** public excitement or commotion.

stîr′rĭng, *adj.* **1.** exciting. **2.** active.

stĭr′rŭp, *n.* foothold hanging from a saddle.

stĭtch, *n.* **1.** single repeated operation in sewing, knitting, etc. **2.** sharp pain. —*v.t.* **3.** sew.

stŏck, *n.* **1.** goods, materials, etc. on hand. **2.** cattle. **3.** any of various parts of guns, implements, etc. **4.** ancestry. **5.** soup or stew base. **6.** dividend-bearing shares. —*adj.* **7.** standard; uniform. —*v.t.* **8.** keep for sale or use. **9.** supply with stock. **10.** supply with live fish, as a pond. —**stock′brok′′er**, *n.* —**stock′**

hold''er, n. —stock'pile'', n. —stock' yard'', n.

stŏck·āde', n., v.t., -aded, -ading. n. 1. barrier of upright stakes. —v.t. 2. put a stockade around.

stŏck'ing, n. clothing for the foot and lower parts of the leg.

stŏck'ў, adj. broad and short of figure.

stŏdg'ў, adj., stodgier, stodgiest. heavy and boring. —stodg'i·ly, adv. —stodg' i·ness, n.

stō'ĭc, n. 1. person who maintains indifference to pain or sorrow. —adj. 2. Also, sto'i·cal, characteristic of a stoic. —sto'i·cal·ly, adv. —sto'i·cism, n.

stōke, v.t., stoked, stoking. keep burning by adding fuel. —stok'er, n.

stōle, n. scarflike garment worn behind the neck and over the shoulders.

stŏl'ĭd, adj. showing no liveliness. —stol' id·ly, adv. —sto·lid'i·ty, n.

stŏm'ach, n. 1. organ of digestion. 2. tolerance. —v.t. 3. take into the stomach. 4. tolerate. —sto·mach'ic, adj. —stom'ach·ache'', n.

stōne, n., pl. stones, adj., v.t., stoned, stoning. n. 1. hard mineral substance. 2. small piece of this. 3. gem. 4. pit of a fruit. 5. hard object formed in a digestive organ. —adj. 6. made of stone. —v.t. 7. attack with stones. 8. pit, as a fruit. —ston'y, adj.

stōōge, n. Informal. 1. comedian's assistant. 2. underling or henchman.

stōōl, n. armless, backless seat.

stōōp, v.i. 1. bend forward. 2. demean oneself. —n. 3. bent posture. 4. small porch.

stŏp, v., stopped, stopping. n. v.t. 1. prevent from starting or going on. 2. clog or plug. —v.i. 3. act or move no further or not at all. 4. stay briefly. —n. 5. act, instance, or place of stopping. 6. device for controlling tone in a musical instrument. —stop'page, n.

stŏp'găp', n., adj. makeshift.

stŏp'ŏv·êr, n. brief pause during a journey.

stŏp'pêr, n. 1. plug, as for a bottle. —v.t. 2. close with a stopper. Also, stop'ple.

stŏp'wătch'', n. watch for measuring elapsed time.

stôr'āge, n. 1. act or instance of storing. 2. condition of being stored.

stôre, n., v.t., stored, storing. n. 1. place for the sale of goods. 2. place of storage. 3. stores, supplies. 4. in store, waiting in the future. —v.t. 5. accumulate and save. 6. put away for future use. —store' front, n. —store'house'', n. —store' keep''er, n. —store'room'', n.

stôrk, n. long-billed, long-legged wading bird.

stôrm, n. 1. high wind, often with rain, snow, etc. 2. sudden attack. —v.t. 3. attack suddenly and violently. —v.i. 4. blow as a storm. 5. rage. —storm'ў, adj. —storm'i·ly, adv.

stôr'ў, n., pl. -ries. 1. account of events, often fictitious. 2. newspaper report. 3. Informal. lie. 4. level in a building.

stoup (stōōp), n. basin for holy water.

stōut, adj. 1. sturdy. 2. courageous; resolute. 3. heavy-set. —n. 4. dark, sweet, beerlike drink. —stout'ly, adv. —stout' ness, n.

stōve, n. device for heating or cooking.

stōw, v.t. 1. put in storage, as on a ship. —v.i. 2. stow away, hide on a ship for a free passage. —stow'age, n. —stow'a· way'', n.

străd'dle, v.t., -dled, -dling, n. v.t. 1. stand over or mount with a leg on each side. —n. 2. straddling posture.

strāfe, v.t., strafed, strafing. fire down upon from an aircraft.

străg'gle, v.i., -gled, -gling. stray or fall behind. —strag'gler, n.

strāight, adj. 1. from point to point in the shortest way; direct. 2. unmodified or undiluted. 3. in good order or condition. 4. honest or unevasive. —adv. 5. directly. 6. without modification. 7. honestly; without evasion. 8. so as to be clearly understood. —straight'ness, n. —straight'en, v.t., v.i.

strāight'a·wāy, n. 1. straight part of racetrack, etc. —adv. 2. Also, straight' way'', at once.

strāight''fôr'wârd, adj. unevasive; honest.

strāin, v.t. 1. tax the strength of. 2. injure or distort through force. 3. run through a filter or sieve. —n. 4. major effort or burden. 5. injury from straining. 6. trying experience. **7.** melody. **8.** chain of ancestors or descendants. **9.** heredity. —**strain′er**, *n.*

strait, *n.* **1.** narrow natural waterway. **2. straits**, difficulties.

strait′en, *v.t.* make narrow or meager.

strand, *n.* **1.** length of fiber for twisting into rope. **2.** length of hair. **3.** river or ocean shore. —*v.t.* **4.** run aground. **5.** put in a helpless position.

strange, *adj., stranger, strangest.* **1.** strikingly unfamiliar; odd. **2.** not known to one. —**strange′ly**, *adv.* —**strange′ness**, *n.*

stran′ger, *n.* unfamiliar person.

stran′gle, *v., -gled, -gling.* *v.t.* **1.** kill by choking. —*v.i.* **2.** choke. —**stran′gler**, *n.* —**stran′′gu·la′tion**, *n.*

strap, *n., v.t., strapped, strapping.* *n.* **1.** band for fastening. —*v.t.* **2.** fasten with a strap.

stra·ta·gem (stra′tə jəm), *n.* plot; trick.

stra·te̅g′ic, *adj.* **1.** pertaining to strategy. **2.** important in a strategy.

strat′e·gy̆, *n., pl. -gies.* **1.** art of planning military operations. **2.** stratagem or series of stratagems. —**strat′e·gist**, *n.*

strat′i·fy̆, *v., -fied, -fying.* *v.t., v.i.* form in layers. —**strat′′i·fi·ca′tion**, *n.*

strat′o·sphēre′′, *n.* atmospheric zone 6 to 15 miles above the earth. —**strat′′o·spher′ic**, *adj.*

stra′tŭm, *n., pl. -ta, -tums.* layers, as of rock.

straw̆, *n.* **1.** stalk of threshed grain. **2.** quantity of such stalks. **3.** tube for sucking liquids.

straw̆′ber′′ry̆, *n., pl. -ries.* red fruit of a vinelike plant.

stray̆, *v.i.* **1.** wander aimlessly. **2.** wander away. —*adj.* **3.** passing or occurring by chance. —*n.* **4.** animal that strays.

streak, *n.* **1.** long mark. **2.** trait of character. **3.** brief period, as of luck. —*v.t.* **4.** mark with streaks. —*v.i.* **5.** move swiftly. **6.** run naked through a public place. —**streak′ing**, *n.*

stream, *n.* **1.** body of running water. **2.** steady flow. —*v.i.* **3.** flow quickly and steadily. **4.** run with moisture.

stream′er, *n.* long, narrow flag or piece of bunting.

stream′line′′, *v.t.* **1.** make with a form minimizing air or water resistance. **2.** purge of unnecessary elements.

street, *n.* road in an urban area.

street′car′′, *n.* rail car for transportation along streets.

strength, *n.* **1.** power of the muscles. **2.** resistance to force. **3.** ability of the mind. **4.** purity.

strength′en, *v.t., v.i.* make or become stronger.

stren′u·ous, *adj.* **1.** involving great effort. **2.** vigorous.

stress, *n.* **1.** emphasis. **2.** difficulties. **3.** force causing a strain. —*v.t.* **4.** put a stress on.

stretch, *v.t., v.i.* **1.** extend or spread. **2.** strain, as a muscle. **3.** pull taut. —*n.* **4.** act or instance of stretching. **5.** unbroken extent.

stretch′er, *n.* **1.** device for carrying a sick person lying down. **2.** device for stretching.

strew̆, *v.t., strewed, strewed or strewn, strewing.* scatter.

stri′āt·ed, *adj.* with closely-spaced grooves or furrows. —**stri·a′tion**, *n.*

strict, *adj.* **1.** demanding exact conformity. **2.** conforming exactly. —**strict′ly**, *adv.* —**strict′ness**, *n.*

stric′tûre, *n.* adverse criticism.

stride, *v.i., strode, stridden, striding, n.* *v.i.* **1.** walk with long steps. —*n.* **2.** long step. **3.** distance covered by such a step.

stri′dent, *adj.* loud and harsh.

strife, *n.* conflict.

strike, *v., struck, struck or stricken, striking, n.* *v.t.* **1.** hit. **2.** make an impression on. **3.** afflict. **4.** discover, as a mineral. **5.** ignite, as a match. —*v.i.* **6.** stop work to enforce demands. —*n.* **7.** act or instance of striking. **8.** *Baseball.* failure to bat. **9.** *Bowling.* perfect score with the first bowl. —**strik′er**, *n.*

strik′ing, *adj.* remarkable.

string, *n., v.t., strung, stringing.* *n.* **1.** thin cord. **2.** cord on a musical instrument. **3. strings**, musical instruments using such cords. **4.** series or row. —*v.t.* **5.** furnish with strings. **6.** hang from a cord. **7.** set in a series or row. —**stringed**, *adj.* —**string′y̆**, *adj.*

string bean, bean with edible pods.

strĭn′gĕnt, *adj.* very strict. **-strin′gent·ly**, *adv.* **—strin′gen·cy**, *n.*

strĭp, *n., v.t.,* **stripped, stripping.** *n.* **1.** long narrow piece. *—v.t.* **2.** remove the clothing or covering from. **3.** remove from an underlying surface. **4.** steal or confiscate the possessions of.

strĭpe, *n.* **1.** long, broad mark. **2.** sort or kind. *—v.t.* **3.** mark with stripes.

strĭp′lĭng, *n.* boy.

strĭve, *v.i.,* **strove, striven, striving.** try hard; strain.

strōke, *v.t.,* **stroked, stroking.** *n. v.t.* **1.** rub or graze gently. *—n.* **2.** act or instance of stroking. **3.** blow. **4.** single movement that is repeated. **5.** sudden attack of illness, esp. apoplexy. **6.** sudden occasion, as of luck. **7.** line made by a pen or pencil. **8.** way of swimming.

strōll, *v.i.* **1.** walk idly. **2.** wander. **—strol′ler**, *n.*

strŏng, *adj.* having strength. **—strong′ly**, *adv.*

strŏng′hōld′′, *n.* place secure against attack.

strŏp, *n., v.t.,* **stropped, stropping.** *n.* **1.** leather strap for sharpening. *—v.t.* **2.** sharpen with a strop.

strŭc′tūre, *n.* **1.** part of a building giving strength. **2.** something built. **3.** basic form, as of a composition. **—struc′tur·al**, *adj.* **—struc′tur·al·ly**, *adv.*

strŭg′gle, *v.i.,* **-gled, -gling.** *n. v.i.* **1.** strive. **2.** fight. *—n.* **3.** strenuous effort. **4.** fight.

strŭm, *v.t.* **strummed, strumming.** play lightly or carelessly, as a piano or plucked string instrument.

strŭt, *v.i.,* **strutted, strutting.** *n. v.i.* **1.** walk affectedly. *—n.* **2.** act or instance of struggling. **3.** postlike brace.

strych·nine (strĭk′nĭn), *n.* poisonous alkaloid.

stŭb, *n., v.t.,* **stubbed, stubbing.** *n.* **1.** short remnant. **2.** stump. *—v.t.* **3.** ram against something, esp. a toe.

stŭb′ble, *n.* **1.** plant stalks mown short. **2.** short growth of beard.

stŭb′bŏrn, *adj.* refusing to obey, give up, etc. **—stub′born·ly**, *adv.* **—stub′born·ness**, *n.*

stŭc′cō, *n., pl.* **-coes, cos,** *v.t.,* **-coed, -coing.** *n.* **1.** coarse exterior plaster. **2.**

fine interior plaster. *—v.t.* **3.** cover with stucco.

stŭd, *n., v.t.,* **studded, studding.** *n.* **1.** projecting feature. **2.** upright wall-framing member. **3.** buttonlike fastener. **4.** collection of horses. **5.** male animal, esp. a horse, for breeding. *—v.t.* **6.** furnish or sprinkle with or as if with studs.

stŭ′dĕnt, *n.* person who studies.

stŭd′iĕd, *adj.* intentional.

stŭ′dĭ·ō, *n.* **1.** artist's workplace. **2.** room for television or radio performers. **3.** place for television or radio performers. **4.** place for making motion pictures.

stŭ′dĭ·oŭs, *adj.* studying diligently. **—stu′di·ous·ly**, *adv.*

stŭd′ÿ, *n., pl.* **studies,** *v.t.,* **studied, studying.** *n.* **1.** methodical acquisition of skill or knowledge. **2.** subject of such activity. **3.** room for reading or writing. **4.** deep thought. *—v.t.* **5.** make a subject of study.

stŭff, *n.* **1.** material. **2.** assorted or worthless objects or materials. *—v.t.* **3.** fill under pressure.

stŭff′ĭng, *n.* material stuffed into a hollow object.

stŭff′ÿ, *adj.,* **stuffier, stuffiest.** **1.** dull and formal. **2.** lacking fresh air.

stŭl′tĭ·fÿ, *v.t.,* **-fied, -fying.** cause to seem foolish.

stŭm′ble, *v.i.,* **-bled, -bling.** trip and begin to fall.

stŭmp, *n.* **1.** remnant of something cut off. *—v.t.* **2.** baffle. *—v.i.* **3.** walk ponderously. **4.** travel on a political campaign.

stŭn, *v.t.,* **stunned, stunning.** **1.** halt with amazement. **2.** knock unconscious.

stŭnt, *n.* **1.** act displaying skill. *—v.t.* **2.** hinder in growing.

stŭ′pe·fÿ, *v.t.,* **-fied, -fying.** **1.** put in a stupor. **2.** amaze. **—stu′′pe·fac′tion**, *n.*

stŭ·pĕn′doŭs, *adj.* astounding.

stŭ′pĭd, *adj.* **1.** low in intelligence. **2.** pointless. **—stu′pid·ly**, *adv.* **—stu·pid′i·ty**, *n.*

stŭ′pŏr, *n.* unconscious or semi-conscious state.

stŭr′dÿ, *adj.* **1.** strong. **2.** vigorous. **—stur′di·ly**, *adv.* **—stur′di·ness**, *n.*

stŭr′geŏn, *n.* large fish whose roe is caviar.

stut'têr, v.i., n. stammer.

stÿ, n., pl. sties. 1. pig shelter. 2. swollen inflammation of the eyelid.

stÿle, n., v.t., styled, styling. n. 1. manner of artistic composition, writing, living, etc. 2. kind or variety. 3. elegance. 4. formal name. —v.t. 5. apply a style to. —stÿ·lis'tic, adj.

stÿl'ish, adj. in style; elegant.

stÿl'ist, n. artist as a possessor of a style.

stÿ'lŭs, n. 1. pointed writing instrument. 2. phonograph needle.

stÿ'miē, v.t., -mied, -mying. hinder.

stÿp'tic, adj. stopping the flow of blood.

suàve (swahv), adj. smoothly polite. —suave'ly, adv. —suav'i·ty, suave'ness, n.

sub'cŏm·mit''tēe, n. committee reporting to a committee.

sub·cŏn'scioŭs, n. 1. part of the mind beyond consciousness. —adj. 2. pertaining to this part of the mind. —subcon'scious·ly, adv.

sub·cŏn'tĭ·nĕnt, n. large land mass within a continent.

sub·dĭ·vīde'', v.t., -vided, -viding. divide still further. —sub'di·vi''sion, n.

sub·dūe', v.t., -dued, -duing. 1. overcome. 2. lower in intensity.

sub'jĕct, n. 1. thing thought, written, etc. about. 2. person or thing acted upon. 3. person ruled by a government. 4. Grammar. person or thing about which a sentence tells. —adj. 5. being a subject. 6. exposed to a specified treatment. —v.t. 7. sub·jĕct', submit to a specified treatment. —sub·jec'tion, n.

sub·jĕc'tīve, adj. existing or originating in one person's mind. —sub·jec'tive·ly, adv. —sub''jec·tiv'i·ty, n.

sub'jŏin', v.t. added at the end.

sub'jŭ·gāte'', v.t., -gated, -gating. conquer. —sub''ju·ga'tion, n.

sub·jŭnc'tīve, Grammar. adj. 1. pertaining to a verbal mode of possibility, etc. —n. 2. subjunctive mode.

sub·lēase', n., v.t., -leased, -leasing. n. 1. lease from a tenant. —v.t. 2. rent with such a lease.

sub'lĕt', v.t., -letted, -letting. sublease.

sub·li·māte'', v.t., -mated, -mating. n. v.t. 1. divert into a more acceptable form. 2. sublime. —n. (sub'lə mət) 3. product of subliming. —sub''li·ma'tion, n.

sub·līme', adj., n., v.t., -limed, -liming. adj. 1. noble and exalted. —n. 2. realm of sublime things. —v.t. 3. vaporize, then solidify. —sub·lime'ly, adv. —sub·lim'i·ty, n.

sub'ma·rīne'', n. 1. underwater vessel. —adj. 2. undersea. 3. pertaining to submarines.

sub·mêrge', v., -merged, -merging. v.t., v.i. sink into a liquid. —sub·mer'gence, n.

sub·mêrse', v.t., -mersed, -mersing. submerge. —sub·mer'sion, n. —sub·mers'i·ble, adj.

sub·mĭt', v., -mitted, -mitting. v.t. 1. offer, as in surrender. 2. offer for consideration. 3. subject to a specified treatment. —v.i. 4. surrender or yield oneself. —sub·mis'sion, n. —sub·mis'sive, adj.

sub·ôr'dĭ·nāte'', v.t. -ated, -ating, adj., n., v.t. 1. subject to the will of another. —adj. (sub ôr'də nət) 2. lower in rank or importance. —n. 3. someone or something subordinate. —sub·or''di·na'tion, n.

sub·ôrn', v.t. induce to commit a wrong.

sub·poe·na (sə pē'nə), n., v.t., -naed, -naeing. n. 1. summons to court. —v.t. 2. serve with such a summons.

sub·scrībe', v., -scribed, -scribing. v.i. 1. pay for continued supply of a periodical, service, etc. 2. promise to contribute money. 3. agree. —v.t. 4. sign. —sub·scrib'er, n. —sub·scrip'tion, n.

sub'sē·quĕnt, adj. occurring after. —sub'se·quent·ly, adv.

sub·sêr'vĭ·ĕnt, adj. 1. servile. 2. subordinate. —sub·ser'vi·ence, n. —sub·ser'vi·ent·ly, adv.

sub·sīde', v.i., -sided, -siding. 1. settle or sink. 2. die down. —sub·sid'ence, n.

sub·sĭd'ĭ·ār''ÿ, adj., n., pl. -ries. adj. 1. subordinate or auxiliary. —n. 2. subsidiary entity.

sub'sĭ·dÿ, n., pl. -dies. monetary aid, esp. from a government. —sub'si·dize'', v.t.

sub·sĭst', v.i. 1. exist. 2. maintain one's existence. —sub·sist'ence, n.

sŭb'stánce, *n.* **1.** material. **2.** essential part or aspect. **3.** basic meaning.

sŭb·stăn'tial, *adj.* **1.** solid. **2.** considerable in amount. **3.** material. **4.** essential. **5.** important in the community. **—sub·stan'tial·ly,** *adv.*

sŭb·stăn'tĭ·ăte, *v.t.,* **-ated, -ating.** show to be true. **—sub·stan''ti·a'tion,** *n.*

sŭb'stan·tǐve, *n.* **1.** noun or word used as a noun. **—adj. 2.** having substance.

sŭb'stǐ·tūte, *v.,* **-tuted, -tuting.** *n. v.t., v.i.* **1.** put or act in another's place. **—n. 2.** person or thing that substitutes. **—sub''sti·tu'tion,** *n.*

sŭb'tẽr·fūge'', *n.* evasive trick or trickery.

sŭb''tẽr·rā'nē·án, *adj.* underground.

sŭb'tle, *adj.* **1.** highly sensitive. **2.** scarcely perceived. **3.** cunning. **—sub'tly,** *adv.* **—sub'tle·ty,** *n.*

sŭb·trăct', *v.t.* remove, as one quantity from another. **—sub·trac'tion,** *n.*

sŭb·trŏp'ǐ·cál, *adj.* close to the tropics.

sŭb'ûrb, *n.* community adjoining or dependent on a city. **—sub·ur'ban,** *adj.*

sŭb·vêrt', *v.t.* undermine or corrupt. **—sub·ver'sion,** *n.* **—sub·ver'sive,** *adj., n.*

sŭb'wāy'', *n.* **1.** underground railroad. **2.** pedestrian underpass.

sŭc·cēed', *v.i.* **1.** obtain good results. **2.** attain success. **—v.t. 3.** follow in an office, inheritance, etc.

sŭc·cĕss', *n.* **1.** favorable outcome of an attempt. **2.** commonly sought goals. **3.** person or thing that attains success. **—suc·cess'ful,** *adj.*

sŭc·cĕs'sion, *n.* **1.** sequential order of things. **2.** act of succeeding another. **—suc·ces'sive,** *adj.* **—suc·ces'sive·ly,** *adv.* **—suc·ces'sor,** *n.*

suc·cinct (suk sinkt'), *adj.* restricted to essential information. **—suc·cinct'ly,** *adv.* **—suc·cinct'ness,** *n.*

sŭc'côr, *n., v.t.* help in need.

sŭc'cô·tăsh, *n.* corn and lima beans cooked together.

sŭc'cū·lént, *adj.* juicy. **—suc'cu·lence,** *n.*

sŭc·cŭmb', *v.i.* **1.** yield. **2.** die.

sŭch, *adj.* **1.** of the kind mentioned. **2.** so much of. **—adv. 3.** so greatly. **—pron. 4.** the kind mentioned. **5.** such a person or thing.

sŭck, *v.t.* **1.** draw by suction. **2.** absorb by capillarity. **3.** lick and absorb.

sŭck'êr, *n.* **1.** person or thing that sucks. **2.** fresh-water fish. **3.** lollipop. **4.** *Informal.* person easily cheated.

sŭck'le, *v.t.,* **-led, -ling.** feed at the breast.

sŭck'lĭng, *n.* unweaned child or animal.

sŭc'tion, *n.* forcing of a fluid into a vacuum by atmospheric pressure.

sŭd'dén, *adj.* quick and unexpected. **—sud'den·ly,** *adv.* **—sud'den·ness,** *n.*

sŭds, *n. pl.* **1.** fine soap bubbles. **2.** soapy water.

sūe, *v.,* **sued, suing.** *v.t.,* **1.** claim damages from court. **—v.i. 2.** make an appeal.

suede (swād), *n.* soft leather with a nap.

sū'ĕt, *n.* hard animal fat.

sŭf'fêr, *v.t.* **1.** undergo. **2.** permit or tolerate. **—suf'fer·er,** *n.*

sŭf'fêr·ánce, *n.* **1.** tacit permission. **2.** endurance.

sŭf·fǐce', *v.i.,* **-ficing.** be enough.

sŭf·fǐ'cĭént, *adj.* enough. **-suf·fi'cient·ly,** *adv.* **—suf·fi'cien·cy,** *n.*

sŭf'fǐx, *n.* *Grammar.* ending added to a word to give a new meaning.

sŭf'fô·cāte, *v.,* **-cated, -cating.** *v.t., v.i.* cut off or be without air for breathing. **—suf''fo·ca'tion,** *n.*

sŭf'frágé, *n.* right to vote.

sŭf·fūse', *v.t.* spread light, color, etc. over.

sŭg'ár, *n.* **1.** sweet carbohydrate. **—v.t. 2.** add sugar to. **—sug'ar·y,** *adj.*

sŭg·gĕst', *v.t.* **1.** offer as advice. **2.** propose. **3.** imply. **—sug·ges'tion,** *n.*

sŭg·gĕs'tive, *adj.* full of implication, esp. of impropriety.

sū'ĭ·cǐde'', *n.* **1.** willful killing of oneself. **2.** person who kills himself willfully. **—su''i·cid'al,** *adj.*

sūit, *n.* **1.** complete set of clothes. **2.** lawsuit. **3.** appeal. **4.** playing cards with a common symbol. **—v.t. 5.** satisfy; please. **6.** adapt. **7.** clothe.

sūit'á·ble, *adj.* right; appropriate. **—suit'a·bly,** *adv.*

sūit'cāse'', *n.* travel case for clothes, etc.

suite (swēt), *n.* **1.** apartment of connected rooms. **2.** set of musical compositions.

sūit'ör, *n.* wooer.

sŭl′fāte, *n.* salt of sulfuric acid.

sŭl·fūr′ĭc, *adj.* pertaining to or containing sulfur. Also, **sul′fur·ous**.

sŭlk, *v.i.* 1. be angry and aloof. —*n.* 2. fit of sulking. —**sulk′y**, *adj.*

sŭl′lĕn, *adj.* 1. quietly resentful. 2. gloomy. —**sul′len·ly**, *adv.* —**sul′len·ness**, *n.*

sŭl′lў̆, *v.t.*, **-lied, -lying.** 1. disgrace. 2. soil or pollute.

sŭl′phŭr, *n.* sulfur.

sŭl′tán, *n.* Muslim ruler.

sŭl′trў̆, *adj.*, **-trier, -triest.** 1. hot and humid. 2. sexually inviting. —**sul′tri·ness**, *n.*

sŭm, *n.*, *v.t.*, **summed, summing.** *n.* 1. number obtained by addition. 2. **in sum**, as a summary. —*v.t.* 3. add up. 4. summarize.

sū′măc, *n.* small tree. Also, **su′mach**.

sŭm′má·rīze, *v.t.*, **-rized, -rizing.** present in a summary.

sŭm′má·rў̆, *n.*, *pl.* **-ries,** *adj.* *n.* 1. presentation of essential information only. —*adj.* 2. without formalities or preliminaries. —**sum′ma·ri·ly**, *adv.*

sŭm·mā′tion, *n.* concluding summary.

sŭm′mêr, *n.* 1. season between spring and autumn, beginning at the summer solstice. —*v.i.* 2. spend the summer. —**sum′mer·y**, *adj.*

sŭm′mĭt, *n.* highest point.

sŭm′mŏn, *v.t.* order or ask to come.

sŭm′mŏns, *n.* 1. order to appear in court. 2. order or request to come.

sŭmp, *n.* pit for collecting ground water.

sŭmp′tū·oŭs, *adj.* costly and luxurious. —**sump′tu·ous·ly**, *adv.* —**sump′tu·ous·ness**, *n.*

sŭn, *n.*, *v.t.*, **sunned, sunning.** *n.* 1. star of the solar system. 2. rays from this star. —*v.t.* 3. expose to the sun. —**sun′ny**, *adj.* —**sun′beam′′**, *n.* —**sun′light′′**, *n.* —**sun′lit′′**, *adj.*

sŭn′bāthe′′, *v.i.*, **-bathed, -bathing.** lie down to receive solar rays. —**sun′bath**, *n.*

sŭn′bûrn′′, *n.*, *v.t.*, **-burned, -burning.** burn from or with the rays of the sun.

sŭn′dāe, *n.* ice cream topped with flavored syrup.

Sŭn′dāy, *n.* first day of the week.

sŭn′dī′′ȧl, *n.* instrument telling time by the shadow of a pointer.

sŭn′dŏwn′′, *n.* time of sunset.

sŭn′dry (sun′drē), *adj.* various.

sŭn′flŏw′′êr, *n.* tall plant with large, yellow-petaled blossoms.

sŭn′glăss′′ĕs, *n.*, *pl.* spectacles tinted to weaken the sun's rays.

sŭn′lămp′′, *n.* ultraviolet lamp.

sŭn′rīse′′, *n.* rise of the sun above the horizon.

sŭn′sĕt′′, *n.* descent of the sun below the horizon.

sŭn′shīne, *n.* rays of the sun.

sŭn′strōke′′, *n.* collapse from overexposure to the sun.

sŭn′tăn′′, *n.* darkening of the skin resulting from sunbathing.

sŭp, *v.i.*, **supped, supping.** have supper.

su·pêrb′, *adj.* admirably excellent. —**su·perb′ly**, *adv.*

su·per·cil·i·ous (soō′′pȯr sil′ē ȧs), *adj.* proudly contemptuous. —**su′′per·cil′i·ous·ly**, *adv.* —**su′′per·cil′i·ous·ness**, *n.*

sū′′pêr·fī′ciȧl, *adj.* 1. on the surface only. 2. lacking depth of thought or feeling. —**su′′per·fi′cial·ly**, *adv.* —**su′′per·fi·ci·al′i·ty**, *n.*

su·pêr′flu·oŭs, *adj.* 1. more than is useful. 2. redundant; useless. —**su·per′flu·ous·ly**, *adv.* —**su′′per·flu′i·ty**, *n.*

sū′′pêr·hū′mȧn, *adj.* beyond ordinary human limitations.

sū′′pêr·ĭm·pōse′, *v.t.*, **-posed, -posing.** place over something else.

sŭ′′pêr·ĭn·tĕnd′′, *v.t.* supervise. —**su′′per·in·ten′dence**, *n.* —**su′′per·in·ten′dent**, *n.*, *adj.* —**su′′per·in·ten′den·cy**, *n.*

sū·pē′rĭ·ŏr, *adj.* 1. better. 2. excellent. 3. proud; haughty. 4. higher in position. —*n.* 5. superior person. 6. head of a religious community. —**su·pe′ri·or′i·ty**, *n.*

sū·pêr′lȧ·tĭve, *adj.* 1. of the highest excellence. 2. *Grammar.* denoting the extreme in a comparison. —*n.* 3. something superlative. —**su·per′la·tive·ly**, *adv.*

sū′′pêr·năt′ū·rȧl, *adj.* 1. outside the laws of nature. —*n.* 2. realm of things outside such laws. —**su′′per·nat′u·ral·ly,** adv.

sü′′pêr·nü′mèr·ār·ÿ, adj., n., pl. **-ries.** adj. **1.** extra; nonessential. —n. **2.** something supernumerary. **3.** nonspeaking actor.

sü′′pêr·scrïbe′′, v.t., **-scribed, -scribing.** write over. —**su′′per·scrip′tion,** n.

sü′′pêr·sēde′, v.t., **-seded, -seding.** replace, esp. in importance or function.

sü′′pêr·sŏn′ĭc, adj. pertaining to speeds faster than that of sound.

sü′′pêr·stï′tion, n. unconfirmed belief, esp. in the supernatural. —**su′′per·sti′tious,** adj. —**su′′per·sti′tious·ly,** adv.

sü′pêr·strúc′tûre, n. upper structure.

sü′′pêr·vēne′, v.i., **-vened, -vening. 1.** arrive or occur in addition. **2.** occur afterward. —**su′′per·ven′tion,** n.

sü′pêr·vïse′′, v.t., **-vised, -vising.** direct and inspect. —**su′per·vis′′or,** n. —**su′′per·vi′so·ry,** adj. —**su′′per·vi′sion,** n.

sü′pïne, adj. **1.** lying on the back. **2.** wrongly passive. —**su′pine·ly,** adv.

sŭp′pêr, n. late dinner.

sŭp·plânt′, v.t. replace, as in favor or function.

sŭp′ple, adj., **-pler, -plest.** flexible. —**sup′ple·ly,** adv. —**sup′ple·ness,** n.

sŭp′ple·mènt, n. **1.** desirable addition. —v.t. (sup′plәment′′) **2.** give a supplement to. —**sup′′ple·men′tal, sup′′ple·men′ta·ry,** adj.

sŭp′plĭ·cāte′′, v.t., **-cated, -cating.** implore. —**sup′′pli·ca′tion,** n. —**sup′′pli·ant, sup′pli·cant,** n.

sŭp·plÿ′, v.t., **-plied, plying,** n., pl. **-plies.** v.t. **1.** provide, as goods. **2.** fill, as a need. —n. **3.** act or instance of supplying. **4.** something supplied. **5.** stock, as of goods. —**sup·pli′er,** n.

sŭp·pôrt′, v.t. **1.** hold up. **2.** provide a livelihood for. **3.** endure. **4.** be loyal to. **5.** confirm. —n. **6.** someone or something that supports.

sŭp·pōse′, v.t., **-posed, -posing. 1.** assume as true. **2.** expect to act as stated. —**sup·pos′ed·ly,** adv. —**sup′′po·si′tion,** n.

sŭp·prëss′, v.t. **1.** force into inaction. **2.** kept from being known or apparent. —**sup·pres′sion,** n.

sup·pu·rate (sup′yә rāt), v.i., **-rated, -rating.** form pus. —**sup′′pu·ra′tion,** n.

sü·prēme′, adj. highest or greatest. —**su·preme′ly,** adv. —**su·prem′a·cy,** n.

sur·charge, n., v.t., **-charged, -charging.** n. (sәr′chahrj) **1.** added or excessive charge. —v.t. (sәr chahrj′) **2.** impose a surcharge on.

sure (shōōr), adj., **surer, surest. 1.** convinced; positive. **2.** reliant. **3.** reliable. **4.** unerring. **5.** Informal. yes, indeed. —**sure′ly,** adv.

sure·ty (shōōr′i tē, shōōr′tē), n., pl. **-ties. 1.** certainty. **2.** security against risk. **3.** guarantor.

sûrf, n. waves breaking against land, shoals, etc.

sûr′fàce, n., adj., v., **-faced, -facing.** n. **1.** outer area. **2.** upper area of a body of water. **3.** outer appearance. —adj. **4.** apparent; specious. —v.t. **5.** finish or dress the surface of. —v.i. **6.** come to the surface, as of a body of water.

sur·feit (sәr′fit), n. **1.** excess, as of eating or drinking. **2.** revulsion from such excess. —v.t. **3.** cause to feel such revulsion.

sûrge, v.i. **surged, surging,** n. v.i. **1.** move in a sudden swell. **2.** gather volume or force suddenly. —n. **3.** act or instance of surging.

sûr′gèon, n. practitioner of surgery.

sûr′gêr·ÿ, n., pl. **-ries. 1.** treatment of illness by physical rather than chemical means. **2.** place where such treatment is given. —**sur′gi·cal,** adj. —**sur′gi·cal·ly,** adv.

sûr′lÿ, adj. **-lier, -liest.** sullenly illtempered. —**sur′li·ness,** n.

sûr·mïse′, v.t., **-mised, -mising,** n. guess.

sûr·mŏunt′, v.t. **1.** get or be on top of. **2.** overcome, as an obstacle. —**surmount′a·ble,** adj.

sûr′nāme′′, n. last name; family name.

sûr·pàss′, v.t. **1.** be superior to. **2.** exceed.

sûr·plĭce n. loose-fitting robe.

sûr′plŭs, adj. **1.** beyond the needed amount. —n. **2.** surplus amount.

sûr·prïse′, v.t., n., **-prised, -prising.** n. **1.** emotion on encountering the unexpected. **2.** unexpected occurrence.

—*v.t.* **3.** fill with surprise. **4.** attack, etc. when not expected.

sûr′′ren′der, *v.t.* **1.** give up. —*v.i.* **2.** yield to superior force. —*n.* **3.** act or instance of surrendering.

sûr′′rep·ti′tious, *adj.* stealthy. —**sur′′rep·ti′tious·ly,** *adv.*

sûr′ro·gāte′′, *n.* **1.** substitute. **2.** judge for legacies and estates.

sûr·round′, *v.t.* enclose or be close to on all sides. —**surrounding,** *adj.*

sûr·round′ings, *n. pl.* things all around; environment.

sûr′tăx′′, *n.* tax added to a tax.

sûr·veil′lance, *n.* close observation.

sur·vey, *v.t., n., pl.* **-veys.** *v.t.* (sər vā′) **1.** measure or evaluate precisely. **2.** view. —*n.* (sər′vā) **3.** act or instance of surveying. **4.** general summary. —**sur′vey′or,** *n.*

sûr·vīve′, *v.,* **-vived, -viving.** *v.i.* **1.** remain alive. —*v.t.* **2.** outlive. —**sur′viv′or,** *n.* —**sur·viv′al,** *n.*

sŭs·cĕp′ti·ble, *adj.* easily affected. —**sus·cep′′ti·bil′i·ty,** *n.*

sŭs·pĕct′, *v.t.* **1.** regard without trust. **2.** guess. —*n.* (sus′pekt) **3.** suspected person. —*adj.* **4.** to be regarded without trust.

sŭs·pĕnd′, *v.t.* **1.** hang. **2.** postpone. **3.** dismiss or expel temporarily.

sŭs·pĕn′dêrs, *n. pl.* straps for holding up the trousers.

sŭs·pĕnse′, *n.* anxiety due to uncertainty.

sŭs·pĕn′sion, *n.* **1.** act or instance of suspending. **2.** postponement. **3.** distribution of particles throughout a fluid.

sŭs·pī′cion, *n.* **1.** feeling of one who suspects. **2.** state of being suspected. **3.** trace.

sŭs·pī′cious, *adj.* **1.** having suspicions. **2.** arousing suspicion. —**sus·pi′cious·ly,** *adv.*

sŭs·tāin′, *v.t.* **1.** maintain; continue. **2.** support. **3.** endure. **4.** suffer. —**sus′tain′er,** *n.*

sŭs′te·nance, *n.* **1.** means of existence. **2.** act or instance of sustaining.

sū·tûre, *n., v.t.,* **-tured, -turing.** *n.* **1.** line of junction. **2.** means by which a wound is sewn. —*v.t.* **3.** join with a suture.

svĕlte, *adj.* slender.

swâb, *n., v.t.,* **swabbed, swabbing.** *n.* **1.** absorbent wiping device. —*v.t.* **2.** wipe with a swab.

swăg′gêr, *v.i.* **1.** walk arrogantly. —*n.* **2.** swaggering gait.

swāle, *n.* **1.** low, marshy area. **2.** valley-like area between slopes.

swâl′lōw, *v.t.* **1.** take down the throat. **2.** suppress, as an emotion. **3.** *Informal.* accept foolishly as true. —*n.* **4.** small, forked-tailed bird. **5.** act or instance of swallowing.

swămp, *n.* **1.** area of wet land and water vegetation. —*v.t.* **2.** drench. **3.** overload, as with work. —**swamp′y,** *adj.*

swăn, *n.* large, long-necked water bird.

swâp, *v.t.,* **swapped, swapping,** *n. Informal.* exchange.

swârm, *n.* **1.** large, unorganized group. —*v.i.* **2.** move in a swarm.

swârth′y, *adj.,* **-ier, -iest.** rather dark-skinned. —**swarth′i·ness,** *n.*

swăsh′bŭck′′ling, *adj.* showily brave or belligerent.

swăs′tī·kà, *n.* cross with end pieces forming right angles: in one form the Nazi symbol.

swăt, *v.t.,* **swatted, swatting,** *n. Informal.* *v.t.* **1.** hit sharply. —*n.* **2.** act or instance of swatting. —**swat′ter,** *n.*

swâth, *n.* mown pathlike area.

swāy, *v.i.* **1.** move unsteadily from side to side. —*v.t.* **2.** influence through argument. —*n.* **3.** act or instance of swaying. **4.** domination.

swear, *v.,* **swore, sworn, swearing.** *v.t.* **1.** affirm with an oath. **2.** bind with an oath. —*v.i.* **3.** utter profanity.

swĕat, *v.i.,* **sweat** or **sweated, sweating,** *n. v.i.* **1.** pass moisture through the pores. **2.** accumulate surface moisture. —*n.* **3.** sweated body moisture. **4.** sweating condition. —**sweat′y,** *adj.*

swĕat′êr, *n.* knitted garment covering the area from waist to neck.

swēep, *v.,* **swept, sweeping.** *v.t.* **1.** free of loose dirt, etc., esp. with brushing motions. **2.** free of enemies or rivals. —*v.i.* **3.** move swiftly and continuously. —*n.* **4.** act or instance of sweeping. **5.** scope.

swēep′stākes′′, *n.* race for a prize given by the competitors.

swēet, *adj.* **1.** somewhat sugarlike in taste.

2. agreeable, esp. to the senses. **3.** gentle. —*n.* **4.** piece of candy, etc. —**sweet'ly**, *adv.* —**sweet'ness**, *n.* —**sweet'en**, *v.t.*, *v.i.*

sweet'heart'', *n.* loved one.

sweet'pea, *n.* fragrant, flowering climbing plant.

sweet potàtò, trailing plant with sweet, edible orange root.

swell, *v.*, **swelled**, **swelled** or **swollen**, **swelling**, *n.*, *adj.* *v.t.*, *v.i.* **1.** expand beyond natural size from pressure. —*n.* **2.** act or instance of swelling. **3.** large rounded ocean wave or waves. —*adj.* **4.** *Informal.* excellent.

swel'ter, *v.i.* suffer from heat.

swerve, *v.*, **swerved**, **swerving**, *n.* *v.t.*, *v.i.* **1.** turn suddenly aside. —*n.* **2.** act or instance of swerving.

swift, *adj.* **1.** quick or prompt. **2.** fast. —*n.* **3.** fast, swallowlike bird. —**swift'ly**, *adv.* —**swift'ness**, *n.*

swig, *n.*, *v.t.*, **swigged**, **swigging**. *Informal.* *n.* **1.** swallow. —*v.t.* **2.** drink in swallows.

swill, *v.t.* **1.** drink greedily. —*n.* **2.** liquified garbage used as pig food.

swim, *v.i.*, **swam**, **swum**, **swimming**, *n.* *v.i.* **1.** move through water by actions of the body. **2.** be drenched or immersed. **3.** be confused or dizzy. —*n.* **4.** occasion of swimming. —**swim'mer**, *n.*

swin'dle, *v.t.*, **-dled**, **-dling**, *n.* *v.t.* **1.** cheat. **2.** fraud. —**swin'dler**, *n.*

swine, *n.*, *pl.* **swine**. pig or hog.

swing, *v.*, **swung**, **swinging**, *n.* *v.t.*, *v.i.* **1.** move back and forth through part of a circle. **2.** move one way in a circular path. —*n.* **3.** suspended seat for swinging. **4.** swinging blow. **5.** act, example, or magnitude of swinging.

swipe, *v.t.*, **swiped**, **swiping**, *n.* *Informal.* *v.t.* **1.** steal. **2.** hit with a swinging blow. —*n.* **3.** act or instance of swiping.

swirl, *v.t.*, *v.i.*, *n.* whirl.

swish, *v.t.*, *v.i.* **1.** whirl through the air with a sound. —*n.* **2.** sound of such whirling.

switch, *n.* **1.** change. **2.** device for controlling electric current. **3.** device for directing train movements. **4.** rodlike whip. —*v.t.* **5.** change or exchange. **6.** control or direct with a switch. **7.** beat with a switch. —**switch'board''**, *n.*

swiv'el, *n.* **1.** rotating support. —*v.t.*, *v.i.* **2.** turn on or as if on a swivel.

swoon, *n.*, *v.i.* faint.

swoop, *v.i.* **1.** descend speedily, as a bird of prey. —*n.* **2.** act or instance of swooping.

sword'fish'', *n.* large salt-water fish with swordlike upper jawbone.

sword, *n.* long, sharp-pointed or -bladed weapon. —**sword'play,''** *n.* —**swords'man**, *n.*

syb'à·rïte'', *n.* lover of luxury. —**syb''à·rit'ic**, *adj.*

syc'á·môre'', *n.* plane tree.

syc·ò·phànt, (sĭk 'ə fənt), *n.* flatterer and parasite. —**syc'o·phan·cy**, *n.*

syl'là·ble, *n.* individual sound that is part of a spoken word. —**syl·lab'ic**, *adj.*

syl'là·bùs, *n.*, *pl.* **-buses**, **-bi**. academic course outline.

sylph, *n.* graceful, slender woman.

syl'vàn, *adj.* **1.** pertaining to forests. **2.** forested.

sym'bòl, *n.* **1.** something representing another thing. **2.** sign representing instructions or orders. —**sym·bol'ic**, **sym·bol'i·cal**, *adj.* —**sym·bol'i·cal·ly**, *adv.* —**sym'bol·ize''**, *v.t.*

sym'bòl·ism, *n.* group of symbols.

sym'me·trÿ, *n.*, *pl.* **-tries**. **1.** mirror-image uniformity on opposite sides. **2.** harmony of arrangement. —**sym·met'ric**, **sym·met'ri·cal**, *adj.* —**sym'met'ri·cal·ly**, *adv.*

sym'pà·thïze'', *v.i.*, **-thized**, **-thizing**. **1.** be in sympathy. **2.** express sympathy. —**sym''pa·thiz'er**, *n.*

sym'pà·thŷ, *n.*, *pl.* **-thies**. **1.** oneness of feeling or opinion. **2.** regret for another's unhappiness. **3.** loyalty. —**sym''pathet'ic**, *adj.* —**sym''pa·thet'i·cal·ly**, *adv.*

sym'phò·nÿ, *n.*, *pl.* **-nies**. major orchestral composition. —**sym·phon'ic**, *adj.*

sym·pō'sï·ùm, *n.*, *pl.* **-siums**, **-sia**. **1.** formal discussion by experts. **2.** collection of papers on a topic.

symp'tòm, *n.* characteristic indication, esp. of an illness. —**symp''to·mat'ic**, *adj.*

syn'á·gŏgue'', *n.* congregation or house of Jewish worship.

sýn'chrȯ·nīze", *v.t.*. -nized, -nizing. 1. cause to occur at the same time or rate of speed. 2. cause to register the same time. —syn''chro·ni·za'tion, *n.* —syn'chro·nous, *adj.*

sýn'cȯ·pāte", *v.t.*, -pated, -pating. *Music.* stress the normally unaccented beat. —syn''co·pa'tion, *n.*

sýn'dĭ·cȧte, *n., v.t.*, -cated, -cating. 1. organization of independent organizations for a major effort. 2. organization selling material to newspapers. —*v.t.* (sin'di kāt'') 3. sell as a syndicate to newspapers. —syn''di·ca'tion, *n.*

syn'drōme", *n.* group of symptoms of a given illness.

sýn'fūel, *n.* synthetic fuel.

sýn'ŏd, *n.* ecclesiastical council.

sýn'ȯ·nŷm, *n.* different word of similar meaning. —syn·on'y·mous, *adj.* —syn·on'y·mous·ly, *adv.*

sýn·ŏp'sĭs, *n., pl.* -ses. summary; brief outline.

sýn'tăx, *n.* arrangement of words, as in a sentence.

sýn'thė·sĭs, *n., pl.* -ses. combination of different parts to form a whole.

sýn'thė·sīze", *v.t.*, -sized, -sizing. make into or as a synthesis.

sýn·thĕt'ĭc, *adj.* 1. imitating a natural material, esp. in composition. 2. pertaining to synthesis. —syn'thet'i·cal·ly, *adv.*

sýph'ĭ·lĭs, *n.* a venereal disease. —syph''i·lit'ic, *adj.*, *n.*

sýr·ĭnge', *n.* plunger-operated device for drawing up and ejecting fluids.

sý'rŭp, *n.* heavy, sweet liquid, esp. one of sugar and water. —syr'up·y, *adj.*

sýs'tĕm, *n.* 1. order or method. 2. coordinated arrangement of working elements. —sys''tem·at'ic, *adj.* —sys''tem·at'i·cal·ly, *adv.*

sýs''tĕm·ȧ·tīze", *v.t.*, -tized, -tizing. arrange according to a system.

sys·to·le (sis'tȧ lē), *n.* rhythmic contraction of the heart. —sys·tol'ic, *adj.*

T

T, t, *n.* twentieth letter of the English alphabet.

tăb, *n.* 1. extension for pulling. 2. bill of charges.

tăb'bŷ, *n., pl.* -bies. house cat.

tăb'ĕr·năc''le, *n.* place of worship.

tā'ble, *n., v.t.*, -bled, -bling. *n.* 1. piece of furniture with a broad horizontal surface. 2. orderly arrangement of data. —*v.t.* 3. postpone, as legislation. —ta'ble·cloth'', *n.* —ta'ble·ware'', *n.*

tăb'leau, *n., pl.* -leaux. picture; scene.

ta·ble d'hôte (tah''bǝl dōt'), *n.* fixed-price meal.

tā'ble·lănd'', *n.* plateau.

tā'ble·spoon'', *n.* spoon of one half a fluid ounce. —ta'ble·spoon''ful, *n.*

tăb'lĕt, *n.* 1. slab for writing or lettering. 2. pill. 3. pad of paper.

tăb'lŏĭd, *n.* small-format newspaper.

tă·bōō', *n., pl.* -boos, *adj., v.t.*, -booed, -booing. *n.* 1. prohibition, as by society. —*adj.* 2. prohibited. —*v.t.* 3. prohibit. Also, ta·bu'.

tăb'ū·lȧr, *adj.* in table form.

tăb'ū·lāte'', *v.t.*, -lated, -lating. arrange in a table. —tab''u·la'tion, *n.* —tab'u·la''tor, *n.*

tăc'ĭt, *adj.* understood though not stated. —tac'it·ly, *adv.*

tăc'ĭ·tûrn'', *adj.* choosing to speak little. —tac''i·turn'i·ty, *n.*

tăck, *n.* 1. short, pointed fastener. 2. change of course. —*v.t.* 3. fasten with tacks. 4. cause to change course. —*v.i.* 5. change course.

tăck'le, *n., v.t.*, -led, -ling. *n.* 1. equipment. 2. system of ropes and pulleys. 3. felling, as in football, by grasping the legs. —*v.t.* 4. undertake. 5. fell with a tackle.

tăck'ŷ, *adj.*, -ier, -iest. 1. sticky. 2. *Informal.* of poor quality.

tâ'cō, *n.* folded and filled fried tortilla.

tăct, *n.* sense of how not to offend. —tact'ful, *adj.* —tact'less, *adj.*

tăc'tĭcs, *n.* 1. science of maneuvering armed forces. 2. connivance; artifice. —tac'ti·cal, *adj.* —tac·ti'cian, *n.*

tăc′tĭle, *adj.* pertaining to touch. —**tac′til′i·ty**, *n.*

tăd′pōle′′, *n.* larva of a frog or toad.

tăf′fe·tá, *n.* stiff silky fabric.

tăf′fў, *n.* chewy candy.

tăg, *n., v.,* **tagged, tagging.** *n.* **1.** label attached with a cord. **2.** chasing game. —*v.t.* **3.** apply a tag to. —*v.i.* **4.** follow closely.

tăil, *n.* **1.** distinct hindmost extremity of an animal. **2.** feature similar in shape or location, as on a vehicle. —**tail′gate′′**, *n.* —**tail′light′′**, *n.* —**tail′less′′**, *adj.*

tāil′ör, *n.* **1.** maker of clothes. —*v.t.* **2.** make as a tailor does.

tāil′spĭn′′, *n.* winding plunge of an airplane.

tāint, *v.t.* **1.** pollute or poison. —*n.* **2.** trace of pollution.

tāke, *v.,* **took, taken, taking.** *v.t.* **1.** carry. **2.** escort. **3.** accept. **4.** seize. **5.** make use of. **6.** select. **7.** require. **8.** react to. **9.** assume. **10.** engage in. —*v.i.* **11.** be effective.

tāke′ŏff′′, *n.* beginning of a flight.

tāke′ō′′vĕr, *n.* assumption of control.

tāk′ĭng, *adj.* **1.** attractive. —*n.* **2.** takings, profits.

tălc, *n.* soft mineral. Also, **tal′cum.**

tāle, *n.* **1.** narrative. **2.** piece of gossip. **3.** lie. —**tale′bear′′er**, *n.*

tăl′ĕnt, *n.* **1.** personal ability. **2.** person or persons of talent. —**tal′ent·ed**, *adj.*

tāles′măn, *n.* person called for jury duty.

tăl′ĭs·măn, *n.* object warding off evil.

tălk, *v.i.* **1.** speak words. **2.** confer. **3.** gossip. —*v.t.* **4.** persuade. —*n.* **5.** conversation. **6.** speech. **7.** gossip or rumor.

tălk′a·tĭve, *adj.* loving to talk.

tălk′ĭng-to′′, *n. Informal.* scolding.

tăll, *adj.* **1.** very high. **2.** of a specified height.

tăl′lŏw, *n.* solid animal fat.

tăl′lў, *n., pl.* **-lies,** *v.,* **-lied, -lying.** *n.* **1.** sum. **2.** account; score. —*v.t.* **3.** add up. —*v.i.* **4.** correspond.

Tăl′mŭd, *n.* compilation of Hebrew law. —**Tal·mud′ic,** *adj.*

tăl′ŏn, *n.* bird claw.

tá·mä′lē, *n.* Mexican dish of meat, red peppers, and corn meal in corn husks.

tăm′bou·rĭne′′, *n.* shallow drumlike instrument.

tāme, *adj.,* **tamer, tamest,** *v.t.,* **tamed, taming.** *adj.* **1.** obedient to a master. **2.** without spirit. —*v.t.* **3.** make tame. —**tame′ly**, *adv.* —**tame′ness**, *n.* —**tam′a·ble, tame′a·ble,** *adj.* —**tam′er,** *n.*

tămp, *v.t.* pack or drive with gentle blows.

tăm′pĕr, *v.i.* interfere wrongly.

tăn, *n., adj.,* **tanner, tannest,** *v.t.,* **tanned, tanning.** *n.* **1.** yellow-brown. **2.** suntan. —*adj.* **3.** yellow-brown. —*v.t.* **4.** convert into leather.

tăn′a·gĕr, *n.* small, colorful American songbird.

tăn′dĕm, *adv., adj.* with one behind the other.

tăng, *n.* penetrating flavor. —**tang′y,** *adj.*

tăn′gĕnt, *n.* line touching a curve. —**tan′gen·tial,** *adj.* —**tan′gen·cy,** *n.*

tăn′′gĕr·ĭne′, *n.* type of orange.

tăn′gĭ·ble, *adj.* **1.** able to be touched. **2.** able to be defined. —**tan′′gi·bil′i·ty,** *n.*

tăn′gle, *v.,* **-gled, -gling,** *n., v.t.* **1.** intertwine in a disorderly way. —*n.* **2.** tangled state.

tăn′gō, *n., pl.* **-gos.** South American dance.

tănk, *n.* **1.** container for fluids. **2.** armored fighting vehicle. —**tank′ful,** *n.*

tănk′ärd, *n.* tall mug with a side handle.

tănk′êr, *n.* ship carrying liquids in bulk.

tăn′nêr, *n.* maker of leather. —**tan′ner·y,** *n.*

tăn′tá·līze′′, *v.t.,* **-lized, -lizing.** torment with gratification withheld. —**tan′′tal·i·za′tion,** *n.*

tăn′tá·moûnt′′, *adj.* equivalent.

tăn′trŭm, *n.* outburst of rage.

tăp, *v.,* **tapped, tapping,** *n. v.t., v.i.* **1.** strike lightly. —*v.t.* **2.** draw off or upon. —*n.* **3.** light blow. **4.** valve or plug.

tăp dănce, dance with light taps of the foot. —**tap′-dance′′,** *v.i.*

tāpe, *n., v.t.,* **taped, taping.** *n.* **1.** thin, flat, long strip. —*v.t.* **2.** bind with tape. **3.** record on tape.

tā′pêr, *n.* **1.** convergence of sides or edges. —*v.t., v.i.* **2.** decrease steadily in thickness. **3.** candle.

tăp′ĕs·trў, *n., pl.* **-tries.** *n.* woven decorative panel.

tāpe′wörm′′, *n.* flat parasitic worm.

tăp″ï·ō′cà, *n.* starchy substance from cassava roots.

tăp′rōōt″, *n.* single, deep-going root.

tăps, *n. Military.* bugle call signifying retirement for the night and also played after military funerals.

târ, *n., v.t.,* **tarred, tarring.** *n.* **1.** thick black liquid distilled from wood, coal, etc. —*v.t.* **2.** coat with tar.

tà·răn′tū·là, *n.* large, hairy spider.

târ′dÿ, *adj.,* **-dier, -diest.** behind the expected time. —**tar′di·ly**, *adv.* —**tar′di·ness**, *n.*

târe, *n.* **1.** container weight. **2.** weed.

târ′gĕt, *n.* something aimed at.

târ′ĭff, *n.* **1.** tax on imports or exports. **2.** price or charge.

târ′nĭsh, *v.t.* **1.** spoil the luster of. —*v.i.* **2.** become tarnished. —*n.* **3.** tarnished state.

tă′rŏt, *n.* set of fortune-telling cards.

târ·pāu′lĭn, *n.* waterproof cloth cover.

târ′pŏn, *n.* large west Atlantic game fish.

târ′rà·gŏn, *n.* seasoning of fragrant leaves.

tar·ry, *v.i.,* **-ried, -rying,** *adj. v.i.* (tar′ē) **1.** linger. —*adj.* (tahr′ē) **2.** covered with or suggesting tar.

târt, *adj.* **1.** acid, as to the taste. —*n.* **2.** small pie.

târ′tàn, *n.* plaid cloth pattern of crisscrossed bands of color.

târ′tàr, *n.* **1.** potassium salt used as a condiment. **2.** deposit on the teeth. —**tar′tar′ic**, *adj.*

tăsk, *n.* **1.** something to be done. —*v.t.* **2.** burden.

tăsk′mäs″tẽr, *n.* person who exacts work of others.

tăs′sĕl, *n.* ornamental gathering of hanging threads.

tāste, *v.,* **tasted, tasting,** *n. v.t.* **1.** sense with the tongue. **2.** experience. —*v.i.* **3.** have a specific flavor. —*n.* **4.** sense operating through the tongue. **5.** flavor. **6.** sense of what is appropriate or seemly. **7.** liking. —**tast′er**, *n.* —**taste′less**, *adj.*

tāste′fŭl, *adj.* in good taste.

tāst′ÿ, *adj.,* **-ier, -iest.** good-tasting. —**tast′i·ness**, *n.*

tăt′tẽr, *n.* **1.** ragged fragment. —*v.t.* **2.** reduce to tatters. —**tat′tered**, *adj.*

tăt′tle, *v.i.,* **-tled, -tling.** gossip.

tăt′tle·tāle″, *n.* betrayer of secrets.

tăt·tōō′, *v.t.,* **-tooed, -tooing,** *n., pl.* **-toos.** *v.t.* **1.** mark with pigments under the skin. —*n.* **2.** tattooed design. **3.** military drum or bugle signal.

taŭnt, *v.t.* **1.** mock. —*n.* **2.** mocking remark.

taŭt, *adj.* tight or tense. —**taut′ly**, *adv.* —**taut′ness**, *n.*

taŭ·tŏl′ō·gÿ, *n., pl.* **-gies.** useless repetition of an idea in a logical argument. —**tau″to·log′i·cal**, *adj.*

tăv′ẽrn, *n.* public drinking place.

tăw′drÿ, *adj.,* **-drier, -driest.** cheap and showy. —**taw′dri·ly**, *adv.* —**taw′dri·ness**, *n.*

tăw′nÿ, *adj.,* **-nier, -niest.** tan.

tăx, *n.* **1.** money exacted by a government. **2.** demand on resources. —*v.t.* **3.** exact a tax on or from. **4.** accuse. —**tax′a·ble**, *adj.* —**tax·a′tion**, *n.* —**tax′pay″er**, *n.*

tăx′ĭ, *n., pl.* **-is,** *v.i.,* **-ied, -iing** or **-ying.** *n.* **1.** Also, **tax′i·cab″**, hired vehicle with metered charges. —*v.i.* **2.** travel by taxi. **3.** move without flying, as an airplane.

tăx′ĭ·dẽr″mÿ, *n.* art of simulating animals using their skins. —**tax″i·der′mist**, *n.*

tēa, *n.* **1.** drink made from the dried leaves of a shrub grown in Asia. **2.** drink made from other leaves and flowers. **3.** meal, etc. at which tea is served. —**tea′cup″**, *n.* —**tea′ket″tle**, *n.* —**tea′pot″**, *n.*

tēach, *v.,* **taught, teaching.** *v.t.* **1.** inform on a subject. **2.** inform students regarding. —*v.i.* **3.** be a teacher. —**teach′a·ble**, *adj.* —**teach′er**, *n.*

tēak, *n.* brown East Indian hardwood.

tēal, *n., pl.* **teals, teal. 1.** freshwater duck. **2.** color of green.

tēam, *n.* **1.** group of animals or persons acting together. —*v.i.* **2.** join or act in a team. —**team′mate″**, *n.* —**team′work″**, *n.*

tear, *v.,* **tore, torn, tearing,** *n., v.t.* (ter) **1.** pull apart by force. **2.** make by piercing or rending. **3.** lacerate or harass. —*v.i.* **4.** be torn. **5.** hurry. —*n.* **6.** torn place. **7.** (tēr) liquid from the weeping eye. —**tear′drop″**, *n.* —**tear′ful**, *adj.*

tēase, *v.t.*, teased, teasing. 1. bother with gentle malice. 2. comb.

tēa'spoon'', *n.* spoon holding one and a third fluid drams. —tea'spoon·ful'', *n.*

tēat, *n.* nipple.

tĕch'nĭ·cal, *n.* 1. pertaining to technology. 2. pertaining to technique. 3. pertaining to specific details. —tech'ni·cal·ly, *adv.* —tech''ni·cal'i·ty, *n.* —tech·ni'cian, *n.*

tĕch·nīque', *n.* 1. working method. 2. proficiency. Also, tech'nic.

tĕch·nŏc'ra·cy, *n.* government by technical experts.

tĕch·nŏl'o·gy, *n.*, *pl.* -gies. application of science, esp. to industry. —tech''no·log'i·cal, *adj.*

tē'dĭ·ŭm, *n.* wearisome or boring quality or state. —te'di·ous, *adj.*

tēe, *n.* stand for a golf ball being driven.

tēem, *v.i.* swarm.

tēen'-āge'', *adj.* pertaining to the teens as an age. Also, teen'age''. —teen'ag''er, *n.*

tēens, *n. pl.* 1. years of life between 13 and 19. 2. numbers in a series between 10 and 19.

tēe'ny, *adj.*, -nier, -niest. *Informal.* tiny.

tēethe, *v.i.*, teethed, teething. grow teeth.

tēe·tō'tal·êr, *n.* total abstainer from alcohol. Also, tee·to'tal·ler.

tĕl·e·căst'', *v.t.*, -cast or -casted, -casting, *n.* broadcast via television. —tel'e·cast''er, *n.*

tĕl'e·grăph'', *n.* 1. apparatus sending messages in code by electrical impulses. —*v.t.* 2. reach by telegraph. 3. send by telegraph. —tel''e·graph'ic, *adj.* —te·leg'ra·phy, *n.* —te·leg'ra·pher, *n.* —tel'e·gram'', *n.*

te·lĕp'a·thy, *n.* extra-sensory communication. —tel''e·path'ic, *adj.* —te·lep'a·thist, *n.*

tĕl'e·phōne'', *n.*, *v.t.*, -phoned, -phoning. *n.* 1. device for transmitting personal spoken messages. —*v.t.* 2. reach by telephone. 3. transmit by telephone. —tel''e·phon'ic, *adj.*

tĕl'e·scōpe'', *n.*, *v.*, -scoped, -scoping. *n.* 1. device for magnifying distant images. —*v.t.*, *v.i.* 2. slide lengthwise into one another. —tel''e·scop'ic, *adj.*

tĕl''e·tȳpe'wrīt''êr, *n.* telegraphic apparatus sending and receiving typed messages.

tĕl'e·vīse'', *v.t.*, -vised, -vising. transmit by television.

tĕl'e·vī''sion, *n.* 1. method of transmitting images by radio waves and electrical impulses. 2. industry using this method. 3. television receiving set.

tĕll, *v.*, told, telling. *v.t.* 1. inform. 2. recount. 3. order. 4. distinguish; recognize. —*v.i.* 5. give a narrative. 6. have an effect. —tel'ling, *adj.* —tel'ling·ly, *adv.*

tĕll'êr, *n.* 1. narrator. 2. bank clerk.

tĕll'tāle'', *adj.* secret-revealing.

te·mĕr'ĭ·tȳ, *n.* audacity.

tĕm'pêr, *n.* 1. mood. 2. anger. 3. control of one's anger. 4. hardness and flexibility, as of steel. —*v.t.* 5. moderate. 6. give toughness to.

tĕm'pêr·à, *n.* paint with egg, glue, etc.

tĕm'pêr·à·mĕnt, *n.* natural mental disposition. —tem''per·a·men'tal, *adj.*

tĕm'pêr·ánce, *n.* moderation, esp. in drinking.

tĕm'pêr·ate, *adj.* 1. moderate. 2. **Temperate**, situated between a tropic and the Arctic or Antarctic Circle.

tĕm'pêr·à·tûre, *n.* 1. relative heat. 2. condition of excessive body heat.

tĕm'pêred, *adj.* 1. modified. 2. having a specified temperament.

tĕm'pĕst, *n.* violent storm. —tem·pes·tu·ous, *adj.*

tĕm'plāte, *n.* pattern for forming.

tĕm'ple, *n.* 1. place of worship. 2. area to either side of the brow.

tĕm'pō, *n.*, *pl.* -pos, -pi. rate of speed, as for music.

tĕm'pò·ral, *adj.* 1. worldly, not spiritual. 2. pertaining to time.

tĕm'pò·rār''ȳ, *adj.* for a limited time. —tem''po·rar'i·ly, *adv.*

tĕm'pò·rīze'', *v.i.*, -rized, -rizing. evade argument or time requirements. —tem''po·ri·za'tion, *n.*

tĕmpt, *v.t.* create an appetite or inclination in. —temp·ta'tion, *n.* —tempt'er, *fem.*, tempt'ress, *n.*

tĕn, *n.* nine plus one.

tĕn'à·ble, *adj.* defensible, as an argument. —ten''a·bil'i·ty, *n.* —ten'a·bly, *adv.*

tĕ·nā′cioŭs, *adj.* **1.** holding firmly. **2.** stubborn. **—te·na′cious·ly,** *adv.* **—te·nac′i·ty,** *n.*

tĕn′ant, *n.* renter of building space or land. **—ten′an·cy,** *n.*

tĕnd, *v.i.* **1.** have a tendency. **—***v.t.* **2.** manage or care for.

tĕn′dĕn·cy, *n., pl.* **-cies.** mild predominance of a certain result, preference, etc.

tĕn·dĕn′tioŭs, *adj.* expressed with a bias. **—ten·den′tious·ly,** *adv.*

tĕn′dĕr, *adj.* **1.** soft. **2.** warmly affectionate. **3.** feeling pain readily. **—***n.* **4.** person who tends. **5.** railroad car for fuel. **6.** something offered in payment. **—***v.t.* **7.** offer. **—ten′der·ly,** *adv.* **—ten′der·ness,** *n.* **—ten′der·heart′ed,** *adj.* **—ten′der·ize′,** *v.t.*

tĕn′dĕr·fŏŏt′′, *n., pl.* **-foots, -feet.** newcomer to out-of-door pursuits.

tĕn′dĕr·loĭn′′, *n.* **1.** tenderest cut of beef or pork loin. **2.** graft-ridden city neighborhood.

tĕn′dŏn, *n.* muscle attachment.

tĕn′drĭl, *n.* attachment on a climbing plant.

tĕn′e·mĕnt, *n.* **1.** shabby apartment building. **2.** apartment in such a building.

tĕn′ĕt, *n.* doctrine accepted as truth.

tĕnnĭs, *n.* game played with rackets and a ball.

tĕn′ŏn, *n.* end of a rail, etc., held in the mortise of another such piece.

tĕn′ŏr, *n.* **1.** highest male singing voice. **2.** gist.

tĕn′pĭns′′, *n.* bowling game.

tĕnse, *adj.,* **tenser, tensest,** *v.,* **tensed, tensing,** *n. adj.* **1.** taut. **2.** nervous: strained. **—***v.t.* **3.** make tense. **—***v.i.* **4.** become tense. **—***n.* **5.** *Grammar.* expression of past, present, future, etc. **—tense′ly,** *adv.* **—ten′sion, tense′ness, ten′si·ty,** *n.*

tĕn′sīle, *adj.* capable of being stretched.

tĕnt, *n.* **1.** fabric shelter spread over poles. **—***v.i.* **2.** lodge in a tent.

tĕn′ta·cle, *n.* grasping or feeling attachment of an invertebrate.

tĕn′ta·tĭve, *adj.* made or done as a trial. **—ten′ta·tive·ly,** *adv.*

tĕn′têr·hŏŏk′′, *n.* **on tenterhooks,** in suspense.

tĕnth, *adj.* **1.** following nine others. **—***n.* **2.** one of ten equal parts.

tĕn′ū·oŭs, *adj.* **1.** thin. **2.** insubstantial. **—ten′u·ous·ly,** *adv.* **—ten·u′i·ty, ten′u·ous·ness,** *n.*

tĕn′ûre, *n.* **1.** right to continuing employment. **2.** occupation, as of public office.

tē′pēe, *n.* conical tent of American Indians.

tĕp′ĭd, *adj.* lukewarm. **—te·pid′ity, tep′id·ness,** *n.* **—tep′id·ly,** *adv.*

te·quĭ′là, *n.* Mexican distilled liquor.

têrm, *n.* **1.** word with a specific meaning. **2.** period of activity. **3. terms, a.** requirements of an agreement. **b.** basis of a relationship.

têr′mĭn·ál, *n.* **1.** station at the end of a railroad, etc. **2.** electrical connecting point. **3.** (computers) work station for data processing. **—***adj.* **4.** coming at the end. **5.** causing death. **—ter′′min·al·ly′,** *adv.*

têr′mĭ·nāte′, *v.,* **-nated, -nating.** *v.t., v.i.* finish. **—ter′mi·na·ble,** *adj.* **—ter′′mi·na′tion,** *n.*

têr′′mĭ·nŏl′ó·gў, *n., pl.* **-gies.** employment of terms.

têr′mĭ·nŭs, *n., pl.* **-ni, -nuses. 1.** end or limit. **2.** station at the end of a railroad, etc.

têr′mīte, *n.* wood-eating insect.

têrn, *n.* gull-like bird.

têr′răce, *n., v.t.,* **-raced, -racing.** *n.* **1.** raised outdoor platform. **—***v.t.* **2.** form in terraces.

tĕr′rà cŏt′tà, earthenware material used in building and decoration.

tĕrrà fĭr′mà, dry land.

têr·raĭn′, *n.* land with its natural features.

têr′rà·pĭn, *n.* type of turtle.

têr·rār′ĭ·ŭm, *n., pl.* **-iums, -ia.** glass box for growing small plants and animals.

têr·rĕs′trĭ·ál, *adj.* pertaining to the earth.

têr′rĭ·ble, *adj.* **1.** bad; poor. **2.** awesome. **—ter′ri·bly,** *adv.* **1.** in a terrible manner. **2.** *Informal.* extremely.

têr′rĭ·êr, *n.* small hunting dog.

têr·rĭf′ĭc, *adj.* **1.** awesome in force. **2.** *Informal.* very good.

têr′rĭ·fў, *v.t.,* **-fied, -fying.** fill with terror.

têr′rĭ·tô′′rў, *n., pl.* **-ries. 1.** region without full political status. **2.** distinct area of land. —**ter''ri·to'ri·al,** *adj.*

těr'ror, *n.* **1.** great fear. **2.** cause of such fear.

těr'ror·ism, *n.* use of terror to enforce demands. —**ter'ror·ist,** *n., adj.,* —**ter''ror·is'tic,** *adj.*

těr'ror·īze'', *v.t.,* -**ized,** -**izing.** intimidate with terror. —**ter''ror·i·za'tion,** *n.*

têrse, *adj., terser, tersest.* short-spoken; concise. —**terse'ly,** *adv.* —**terse'ness,** *n.*

têr'ti·ār'y̆, *adj.* third in order.

těst, *n.* **1.** act or event that reveals qualities, accomplishments, illnesses, etc. —*v.t.* **2.** subject to a test. —*v.t.* **3.** perform a test. —**test'er,** *n.*

těs'ta·měnt, *n.* **1.** *Law.* will. **2.** part of the Bible. —**tes''ta·men'ta·ry,** *adj.*

těs'tā·tŏr, *n.* maker of a will.

těs'tĭ·cle, *n.* male sex gland.

těs'tĭ·fy̆'', *v.,* -**fied,** -**fying.** *v.t., v.i.* bear witness.

těs''tĭ·mō'nĭ·ăl, *adj.* **1.** expressing gratitude. —*n.* **2.** recommendation.

těs'tĭ·mō''ny̆, *n., pl.* -**nies.** declaration.

těs'ty̆, *adj.,* -**tier,** -**tiest.** irritable. —**tes'ti·ly,** *adv.* —**tes'ti·ness,** *n.*

tět'a·nŭs, *n.* acute spasmodic disease.

tête-a-tête, *n.* intimate conversation.

těth'ĕr, *n.* **1.** long tying rope. —*v.t.* **2.** fasten with a tether.

tět''rä·hē'drŏn, *n., pl.* -**drons,** -**dra.** four-sided solid.

těxt, *n.* **1.** written matter. **2.** textbook. —**tex'tu·al,** *adj.*

těxt'bŏŏk'', *n.* school book.

těx'tĭle, *n.* cloth.

těx'tūre, *n.* surface quality. —**tex'tur·al,** *adj.*

thăn, *conj.* introduces a basis of comparison.

thănk, *v.t.* express gratitude to. —**thank'ful,** *adj.* —**thank'ful·ly,** *adv.* **thank'less,** *adj.* —**thank'less·ly,** *adv.*

thănks, *n.* **1.** gratitude. —*interj.* **2.** I thank you.

thănks'gĭv''ĭng, *n.* **1.** expression of thanks to God. **2. Thanksgiving,** U.S. holiday.

thăt, *pron., adj., pl.* **those,** *conj. pron., adj.* **1.** the one. **2.** the other. —*pron.* **3.**

which. —*conj.* **4.** (used to introduce noun and adverbial clauses). —*adv.* **5.** to such an extent.

thătch, *n.* **1.** roof surface of straw, reeds, etc. —*v.t.* **2.** cover with such a surface.

thăw, *v.i.* **1.** warm above freezing. —*n.* **2.** state of thawing.

thė, *def. article.* (refers to a particular person, thing, or type.)

thē·ā·têr, *n.* **1.** place for plays, etc. **2.** theatrical profession. Also, **the'a·tre.** —**the·at'ri·cal,** *adj.* —**the·at'ri·cal·ly,** *adv.*

thěft, *n.* stealing.

thěir, *adj.* pertaining to them.

thěirs, *pron.* something pertaining to them.

thěm, *pron.* objective of they.

thēme, *n.* **1.** subject. **2.** basic melody. —**the·mat'ic,** *adj.*

thěm·sělves', *pron.* **1.** (intensive and reflexive of they). **2.** their true selves.

thěn, *adv.* **1.** at that time. **2.** and after. **3.** in that case. —*n.* **4.** that time.

thěnce, *adv.* from there or then.

thěnce''fôrth', *adv.* from then on. Also, **thence''for'ward.**

thē·ŏc'ra·cy̆, *n., pl.* -**cies.** rule by priests. —**the''o·crat'ic,** *adj.*

thē·ŏl'ŏ·gy̆, *n., pl.* -**gies.** study of religious doctrine. —**the''o·log'i·cal,** *adj.* —**the''o·lo'gian,** *n.*

thē'ŏ·rěm, *n.* something to be proved.

thē'ŏ·ry̆, *n., pl.* -**ies. 1.** statement of a possible truth. **2.** untried assumption. —**the''o·ret'i·cal,** *adj.* —**the''o·ret'i·cal·ly,** *adv.* —**the'o·rize'',** *v.i.* —**the'o·rist,** *n.*

thē·ōs'ŏ·phy̆, *n.* mystical religion. —**the''o·soph'ic,** *adj.* —**the·os'o·phist,** *n.*

thěr''a·peū'tĭc, *adj.* aiding health. —**ther''a·peu'tics,** *n.*

thěr'a·py̆, *n., pl.* -**pies.** healing process. —**ther'a·pist,** *n.*

thěre, *adv.* **1.** at or to that place. **2.** in that respect. **3.** used to introduce expressions of existence or nonexistence.

thěre·ăf'têr, *adv.* from then on.

thěre'by̆, *adv.* in connection with that.

thěre'fôre'', *adj.* for this reason.

thěre·ĭn', *adv.* in that.

thěre·ŏf', *adv.* of that.

thĕre·ŏn′, *adv.* **1.** on that. **2.** just afterward.

thĕre·to′, *adv.* to that place.

thĕre′ŭp·ŏn′, *adv.* **1.** just afterward. **2.** in consequence.

thĕr′mǎl, *adj.* pertaining to heat.

thĕr·mŏm′ĕ·tĕr, *n.* heat-measuring device.

thĕr′′mō·nū′clē·ǎr, *adj.* pertaining to atomic fusion at high heat.

thĕr′mŏs, *n.* heat-insulated bottle.

thĕr′mo·stắt′′, *n.* heating control.

thē·sāū′rŭs, *n.*, *pl.* **-ri**, **-ruses.** *n.* book of synonyms and antonyms.

thē′sĭs, *n.*, *pl.* **-ses.** **1.** belief to be defended. **2.** research paper.

thĕs′pĭ·ăn, *n.* **1.** actor or actress. —*adj.* **2.** pertaining to the theater.

they, *n.* plural of *he, she,* or *it.*

thĭck, *n.* **1.** deep from front to back. **2.** dense. —**thĭck′ly**, *adv.* —**thĭck′ness**, *n.* —**thĭck′en**, *v.t., v.i.*

thĭck′ĕt, *n.* thick clump of shrubbery.

thĭck′sĕt′, *adj.* stout.

thĭck′-skĭnned′, *adj.* coarse; insensitive.

thĭef, *n.*, *pl.* **thieves.** person who steals. —**thiev′er·y**, *n.* —**thiev′ish**, *adj.*

thĭgh, *n.* upper leg. —**thĭgh′bone′′**, *n.*

thĭm′ble, *n.* fingertip protector.

thĭn, *adj.*, **thinner, thinnest,** *v.t.*, **thinned, thinning.** *adj.* **1.** shallow from front to back. **2.** not dense; meager. —*v.t.* **3.** make thin. —**thĭn′ly**, *adv.* —**thĭn′ness**, *n.* —**thĭn′ner**, *n.*

thĭng, *n.* inanimate entity.

thĭnk, *v.*, **thought, thinking.** *v.t.* **1.** have in the mind. **2.** believe. —*v.i.* **3.** employ the mind. —**think′er**, *n.*

thĭn′-skĭnned′, *adj.* sensitive to insult.

thĭrd, *adj.* **1.** being number three. —*n.* **2.** one of three equal parts.

thĭrst, *n.* desire to absorb liquids. —**thirst′y**, *adj.* —**thirst′i·ly**, *adv.*

thĭr·tēen′, *adj.*, *n.* ten plus three. —**thir′teenth′′**, *adj.*

thĭr′tÿ, *adj.*, *n.* three times ten. —**thir′ti·eth**, *adj.*, *n.*

thĭs, *pron.*, *adj.*, *pl.* **these,** *adv. pron.*, *adj.* **1.** designating something near at hand. —*adv.* **2.** to this extent.

thĭs′tle, *n.* prickly plant.

thĭth′ĕr, *adv.* to that place.

thŏng, *n.* small flexible strap.

thō′răx, *n.*, *pl.* **-raxes, -races.** center of the body. —**tho·rac′ic**, *adj.*

thŏrn, *n.* spike of a plant stalk. —**thorn′y**, *adj.*

thŏr′ough, *adj.* complete in every detail. —**thor′ough·ly**, *adv.* —**thor′ough·ness**, *n.*

thŏr′ough·brĕd′′, *adj.* pedigreed.

thŏr′ough·fāre′′, *n.* way through.

thŏr′ough·gō′ing, *adj.* thorough.

thŏū, *pron.* Archaic. you.

thŏugh, *conj.* **1.** despite the fact that. —*adv.* **2.** however.

thŏught, *n.* **1.** thinking process. **2.** something thought. **3.** something to consider. —**thought′ful**, *adj.* —**thought′ful·ly**, *adv.* —**thought′ful·ness**, *n.* —**thought′less**, *adj.* —**thought′less·ly**, *adv.* **thought′less·ness**, *n.*

thŏū′sǎnd, *adj.*, *n.* ten times one hundred. —**thou′sandth**, *adj.*, *n.*

thrăsh, *v.t.* beat vigorously.

thrĕad, *n.* **1.** length of spun fiber. **2.** ridge on a screw. —*v.t.* **3.** put a thread through.

thrĕad′bāre′′, *adj.* worn thin.

thrĕat, *n.* warning of revenge or danger.

thrĕat′ĕn, *v.t.* make or constitute a threat against.

thrēe, *n.* two plus one.

thrĕsh, *v.t.* separate from husks. —**thresh′er**, *n.*

thrĕsh′ŏld, *n.* doorway pavement.

thrīce, *adv.* three times.

thrĭft, *n.* saving of money, etc.

thrĭft′ÿ, *adj.*, **-ier, -iest.** characterized by thrift. —**thrift′i·ly**, *adv.*

thrĭll, *v.t.* **1.** excite emotionally. —*v.i.* **2.** be excited emotionally. —*n.* **3.** act or instance of thrilling.

thrīve, *v.i.*, **thrived** or **throve, thrived** or **thriven, thriving.** be prosperous or healthy.

thrōat, *n.* interior of the neck.

thrŏb, *v.i.*, **throbbed, throbbing.** *n.*, *v.i.* **1.** beat, as the heart or pulse, with more than usual force. —*n.* **2.** act or instance of throbbing.

thrōe, *n.* pang.

thrŏm·bō′sĭs, *n.* clotting of blood.

thrōne, *n.* chair of state.

thrŏng, *n.*, *v.i.* crowd.

throt'tle, *n.*, *v.t.*, **-tled, -tling**. *n.* **1.** valve. *v.t.* **2.** squeeze and choke.

through, *prep.* **1.** from end to end of. **2.** by means of. —*adv.* **3.** from end to end. —*adj.* **4.** from end to end. **5.** finished.

through·out', *prep.* **1.** in every part of. —*adv.* **2.** in every part.

throw, *v.t.*, **threw, thrown,** *n.*, *v.t.* **1.** propel unsupported. **2.** send forcefully. —*n.* **3.** act or instance of throwing. **4.** distance of throwing. —**throw'er,** *n.*

throw'back'', *n.* reversion.

thru, *prep.*, *adv.*, *adj.* through.

thrush, *n.* songbird.

thrust, *v.*, **thrust, thrusting,** *n.* *v.t.*, *v.i.*, *n.* push.

thud, *v.i.*, **thudded, thudding,** *n.* boom with a dull sound.

thug, *n.* hoodlum.

thumb, *n.* **1.** innermost hand digit. —*v.t.* **2.** move with the thumb.

thumb'tack'', *n.* broad-headed tack.

thump, *n.* **1.** heavy blow. **2.** sound produced by such a blow.

thun'der, *n.* **1.** sound following lightning. —*v.t.* **2.** say loudly or vehemently. —**thun'der·ous,** *adj.* —**thun'der·bolt'',** *n.* —**thun'der·clap'',** *n.* —**thun'der·cloud'',** *n.* —**thun'der·show''er,** *n.* —**thun'der·storm'',** *n.*

thun'der·struck', *adj.* stupefied with amazement. Also, **thun'der·strick''en.**

Thurs'day, *n.* fifth day of the week.

thus, *adv.* **1.** in this way. **2.** to this extent. **3.** therefore.

thwart, *v.t.* obstruct.

thy, *adj. Archaic.* your.

thyme (tīm), *n.* herb plant used for seasoning.

thy'roid gland, ductless gland regulating growth.

thy·self', *pron. Archaic.* yourself.

ti·ar'a, *n.* woman's decorative coronet.

tic, *n.* repeated muscular spasm.

tick, *n.* **1.** sound of a mechanical clock. **2.** bloodsucking insect. **3.** mattress cloth. —*v.i.* **4.** make a ticking sound. —**tick'er,** *n.*

tick'et, *n.* **1.** paper giving admission. **2.** list of candidates.

tick'le, *v.*, **-led, -ling.** *v.t.* **1.** cause to

twitch by light stroking. **2.** amuse. —*v.i.* **3.** cause tickling.

tick'lish, *adj.* **1.** susceptible to tickling. **2.** needing caution.

tid'bit', *n.* small morsel.

tide, *n.* periodic fluctuation of sea level. —**tid'al,** *adj.* —**tide'wa''ter,** *n.*, *adj.*

ti'dings, *n. pl.* news.

ti'dy, *adj.*, **-dier, -diest,** *v.t.*, **-died, -dying.** *adj.* **1.** orderly. —*v.t.* **2.** make orderly. —**ti'di·ness,** *n.* —**ti'di·ly,** *adv.*

tie, *v.t.*, **tied, tying,** *n.* *v.t.* **1.** fasten with ropes, etc. **2.** equal in scoring. —*n.* **3.** something that ties. **4.** something that prevents spreading. **5.** equal score. **6.** necktie.

tier, *n.* horizontal row.

tie'-up'', *n.* stoppage.

tiff, *n.* slight quarrel.

ti'ger, *n.* large catlike African and south Asian animal. Also, *fem.*, **ti'gress.**

tight, *adj.* **1.** preventing movement. **2.** fully stretched. —*adv.* **3.** securely. —*n.* **4. tights,** tight-fitting hose. —**tight'ly,** *adv.* —**tight'ness,** *n.* —**tight'en,** *v.t.*, *v.i.* —**tight'-fit''ting,** *adj.*

tight'-fist''ed, *adj.* stingy.

tight'rope'', *n.* taut rope for balancing acrobats.

tile, *n.*, *v.t.*, **tiled, tiling.** *n.* **1.** thin piece of material, originally baked earth. —*v.t.* **2.** furnish with tiles. —**til'ing,** *n.*

till, *prep.*, *conj.* **1.** until. —*v.t.* **2.** prepare for growing crops. —*n.* **3.** money drawer. —**till'age,** *n.*

til'ler, *n.* steering lever.

tilt, *v.t.*, *v.i.* **1.** slant from an upright position. —*n.* **2.** act or instance of tilting.

tim'ber, *n.* **1.** cut wood. **2.** trees collectively. —**tim'bered,** *adj.*

tim·bre (tam'bər), *n.* distinctive quality of sound.

time, *n.*, *v.t.*, **timed, timing.** *n.* **1.** past, present, and future. **2.** Often, **times,** period of occurrence. **3.** instance. —*prep.* **4. times,** multiplied by. —*v.t.* **5.** determine the time or duration of. —**tim'er,** *n.*

time'-hon''ored, *adj.* honored because of long duration or usage.

time'less, *adj.* eternal.

time'ly, *adj.*, **-lier, -liest.** coming at the right time. —**time'li·ness,** *n.*

tīme′piĕce′′, *n*. clock or watch.

tīme′sĕrv′′ĕr, *n*. exploiter of popular trends. —**time′serv′′ing**, *n., adj.*

tīme′tā′′ble, *n*. schedule of times.

tīme′wôrn′′, *adj*. worn or hackneyed by long use.

tĭm′ĭd, *adj*. lacking self-confidence. —**tim·id·ly**, *adv*. —**ti·mid′i·ty**, *n*.

tīm′ĭng, *n*. performance with regard to time.

tĭm′ŏr·oŭs, *adj*. fearful. —**tim′or·ous·ly**, *adv*.

tĭm′o·thȳ, *n*. grass used for hay.

tĭm′pá·nĭ, *n. pl.* kettledrums. —**tim′pa·nist**, *n*.

tĭn, *n., v.t.*, **tinned**, **tinning**. *n*. **1.** white metallic element. —*v.t.* **2.** plate with tin. —**tin′foil′′**, *n*. —**tin′smith′′**.

tĭnc′tûre, *n*. **1.** tinge. **2.** medicine in alcohol.

tĭn′dĕr, *n*. dry flammable material. —**tin′der·box′′**.

tīne, *n*. fork prong.

tĭnge, *n., v.t.*, **tinged**, **tingeing** or **tinging**. *n*. **1.** slight color or trace. —*v.t.* **2.** give a tinge to.

tĭn′gle, *v.i.*, **-gled**, **-gling**. feel a slight prickle.

tĭn′kĕr, *v.i.* work inexpertly.

tĭn′kle, *v.i.*, **-kled**, **-kling**, *n. v.i.* **1.** ring lightly. —*n*. **2.** light ringing sound.

tĭn′sĕl, *n*. metal foil.

tĭnt, *n*. **1.** light color or shade. —*v.t.* **2.** give a tint to.

tī′nȳ, *adj.*, **-nier**, **-niest**. very small.

tĭp, *n., v.*, **tipped**, **tipping**. *n*. **1.** outermost point. **2.** reward for a service. —*v.t., v.i.* **3.** overturn. —*v.t.* **4.** give a tip to. —**tip′per**, *n*.

tĭp′sȳ, *adj.*, **-sier**, **-siest**. intoxicated. —**tip′si·ly**, *adv*.

tĭp′tōe′′, *v.i.*, **-toed**, **-toing**. walk on the balls of the feet.

tĭp′tŏp′′, *adj*. **1.** highest. **2.** best.

tī′rāde, *n*. vehement speech.

tīre, *v.*, **tired**, **tiring**, *n. v.t.* **1.** make tired. —*v.i.* **2.** become tired. —*n*. **3.** wearing surface of a wheel.

tīred, *adj*. without strength because of exertion. —**tired′ly**, *adv*.

tīre′lĕss, *adj*. without becoming tired. —**tire′less·ly**, *adv*.

tīre′sŏme, *adj*. annoying; tedious. —**tire′some·ly**, *adv*. —**tire′some·ness**, *n*.

tĭs′sūe, *n*. **1.** thin cloth or paper. **2.** organic matter.

tī′tán, *n*. giant. —**ti·tan′ic**, *adj*.

tĭt′ĭl·lāte′′, *v.t.*, **-lated**, **-lating**. excite pleasantly. —**tit′′il·la′tion**, *n*.

tī′tle, *n., v.t.*, **-tled**, **-tling**. *n*. **1.** formal name. **2.** right of ownership. —*v.t.* **3.** give a title to. —**ti′tled**, *adj*.

tĭt′tĕr, *v.i., n*. giggle.

tĭt′tle, *n*. minute amount.

tĭt′u·lár, *adj*. **1.** having a title. **2.** in name only. —**tit′u·lar·ly**, *adv*.

tĭz′zȳ, *n., pl.* **-zies**. *Informal*. excited state.

to, *prep*. **1.** as far as. **2.** in the direction of. **3.** until; before. **4.** being supported or held by. **5.** along with. **6.** in compassion or equivalence with.

tōad, *n*. froglike animal.

tōad′stōol′′, *n*. inedible mushroom.

tōast, *n*. **1.** browned sliced bread. **2.** drink in honor of someone. —*v.t.* **3.** brown with heat. **4.** drink in honor of. —**toast′er**, *n*. —**toast′mas′′ter**, *n*.

to·băc′cō, *n., pl.* **-cos.** leaves prepared for smoking, chewing, etc. —**to·bac′co·nist**, *n*.

to·bŏg′gán, *n*. **1.** long, flat sled. —*v.i.* **2.** coast on such a sled.

to·dāy, *adv*. **1.** on the present day. —*n*. **2.** present day. **3.** modern times.

tŏd′dle, *n., v.i.*, **-dled**, **-dling**. *n*. **1.** unsteady walk. —*v.i.* **2.** walk in a toddle.

tŏd′dȳ, *n., pl.* **-dies.** hot alcoholic drink.

tōe, *n*. foot digit. —**toed**, *adj*. —**toe′nail′′**, *n*.

to·gĕth′ĕr, *adv*. one with another.

tŏil, *n., v.i.* labor. —**toil′er**, *n*. —**toil′some**, *adj*.

tŏi′lĕt, *n*. **1.** dress and grooming. **2.** place or fixture for excretion.

tŏil′ĕt·rȳ, *n., pl.* **-ries.** aid to grooming.

tŏils, *n. pl.* snare.

tō′kĕn, *n*. **1.** souvenir. **2.** indication. **3.** metal disk used in payment. —*adj*. **4.** intended as a gesture.

tŏl′ĕr·ánce, *n*. **1.** patience or understanding. **2.** permissible deviation. **3.** resistance to poison, etc. —**tol′er·ant**, *adj*.

tŏl′ĕr·āte′′, *v.t.*, **-ated**, **-ating**. **1.** be patient with. **2.** endure. —**tol′′er·a′tion**, *n.* —**tol′er·a·ble,** *adj.* —**tol′er·a·bly,** *adv.*

tōll, *n.* **1.** tariff. *v.t.,* *v.i.* **2.** ring solemnly. —**toll′gate′′,** *n.*

tŏm, *adj.* male.

tŏm′a·hāwk′, *n.* Native American ax.

to·mā′tō, *n., pl.* -**toes.** juicy red or yellow vegetable.

tomb, *n.* burial place. —**tomb′stone,′′** *n.*

tŏm′bŏy′′, *n.* boyish girl.

to·mŏr′rōw, *n., adv.* day after this.

tŏm′-tŏm′′, *n.* hand drum.

tŏn, *n.* U.S. unit of 2,000 pounds.

tōne, *n.* **1.** sound of a certain pitch. **2.** shade of color. **3.** air or appearance. —**ton′al,** *adj.* —**to·nal′i·ity,** *n.* —**tone′ deaf′′,** *adj.*

tŏngs, *n. pl.* pincers.

tŏngue, *n.* **1.** flexible licking and tasting organ in the mouth. **2.** language. **3.** projection.

tŏngue′-lăsh′′ĭng, *n.* severe scolding.

tŏngue′-tīed′′, *adj.* rendered speechless.

tŏn′ĭc, *n.* **1.** invigorating medicine. **2.** *Music.* keynote.

to′nĭght′, *n., adv.* this night.

tŏn′nage, *n.* shipping, esp. in terms of cargo capacity.

tŏn′sĭl, *n.* oval growth at the back of the throat. —**ton′′sil·li′tis,** *n.*

tŏn·sŏ′ri·al, *adj.* pertaining to barbering.

tōō, *adv.* **1.** also. **2.** excessively.

tōōl, *n.* **1.** object for shaping, fastening, etc. **2.** something or someone used. —*v.t.* **3.** shape with a tool.

tōōt, *v.i.* **1.** give a shrill whistle. —*n.* **2.** shrill whistle.

tōōth, *n., pl.* **teeth.** **1.** hard white growth used for biting. **2.** similar object in a gear, etc. —**tooth′ache′′,** *n.* —**tooth′ brush′′,** *n.* —**toothed,** *adj.* —**tooth′ less,** *adj.* —**tooth′pick′′,** *n.* —**tooth′y,** *adj.*

tōōth′sŏme, *adj.* tasty.

tŏp, *n., v.t.,* **topped, topping.** *n.* **1.** uppermost point or part. **2.** spinning toy. —*v.t.* **3.** put a top on. **4.** remove a top from. **5.** surpass.

to′p̄ăz, *n.* yellow gem.

tŏp′cōat′′, *n.* light overcoat.

tŏp′-drăw′ĕr, *adj. Informal.* first-rate. Also, **top′-flight′, top′-notch′.**

tŏp′-hēav′′y, *adj.* liable to tip.

tŏp′ĭc, *n.* subject of discussion. —**top′i· cal,** *adj.*

tŏp′mōst′′, *adj.* at the very top.

tŏp′nŏtch′, *adj. Informal.* among the best.

to·pŏg′ra·phy̆, *n., pl.* -**phies.** **1.** study of the earth's surface. **2.** terrain. —**top′′o· graph′i·cal, top′′o·graph′ic,** *adj.* —**to·pog′ra·pher,** *n.*

tŏp′ping, *n.* something put on top.

tŏp′ple, *v.,* -**pled,** -**pling.** *v.t., v.i.* overturn.

tŏp′sāil′′, *n. Nautical.* second sail up.

tŏp′sŏil′′, *n.* fertile surface soil.

tŏp′sy̆-tûr′vy̆, *adj., adv.* in disorder.

Tō′rah, *n.* Hebrew scriptures.

tŏrch, *n.* flame-bearing object. —**torch′ light′′,** *n., adj.*

tôr′ē·a·dôr′′, *n.* bullfighter.

tor′ment, *v.t.* (tor ment′) **1.** harass or torture. —*n.* (tor′ment) **2.** tormented state. **3.** something that torments. —**tor′men′ tor, tor·men′ter,** *n.*

tôr·nā′dō, *n., pl.* -**does,** -**dos.** violent whirlwind.

tor·pē′dō, *n., pl.* -**does,** *v.t.,* -**does,** -**doing.** *n.* **1.** explosive water projectile. —*v.t.* **2.** hit with a torpedo.

tôr′pĭd, *adj.* without energy. —**tor′pid· ly,** *adv.* —**tor′por, tor·pid′i·ty,** *n.*

tôrque, *n.* twisting force.

tôr′rent, *n.* rush of fluid. —**tor·ren′tial,** *adj.*

tôr′rĭd, *adj.* **1.** hot. **2. Torrid,** between the tropics on either side of the equator.

tôr′sion, *n.* twisting. —**tor′sion·al,** *adj.*

tôr′sō, *n., pl.* -**sos.** trunk of the human body.

tôrt, *n. Law.* basis of a civil suit.

tor′til·la (tôr tē′yà), *n.* flat Mexican cake of corn meal.

tôr′toĭse, *n.* land turtle.

tôr′tū·oŭs, *adj.* winding; involved. —**tor′ tu·ous·ly,** *adv.* —**tor′tu·ous·ness,** *n.*

tôr′tūre, *n., v.t.,* -**tured,** -**turing.** *n.* **1.** application of severe pain, etc. —*v.t.* **2.** subject to torture. —**tor′tur·er,** *n.*

tŏss, *v.t.* **1.** throw lightly. **2.** jerk upward. —*n.* **3.** act or instance of tossing.

tŏss′ŭp′′, *n.* even chance.

tŏt, *n.* small child.

to′tăl, *adj.* **1.** being a sum. **2.** complete.

—*n.* **3.** sum. —**to'tal·ly**, *adv.* —**to·tal'i·ty**, *n.*

tō"**tär'ism**, *n.* absolute control by one political group. —**to·tal"i·tar'i·an**, *n., adj.*

tōte, *v.t.*, **toted, toting.** carry.

to'tem, *n.* natural object used as a clan symbol. —**to·tem'ic**, *adj.*

tŏt'têr, *v.i.* walk unsteadily.

touch, *v.t.* **1.** tap, pat, or feel. **2.** move emotionally. —*n.* **3.** act or instance of touching. **4.** distinctive manner. **5.** slight amount. —**touch'ing**, *adj.* —**touch'ing·ly**, *adv.*

touch and gō, precarious situation.

touch'dŏwn, *n.* football score.

touched, *adj.* **1.** emotionally moved. **2.** insane.

touch'stōne", *n.* test of genuineness or worth.

touch'y, *adj.*, **-ier, -iest.** readily hurt or annoyed. —**touch'i·ness**, *n.*

tough, *adj.* **1.** resistant to injury. **2.** enduring. **3.** brutal. **4.** difficult. —**tough'ness**, *n.* —**tough'en**, *v.t., v.i.*

tou·pee (tōo pā'), *n.* small wig worn esp. by men.

toûr, *n.* **1.** trip with many stops. —*v.t.* **2.** make a tour through.

toûr de fôrce, *n., pl.* **tours de force.** example of high skill.

toûr'ĭst, *n.* person on a pleasure tour. —**tour'ism**, *n.*

toûr'nà·mênt, *n.* **1.** knightly contest. **2.** series of athletic contests.

toûr'nĭ·quêt, *n.* twisted device to stop bleeding.

tou'sle, *v.t.*, **-sled, -sling.** muss.

tŏut, *Informal. v.t.* **1.** praise highly. **2.** sell bets. —*n.* **3.** person who touts.

tōw, *v.t.* **1.** pull with a line. —*n.* **2.** act or instance of towing. —**tow'line**", **tow'rope**", *n.* —**tow'path**", *n.*

tō·wârd', *prep.* in the direction of. Also, **to·wards'.**

tŏw'ĕl, *n.* drying cloth.

tŏw'êr, *n.* **1.** tall construction. —*v.i.* **2.** stand high.

tŏw'êr·ing, *adj.* **1.** standing high. **2.** violent.

tŏwn, *n.* **1.** large community. **2.** urban center. —**towns'man**, *n.* —**towns'-peo"ple**, *n., pl.*

tŏwn'shĭp", *n.* unit of local government.

tŏx'ĭc, *adj.* poisonous. —**tox·ic'i·ty**, *n.*

tŏx"ĭ·cŏl'o·gy̆, *n.* study of poisons. —**tox"i·col'o·gist**, *n.*

tŏx'ĭn, *n.* poison from organisms.

tŏy̆, *n.* **1.** something to play with. —*v.i.* **2.** play; trifle.

trāce, *n., v.t.*, **traced, tracing.** *n.* **1.** faint sign or trail. —*v.t.* **2.** follow the trail of. **3.** copy by following the lines of. —**trace'a·ble**, *adj.* —**trac'er**, *n.* —**trac'ing**, *n.*

trăc'êr·y̆, *n., pl.* **-ies.** decorative frame in a window.

trăck, *n.* **1.** trail or trace. **2.** pair of rails, etc. used as a guide. —*v.t.* **3.** follow or trace. —**track'less**, *adj.*

trăct, *n.* **1.** expanse of land. **2.** series of bodily organs. **3.** religious leaflet.

trăc'ta·ble, *adj.* readily managed. —**trac'ta·bly**, *adv.* —**trac"ta·bil'i·ty**, *n.*

trăc'tion, *n.* **1.** pulling effort. **2.** friction between a foot or wheel and a surface.

trăc'tôr, *n.* pulling vehicle.

trāde, *v.*, **traded, trading**, *n. v.t.* **1.** exchange. —*v.i.* **2.** have business dealings. **3.** make an exchange. —*n.* **4.** buying and selling. **5.** skilled occupation. **6.** swap. —**trad'er**, *n.*

trāde'-ĭn", *n.* return of a used object in partial payment for a new one.

trāde'mârk", *n.* symbol of a business or product.

trāde'ôff", *n.* sacrifice of one advantage for another.

trādes'màn, *n.* **1.** skilled worker. **2.** merchant.

trāde wĭnd, tropical wind blowing toward the equator.

trà·dī'tion, *n.* long-accepted custom or belief. —**tra·di'tion·al**, *adj.* —**tra·di'tion·al·ly**, *adv.* —**tra·di'tion·al·ist**, *n., adj.*

trà·dūce', *v.t.*, **-duced, -ducing.** slander.

trăf'fĭc, *n., v.i.*, **-ficked, -ficking.** *n.* **1.** movement along roadways. **2.** commerce. —*v.i.* **3.** have dealings. —**traf'fick·er**, *n.*

trăg'e·dy̆, *n., pl.* **-ies.** **1.** drama ending unhappily. **2.** disastrous event. —**tra·ge'di·an**, *n., fem.*, **tra·ge'di·enne'.**

—**trag′ic, trag′i·cal**, *adj.* —**trag′i· cal·ly**, *adv.*

trail, *n.* **1.** mark left in passing. **2.** route, esp. in wild country. —*v.t.* **3.** trace. **4.** drag. —*v.i.* **5.** drag or grow along the ground.

trail′ér, *n.* vehicle pulled by another.

train, *n.* **1.** string of railroad cars. **2.** trailing skirt or cape. **3.** connected series. **4.** procession. —*v.t.* **5.** educate for a purpose. **6.** exercise for sports. —**train·ee′**, *n.* —**train′er**, *n.* —**train′ing**, *n.*

traipse, *v.i.* **traipsed, traipsing.** *Informal.* walk.

trait, *n.* distinctive quality.

trai′tor, *n.* betrayer. —**trai′tor·ous**, *adj.*

tra·jec′to·rÿ, *n., pl.* **-ries.** path of a missile.

tram, *n.* car on rails.

tram′mel, *n.* **1.** Usually **trammels**, hindrance or restraint. —*v.t.* **2.** hinder or restrain.

tramp, *v.i.* **1.** walk heavily. **2.** travel on foot. —*n.* **3.** vagrant. **4.** hike. **5.** unscheduled freighter.

tram′ple, *v.,* **-pled, -pling.** *v.i.* **1.** tread heavily. —*v.t.* **2.** crush under foot.

tram·po·line (tram′pə lēn′′), *n.* stretched horizontal sheet used by gymnasts.

trance, *n.* sleeplike or abstracted state.

tran′quil, *adj.* serene; relaxed. —**tran′ quil·ly**, *adv.* —**tran·quil′i·ty**, *n.* —**tran′quil·ize′′**, *v.t.* —**tran′quil·iz′′ er**, *n.*

trans·act′, *v.t.* complete, as a business deal. —**trans·ac′tion**, *n.* —**trans·ac′ tor**, *n.*

trans′′at·lăn′tĭc, *adj.* **1.** from across the Atlantic Ocean. **2.** across the Atlantic Ocean.

tran·scěnd′, *v.t.* **1.** go outside the limits of. **2.** surpass. —**tran·scend′ent**, *adj.*

tran′′scén·děn′tal, *adj.* beyond the limits of the apparent world. —**tran′′scen· den′tal·ism**, *n.* —**tran′′scen·den′tal· ist**, *n., adj.*

trans′′cŏn·tĭ·nĕn′tal, *adj.* across a continent.

tran·scrībe′, *v.t.,* **-scribed, -scribing.** copy elsewhere or in another medium.

tran′script, *n.* copy of a document.

tran·scrip′tion, *n.* **1.** transcript. **2.** ar-

rangement of a musical score. **3.** radio or television recording.

tran′sěpt, *n.* arm of a church crossing the nave.

trans′fěr′, *v.,* **-ferred, -ferring.** *n. v.t., v.i.* **1.** move to another place. —*n.* **2.** act or instance of transferring. **3.** authorization for transferring. —**trans·fer′a·ble**, *adj.* —**trans·fer′ence**, *n.*

trans·fĭg′ûre, *v.t.,* **-ured, -uring.** make glorious. —**trans·fig′′u·ra′tion**, *n.*

trans·fĭx′, *v.t.* **1.** pierce. **2.** halt in one's tracks.

trans·fôrm′, *v.t., v.i.* change in nature. —**trans′′for·ma′tion**, *n.* —**trans· form′er**, *n.*

trans·fūse′, *v.t.,* **-fused, -fusing. 1.** instill. **2.** admit to a blood vessel. —**trans· fu′sion**, *n.*

trans·grěss′, *v.t.* **1.** sin against. **2.** go beyond. —**trans·gres′sion**, *n.* —**trans· gres′sor**, *n.*

tran′sĭent, *adj.* **1.** temporary. —*n.* **2.** temporary lodger. —**tran′sient·ly**, *adv.* —**tran′science, tran′scien·cy**, *n.*

tran·sĭs′tor, *n.* device controlling electrical current flow. —**tran·sis′tor·ize′′**, *v.t.*

tran′sĭt, *n.* **1.** movement from place to place. **2.** public transportation.

tran·sĭ′tion, *n.* gradual change of nature or condition. —**tran·si′tion·al**, *adj.*

tran′sĭ·tĭve, *adj. Grammar.* taking a direct object.

tran′sĭ·tô′′rÿ, *adj.* impermanent. —**tran′si·to′′ri·ness**, *n.*

trans·lāte′, *v.t.,* **-lated, -lating. 1.** alter in language. **2.** alter in condition. —**trans· la′tion**, *n.* —**trans·la′tor**, *n.* —**trans· lat′a·ble**, *adj.*

trans·lĭt′ēr·āte′′, *v.t.,* **-ated, -ating.** put into a different alphabet, etc. —**trans· lit′′er·a′tion**, *n.*

trans·lū′cent, *adj.* passing light but not images. —**trans·lu′cence, trans·lu′ cen·cy**, *n.*

trans·mĭ′grāte, *v.i.,* **-grated, -grating.** enter a new body after death. —**trans′′ mi·gra′tion**, *n.*

trans·mĭs′sion, *n.* **1.** act or instance of transmitting. **2.** something transmitted. **3.** gear assembly.

trans·mĭt′, *v.t.,* **-mitted, -mitting. 1.** convey through a medium. **2.** send out in radio waves. **3.** hand down, as to a new generation. —**trans·mit'tal, trans·mit'tance,** *n.* —**trans·mit'ti·ble, trans·mit'ta·ble,** *adj.* —**trans·mit'ter,** *n.*

trăns·mūte', *v.t.,* **-muted, -muting.** alter in nature. —**trans''mu·ta'tion,** *n.* —**trans·mut'a·ble,** *adj.*

trăns''ō·cē·ăn'ĭc, *adj.* across the ocean.

trăn'sŏm, *n.* **1.** crosspiece. **2.** window over a door.

trăns''pȧ·cĭf'ĭc, *adj.* **1.** from across the Pacific Ocean. **2.** across the Pacific Ocean.

trăns·pār'ĕnt, *adj.* **1.** passing light and images. **2.** obvious. —**trans·par'ent·ly,** *adv.* —**trans·par'en·cy,** *n.*

trăn·spīre', *v.i.,* **-spired, -spiring. 1.** become known. **2.** *Informal.* occur. —**tran''spi·ra'tion,** *n.*

trăns·plănt', *v.t.* **1.** plant in a new place. **2.** graft surgically. —*n.* **3.** act or instance of transplanting. —**trans''plan·ta'tion,** *n.*

trăns·pôrt', *v.t.* **1.** carry. —*n.* (trans'port) **2.** transportation. **3.** state of rapture. **4.** carrier for troops. —**trans''por·ta'tion,** *n.*

trăns·pōse', *v.,* **-posed, -posing.** *v.t., v.i.* change in order or position. —**trans''po·si'tion,** *n.*

trăns·sĕx'ū·ȧl, *n.* person who identifies with or undergoes surgery to become the opposite sex.

trăns·shĭp', *v.t.,* **-shipped, -shipping.** put on a new conveyance. —**trans·ship'ment,** *n.*

trăns·vêrse', *adj.* crosswise. —**trans·verse'ly,** *adv.*

trăns·vĕs'tīte, *n.* dresser in clothes of the opposite sex.

trăp, *n., v.t.,* **trapped, trapping.** *n.* **1.** device for catching animals. **2.** trick for detection or capture. —*v.t.* **3.** catch. **4.** adorn. —**trap'per,** *n.* —**trap'pings,** *n. pl.*

trăp'dôor'', *n.* horizontal door.

trȧ·pēze', *n.* swing with a bar.

trăp'e·zoĭd'', *n.* four-sided figure with two parallel sides. —**trap''e·zoi'dal,** *adj.*

trăsh, *n.* discarded matter. —**trash'y,** *adj.*

traū'mȧ, *n., pl.* **-mas, -mata.** bodily or emotional shock. —**trau·mat'ic,** *adj.* —**trau'ma·tize'',** *v.t.*

trȧ·vāil', *n.* agony.

trăv'ĕl, *v.i.,* **-eled** or **-elled, -eling** or **-elling,** *n. v.i.* **1.** go on a journey. —*n.* **2.** traveling, esp. for pleasure. —**trav'el·er, trav'el·ler,** *n.*

trăv·êrse', *v.t.,* **-ersed, -ersing.** pass across.

trăv'ĕs·tȳ, *n., pl.* **-ties,** *v.t.,* **-tied, -tying.** *n.* **1.** mocking imitation. —*v.t.* **2.** make a travesty of.

trāwl, *n.* **1.** dragged fish net. —*v.i.* **2.** use a trawl. —**trawl'er,** *n.*

trāy, *n.* shallow, broad receptacle.

trĕach'êr·ȳ, *n., pl.* **-ies.** betrayal of trust. —**treach'er·ous,** *adj.*

trĕad, *v.,* **trod, trodden, treading.** *v.i.* **1.** walk deliberately. —*v.t.* **2.** press, make, etc. by treading. —*n.* **3.** manner of treading. **4.** step. **5.** surface of a wheel, tire, etc. that touches the ground.

trĕa'dle, *n.* foot-operated lever.

trĕa'sŏn, *n.* betrayal of one's country. —**trea'son·a·ble, trea'son·ous,** *adj.*

trĕas'ūre, *n., v.t.,* **-ured, -uring.** *n.* **1.** precious possession. —*v.t.* **2.** regard as a treasure.

trĕas'ūr·êr, *n.* handler of funds.

trĕas'ūre-trōve'', *n.* discovered treasure.

trĕas'ūr·ȳ, *n., pl.* **-ies.** department or place for storing money.

trēat, *v.t.* **1.** act toward as specified. **2.** handle as specified. **3.** give medical care to. **4.** have as a guest. —*n.* **5.** something offered a guest. **6.** source of pleasure. —**treat'ment,** *n.*

trēa'tīse, *n.* paper on a subject.

trēa'tȳ, *n., pl.* **-ties.** agreement between nations.

trĕ'ble, *adj., v.t.,* **-bled, -bling.** *adj.* **1.** triple. **2.** high-pitched. —*v.t.* **3.** multiply by three. —**treb'ly,** *adv.*

trēe, *n., v.t.,* **treed, treeing.** *n.* **1.** tall plant with a woody stem and branches. —*v.t.* **2.** chase up a tree. —**tree'less,** *adj.*

trĕk, *v.i.,* **trekked, trekking,** *n. v.i.* **1.** travel with difficulty. —*n.* **2.** long, difficult journey.

trĕl'lĭs, *n.* frame for climbing plants.

trĕm′ble, *v.i.,* **-bled, -bling. 1.** shiver. **2.** be in fear or awe.

tré·mĕn′doŭs, *adj.* huge. **—tre·men′dous·ly,** *adv.*

trĕm′ó·lō′′, *n., pl.* **-os.** wavering of a musical tone.

trĕm′ór, *n.* quiver.

trĕm′ū·loŭs, *adj.* timid.

trĕnch, *n.* deep, narrow ditch.

trĕnch′ánt, *adj.* incisive.

trĕnd, *n.* current style or tendency.

trĕp′′ĭ·dā′tion, *n.* fear and doubt.

trĕs′păss, *v.i.* **1.** enter property without right. **—***n.* **2.** sin. **—tres′pas·ser,** *n.*

trĕss, *n.* lock of hair.

trĕs′tle, *n.* **1.** transverse frame. **2.** viaduct on framed towers.

trī′ăd, *n.* group of three.

trī′ál, *n.* **1.** test, as for value. **2.** annoyance or source of annoyance. **3.** examination in a law court.

trī′ăn·gle, *n.* three-sided figure. **—tri·an′gu·lar,** *adj.*

tribe, *n.* group of related persons under one leader. **—trib′al,** *adj.* **—tribes′man,** *n.*

trĭb′′ū·lā′tion, *n.* distress.

trī·bū′nál, *n.* court of justice.

trĭb′ūne, *n.* speaking platform.

trĭb′ū·tăr′′ÿ, *adj., n., pl.* **-ies.** *adj.* **1.** paying tribute. **2.** flowing into a larger stream. **—***n.* **3.** tributary stream or river.

trĭb′ūte, *n.* **1.** compulsory payment. **2.** expression of gratitude or honor.

trice, *n.* instant.

trick, *n.* **1.** cunning or treacherous act. **—***v.t.* **2.** cheat. **—trick′er·y,** *n.* **—trick′ster,** *n.*

trick′le, *v.i.,* **-led, -ling.** flow in a thin, slow stream.

trĭck′ÿ, *adj.,* **-ier, -iest. 1.** treacherous; wily. **2.** challenging the skill or cunning.

trī′cÿ·cle, *n.* three-wheeled vehicle.

trī′dĕnt, *n.* three-pronged spear.

tried, *adj.* proved, esp. as trustworthy.

trī′fle, *n., v.i.,* **-fled, -fling.** *n.* **1.** something of little importance. **—***v.i.* **2.** talk or act frivolously. **—tri′fler,** *n.*

trī′flĭng, *adj.* unimportant; insignificant.

trī′fō′′cáls, *n.* spectacles with three focuses.

trĭg′gĕr, *n.* **1.** lever for firing a gun. **—***v.t.* **2.** precipitate; cause to happen.

trĭg′′ó·nŏm′é·trÿ, *n.* mathematics based on the triangle. **—trig′′o·no·met′ric,** *adj.*

trĭll, *n.* **1.** high, warbling sound. **—***v.i.* **2.** emit a trill.

trĭl′lión, *n.* one thousand billion.

trĭl′ó·gÿ, *n., pl.* **-gies.** trio of related novels, etc.

trĭm, *v.t.,* **trimmed, trimming,** *n., adj.,* **trimmer, trimmest.** *v.t.* **1.** make neat. **2.** decorate. **3.** balance. **—***n.* **4.** good condition. **—***adj.* **5.** neat. **—trim′ly,** *adv.* **—trim′mer,** *n.*

trī·mĕs′têr, *n.* three months.

trĭm′mĭng, *n.* something added, as a decoration.

trĭn′ĭ·tÿ, *n., pl.* **-ties. 1.** set of three. **2. the Trinity,** God as Father, Son, and Holy Spirit.

trĭn′kĕt, *n.* small ornament.

trĭ·o (trē′ō), *n., pl.* **-os.** group of three.

trĭp, *v.,* **tripped, tripping,** *n. v.i.* **1.** stumble and lose balance. **—***v.t.* **2.** cause to stumble. **3.** set in motion. **—***n.* **4.** act or instance of tripping. **5.** journey.

trī·pär′tīte, *adj.* in three parts.

tripe, *n.* **1.** edible part of an animal stomach. **2.** *Informal.* drivel.

trĭp′hăm′′mêr, *n.* heavy mechanical hammer.

trī′ple, *adj., v.,* **-pled, -pling.** *adj.* **1.** in three parts. **2.** three times normal size. **—***v.t., v.i.* **3.** multiply three times. **—tri′ply,** *adv.*

trĭp′lĕt, *n.* one of three siblings born at the same time.

trĭp′lĭ·căte, *n.* threefold form.

trī′pŏd, *n.* three-legged support.

trī·sĕct′, *v.t.* divide in three. **—tri·sec′tion,** *n.*

trīte, *adj.,* **triter, tritest.** overly familiar. **—trite′ly,** *adv.* **—trite′ness,** *n.*

trī′ŭmph, *n.* **1.** victory. **2.** delight in victory. **—***v.i.* **3.** be victorious. **—tri·um′phal,** *adj.* **—tri·um′phant,** *adj.*

trī·ŭm′vĭ·rāte, *n.* trio in power.

trĭv′ĕt, *n.* stand for hot things.

trĭv′ĭ·à, *n., pl.* trivial things.

trĭv′ĭ·ál, *adj.* petty and unimportant. **—triv′′i·al′i·ty,** *n.* **—triv′i·al·ly,** *adv.*

trŏll, *n.* supernatural cave dweller.

trŏl′lĕy, *n., pl.* **-leys. 1.** raised structure for collecting electricity. **2.** streetcar with such a structure. 3. wheeled container.

trŏm·bŏne′, brass musical instrument. —**trom·bon′ist**, *n.*

trŏŏp, *n.* 1. uniformed group. —*v.i.* 2. move in a group. —**troop′er**, *n.*

trŏ′phў, *n., pl.* **-phies.** memento of victory.

trŏp′ĭc, *n.* 1. boundary of the Torrid Zone. 2. **tropics**, Torrid Zone or nearby areas. —*adj.* 3. Also, **trop′i·cal**, pertaining to the Torrid Zone.

trŏ′pĭsm, *n. Biology.* response, as in growth, to stimuli.

trŏt, *v.i.*, **trotted, trotting**, *n. v.i.* 1. run at moderate speed. —*n.* 2. trotting gait. —**trot′ter**, *n.*

troŭ′bà·dôur′′, *n.* medieval singer.

troŭ′ble, *n., v.,* **-bled, -bling.** *n.* 1. worry or exertion. 2. source of these. —*v.t.* 3. cause trouble to. —*v.i.* 4. go to trouble. —**trou′ble·some**, *adj.* —**trou′ble·mak′′er**, *n.*

trŏugh, *n.* long, open container.

troŭnce, *v.t.*, **trounced, trouncing.** beat.

troŭpe, *n.* group of performers. —**troup′er**, *n.*

troŭ′sêrs, *n. pl.* pants.

troŭs′seau, *n., pl.* **-seaux, -seaus.** bride's clothing, etc.

trŏut, *n., pl.* **trout, trouts.** edible freshwater fish.

trŏw′ĕl, *n.* spreading or scooping hand tool.

trŏў, *adj.* pertaining to a jeweler's weight with a twelve-ounce pound.

trū′ànt, *n.* unauthorized absentee from school. —**tru′an·cy**, *n.*

trūce, *n.* temporary suspension of hostilities.

trŭck, *n.* 1. freight motor vehicle. 2. hand cart for loads. —*v.t.* 3. carry by truck. —**truck′er**, *n.*

trŭck′le, *v.i.*, **-led, -ling.** be servilely submissive.

trŭc′ū·lĕnt, *adj.* fierce. —**truc′u·lent·ly**, *adv.* —**truc′u·lence**, *n.*

trŭdge, *v.i.*, **trudged, trudging**, *n. v.i.* 1. walk laboriously. —*n.* 2. laborious walk.

trūe, *adj.*, **truer, truest.** 1. according with truth. 2. faithful. —**tru′ly**, *adv.* —**true′ness**, *n.*

trū′ĭsm, *n.* tritely true statement.

trŭmp, *n.* highest-ranking card.

trŭmp′ĕr·ў, *n., pl.* **-ies.** worthlessly pretentious things.

trŭm′pĕt, *n.* brass musical wind instrument. —**trum′pet·er**, *n.*

trŭn′cāte, *v.t.*, **-cated, -cating.** remove part of. —**trun′ca′tion**, *n.*

trŭn′cheŏn, *n.* club.

trŭn′dle, *v.t.*, **-dled, -dling.** roll out or along.

trŭnk, *n.* 1. large piece of luggage. 2. main stem of a tree. 3. body apart from head and limbs.

trŭss, *n.* 1. frame of triangular parts. 2. support for the ruptured. —*v.t.* 3. bind up. 4. support with a truss.

trŭst, *n.* 1. reliance; faith. 2. custody. 3. monopolistic combination. —*v.t.* 4. have reliance or faith in. —**trust′ful**, **trust′ing**, *adj.* —**trust′worth′′y**, **trust′y**, *adj.*

trŭst·ēe′, *n.* person to whom property is entrusted. —**trus·tee′ship**, *n.*

trŭst′ў, *adj.*, **-ier, -iest.** trustworthy.

trŭth, *n.* 1. that which is actually so. 2. accuracy. —**truth′ful**, *adj.* —**truth′ful·ly**, *adv.* —**truth′ful·ness**, *n.*

trў, *v.t.*, **tried, trying**, *n. v.t.* 1. attempt. 2. test. 3. examine in a court of law. 4. annoy or afflict. —*n.* 5. attempt or test. —**try′ing**, *adj.*

trў′ŏut′′, *n. Informal.* test operation.

trўst, *n.* lovers' appointment.

tsâr, *n.* Slavic emperor, variant of czar.

tŭb, *n.* broad, deep vessel.

tū′bà, *n.* large brass wind musical instrument.

tŭb′bў, *adj.*, **-bier, -biest.** chubby.

tūbe, *n.* hollow cylinder. —**tub′ing**, *n.* —**tub′u·lar**, *adj.*

tū′bêr, *n.* swelling part of an underground plant stem. —**tu′ber·ous**, *adj.*

tū·bêr′′cū·lō′sĭs, *n.* illness with swelling lesions. —**tu·ber′cu·lar**, **tu·ber′cu·lous**, *adj.*

Tūes′dāў, *n.* third day of the week.

tŭft, *n.* cluster of fibers, threads, etc.

tŭg, *v.t.*, **tugged, tugging**, *n. v.t.* 1. pull forcefully. —*n.* 2. act or instance of tugging. —**tug′boat′′**, *n.*

tū·ĭ′tion, *n.* fee for teaching.

tū′lĭp, *n.* plant with a cup-shaped flower.

tŭm′ble, *v.i.,* **-bled, -bling. 1.** fall or roll helplessly. **2.** perform acrobatics on a flat surface.

tŭm′blêr, *n.* **1.** drinking glass. **2.** acrobat who tumbles.

tū′mĭd, *adj.* swollen.

tŭm′mў, *n., pl.* **-mies.** *Informal.* stomach.

tū′mŏr, *n.* abnormal growth.

tū′mŭlt, *n.* commotion. **—tu·mul′tu·ous,** *adj.*

tŭn, *n.* large cask.

tū′ná, *n., pl.* **-na, nas.** large ocean fish.

tŭn′drá, *n.* barren Arctic plain.

tūne, *n., v.t.,* **-tuned, tuning.** *n.* **1.** melody. **2.** harmony. **—v.t. 3.** put in tune. **—tune′ful,** *adj.* **—tune′less,** *adj.*

tūn′ĭc, *adj.* jacket, often belted.

tŭn′nĕl, *n., v.i.,* **-neled, -neling.** *n.* **1.** route cut underground. **—v.i. 2.** dig a route.

tûr′bàn, *n.* headdress of wound cloth.

tûr′bĭd, *adj.* cloudy or muddy. **—tur·bid′i·ty,** *n.*

tûr′bīne, *n.* rotary engine driven by the passing of a fluid.

tûr′bō·jĕt′′, *n.* jet engine using turbine-compressed air.

tûr′bū·lĕnt, *adj.* in disturbed motion. **—tur′bu·lence,** *n.*

tū·rēen′, *n.* covered soup container.

tûrf, *n.* earth held by grass roots. **—turf′y,** *adj.*

tûr′gĭd, *adj.* pompously or excessively worded. **—tur′gid·ly,** *adv.* **—tur·gid′i·ty, tur·gid′ness,** *n.*

tûr′kĕy, *n.* large North American fowl.

tûr′mŏĭl, *n.* confused activity.

tûrn, *v.t., v.i.* **1.** change in direction. **2.** change in nature. **—n. 3.** curve. **4.** loop. **5.** place in a sequence. **6.** act toward another. **—turn′ing,** *n.*

tûrn′á·bŏut′′, *n.* reversal of conditions.

tûrn′cŏat′′, *n.* renegade.

tûr′nĭp, *n.* edible root.

tûrn′ŏut′′, *n.* attendance at a meeting.

tûrn′ō′′vêr, *n.* **1.** rate of sale, replacement, etc. **2.** baked dish of crust folded over filling.

tûrn′pīke′′, *n.* toll road.

tûrn′stīle′′, *n.* rotating gate.

tûrn′tā′′ble, *n.* rotating platform.

tûr′pén·tīne′′, *n.* oil from coniferous trees.

tûr′pĭ·tūde′′, *n.* vileness.

tûr′quoĭse, *n.* greenish-blue stone.

tûr′rĕt, *n.* **1.** small tower. **2.** housing for cannon.

tûr′tle, *n.* shell-encased reptile.

tŭsk, *n.* long, projected tooth.

tŭs′sle, *n., v.i.,* **-sled, -sling.** struggle.

tū′tê·làge, *n.* **1.** guardianship. **2.** education. **—tu′te·lar, tu′te·lar′′y,** *adj.*

tū′tŏr, *n.* **1.** private teacher. **—v.t. 2.** teach privately. **—tu·to′ri·al,** *adj., n.*

tŭx·ē′dō, *n.* semiformal evening suit.

TV, television.

twăng, *n.* **1.** sound of a plucked string. **2.** nasal accent.

twēak, *v.t., n.* pinch with a twist.

twēed, *n.* rough woolen cloth.

twēet, *n., v.i.* chirp.

twēez′êrs, *n. pl.* small pincers.

twĕlve, *n., adj.* ten plus two. **—twelfth,** *adj., n.*

twĕn′tў, *adj., n.* two times ten. **—twen′ti·eth,** *adj.*

twīce, *adv.* two times.

twĭd′dle, *v.t.,* **-dled, -dling.** play with absently.

twĭg, *n.* tiny plant branch.

twī′līght′′, *n.* half-light, as between day and night.

twĭll, *n.* cloth with a diagonal pattern.

twĭn, *n.* **1.** one of two siblings born at the same time. **2.** exact match. **—adj. 3.** matching another or each other exactly.

twīne, *n., v.,* **twined, twining.** *n.* **1.** string. **—v.t., v.i. 2.** twist together.

twĭnge, *n.* stab of pain.

twĭn′kle, *v.i.,* **-kled, -kling,** *n. v.i.* **1.** gleam intermittently. **2.** show amusement. **—n. 3.** act or instance of twinkling.

twĭn′klĭng, *n.* instant.

twîrl, *v.t., v.i.* rotate rapidly.

twĭst, *v.t.* **1.** wind around, rotate, or bend into a helical form. **2.** distort the actuality of. **—v.i. 3.** assume a twisted form. **4.** squirm. **—n. 5.** act or instance of twisting.

twĭt, *v.t.,* **twitted, twitting.** address teasingly.

twĭtch, *v.i.* **1.** jerk spasmodically. **2.** pluck. **—n. 3.** spasmodic jerk.

twĭt′tĕr, *v.i.* chirp rapidly.

two, *n., adj.* one plus one. **—two′fold′′,** *adj., adv.* **—two′some,** *n.*

two′-ĕdged′, *adj.* interpretable two ways.

tȳ·cōon′, *n.* man of great wealth and power.

tȳpe, *n., v.t.,* **typed, typing.** *n.* **1.** variety; sort. **2.** reproducible characters used in printing. **—v.t. 3.** classify. **4.** produce with a typewriter.

tȳpe′wrīt′ẽr, *n.* machine for producing letters by mechanical means.

tȳ′phoĭd, *n.* acute infectious disease.

tȳ·phoon′, *n.* violent storm of the west Pacific Ocean.

tȳ′phŭs, *n.* acute infectious disease.

tȳp′ĭ·cǎl, *n.* **1.** representative of a type. **2.** customary. **—typ′i·cal·ly,** *adv.*

tȳp′ĭ·fy′′, *v.t.,* **-fied, -fying.** be typical of.

tȳp′ĭst, *n.* user of typewriters.

tȳ·pŏg′rȧ·phȳ, *n.* art of composing and printing with type. **—ty′′po·graph′ic,** *adj.* **—ty·pog′ra·pher,** *n.*

tȳ′rȧnt, *n.* harsh, arbitrary ruler. **—tyr′an·ny,** *n.* **—ty·ran′ni·cal,** *adj.* **—tyr′an·nīze′′,** *v.i., v.t.*

tȳ′rō, *n., pl.* **-ros.** beginner; novice.

U

U, u, *n.* twenty-first letter of the English alphabet.

ū·bĭq′uī·tȳ, *n.* presence everywhere simultaneously. **—u·biq′ui·tous,** *adj.*

ŭd′dẽr, *n.* mammary gland of a cow.

ŭg′lȳ, *adj.,* **-lier, -liest. 1.** unattractive. **2.** discomforting; difficult. **—ug′li·ness,** *n.*

ū·kāse′, *n.* arbitrary command.

ŭl′cẽr, *n.* open break in tissue. **—ul′cer·ous,** *adj.* **—ul′cer·āte′′,** *v.i., v.t.*

ŭl′nȧ, *n.* large bone of the forearm. **—ul′nar,** *adj.*

ŭl·tē′rĭ·ŏr, *adj.* **1.** further; beyond. **2.** concealed; disguised.

ŭl′tĭ·mȧte, *adj.* **1.** final; conclusive. **2.** fundamental; basic. **—ul′ti·mate·ly,** *adv.*

ŭl′′tĭ·mā′tŭm, *n., pl.* **-matums, -mata.** final, decisive demand.

ŭl′tĭ·mō, *adj.* of or occurring in the preceding month.

ŭl′trȧ·līght, *n.* miniature aircraft for solo, powered flight.

ŭl′′trȧ·mȧ·rīne′, *adj.* deep blue.

ŭl′′trȧ·vī′ō·lĕt, *adj.* beyond the visible spectrum at its violet end.

ŭm′bĕl, *n.* cluster of flowers with the stalks having a common center.

ŭm′bẽr, *n.* reddish brown.

ŭm·bĭl′ĭ·cŭs, *n.* navel. **—um·bil′i·cal,** *adj.*

ŭm′brȧge, *n.* resentment; pique.

ŭm·brĕl′lȧ, *n.* collapsible device with a fabric-covered frame, carried for protection against the weather.

ŭm′pīre, *n., v.t.,* **-pired, -piring.** *n.* **1.** final authority; judge. **—v.t. 2.** to serve as umpire for.

ŭn-, prefix indicating "not." **unable, unassuming, unavoidable, unaware, unbalanced, unbend, unborn, unbridled, uncertain, uncivil, unclean, unclothe, uncommon, unconcern, unconscious, uncork, undeniable, undeclared, undress, undue, unduly, uneasy, unequal, unerring, unexpected, unfailing, unfaithful, unfasten, unfit, unfold, unfortunate, unfriendly, ungodly, unhinge, unholy, unlike, unlock, unnatural, unpack, unroll, unscrew, unsettle, unshackle, unsightly, untangle, untouchable, untrue, untruth, untypical, unusual, unveil, unwell, unwind, unwise, unyoke.**

ū′′năn′ĭ·moŭs, *adj.* totally agreed. **—u·na·nim′i·ty,** *n.* **—u′′nan′i·mous·ly,** *adv.*

ŭn′′ȧ·wāres′, *adv.* not aware.

ŭn·bó′sŏm, *v.t.* disclose; reveal.

ŭn·cälled′-fōr′′, *adj.* unwarranted; unneeded.

ŭn·căn′nȳ, *adj.* unnatural; eerie.

ŭn′cle, *n.* brother of one's mother or father, or husband of one's aunt.

Ŭncle Săm, the United States.

ŭn·cŏn′scion·ȧ·ble, *adj.* excessive; unreasonable. **—un·con′scion·a·bly,** *adv.*

ŭn·coŭth′, *adj.* lacking grace; clumsy.

ŭnc′tion, *n.* consecration with oil.

ŭnc′tū·oŭs, *adj.* 1. oily. 2. unpleasantly suave.

ŭn′dẽr, *prep., adj., adv.* 1. below; beneath. 2. less than. —*adj.* 3. lower.

ŭn′dẽr·brŭsh′′, *n.* low-growing forest shrubs and grass.

ŭn′dẽr·cŏv′′ẽr, *adj.* disguised; secret.

ŭn′dẽr·cŭt′′, *v.t.,* -cut, -cutting. offer at a lower price than.

ŭn′dẽr·dŏg′′, *n.* predicted loser.

ŭn′′dẽr·ĕs′tĭ·māte′, *v.t.,* -ated, -ating. value or estimate too low.

ŭn′′dẽr·gō′, *v.t.* -went, -gone, -going. endure; experience.

ŭn·dẽr·grăd′ū·āte, *n.* college student working toward a bachelor's degree.

ŭn′dẽr·groŭnd′′, *adj.* 1. below the ground. 2. secret; confidential. —*adv.* 3. below the ground. —*n.* 4. secret army of resistance.

ŭn′dẽr·hănd′′, *adj.* secret; sly. Also, ŭn′der·hand′′ed.

ŭn′dẽr·mīne′, *v.t.* -mined, -mining. weaken; sabotage.

ŭn·dẽr·nēath′, *prep., adv.* beneath.

ŭn·dẽr·stănd′, *v.t., v.i.* -stood, -standing. *v.t.* 1. comprehend; take the meaning of. —*v.i.* 2. sympathize. —ŭn′dẽr·stand′ing, *n., adj.*

ŭn·dẽr·stood′, *adj.* assumed; agreed upon.

ŭn′dẽr·stŭd·ÿ, *n., pl.* -dies. performer on call for emergencies.

ŭn·dẽr·tāke′, *v.t., v.i.* -took, -taken. 1. set about; enter upon. 2. accept as an obligation.

ŭn′dẽr·tāk′′ẽr, *n.* director of funerals.

ŭn′dẽr·world′′, *n.* world of criminals.

ŭn′dẽr·wrīte′′, *v.t.* -wrote, -written, -writing. accept, as an expense or liability. —ŭn′der·writ′′er, *n.*

ŭn′′do′, *v.t.* -did, -done, -doing. 1. unfasten. 2. nullify. 3. ruin.

ŭn′′dū·lāte′′, *v.i., v.i.* -lated, -lating. 1. move or form in waves. 2. fluctuate in pitch and cadence. —ŭn′′du·la′tion, *n.*

ŭn·earth′, *v.t.* discover; reveal.

ŭn′guĕnt, *n.* ointment; salve.

u·ni·corn (yōō′ ni korn), *n.* mythical horselike animal with a single horn.

ū′nĭ·fŏrm′′, *adj.* 1. alike; similar. *n.* 2.

distinctive or stylized dress for a particular group. —*v.t.* 3. clothe with a uniform. —ū·nĭ·fŏrm′ĭ·ty, *n.*

ū′′nĭ·fÿ′′, *v.t.* -fied, -fying. make into a whole; unite. —ū′′ni·fi·ca′tion, *n.*

ū·nĭ·lăt′ẽr·ăl, *adj.* one-sided.

ŭn′iŏn, *n.* 1. act or instance of uniting. 2. labor group organized for mutual aid. —ŭn′ion·īze′′, *v.t., v.i.*

Ūn′ion Jăck, British flag.

ū′nīque′, *adj.* 1. single; only. 2. rare; unusual. —ū·nīque′ly, *adv.*

ū′nĭ·sŏn′′, *n.* agreement; harmony.

ū′nĭt, *n.* single amount, item, etc.

ū·nīte′, *v.t., v.i.* -nited, -niting. join into one group or entity.

ū′nĭ·tÿ, *n.* 1. state of being united; oneness. 2. agreement.

ū′′nĭ·vẽr′săl, *adj.* including all. —ū′′nĭ·ver·sal′ĭ·ty, *n.*

ū′nĭ·vẽrse′′, *n.* entirety of physical creation.

ū′′nĭ·vẽr′sĭ·tÿ, *n., pl.* -ties. large institution of higher learning.

ŭn·kĕmpt′, *adj.* untidy; shabby; messy.

ŭn·lĕss′, *conj., prep.* if not; except.

ŭn·răv′ĕl, *v.t.* 1. disentangle; undo. 2. solve.

ŭn·rĕst′, *n.* 1. uneasy state. 2. discontent.

ŭn·rū′lÿ, *adj.* undisciplined; rebellious. —ŭn·rul′i·ness, *n.*

ŭn·tīe′, *v.t., v.i.* -tied, -tying. loosen or undo.

ŭn·tĭl′, *conj., prep.* 1. up to the time when. 2. before.

ŭn′to, *prep. Archaic.* to.

ŭn·tōld′, *adj.* vast; incalculable.

ŭn·tō·ward′, *adj.* 1. improper. 2. adverse.

ŭn·wĭeld′ÿ, *adj.* awkward; bulky.

ŭn·wĭt′tĭng, *adj.* unintentional; inadvertent. —ŭn·wit′ting·ly, *adv.*

ŭn·wŏnt′′ĕd, *adj.* not usual; uncharacteristic.

ŭp, *adv., adj., prep., v.t.,* -ped, -ping. *adv.* 1. to a higher level or location. 2. straight; erectly. 3. at bat. 4. awake; out of bed. 5. (computers) operating. —*prep.* 6. to a higher level or place in or on. —*v.t.* 7. increase.

ŭp·brăid′, *v.t.* scold; chide.

ŭp·hēav′ăl, *n.* turmoil; unrest; agitation.

ŭp·hŏld′, *v.t.* -held, -holding. support; advocate.

ŭp·hŏl'stêr, *v.t.* furnish with padding and fabric covering. **—up·hol'ster·er**, *n.*

ŭp'kēep', *n.* maintenance; support.

ŭp·lĭft', *v.t.* **1.** elevate; exalt. *—n.* **2.** edification.

ŭp·ŏn', *prep.* on; onto.

ŭp'pêr, *adj.* higher. **—up'per·most''**, *adj.*

ŭp'rĭs''ĭng, *n.* rebellion; revolt.

ŭp'rōar'', *n.* tumult; din.

ŭp·rōot'', *v.t.* **1.** to pull up by the roots. **2.** displace from a home or homeland.

ŭp·sĕt', *v.*, **-set, -setting**, *adj.*, *n. v.t.* (up set') **1.** overturn. **2.** defeat. **3.** put in confusion or distress. *—v.i.* **4.** be overturned. *—adj.* **5.** distressed in mind. *—n.* (up'set'') **6.** act or instance of upsetting.

ŭp'shŏt', *n.* final result.

ŭp''stāirs', *adj.* **1.** situated on an upper floor. *—adv.* **2.** to or on an upper floor. *—n.* **3.** floor above a ground floor.

ŭp'stärt'', *n.* person of recent power or wealth.

ŭp'-tò-dāte', *adj.* latest; modern; current.

ŭp'wård, *adv.* **1.** Also, **up'wards**, to a higher level or place. *—adj.* **2.** toward a higher level or place.

ū·rā'nĭ·ŭm, *n.* radioactive metallic element used as a source for atomic energy.

ûr'bån, *adj.* pertaining to cities.

ûr·bāne', *adj.* sophisticated; polite. **—ur·ban'i·ty**, *n.*

ûr'chĭn, *n.* unkempt child; ragamuffin.

ûrge, *v.t.*, **urged, urging**, *n. v.t.* **1.** advocate. **2.** implore. *—n.* **3.** impulse; desire; longing.

ûr'gĕnt, *adj.* pressing; vital; crucial. **—ur'gen·cy**, *n.* **—ur'gent·ly**, *adv.*

ū'rĭ'nāte', *v.i.* **-nated, -nating.** pass urine. **—u''ri'na'tion**, *n.*

ū'rĭne, *n.* fluid waste from kidneys.

ûrn, *n.* vase.

ŭs, *pron.* objective case of we.

ūs'åge, *n.* **1.** custom. **2.** treatment; handling.

use, *v.t.*, **used, using**, *n. v.t.* (yōōz) **1.** employ or engage for a purpose. **2.** expend; consume. **3.** behave toward; treat. **4.** do regularly. **5.** accustom; habituate. *—n.* (yōōs) **6.** application; employment. **7.** value; service. **—us'a·ble**, *adj.* **—use'ful**, *adj.* **—use'less**, *adj.*

ūs'êr-frĭend'lÿ, *adj.* (computers) designed for ease of use.

ŭsh'êr, *n.*, *v.t.* escort; guide.

ū'su·ål, *adj.* **1.** habitual; customary. **2.** ordinary; common. **—u'su·al·ly**, *adv.*

ū·sûrp', *v.t.* take or assume without right. **—u·surp'er**, *n.*

ū'su·rÿ, *n.* lending of money at excessive interest. **—u'sur·er**, *n.*

ū·tĕn'sĭl, *n.* implement or vessel useful esp. in the kitchen.

ū'têr·ŭs, *n.* female bodily organ in which fetuses develop.

ū·tĭl''ĭ-tār'ĭ-ån, *adj.* practical; useful; functional.

ū·tĭl'ĭ·tÿ, *n.*, *pl.* **-ties. 1.** usefulness; function. **2.** service provided for public use.

ū'tĭ·līze, *v.t.*, **-lized, -lizing.** make use of. **—u''ti·li·za'tion**, *n.*

ŭt'mōst'', *adj.* **1.** furthest. **2.** greatest.

ū·tō'pĭ·ån, *adj.* impossibly ideal.

ŭt'têr, *v.t.* **1.** say; speak; enunciate. *—adj.* **2.** total; complete. **—ut'ter·ance**, *n.* **—ut'ter·ly**, *adv.*

ū'vū·là, *n.* fleshy pendant lobe of the soft palate.

ux·o·ri·ous (ōok sōr'i əs), *adj.* excessively fond of one's wife.

V

V, v, *n.* twenty-second letter of the English alphabet.

vă'cån·cÿ, *n.*, *pl.* **-cies. 1.** state of being vacant. **2.** void. **3.** available rental space.

vă'cånt'', *adj.* **1.** empty; uninhabited. **2.** stupid; foolish. **3.** expressionless. **—va'cant''ly**, *adv.*

vă'cāte'', *v.*, **-cated, -cating.** *v.t.* **1.** deprive of an occupant or incumbent. **2.** leave. **3.** void; annul. *—v.i.* **4.** vacate a tenancy, office, or post.

vă·cā'tion, *n.* **1.** respite from duty or occupation. **2.** period of rest and relaxation. *—v.i.* **3.** take a vacation. **—va·ca'tion·er, va·ca'tion·ist**, *n.*

văc'cĭ·nāte'', *v.t.*, **-nated, -nating.** inoculate with serum for immunity to disease. —**vac''ci·na'tion**, *n.*

văc'cĭne', *n.* substance used for vaccinating. —**vac'ci·nal**, *adj.*

văc'ĭl·lāte'', *v.i.* **-lated, -lating. 1.** sway; oscillate; fluctuate. **2.** waver; hesitate. —**vac''il·la'tion**, *n.*

vă·cū'i·tў, *n., pl.* **-ties. 1.** emptiness. **2.** emptyheadedness. —**vac'u·ous**, *adj.* —**vac'u·ous·ly**, *adv.*

văc'ū·um, *n.* **1.** space devoid of matter. —*v.t.* **2.** use a vacuum cleaner on.

văg'ă·bŏnd'', *adj.* **1.** wandering; rootless. —*n.* **2.** person leading a vagabond life.

vă·gār'ў, *n., pl.* **-garies.** capricious action or notion.

va·gin·a (və jī'nə), *n.* canal in the female from the vulva to the uterus. —**vag'i·nal**, *adj.*

vă'grănt, *n.* **1.** wanderer, esp. without visible means of support. —*adj.* **2.** wandering; itinerant. **3.** random; wayward. —**va'gran·cy**, *n.*

vāgue, *adj.,* **vaguer, vaguest. 1.** not definite; imprecise. **2.** indistinct; blurred. —**vague'ly**, *adv.* —**vague'ness**, *n.*

văin, *adj.* **1.** futile. **2.** conceited. —**vain'ly**, *adv.*

val·ance (văl'əns), *n.* drapery or frame disguising the top of a window.

vāle, *n.* valley.

văl·ė·dĭc'tion, *n.* act of bidding farewell. —**val''e·dic'to·ry**, *adj.*

vă'lence, *n. Chemistry.* combining power of an element or radical.

văl'ĕn·tīne, *n.* **1.** sentimental greeting on St. Valentine's Day. **2.** sweetheart chosen on St. Valentine's Day.

val·et (val'it, val'ā), *n.* man's personal servant.

văl'ĭant, *adj.* possessing valor; courageous. —**val·ian·tly**, *adv.*

vă'lĭd, *adj.* **1.** reasonable. **2.** having legal force. —**va·lid'i·tў**, *n.* —**val'id·ly**, *adv.* —**val'i·date**, *v.t.*

va·lise, *n.* traveling bag; suitcase.

văl'lēy, *n.* long depression between mountains, plateaus, etc.

văl'ör, *n.* courage; bravery. —**val'o·rous**, *adj.* —**val'o·rous''ly**, *adv.*

văl'ū·ȧ·ble, *adj.* **1.** having worth or usefulness. —*n.* **2.** **valuables,** valuable possessions. —**val'u·ȧ·bly**, *adv.*

văl·ū·ā'tion, *n.* estimated value.

văl'ūe, *n., v.t.* **-ued, -uing.** *n.* **1.** importance; worth. **2.** relative worth. **3.** basic principle. —*v.t.* **4.** estimate the worth of. **5.** prize; esteem. —**val'ue·less**, *n.*

vălve, *n.* device for regulating the flow of a fluid. —**val'vu·lar**, *adj.*

vămp, *n.* **1.** uppermost front part of a shoe, etc. **2.** seductive woman. **3.** repeated introductory musical passage. —*v.i.* **4.** play a musical vamp.

văm'pīre'', *n.* **1.** corpse believed to rise and suck the blood of sleepers at night. **2.** Also, **vampire bat,** South American bat subsisting on blood.

văn, *n.* **1.** foremost part; vanguard. **2.** enclosed truck.

văn'dăl, *n.* person who willfully damages property. —**van'dal·ism**, *n.* —**van'dal·ize**, *v.t.*

Văn·dўke', *n.* short, pointed, trimmed beard.

vāne, *n.* blade rotated by moving air, steam, etc.

văn'guård'', *n.* **1.** advance troops. **2.** forefront of an action, movement, or cause.

vă·nĭl'là, *n.* extract of a tropical American orchid used in cookery.

văn'ĭsh, *v.i.* disappear.

văn'ĭ·tў, *n., pl.* **-ties.** inflated pride; conceit.

văn'quĭsh, *v.t.* defeat; conquer.

văn'tȧge, *n.* position giving strategic advantage.

vă'pĭd, *adj.* dull; uninteresting; flat. —**vap'id·ly**, *adv.* —**va·pid'i·tў**, *n.*

vă'pör, *n.* gaseous substance, as steam or mist. —**va'por·ous**, *adj.*

vă'pör·īze'', *v.,* **-ized, -izing.** *v.t., v.i.* turn into vapor. —**va''por·i·za'tion**, *n.* —**va'por·i''zer**, *n.*

văr'ĭ·ȧ·ble, *adj.* **1.** changeable; fluctuating. **2.** inconstant; fickle. —**var''i·a·bil'i·tў**, *n.* —**var'i·a·bly**, *adv.*

văr'ĭ·ănce, *n.* **1.** divergence. **2.** disagreement.

văr'ĭ·ănt, *adj.* **1.** varying. **2.** altered in form. —*n.* **3.** variant form or structure.

văr''ĭ·ā'tion, *n.* **1.** change; alteration. **2.** degree of change. **3.** elaboration of a musical theme. —**var''i·a'tion·al**, *adj.* —**var''i·a'tion·al·ly**, *adv.*

vãr'ĭ·ĕ·gāte'', *v.t.*, **-gated, -gating. 1.** add different colors to; dapple. **2.** add variety to. —**var''i·e·gat'ed**, *adj.* —**var''i·e·ga'tion**, *n.*

vä·rī'ė·tў, *n., pl.* **-ties. 1.** diversity. **2.** assortment. **3.** category; kind; type. —**va·ri'e·tal**, *adj.*

vä·rī'ō·lå, *n.* smallpox; cowpox.

vãr'ĭ·oŭs, *adj.* **1.** several. **2.** diverse; different. —**var'i·ous·ly**, *adv.*

vãr'nĭsh, *n.* **1.** resinous liquid preparation drying to a hard, glossy surface. **2.** outward appearance; gloss. —*v.t.* **3.** apply varnish to. **4.** gloss over; conceal.

vãr'ў, *v.*, **varied, varying.** *v.t.*, *v.i.* **1.** change; fluctuate. **2.** differ. —**var'i·ance**, *n.*

väse, *n.* ornamental vessel often used to hold flowers.

vǎs'sal, *n.* **1.** landholder subservient to a feudal lord. **2.** person under domination of another. —**vas'sal·age**, *n.*

vǎst, *adj.* enormous; huge; immense. —**vast'ly**, *adv.* —**vast'ness**, *n.*

vǎt, *n.* large vessel for holding fluids.

vaŭde'vĭlle, *n.* stage entertainment with a series of acts. —**vaude·vil'lian**, *n.*

vault, *n.* **1.** arched structure forming a ceiling. **2.** space covered by such a structure. **3.** burial chamber. **4.** room or container for valuables. —*v.t.* **5.** form or cover with a vault. **6.** leap over. —*v.i.* **7.** perform a leap; jump.

vaŭnt, *v.i.* **1.** brag; boast. —*v.t.* **2.** call attention to boastfully. —*n.* **3.** boast.

VCR, video cassette recorder.

vēal, *n.* flesh of a young calf.

vēer, *v.i.* **1.** change direction or course. —*n.* **2.** act or instance of veering.

vĕg'ė·tà·ble, *n.* **1.** partly edible plant. —*adj.* Also, **veg'e'tal. 2.** being a vegetable. **3.** pertaining to plants.

vĕg''ė·tãr'ĭ·àn, *n.* **1.** abstainer from meat. —*adj.* **2.** advocating the exclusion of meat in the diet. **3.** consisting solely of vegetables. —**veg''e·tar'i·an·ism**, *n.*

vĕg'ė·tāte'', *v.i.*, **-tated, -tating. 1.** grow in the manner of a plant. **2.** lead a passive life. —**veg·e'ta''tive**, *adj.*

vē'hė·mĕnt, *adj.* **1.** passionate; emotional; fervid. **2.** violent. —**ve'he·ment·ly**, *adj.* —**ve'he·mence**, *n.*

vē'hĭ·cle, *n.* **1.** inert medium containing an active agent. **2.** means of transporting or conveying. —**ve·hic'u·lar**, *adj.*

veil, *n.* **1.** net-like cloth for covering the face. **2.** outer covering of a nun's headdress. **3.** screen; cover-up. —*v.t.* **4.** cover with or as if with a veil.

vein, *n.* **1.** tubular vessel conveying blood within the body. **2.** tubular thickening in an insect wing or a leaf. **3.** stratum of mineral, ore, or ice. **4.** spirit; mood. —*v.t.* **5.** pattern with or as if with veins.

vĕl'lŭm, *n.* parchment.

vė·lŏc'ĭ·tў, *n., pl.* **-ties.** speed.

vĕl'vĕt, *n.* fabric with a thick, short, soft pile. —**vel'vet·y**, *adj.*

vē'nàl, *adj.* open to bribery or corruption; mercenary. —**ve'nal·ly**, *adv.* —**ve·nal'i·ty**, *n.*

vĕnd, *v.t.* sell; peddle. —**ven'dor**, *n.*

vé·nēer', *n.* **1.** facing of fine material. **2.** outer appearance. —*v.t.* **3.** cover with or as with a veneer.

vĕn'ĕr·à·ble, *adj.* worthy of or commanding reverence. —**ven·er·a·bil'i·ty**, *n.*

vĕn'ĕr·āte'', *v.t.*, **-ated, -ating.** respect deeply; worship; revere. —**ven''er·a'tion**, *n.*

vé·nē'rē·ăl, *adj.* relating to or resulting from sexual activity.

vĕnge'ance, *n.* retaliation; retribution.

vĕnge'fŭl, *adj.* seeking revenge; vindictive. —**venge'ful·ly**, *adv.*

vē'nĭ·ăl, *adj.* pardonable; forgivable. —**ve'ni·al·ly**, *adv.*

vĕn'ĭ·sŏn, *n.* deer meat.

vĕn'ŏm, *n.* **1.** poisonous secretion. **2.** malice; spite. —**ven'om·ous**, *adj.*

vĕnt, *n.* **1.** means of outlet or escape. —*v.t.* **2.** provide or serve as a vent. **3.** give free expression to.

vĕn'tĭ·lāte, *v.t.*, **-ated, -ating. 1.** provide with or expose to fresh air. **2.** express openly and freely. —**ven·ti·la'tion**, *n.*

vĕn·trĭl'ō·quĭsm, *n.* technique of projecting the voice so that it seems to emanate from a source other than the speaker. —**ven·tril'o·quist**, *n.*

vĕn'tūre, *v.t.*, **-tured, -turing.** *n.* *v.t.* **1.** expose to hazard; risk. **2.** offer at risk of rejection. —*n.* **3.** challenging or risky

undertaking. **—ven′ture·some, ven′
tur·ous,** adj.

Vē′nŭs, n. 1. goddess of love. 2. second
planet in distance from the sun.

vé·rā′cioŭs, adj. openly honest; truthful.
—ve·ra′cious·ly, adj. **—ve·rac′i·ty,** n.

vé·răn′dá, n. an open portico attached to a
building; porch. Also, **ve·ran′dah.**

vêrb, n. Grammar. part of speech indicating action, occurrence, being, etc.

vêr′bál, adj. 1. relating to or formed of
words. 2. oral; spoken. 3. relating to or
constituting a verb or form of a verb.
—ver′bal·ly, adv.

vêr′bál·īze″, v., **-ized, -izing.** v.t. 1. express in words. **—**v.i. 2. speak in words.
—ver″bal·i·za′tion, n.

vêr·bā′tĭm, adv. word for word; literally.

vêr′bi·áge, n. excess of words.

vêr·bōse′, adj. wordy; loquacious. **—ver·
bose′ness, ver·bos′i·ty,** n.

vêr′dánt, adj. green. **—ver′dant·ly,** adj.
—ver′dan·cy, n.

vêr′dĭct, n. decision.

vêr′dūre, n. 1. greenery. 2. greenness.

vêrge, n., v.i., **verged, verging.** n. 1. margin; edge. **—**v.i. 2. border; surround. 3.
tend; incline.

vêr′ĭ·fy, v.t., **-fied, -fying.** prove or ascertain the correctness of. **—ver·i·fi′a·ble,**
adj. **—ver·i·fi·ca′tion,** n.

vêr′ĭ·lÿ, adv. truly.

vêr″ĭ·sĭm·ĭl′ĭ·tūde, n. appearance of
truth or reality.

vêr′ĭ·tá·ble, adj. true; genuine. **—ver′i·
ta·bly,** adj.

vêr′ĭ·tÿ, n., pl. **-ties.** truth.

vêr′mĭn, n. pl. obnoxious animals or
creatures collectively. **—ver′min·ous,**
adj.

vêr·năc′ū·lár, adj. 1. locally native. **—**n.
2. language characteristic, esp. of a particular group or class.

vêr′nál, adj. pertaining to spring.

vêr′sá·tĭle, adj. changing tasks or activities easily. **—ver·sa·til′i·ty,** n.

vêrse, n. 1. poetry. 2. part of a poem, esp.
when rhymed. 3. passage from the Bi-
ble.

vêrsed, adj. accomplished; skilled;
knowledgeable.

vêr·sĭ·fÿ, v., **-fied, -fying.** v.t. 1. put into

verse. **—**v.i. 2. compose verse. **—ver″
si·fi·ca′tion,** n. **—ver′si·fi″er,** n.

vêr′siŏn, n. 1. account. 2. translation.

vêr′tè·brá, n., pl. **-bras, -brae.** segment
of the spinal column. **—ver′te·bral,**
adj.

vêr′tè·brāte, adj. 1. having vertebras.
—n. 2. creature having vertebras.

vêr′tĭ·cál, adj. 1. perpendicular to the horizon. **—**n. 2. vertical plane, line, etc.
—ver′ti·cal·ly, adv.

vêr′tĭ·gō″, n., pl. **-gos.** dizziness.

vêr′ÿ, adv., adj., **-ier, -iest.** adv. 1. to a
great extent. **—**adj. 2. identical; actual.
3. absolute.

vĕs′pêrs, n. sing. evening religious service.

vĕs′sél, n. 1. ship, boat, etc. 2. container
for fluid. 3. channel for blood.

vĕst, n. 1. sleeveless garment worn under a
coat or jacket. **—**v.i. 2. put in possession
or control of. 3. endow with authority.

vĕs′tĭ·būle, n. antichamber. **—ves·ti·bu·
lar,** adj.

vĕs′tīge, n. remnant; trace. **—ves·tig′i·
al,** adj.

vĕst′mĕnt, n. gown; robe.

vĕst·pŏckĕt, adj. small enough for a
pocket.

vĕs′trÿ, n., pl. **-tries.** 1. auxiliary room of
a church. 2. church committee. **—ves′
try·man,** n.

vĕt′êr·án, n. 1. person who has served,
esp. in the military forces. **—**adj. 2.
greatly experienced.

vĕt′êr·ĭ·năr″ÿ, adj., n., pl. **-ies.** adj. 1.
pertaining to the healing of animals.
—n. 2. Also, **vet″er·i·nar′i·an,** doctor for animals.

vē′tō, n., pl. **-toes,** v.t., **-toes, -toing.** n.
1. power to reject, prohibit, or ignore.
2. prohibition. **—**v.t. 3. reject or prohibit
by veto.

vĕx, v.t. 1. irritate. 2. trouble. **—vex′a′ti·
ous,** adj. **—vex′ed·ly,** adj.

vĕxed, adj. controversial.

vī′á, prep. by way of.

vī′á·ble, adj. capable of or fit for living.
—vi′a·bly, adv.

vī′á·dŭct″, n. long road bridge.

vī′ánd, n. item of food, esp. when very
choice or tasty.

vī′bránt, adj. 1. oscillating; fluctuating.

2. vigorous; energetic. —**vi′brant·ly**, adj. —**vi′bran·cy**, n.

vī′brāte, v., **-brated, -brating**. v.t., v.i. **1.** move rapidly back and forth. —v.i. **2.** shiver. **3.** resound. —**vi·bra′tion**, n. —**vi′bra·to′ry**, adj. —**vi·bra·tor**, n.

vic′ǎr, n. **1.** parish priest. **2.** representative of the pope or of a bishop. **3. Vicar of Christ**, pope. —**vic′ar·ship′′**, n.

vi·cǎr′i·oŭs, adj. **1.** serving in the place of another. **2.** experienced in imagination only. —**vi·car′i·ous·ly**, adv. —**vi·car′i·ous·ness**, n.

vīce, n. **1.** moral depravity. **2.** habitual personal shortcoming.

vice′-prĕs′i·dĕnt, n. official next in rank below president. —**vice′-pres′′i·den′tial**, adj. —**vice′′-pres·i·den·cy**, n.

vice′rôў, n. deputy sovereign; representative ruler. —**vice-re′gal**, adj.

vī′ce vêr′sà, with the order changed; conversely.

vi·cĭn′i·tў, n., pl. **-ties.** local area; neighborhood.

vī′cioŭs, adj. **1.** depraved; immoral. **2.** spiteful; malicious. **3.** evil. —**vi′cious·ly**, adv. —**vi′cious·ness**, n.

vi·cis·si·tude (vǝ sĭs′ǝ tōōd′′), n. unpredictable change.

vĭc′tĭm, n. **1.** sufferer from a force or action. **2.** dupe. —**vic′tim·ize′′**, v.t.

vĭc′tôr, n. winner; conqueror.

vĭc′tô·rў, n., pl. **-ries.** success in a contest; triumph. —**vic·to′ri·ous**, adj. —**vic·to′ri·ous·ly**, adv.

vict·ual (vǐ′tǝl), n. **1. victuals**, food. —v.t. **2.** provision.

vĭd′e·ō, n., adj. **1.** television. **2.** a short, visual performance featuring a rock music soundtrack.

vĭd′′e·ō·tāpe′, n. electromagnetic tape for recording visual images.

vīe, v.i. **vied, vying.** contend; compete.

vieŵ, n. **1.** seeing; beholding. **2.** area or range of vision. **3.** landscape. **4.** purpose. **5.** opinion; attitude. —v. **6.** look at; regard. —**view′er**, n. —**view′less**, adj.

vĭg′ĭl, n. act of keeping awake and alert.

vĭg′i·lǎnt, adj. alert; keenly aware. —**vig′i·lant·ly**, adv. —**vig′i·lance**, n.

vĭg′ŏr, n. robust health, energy, or strength. —**vig′or·ous**, adj. —**vig′or·ous·ly**, adv.

vīle, adj., **viler, vilest. 1.** of little account; mean. **2.** nasty; contemptible. —**vile′ly**, adv. —**vile′ness**, n.

vĭl′i·fў′′, v.t. **-fied, -fying.** denounce; defame. —**vil′′i·fi·ca′tion**, n.

vĭl′là, n. country or suburban house.

vĭl′lâge, n. small town; hamlet. —**vil′lag·er**, n.

vĭl′lǎin, n. wicked person; scoundrel. —**vil′lain·ous**, adj. —**vil′lain·y**, n.

vĭm, n. vigor; robustness.

vĭn′dĭ·cāte′′, v.t. **-cated, -cating.** absolve from suspicion or doubt. —**vin′′di·ca′tion**, n. —**vin′di·ca·ble**, adj.

vĭn·dĭc′tĭve, adj. holding a grudge. —**vin·dic′tive·ly**, adj. —**vin·dic′tive·ness**, n.

vīne, n. slender, creeping or climbing plant.

vĭn′e·gǎr, n. sour fermented liquid. —**vine′gar·y**, adj.

vīne′yàrd, n. garden or plantation for the growth of vines.

vĭn′tâge, n. **1.** wine extracted from a single harvest of grapes. **2.** harvest of grapes.

vī′ō·lāte′′, v.t., **-lated, -lating. 1.** break; transgress. **2.** desecrate. **3.** rape. —**vi′′o·la′tion**, n. —**vi′o·la′′tor**, n.

vi·ō′là′, n. string instrument with a pitch slightly below that of a violin.

vī′ō·lĕnt, adj. **1.** physically aggressive. **2.** severe; turbulent. —**vi′o·lent·ly**, adv. —**vi′o·lence**, n.

vī′ō·lĕt, n. **1.** low-growing herb bearing purplish or bluish blossoms. **2.** bluish purple.

vī′ō·lĭn, n. small, stringed musical instrument played with a bow. —**vi′′o·lin′ist**, n.

vī′′ō·lòn·cĕl′lō, n., pl. **-los.** cello. —**vi′′o·lon·cel′list**, n.

vī′pêr, n. **1.** venomous snake. **2.** ill-tempered, malicious person. —**vi′per·ous**, adj.

vi·rã′gō, n., pl. **-gos, -goes.** malicious woman; shrew; witch.

vĭr′gĭn, n. **1.** sexually inexperienced person. —adj. **2.** being a virgin. **3.** unexplored, unexploited, etc. —**vir′gin·al**, adj.

vir′īle, *adj.* **1.** capable of siring offspring. **2.** vigorous; manly; potent. —**vi·ril′i·ty,** *n.*

vir′tū·al, *adj.* so in effect. —**vir′tu·al·ly,** *adv.*

vir′tūe, *n.* **1.** morality. **2.** chastity. **3.** merit. —**vir′tu·ous,** *adj.* —**vir′tu·ous·ly,** *adv.* —**vir′tu·ous·ness,** *n.*

vir″tū·ō′sō, *n., pl.* **-sos, -si.** musician, etc., of outstanding skill. —**vir″tu·os′i·ty,** *n.*

vir′u·lent, *adj.* **1.** poisonous; deadly. **2.** hostile. —**vir′u·lence, vir′u·len·cy,** *n.* —**vir′u·lent·ly,** *adv.*

vī′rŭs, *adj.* infectious agency. —**vi′ral,** *adj.* —**vī′ral·ly,** *adv.*

vīs′āge, *n.* **1.** face. **2.** aspect; look.

vī·sá, *n.* endorsement to a passport.

vīs·cēr′·à, *n. pl.* internal bodily organs. —**vis′cer·al,** *adj.*

vīs·cĭd, *adj.* sticky to the touch; tacky. Also, **vis′cous.** —**vis·cos′i·ty,** *n.*

vīse, *n.* holding tool attached to a work bench, etc.

vīs′ī·ble, *adj.* **1.** capable of being seen. **2.** perceptible. —**vis′i·bly,** *adv.* —**vis·i·bil′i·ty,** *n.*

vī′sion, *n.* **1.** sense of sight. **2.** supernatural apprehension. **3.** foresight. —**vi′sion·al,** *adj.*

vī′sion·ār″ÿ, *adj.* **1.** fanciful. **2.** apprehended by or as by supernatural means. **3.** unreal; fancied. —*n.* **4.** person seeing visions. **5.** impractical person; dreamer.

vī′sĭt, *v.t.* **1.** go to and stay briefly at. **2.** afflict. —*n.* **3.** brief stay, esp. as a guest. —**vis′i·tor,** *n.* —**vis′i·tant,** *adj.* —**vis″i·ta′tion,** *n.*

vī′sŏr, *n.* forward projecting part, as of a helmet or cap.

vīs′tá, *n.* panoramic view.

vīs′ū·àl, *adj.* pertaining to sight. —**vis′u·al·ly,** *adj.*

vīs′ū·à·līze″, *v.t.,* **-ized, -izing.** obtain or create a picture or conception of. —**vis″u·al·i·za′tion,** *n.*

vī′tál, *adj.* **1.** pertaining to life or existence. **2.** extremely important. **3.** full of exuberance, creativity, etc. —**vi′tal·ly,** *adv.* —**vi·tal′i·ty,** *n.*

vī′tá·mĭn, *n.* organic substance vital in small quantities to proper nutrition. —**vi″ta·min′ic,** *adj.*

vi·ti·ate (vish′i āt″), *v.t.,* **-ated, -ating. 1.** impair. **2.** invalidate; negate. —**vi″ti·a′tion,** *n.*

vĭt′rē·oŭs, *adj.* glazed or glassy.

vĭt′rĭ·ŏl, *n.* sulfuric acid.

vĭt″rĭ·ŏl′ĭc, *adj.* **1.** pertaining to vitriol. **2.** caustic, as criticism.

vī·tū′pēr·āte″, *v.t.,* **-ated, -ating. 1.** criticize harshly or abusively. **2.** revile. —**vi·tu″per·a′tion,** *n.* —**vi·tu′per·a·tive,** *adj.*

vī·vā′cioŭs, *adj.* animated; lively. —**vi·va′cious·ly,** *adv.* —**vi·vac′i·ty, vi·va′cious·ness,** *n.*

vĭv′ĭd, *adj.* **1.** bright; brilliant. **2.** intense. —**viv′id·ly,** *adv.* —**viv′id·ness,** *n.*

vĭv′ī·sĕct″, *v.t.* dissect while alive. —**viv″i·sec′tion,** *n.* —**viv″i·sec′tion·ist,** *n.*

vīx′ĕn, *n.* **1.** female fox. **2.** mischievous girl or woman.

vō·căb′ū·lār·ÿ, *n., pl.* **-ies. 1.** stock of words used by a person, people, or group. **2.** collection of words in alphabetical order.

vō′cál, *adj.* **1.** pertaining to the voice. **2.** pertaining to singing. **3.** articulate; outspoken. —**vo′cal·ly,** *adj.* —**vo′cal·ize,** *v.t., v.i.* —**vo″cal·i·za′tion,** *n.*

vō·cā′tion, *n.* profession; occupation. —**vo·ca′tion·al,** *adj.*

vŏc′ä·tĭve, *adj.* **1.** relating to a grammatical case indicating person or thing addressed. —*n.* **2.** vocative case.

vō·cĭf′·ĕr·āte, *v.,* **-ated, -ating.** *v.i., v.t.* shout. —**vo·cif″er·a′tion,** *n.* —**vo·cif″er·ous,** *adj.*

vōgue, *n.* **1.** fashion; trend. **2.** popular favor or approval.

voīce, *n., v.t.* **voiced, voicing.** *n.* **1.** sound uttered through the mouth. **2.** singing or speaking voice. **3.** expression. **4.** choice. **5.** right to express one's opinion. **6.** *Grammar.* verbal inflection indicating whether subject is acting or acted upon. —*v.t.* **7.** express; declare. —**voice′less,** *adj.*

voĭd, *adj.* **1.** without legal power. **2.** useless; fruitless. **3.** empty; hollow. —*n.* **4.** empty or hollow space. —*v.t.* **5.** cancel; invalidate. —**void′a·ble,** *adj.* —**void′ance,** *n.*

vŏl′á·tĭle, *adj.* **1.** evaporating rapidly. **2.**

energetic; lively. **3.** tending to erupt into violence. **—vol·a·til'i·ty,** *n.*

vol·cā'nō, *n., pl.* **-noes, -nos.** mountain that ejects molten lava, rock, and steam. **—vol·can'ic,** *adj.* **—vol·can'i·cal·ly,** *adv.*

vo·lī'tion, *n.* **1.** power of choosing or determining; will. **2.** act of willing. **—vo·li'tion·al,** *adj.*

vol'ley, *n., pl.* **-leys,** *v.t. n.* **1.** simultaneous discharge of a number of missiles. **—v.t. 2.** fire in a volley.

volt, *n.* unit of electromotive force.

vol'u·ble, *adj.* fluent; talkative. **—vol'u·bly,** *adv.* **—vol·u·bil'i·ty,** *n.*

vol'ume, *n.* **1.** size in three dimensions. **2.** quantity; mass. **3.** degree of loudness. **4.** book.

vo·lū'mi·noŭs, *adj.* **1.** great in size or degree. **2.** consisting of or filling many books. **—vo·lu'min·ous·ly,** *adv.*

vol'ŭn·tār''ÿ, *adj.* **1.** performed or acted on by choice. **2.** controlled by the will. **—vol''un·tar'i·ly,** *adv.*

vol''ŭn·tēer', *v.t.* **1.** offer freely or spontaneously. **—v.i. 2.** volunteer oneself. **—n. 3.** person who volunteers.

vo·lŭp'tū·oŭs, *adj.* sensuous; sensual; luxurious. **—vo·lup'tu·ous·ly,** *adv.* **—vo·lup'tu·ous·ness,** *n.*

vŏm'ĭt, *v.i.* **1.** disgorge the contents of the stomach through the mouth. **—v.t. 2.** eject with force. **—n. 3.** matter ejected by vomiting.

vô·rā'cioŭs, *adj.* ravenous; greedy. **—vo·ra'cious·ly,** *adv.* **—vo·ra'ci·ty, vo·ra'cious·ness,** *n.*

vôr'těx, *n., pl.* **-tices, -texes.** whirling mass drawing objects to a central cavity.

vōte, *n., v.,* **voted, voting.** *n.* **1.** formal expression of opinion or choice, as by ballot. **2.** right to such opinion or choice. **3.** votes collectively. **—v.t. 4.** express or endorse by vote. **—v.i. 5.** cast one's vote. **—vot'er,** *n.*

voŭch, *v.i.* **1.** give a guarantee or surety. **2.** give personal assurance.

voŭch'ĕr, *n.* **1.** person who vouches. **2.** document certifying the occurrence of a transaction.

voŭch·sāfe', *v.t.,* **-safed, -safing.** permit; grant; allow.

vōw, *n.* **1.** pledge; solemn promise. **—v.t.**

2. promise solemnly; swear. **—v.i. 3.** make a vow.

vōw'ĕl, *n.* **1.** speech sound made with the central part of the breath channel unblocked. **2.** letter representing a vowel: *a, e, i, o, u* and sometimes *y.*

voy'āge, *n., v.,* **-aged, -aging.** *n.* **1.** an extended journey, esp. by sea. **—v.i. 2.** make a journey; travel. **—v.t. 3.** traverse; sail. **—voy'ag·er,** *n.*

vŭl'căn·īze'', *v.t.,* **-ized, -izing.** treat crude or synthetic rubber chemically to give it elasticity and strength. **—vul''can·i·za'tion,** *n.* **—vul'can·i''zer,** *n.*

vŭl'går, *adj.* **1.** lacking taste or breeding; unrefined. **2.** ordinary; plebian. **3.** ostentatiously showy. **4.** indecent; obscene. **5.** vernacular. **—vul'gar·ly,** *adv.* **—vul'gar'i·ty, vul'gar'ness,** *n.*

vŭl'nĕr·a·ble, *adj.* **1.** capable of being physically or emotionally wounded. **2.** open to damage or attack. **—vul'ner·a·bly,** *adv.* **—vul''ner·a·bil'i·ty,** *n.*

vŭl'tūre, *n.* **1.** large bird subsisting chiefly on carrion. **2.** predatory or rapacious person. **—vul'tur·ous,** *adj.*

vŭl'và, *n., pl.* **-vas, -vae.** external female genital organs. **—vul'val, vul'var,** *adj.*

vȳ'ĭng, *adj.* competing; competitive.

W

W, w, *n.* twenty-third letter of the English alphabet.

wăck'ÿ, *adj.* **-ier, -iest.** *Informal.* odd, erratic, crazy. **—wack'i·ly,** *adv.* **—wack'i·ness,** *n.*

wăd'dle, *v.i.,* **-dled, -dling,** *n. v.i.* **1.** walk like a duck. **—n. 2.** waddling gait.

wāde, *v.,* **waded, wading.** *v.i.* **1.** walk through water. **—v.t. 2.** cross by wading. **—wad'er,** *n.*

wā'fēr, *n.* **1.** thin, crisp cracker or cookie. **2.** thin disk of bread used in the Eucharist.

wâf'fle, *n.* crisp batter cake baked in a double griddle.

wâft, *v.t., v.i.* float through air or over water.

wăg, *v.*, **wagged, wagging.** *n. v.t., v.i.* **1.** shake in an arc. —*n.* **2.** wit, joker. —**wag´ger·y**, *n.* —**wag´gish**, *adj.*

wāge, *n., pl.* **wages,** *v.t.*, **waged, waging.** *n.* **1.** pay. —*v.t.* **2.** carry on, as war.

wā´gĕr, *n., v.t., v.i.* bet.

wăg´gle, *v.*, **-gled, -gling.** *n. v.t., v.i.* **1.** shake. —*n.* **2.** shake.

wăg´on, *n.* four-wheeled draft freight vehicle.

wāif, *n.* homeless child or animal.

wāil, *v.i., v.t.* **1.** cry mournfully. —*n.* **2.** mournful cry. —**wail´er**, *n.*

wāin´scŏt, *n.* **1.** woodwork along an interior wall. —*v.t.* **2.** line with woodwork.

wāist, *n.* part of the body between ribs and hips. —**waist´band´´**, *n.* —**waist´line´´**, *n.*

wāit, *v.i.* **1.** stop briefly; pause. **2.** be in expectation. **3.** be patient. **4.** remain undone. **5.** serve food, etc. —*n.* **6.** act, instance, or period of waiting. **7. in wait,** in ambush.

wāit´er, *n.* **1.** person who waits. **2.** Also, *fem.*, **wait´ress,** server of diners.

wāive, *v.t.*, **waived, waiving.** give up; relinquish.

wāiv´er, *n.* document that relinquishes.

wāke, *v.i.*, **waked** or **woke, woken, waking,** *n. v.i.* **1.** awake. **2.** be alert. —*v.t.* **3.** arouse. —*n.* **4.** vigil, as over a corpse. —**wake´ful**, *adj.* —**wake´ful·ly**, *adv.* —**wake´ful·ness**, *n.*

wāle, *n., v.t.*, **waled, waling.** *n.* **1.** welt as from a whip. —*v.t.* **2.** mark with wales.

wălk, *v.i.* **1.** go on foot. —*v.t.* **2.** cause to walk. **3.** accompany on foot. —*n.* **4.** act or instance of walking. **5.** place for walking. —**walk´er**, *n.*

wălk´ĭe-tälk´ĭe, *n.* portable two-way radio.

wăll, *n.* **1.** upright enclosure. —*v.t.* **2.** enclose or separate.

wăll´bôard´´, *n.* light material for covering interior walls or ceilings.

wăl´lĕt, *n.* pocket case for money, cards, etc.

wăll´flŏw´´êr, *n. Informal.* **1.** girl onlooker at a party. **2.** sweet-scented flowering plant that sometimes grows on walls.

wăl´lŏp, *v.t.* **1.** beat or thrash. —*n.* **2.** powerful blow.

wăl´lōw, *v.i.* **1.** roll about, as in mud. **2.** indulge oneself. —*n.* **3.** muddy area.

wăll´pā´´pêr, *n.* **1.** decorative paper for interior walls. —*v.t.* **2.** put wallpaper on.

Wăll Strēet, U.S. financial world.

wăl´nŭt´´, *n.* edible nut from a northern tree.

wăl´rŭs, *n.* large sea mammal with two tusks.

wăltz, *n.* **1.** dance in three-quarter time. —*v.i.* **2.** dance a waltz. —*v.t.* **3.** *Informal.* lead briskly. —**waltz´er**, *n.*

wăm´pŭm, *n.* shell beads used by Native Americans as money or ornaments.

wăn, *adj.*, **wanner, wannest.** pale or sicklooking. —**wan´ly**, *adv.*

wănd, *n.* rod with supposed magical power.

wăn´dêr, *v.i.* **1.** move about aimlessly. **2.** stray. —*v.t.* **3.** travel over. —**wan´der·er**, *n.*

wăn´dêr·lŭst´´, *n.* desire to wander or travel.

wāne, *v.i., n.*, **wane, waning.** *v.i.* **1.** grow dim, as the moon's light. **2.** decline in strength or power. —*n.* **3.** decrease or decline.

wăn´gle, *v.t.*, **-gled, -gling.** *Informal.* get by scheming or persuasion.

wănt, *v.t.* **1.** wish for. **2.** desire, crave, demand. —*v.i.* **3.** be lacking or deficient. —*n.* **4.** something needed. **5.** deficiency or lack. —**want´ing**, *adj., prep.*

wăn´tŏn, *adj.* **1.** gratuitous. **2.** sexually loose. —*n.* **3.** lascivious woman. —*v.t.* **4.** squander. —**wan´ton·ly**, *adv.* —**wan´ton·ness**, *n.*

wăp´ĭ·tī, *n., pl.* **-tis, -ti.** elk with wide antlers.

wâr, *n., v.i.*, **warred, warring.** *n.* **1.** armed conflict, as between nations. **2.** hostility or struggle. —*v.i.* **3.** be in conflict. —**war´fare´´**, *n.* —**war´like**, *adj.*

wâr´ble, *v.*, **-bled, -bling.** *n. v.t., v.i.* **1.** sing with trills, as a bird. —*n.* **2.** warbling. —**war´bler**, *n.*

wârd, *n.* **1.** administrative division of a city. **2.** division of a hospital. **3.** person under the care of a guardian. —*v.t.* **4.** repel or avert.

wâr´dĕn, *n.* **1.** chief officer of a prison. **2.**

person in charge of others or things, keeper.

wård´êr, n. guard.

wård´rōbe´´, n. **1.** collection for clothes. **2.** closet of clothes.

wård´rōōm´´, n. living and dining area for commissioned officers on a warship.

wāre, n. goods for sale.

ware´hōuse´´, n., v.t., **-housed, -housing.** n. **1.** storage building. —v.t. **2.** store in a warehouse.

wår´hĕad´´, n. explosive front part of a bomb, missile, or torpedo.

wår´hôrse´´, n. **1.** veteran of many conflicts. **2.** overfamiliar concert number.

wår´lŏck´´, n. male with magical power; sorcerer.

wår´lôrd´´, n. military ruler.

wårm, adj. **1.** having or giving moderate heat. **2.** friendly or affectionate. **3.** irritated or angry. —v.t., v.i. **4.** heat moderately. **—warm´ly,** adv. **—warmth,** n. **—warm´ness,** n. **—warm´ish,** adj.

wårm´heârt´ĕd, adj. friendly; sympathetic.

war´mon·ger (wor´mun´´gər), n. inciter of war.

wårn, v.t. give notice of danger, caution. **—warn´ing,** n., adj.

wårp, n. **1.** distortion. **2.** lengthwise threads in cloth. —v.t., v.i. **3.** distort.

wår´rånt, n. **1.** authorization, as by law. **2.** guarantee. —v.t. **3.** authorize. **4.** guarantee. **—war´rant·a·ble,** adj.

wår´rån·tў, n., pl. **-ties.** guarantee on something used.

wår´rĭ·or, n. soldier.

wårt, n. small hard protuberance on the skin. **—wart´y,** adj.

wår´ў, adj., **warier, wariest.** cautious; watchful. **—war´i·ly,** adv. **—war´i·ness,** n.

wås, v. 1st and 3rd person singular, past indicative of be.

wåsh, v.t. **1.** clean with or in water or a solution. **2.** flow over. —v.i. **3.** wash oneself. **4.** undergo washing. —n. **5.** washing, as of clothes. **6.** current behind a moving ship or plane. **—wash´a·ble,** adj. **—wash´board´,** n. **—wash´bowl´,** n. **—wash´cloth´,** n. **—wash´stand´,** n.

wåsh´êr, n. **1.** washing machine. **2.**

pierced disk for tightening a joint to prevent leakage, etc.

wåsh´ōut´´, n. **1.** washing away of earth, soil, etc. **2.** Informal. failure.

WASP, n. white Anglo-Saxon Protestant. Also, **W.A.S.P., Wasp.**

wåsp, n. stinging insect. **—wasp´ish,** adj.

wăs´sail (wos´əl), n. **1.** drinking or toasting a person's health, as with a spiced ale. **2.** drinking festivity. **3.** hot drink made with beer, wine, or cider and spices. —v.i., v.t. **4.** toast.

wāste, v., **wasted, wasting,** n., adj. v.t. **1.** use up needlessly. **2.** ruin. —v.i. **3.** be used up gradually. —n. **4.** needless consumption or expenditure. **5.** unused remains. **6.** neglect. **7.** ruin. —adj. **8.** unused. **—waste´bas´ket,** n. **—waste´ful,** adj. **—waste´pa´per,** n.

wast·rel (wās´trəl), n. wasteful person; spendthrift.

wåtch, v.i. **1.** observe; be on the alert. —v.t. **2.** observe. **3.** guard or tend. —n. **4.** period of watching; observation. **5.** small timepiece worn on the person. **—watch´band,** n. **—watch´dog,** n. **—watch´ful,** adj. **—watch´man,** n. **—watch´tow´er,** n.

wåtch´wôrd´´, n. **1.** password. **2.** motto; slogan.

wä´têr, n. **1.** colorless, odorless liquid forming rain, rivers, etc. —v.t. **2.** supply with water. —v.i. **3.** discharge water or tears. **—wa´ter·y,** adj.

wä´têr·bĕd´´, n. heavy water-filled bag used as a bed.

wåtêr clŏsĕt, toilet.

wä´têr·cŏl´´or, n. **1.** pigment mixed with water. **2.** painting with such pigments.

wä´têr·côurse´´, n. channel for water, as a river, canal, etc.

wä´têr·făll´´, n. steep fall of water, as over a precipice.

wä´têr·fōwl´´, n. water bird.

wåtêr glåss, drinking glass.

wåtêr lĭlў, aquatic plant with floating leaves and flowers.

wä´têr·lŏgged´´, adj. saturated with water.

wä´têr·mårk´´, n. **1.** mark showing height of water, as of a river, etc. **2.** manufacturer's impression on paper. —v.t. **3.** mark with a watermark.

wä′têr·mĕl′′ŏn, *n.* large fruit with juicy, red pulp.

wä′têr·prŏŏf′′, *adj.* **1.** impervious to water. —*v.t.* **2.** make waterproof.

wä′têr·shĕd′′, *adj.* **1.** ridge between two drainage areas. **2.** drainage area.

wä′têr·skī′′, *v.,* **-skied, -skiing,** *n.* *v.i.* **1.** skim over water on ski-like boards drawn by a line attached to a speedboat. —*n.* **2.** short, broad board for water-skiing.

wä′têr·spŏut′′, *n.* **1.** pipe for discharging water. **2.** tubelike column of air and water occurring over water.

wätêr tāble, *n.* level below which the ground is saturated.

wä′têr·whēel′′, *n.* mill wheel moved by water.

wâ′têr·wörks′′, *n.* plant for supplying water.

wätt, *n.* unit of electric power. —watt′age, *n.*

wät′tle, *n.* **1.** stakes interwoven with twigs, as for fences, walls, etc. **2.** fleshy skin hanging from the throat or chin.

wāve, *n., v.,* **waved, waving.** *n.* **1.** ridge along the ocean's surface. **2.** undulation. **3.** movement back and forth, as of a hand or flag. —*v.i., v.t.* **4.** move to and fro. —*v.t.* **5.** signal with the hand. —wav′y, *adj.*

wā′vêr, *v.i.* **1.** hesitate. **2.** sway. —*n.* **3.** wavering.

WAVES, *n.* W(omen) A(ccepted for) V(oluntary) E(mergency) S(ervice); women in the U.S. Navy.

wăx, *n.* **1.** readily melted, molded, and burned substance. —*v.t.* **2.** treat with wax. —*v.i.* **3.** increase, as the moon. **4.** *Archaic.* become. —wax′en, *adj.* —wax′er, *n.* —wax′y, *adj.*

wăx′wĭng′′, *n.* crested bird with scarlet wings' ends.

wāy, *n.* **1.** manner, custom, or fashion. **2.** plan. **3.** direction or route. **4.** ways, tracks for launching a ship.

wāy′fär′′êr, *n.* traveler or rover.

wāy′lāy′′, *v.t.,* **-laid, -laying.** lie in wait for; ambush.

wāy′wärd, *adj.* **1.** willful. **2.** capricious. —way′ward·ness, *n.*

wē, *pron.* nominative plural of *I.*

wēak, *adj.* **1.** not strong physically. **2.** lacking moral or mental strength. **3.** easily broken. —weak′ly, *adj., adv.* —weak′en, *v.t., v.i.* —weak′ling, *n.* —weak′ness, *n.*

wĕalth, *n.* **1.** abundance of money or property. **2.** large and valuable amount. —wealth′y, *adj.*

wēan, *v.t.* **1.** accustom to food other than mother's milk. **2.** cure of a dependency or delusion.

wĕap′ŏn, *n.* instrument for fighting. —weap′on·ry, *n.*

wear, *v.,* **-wore, worn, wearing.** *v.t.* **1.** have on the body, as clothing. **2.** diminish by use. —*v.i.* **3.** deteriorate as through use. —*n.* **4.** diminution or impairment through use. **5.** clothing. —wear′a·ble, *adj.* —wear′er, *n.*

wēa′rĭ·sŏme, *adj.* tiresome.

wēar′ў, *adj.,* **-rier, -riest,** *v.t.,* **-rying, -ried.** *adj.* **1.** very tired. **2.** causing fatigue. —*v.t.* **3.** tire. —wear′i·ly, *adv.* —wear′i·ness, *n.*

wēa′sĕl, *n.* small, flesh-eating mammal.

wĕath′êr, *n.* **1.** condition of the sky. **2.** storms, rains, etc. —*v.t.* **3.** withstand. **4.** expose to the weather. —*adj.* **5.** toward the wind.

wĕath′êr·bēat′′ĕn, *adj.* showing the effect of weather.

wēave, *v.,* **wove, woven** or **weaved, weaving,** *n.* *v.t.* **1.** interlace threads, etc., as on a loom. **2.** construct, as in the mind. —*v.i.* **3.** become interlaced. —*n.* **4.** type of weaving. —weav′er, *n.*

wĕb, *n., v.t.,* **webbed, webbing.** *n.* **1.** something woven. **2.** network spun by spiders. **3.** trap. —*v.t.* **4.** join or cover, as by or with a web. —webbed, *adj.* —web′bing, *n.*

wĕb′fŏŏt′′, *n., pl.* **-feet.** foot with webbed toes. —web′-foot′′ed, web′-toed′′, *adj.*

wĕd, *v.,* **wedded, wedded** or **wed, wedding.** *v.t., v.i.* **1.** marry. **2.** join. —wed′ding, *n.*

wĕdge, *n., v.,* **wedged, wedging.** *n.* **1.** object with two faces meet at a sharp angle. —*v.t.* **2.** force or fix with a wedge. —*v.i.* **3.** become wedged.

wĕd′lŏck, *n.* state of marriage.

Wĕdnes′dāy, *n.* fourth day of the week.

wēe, *adj.* tiny.

wēed, n. 1. useless plant. —v.i. 2. free from weeds. —**weed′er**, n. —**weed′y**, adj.

wēek, n. 1. period of seven days, esp. starting from Sunday. 2. working days of the week.

wēek′dāy″, n. 1. any day except Saturday or Sunday. —adj. 2. pertaining to such days.

wēek′ėnd″, n. Saturday and Sunday.

wēek′lў̄, adj., adv., n., pl. **-lies.** adj. 1. appearing or occurring once a week. 2. lasting a week. —adv. 3. every week. —n. 4. weekly periodical.

wēep, v.i., **wept, weeping.** mourn or shed tears. —**weep′er**, n.

wēe′vĭl, n. beetle destructive to grain, fruit, etc.

weigh, v.t. 1. measure the heaviness of. 2. consider carefully. —v.i. 3. have significance. 4. be a burden. —**weigh′er**, n.

weight, n. 1. heaviness or pressure. 2. burden, influence, or importance. —v.t. 3. burden. —**weight′y**, adj. —**weight′i·ness**, n.

wēird, adj. strange, uncanny, or queer. —**weird′ly**, adv. —**weird′ness**, n.

wĕl′cŏme, n., v.t., **-comed, -coming,** adj. n. 1. friendly greeting. —v.t. 2. greet with pleasure. —adj. 3. happily or readily received. 4. freely permitted.

wĕld, v.t. 1. unite, as by heat or pressure. —n. 2. welded joint. —**weld′er**, n.

wĕl′fāre″, n. 1. well-being. 2. aid for the poor.

wĕll, adv., **better, best,** adj., n., v.i., interj. adv. 1. in a benevolent, good, or thorough manner. —adj. 2. in good health. 3. suitable. —n. 4. opening in the earth as a source of water, oil, etc. —v.i. 5. flow or gush. —interj. 6. (exclamation denoting surprise or introducing a sentence).

wĕll- prefix meaning "in a good or thorough manner." **well-accomplished, well-adjusted, well-aimed, well-argued, well-armed, well-arranged, well-attended, well-aware, well-behaved, well-built, well-considered, well-contented, well-controlled, well-developed, well-disciplined, well-documented, well-earned, well-educated, well-equipped, well-governed, well-hidden, well-justified, well-kept, well-liked, well-loved, well-managed, well-planned, well-prepared, well-protected, well-qualified, well-regulated, well-remembered, well-respected, well-satisfied, well-secured, well-situated, well-spent, well-stated, well-suited, well-taught, well-trained, well-traveled, well-treated, well-understood, well-used.**

wĕll′-bē-ĭng, n. state of being well and happy.

wĕll′-brĕd′, adj. with good manners.

wĕll′-ės·tăb′lĭshed, adj. settled; firmly in place.

wĕll′-fŏund′ėd, adj. based on good reason. Also, **well′-ground′ed**, adj.

wĕll′hĕad″, n. fountainhead; source.

wĕll′-măn′nêred, adj. polite; courteous.

wĕll′-mēan′ĭng, adj. having good intentions. —**well′-meant′**, adj.

wĕll′-nĭgh′, adv. almost.

wĕll′-ŏff′, adj. 1. in a good condition. 2. prosperous.

wĕll′-prē·sêrved′, adj. 1. in good condition. 2. youthful for one's age.

wĕll′-rŏund′ėd, adj. 1. having varied abilities. 2. well-diversified.

wĕll′-spō′kĕn, adj. speaking well or pleasantly.

wĕll′sprĭng″, n. source.

wĕll′-tô-dô′, adj. wealthy.

wĕll′-wĭsh″êr, n. person who wishes well to another.

wĕlt, n. 1. ridge or wale on the body from a blow. 2. leather strip on the seam of a shoe. —v.t. 3. beat soundly.

wĕlt′êr, v.i. 1. roll or heave, as waves. 2. wallow. —n. 3. jumble or muddle.

wĕn, n. skin cyst or tumor.

wĕnch, n. 1. young woman. 2. strumpet. —v.i. 3. associated with promiscuous women.

wĕnt, v.i. past form of go.

wêre, v. past plural form of be.

wêre′wolf″, n., pl. **-wolves.** person changed into a wolf.

wĕst, n. 1. compass point to the left of north. 2. direction of such point. 3. Also, **West,** the Occident. —adj., adv. 4. toward or from the west. —**west′ern**, adj. —**west′ern·er**, n.

wĕst′êr·lў, *adj., adv.* **1.** from the west, as wind. **2.** toward the west.

wĕst′ẽrn·īze′′, *v.t.,* **-ized, -izing.** make Occidental in culture.

wĕst′ward, *adj.* **1.** toward the west. —*adv.* **2.** Also, **west′wards, toward the west.** —*n.* **3.** westward direction.

wĕt, *adj.,* wetter, wettest, *n., v. adj.* **1.** covered with water or liquid. —*n.* **2.** water or moisture. —*v.t.* **3.** make wet. —*v.i.* **4.** become wet. —**wet′ness,** *n.*

whăck, *Informal. v.t., v.i.* **1.** slap or strike. —*n.* **2.** sharp blow.

whāle, *n., v.i.,* **whaled, whaling.** *n.* **1.** large sea mammal. —*v.i.* **2.** hunt whales. —**whal′er,** *n.*

whāle′bōne′′, *n.* elastic material in the upper jaw of some whales.

whârf, *n., pl.* **wharves.** pier or quay.

whät, *pron., adj., pl.* **what,** *adj., adv., interj. pron.* **1.** which one? **2.** that which. —*adj.* **3.** which kind of. —*adv.* **4.** how? **5.** partly. —*interj.* **6.** (exclamation of surprise).

whät·ĕv′êr, *pron.* **1.** anything that. —*adj.* **2.** of any kind.

whät′nŏt′′, *n.* open cupboard, as for bric-a-brac.

whēal, *n.* small swelling, as from an insect bite.

whēat, *n.* cereal grass used in flour, etc.

whee′dle, *v.t.,* **-dled, -dling.** persuade by coaxing.

wheel, *n.* **1.** rotating disk that transmits power or facilities movement. —*v.t., v.i.* **2.** move on wheels. **3.** revolve.

wheel′bär′′rōw, *n.* one-wheeled container for moving loads.

wheel′base′′, *n.* distance between the front and rear wheel hubs of an automobile.

wheel′êr-dēal′êr, *n. Informal.* person skillful in business deals.

whēeze, *v.i.,* **wheezed, wheezing.** *n. v.i.* **1.** breathe with a whistling sound. —*n.* **2.** a wheezing sound. —**wheez′y,** *adj.*

whĕlm, *v.t.* **1.** submerge. **2.** overwhelm.

whĕlp, *n.* **1.** young of a dog, bear, etc. —*v.i., v.t.* **2.** give birth to.

whĕn, *adv.* **1.** at what time? —*conj.* **2.** at the time that. —*pron.* **3.** what or which time.

whĕnce, *adv.* from what place, cause, etc.

whĕn·ĕv′êr, *adv.* **1.** when. —*conj.* **2.** at whatever time.

whêre, *adv.* **1.** at what place? **2.** in what way? —*conj.* **3.** at which place; wherever. —*pron.* **4.** the place at which.

whêre′a·bŏuts′′, *adv.* **1.** where. —*n.* **2.** location.

whêre·ăs′, *conj.* **1.** considering that. **2.** on the contrary.

whêre′fōre′′, *adv., conj.* for what.

whêre·ĭn′, *conj.* in which.

whêre′′ŭp·ŏn′, *conj.* upon which.

whêre′′wĭth·ăl′, *n.* means.

whêr′rў, *n., pl.* **-ries.** light rowboat.

whĕt, *v.t.,* **whetted, whetting.** **1.** sharpen. **2.** stimulate, as the appetite. —**whet′stone′**, *n.*

whĕth′êr, *conj.* **1.** if it is so that. **2.** if either.

whēy, *n.* water part of curdled milk.

whĭch, *pron.* **1.** what one? **2.** that. —*adj.* **3.** what one.

whĭch·ĕv′êr, *pron., adj.* **1.** any. **2.** regardless of which.

whĭff, *n.* light odor or puff.

whĭf′fle·trēe′′, *n.* crossbar to which harness traces are fastened.

whīle, *n., conj., v.t.,* **whiled, whiling.** *n.* **1.** time. —*conj.* **2.** during the time that. **3.** although. —*v.t.* **4.** spend pleasantly, as time.

whĭm, *n.* sudden fancy; caprice. —**whim′si·cal,** *adj.* —**whim′sy,** *n.*

whīne, *v.i.,* **whined, whining.** **1.** complain childishly. **2.** make a high-pitched, nasal sound. —**whin′ing·ly,** *adv.* —**whin′y,** *adj.*

whĭn′nў, *v.i.,* **-nied, -nying,** *n., pl.* **-nies.** neigh.

whĭp, *v.,* **whipped, whipping,** *n. v.t.* **1.** strike or lash. —*v.i.* **2.** move quickly. —*n.* **3.** instrument for whipping.

whĭp′côrd′′, *n.* hard, braided cord.

whĭp′lăsh′′, *n.* neck injury from jerking of the head as in an automobile accident.

whĭp′′pêr·snăp′′pêr, *n.* presumptuous person.

whĭp′pĕt, *n.* fast dog.

whĭp′′pōor·wĭll′′, *n.* gray bird with nocturnal cry.

whĭr, *v.,* **whirred, whirring,** *n. v.i., v.t., n.* hum or buzz. Also, **whirr.**

whĭrl, *v.i., v.t.* **1.** move or revolve rapidly.

—*n.* **2.** whirling movement. **3.** uproar or confusion.

whirl'pool'', *n.* whirling current of water.

whirl'wind'', *n.* whirling current of air.

whisk, *v.t., v.i.* **1.** brush with a quick motion. —*n.* **2.** act or instance of whisking. —**whisk'broom''**, *n.*

whisk'er, *n.* **1.** a facial hair. **2.** long bristle, as on a cat.

whis'key, *n., pl.* **-keys, -kies.** liquor distilled from fermented grain. Also, **whis'ky.**

whis'per, *v.i., v.t.* **1.** speak softly. **2.** make a low rustling. —*n.* **3.** act or instance of whispering.

whist, *n.* card game.

whis'tle, *v.i.,* **-tled, -tling,** *n. v.i.* **1.** make a high-pitched sound through pursed lips. —*n.* **2.** act or instance of whistling. **3.** noise-making device using steam or air.

whit, *n.* small bit.

white, *adj.* **1.** of the color of snow. **2.** pale. **3.** pure. —*n.* **4.** opposite to black. **5.** Caucasoid. —**white'ness**, *n.* —**whit'ish**, *adj.* —**whit'en**, *v.t., v.i.*

white élephánt, **1.** albino elephant. **2.** awkward, useless possession.

white'fish'', *n.* edible lake fish.

White House, **1.** residence of the U.S. president. **2.** executive branch of the U.S. government.

white lie, small, pardonable lie.

white slave, woman forced into prostitution. —**white slavery.**

white'wash'', *n.* **1.** mixture for whitening walls. —*v.t.* **2.** apply whitewash to. **3.** *Informal.* conceal the guilt of.

whith'er, *adv., conj. Archaic.* to what place.

whit'ing, *n.* **1.** food fish. **2.** chalk for paints.

whit'low, *n.* inflammation of a finger or toe.

whit'tle, *v.,* **-tled, -tling.** *v.t., v.i.* **1.** cut or carve, as from wood. —*v.t.* **2.** reduce the amount of.

whiz, *v.i.,* **whizzed, whizzing,** *n. v.i.* **1.** make a buzzing sound in motion. —*n.* **2.** such a sound. **3.** *Informal.* expert. Also, **whizz.**

who, *pron.* **1.** which person? **2.** person that.

whoa, *interj.* stop!

who·ev'er, *pron.* anyone that.

whole, *adj.* **1.** entire. **2.** intact. **3.** *Math.* not a fraction. —*n.* **4.** all the amount. —**whole'ly**, *adv.* —**whole'ness**, *n.*

whole'heart'ed, *adj.* enthusiastic; dedicated. —**whole'heart'ed·ly**, *adv.*

whole'sale'', *n., adj., v.,* **-saled, -saling.** *n.* **1.** sale of goods in quantity, as to retailers. —*adj.* **2.** selling by wholesale. —*v.t., v.i.* **3.** sell wholesale. —**whole'sal'er**, *n.*

whole'some, *adj.* healthful, salutary. —**whole'some·ly**, *adv.* —**whole'some·ness**, *n.*

whom, *pron. Grammar.* objective case of who.

whoop, *n.* **1.** shout of joy. **2.** sound in whooping cough. —*v.t., v.i.* **3.** utter with whooping.

whop'per, *n. Informal.* **1.** something unusually large. **2.** outrageous lie. —**whop'ping**, *adj.*

whore, *n., v.i.,* **whored, whoring.** *n.* **1.** prostitute. —*v.i.* **2.** consort with whores. —**whor'ish**, *adj.*

whorl, *n.* spiral or circular arrangement.

whose, *pron. Grammar.* possessive case of who.

who·so·ev'er, *pron.* whoever.

why, *adv., n., pl.* **whys,** *interj. adv.* **1.** for what reason or cause. —*n.* **2.** reason, cause, or purpose. —*interj.* **3.** exclamation of surprise.

wick, *n.* length of fiber that absorbs fuel to burn.

wick'ed, *adj.* **1.** bad, evil. **2.** mischievous. —**wick'ed·ly**, *adv.* —**wick'ed·ness**, *n.*

wick'er, *n.* **1.** flexible twig. —*adj.* **2.** made of wicker. —**wick'er·work''**, *n.*

wick'et, *n.* **1.** small gate. **2.** upright frame used in cricket or croquet.

wide, *adj.,* **wider, widest.** *adj.* **1.** broad. —*adv.* **2.** far. —**wide'ly**, *adv.* —**wide'ness**, *n.* —**wid'en**, *v.t., v.i.* —**wide'spread'**, *adj.*

wide'-a·wake', *adj.* alert.

widg'eon, *n.* fresh-water wild duck. Also, **wig'eon.**

wid'ow, *n.* **1.** unmarried woman whose husband has died. —*v.t.* **2.** make into a widow. Also, *masc.*, **wid′ow·er. —wid′ow·hood′′**, *n.*

width, *n.* breadth.

wield, *v.t.* **1.** handle or manage. **2.** exercise, as authority or power. **—wield′er**, *n.*

wie′ner, *n.* frankfurter. Also, *Informal*, **wee′nie** or **wie′nie.**

wife, *n.*, *pl.* **wives.** married woman. **—wife′less**, *adj.* **—wife′ly**, *adj.*

wig, *n.*, *v.*, **wigged, wigging.** *n.* **1.** artificial hair piece. *—v.t.* **2.** furnish with a wig.

wig′gle, *v.*, **-gled, -gling**, *n.* *v.i.*, *v.t.* **1.** move with quick motions from side to side. *—n.* **2.** act or instance of wiggling. **—wig′gly**, *adj.*

wig′wag′′, *v.*, **-wagged, -wagging**, *n. v.t.*, *v.i.* **1.** signal with swung flags. *—n.* **2.** act or instance of wigwagging.

wig′wäm, *n.* Native American hut.

wild, *adj.* **1.** uncivilized. **2.** uncontrollable. **3.** lacking restraint; dissolute. *—n.* **4.** desolate region. **—wild′ly**, *adv.* **—wild′ness**, *n.*

wild′cät′′, *n.*, *v.*, **-catted, -catting**. *n.* **1.** large, fierce feline. **2.** savage person. **3.** exploratory oil or gas well. *—v.i.*, *v.t.* **4.** search for oil or gas.

wil′dêr·ness, *n.* uninhabited region.

wild′-gōōse′ chäse, search for a nonexistent thing.

wile, *n.*, *v.t.*, **wiled, wiling**. *n.* **1.** sly trick. *—v.t.* **2.** beguile. **3. wile away**, pass leisurely, as time.

will, *n.*, *v.*, **willed, willing.** *n.* **1.** power of conscious choice or action. **2.** determination. **3.** disposition toward another. **4.** legal document of one's wishes after death. *—v.i.*, *v.t.* **5.** desire, wish or want. **6.** bequeath by a will. *—auxiliary v.* **7.** am, is, or are about to. **8.** am, is, or are willing to. **9.** am, is, or are expected to. **—will·a·ble**, *adj.*

will′fül, *adj.* **1.** intentional. **2.** stubborn. Also, **wil′ful. —will′ful·ly**, *adv.* **—will′ful·ness**, *n.*

will′ing, *adj.* **1.** favorably inclined. **2.** cheerfully done. **—will′ing·ly**, *adv.* **—will′ing·ness**, *n.*

will′′-ó′-thē-wisp′, **1.** elusive light. **2.** anything that deludes.

wil′löw, *n.* slender tree with flexible limbs and narrow leaves. **—wil′low·y**, *adj.*

wil′lÿ-nil′lÿ, *adv.*, *adj.* whether willingly or not.

wilt, *v.i.* **1.** become limp or weak; droop. *—v.t.* **2.** cause to wilt. *—n.* **3.** wilted state.

wil′ÿ, *adj.*, **-lier, -liest.** sly. **—wi′li·ness**, *n.*

win, *v.*, **won, winning**, *n. v.i.* **1.** succeed. *—v.t.* **2.** gain, as a victory, favor, etc. **3.** influence. *—n.* **4.** victory.

wince, *v.i.*, **winced, wincing**, *n. v.i.* **1.** shrink, as from a blow or pain. *—n.* **2.** act or instance of wincing.

winch, *n.* **1.** crank. **2.** windlass. *—v.t.* **3.** hoist or haul by a winch.

wind, *v.*, **wound, winding**, *n. v.t.* (wīnd) **1.** turn. *—v.i.* **2.** coil. **3.** make one's way, as along a path. *—n.* (wind) **4.** air in motion, as a gale. **5.** breath. **6.** intestinal gas. **—wind′er**, *n.* **—wind′y**, *adj.*

wind′båg′′, *n. Informal.* empty talker.

wind′break′′, *n.* shield against the wind.

wind′bûrn′′, *n.* inflammation of the skin from the wind. **—wind′burned′′**, *adj.*

wind′ed, *adj.* out of breath.

wind′fäll′, *n.* **1.** unexpected good fortune. **2.** something blown down by the wind.

wind instrument, musical instrument sounded by the breath.

wind′jäm′′mêr′, *n.* large sailing ship.

wind′läss, *n.* winch.

wind′mïll′′, *n.* wind-driven machine.

win′döw, *n.* opening in a wall for light, air, etc. **—win′dow·pane′′**, *n.* **—win′dow·sill′′**, *n.* **—window shade.**

window dressing, **1.** store display. **2.** specious display.

wind′pïpe′′, *n.* trachea.

wind′röw′′, *n.* row of leaves, hay, etc.

wind′shield′′, *n.* glass above and across a car's dashboard.

wind′ŭp′′, *n.* **1.** conclusion or end. **2.** *Baseball.* pitcher's arm and body movements before throwing.

wind′wärd, *n.* **1.** direction from which the wind blows. *—adj.* **2.** moving to windward. *—adv.* **3.** toward the wind.

wine, *n.*, *v.*, **wined, wining**. *n.* **1.** fermented juice from grapes, other fruits, or plants. *—v.i.* **2.** entertain with wine. **—win′y**, *adj.*

wĭn′ĕr·y, *n.*, *pl.* **-ies.** wine-making place.

wĭng, *n.* **1.** organ for flight of birds, insects, bats, etc. **2.** supporting surface of an airplane. **3.** distinct section. —*v.t.* **4.** shoot in an arm or wing. —*v.i.* **5.** travel on wings. —**wĭng′ed**, *adj.* —**wĭng′less**, *adj.* —**wĭng′like**, *adj.* —**wĭng′tip″**, *n.*

wĭng′spăn″, *n.* distance between an airplane's wingtips.

wĭng′spread″, *n.* distance between the tips of extended wings.

wĭnk, *v.t.*, *v.i.* **1.** close and open quickly, as one eye. **2.** signal by winking. —*v.i.* **3.** shine or twinkle. —*n.* **4.** winking, as a signal. **5.** instant.

wĭn′nêr, *n.* person or thing that wins.

wĭn′nĭng, *adj.* **1.** pleasing; charming. **2.** victorious. —*n.* **3.** Often **winnings**, something won, as money. —**win′ning·ly**, *adv.*

wĭn′nŏw, *v.t.*, *v.i.* **1.** blow away from grain. **2.** separate.

wĭn·ō, *n.*, *pl.* **-os.** *Informal.* alcoholic who drinks cheap wine.

wĭn′sŏme, *adj.* attractive. —**win′some·ly**, *adv.* —**win′some·ness**, *n.*

wĭn′têr, *n.* **1.** cold season between autumn and spring. **2.** time like winter, as of decline, cold, etc. —*v.i.* **3.** spend the winter. —**win′ter·time″**, *n.* —**win′try**, **win′ter·y**, *adj.*

wĭn′têr·grēen″, *n.* small evergreen aromatic shrub with white flowers.

wĭn′têr·īze″, *v.t.*, **-ized**, **-izing.** prepare for winter.

wīpe, *v.t.*, **wiped**, **wiping**, *n.*, *v.t.* **1.** clean or rub. —*n.* **2.** act or instance of wiping. —**wip′er**, *n.*

wīre, *n.*, *v.*, **wired**, **wiring.** *n.* **1.** stringlike piece of metal. **2.** *Informal.* telegram. —*v.t.* **3.** install or bind with wire. —*v.t.*, *v.i.* **4.** telegraph.

wīre′hâir″, *n.* fox terrier.

wīre′lĕss, *adj.* *Archaic.* pertaining to radio.

wīre′tăp″pĭng, *n.* listening secretly to the telephone calls of others.

wīr′ÿ, *adj.*, **-ier**, **-iest.** lean and tough.

wĭs′dŏm, *n.* **1.** knowledge and good judgment. **2.** wise teachings.

wĭsdŏm tōoth, back molar.

wīse, *adj.*, **wiser**, **wisest. 1.** showing knowledge and judgment. **2.** erudite or informed. **3.** *Informal.* insolent. —**wise′ly**, *adv.*

wīse′ā·crē, *n.* person who affects to have wisdom. Also, *Informal*, **wise guy.**

wīse′crăck″, *Informal.* *n.* **1.** flippant remark. —*v.i.* **2.** make wisecracks.

wĭsh, *v.t.* **1.** want or desire. —*v.i.* **2.** yearn. —*n.* **3.** desire; longing. —**wish′er**, *n.* —**wish′ful**, *adj.* —**wish′ful·ly**, *adv.* —**wish′ful·ness**, *n.*

wĭsh′bōne″, *n.* forked breastbone of a bird.

wĭsh′ÿ-wăsh′ÿ, *adj.* weak and vacillating.

wĭsp, *n.* thin film or strand. —**wisp′y**, *adj.*

wĭs·tē′rĭ·à, *n.* climbing shrub with showy flowers.

wĭst′fŭl, *adj.* longing or yearning. —**wist′ful·ly**, *adv.* —**wist′ful·ness**, *n.*

wĭt, *n.* **1.** intelligence. **2.** cleverness of expression. **3.** person clever with words. —**wit′less**, *adj.* —**wit′less·ly**, *adv.* —**wit′ty**, *adj.* —**wit′ti·ly**, *adv.*

wĭtch, *n.* **1.** woman with supposed supernatural power. **2.** ugly woman. —**witch′craft″**, *n.* —**witch′er·y**, *n.*

wĭtch dŏctŏr, man who uses magic to cure sickness.

wĭtch hāzĕl, **1.** shrub with yellow leaves. **2.** liquid extracted from it.

wĭth, *prep.* **1.** accompanied by. **2.** characterized by. **3.** against. **4.** in regard to.

wĭth·drāw′, *v.*, **-drew**, **-drawn**, **-drawing.** *v.t.* **1.** take back. **2.** retract, as a statement, etc. —*v.i.* **3.** remove oneself. —**with·draw′al**, *n.*

wĭthe, *n.* willow twig.

wĭth′ĕr, *v.t.*, *v.i.* **1.** shrivel. —*v.t.* **2.** confuse and humiliate. —**with′er·ing·ly**, *adv.*

wĭth′ĕrs, *n. pl.* lower nape of the neck of a sheep, horse, etc.

wĭth·hōld′, *v.t.*, **-held**, **-holding. 1.** hold back. **2.** deduct, as taxes.

wĭth·ĭn′, *adv.* **1.** inside; indoors. —*prep.* **2.** inside. **3.** in the area of.

wĭth·out′, *prep.* **1.** lacking; not with. **2.** outside. —*adv.* **3.** outside; externally.

wĭth·stănd′, *v.t.*, **-stood**, **-standing.** resist or oppose.

wĭt′nĕss, *n.* **1.** person who sees. **2.** testimony. —*v.t.* **3.** see. **4.** attest.

wĭt′tĭ·cĭsm″, *n.* witty remark.

wĭt′tĭng, *adj.* knowing; intentional. —**wit′ting·ly**, *adv.*

wĭz′ärd, *n.* magician; sorcerer. —**wiz′ard·ry**, *n.*

wĭz′ened, *adj.* withered.

wŏb′ble, *v.*, **-bled, -bling**, *n. v.i., v.t.* **1.** shake. —*n.* **2.** wobbling motion. —**wob′bly**, *adj.* —**wob′bli·ness**, *n.*

wŏe, *n.* **1.** grief. **2.** trouble. —*interj.* **3.** alas! —**woe′ful**, *adj.* —**woe′ful·ly**, *adv.* —**woe′ful·ness**, *n.*

wŏe′bē·gŏne′′, *adj.* showing woe. —**woe′be·gone′′ness**, *n.*

wŏlf, *n., pl.* **wolves. 1.** wild, doglike mammal. **2.** *Informal.* man who flirts with women. **3.** cruel person. —*v.t.* **4.** devour greedily. —**wolf′hound′′**, *n.* —**wolf′ish**, *adj.* —**wolf′like′′**, *adj.*

wŏl′′vēr·īne′, *n.* stocky, carnivorous mammal.

wŏm′ăn, *n., pl.* **women.** female human being. —**wom′an·hood′′**, *n.* —**wom′an·ish**, *adj.* —**wom′an·like′′**, *adj.* —**wom′an·ly**, *adj.* —**wom′an·li·ness**, *n.*

wŏm′ăn·īze′′, *v.* **-ized, -izing.** *v.t.* **1.** make effeminate. —*v.t.* **2.** pursue women habitually. —**wom′an·iz′′er**, *n.*

womb, *n.* **1.** uterus. **2.** source of being.

wŏn′dēr, *n.* **1.** awe or amazement. **2.** source of such an emotion. —*v.i.* **3.** be curious. **4.** be filled with wonder. —**won′der·ful**, *adj.* —**won′der·ful·ly**, *adv.* —**won′der·ing·ly**, *adv.* —**won′der·ment**, *n.* —**won′drous**, *adj.* —**won′drous·ly**, *adv.*

wŏnt, *adj.* **1.** Also, **wont′ed**, accustomed. —*n.* **2.** habit.

wŏn′t, *v.* contraction of *will not.*

wŏō, *v.i., v.t.* solicit for love or favor. —**woo′er**, *n.*

wŏŏd, *n.* **1.** hard substance beneath the bark of trees. **2.** Also, **woods**, forest. **3.** lumber. —*adj.* **4.** wooden; made of wood. —**wood′en**, *adj.* —**wood′en·ness**, *n.* —**wood′craft′′**, *n.* —**wood′cut′′ter**, *n.* —**wood′ed**, *adj.* —**wood′pile′′**, *n.* —**wood′shed′′**, *n.* —**woods′man**, *n.* —**woods′y**, *adj.* —**wood′y**, *adj.*

wŏŏd′bīne′′, *n.* honeysuckle or the Virginia creeper.

wŏŏd′chŭck′′, *n.* burrowing and hibernating marmot.

wŏŏd′cŏck′′, *n.* snipelike game bird.

wŏŏd′cŭt′′, *n.* **1.** carved block of wood. **2.** print from this block.

wŏŏd′en, *adj.* **1.** made of wood. **2.** without natural feeling or expression. —**wood′en·ly**, *adv.*

wŏŏd′lănd′′, *n.* land covered with trees.

wŏŏd′pĕck′′êr, *n.* bird with a hard bill for pecking.

wŏŏd′wĭnd′′, *n.* musical non-brass wind instrument.

wŏŏd′wŏrk′′, *n.* **1.** objects made of wood. **2.** wooden fittings of a house, as doors, moldings, etc. —**wood′work′′er**, *n.* —**wood′work′′ing**, *n.*

wŏŏf, *n.* cross-threads of a fabric.

wŏŏf′êr, *n.* loudspeaker for reproducing low frequencies.

wŏŏl, *n.* **1.** soft, curly hair, as from sheep, goats, etc. **2.** yarn or garments made from such. —**wool′en, wool′len**, *adj.* —**wool′y, wool′ly**, *adj.* —**wool′i·ness, wool′li·ness**, *n.*

wŏŏl′gäth′′êr·ing, *n.* absentmindedness or daydreaming.

wŏŏz′ў, *adj.*, **-ier, -iest.** *Informal.* muddled or dizzy. —**wooz′i·ly**, *adv.* —**wooz′i·ness**, *n.*

wŏrd, *n.* **1.** spoken or written sounds with meaning as a unit of language. **2.** words, speech or talk. **3.** promise or assurance. **4.** news or information. **5.** (computers) several bits of data treated as a unit. —*v.t.* **6.** express in words. —**word′′age**, *n.* —**word′′ing**, *n.* —**word′′less**, *adj.* —**word′′y**, *adj.* —**word′′i·ness**, *n.*

wŏrk, *n., v.*, **worked** or **wrought, working**, *n.* **1.** labor or toil. **2.** occupation. **3.** something on which one is working. —*v.i.* **4.** do work. **5.** act or operate. —*v.t.* **6.** manage or manipulate. **7.** solve. **8.** cultivate, as the soil. **9.** provoke or excite. —**work′a·ble**, *adj.* —**work′bench′′**, *n.* —**work′book′′**, *n.* —**work′er**, *n.* —**work′day′′**, *n.* —**work′ing·man′′**, *n.* —**work′man**, *n.* —**work′shop′′**, *n.* —**work′week′′**, *n.*

wŏrk′dāy, *n.* **1.** day on which work is done. **2.** part of the day one works.

wörk′màn·līke″, *adj.* skillful.

wörk′màn·shĭp″, *n.* **1.** workman's art or skill. **2.** quality of work.

wörk′ōut″, *n.* practice athletic session.

wörld, *n.* **1.** earth; universe. **2.** people; mankind. **3.** part of the earth. **4.** great quantity or extent. **—world′wide′**, *adj.*

wörld′lў, *adj.*, **-lier, -liest. 1.** secular. **2.** Also, **world′ly-wise′**, sophisticated. **—world′li·ness**, *n.*

wörm, *n.* **1.** long, soft, legless, creeping animal. **2.** something like this creature. **3.** *Informal.* contemptible person. **4.** **worms**, intestinal disease from parasitic worms. *—v.i.* **5.** move or act stealthily. *—v.t.* **6.** get by insidious efforts. **7.** free from worms. **—worm′y**, *adj.* **-ier, -iest. —worm′i·ness**, *n.*

wörm′wōod″, *n.* **1.** bitter, strong-smelling herb. **2.** something bitter or unpleasant.

wörn, *adj.* **1.** used by wear, handling, etc. **2.** exhausted; tired. **—worn′-out′**, *adj.*

wör′rў, *v.*, **-ried, -rying**, *n.*, *pl.* **-ies.** *v.i.* **1.** feel anxious. *—v.t.* **2.** make anxious. *—n.* **3.** anxiety. **4.** cause of anxiety. **—wor′ri·er**, *n.* **—wor′ri·some**, *adj.*

wörse, *adj.* **1.** bad in a greater or higher degree. **2.** in poorer health. *—n.* **3.** that which is worse. *—adv.* **4.** in a worse manner. **—wors′en**, *v.t.*, *v.i.*

wör′shĭp, *n.*, *v.*, **-shiped**, or **-shipped**, **-shiping** or **-shipping**. *n.* **1.** reverence for a deity. **2.** admiration or love. *—v.t.*, *v.i.* **3.** show religious reverence. **—wor′ship·er, wor′ship·per**, *n.* **—wor′ship·ful**, *adj.*

wörst, *adj.* **1.** bad in the highest degree. **2.** least well. *—n.* **3.** that which is worst. *—adv.* **4.** in the worst manner. *—v.t.* **5.** beat; defeat.

wor·sted (wŏŏs′tĭd), *n.* **1.** firmly twisted wool yarn. **2.** garment made of it. *—adj.* **3.** consisting of worsted.

wört, *n.* infusion with malt before fermentation, as in making beer or mash.

wörth, *n.* **1.** material value, as in money. **2.** importance; value. *—adj.* **3.** worthy of; justifying. **4.** having equal value. **—worth′less**, *adj.* **—worth′less·ness**, *n.*

wörth′whīle′, *adj.* worthy of doing, etc.

wörth′ў, *adj.*, **-ier, -iest.** deserving. **—worth′i·ly**, *adv.* **—worth′i·ness**, *n.*

wōuld, *auxiliary v.* expressing condition, futurity, habitual action, or request.

wōuld′-bē″, *adj.* wishing or intending to be.

wōund, *n.* **1.** physical injury. **2.** injury to feelings, sensibilities, etc. *—v.t.* **3.** injure. **—wound′ed**, *adj.*, *n.*, *pl.*

wrăck, *n.* ruin or destruction.

wrāith, *n.* ghost.

wrăn′gle, *v.t.*, *v.i.*, **-gled, -gling**, *n.* dispute.

wrăp, *v.*, **wrapped** or **wrapt, wrapping**, *n.* *v.t.*, *v.i.* **1.** wind or fold, as around something. *—v.t.* **2.** enclose or envelop. *—n.* **3.** outer garment wrapped around the body. **—wrap′ping**, *n.*

wrăp′pêr, *n.* **1.** person who wraps. **2.** something wrapped around as a cover.

wrăth, *n.* **1.** anger; rage. **2.** vengeance. **—wrath′ful**, *adj.* **—wrath′ful·ly**, *adv.*

wrēak, *v.t.* inflict.

wrēath, *n.*, *pl.* **wreaths.** circular formation, as of flowers, etc.

wrēathe, *v.t.*, **wreathed, wreathing. 1.** form into a wreath. **2.** encircle.

wrĕck, *n.* **1.** structure or object in ruins. **2.** run-down person. *—v.t.* **3.** tear down or destroy. **—wreck′age**, *n.* **—wreck′er**, *n.*

wrĕn, *n.* small active songbird.

wrĕnch, *n.* **1.** sudden twist or pull, as to the arms, back, etc. **2.** sudden emotional strain. **3.** tool for turning bolts, etc. *—v.t.*, *v.i.* **4.** turn suddenly. *—v.t.* **5.** overstrain or injure.

wrĕst, *v.t.* **1.** pull violently. **2.** usurp. *—n.* **3.** twist.

wrĕs′tle, *v.*, **-tled, -tling.** *v.t.* **1.** grapple and attempt to throw down. *—v.i.* **2.** engage in wrestling. **3.** struggle. **—wrest′ler**, *n.*

wrĕtch, *n.* **1.** unhappy person. **2.** despicable person.

wrĕtch′ĕd, *adj.* **1.** pitiful. **2.** contemptible. **3.** worthless. **—wretch′ed·ly**, *adv.* **—wretch′ed·ness**, *n.*

wrĭg′gle, *v.i.*, *n.*, **-gled, -gling.** *v.i.* **1.** squirm; twist and turn. *—n.* **2.** act or instance of wriggling. **—wrig′gly**, *adj.*

wrĭght, *n.* carpenter.

wrĭng, *v.t.*, **wrung, wringing**, *n.*, *v.t.* **1.**

twist; press; squeeze. —*n.* **2.** act or instance of wringing. —**wring'er**, *n.*

wrin'kle, *n., v.,* **-kled, -kling.** *n.* **1.** ridge or furrow on a surface. **2.** ingenious trick or device. —*v.t., v.i.* **3.** crease or furrow. —**wrin'kly**, *adj.*

wrist, *n.* joint between the hand and forearm. —**wrist'band''**, *n.* —**wrist' watch''**, *n.*

writ, *n.* **1.** *Law.* formal legal order or document. **2.** something written.

write, *v.,* **wrote, written, writing.** *v.i.* **1.** form letters, words, etc., as with a pen, pencil, etc. —*v.t.* **2.** compose. **3.** communicate with. —**writ'er**, *n.*

writhe, *v.,* **writhed, writhing,** *n. v.t., v.i.* **1.** squirm, twist, or bend, as in pain. —*n.* **2.** act or instance of writhing.

wrong, *adj.* **1.** not right or good. **2.** not truthful or factual. **3.** inappropriate. —*n.* **4.** injustice; evil. —*v.t.* **5.** do wrong to. —**wrong'ly**, *adv.* —**wrong'ness**, *n.* —**wrong'do''er**, *n.* —**wrong'do''ing**, *n.* —**wrong'ful**, *adj.* —**wrong'ful·ly**, *adv.*

wrong'head''ed, *adj.* deeply erroneous.

wroth, *adj. Archaic.* angry.

wrought, *adj.* **1.** worked. **2.** shaped by beating.

wrought'-ŭp', *adj.* upset; excited.

wry, *adj.,* **wrier, wriest. 1.** distorted or lopsided. **2.** misdirected or perverse. **3.** bitterly ironic. —**wry'ly**, *adv.* —**wry' ness**, *n.*

wûrst, *n.* sausage.

X

X, x, *n.* twenty-fourth letter of the English alphabet.

xē'nŏn, *n.* chemically inactive gaseous element.

xĕn''ŏ·phō'bĭ·á, *n.* irrational fear of that which is foreign or strange. —**xen''o· pho'bic**, *adj.*

Xmás, *n.* Christmas.

x'-rāy, *n.* **1.** electromagnetic radiation which penetrates solids. **2.** picture made by x-rays. —*v.t.* **3.** treat or photograph with x-rays.

xȳ'lĕm, *n.* woody tissue of plants and trees.

xȳ'lö·phōne'', *n.* musical instrument with wooden sounding bars struck by small hammers.

Y

Y, y, *n.* twenty-fifth letter of the English alphabet.

yächt, *n.* pleasure ship. —**yachts'man**, *n.*

yä·hōō', *n.* coarse or rowdy person.

Yäh'weh, *n.* God of the Hebrews.

yăk, *n.* long-haired Tibetan ox.

yăm, *n.* edible potatolike root; sweet potato.

yăm'mêr, *v.i.,* **-mered, -mering. 1.** complain or whine. **2.** talk persistently; chatter.

yănk, *v.t., v.i.* **1.** pull strongly and abruptly. —*n.* **2.** strong, abrupt pull. **3. Yank,** Yankee.

Yăn'kee, *n.* native or inhabitant of the U.S., the northeastern U.S., or New England.

yăp, *v.i.,* **yapped, yapping,** *n. v.i.* **1.** yelp; bark shrilly. —*n.* **2.** shrill bark.

yârd, *n.* **1.** linear unit of measure equal to 3 feet. **2.** open area. **3.** long spar that supports a sail.

yârd'áge, *n.* amount in yards.

yârd'stick'', *n.* one-yard measuring stick.

yârn, *n.* **1.** multi-stranded thread for sweaters, etc. **2.** story; tall tale.

yäw, *v.i.* **1.** deviate from a course. —*n.* **2.** deviation.

yäwl, *n.* two-masted sailboat.

yäwn, *v.i.* **1.** involuntarily open the mouth wide as from drowsiness. —*n.* **2.** act or instance of yawning.

yeá, *adv., n.* yes.

yēar, *n.* **1.** time period equal to 365 or 366 days. **2. years,** age. —**year'ly**, *adv., adj.*

yêar'lĭng, *n.* year-old animal.

yêarn, *v.i.* **1.** desire earnestly or strongly.

2. feel affection or tenderness. **—yearn′ ing,** n., adj.

yĕast, n. fungous substance used to leaven bread, etc.

yĕll, v.i., n. cry; shout.

yĕl′lōw, n. **1.** bright color of butter, etc. —adj. **2.** of the color yellow. **3.** Informal. cowardly; chicken.

yĕl′lōw fē′vēr, n. tropical disease.

yĕlp, v.i. **1.** cry quickly or shrilly like a dog. —n. **2.** quick, sharp bark.

yĕn, n. Informal. desire; urge.

yeō′mȧn, n. **1.** naval petty officer. **2.** small independent farmer. —adj. **3.** valiant.

yĕs, adv., n. expression of assent, agreement or affirmation.

yĕs′tēr·dȧy, adv., n. day before today.

yĕt, adv. **1.** up to now. **2.** besides. **3.** nevertheless. **4.** eventually. —conj. **5.** but; still.

yĕw, n. coniferous evergreen tree or bush.

yĭeld, v.t., v.i. **1.** produce. **2.** surrender. **3.** concede. —v.i. **4.** give way to force. —n. **5.** amount produced.

yō·dĕl, v., -deled, -deling, n. v.t., v.i. **1.** shout or sing alternating falsetto with chest voice. —n. **2.** act or instance of yodeling.

yō′gȧ, n. **1.** Hindu philosophy teaching suppression of the body to free the soul. **2.** system of exercises for total bodily control.

yō′gĭ n. adherent of yoga.

yō′gûrt, n. fermented milk food.

yōke, n., v., yoked, yoking. n. **1.** device for joining oxen. **2.** pair, esp. of oxen. **3.** something oppressive. —v.t. **4.** put a yoke on.

yō′kĕl, n. rustic; bumpkin.

yōlk, n. yellow part of the egg.

Yŏm Kĭp·pūr (yom kē poŏr′), n. Jewish Day of Atonement.

yŏn′dêr, adj., adv. over there.

yōre, adv., adj. Archaic. long ago.

yoŭ, pron. **1.** person or persons addressed. **2.** any person.

yŏung, adj. **1.** in the early stages of life, etc. **2.** pertaining to youth. —n. **3.** children; young people. **—young′ish,** adj.

yŏung′stêr, n. child; youth.

yoŭr, adj. pertaining to you.

yoŭrs, pron., belonging to you.

yoŭr·sĕlf′, pron., pl. -selves. **1.** form of you used reflexively or emphatically. **2.** your true self.

yoŭth, n. **1.** young state. **2.** child; young person. **—youth′ful,** adj. **—youth′ful·ly,** adv. **—youth′ful·ness,** n.

yōwl, v.i., n. howl.

yŭc′cȧ, n. tropical American plant.

yūle, n. Christmas.

yūle′tīde′′, n. Christmas season.

Z

Z, z, n. twenty-sixth letter of the English alphabet.

zä′nÿ, n., pl. -nies, adj. n. **1.** clown. **2.** silly person. —adj. **3.** crazy; foolish.

zĕal, n. intense or eager interest. **—zeal′ ous,** adj. **—zeal′ous·ly,** adv. **—zeal′ ous·ness,** n.

zĕal·ŏt (zel′ot), n. enthusiast; fanatic. **—zeal′ot·ry,** n.

zē′brȧ, n. black and white striped horselike African mammal.

Zĕn, n. Buddhist sect.

zē′nĭth, n. **1.** celestial point directly overhead. **2.** highest point.

zĕph′ýr, n. mild or gentle breeze.

zĕp′pe·lĭn, n. large dirigible. Also, **Zep′ pe·lin.**

zē′rō, n. **1.** numerical symbol, 0, denoting the absence of quantity. **2.** nothing.

zĕst, n. **1.** something enhancing enjoyment. **2.** enjoyment. **—zest′ful,** adj. **—zest′ful·ly,** adv.

zĭg′zȧg′′, n., adj., adv., v.i., -zagged, -zagging. n. **1.** short sharp alternations in a line. —adj., adv. **2.** with or having sharp back and forth turns. —v.i. **3.** proceed in a zigzag.

zĭnc, n. bluish metallic element.

zĭnc ŏx′īde, n. zinc and oxygen salve.

zĭng, n. **1.** sharp singing or whistling sound. **2.** vitality. —v.i. **3.** move with or make a zinging sound.

zĭn′ni·ȧ, n. colorful annual garden flower.

Zi′ŏn·ism′′, n. political movement for reestablishment of the Jewish Biblical homeland. **—Zi′on·ist,** n.

zip, *v.,* **zipped, zipping,** *n. v.i.* **1.** act or move speedily or energetically. —*v.t.* **2.** fasten with a zipper. —*n.* **3.** energy.

zip′pêr, *n.* slide fastener with interlocking teeth.

zĭth′êr, *n.* stringed musical instrument.

zō′dĭ·ăc, *n.* imaginary heavenly region including the paths of all planets except Pluto, with divisions for the twelve constellations.

zŏm′bĭ, *n.* reanimated dead body. Also, **zom′bie.**

zōne, *n., v.t.,* **zoned, zoning.** *n.* **1.** special area or region. —*v.t.* **2.** mark off or arrange in zones.

zōō, *n.* park where animals are exhibited.

zō·ŏl′ö·gў, *n.* study of animals. —**zo·o·log′i·cal,** *adj.* —**zo·ol′o·gist,** *n.*

zōōm, *v.i.* **1.** move quickly with a humming sound. **2.** fly upward sharply and at great speed.

zūc·chĭ′nĭ, *n.* green cylindrical summer squash.

zў·gōte′, *n.* fertilized egg cell.

FOR GIFT GIVING

WEDDING ANNIVERSARY SYMBOLS

	TRADITIONAL	MODERN
1st	paper	clocks
2nd	cotton	china
3rd	leather	crystal, glass
4th	books	electrical appliances
5th	wood	silverware
6th	sugar, candy	wood
7th	wool, copper	desk sets
8th	bronze, pottery	linens, laces
9th	pottery, willow	leather
10th	tin, aluminum	diamond jewelry
11th	steel	fashion jewelry
12th	silk, linen	pearls, colored gems
13th	lace	textiles, furs
14th	ivory	gold jewelry
15th	crystal	watches
20th	china	platinum
25th	silver	silver
30th	pearl	diamond
35th	coral	jade
40th	ruby	ruby
45th	sapphire	sapphire
50th	gold	gold
55th	emerald	emerald
60th	diamond	diamond
75th	diamond	diamond

BIRTHSTONES

January	Garnet	July	Ruby
February	Amethyst	August	Sardonyx or Peridot
March	Bloodstone or Aquamarine	September	Sapphire
		October	Opal or Tourmaline
April	Diamond	November	Topaz
May	Emerald	December	Turquoise or Zircon
June	Pearl or Alexandrite		

313

WEIGHTS AND MEASURES

Cubic Measure

1.728 cubic inches	1 cubic foot
27 cubic feet	1 cubic yard
128 cubic feet	1 cord (wood)
40 cubic feet	1 ton (shipping)
2,150.42 cubic inches	1 standard bushel
231 cubic inches	1 U.S. standard gallon
1 cubic foot	about $\frac{4}{5}$ of a bushel

Dry Measure

2 pints	1 quart
8 quarts	1 peck
4 pecks	1 bushel

Liquid Measure

4 gills	1 pint
2 pints	1 quart
4 quarts	1 gallon
31½ gallons	1 barrel

Imperial Liquid Measure

1 U.S. gallon	0.833 Imperial gallon
1 U.S. gallon	3.785 liters
1 Imperial gallon	1.201 U.S. gallons
1 Imperial gallon	4.546 liters
1 liter	0.264 U.S. gallon
1 liter	0.220 Imperial gallon

Long Measure

12 inches	1 foot
3 feet	1 yard
5½ yards	1 rod
40 rods	1 furlong
8 furlongs	1 statute mile
3 miles	1 league

Mariner's Measure

6 feet	1 fathom
120 fathoms	1 cable length
7½ cable lengths	1 mile
5,280 feet	1 statute mile
6,080.2 feet	1 nautical mile

Square Measure

144 square inches	1 square foot
9 square feet	1 square yard
30¼ square yards	1 square rod
40 square rods	1 rood
4 roods	1 acre
640 acres	1 square mile

Avoirdupois Weight

27¹¹⁄₃₂ grains	1 dram
16 drams	1 ounce

16 ounces	1 pound
25 pounds	1 quarter
4 quarters	1 cwt
2,000 pounds	1 short ton
2,240 pounds	1 long ton

Troy Weight

24 grains	1 pwt
20 pwt	1 ounce
12 ounces	1 pound

Used for weighing gold, silver and jewels

METRIC EQUIVALENTS

Linear Measure

1 centimeter		0.3937 inch
1 inch		2.54 centimeters
1 decimeter	3.937 inches	0.328 foot
1 foot		3.048 decimeters
1 meter	39.37 inches	1.0936 yards
1 yard		0.9144 meter
1 dekameter		1.9684 rods
1 rod		0.5029 dekameter
1 kilometer		0.621 mile
1 mile		1.609 kilometers

Square Measure

1 square centimeter	0.1550 square inch
1 square inch	6.452 square centimeters
1 square decimeter	0.1076 square foot
1 square foot	9.2903 square decimeters
1 square meter	1.196 square yards
1 square yard	0.8361 square meter
1 acre	160 square rods
1 square rod	0.00625 acre
1 hectare	2.47 acres
1 acre	0.4047 hectare
1 square kilometer	0.386 square mile
1 square mile	2.59 square kilometers

Weights

1 gram	0.03527 ounce
1 ounce	28.35 grams
1 kilogram	2.2046 pounds
1 pound	0.4536 kilogram
1 metric ton	0.98421 English ton
1 English ton	1.016 metric tons

Measure of Volume

1 cubic centimeter	0.061 cubic inch
1 cubic inch	16.39 cubic centimeters
1 cubic decimeter	0.0353 cubic foot
1 cubic foot	28.317 cubic decimeters
1 cubic meter	1.308 cubic yards
1 cubic yard	0.7646 cubic meter

```
1 stere . . . . . . . . . . . . . . . . . . . . . . . . . . . . . . . . . . . . . . . . . . 0.2759 cord
1 cord . . . . . . . . . . . . . . . . . . . . . . . . . . . . . . . . . . . . . . . . . . . 3.624 steres
1 liter . . . . . . . . . . . 0.908 dry quart . . . . . . . . . 1.0567 liquid quarts
1 quart dry . . . . . . . . . . . . . . . . . . . . . . . . . . . . . . . . . . . . . . . 1.101 liters
1 quart liquid . . . . . . . . . . . . . . . . . . . . . . . . . . . . . . . . . . . . 0.9463 liter
1 dekaliter . . . . . . . . . . . 2.6417 gallons . . . . . . . . . . . . . 1.135 pecks
1 gallon . . . . . . . . . . . . . . . . . . . . . . . . . . . . . . . . . . . . . . . 0.3785 dekaliter
1 peck . . . . . . . . . . . . . . . . . . . . . . . . . . . . . . . . . . . . . . . . 0.881 dekaliter
1 hektoliter . . . . . . . . . . . . . . . . . . . . . . . . . . . . . . . . . . . . 2.8375 bushels
1 bushel . . . . . . . . . . . . . . . . . . . . . . . . . . . . . . . . . . . . . . . 0.3524 hektoliter
```

APPROXIMATE METRIC EQUIVALENTS

```
1 decimeter . . . . . . . . . . . . . . . . . . . . . . . . . . . . . . . . . . . . . . . 4 inches
1 liter . . . . . . . . . . . 1.06 quarts liquid . . . . . . . . . . 0.9 quart dry
1 meter . . . . . . . . . . . . . . . . . . . . . . . . . . . . . . . . . . . . . . . . . 1.1 yards
1 kilometer . . . . . . . . . . . . . . . . . . . . . . . . . . . . . . . . . . . ⅝ of a mile
1 hektoliter . . . . . . . . . . . . . . . . . . . . . . . . . . . . . . . . . . . 2⅝ bushels
1 hectare . . . . . . . . . . . . . . . . . . . . . . . . . . . . . . . . . . . . . 2½ acres
1 kilogram . . . . . . . . . . . . . . . . . . . . . . . . . . . . . . . . . . . . 2⅕ pounds
1 stere, or cubic meter . . . . . . . . . . . . . . . . . . . . . . . . ¼ of a cord
1 metric ton . . . . . . . . . . . . . . . . . . . . . . . . . . . . . . . . . 2,204.6 pounds
```

States and Territories of the United States with Their Post Office Abbreviations and Capitals

Alabama (AL)	Montgomery	Nevada (NV)	Carson City
Alaska (AK)	Juneau	New Hampshire (NH)	Concord
Arizona (AZ)	Phoenix	New Jersey (NJ)	Trenton
Arkansas (AR)	Little Rock	New Mexico (NM)	Santa Fe
California (CA)	Sacramento	New York (NY)	Albany
Colorado (CO)	Denver	North Carolina (NC)	Raleigh
Connecticut (CT)	Hartford	North Dakota (ND)	Bismarck
Delaware (DE)	Dover	Ohio (OH)	Columbus
District of Columbia (DC)		Oklahoma (OK)	Oklahoma City
Florida (FL)	Tallahassee	Oregon (OR)	Salem
Georgia (GA)	Atlanta	Pennsylvania (PA)	Harrisburg
Hawaii (HI)	Honolulu	Rhode Island (RI)	Providence
Idaho (ID)	Boise	South Carolina (SC)	Columbia
Illinois (IL)	Springfield	South Dakota (SD)	Pierre
Indiana (IN)	Indianapolis	Tennessee (TN)	Nashville
Iowa (IA)	Des Moines	Texas (TX)	Austin
Kansas (KS)	Topeka	Utah (UT)	Salt Lake City
Kentucky (KY)	Frankfort	Vermont (VT)	Montpelier
Louisiana (LA)	Baton Rouge	Virginia (VA)	Richmond
Maine (ME)	Augusta	Washington (WA)	Olympia
Maryland (MD)	Annapolis	West Virginia (WV)	Charleston
Massachusetts (MA)	Boston	Wisconsin (WI)	Madison
Michigan (MI)	Lansing	Wyoming (WY)	Cheyenne
Minnesota (MI)	St. Paul		
Mississippi (MI)	Jackson	American Samoa (AS)	Pago Pago
Missouri (MO)	Jefferson City	Guam (GU)	Agaña
Montana (MT)	Helena	Puerto Rico (PR)	San Juan
Nebraska (NE)	Lincoln	Virgin Islands (VI)	Charlotte Amalie